SPYING
FOR
AMERICA

BOOKS BY NATHAN MILLER

SPYING FOR AMERICA:
The Hidden History of U.S. Intelligence

FDR: An Intimate History

The Naval Air War: 1939–1945

The Roosevelt Chronicles

The U.S. Navy: An Illustrated History

The Founding Finaglers:
A History of Corruption in America

Sea of Glory: The Continental Navy
Fights for Independence, 1775–1783

The Belarus Secret (with John Loftus)

Stealing From America

SPYING
FOR
AMERICA

The
Hidden History
of U.S. Intelligence

NATHAN MILLER

MARLOWE & COMPANY
NEW YORK

Published in the United States by

Marlowe & Company
632 Broadway, Seventh Floor
New York, NY 10012

Library of Congress Cataloging-in-Publication Data

Miller, Nathan, 1927–
    Spying for America : the hidden history of U.S. intelligence/
Nathan Miller.—1st ed.
    p.   cm.
    Bibliography: p.
    Includes index.
    ISBN 1-56924-721-8
    1. Military intelligence—United States—History   I. Title.
UB251.U5M56   1989
327.1'273—dc19   88-26779
Second Printing   CIP

Manufactured in the United States of America

Secrets are edged tools
That must be kept from children
and from fools.
—JOHN DRYDEN

Contents

I

The Spy As Amateur

$$\boxed{\textbf{II}}$$

The Spy As Professional

$$\boxed{\textbf{III}}$$

The Spy As Bureaucrat

Preface

This book is a first. Several years ago, while working with a young Justice Department investigator named John Loftus on *The Belarus Secret*, in which we were the first to reveal that American intelligence agencies had secretly recruited ex-Nazi collaborators during the Cold War and then smuggled them into the United States, I looked for a history of American intelligence operations. Romanticized accounts of spying during the American Revolution and the Civil War, books glorifying the cloak-and-dagger Office of Strategic Services, and muckraking attacks on the Central Intelligence Agency were readily available. But there was no overall account of American intelligence that placed it within the context of two centuries of national history.

Spying for America is a pioneering attempt to begin to fill this gap. The story of American intelligence operations is an important, dramatic, and largely unknown part of our heritage. It is a story well worth telling, not only for the perspective it affords on current events, but for the human drama of men and women caught inside the espionage maze. Bravery, imagination, and technical wizardry are all part of the tale. And so are treachery and double-dealing, as well as incompetence and stupidity that verge on the slapstick.

Today's headlines have their roots in the past. The purpose of this book is to examine that past so that it may be used to understand the present and guide the future. History permits no reruns, but a knowledge of the past may prevent policymakers and the public from seeing the present as unique and myopically repeating old mistakes. If we are to bring the intelligence services under responsible control, we must develop a fuller understanding of the process that created them and the men and women they employ. As Winston S. Churchill pointed out "History is the one sure guide to the future—that, and imagination."

My book focuses on individual men and women—those who directed and carried out American intelligence operations over the past two centuries, and some of those who were their adversaries in the shadows. Along the way it provides an overview of the political and legal underpinning of intelligence activities, the incessant bureaucratic infighting for the control of intelligence, and the evolving relations within the intelligence community itself and between that community and the executive branch and Congress. From this overview three distinct themes emerge in sharp relief:

- The professionalization of the nation's military and diplomatic establishments has been matched by a similar trend in intelligence operations as the flamboyant amateur has given way to the systems analyst and the bureaucratic manager. Nevertheless, remnants of the older tradition of derring-do persist today, not always to the advantage of the intelligence community or the nation.
- The growth of intelligence organizations in size and influence has been matched by a corresponding increase in the tendency to become involved in areas that are as murky morally as they are legally. This tendency has raised a vital question: In a free society, how far can a government reasonably pry into the private affairs of its citizens to oppose threats to the national security? As pressing as this issue is today, the broader question of reconciling national security with constitutional guarantees is nearly as old as the nation itself. From the Alien and Sedition Acts through Lincoln's suspension of habeas corpus in the Civil War to black-bag jobs by the FBI, the tension between freedom and security has troubled the American experiment.
- With a secret apparatus in place, high officials have been all too tempted to use it as a shortcut in dealing with seemingly intractable domestic and international problems. Secret intelligence agencies have been transformed in the public imagination from the shield of the Republic to a threat to democratic institutions. Yet for this development, too, there is an ample "tradition" at least as far back as American presidents' use of personal secret agents and covert operations in the early nineteenth century.

Some definitions are in order here. Intelligence is information about what other nations, especially potential adversaries, are doing that has been subjected to sound assessment. Positive intelligence is the gathering of information, in contrast to the safeguarding of one's own secrets, or counterintelligence. Positive intelligence may be collected by either overt or clandestine means. Overt sources include research and observation, while clandestine techniques run the gamut from the tradecraft of the solitary spy to complex electronic eavesdropping and other forms of technological espionage. Covert operations include deceptive and often violent actions resorted to by one nation to affect the affairs of another, and are sometimes regarded as of questionable legality.

Although most Americans believe the United States did not become deeply involved in intelligence operations until the creation of the Office of Strategic Services (OSS) during World War II, this book demonstrates that we have participated in such activities—with varying degrees of success—since the Revolution. Probably the reason the early history of U.S. intelligence has remained obscure is our unwillingness to reconcile political realities with our ideals. Americans have never been comfortable with clandestine activities. Other nations spied or committed "dirty tricks," but not the United States. *Spying for America* provides essential material for filling in the details of this missing chapter in the accepted version of American history.

Upon learning that I was working on a history of American intelligence operations, most people expressed both a strong interest in the book and doubts about its feasibility. Finding documentation about intelligence operations is indeed difficult, because excessive secrecy is the occupational disease of the intelligence profession. Records are frequently destroyed after use; mistakes are quietly buried. Nevertheless, I was able to discover much surviving material as well as to draw threads from many published sources.

While this book was written without the official cooperation or blessing of the intelligence community, I have had the voluntary assistance of some of its former members. I also wish to express my appreciation to Lisa Drew, who provided early support for this project; to Anne Hukill Yeager, who guided it through much of its progress; and especially to my editor at Paragon House, Don Fehr, who put the finishing touches upon it. And once again, I wish to acknowledge the help of my wife, Jeanette, without whose support this book could not have been written.

Many thanks to all.

NATHAN MILLER
Washington, D.C.

THE SPY AS AMATEUR

1

George Washington, Spymaster

John Honeyman was an unlikely spy.

A giant of a man—burly and well over six feet tall—he lustily proclaimed his loyalty to King George III in the west Jersey taverns and served the British army in the rebellious American colonies as a cattle trader and butcher. Sometimes he also supplied them with bits of information. So no one paid much attention as he wandered about the Hessian outposts near Trenton toward the end of December 1776. But Honeyman took careful note of the alertness of sentries, the disposition of troops, and the placement of artillery—for John Honeyman, Tory butcher, was one of George Washington's most valued secret agents.

Blowing in off the mackerel-gray waters of the Delaware River, the sharp wind forced Honeyman to huddle in his cloak as he moved about the back roads. Snow crusted the fields; patches of ice glinted like diamonds in the wintry sunlight. European armies did not campaign in cold weather, and not long before, General Sir William Howe, commander of the British forces, had ordered his troops into winter quarters. While the British settled into the comfort of the towns and villages, the remnant of Washington's army encamped in the freezing cold just a few miles to the north, on the Pennsylvania side of the river. Casualties and desertion had taken a heavy toll, and of the men who remained many were without shoes or blankets—or hope. Five months after the signing of the Declaration of Independence, the flame of American liberty was flickering low.

The British had seized New York and driven Washington's army across New Jersey like wild game. Fearing that the enemy would soon occupy Philadelphia, a panic-stricken Congress had fled to Baltimore. "These are the times that try men's souls," Thomas Paine observed in

3

words like drum taps during the demoralizing retreat. Even the commander in chief agreed with this dismal assessment. If something were not done to keep soldiers whose enlistments were running out from going home, he wrote his brother, John Augustine Washington, "I think the game will be pretty near up."

Nevertheless, Washington clung to a feeble hope. The British were scattered about the area, with strong points at Trenton, Bordentown, and Burlington. A successful surprise attack against one of these posts would provide his army with an emotional lift and revive the American cause. But he desperately needed information on the strength of the enemy's positions. "Expense must not be spared in procuring such Intelligence," he told his commanders. Word was secretly passed to Honeyman of the general's requirements, and Washington impatiently awaited news from his spy. When sufficient time had passed, orders were issued for the arrest of the Tory butcher. Washington carefully stipulated, however, that he was to be brought in alive.

Washington and Honeyman had established their arrangements for making contact the year before in Philadelphia, when the general had been named to lead the Continental Army. Honeyman, a Scotch-Irishman who had served in the British army at the capture of Quebec during the French and Indian War, had volunteered his services as a spy. He would adopt the cover of a Tory and, when he had important information, allow himself to be captured by American troops and hustled before the commander in chief for interrogation.

On December 22, Honeyman was ready to report. Trenton was vulnerable to a surprise attack: the Hessians had not prepared proper redoubts, and security was lax. Working his way close to the Delaware looking for a chance to be taken prisoner, he spotted two American cavalrymen who had dismounted to rest. To maintain his cover as a Tory butcher, Honeyman appropriated a cow from a nearby pasture and with much shouting and cracking of his whip drove her toward the troopers. They recognized him as the rogue being sought by General Washington and ambushed him. Honeyman pretended to fight vigorously for his freedom but conveniently slipped on some ice and was overpowered.

The scouts triumphantly brought their prize to headquarters, where they were rewarded for their good work. Washington ordered his office cleared so that he could question the prisoner in private. Alone with the general, Honeyman provided detailed information on the situation in Trenton that confirmed reports Washington had gathered from other sources. About a half-hour later, he was taken to the guardhouse to be tried by a court-martial the next morning. Not long after he had been locked up, a fire broke out in the camp, and the sentries left their post to help fight the blaze. When they returned, the prisoner was gone. No one seemed to know how he had escaped.

Honeyman made his way back across the partially frozen Delaware to report to Colonel Johann Rhall, the commander of the Hessians quartered at Trenton. Wet and exhausted, he told Rhall of his capture and escape. From his own observation, he assured the colonel, the American army was hopelessly disorganized and incapable of launching an attack. This report confirmed Rhall's low opinion of the enemy, and he saw no reason to alter the elaborate Christmas celebration planned by his men. Honeyman, having planted this bit of disinformation at the instruction of General Washington, left Rhall's quarters and quickly faded into the darkness.

Late on Christmas night, Washington recrossed the Delaware in a blinding snow storm to attack Trenton.* Within an hour after the attack was launched, it was all over. As Honeyman had reported, the Hessians were completely unprepared to resist. Many were sleeping off monumental hangovers. In the wake of this debacle, the British hastily evacuated Bordentown, Burlington, and Mount Holly, while Washington followed up his victory with a successful attack on Princeton. Thanks in no small part to the work of a spy, faith in the American cause was rekindled, some of the troops whose enlistments were up extended them, and the revolution was saved.

■ ■ ■

George Washington was America's first spymaster. Probably no American military commander since has surpassed him in the attention given to intelligence operations. From the outset Washington understood the need for wartime intelligence: within a few days of taking command of the troops besieging the British in Boston on July 2, 1775, he began building a network of spies. In fact, the first substantial expenditure entered in the account book he kept throughout the war (for $333.33) was for an agent "to go into the town of Boston to establish secret correspondence for the purpose of conveying intelligence of the Enemys movements and designs." Soon other secret agents were sent to join him. To protect these spies, Washington carefully refrained from naming them in case the record book fell into enemy hands.

Accurate intelligence was crucial to Washington because of a poverty of resources with which to battle the British. Unable to muster a large, well-trained army, he resorted to a strategy of surprise attacks and hit-and-run raids on British outposts, such as the Christmas night descent upon the unwary Hessians. Intelligence enabled him to perceive

---

*Few episodes are more familiar to Americans than Washington's crossing of the Delaware as memorialized in Emmanuel Leutze's nineteenth-century painting—a canvas filled with inaccuracies. Large, flat-bottomed freight boats pushed by men with poles were used rather than Leutze's rowboats. And had Washington been foolish enough to stand in a rowboat with a foot on the gunwale, it would have quickly capsized.

the strengths and weaknesses of both his own forces and those of the enemy. With this knowledge, he was able to mask his own weaknesses while exploiting those of his adversaries. "Everything, in a manner, depends upon obtaining intelligence," he observed. "Secrecy and dispatch may prove the soul of success. . . ."

Regarding the accumulation of accurate intelligence as one of his most important duties, Washington served as his own chief of intelligence throughout the war and showed a remarkable flair for the role. Spies, double agents, counterintelligence, covert operations, disinformation, propaganda, and codes and ciphers* were all part of his astonishingly contemporary tradecraft. He personally recruited agents, issued them instructions, and analyzed and acted upon their reports. Although this system added to his burdens as commander in chief, it made certain that—unlike later periods in the nation's history—intelligence received the prompt attention of those in authority.

Washington's early intelligence techniques were primitive, based mostly on the activities of daring, sometimes flamboyant amateurs. As the war continued, his methods became increasingly sophisticated. An examination of Washington's correspondence reveals that he was in almost daily contact with his intelligence officers and agents in the field. Networks of spies—or "chains"—were organized. Special emphasis was placed on the recruitment of "stay-behind" agents who remained in place in the enemy's rear after the Continental Army had been driven from an area. "The greatest benefits are to be derived from persons who live on the other side," Washington said on the basis of four years of war.

Many of Washington's instructions could have come from a modern chief of intelligence. Realizing that even the smallest shreds of information could form a mosaic when fitted together with other information, the general exhorted his commanders to overlook nothing. "Even minutiae should have a place in our collection, for things of a seemingly triffling nature when enjoined with others of a more serious cast may lead to valuable conclusions," he declared. His instructions to his secret agents were precise, and he insisted that their reports be swift and accurate. They were to obtain exact details on British military and naval movements, the location and condition of fortifications and bases, and, not least, the health and morale of enemy troops. The general demanded hard intelligence, not speculation: "I would not have you pay any attention to vague calculations that may be made by those of whom you inquire," he told Colonel Elias Dayton, one of his aides. "If only you can

---

*Although the words are used interchangeably by the uninitiated, codes and ciphers are different systems of secret writing. A code is a system of choosing words, numbers, or signs that directly substitute for plain language, whereas a cipher usually substitutes a number, letter, or sign for a single letter of the standard alphabet. In practice the two systems can, of course, be intertwined.

ascertain with certainty, the particular Regiments and Corps, we should be able to estimate their numbers better by that, than by any conjectures they can form."

Silence made Washington uneasy. If regular communication with an agent was interrupted, he quickly inquired into the situation and impressed upon his officers the need to keep information flowing. "It is now 3 days since I have received any intelligence," he wrote one of his generals. "This makes me the more uneasy as my movements depend altogether upon the indications you give me of those of the enemy. It is of such importance to me to be regularly informed that I must request you will send expresses daily, acquainting me precisely with the enemy's position and communicating such intelligence as you may collect from spies, deserters and &c."

Aware of the danger that reports could become garbled in transmission, the general preferred written to verbal reports. Some agents were supplied with a "sympathetic stain," or invisible ink, developed by Sir James Jay, a physician and elder brother of John Jay who was then living in London. When war seemed inevitable, Sir James sent his brother a supply of the ink and the counterpart used to develop it. Unlike lemon juice and milk, which were commonly used for secret writing, Jay's ink could not be made visible by being held up to a candle flame.

Washington kept a careful eye on the material turned in by each of his agents and made sure their reports were checked against those submitted by others. Sometimes he sent two spies to work in the same area without telling either of the other agent's presence. "If they have no knowledge of the business entrusted to each other the better chance would there be to come at the truth by comparing their Acts," he noted. Even though money was always in short supply, he made certain his agents received some reward. Still, the general was wary of those who took up espionage for the money. "The enemy," he observed wryly, "can purchase their fidelity at a higher price than we can."

■ ■ ■

Spying on adversaries was not, of course, Washington's invention. Espionage was an accepted fact of eighteenth-century warfare, and when discontent flared in the American colonies, both sides quickly resorted to the use of spies. The American cause was assisted by several secret societies, the best known being the Sons of Liberty, which had been formed in 1765 to oppose the Stamp Act. The organization served as an underground network that extended throughout the colonies and sometimes resorted to violence to emphasize resistance to British policy. On the other side, Loyalists kept the King's officers informed about the conspiracies undertaken by their neighbors.

Boston became the center of this twilight war because Britain's restrictive colonial policies threatened the town's commercial interests. The flashpoint occurred on June 1, 1774, when the British government ordered the Port of Boston closed until the townspeople paid for three shiploads of tea that had been dumped in the harbor in protest against a tax upon it. General Thomas Gage was appointed military governor of the colony, and the narrow streets echoed to the thumping of drums as the number of resident redcoats swelled until they equaled a third of the civilian population.

One of the most vigilant of the groups keeping an eye on the occupying forces was a band of about thirty townspeople headed by Paul Revere, a prominent silversmith. Every evening they met at the Green Dragon Tavern, and two or three men would slip away to patrol the streets, noting the number of troops as well as their movements and dispositions. Revere and his men also gathered information from hundreds of seamen who had been thrown out of work by the closing of the Port and who eagerly passed along gossip they picked up from British soldiers and sailors while loafing about the wharves. This information was passed on to John Hancock, head of the Committee of Public Safety that had been established by the Provincial Congress. Other members of the committee included such leading patriots as Samuel and John Adams, Dr. Joseph Warren, and a man we shall hear more of shortly, Dr. Benjamin Church.

Gage had his spies, too, both in Boston and in the surrounding countryside. There was even a leak in the Revere spy ring. "A Gentleman who had connections with the Tory party, but was a Whig at heart, acquainted me that our meetings were discovered," its leader wrote, "& mentioned the exact words spoken among us the night before." Alarmed, the conspirators abruptly abandoned the Green Dragon but found that their meetings were no more secure. Revere was convinced that there was a "Traytor" in the Provincial Congress.

Early in April 1775, Gage's network of informers reported that the Yankees had gathered a large stock of military supplies at Concord, twenty-one miles outside Boston. "A sudden blow struck now . . . would oversett all their plans," one spy observed. Troops were detached for a raid, with Gage masking his intentions by spreading rumors that they were being assigned to special training. But on April 16 Revere realized that something big was in the wind. The transports in the harbor had swung out their boats, and they bobbed in readiness astern of the vessels. A groom at British headquarters overheard some officers talking about Gage's plan to surprise the rebels and discussed it with a friend who pretended to be a supporter of the Crown. The following day, Revere rode to Concord with a warning of the British plans. He also stopped at Lexington to alert John Hancock and Samuel Adams, who were on their way to Philadelphia, where the Second Continental Congress was to convene.

Forewarned, the colonists hastily shifted their cache of weapons and powder to fresh hiding places in out-of-the-way barns and swamps. The task was accomplished so swiftly that General Gage's spies were unable to warn him of the changes before the troops left Boston. Meanwhile, word was passed to the local militiamen to keep their guns at hand and to be ready to turn out at a moment's notice. Before returning to Boston, Revere stopped in Charlestown to arrange a signal that the British had begun to move.* Noting that the steeple of Christ's Church—now known as the Old North Church—was clearly visible across the Charles River, he told a fellow conspirator that a single lantern would be shown if the British went by land over Boston Neck, two lanterns if they crossed the river.

Shortly after ten o'clock on the night of April 18, 1775, seven hundred British soldiers pushed off in longboats from the foot of Boston Common and rowed with muffled oars across the black waters of the Charles. The tide was in, and they were forced to wade ashore near Cambridge in water up to their chests. Early the next morning, tired and chilled, their feet sloshing in their boots, the troops were streaming along the road to Lexington and Concord—and the shot heard 'round the world.

■ ■ ■

Toward the end of September 1775, Brig. Gen. Nathanael Greene, commander of the Rhode Island troops in Washington's army, sought a private meeting with the commander in chief. Greene came to Washington's headquarters on Brattle Street in Cambridge with a civilian in tow. As soon as the general had dismissed his aides and they were alone behind closed doors, Greene introduced his companion, a prosperous baker named Godfrey Wenwood, who had brought a mysterious communication with him from his home in Newport.

Washington was puzzled by the document. He turned it this way and that but could make no sense of it. Addressed to an officer on General Gage's staff, it was written in unintelligible clusters of characters that were obviously intended as a cipher. Washington had little experience with "secret writing," but he was alarmed. The document smacked of treason.

Questioned about the origins of the document, Wenwood related with some embarrassment that about two months before a lady of easy

*Contrary to Henry Wadsworth Longfellow's poem, Revere was not waiting on the opposite shore for the signal when it came but was in Boston helping hang the lanterns. William Dawes was ordered by Dr. Joseph Warren to carry the news that the British were on the move, and he made his way out of town over Boston Neck. Later that night, Warren, fearing that Dawes might be captured, instructed Revere to alert the countryside as well. Revere crossed the Charles River in a small boat and galloped off to Lexington with a warning for Hancock and Adams. He was captured by the British before he reached Concord but was freed after being deprived of his horse.

virtue he had known in Boston had unexpectedly called upon him in Newport. The woman asked him to arrange a meeting with either Captain James Wallace, of the British frigate *Rose,* then prowling off Newport, or some well-known Loyalists. Surprised, the baker asked the purpose of the meeting. The woman told him that a friend in Cambridge had given her a letter to be turned over to one of these men so that it could be transmitted to Boston. Who was this friend? She declined to say. Fearing that he was being involved in a Tory plot, Wenwood stalled until the woman grew weary of the delay and left a sealed packet with him for future delivery.

The uneasy baker showed the mysterious packet to a friend named Maxwell, who unhesitatingly broke the seal. Wenwood's worst fears were confirmed. Inside was a letter in cipher addressed to "Major Cane in Boston on his magisty's sarvice." Instead of turning the message over to the colonial authorities for investigation, the frightened Wenwood said nothing. Several weeks later, he received a note from the woman asking why he had not forwarded the letter to Boston and giving an address in Cambridge where she could be reached. Shrewdly concluding that the cipher's author could not have known that the letter had failed to reach its destination unless he was in communication with Boston, Wenwood finally showed it to the Rhode Island authorities. Convinced that mischief was afoot, they lost no time in sending Wenwood to Cambridge with a letter to General Greene.

Upon hearing Wenwood's tale, Washington immediately ordered the arrest of the woman who had given him the letter. She was found at the address she had supplied Wenwood and was brought in for questioning that evening. The commander in chief conducted the interrogation himself. Stern-faced and standing six feet tall in his blue-and-buff uniform, he was an impressive figure certain to arouse fear in the heart of any conspirator. Who had given her the letter? he demanded. Why was it in cipher? What did it say?

Tears and protestations of innocence and ignorance followed. The woman was warned that she had been caught red-handed trying to send information to the enemy and that the penalty for spying was death. Still, as Washington later told John Hancock, now the president of the Continental Congress, "for a long time she was proof against every threat and persuasion." The inquisition continued throughout the night and into the next day. At last the woman broke down and revealed who had given her the letter: Dr. Benjamin Church.

Washington reacted as if he had been slapped in the face. Church not only was a member of the Provincial Congress but, as Director-General of Hospitals, was now the Continental Army's chief medical officer with an office just across the street from the commander in chief's own headquarters. Stunned and disbelieving, Washington nevertheless had Church summoned for questioning. Meanwhile, two officers with some experience in deciphering were found and put to work on the letter as Church underwent interrogation.

Church was affability itself. He readily acknowledged authorship of the letter and said his mistress had carried it to Newport for transmittal to his brother, Fleming Church, who was living in Boston. Why was it in cipher? Purely because personal matters were discussed. There was nothing sinister about sending messages into Boston, Church argued; letters were regularly being exchanged with persons inside British lines. Icily, Washington pointed out that it would have been easy enough to transmit a message about personal matters under a flag of truce. Sending a letter by way of Newport—and in cipher, at that—invited suspicion. Further, he noted, despite Church's vehement protestations of loyalty he had not volunteered to put the letter into plain language.

Washington's suspicions were substantiated on October 3, when the letter was deciphered. It contained an account of a recent visit by Church to Philadelphia, where Congress was in session. Church told his correspondent, with whom he appeared to be in regular contact, that the mood there was "united, determined in opposition." Estimates of the number, equipment, and readiness of the colonial forces were supplied, as well as details of plans to mobilize an army for the invasion of Canada. It was obvious that the writer realized the dangerous nature of the letter, for he implored the recipient to "make use of every precaution" to keep it from falling into the wrong hands, "or I perish."

Faced with this overwhelming evidence of his treachery, Church tried to bluff his way out of the hangman's noose. He now claimed that he had been in contact with the British only to assist the American cause. The estimates of Continental strength in his letter were purposely overstated, he said. The idea was to deter General Gage from launching an attack at a time when the supply of ammunition was so low that Washington had forbidden the firing of salutes out of fear they might touch off a bombardment by the British that could not be answered by his own artillery.* Rather than being guilty of treason, Church argued glibly, he had really been furthering the American cause. Washington was not amused. Church was ordered held for a court-martial on charges of having criminal communication with the enemy.

Little time was lost in determining Church's guilt, and it was expected that he would be hanged as a spy. Much to Washington's chagrin, it was discovered that in drafting the Continental Army's regulations, Congress had overlooked the possibility of espionage. The stiffest penalty

*Pickets guarding the roads outside Boston were often issued pikes and spears instead of muskets because of the shortage of arms and powder. Benjamin Franklin suggested that the troops be armed with bows and arrows, reasoning that a man could shoot four arrows in the time it took to load and fire a musket just once.

that could be ordered by a court-martial was thirty-nine lashes and dismissal from the service. Eventually Congress closed this loophole by approving the death penalty for spying—but too late for the penalty to be applied to Church.*

Thinking it inconceivable that this blatant rascal should escape his deserved punishment, Washington turned Church over to the Provincial Congress so that it could deal with its treacherous member. Church was expelled from the Congress and jailed until a decision could be made about what to do with him. Following his arrest, people began to recall suspicious conduct on his part they had previously ignored, including the fact that he seemed to have come into a large sum of money shortly after the Battle of Lexington. When the British offered to give up several American officers they were holding in exchange for Church, they only convinced his captors that he was too dangerous to be freed. The Americans did not relent until mid-1777, when Church was ordered to leave the country and never return. Whatever reward was due him from the British went uncollected, for the ship carrying him to the West Indies went down in a storm with all on board.

The full extent of Church's betrayal was not discovered until Gage's papers were opened a century and a quarter later. They revealed that the doctor had been supplying the British with inside information on American political secrets and preparations for resistance since 1774, and perhaps even earlier. Like many others before and since, Church claimed to have acted out of unselfish motives—"the salvation of his country." But there is no mistaking the meaning of a sentence in one of his secret reports to General Gage: "The 25th of the month finishes a quarter." It was a plain reminder that, in keeping with the custom of the time, three months' wages were due.

■ ■ ■

Early in 1776, following months of frustration, Washington obtained the weapons he needed to drive the British from Boston: fifty-nine cannon captured at Fort Ticonderoga on Lake Champlain arrived in Cambridge after being dragged overland on sledges. The elated commander in chief ordered them mounted on Dorchester Heights, which dominated the town and its harbor. For three nights, beginning on March 2, 1776, the Americans shelled Boston to draw British attention away from their efforts to fortify the heights. Duped by the bombardment, the British paid

---

*Congress appointed a five-member Committee on Spies, which included John Adams and Thomas Jefferson, to "consider what is proper to be done with persons giving intelligence to the enemy or supplying them with provisions." The committee produced the nation's first Espionage Act, which established the death penalty for spying. It was enacted on August 21, 1776.

no attention to the work of entrenchment until it was too late. Looking into the muzzles of the massed batteries, General Sir William Howe, the new British commander, decided that his only choice was to abandon the town. On March 17—St. Patrick's Day—the last of Howe's troops and about a thousand dejected Loyalists boarded ship and sailed away to Halifax, in Nova Scotia.

Washington did not remain in Boston to celebrate his triumph. Expecting the British to strike next at New York City, he immediately marched south with the bulk of his army. Political considerations played as much a part as military ones in this decision to defend New York. A sizable proportion of the city's citizenry harbored Tory sympathies, particularly the well-to-do, and the city teetered on the fence between adherence to the Crown and independence. Manhattan could not be defended against a large army supported by a fleet that could land troops anywhere at will, but Congress insisted that the attempt be made in hopes of stirring support for the American cause.

Anxiously anticipating the appearance of the British, Washington built forts on both sides of the Hudson and on Brooklyn Heights, across the East River, to prevent the enemy from enveloping his exposed flanks on Manhattan. To add to his worries, plots against his safety and that of his army flourished. William Tryon, the deposed royal governor, directed conspiracies from a British man-of-war lying offshore. Guerrilla bands were being raised on Long Island and in the countryside to the north of the city, and "fifth columnists" moved about freely. In May 1776, British spies obtained a report containing a full description of the American defenses and a detailed account of every battery.

The most sinister plot came to light a month later, when a man awaiting trial on counterfeiting charges tried to bargain his way out of jail by informing on his fellow prisoners. He told the authorities that two soldiers who had been arrested for passing counterfeit money had tried to enlist him in a Tory legion being formed by Governor Tryon and David Matthews, the Loyalist mayor of New York. The men were identified as Sergeant Thomas Hickey and Private Michael Lynch, both members of General Washington's own guard. Other sources provided confirmation of this alarming report, and additional members of Washington's guard were taken into custody.

Rumors of plots to murder or kidnap the commander in chief buzzed about New York. Washington, it was said, had declined a dish of peas, of which he was fond—and when his housekeeper scattered them to the chickens, they all died. Other tales had it that Washington was to have been kidnapped by a band led by Hickey and turned over to the British for punishment as a traitor or that Hickey was supposed to stab the general when the British invaders arrived. Each day the rumors grew wilder. The

Tories were planning a mass uprising. The powder magazine was to be blown up. The arsenal was to be looted and the Continental Army attacked from the rear with its own artillery.

Washington ordered a court-martial for Hickey and "others," but no one besides Hickey was brought to trial. The "others" may have saved themselves by providing evidence against the sergeant. Though he was charged with "exciting and joining in a mutiny and sedition," no testimony was produced regarding plots to assassinate or kidnap Washington. Perhaps the general thought it better not to alarm the already nervous population of New York. Witnesses did testify that Mayor Matthews had put up a hundred pounds to bankroll the recruitment of men for the Tory legion and that Hickey had promised money to prospective recruits. In his defense, Hickey claimed he had gone along with the plot merely to defraud the Tories of their money. The court-martial wasted little time in ordering him hanged.

Washington used the execution of Thomas Hickey as an opportunity to press home the moral lesson to the army. Promptly at eleven o'clock on the morning of June 28, 1776, the mournful beat of drums was heard and the condemned man was marched across Chatham Square to an open field off the Bowery Lane. The insignia of his rank had been ripped from his right shoulder, and his uniform coat, its buttons slashed off, flapped open. With a sullen smile on his face, Hickey mounted the gallows. A noose was draped over his neck, a blindfold was adjusted about his eyes, and he was abruptly turned off into thin air. The body dropped to the end of the rope, jolted upward, and swung in a dreadful little arc in the sunshine, a gruesome reminder of the perils of treason.

2

Spies Who Went Out Into the Cold

Outside the entrance to the Central Intelligence Agency, in the rolling Virginia countryside near Washington, D.C., stands a bronze, life-sized statue of Nathan Hale. A duplicate of a memorial at Yale, Hale's alma mater, it portrays the martyred Revolutionary War spy with his arms pinioned, courageously awaiting execution at the hands of his British captors. Although the statue is obviously intended to remind today's spies of their predecessor's patriotism and readiness to sacrifice himself, Hale is hardly the model of a successful secret agent.

Probably no mission in the history of American espionage was more amateurishly conceived and carried out than Hale's attempt to determine British strength on Long Island. The young officer was completely without experience in intelligence. He had no training, no contacts behind British lines, no cipher or code to hide any information he might be able to gather, and no means of communicating it to his superiors except in person. This meant he had to make and carry notes that would instantly condemn him to death as a spy if he was caught. Further, Hale had an openness that made him particularly ill-suited for clandestine operations. Only a commander desperate for intelligence could have sent such a poorly prepared secret agent into the field.

The return of the British to New York placed George Washington in just such a predicament. On June 29, 1776, the day after the execution of Thomas Hickey, lookouts stationed at Sandy Hook sighted a cloud of sails coming up over the horizon. Within a few days, thirty-five thousand British troops, many of them German mercenaries, had been put ashore on Staten Island. The assemblage was the largest British expeditionary force of the eighteenth century—and nearly double the size of Washington's own army. Yet, to Washington's surprise, Sir William Howe, the

British commander, did not immediately try to drive the Continental Army from the city. He seemed more interested in drinking, gambling, and making love to his blonde mistress, Mrs. Joshua Loring.

Late in August, after two months of delay, Howe finally leapfrogged from Staten Island to the beaches of Gravesend Bay on Long Island. Working with information supplied by a spy who knew the back roads, he outflanked the Americans and inflicted heavy losses as he drove them back upon Brooklyn Heights, across the East River from Manhattan. Washington could not afford to wait for what could be a crushing blow. On the night of August 29, under cover of darkness and fog, the remainder of his troops—some 9,000 men—withdrew across the river in small boats. The British awoke the next morning to find the Americans gone.

Although Washington had extricated his army, the British were certain to strike again. Completely in command of the waters about New York City, they could land anywhere from the tip of Manhattan to Westchester, where they could seal off the only escape route from the island. Frantic over the need for intelligence, Washington peppered his commanders with demands for information. "Leave no stone unturned, nor stick at expense," he declared, "as I was never more uneasy than on account of my want of knowledge." Disturbed by the conflicting information that did reach him, he decided to risk sending a spy into the British lines on Long Island to fathom the enemy's intentions.

No one could be ordered to undertake such a hazardous mission, so Washington asked Lt. Col. Thomas Knowlton, commander of an elite unit known as Knowlton's Rangers, to secure a volunteer. On September 10 Knowlton called a meeting of officers, told them of Washington's need for accurate intelligence, and asked for a volunteer. This service was not only out of the usual line of duty, he cautioned, but dangerous in the extreme. If caught, the spy would certainly be hanged. When he had finished, Knowlton looked about the room. The faces of his officers were impassive, Lieutenant James Sprague, a veteran of the French and Indian War, summed up their feelings. "I am willing to go and fight them," he declared, "but as far as going among them and being taken and hung up like a dog, I will not do it." Finally Nathan Hale, a twenty-one-year-old captain who had only recently joined the Rangers, volunteered for the mission.

■ ■ ■

Nathan Hale is the prototype of a relatively modern phenomenon— the "patriot spy." Historically, spying was considered a dirty business, and most spies worked either for adventure or for personal gain. Now men and women to whom spying was personally repugnant accepted the task because their country's needs outweighed their own reluctance to engage in such activities. They were, in effect, among history's first ideological spies.

Hale was hardly the type of person usually associated with espionage. A native of Coventry, Connecticut, he was a member of a family prominent in the affairs of the colony. Handsome, intelligent, and athletic, he was popular at Yale College, where he had enrolled with the intention of becoming a teacher of Latin. Among his friends and classmates was Benjamin Tallmadge, who was to play a key role in General Washington's intelligence operations. Following his graduation in 1773, Hale became a schoolmaster, first in East Haddam, Connecticut, and then in New London. When news of the fighting around Boston reached the town, he immediately enrolled in a local regiment and was made a lieutenant. In his first taste of action, Hale distinguished himself by seizing a small vessel loaded with supplies from under the guns of a British warship. His resourcefulness brought him promotion and an invitation from Colonel Knowlton to join the Rangers.

After agreeing to undertake the mission, Hale visited a Yale classmate and friend, Captain William Hull, who was stationed nearby with his old regiment. Surprised by Hale's decision, Hull tried to persuade him to change his mind, but the young man was adamant. Years later, Hull put down his recollections of that conversation. Hale told him that "he owed to his country the accomplishment of an object so important, and so much desired by the Commander of her armies, and he knew of no other mode of obtaining the information, than by assuming a disguise and passing into the enemy's camp."

On September 12, Hale left the camp at Harlem Heights,* accompanied by Sergeant Stephen Hempstead, an old friend. The two men proceeded along the northern shore of Long Island Sound, looking for a vessel to carry them across to Long Island. They found a suitable craft— the privateer *Schuyler*—at Norwalk. A few nights later, hidden by an overcast that hung over the dark waters of the Sound, the sloop eased into Huntington Bay. Having decided to disguise himself as a Tory schoolmaster looking for work—he was carrying his Yale diploma to serve as his credentials—Hale changed into a brown civilian suit and a round, flat-brimmed hat before going ashore. Hempstead wanted to accompany his friend into enemy territory, but Hale instructed him to return to Norwalk, wait a few days, and then send a boat back to Long Island to pick him up. With that, he disappeared into the darkness.

■ ■ ■

"A spy from the enemy by his own full confession, apprehended last night, was executed [this] day at 11 o'clock in front of the Artillery Park."

---

*At about the present site of 127th Street.

These laconic words, entered in General Howe's orderly book on September 22, 1776, are the only official comment on the tragic end of Nathan Hale's mission. No surviving letter, no personal diary, no court-martial record provides an account of his movements from the time he landed on Long Island until his capture, so we can only try to reconstruct them.

Had Hale been a less conscientious spy, he might have turned back for the reason for his mission disappeared even before it was well underway. On September 15, the British landed on Manhattan at Kip's Bay, and the panicked Yankee troops fled for their lives. Having been driven from all but the upper reaches of Manhattan, General Washington no longer had a pressing need for information about enemy movements on Long Island, so Hale could have recrossed the Sound to safety without criticism. On his own initiative, however, he went into New York City to gather intelligence on British troop dispositions and fortifications. There he was arrested on September 21; following a search, his incriminating notes were discovered. Hale was either betrayed by a Tory cousin who recognized him, or he was captured while trying to make his way to the American lines on Harlem Heights or on the shore of the East River while awaiting a boat to take him away.

Hale was brought to British Army headquarters in the Beekman mansion,* where he was interrogated by General Howe. He gave his name and rank and readily admitted his mission. Having ascertained that the prisoner was an American officer out of uniform, Howe ordered him hanged the next morning. Hale was placed in the custody of William Cunningham, a Loyalist refugee who served as provost marshal, and was held overnight in the greenhouse of the Beekman mansion. The following morning, he was taken to an artillery park in an apple orchard and hanged.†

That evening, Captain John Montresor, the British Army's chief engineer, carried a flag of truce into the American lines on other business and in passing told Captain Alexander Hamilton of the execution of a spy named Hale earlier that day. Knowing of William Hull's friendship with Hale, Hamilton passed on the sad news. Hull was stunned at the death of his friend and obtained permission from Washington to seek out Captain Montresor. In his memoirs, Hull set out an account of Hale's final moments, which he learned from the British officer.

Hale was brought to the artillery park shortly before 11 A.M. The day was already hot, so Montresor, pitying the young man who was about to die, asked Cunningham to allow him to await the execution in his nearby

---

*Near what is now the intersection of First Avenue and Fifty-ninth Street.

†The orchard was located near the present intersection of Third Avenue and Sixty-sixth Street. The plaque on the Yale Club near Grand Central Station marking the site of Hale's execution is off by twenty blocks.

tent. "Captain Hale entered; he was calm, and bore himself with gentle dignity, in the consciousness of rectitude and high intentions. He asked for writing materials, which I furnished him: he wrote two letters, one to his mother and another to a brother officer. He was shortly after summoned to the gallows. But a few persons were around him, yet his characteristic dying words were remembered. He said 'I only regret that I have but one life to lose for my country.'"*

■ ■ ■

Nathan Hale's useless sacrifice convinced Washington of the need for an organized intelligence system. Over the next several months, the general established the first real spy networks of the war. Not even the most effective and speedy intelligence could compensate for the weakness of the Continental Army, but on several occasions the alertness of Washington's secret agents saved the army from surprise and annihilation. The vital role of spies such as John Honeyman in the victories at Trenton and Princeton is clear evidence of the improvement in the quality of Washington's intelligence.

This is not to say that Washington's spies were professionals. Most of them were ordinary folk who volunteered their services. Some were farmers and hucksters who sold provisions and other goods to the British; a handful were gentry who mingled easily with British officers. Few clues exist to their identities: a surviving letter here, a local legend there, an old soldier's pension claim. For the most part, their only reward was the knowledge that they had made significant contributions to the eventual American victory.

Among those who gathered information for General Washington were the Darraghs, a family of respectable Philadelphia Quakers whose home on Second Street had been requisitioned by the British for General Howe's staff. Since most Quakers took no part in the war, Howe's officers saw no danger in talking freely before the family. The Darraghs, however, were deeply committed to the American cause. William Darragh secretly transcribed whatever information the family gleaned from these conversations in shorthand on bits of paper. His wife, Lydia, concealed the scraps of paper in large, cloth-covered buttons, commonly worn in those days, and sewed the buttons onto the coat of their fourteen-year-old son, John. This youthful secret agent then slipped out of town and made his way to the American camp at Whitemarsh, where he sought out his older brother, Charles, a lieutenant in the American army. Charles, who knew shorthand, transcribed his father's notes and delivered the intelligence to General Washington.

*These words are similar to a line from Joseph Addison's play *Cato,* which was well known to educated Americans: "What a pity is it / That we can die but once to serve our country!"

On the evening of December 2, 1777, the British held a staff meeting at the house and ordered the Darraghs to go to bed to prevent them from overhearing the discussions. For Lydia Darragh, the order was an invitation to eavesdrop. Hidden in a closet in an adjoining room with her ear pressed against the thin wall, she learned that Howe was planning a surprise attack on Washington's army two nights later. When the scraping of chairs being pulled back indicated the end of the meeting, she hurried to her bed. The officer who summoned the lady of the house to lock up found that he had to knock loudly on her door to awaken her from her sound sleep.

With the surprise attack due in less than forty-eight hours, the Darraghs worried about how to transmit the vital information to General Washington. There was no time for their usual method of sending secret messages, and with the British on the alert William Darragh stood little chance of getting out of Philadelphia. Courageously, Lydia decided to carry the message herself. Early the next morning, empty flour sack in hand, she made her way past the sentries by telling them that she was going to the Frankford mill to obtain flour. Once through the British perimeter, she headed for the nearby Rising Sun Tavern, which was used by the Americans as a listening post.

When Lydia Darragh's message reached Washington, it confirmed earlier reports that the British were planning some sort of troop movement. As so often is the case in intelligence, bits and pieces of information had to be gathered and sorted out before an accurate picture of enemy intentions could be assembled. Forewarned by these reports, the Continental Army was on the alert when Howe launched his "surprise" attack. Thwarted, the British marched back to Philadelphia—"like a parcel of damned fools," said one officer. Considering the fragile state of the American army, had the attack succeeded it might have meant the end of the war.

■ ■ ■

The Darraghs' work confirmed the value of Washington's efforts to gather information from as many sources as he could. But, as Washington had reason to know, the importance of trustworthy intelligence soon leads to further complications in the murky war-within-the-war of spy and counterspy. One complication is the need for vigilant counterintelligence: active measures to protect one's own secrets and ferret out the spies and traitors who would betray them to the enemy. A second is the more creative possibility of turning the tables on one's adversary by using deception to feed him *in*accurate intelligence. While the word "disinformation" might be a modern invention, the practice itself is not—and Washington made masterful use of it to confound the British.

One of the most effective cases occurred during the winter of 1777. The Continental Army, which had gone into winter quarters in Morristown, New Jersey, had dwindled to some 4,000 men, fewer than the British detachment at Amboy, only a few miles away. To prevent Tories from discovering his weakness and passing the news on to General Howe, Washington billeted his men by twos and threes in a number of houses in the surrounding countryside, making his army appear much larger than it was. Presently, a merchant arrived in camp loudly complaining of having been mistreated by the British. The Americans had been warned by their own agents that he was a spy sent to obtain an accurate estimate of Washington's strength. Some officers wanted to summarily arrest him, but the wily commander in chief sensed a heaven-sent opportunity to fool the enemy.

Every brigadier was told to prepare grossly inflated reports of the strength of his unit, all of which were forwarded to a staff officer who had purposely become friendly with the "merchant" and shared quarters with him. The two men were having supper together when the officer was called away at Washington's orders, leaving the brigadiers' reports on his desk. When he returned, the spy was gone. Back in New York, Howe's spy provided the British commander with the stolen information that placed the Continental Army's force at triple its actual strength. Colonel Elias Boudinot, who had helped stage the affair, said it convinced the British commander "that we were too strong to attack & saved us thro' the Winter." In fact, Howe was so convinced of the accuracy of his intelligence that when an escaped British prisoner provided him with the correct figures, he refused to believe them.

■ ■ ■

In the spring of 1778, the war took a new turn. Leaving his plump mistress and his misfortunes behind, Sir William Howe returned to England to try to explain why he had so utterly failed to suppress the rebellion. General Sir Henry Clinton, his successor as British commander in America, wasted no time in abandoning Philadelphia and consolidating his forces in New York City. This move marked a complete change in strategy. The British now concentrated on naval operations against the French, who had entered the war on the side of the Americans, and on operations in the Carolinas, where Loyalist sentiment was strong.

As both armies concentrated about New York, the city and the surrounding area became a focus of intrigue. Like Bern in World War II and Bangkok during the Vietnamese conflict, New York became the stage for an undercover war that never ceased. Spies and counterintelligence agents fought a silent struggle in the coffeehouses and taverns, in British headquarters, at the ferries leading in and out of town, and in the lawless "neutral ground" between the armies. Bribery, subversion, and treachery were the weapons of this war—and the penalty for failure was sudden death.

Washington, who transferred his headquarters to White Plains, in Westchester, needed complete and regular reports from New York and Long Island more than ever, but the channels that had previously supplied information were silent. Reports brought in by cavalry patrols and picked up from refugees and deserters was sketchy and uncertain. Spies, disguised as black-market traders, were sent into the city, but the quality of the intelligence obtained was disappointing.

Fortunately, Washington now obtained the services of young Major Benjamin Tallmadge to take over the management of espionage activities. During his long life—he lived until 1835—the taciturn Tallmadge rarely mentioned his career as chief of Washington's spies. In one of his rare public comments he stated tersely, "That year [1778] I opened a private correspondence with some persons in New York." In point of fact, he organized the most successful American spy network of the Revolution. Operating under the noses of the British, Tallmadge's agents—known as the "Culper Ring"—provided General Washington with abundant, accurate, and detailed information from New York City and Long Island for the rest of the war.

Tallmadge's most valuable asset was an intimate knowledge of the people and of the area in which he conducted operations. The 24-year-old officer was a member of a leading Long Island family whose father had been minister of the Presbyterian church at Setauket, on the north shore. As a boy, Tallmadge had fished and sailed in the secluded inlets and hidden harbors that honeycombed the district and that were later to become havens for his secret agents. At Yale, he and Nathan Hale had been close friends. Like Hale, Tallmadge taught school after graduation and abandoned teaching for the army at the outbreak of the war.

Tallmadge proved a brave soldier, and in April 1777 he was promoted to major in the Second Dragoons. An elite unit, the regiment was mounted on matched dapple-gray horses, officers and troopers alike wearing helmets topped by waving horse-tail plumes. Impressed by the young officer's daring and the accuracy of his reports during the Philadelphia campaign, Washington detailed him to intelligence. Unlike Hale, who became a spy from patriotic motives, Tallmadge had reason to hate the British. Not only had they summarily hanged his best friend, but his brother, William, had died of mistreatment after being taken prisoner. Further, British troops had used his father's church as a stable for their horses and had forced the old man to flee to Connecticut because of his outspoken support of the American cause.

Tallmadge forged a spy chain that cut across class and social lines. Late in August 1778, he ventured over to Long Island from his headquarters at Fairfield, probably in a small boat, with Caleb Brewster, an old Setauket neighbor. Brewster, a big, swashbuckling ex-whaler, specialized in harassing British shipping in the Sound and gathering information on the enemy's movements. The first agent Tallmadge recruited, Abraham Woodhull, was another former neighbor and a member of a well-to-do Setauket family that had suffered at the hands of the British. Four years older than Tallmadge, he had recently resigned a commission in the militia to help his aged parents run their farm. Woodhull hardly fitted the popular image of a cloak-and-dagger operative: timid and something of a hypochondriac, he was sent into paroxysms of fear by an unexpected challenge or a sharp glance from a stranger.

Returning to headquarters, Tallmadge submitted his plan for a spy network to the commander in chief for approval. Woodhull was to go in and out of New York City to gather intelligence that would be transmitted to Brewster, who would then carry it across the Sound to Tallmadge in one of his armed whaleboats. The major, who kept a squadron of dragoons on the alert for such missions, would then send the information to Washington. Tallmadge suggested a face-to-face meeting with Woodhull so the general could take his measure, but Washington declined on security grounds: "You should be perfectly convinced of the Integrity of _____ previous to his imbarking in the business proposed—this being done I shall be happy in employing him—but there will be an impropriety in his coming with you to head Quarters, as a knowledge of the circumstances in the enemy might blast the whole design."

To protect Woodhull, it was agreed that he would henceforth be known in all correspondence as "Samuel Culper," while Tallmadge would assume the identity of "John Bolton." Only Washington and Tallmadge were to know Culper's true identity and to have access to his reports. The general's other aides knew only that he had a shadowy "confidential correspondent" in New York who provided him with vital intelligence.

By early 1779 Washington had become so dependent upon Culper's reports that he suggested the spy permanently establish himself in New York. Since "all great movements, and the fountain of all intelligence must originate at, and proceed from the head Quarters of the enemy's army," the general wrote Tallmadge, Culper "had better reside at New York, mix with, and put on the airs of a Tory to cover his real character and avoid suspicion." He was to pay particular attention to movements of the British fleet, the placement of troops, the arrival of reinforcements, and the morale of the garrison. Washington enclosed fifty guineas for expenses, along with "an earnest exhortation to use them with all possible economy, as I find it very difficult to obtain hard money."

■ ■ ■

Within a few weeks, Abraham Woodhull was installed at a boarding house operated by his sister and her husband, Amos Underhill, on Queen Street, only a few blocks from General Clinton's headquarters on Broadway. Most of the other guests were British officers, but they paid little attention to the self-effacing Tory refugee who occupied a tiny room at the top of the house. Woodhull's best defense was his bland anonymity. Throughout his service as a spy, he lived in perpetual dread of discovery: "I am perfectly acquainted with a full year's anxiety, which no one can scarcely have any idea but those that experience" it, he wrote Tallmadge on one occasion. "Not long since there was not the breadth of your finger betwixt me and death. . . ."

Yet every morning he went out into the narrow, bustling streets of New York, to visit the market places, tarry at the coffeehouses with the hope of eavesdropping on unwary British officers, inspect encampments and fortifications. When he had seen enough, he returned to his room to write lengthy letters to "John Bolton." Hidden between the lines of these letters were secret messages written in the "sympathetic stain," or invisible ink, invented by Sir James Jay and supplied to Woodhull by Tallmadge.

One night, while Woodhull was at work in his room on a secret dispatch, the door suddenly burst open. Startled, he sprang to his feet, upsetting the precious vial of invisible ink. Woodhull was so terrified that he was about to be arrested that it took him several moments to absorb the identity of his visitors: two women who also lived in the house and who playfully had wished to surprise him. "Such excessive fright and so great a turbulance of passions so wrought on poor Mr. C. that he has hardly been in tolerable health since," Tallmadge reported to General Washington in explaining a lapse in communication with the secret agent.

The terror-stricken Woodhull soon became convinced that he had become "a suspected person" and begged to be allowed to leave New York. He recruited "an intimate friend" to take his place—Robert Townsend, a Quaker dry-goods merchant from Oyster Bay. Townsend was in a good position to be a spy, because a merchant could travel freely about Manhattan and Long Island on business without attracting attention. His opportunities for espionage were enhanced by a second career as a gatherer of gossip for the *Royal Gazette,* a newspaper published by a notorious Tory named James Rivington. General Washington accepted this new agent—designated "Samuel Culper, Jr."—and Woodhull, undoubtedly with a deep sigh of relief, returned to Setauket to serve as a link between his successor and Major Tallmadge.

Unlike Woodhull, who clung to the shadows, Townsend affected the style of a lively young man about town despite his Quaker background. He frequented the taverns and the Theatre Royal on John Street and made his headquarters at the coffeehouse operated by Rivington near the *Gazette's* offices, a place popular with British officers and Loyalist hangers-on. The debonair Major John André, deputy adjutant general of the British army in America and Sir Henry Clinton's chief spymaster, sometimes shared a bottle of old Madeira with him.* Townsend was Rivington's silent partner in the coffeehouse, although it is doubtful that the Tory printer ever knew his true loyalties.

And vice versa: unknown to Townsend, James Rivington was himself one of George Washington's secret agents. The *Gazette* provided excellent cover, for it was a violently pro-Tory publication whose editor poked fun at the American cause and its leaders. After the French alliance, Rivington had had a change of heart. Motivated perhaps by financial reverses, or perhaps by a well-honed survivor's instinct that told him the war was going against the British, he secretly began supplying Washington with intelligence. Rivington communicated his information by binding messages written on tissue paper in the covers of books sent to the general. In 1781, he succeeded in stealing a copy of the Royal Navy's signal book, which was turned over to the Comte de Grasse, commander of the French fleet, when the fleet arrived off Yorktown.†

Sometimes Culpers ran out of invisible ink, so Tallmadge prepared a comprehensive code for the use of his agents. The words most likely to be needed were selected from the widely circulated *Entick's Dictionary* and given corresponding numbers. For example, 73 meant camp; 178, enemy; 286, ink; 585, refugees; 592, ships. Washington was 711, Tallmadge, 721. Culper, Sr., was designated 72; Culper, Jr., 723; Rivington, 726; New York, 727; Setauket, 729. An unidentified female spy was codenamed 355. Words and phrases not included in the code were accommodated by a cipher of the substitution type in which one letter stood for another.‡

Townsend's reports were carried out of New York City by Austin Roe, another Tallmadge friend from Setauket, who operated a tavern in the village. Posing as a deliveryman for Townsend's dry-goods business, Roe

---

*André's actual rank was captain; he was an acting major.

†Although Rivington's services to the American cause remained secret, he was allowed to stay in New York after independence was won in 1783. With his pro-Tory reputation, this could not have been permitted unless someone in authority—perhaps Washington himself—gave silent approval. There is a story, perhaps apocryphal, that when Washington arrived in New York after the British evacuation, he visited Rivington and gave him two heavy purses of gold.

‡Tallmadge's substitution code was as follows:

```
a b c d e f g h i j k l m n o p q r s t u v w x y z
e f g h i j a b c d o m n p q r k l u v w x y z s t
```

There is a copy of his number code in the George Washington Papers in the Library of Congress.

was permitted to travel freely between Long Island and New York. The British even allowed him to stable remounts along the fifty-five-mile route—horses purchased with funds supplied by General Washington. When he had a message for the commander in chief, Townsend wrote it in invisible ink on a blank sheet of paper and, counting down a prearranged number of sheets, slipped it into a ream of similar paper that was disguised as a parcel being delivered by Roe.

Upon his arrival in Setauket, Roe proceeded to a pasture he rented from Abraham Woodhull, where he had hidden a small wooden box. There he placed Townsend's report in the box to be picked up by Woodhull as he passed that way. After retrieving the message, Woodhull strolled over to nearby Strong's Neck to chat with Anna Strong. Shortly afterward, she hung out her wash. If it included a black petticoat and several handkerchiefs, Caleb Brewster, who was usually lying offshore in one of his whaleboats, came in and picked up Woodhull's message. The number of handkerchiefs indicated the inlet where they were to meet. Brewster then carried the communication across the Sound to Major Tallmadge, who developed the invisible ink to see if there was any information intended for him and then passed the message to a waiting dragoon to be carried with all speed to the commander in chief.

Washington consistently sought a speedier line of communication with the Culpers but was unable to develop one. In June 1779, delays resulting from the circuitous route almost led to the detection of the ring. Townsend had dispatched a warning to Washington that the British were planning a surprise attack on American positions in Connecticut, but it arrived too late. The British captured most of Tallmadge's personal baggage as well as confidential papers that Washington had instructed him to send to the Culpers. One mentioned "S_____ C_____" and his successor "C_____," providing the British with evidence of the existence of a spy ring within their camp. Fortunately for the Culpers, they failed to follow it up.*

■ ■ ■

Much of the intelligence supplied by the Culper Ring* was routine, but a steady stream of accurate information was a vital factor in Washington's operational planning. The single most important achievement of the network was the thwarting of a British attack upon a newly arrived

---

*Washington used the incident to impress upon Tallmadge the need for tighter security. "The loss of your papers . . . shows how dangerous it is to keep papers of any consequence at an advanced post," he wrote. "I beg you will take care to guard against the like in the future."

*Washington had other spies in New York who apparently were unconnected to the Culper Ring. Among them were Hercules Mulligan, a fashionable tailor, and Hyam Solomon, a Polish-born financier.

French army as it disembarked from its transports at Newport in July 1780—a crucial operation, because British destruction of the first French expeditionary force sent to America would have had untold consequences for the course of the war.

From sources within British headquarters, Townsend learned that General Clinton intended to pounce upon the French before they could organize their defenses. Ten British warships had sailed for Newport, and some eight thousand men were being loaded on the transports at that very moment. How was he to get this vital information to Washington? With a major operation underway, the British were keeping a close watch on all the roads and ferries out of town. The usual procedure of secreting a message among parcels to be delivered by Austin Roe was too slow; a single package would invite suspicion. Townsend's solution was to write a business letter that appeared to be intended for a well-known Long Island Tory, with a secret message inscribed on the back in invisible ink.

By nightfall, Townsend's message was on its way across the Sound to Washington's headquarters. The commander in chief was away on an inspection trip, but Captain Alexander Hamilton, one of his aides, knew the secret of the "sympathetic stain." After developing Townsend's message, he rushed a warning to the Comte de Rochambeau, the French commander. Upon his return, Washington assessed the situation. Unfortunately, he did not have enough men either to strike the weakened garrison in New York or to interfere with the British force before it reached Newport. But what if Clinton could be convinced that an attack upon New York was imminent? Lacking the resources to fight, Washington seized on the one weapon he had—disinformation.

"Secret" documents soon fell into British hands purporting to show that the Americans were planning to sweep down upon New York from the Hudson highlands. Alarmed, Clinton scrambled back to the city to protect his base of operations. Not long afterward, he wrote officials at home to explain why he had failed to attack the French at Newport. "During this time," he reported, "Washington, by a rapid movement, had with an army increased to 12,000 men, passed the North-river, and was moving toward Kingsbridge. . . ." For his part, the normally reserved General Washington warmly expressed his gratitude to Major Tallmadge for the services of his New York spies: "I am engaging in behalf of the United States a liberal reward for the services of the C_____s (of whose fidelity and ability I entertain a high opinion)."

Not every American agent fared so well, however. One member of the Culper Ring—the woman known only as 355—was caught and is thought to have died while in captivity. Abraham Woodhull, who had recruited the woman, told Tallmadge that she was "one who hath been ever serviceable to this correspondence." While working with Townsend, 355 became his mistress as well as his spy, but nothing is known of her identity. Possibly she was a member of a high-ranking Tory family with access to British headquarters and the secrets of Major André, who enjoyed the company of pretty women.

The only thing known for certain is that she was arrested in October 1780, shortly after the defection of Benedict Arnold to the British— possibly on the basis of information supplied by the traitor. Pregnant with Townsend's child, she is believed to have been held on the notorious prison ship *Jersey*, which lay grounded on a mud bank off Brooklyn. For all practical purposes, confinement on the *Jersey* was a sentence of death; substantial numbers of the prisoners held on the old hulk did not survive long. The grief-stricken Townsend, who expected his own arrest to occur momentarily, never saw her again. The secret of the Culper Ring had been guarded well, however, and none of its chief operatives were snared. Not long after her arrest, 355 died, apparently in giving birth to a son. The boy survived and was christened Robert Townsend, Jr.

■ ■ ■

When Major André took up his post as Sir Henry Clinton's spymaster, he made a list of the American military leaders most likely to switch sides if offered the right price in honors or hard cash. Paradoxically, the name of Benedict Arnold was not among them. Rated by the British as one of the Continental Army's best combat generals, he had been wounded twice and was considered an incorruptible patriot.* "Surely a more active, a more spirited and more sensible officer [than Arnold] fills no department of the army," wrote General Washington. Short, swarthy and hawk-nosed, Arnold had a fiery courage, but his personality was marred by towering pride and unchecked ambition.

Why did Arnold commit treason? He was in trouble with Congress over the state of his accounts, angry at what he saw as its refusal to grant proper recognition of his exploits and facing a court-martial because of irregularities in the handling of supplies while in command at Philadelphia. Arnold later claimed that his experiences with the politicians proved that independence was a mistake and said he mistrusted the alliance with France—but that was after he had gone over to the British. In reality, the bottom line was his need for money. Always extravagant, Arnold found his financial difficulties increased by marriage to a beautiful and ambitious young wife.

A member of a prominent Philadelphia family, Peggy Shippen Arnold had found the British occupation a most enjoyable experience, largely

---

*The modern American military commander whom Arnold most resembles is General George S. Patton. Both men loved parading in fine uniforms and taking the offensive, and preferred the slam-bang of combat to the semi-academic cerebrations of staff work. Too, they were both high-strung, irascible, and beloved and hated at once by their own troops, though Arnold probably enjoyed a degree more affection from his.

because of the presence of the charming John André. Whether she and André were lovers is an unresolved question, but she kept up a correspondence with him after he returned to New York. Arnold, a widower of thirty-seven, was captivated by the vivacious Peggy, who was half his age, and they were married after a whirlwind courtship. Although she knew of his plan to switch sides, it is unlikely that she actually influenced Arnold to become a traitor. More than likely, she merely confirmed his own inclinations.

Arnold made his first overtures to the British in May 1779, offering to sell his services for proper consideration, "either by immediately joining the British army, or cooperating on some concerted plan with Sir Henry Clinton." With Clinton's approval, Major André opened a correspondence with Arnold as both sides cautiously felt each other out. They used a number code in which the first of three numbers referred to a page, the second to a line and a third to a word in Blackstone's *Commentaries*. André used the cover name "John Anderson," while Arnold called himself "Mr. Moore" or "Monk"—a reference to General George Monk, who had helped restore the exiled King Charles II to the throne after the death of Oliver Cromwell. Monk had received a dukedom for switching sides; undoubtedly Arnold hoped for comparable rewards for himself. The letters exchanged with André make it clear that Peggy Arnold was a party to the conspiracy almost from the beginning. André suggested that she send gossipy letters to a woman friend in New York that would contain messages from her husband written between the lines in invisible ink. The friend would turn the letters over to him.

Arnold persuaded General Washington to give him command of West Point, which controlled the Hudson River north of New York City, and agreed to sell out the post to the British in exchange for twenty thousand pounds and a general's commission. In New York, candles burned late in British headquarters as Clinton and André huddled behind locked doors, putting the finishing touches on the plot. Culper, Jr., sensed something was up but could not penetrate the tight security. The final details of the surrender of West Point were to be worked out at a meeting between Arnold and André near the post. Reluctantly, Clinton gave his ambitious young aide permission to keep the rendezvous but warned him not to enter the American lines or to remove his uniform, to avoid the risk of being treated as a spy if captured.

Following two failed attempts, the two men met at Haverstraw on the night of September 21, 1780. André was rowed ashore from the sloop *Vulture*, and he and Arnold conferred in a grove of fir trees until about 4 A.M. Arnold gave André the plans for West Point and a detailed accounting of ordnance and the number of men present for duty. With daybreak coming, the oarsmen refused to take André back to the ship, so Arnold escorted him to a nearby farmhouse to rest. A sentry's challenge was the first notice that, contrary to Clinton's orders, he had gone behind American lines.

Shortly after daybreak, Arnold and André were startled by the distant boom of a heavy gun from the Hudson, followed by another. They sprang to a window, and what they saw must have chilled their blood. Without permission from Arnold, American artillery had opened up on the *Vulture,* and the vessel was dropping back down the river. André was stranded and would have to return to New York over land.

Removing his uniform, the major changed into civilian clothes and stuffed the papers he had been given inside his stockings. With Arnold's written order permitting "Mr. John Anderson" to pass through the American lines, he proceeded south on horseback into the "neutral ground" between the two armies. The area was infested with freebooting marauders more interested in plunder than in harassing each other. Only a few miles stood between André and safety on the morning of September 23, and he must have been thinking about the rewards awaiting him when he was halted near Tarrytown by a trio of rough-looking fellows who leveled their muskets at him.

Seeing that one of the men was wearing a Hessian uniform coat, André assumed they were Loyalists and identified himself as a British officer. It was a fatal mistake. To his dismay, the bushwhackers turned out to be Yankees, and he was ordered to dismount. André flourished the pass signed by General Arnold. Their suspisions already aroused, his captors searched him—"rifled me" were André's words—and took his watch and a small amount of money. They were convinced he had more money secreted in his boots and forced him to remove them. Instead of money, they found packets of papers. The only one of the men who could read did not understand the significance of the documents, but in hopes of collecting a reward, they decided to take their prisoner to a nearby outpost at North Castle.

That evening Benjamin Tallmadge, who was returning from a scouting mission, was told by Lt. Col. John Jameson, the commander of the North Castle outpost, that a man who called himself John Anderson had been caught earlier in the day with suspicious papers. Upon examination, they had proved to be notes and sketches detailing the defenses of West Point. Assuming "Anderson's" pass from General Arnold to be a forgery, Jameson said, he had sent the prisoner to Arnold's headquarters, preceded by a courier bearing a dispatch explaining what had happened. At the same time, he had forwarded the incriminating documents to General Washington, who, following a conference with the French at Hartford, was on his way to West Point.

John Anderson? That name rang a bell in Tallmadge's mind. Only two weeks before, Arnold had instructed him to keep an eye out for a man named John Anderson who was coming up from New York City and to escort him to headquarters. Now, someone with the same name had been caught with the plans for West Point. And rather than coming up from Manhattan, he was heading in the other direction. The incredible truth dawned on Tallmadge. Anderson was a British spy, and Benedict Arnold was a traitor!

The courier carrying the letter to Arnold was too far ahead to be recalled, but with some difficulty Tallmadge persuaded Jameson to order "Anderson" brought back to North Castle. Arms bound behind him, André was cheerfully trudging along toward Arnold's headquarters—and freedom—when a dragoon trotted up with the order to return to North Castle. André was dumbfounded as he suddenly found himself turned about and led away from sanctuary.

Arnold was having breakfast with two of Washington's staff officers who had preceded the commander in chief to West Point when Jameson's messenger arrived. Opening the dispatch, he read that a suspicious person named John Anderson, carrying a pass signed by him, had been captured and that documents found hidden on the prisoner had been sent to General Washington. Arnold was visibly shaken—one of the officers noted an "embarrassment" on his face—but he rapidly regained control of himself. Murmuring apologies, Arnold excused himself and issued orders for his horse to be saddled and the crew of his boat alerted to stand by.

Peggy was breakfasting in bed when her husband burst in upon her. Everything was lost, he whispered, and he must flee for his life. She gave a little cry, but before Arnold could tell her more an aide tapped at the door to announce that Washington was expected momentarily. Arnold dashed from the room, almost bowling the man over. Leaping into the saddle, he spurred his horse across the lawn and down a sharp incline to the Hudson. He boarded his waiting boat and was rowed out to the *Vulture,* which had returned to await André. Soon the traitor was on his way to a haven in New York City—and infamy.

As for André, he was placed in Tallmadge's custody at North Castle. Although the prisoner refused to provide any information regarding his true identity, Tallmadge was convinced that he was a soldier, particularly after watching him pace the floor. "I communicated my suspicion to Lieut.-Col. Jameson and requested him to notice his gait, especially when he turned on heel to retrace his course across the room," he wrote in his memoirs. Told that the papers found upon him were in Washington's hands, André realized it was useless to maintain silence. In a brief letter to the general, he acknowledged having come into the American lines to gain intelligence, but claimed to have been involuntarily "betrayed into the vile condition of an enemy in disguise within your posts."

Washington ordered André brought to his headquarters at Tappan to be tried on charges of being a spy. On the way, André and Tallmadge spent many hours talking. The prisoner was naturally curious about his fate. "I endeavored to evade the question, unwilling to give him a true answer," Tallmadge said. "When I could no longer evade this Importunity, I said to him that I had a much loved Classmate in Yale College by the name of Nathan Hale, who entered the army with me. After the British Troops had entered N. York, Genl Washington wanted Information respecting the strength, position & probable movements of the enemy. Capt. Hale tendered his services, went into N. York & was taken just as he was passing the outposts of the Enemy.

"Said I with Emphasis, do you remember the sequel of this Story.

"Yes, said André; he was hanged as a Spy; but you surely do not consider his case & mine alike.

"I replied, precisely similar, and similar will be your fate."

Tragically, Tallmadge's prediction proved to be correct. André was found guilty by a court-martial and condemned to be hanged. Efforts were made to exchange him for Arnold—whom General Washington regarded as "hackneyed in villainy"—but Clinton refused to give him up. The unlucky André was executed on October 2, 1780. Although Arnold had failed to deliver West Point, he received part of the cash reward for which he had bargained and a general's commission. With the same zeal that he had shown in the Continental Army, he organized a Loyalist regiment that devastated New London in his native Connecticut and led a destructive raid on tidewater Virginia. Washington never gave up hope of bringing the traitor to justice, however, and several attempts were made to kidnap him. Should the rascal be captured, Washington instructed his officers, he was to be summarily executed.*

■ ■ ■

Undoubtedly Washington's most brilliant use of intelligence and disinformation occurred in the preliminaries to the Yorktown campaign that brought the War of Independence to a victorious end. In May 1781, the Comte de Rochambeau, the commander of French troops in America, met with Washington at Weathersfield, Connecticut, to plan joint strategy for the summer. Rochambeau reported that a French fleet under the Comte de Grasse was coming north from the West Indies, and Washington proposed an all-out attack upon New York. Rochambeau did not share Washington's enthusiasm for an assault on the city and argued for a march south to deal with Lord Cornwallis, whose army was raising havoc in the Carolinas and Virginia.

Washington's strategy prevailed, but a full transcript of the Weathersfield meeting fell into Sir Henry Clinton's hands. The British

---

*Arnold died in obscurity in England in 1801. The legend that on his deathbed he asked to be buried in his old Continental Army uniform is false. Peggy joined him in death three years later.

braced for an attack on New York and beat back several attempts to probe their positions. Suddenly, just as the allies were settling in for a siege, the entire campaign changed. Cornwallis retreated with his battle-weary army to Yorktown, on Chesapeake Bay, to await relief from the Royal Navy. Meanwhile word was received that the French fleet was due momentarily off the American coast. Washington and Rochambeau immediately saw an opportunity to trap Cornwallis between the hammer of the allied armies and the anvil of the fleet. On August 20, 1781, they began shifting their troops to the south.

To prevent Clinton from learning of the movement and either reinforcing Cornwallis or attacking the French and Americans while they were on the move, Washington launched a massive campaign of deception. Tight security was imposed upon the army; only the senior generals knew its actual destination. Thanks to the captured documents in his possession, Clinton fell headlong into the trap set for him. He seems to have ignored the possibility that the allied commanders might change their plans. Reports from spies on the Jersey side of the Hudson confirmed his belief that New York was the allied objective: the enemy, they said, was building ovens to bake bread for a large army, and roads were being improved in preparation for a long siege. Instructions to American secret agents that conveniently fell into British hands told the agents to "inquire minutely" into enemy troop strength and placement in New York City. Boats were being gathered at Sandy Hook—obviously for a landing on Staten Island. The evidence all pointed to an attack on New York, but as days passed the expected assault failed to materialize. Some British officers informed Clinton that the French and Americans were bypassing New York for the Chesapeake, but the general scoffed. By the time he began to realize that he had been hoodwinked, it was too late.

On September 5, Rochambeau and his staff were approaching a wharf at Chester, Pennsylvania, after an inspection of the Delaware forts. They saw a tall officer in Continental uniform jumping up and down, waving his hat in one hand and his handkerchief in the other. Much to their astonishment, the jubilant figure appeared to be George Washington. That, of course, was impossible; the commander in chief was a cold, austere figure. But it *was* Washington. And he was not only jumping up and down and waving his hat but was shouting exuberantly. The Frenchmen heard the name "de Grasse!" The French fleet had arrived in the Chesapeake five days before, Washington shouted.

The trap had snapped shut on Cornwallis.

3

"Surrounded by Spies"

Benjamin Franklin radiated an aura of good will. Scientist, statesman, and sage, he seemed to look out upon the world with a bemused benevolence. But behind this facade lurked a master of intrigue. A skilled manipulator of men and ideas, for nearly two decades Franklin had served in London in the quasi-diplomatic post of colonial agent for Pennsylvania and several other colonies. When the Continental Congress launched a covert campaign to win foreign backing for American independence, it naturally turned to the new nation's most experienced diplomat. Franklin thus became the key figure in a clandestine struggle—a struggle fought not on the battlefield, but in the brilliant courts and shadowy back stairs of European capitals.

Though sometimes characterized as "un-American," involvement in foreign intrigue is as old as the nation itself. The Secret Committee of Correspondence organized in November 1775—Franklin, John Jay of New York, Benjamin Harrison of Virginia, Thomas Johnson of Maryland and John Dickinson of Pennsylvania—was not only responsible for the nation's foreign relations but also constituted its first foreign intelligence directorate. Working in conjunction with a Secret Committee previously established by Congress to procure arms and supplies, the committee employed secret agents, conducted covert operations, engaged in gunrunning, originated codes and ciphers, established a courier system that included dispatch vessels, funded propaganda activities, and provided "gratuities" for foreign officials whose influence it thought worth buying.*

---

*The Secret Committee of Correspondence became the Committee on Foreign Affairs in 1777 and was the direct forerunner of the Department of State. The Secret Committee became the Committee of Commerce the same year.

The secret committees and the Continental Congress established a number of precedents for the conduct of intelligence operations. They originated the first oaths pledging members and staff to secrecy. While providing for some measure of legislative oversight, they took steps to protect intelligence methods and sources. For example, on May 10, 1776, the Committee of Secret Correspondence was directed to lay its proceedings before Congress but obtained permission to withhold the names of secret agents. Secret journals were kept in which intelligence and foreign relations matters were recorded, and access to them was severely restricted. On one occasion, the secrecy of intelligence data was enforced to the point of approving a false resolution. Revolutionary propagandist Thomas Paine, serving as clerk to one of the committees, earned the distinction of being one of the first government officials to be fired for leaking classified information.

Clandestine operations are hardly a task for the novice, however. Despite the fetish for secrecy, the secret committees and their successors were often unable to keep their activities hidden from view. As in our day, the most serious leakers were the members of Congress themselves. For example, on October 1, 1776, a courier brought a report from Dr. Arthur Lee, the resident American agent in London and brother of Richard Henry Lee, a delegate to Congress from Virginia. Franklin and Robert Morris, who had recently joined the Committee, were the only members in Philadelphia. "We agree in opinion that it is our indispensable duty to keep it a secret even from Congress," they wrote of the report. "We find, by fatal experience, the Congress consists of too many members to keep secrets."

When Richard Lee returned to Philadelphia, he was briefed on his brother's report. Although he promised not to divulge anything he was told, Lee leaked the information to a friend. This breach of security came to the attention of John Jay, who was engaged in counterintelligence operations in upstate New York. His response strikes a familiar chord: "Communicate no other intelligence to Congress at large than what may be necessary to promote the common weal, not to gratify the curiosity of individuals," he admonished Morris angrily.

The Continental Congress also learned the hard way about the need for the centralization of intelligence. In mid-1775, Franklin and Morris were informed by American sympathizers in Bermuda that a respectable amount of gunpowder was stored, unguarded, in the royal arsenal at St. George's. A successful "smash and grab" operation was engineered, and more than a ton of powder was landed in Philadelphia. Unfortunately, no one in Congress had bothered to inform General Washington of the raid. Having learned independently of the powder, he prevailed upon Rhode Island, which had its own navy, to send a vessel to capture it. By the time the Rhode Islanders arrived in October, British warships were on patrol off the island, and they were nearly captured.*

■ ■ ■

Soon after the Secret Committee of Correspondence set up shop, it received feelers from a mysterious stranger named Julien Achard de Bonvouloir. In a cloak-and-dagger atmosphere insisted upon by the visitor, the well-muffled members—including the seventy-year-old Franklin—proceeded at dusk to a quiet house on the outskirts of Philadelphia, each alone and by a different route. Bonvouloir claimed to be a Flemish merchant who had come to America to explore the possibility of making a business deal to supply the Americans with weapons. Franklin, however, immediately sensed the familiar aura of international intrigue.

Bonvouloir had been dispatched by the Comte de Vergennes, the French foreign minister, who harbored a passionate hatred of England and a desire to avenge the humiliations France had suffered at her hands. The agent had been instructed to gather information about the situation in America and to provide the rebel leaders with unofficial assurances of French sympathy. As soon as these polite preliminaries were out of the way, the bargaining began. The Americans hoped to persuade France to enter the war against Britain, but the French, fearing that the British might eventually conciliate the colonies, were reluctant to take the plunge until convinced that the break was irrevocable.

Franklin made telling use of France's desire for revenge against Britain. Although he lived long before the age of psychological warfare, he understood its principles well and skillfully manipulated the vacillating powers of Europe. Assuring Bonvouloir that independence was merely a matter of time, Franklin made certain that the Frenchman was spoon-fed information casting the rebel cause in the best possible light. Bonvouloir was seduced by what he was told. Although Washington's army, then besieging Boston, was short of men and ammunition, he glowingly reported to Vergennes that "the troops were well clothed, well paid and well commanded. . . . They are stronger than others thought. . . . Take your measures accordingly."

Franklin was under no illusions about the generosity of the Europeans' motives, coolly analyzing them in a letter to the Reverend Samuel

---

*Even then, Congress was concerned about the Russian "menace." Tobacco sales abroad were to furnish the funds to pay for military equipment, and William Carmichael, an agent of the Secret Committee of Correspondence, was given the task of determining whether Russian tobacco exports would hinder these plans. Carmichael's report from Amsterdam in November 1776 was reassuring. "I have seen some of [the Russian] tobacco here," he told Congress, "and the best of it is worse than the worst of our ground leaf."

Cooper: "Europe has its reasons. . . . It fancies itself in some danger from the growth of British power, and would be glad to see it divided against itself." Economic interests were also influential, for the Europeans hoped that by humbling Britain they could divert the lucrative commercial trade of the colonies from London and Bristol to Nantes, Amsterdam and Bilbao. Even before the outbreak of the Revolution, gunrunning from the ports of the Bay of Biscay and the West Indies had become big business. This illicit enterprise was so effective that a British diplomat in Paris estimated that by July 1775, French trading houses had supplied the American colonists with at least six million dollars' worth of military equipment.

Following through on a discreet nudge from Bonvouloir, the Committee decided on March 3, 1776, to send an agent to Paris. Silas Deane, a Connecticut businessman and former delegate to Congress, was appointed to the post. He was also named an agent of the Secret Committee, charged with making purchases of arms and supplies. The committee might have made a better selection; Deane was ignorant of French, and even he acknowledged that "people here, members of Congress and others, have unhappily and erroneously thought me a schemer." The ascerbic John Adams, who held a low opinion of Deane, later suggested that the real reason for sending him abroad was to provide a congressional "lame duck" with a job.

Deane's instructions, written by Franklin, ordered him to assume the cover of a merchant buying goods for the Indian trade. His real objective was to secure military and financial assistance while sounding out the French on the possibilities of an alliance. The first task assigned Deane was to procure arms and uniforms for twenty-five thousand men. Free access to the commerce of an "independent" America—the Declaration of Independence was still four months away—was to be dangled before the French as bait. Franklin also instructed Deane to make contact with Dr. Edward Bancroft, an American living in London who was known to both men, and to employ him as an informant on political and commercial matters. And so the new nation launched its first frail craft on the sea of international relations—and foreign intrigue.

■ ■ ■

Arriving in Paris in July 1776, Silas Deane was immediately enmeshed in a web of intrigue. Inexperienced in the wiles of diplomacy and overimpressed with titles and aristocratic pretensions, Deane was out of his depth in the world's most brilliant, frivolous, and corrupt capital. Fearful of the British spies who swarmed about Paris, he adopted the name "Jones," wrote his letters in invisible ink, and vowed that in the presence of English-speaking people he would speak only in French. "He must be the most silent man in France," remarked one caustic observer, "for I defy him to say more than six consecutive words in French."

Deane was hardly off the ship that brought him to France before a British agent attached himself to him. Jacobus van Zandt, a New Yorker who used the code name "George Lupton," discovered that the American lacked the slightest conception of security and talked freely. He reported that Deane had taken rooms in a fashionable district "where he struts about like a Cock on his Dunghill, and is as well pleased as a Child with a new plaything, but I perfectly join with you in the opinion that his pride must have a downfall." Once, when Deane stepped out of the room, "Lupton" rifled his desk. Fortunately for Deane, the spy was put out of action by venereal disease, having, as he put it, "been deceived by a Girl."

In the meantime, Deane obtained a secret audience with the Comte de Vergennes. Through an interpreter, the foreign minister carefully emphasized that open aid to the American colonies would disrupt France's relations with Britain. Of course, he added—undoubtedly with an expressive Gallic shrug—as a private citizen Deane was free to conduct his own business in France. Unknown to Deane, however, Vergennes had already decided to funnel arms and supplies to the Americans covertly through a fictitious trading company, Roderique Hortalez & Company, established by Pierre Augustine Caron de Beaumarchais, the author of the popular comedy *The Barber of Seville*. The French and Spanish governments were Beaumarchais' silent partners and the financial backers of the enterprise.

Playwright, secret agent, blackmailer, and suspected murderer, Beaumarchais had an adventurous career that rivalled his own plays for theatricality. On one occasion, the Chevalier d'Eon, a French agent who dressed as a woman, fled to England, taking secret contingency plans for the invasion of Britain with him. Worried that "Mademoiselle" might sell the papers to the British, the government assigned Beaumarchais the delicate task of getting them back. The playwright played court to this "lady"—who, he said, "drank and smoked like a German trooper"—and returned the plans to Paris in triumph.

While on another trip to London, Beaumarchais—who used the code name "Norac," or Caron spelled backward—had met Arthur Lee, the American resident agent, with whom he discussed the prospects for the rebellion. Beaumarchais quickly convinced himself that Britain's colonial empire was tottering. Seeing an opportunity to make his own fortune, he bombarded the young King Louis XVI with position papers designed to break down royal scruples against aiding rebels. There was strong prejudice at Versailles against assisting the Americans, especially from Baron Turgot, the controller general of finance, who warned that the measures advocated by Vergennes and Beaumarchais would lead to financial catastrophe.*

The king, however, sided with Beaumarchais. On April 22, 1776, nearly three months before Silas Deane's arrival in Paris, he issued orders for the procurement of new equipment for the army—and the release of a vast stock of surplus arms to Hortalez & Co. To prevent British spies from linking this arrangement to the government, Vergennes had his fifteen-year-old son write the note informing Beaumarchais of the decision so that his own handwriting or that of his clerks would not tip off British spies. "It was slippery business in the face of the English," the foreign minister noted.

Establishing his headquarters in a large building that had once been the Dutch embassy, Beaumarchais zestfully plunged into the task of accumulating a mountain of supplies and a fleet of ships to transport them to America. When Deane arrived with authority to pay in tobacco, furs, rice, and other commodities for arms and other supplies shipped to America, Beaumarchais gleefully rubbed his hands in anticipation. He immediately dispatched a note to Deane in which he touchingly claimed to have long "cherished a desire to aid the brave Americans to shake off the British yoke." The resulting partnership of the prince of conspirators and the down-to-earth Connecticut businessman proved invaluable to the American cause. Much of the arms and munitions that made the decisive victory at Saratoga possible—and with it France's decision to recognize the new nation—was provided by Hortalez & Co.

Nor did the conspiracy end there. Although Vergennes issued proclamations and statements to the contrary for the benefit of the angry British, American privateers were clandestinely permitted to fit out in French ports and to prey upon British commerce. Well aware of these unneutral activities, Lord Stormont, the British ambassador, repeatedly demanded that the American agents be expelled and the vessels taken by the Yankees returned. When the pressure eventually became too great, the French authorities ordered the privateers seized. Later, the Americans were compensated for their losses or their ships were allowed to escape.

Beaumarchais' decision to deal with Deane rather than with Arthur Lee infuriated Lee. To all who would listen, he charged that France had intended the supplies as an outright gift but that Deane and Beaumarchais were trying to extract payment in order to line their own pockets. Conflict of interest was rampant in the eighteenth century, and

---

*Turgot was proven correct. The desperate financial condition of France after the American Revolution contributed to the outbreak of the French Revolution in 1789. If Louis XVI had followed the advice of Turgot rather than that of Vergennes and Beaumarchais, he might not have lost his head.

the business ethics of the day did not preclude the use of government property for private ends so long as the government's interests were not betrayed. In keeping with this practice, Beaumarchais and Deane did take a rake-off on the supplies shipped to America, but Lee's charges were the product of jealousy and a suspicious mind. Nevertheless, Lee's complaints found ready ears in Congress, including those of his influential brother and the New England faction headed by Samuel Adams.*

■ ■ ■

Three months after the signing of the Declaration of Independence, Congress sent a mission to Paris with instructions to seek formal recognition of the new nation and an alliance with France. Benjamin Franklin, Silas Deane, and Thomas Jefferson were named commissioners, but Jefferson declined the appointment and Arthur Lee was told to move from London to Paris in his place. Suffering from gout and feeling the burden of his years, Franklin had grave doubts about his usefulness. "I am old and good for nothing; but as the storekeepers say of their remnants of cloth, I am but a fag end, and you may have me for what you please to give," he declared. Despite his misgivings, Franklin was to become the key member of the delegation, and the next three years proved to be the most noteworthy in his remarkable career.

Franklin arrived in Paris in December 1776 and took the city by storm. A master of public relations, he dressed simply, wore an old fur cap rather than an elaborate wig, and to the French seemed at once the embodiment of Rousseau's natural man and the very personification of the American cause. Voltaire, for example, spoke of the American army as "Franklin's troops." No social affair was a success without his presence; crowds gathered whenever he appeared; the curious even paid to secure vantage points from which to watch him pass. Portraits of Franklin appeared everywhere—on rings, snuffbox lids, medallions, and even chamber pots—and his almanacs were translated as *Les Maximes du Bonhomme Richard.** The British, however, took a less exalted view. "I look upon him as a dangerous engine," wrote Lord Stormont, the British ambassador, "and am very sorry that some English frigate did not meet him by the way."

---

*Eventually, Deane was recalled for an examination of his accounts, but attempts to unravel them were largely unsuccessful. The situation was even more tangled by the fact that Deane, working with Robert Morris, used his position to trade in supplies for their own account. In fact, Morris, who ran the Continental procurement program as an adjunct to his mercantile house, profited so much from government contracts that he emerged from the war America's richest man. When critics demanded an audit of his books, they were found to be in such a confused state it was impossible to make sense of them.

*Unlike his fellow commissioners, Franklin spoke French—although, as he acknowledged, he paid little attention to the grammatical details.

From the moment of his arrival, Franklin used his popularity to promote the American cause. Newspaper articles and pamphlets casting discredit upon the British flowed from his facile pen, among them a forged document purporting to show that the British were buying bales of American scalps from the Indians, including those of women and children. He also plotted an attack on British commerce by privateers sailing from French ports in the hope of forcing an outraged Britain to declare war on France.

Making his headquarters in a pleasant villa in suburban Passy provided by a contractor doing business with the Americans, Franklin held court for a colorful array of political adventurers, soldiers of fortune, diplomats, spies, bankers, scientists, and philosophers. And there were also his women friends. Most in evidence were Madame Helvetius, to whom Franklin proposed marriage at seventy-two, and Madame Brillon, who allowed him to join her for chess while she was in her bath.† Silas Deane, who enjoyed the company of the venerable doctor, came almost every day to Passy, but Lee, angry at being overshadowed by the old man, kept his distance and grumbled about the venality of his fellow Americans.

The commissioners lived in a world of intrigue. For their part, they maintained agents in various ports along the French coast to keep them informed of changes in French attitudes and regulations, to speed privateers and merchantmen to sea, to recruit French seamen to fill vacant berths on these vessels, and to find ships for masters and masters for ships. The British Secret Service surrounded the commissioners with a net of spies and double agents (Franklin was referred to in the British code as "72" and "Moses"). While British agents spied on the Americans, the spies of Vergennes and Beaumarchais were on the lookout for suspicious Englishmen in France—and the French police kept an eye on everyone.

Franklin's most dangerous adversary was William Eden, the operational chief of the British Secret Service.* Eden, who used the cover of an under secretary of state, was the most effective British spymaster since Sir Francis Walsingham, who had founded the organization under Queen Elizabeth. Reaching from Gibraltar to the Elbe, his network of spies compares favorably in resources and activity to the clandestine intelligence organizations of our own day. The British spent 115,900 pounds on gathering information in 1775; by 1778, these expenditures

---

†Madame Helvetius once upbraided *"cher Papa"* for having put off a visit to her. "Madame," he replied, ever the diplomat, "I am waiting until the nights are longer."

*Eden, later Lord Auckland, was the brother of Sir Robert Eden, the last royal governor of Maryland, and an ancestor of Anthony Eden, Lord Avon.

had reached 200,000 pounds. This amount did not include nearly un-limited contingency funds and the support of other agencies such as the Royal Navy and the Post Office. The latter not only intercepted mail but had some of Britain's most talented forgers on its payroll.*

Eden recruited many of his agents from among the American Loy-alists living in England, men who could easily pose as rebel sym-pathizers. The most important of them was Paul Wentworth, who headed the spy network targeted on the American agents in Paris. Related to a wealthy and politically influential New Hampshire family, Wentworth once operated a plantation in Surinam on the north coast of the South American continent. Named the London agent for his native province in 1770, he was a heavy plunger on the stock market. Shrewd, smooth, and unscrupulous—he had at least a dozen aliases—Wentworth bristled at being accused of spying and professed to be a Loyalist out of conviction. In reality, he was motivated by his constant need for money and hoped to be rewarded for his intelligence work with a knighthood, a safe seat in Parliament, and a government sinecure.

Provided with a generous expense account, Wentworth established himself in Paris with a pretty mistress, handsome lodgings, and an elaborate coach. "This Mr. Wentworth speaks French like you, and better than I do," Beaumarchais warned Vergennes. "He is one of the cleverest men in England." Although his task was to run a network of agents, he turned any opportunity to his advantage. On one occasion, he called on William Lee, brother of Arthur Lee and the American agent in Nantes; finding him out, he pocketed Lee's calling card and seal for use in concocting forgeries. Wentworth's most important move was to recruit Dr. Edward Bancroft, the private secretary of both Silas Deane and Benjamin Franklin, into the Secret Service. Bancroft became one of the most remarkable double agents in the history of espionage—and so successful that his treason remained a secret for a century.*

Shortly after his arrival in Paris, Deane had summoned Dr. Bancroft to Paris, not only to obtain information but to renew an old friendship. Years before, Deane had taught school in Connecticut; Bancroft, a native

---

*In fact, the law enacted in 1657 establishing the British postal system included the observation that the "best means of discovering dangerous and wicked designs against the Commonwealth" was through the interception of mail. Men of affairs in England and on the Continent were aware of the interception and opening of private letters, but not until after the Napoleonic wars did the general public perceive this sort of activity as an infringement of their personal liberties.

*Bancroft's double-dealing was not proven until B. F. Stevens began publishing his *Fac-similes of Manuscripts in European Archives Relating to America* in 1889. Included in the twenty-five volumes are the Secret Service papers of William Eden, which made it possible to pinpoint Bancroft's activities. In 1784, the doctor submitted a memorial to the foreign secretary protesting delays in paying his salary. The memorial described his services to the Crown in detail.

of Westfield, Massachusetts, was his star pupil. Later, Bancroft studied medicine and practiced in the West Indies before going to Surinam, where Paul Wentworth engaged him as a plantation doctor and took him into the "big house" as a member of the family. Feeding pills to Wentworth's slaves required little effort, and Bancroft spent much of his time studying tropical plants and experimenting with medicinal herbs and other compounds, including the deadly poison curare, which he called "Woowara."

In 1767, the ambitious young physician went to London, where he talked his way onto the staff at St. Bartholomew's Hospital and also found time to write learned treatises on the flora and fauna of Surinam as well as a lengthy novel. These accomplishments brought him to the attention of Benjamin Franklin, the most prominent American living in London. Regarding Bancroft as a "very intelligent, sensible man," Franklin sponsored him for election as a fellow of the Royal Society. Franklin also introduced him to politics and land speculation. Bancroft wrote pamphlets supporting the American cause against Britain and invested in the Vandalia Company, a speculative scheme designed by Franklin to carve a new colony out of the vast area to the north of the Ohio River. The outbreak of revolution in America dashed the hopes of the speculators, however, and Bancroft, perennially in need of funds to finance his stock market operations and to support a large family, was left seeking new opportunities.

Over a convivial supper—undoubtedly paid for by the talkative Deane—Bancroft was taken into his host's confidence. Deane revealed the details of his instructions from the Continental Congress and filled the doctor in on his accomplishments in France. The friends soon worked out an arrangement whereby Bancroft agreed to act as Deane's confidential agent in London and to forward regular reports on political and military matters in return for payment for services rendered. Almost immediately after his return to London, the doctor, whose letters had been opened in the Post Office, was persuaded by Wentworth to enter the employ of the British Secret Service.

For the next several months, Bancroft traveled back and forth between London and Paris, supplying Eden with reports on Deane's activities. He had the full details of the American's interview with Vergennes well before word of Deane's arrival in France had even reached Congress. To allay any suspicions Deane may have had, he brought back from London seemingly important but inconsequential information—"chicken feed," in today's lingo—given him by the Secret Service.

Soon Bancroft and Deane were using inside information to enrich themselves by speculating heavily in the London insurance market, the eighteenth-century equivalent of Las Vegas. Anyone could take out "insurance"—actually a bet—against a certain event's taking place. Wagers were made on almost anything: what army would win a battle, which politician would fall from power, whether a particular noble lord would die before the year was out. Insiders such as Bancroft and Deane could win fortunes by using official information, and in all they may have shared profits of as much as ten thousand pounds. Like most gamblers, however, Deane also lost, and in the end netted little for his efforts.

Eden and Wentworth eventually concluded that Bancroft would be more useful if he were in Paris full-time. The Secret Service accordingly arranged to have him "arrested" under suspicion of involvement in a rebel plot. Upon his release, Bancroft "fled" to Paris with a contract in his pocket for five hundred pounds up front, a yearly salary of five hundred pounds, and a promise of a lifetime pension of two hundred pounds annually. There he became Deane's private secretary and shared quarters with William Carmichael, another of Deane's assistants. They maintained, said Carmichael, "a very decent house. We have none but Ladies of the 1st quality—I have not seen a Strumpet here in 3 weeks."*

Upon his arrival in Paris, Benjamin Franklin made Bancroft general secretary of the American mission. Invited to make his home at Passy, he had full access to the commission's private conversations and secret papers. Indifferent to security, Franklin left secret documents lying around even though friends frequently warned that he was "surrounded by spies." Shrugging off these warnings, he replied: "I have long observ'd one Rule which prevents any Inconvenience from such Practices. It is simply this, to be concern'd in no Affairs that I should blush to have made publick, and to do nothing but what Spies may see & welcome. . . . If I was sure, therefore, that my Valet de Place was a Spy, as probably he is, I think I should not discharge him for that, if in other Respects I lik'd him."

Bancroft, known by the code name "Mr. Edwards," supplied the Secret Service with details of the negotiations for an alliance between France and America, the names of American agents in Europe and the Caribbean, and copies of Franklin's correspondence with the Continental Congress. Exhaustive reports on ship movements enabled the Royal Navy to intercept shipments of arms and supplies and provided Lord Stormont with accurate details upon which to base protests against French violations of neutrality. If the Americans attended a salon or a reception, Wentworth knew the details of every conversation soon after the doors closed on the last departing guest.

Bancroft wrote his reports in invisible ink between the lines of love letters addressed to a "Mr. Richardson" and left them in a sealed bottle in

*Bancroft later diverted suspicion from himself to Carmichael. Vergennes, suspecting Carmichael of being a British agent, insisted that he be sent home to America. Modern research indicates that while Carmichael was often less than discreet, he was not in Eden's pay.

a hole in a box tree of the south garden of the Tuileries. Promptly at half-past nine every Tuesday evening, Lord Stormont sent a messenger to the "drop." The messenger pulled up the bottle by a long string attached to it and replaced it with another containing communications for Bancroft. Periodically, Bancroft went to London on the excuse of seeing his family or attending to business affairs. Although this should have set off an alarm, Franklin and Deane maintained the information he brought back to Paris was invaluable. Indeed, Congress was so impressed by Bancroft's reports that it voted him a salary in addition to that paid by the commissioners. When his pay was late, he had the effrontery to threaten to quit.

Neither Franklin nor Deane ever professed to suspect Bancroft of transmitting their innermost secrets to the British. But the irascible Arthur Lee, who suspected everybody but his own secretary—who *was* a British spy—claimed to have evidence that the doctor met with the British privy council while in London. He told Bancroft to his face that he suspected him of treason, and a duel almost ensued. Luckily for Bancroft, who lived in terror of discovery and kept an extra passport at hand so that he could flee at any moment, Lee and the other commissioners were constantly at sword's point, and no one paid any attention to his charges.

To get rid of Lee, the commissioners sent him to Prussia to convince Frederick the Great to recognize American independence. On the face of it, Frederick seemed a likely ally, for he hated the British and was contemptuous of the German princelings who had sold them mercenaries. But the mission ended in a farce worthy of the pen of Beaumarchais. Frederick refused to receive Lee, having decided to wait and see on which side "fortune shall declare herself." Not to be put off, the terrible-tempered Lee dogged the foreign minister so persistently that the harried Prussian became apoplectic at the mere sight of the American.

Adding to Lee's problems, Hugh Elliott, the British minister to Berlin, personally burglarized his desk and stole a portfolio of confidential documents. Elliott put several clerks to work copying the papers and then returned the originals to their owner with the hope they had not been missed. They included Lee's private journal and a record of all the transactions of the American commissioners in Paris. Frederick thundered against this breach of diplomatic decorum by *"votre Gott Damme Elliott,"* but the papers were already on their way to London.* As a result of the disclosures, the commissioners had to abandon the building of a frigate in Amsterdam, and their difficulties in shipping supplies from France were doubled.

■ ■ ■

---

*To mollify Frederick, Elliott was recalled from Berlin and given a gentle public reprimand. He was also rewarded with a secret gift of one thousand pounds.

Bancroft was not the only double-dealer installed by the Secret Service at Passy. Captain Joseph Hynson, a Maryland shipmaster, was involved in a clandestine operation that became one of the most bizarre of the war—with a touch of romantic farce in the bargain.

Alerted by Bancroft, the Royal Navy was having little trouble seizing ships and mail destined for America. The commissioners therefore decided to secure a fast cutter to carry important dispatches. Early in 1777 another Marylander, Captain Samuel Nicholson, who had two brothers serving in the Continental Navy, was given the task of procuring the vessel. Hynson, who was on the beach in London, was selected to command the cutter at the recommendation of his step-brother, Captain Lambert Wickes, the most successful American naval officer then operating in European seas.

Although Nicholson was expected to have little trouble obtaining a satisfactory craft in one of the ports on the French coast, his instructions gave him leeway to cross the English Channel to Dover and try his luck there if necessary. Unknown to the commissioners, however, Nicholson had a mistress in London, Mrs. Elizabeth Carter. After a perfunctory search for a suitable cutter in France, he dashed off to London, as much in quest of his mistress as of a vessel. The crossing presented little difficulty: even though the coastal ports were closely watched by both French and British agents, knowledgeable men moved back and forth with ease. Smugglers operated freely between Dover and Deal on the English side and Dunkirk and Calais on the French. It was a simple matter for a well-paying stranger to take his place among the barrels of brandy and bundles of lace, and no questions were asked at either end of the trip.

Immediately upon his arrival at Mrs. Carter's house on Portland Street, Nicholson sent off a quick note to Joe Hynson. "Take a coach and come immediately," he wrote, because "my Business are of Such a Nature, won't bare putting to Paper." Hynson hastened to see Nicholson and was bedazzled when told that Benjamin Franklin had selected him to carry the commissioners' dispatches to Congress. Although he was sworn to secrecy, he could not resist telling Mrs. Elizabeth Jump, his landlady and good friend, of the sudden turn in his fortunes. Mrs. Jump's boarding house in Stepney was a snug harbor for American seamen between voyages. She offered good food, good grog, and good company, including the presence of several unattached young ladies. Hynson's attention was centered upon Isabella Cleghorn, and he could not resist letting *her* know, too, what an important fellow he had become. The hospitable Mrs. Jump, however, was no friend of the American cause. Alarmed at what she and Isabella had been told, she went off to tell her story to the Reverend John Vardill.

Vardill was no ordinary parson. He had served as assistant rector of

Trinity Church in New York City and professor of natural law at King's College (now Columbia University). In London at the outbreak of the Revolution, he joined the Secret Service in return for a stipend of two hundred pounds a year and hints that he would have an endowed chair of divinity at King's after the rebellion had been suppressed. Vardill specialized in spying on the American colony in London. Mrs. Jump was not in his social class, but he cultivated her because she was an excellent source of information about the comings and goings of Yankee sea captains.

As soon as the landlady had unburdened herself of her fears, Vardill went to Stepney, where he invited Hynson into his coach for a chat. "I expostulated with Him & found him disposed to be made any use of that might be thought expedient," Vardill told William Eden with evident understatement. Probably the threat of a treason charge and the gallows made the talkative Hynson even more malleable.

As a result of this meeting, the British counter-plan was put in place. Hynson and Nicholson were to be permitted to purchase a cutter in England and take it to Havre on the French coast. As soon as Hynson had possession of the American commissioners' dispatches, he was to sail into the waiting arms of several British men-of-war. In return, Hynson was promised a small pension that would keep him comfortably in England for the rest of his life. Mrs. Jump and Isabella were not told of Hynson's change of loyalties, and he continued to spout pro-rebel sentiments. Hynson rejoined Nicholson, and in company with Mr. Carter, they went to Dover in mid-February 1777 to search for a suitable cutter. Isabella was left to languish in London. Hynson wrote her a carefully worded letter about his travels with "my companion and wife," noting, "we have a fine time of it, nothing to do but Drive from one place to another." On the back of the letters the distraught Isabella scrawled, "I have not Slept one hour since you left. For God's sake write to me . . . I am wreatched."

Before the mission could be completed, Nicholson was unexpectedly recalled to Paris, leaving Hynson—and the Secret Service—to provide the cutter. The craft finally chosen was a discarded Customs vessel that could "neither fight nor run away," as Nicholson later observed. She was renamed the *Dolphin,* and Hynson sailed her across the Channel to Havre. Following along was Colonel Edward Smith, detailed by Eden to be Hynson's case officer. Smith soon reported that Hynson was to sail for America on March 10, 1777, with dispatches for Congress and a cargo of dry goods. Seven British warships were placed where they could easily pick up the cutter.

But the date of sailing came and went, and the *Dolphin* remained in harbor. The cruisers remained on station, relentlessly patrolling the area while nerves were stretched taut in Eden's headquarters in Downing Street. What had gone wrong? At the end of the month, Smith reported that the plan was off. A schooner had arrived from Baltimore bringing news of Washington's victories at Trenton and Princeton, and Franklin and Deane had decided to delay sending dispatches until they had more to report on French reaction to the victories. Further, the pouches would then be sent on the Baltimore schooner, while Hynson and the *Dolphin* were held for other tasks. The whole elaborate plot had collapsed, leaving the rebels in possession of a cutter that had been placed in their hands by British intelligence.*

King George III, who as nominal head of the Secret Service had been closely watching the unfolding of the conspiracy, sent Eden a caustic memorandum: "I have ever doubted whether any trust could be reposed in Hynson; I am now quite settled in my opinion that He as well as every other Spy from N. America is encouraged by Dean & Franklin and only give intelligence to deceive."

■ ■ ■

Benjamin Franklin's most important coup, however, was to use the British Secret Service as an unwitting ally in tumbling France into the war against Britain. Although there was a steady flow of secret French loans and supplies to America, Vergennes had resisted every effort to persuade the French to enter an alliance with the United States. Recognition meant war with Britain. Cautious and prudent, Vergennes was reluctant to proceed without the support of Spain and also awaited a Yankee military success to be certain there would be no last-minute reconciliation that would forestall independence. The surprising American victory at Saratoga, on October 17, 1777, removed the last shred of doubt from his mind. He now suggested that the American commissioners renew their proposals for an open alliance.

Saratoga, which began a string of events that was to end at Yorktown, was greeted with as much joy in France "as if it had been a victory of their own troops over their own enemies," the commissioners reported. No one was more elated at the humbling of Britain than Beaumarchais. In his haste to get to King Louis with the glad tidings—or perhaps to engage in a quick speculation—his carriage overturned and he was injured. Such was the change in the war's momentum that Vergennes began to fear the disaster at Saratoga might spur Britain into an attempt at reconciliation. Early in December he told the king that the time had come to recognize the United States.

---

*This was not the last of Joe Hynson, however. In 1778, he was sent to Havre to deliver several packets of dispatches to the captain of a ship about to sail for America. When the packets were opened by Congress, they were found to contain only blank paper. Hynson had removed the secret documents and turned them over to the British. He was given a reward of two hundred pounds and an annual pension of an equal amount. "He was an honest rascal, and no fool though apparently stupid," observed Eden.

Bancroft sent repeated warnings of an impending treaty of alliance between France and the colonies to the British government, but King George refused to credit the intelligence. Poring over the reports supplied by Eden's agents with the dogged industry of his German ancestors, the monarch labored under a severe handicap. He was a man of high moral standards and refused to credit reports from agents whose personal lives he regarded as tinged with scandal—and those of Wentworth, Bancroft, and many of the other agents employed by Eden were decidedly mottled.

Although Eden and Wentworth urged the king to conciliate the Americans before it was too late, he remained adamant. *"Edwards* [Bancroft] is a stock jobber as well as a double spy," he retorted. "No faith can be placed in his intelligence but that it suits his private views to make us expect the French Court means war." Nevertheless, Lord North, the prime minister, eventually persuaded his royal master to allow Wentworth to sound out Deane and Franklin on the possibility of peace on terms short of independence before the Americans committed themselves to an alliance with France.

Such meetings between the belligerents were not uncommon. On several occasions Franklin rendezvoused with unofficial representatives of the British government and the Whig opposition, sometimes in a bathhouse on the Seine where he sat shrouded in steam, safe from the prying eyes of spies. Wentworth and Franklin had known each other in London before the war, and British Secret Service files indicate that Franklin had called upon the master spy in his lodgings in Paris, while Wentworth had been a visitor to Passy.

Wentworth arrived in Paris on December 12, 1777. Finding that Bancroft had gone "on the wing" to England to collect the rewards of his latest speculations, he had to contact the commissioners on his own. Overtures were made to Deane with an unsigned note reading: "A Gentleman who has some acquaintance with Mr. Deane wishes to improve it." Another followed, signed with Wentworth's initials. Immediately recognizing the identity of his correspondent, Deane agreed to a series of "secret and confidential" meetings. Wentworth unveiled a plan calling for peace without victory—the colonies to give up independence in return for repeal of the measures that had led to the rebellion. Vividly he described to Deane the panorama of honors ("Governors General—Privy Seals—Great Seals—Treasurers—Secretaries—Councillors—Local barons and knights") awaiting those who led the way to such a reconciliation.

With his usual deviousness, Franklin had, in the meantime, carefully notified Vergennes of the arrival of an English businessman with whom the Americans would be dealing, while supplying few details about the mysterious visitor or the purpose of his mission. The French already knew that Wentworth was in Paris, however, for he was being shadowed both by the police and by agents of Beaumarchais. Just as Franklin had calculated, Vergennes had guessed the purpose of Wentworth's mission and was concerned that the war-weary Americans might make peace with Britain if an alliance was not immediately agreed upon.

Negotiations had been delayed at the insistence of King Louis while efforts were made to convince Spain to join in the war against Britain. The Spaniards, reluctant to support a revolution in the Western Hemisphere that might inflame their own colonies, dragged their feet, and no answer was forthcoming from Madrid. Worried that the delay might drive the Americans into the arms of the British, on December 17 the French acted unilaterally. Vergennes hastily offered the commissioners recognition and a treaty of friendship and commerce in exchange for the promise that the United States would not make a separate peace with Britain.

With Bancroft absent, Wentworth was unable to confirm the persistent rumors that the French were preparing to recognize the United States, but he was convinced of their accuracy. "Take care that America and the West Indies don't glide through our fingers," he warned Eden. Two anxious weeks passed in which he feared arrest or even assassination by the French. Finding that someone had tried to force his strongbox, he burned all his letters. Finally, Bancroft returned, flush with his latest winnings, and arranged a meeting with Franklin on January 6, 1778. Undoubtedly, the crafty doctor agreed to meet Wentworth for the effect it would have on the French in case they were reconsidering their rash decision to act without Spain.

"72 received me very kindly," Wentworth reported to Eden, using Franklin's code number. But the rest of the rambling two-hour meeting must have been disappointing to the British agent. Franklin emphatically told his visitor that the American commissioners would not consent to peace without independence and that he had no power to conclude a truce. Wentworth also found the old man, usually so clear and pungent, curiously fuzzy and indefinite. When Wentworth suggested that Franklin and Deane might be given a safe conduct to England for talks with government representatives, Franklin was cagey.

If the interview was unsatisfactory from Wentworth's point of view, it was wildly successful as far as Franklin was concerned. The dread spectre of American reconciliation with Britain caused a tremor in the French court. The next day, the Royal Council unanimously agreed to enter into an alliance with the United States without waiting for Spain to act.

The commissioners were informed of the momentous decision by a French official who put a question to them that testifies eloquently to the effectiveness of Franklin's tactics of deception: "What is necessary to be done to give such satisfaction to the American Commissioners as to engage them not to listen to any propositions from England for a new connection with that country?" Franklin's reply was simple and direct:

"The immediate conclusion of [a] treaty will remove the uncertainty they are under with regard to it, and give them such a reliance on the friendship of France as to reject firmly all propositions made to them of peace from England."

The formal signing of the treaty that guaranteed American independence took place in great secrecy on February 6, 1778. Benjamin Franklin was the first American to sign; Silas Deane and Arthur Lee followed. When the ceremony had been concluded, the documents were given to Franklin for safekeeping. He handed them to Dr. Bancroft, who stood by, silently observing the ceremony. Forty-two hours later, a copy was being studied in Whitehall by a distressed King George and Lord North. Britain's offer was too little and too late. What had begun as a colonial uprising was now a global war that ranged from the Caribbean to the Indian Ocean.

■ ■ ■

Franklin remained in Paris until 1785, America's senior diplomat and the physical embodiment of the alliance with France he had done so much to bring to life. The old man's crowning achievement was the negotiation of the Treaty of Paris of 1783, which ended the Revolution with British recognition of the independence of the United States. "May we never see another war," he declared, "for in my opinion there never was a good war or a bad peace."

By that time, Silas Deane and Arthur Lee had returned home to continue their bitter brawl on another stage (they were replaced by John Adams and John Jay). Deane was recalled from Paris in 1778 to answer Lee's charges that he had used government funds to enrich himself. Two years later, embittered at his treatment by Congress, he returned to Europe and agreed to write a series of letters to old friends in America recommending reconciliation with Britain. These letters were forwarded through Bancroft to Wentworth and were sent to New York, where they were published by James Rivington in the *Royal Gazette* under the guise of having been captured at sea by a British warship. As a reward, the author was to receive three thousand pounds in merchandise to be sold in America. Unfortunately for Deane, the letters appeared at about the same time as the victory at Yorktown, and he was branded a traitor.

With Bancroft as his only friend, Deane lived in Europe on the verge of poverty until 1789, when he decided to return home. Just as he was to embark, however, he died under mysterious circumstances. Bancroft indicated that he was a suicide, but Julian P. Boyd, a professor of history at Princeton, made a provocative case in 1959 that Bancroft poisoned him with curare out of fear that he might reveal Bancroft's own treasonable activities.

Throughout the war and the negotiations for peace, Bancroft had remained at Franklin's side, serving the commissioners, his masters in Downing Street—and himself. When the French considered an invasion of a restive Ireland in 1779, Franklin sent Bancroft to survey conditions there. Upon his return to France, the double agent reported that "the fruit is not ripe" and advised that the expedition be postponed, undoubtedly a recommendation prepared by the British Secret Service.

Franklin's continued confidence in Bancroft despite the persistent charges that he had sold out to the British, combined with his complete disdain for the most elementary security precautions, have raised questions about the American statesman's own loyalty. Surely Bancroft's repeated journeyings across the Channel—not to mention the fact that secret documents entrusted to him had the curious habit of falling into the waiting hands of Lord Stormont—should have aroused Franklin's suspicions. But instead of rooting out the spy, he did nothing except mutter aphorisms from Poor Richard's ready stock. Was the old man duped? Was he senile? Or was Benjamin Franklin really the greatest traitor of them all?

Let's examine each of these possibilities. Franklin was well over seventy, but his masterful handling of the negotiations for both the alliance with France and the peace with Britain make it abundantly clear that time had not dulled his astuteness. With remarkable aplomb, he outmaneuvered and outbargained experienced French and British diplomats and even turned the surveillance of the British Secret Service to his own advantage. Clearly, his failures on the security front cannot be laid to the dimness of age. Nor is it likely that he was duped. Franklin was too experienced in the game of international intrigue to have been lulled by Bancroft's denials. It is impossible to believe he did not know what was going on about him.

Was he, then, a turncoat who secretly served the British?

Talk of shifting loyalties swirled about Franklin throughout the Revolution—he had lived in London for nearly twenty years, and critics charged he was more English than American—and in 1781 he was almost recalled from Paris.

Arthur Lee, John Adams, and Ralph Izard, another American representative in Europe, all had their doubts about him. Lee can be dismissed as paranoid, but Adams and Izard cannot be brushed off so easily. While none of these men actually accused Franklin of treason, Adams thought the "old conjurer" was hand in glove with Silas Deane in his speculations at the expense of the American government—and Deane turned out a traitor. For his part, Izard claimed that "the salvation of America depends upon the recalling of Dr. Franklin."

Two modern writers, Richard Deacon and Cecil B. Currey, have contended that Franklin was linked to the British Secret Service. Both writers emphasize that Franklin was close to Deane and Bancroft, who were later proven to be British agents, and that he was insensitive to security and lax in accounting for government funds. Currey made his well-publicized charge that Franklin may have been a British agent in *Code Number 72/ Ben Franklin: Patriot or Spy?*, published in 1972. Deacon is less circumspect in his *History of British Secret Service*, flatly stating that "Franklin used many code-names to cover his tracks and the British Secret Service referred to him as 'Agent No. 72.' "

There is no question that the British referred to Franklin as "72." The number appears several times in the Secret Service papers, most prominently in the previously quoted report filed by Paul Wentworth on his meeting with Franklin on January 6, 1778: "72 received me very kindly," Wentworth wrote. That he was referring to Franklin is certain; either Eden or his secretary carefully wrote "Dr. Franklin" above the number every time it appears in Wentworth's letter.* ("Mr. Deane" is written above the number "51.")

So far so good. But Currey's theory that these are agent numbers quickly falls apart upon further examination of Wentworth's annotated dispatch. The page is filled with numbers that, on this interpretation, would indicate that almost everyone at Passy was a British agent. Upon closer examination, however, "107" turns out to be "Independency," "64" to be "England," and "45" to be "Congress." Obviously, Currey has constructed a crucial element of his case on a misreading of the British code. Rather than constituting a list of secret agents, it is merely a substitution code in which numbers take the place of words.

But if Franklin was not senile, not a dupe, and not a British agent, why did he allow Bancroft to continue his espionage activities unmolested? The answer is obvious. Franklin *knew* Bancroft was a spy and wished him to have access to secret information. In present-day parlance, the entire operation was a calculated leak. Realizing full well that American independence turned on open French participation in the war, the crafty old fellow wanted the British to know all about French assistance to the embattled Americans. The more the British raged about this aid, the better the prospects for war between France and Britain. Under these circumstances, Bancroft was too valuable to be unmasked.

In fact, had Edward Bancroft not existed, Benjamin Franklin might have had to invent him.

---

*A photostat of the letter is in Stevens, *Facsimiles*, No. 489 (see Bibliography).

4

A More Perfect Union

Pushing out into the Cooper River, the small boat dropped down past a line of ships anchored off Charleston late in February 1799 and bumped with a hollow thud against the side of a Danish brig. Hand over hand, a band of heavily armed men clambered up a Jacob's ladder to the deck of the brig, determined to save the nation from subversion and slave rebellion. Three mulattoes, including Matthew Salmon, a former member of the revolutionary French National Convention, were placed under arrest. Several wooden tubs found amid their baggage were broken open; hidden in the false bottoms were mysterious-looking documents written in French.

"The horrors of guilt were depicted strongly on the countenances of the guilty wretches," witnesses reported. For a brief moment, the travelers were in danger of being thrown overboard, but cooler heads prevailed. They had been seized at the direct order of Timothy Pickering, secretary of state under President John Adams. The American consul in Hamburg had reported that Salmon had sailed for Charleston with dispatches from the Directory, which was then running the French government, concealed in false-bottomed tubs. The United States was engaged in an undeclared naval war with its former ally, and imagination leaping ahead of the facts, Pickering concluded that this report was clear evidence of a French conspiracy to overthrow the government. Because Salmon was a mulatto, it was also assumed that he had been sent by the Directory to stir up a slave revolt in the southern states similar to that which had occurred in Santo Domingo (now Haiti).

Pickering and the Carolinans were hailed as saviors of the Republic. Had it not been for their providential discovery of this latest example of French perfidy, proclaimed the Newport *Mercury*, "throats might have been cut: Carnage and devastation roaming thro' our Land, and our City one Pile of Ruins." In other towns solemn thanks were offered for the country's narrow escape from the murderous conspiracy.

The "Tub Plot" soon fell apart, however. An inquiry revealed that, far from being secret agents of the Directory, the people arrested at Charleston were actually hostile to the current French regime. Rather than planning to instigate a slave revolt in the United States, they had intended to proceed to Santo Domingo to warn the blacks that the Directory was plotting to again reduce them to slavery.

Like espionage itself, panic over the real or imagined activities of foreign or home-grown agents has been part of the American scene from the nation's earliest days. The "Tub Plot" was typical of the periodic spy manias that swept the United States in the first years of independence. Like most nations born in the fires of revolution, the new republic was haunted by the fear of conspiracies against its security. Some were fanciful; others were all too real. Uncertainty was heightened by the continued presence maintained by Britain and Spain on the nation's borders. The British held frontier forts to the north of the Ohio River, in defiance of the Treaty of Paris, which had ended the War of Independence; the Spaniards were in possession of Louisiana and East and West Florida.* In addition, relations with France had deteriorated steadily in the wake of the French Revolution.

If some Americans felt encircled and insecure, they had reason to. Up and down the great arc of the frontier from New Hampshire to Georgia, settlers talked of breaking their bonds to the Union and coming to terms with the nations that could protect their interests. The American government had almost no intelligence regarding the intentions of these foreign powers; all that had been learned about such operations during the war had been promptly forgotten. The United States Army had established an elementary general staff that might have taken intelligence into account, but it was never properly manned, and intelligence functions were limited to scouting and mapping.

To add to the turmoil, until George Washington's inauguration in 1789, the nation was not so much governed as maintained in a caretaker status by the loosely drawn Articles of Confederation. Far from being united as Americans, the former colonists feared that a strong central government might lead to a new tyranny no better than the one they had just escaped. Consequently, a weak Congress functioned as little more than a council of ambassadors of an uneasy league of thirteen more or less sovereign republics. Money was short, there was only a shadow of an army, and there was no navy at all.

---

*Florida was divided into East and West Florida at the Perdido River near Pensacola. West Florida included the southern parts of what are now Alabama and Mississippi as well as part of Louisiana, while East Florida approximated the current state.

For their part, the British maintained an extensive intelligence network in America under the control of Lord Dorchester, the governor-general of Canada. These agents gathered information, established links with influential Americans, and cultivated pro-British sentiments. They received considerable assistance from Americans of varying degrees of loyalty—or disloyalty—to the new republic: Americans who may have been critical of the mother country during the Revolution but who were now friendly to Britain. "There is not a gentleman from New Hampshire to Georgia," wrote one informant, "who does not view the present government with contempt, who is not convinced of its inefficiency, and who is not desirous of changing it for a Monarchy."

The political and economic inadequacies of the Articles of Confederation led to the Constitutional Convention that opened in Philadelphia in May 1787. Throughout that stifling summer, the fifty-five delegates struggled to find a compromise between conflicting interests—shipowners against manufacturers, planters against merchants, small states against big states. The delegates wanted a stable, secure government—""a more perfect union"—badly enough to submerge class, economic, and political differences in favor of an agreement that distributed power among all the competing interests.

The resulting Federal Constitution makes no direct reference to intelligence activities, and the subsequent Bill of Rights, with its guarantees of individual liberties, protects the citizenry from domestic espionage. But the Constitution does contain provisions granting implied authority for an intelligence function. Article II, Section 2, names the president as commander in chief of the army and navy, while Section 3 directs the chief executive to "take care that the laws be faithfully executed." Presidents ever since have relied upon this broad and vague authority to justify intelligence activity—from the extemporaneous operations of the early Republic to the establishment of the modern intelligence structure.

Writing in *The Federalist Papers*, John Jay, one of the few American political leaders with actual experience in intelligence during the War of Independence,* emphasized the necessity for the new government to have such a capability:

> There are cases where the most useful intelligence may be obtained, if the persons possessing it can be relieved from apprehensions of discovery. Those apprehensions will operate on those persons whether they are actuated by mercenary or friendly motives; and there doubtless are

---

*Jay had run a wide-ranging spy-catching operation in Westchester, to the north of New York City, that sniffed out British spies and Tory sympathizers with considerable success. Among Jay's people was Enoch Crosby, thought to be the inspiration for J. Fenimore Cooper's novel, *The Spy*.

many of both descriptions who would rely on the secrecy of the President, and would not confide in that of the Senate, and still less in that of a largely popular assembly. The Convention have done well, therefore, in so disposing of the making of treaties that although the President must, in forming them, act by the advice and consent of the Senate, yet he will be able to manage the business of intelligence in such a manner as prudence may suggest.

In fact, the first appropriation approved by Congress—on July 1, 1790—provided President Washington with a "Contingent Fund of Foreign Intercourse" that was obviously to be used for secret diplomacy. There can be no other explanation for the provisions authorizing the president to account for funds expended by voucher without revealing either their purpose or the person to whom the money was paid.* The secret service fund amounted to forty thousand dollars in 1790; within three years, it had grown to one million dollars; or about twelve percent of the national budget. Most of this money was used for ransoming Americans held hostage by the Barbary pirates, for paying off foreign officials, and, in effect, for buying peace.

Washington also established the practice followed by later presidents of bypassing both Congress and the State Department and sending executive agents abroad to gain intelligence and conduct negotiations. In many cases, the president's men were paid from the "contingent fund" and acted as secret agents. The president did not even wait until the fund was approved to send Gouverneur Morris to Britain to inquire into the continued British occupation of the frontier forts. Morris was, in effect, the first intelligence agent sent abroad under the Constitution. David Humphreys, who was dispatched to Lisbon to make arrangements for a diplomatic office in the Portuguese capital, was instructed to "avoid all suspicion of being on public business."

Even at this early date, however, Congress was unhappy with being shunted aside in the conduct of foreign affairs. Upon being notified of Humphreys' mission, Senator William Maclay of Pennsylvania observed that "the President sends first and asks our advice and consent afterwards." Maclay was even more caustic about Morris: "He has acted in a strange kind of capacity, half pimp, half envoy, or perhaps more properly a kind of political eavesdropper about the British Court."

■ ■ ■

The French Revolution splintered the fragile alliance of former colonists and precipitated a virulent outbreak of spy fever in the United States. In the beginning, most Americans were sympathetic to the revo-

*A century and a half later, the director of central intelligence was given the same authority by the Central Intelligence Agency Act of 1949.

lution, seeing it as a continuation of their own revolt against the despotism of kings. Lafayette even presented President Washington with the key to the Bastille to signify the link between the two revolutions. In the "love-frenzy for France," honorifics such as "Judge" and "Mister" temporarily became in the new French style, "Citizen." But when the revolution spawned the Reign of Terror, American public opinion split along class and political lines.

Partly as a result of differences over the French Revolution two political parties crystallized during Washington's first administration: the Federalists, led by Alexander Hamilton, the secretary of the treasury, and the Republicans—forerunners of the modern Democratic party—led by Thomas Jefferson, the secretary of state. These two brilliant, strong-willed men had clashed almost from the beginning. They were, in Jefferson's words, "daily pitted in the cabinet like two cocks." To guarantee the future stability of the new nation, Hamilton believed it should be grounded upon the mercantile and manufacturing class and looked to England for his model. In essence, he felt those who owned the country should govern it. Jefferson, suspicious of a government founded on commercial interests, held aloft a vision of an America of yeoman farmers and artisans, and sympathized with France when she went to war with Britain early in 1793. By no means for the last time, different visions of America governed how its leaders viewed foreign "friends" and "enemies."

■ ■ ■

Political passions ran high. Federalists were branded as "British bootlickers," while Republicans were called "a despicable mobocracy" who wanted to set up guillotines in the town squares. Although sympathetic to Hamilton's views, Washington tried to steer a middle course between the belligerents. In effect the president used the four members of his cabinet—besides Hamilton and Jefferson, Edmund Randolph, the attorney general, and Henry Knox, the secretary of war—as an early version of the National Security Council,* obtaining a variety of advice upon which to base his decisions.

The process was made more difficult by the activities of the new French minister, Edmond Charles Genet. Even before arriving at the capital at Philadelphia to present his diplomatic credentials, "Citizen" Genet demanded that the United States live up to its obligations under the Franco-American treaty of 1778 by allowing its territory to be used as a base for operations against the British. Genet commissioned fourteen

*The National Security Council was created in 1947 to provide a unified, high-level body to create and coordinate politico-military policy.

privateers to prey upon British commerce, and he recruited armed expeditions for the conquest of Canada, as well as Louisiana and East and West Florida, which were both controlled by Spain, a British ally.

Jefferson and his followers gave Genet an enthusiastic welcome, and they aided and abetted his plans. André Michaux, a leading French botanist, was among the undercover agents sent out by Genet to organize American frontiersmen for the foray into enemy territory. Jefferson fully realized that Michaux had other business in the West than collecting specimens, but he placed no restrictions upon him. He justified this unneutral conduct with the hope that, as a reward for its complicity, the United States would receive the Floridas, and France, after seizing control of Louisiana, would permit Americans to enjoy free navigation of the Mississippi River, a privilege denied by the Spaniards.

Swarming out of American ports, Genet's privateers snatched up over eighty British prizes. The British strongly protested this flagrant violation of neutrality, but offenders were freed by pro-French juries. With his efforts crowned by success, the irrepressible Genet became more and more indiscreet. Jefferson began to worry that his activities might backfire on the Republicans and eventually embroil the United States in a war with Britain. "Citizen" Genet was finally neutralized by a change of regime in France, though not before threatening to appeal to the American people over the head of the president.* These blunders increased the ill will between the United States and France while exacerbating domestic disputes as well.

Meanwhile, pro-British Americans could take heart in a temporary easing of tensions with Britain. In 1794, John Jay, taking leave of his post as chief justice, was sent to London to negotiate a treaty with the British aimed at settling the problems outstanding between the two nations. Jay did not have a strong hand, but he did have one ace—the possibility that America might join a group of neutral nations in resisting Britain's arbitrary interference with maritime trade. This was merely a bluff, however, for the administration had already decided to steer clear of the so-called Armed Neutrality. Jay's mission was partially undone by intrigue: Hamilton leaked news of the administration's real position to George Hammond, the British minister in Philadelphia, allowing the British negotiators to trump Jay's best card before he could play it. It was, to say the least, a time of complex and sometimes confused loyalties.

In fact, Hamilton's relations with Hammond—and before him with

---

*The faction that assumed power in France wanted to cut off not only the minister's diplomatic career but his head as well. Terrified, Genet threw himself upon the mercy of the administration he had threatened to overthrow. Washington granted him asylum in the United States. Not long afterward, he married the daughter of Governor George Clinton of New York and settled down to the quiet life of a country squire.

Major George Beckwith, a British secret agent*—have raised the question of whether or not Hamilton himself was a British agent. If Jefferson had all but actively assisted Genet's machinations, Hamilton maintained a relationship with Beckwith and Hammond that could not have been closer had Britain and the United States been allies. There were few state secrets to which they did not have access because of their ties to the treasury secretary. (In his reports, Beckwith referred to Hamilton by the code name "Number 7" to protect his informant.) Jefferson suspected that his cabinet colleague was undermining his foreign policy but never grasped the extent of the betrayal.

The only real concessions obtained by Jay from the well-informed British were promises to abandon the frontier forts they were to have relinquished in 1783 and to open the West Indian islands to American trade. The treaty was highly unpopular, and Jay was denounced as a traitor and hanged in effigy. In March 1796, the House of Representatives requested the executive branch to furnish it with all documents pertaining to the negotiations. Establishing a pattern for the future, Washington declined the request and reminded Congress that diplomatic negotiations depend on secrecy "and even when brought to a conclusion a full disclosure of all the measures, demands, or eventual concessions which may have been proposed or contemplated would be extremely impolitic."

Nevertheless, Jay's treaty reduced the possibility that the United States and Britain might stumble into another war. But the French Directory claimed the agreement was detrimental to the interests of France and stepped up harassment of American shipping. Over a nine-month period, the French seized 316 Yankee vessels, some in American waters. Now the danger of a clash with France loomed on the horizon. Hoping to avert war, President John Adams, who had taken office in 1797, dispatched a special mission to Paris in the latter part of the year. For several months, the commissioners were given the runaround, but just as they were ready to return home in failure, they were approached by three agents of Charles Maurice de Talleyrand-Perigord, the apostate bishop who had become the French foreign minister. These agents, accompanied by a woman (without whom no European diplomatic intrigue was complete), demanded a $250,000 bribe for the minister and a large loan to the French government as a prerequisite for negotiations. The Americans flatly refused to pay, but they could hardly have been shocked by the proposal. Bribery was a customary adjunct to eighteenth-

---

*Beckwith, who had been on Sir Henry Clinton's staff during the war, had assisted John André in his correspondence with Benedict Arnold and had a wide acquaintanceship with the Loyalist families of New York. He returned to America in 1787 as an agent for the intelligence network that reported to Lord Dorchester in Canada and stayed on after the establishment of the new American government.

century statecraft, and Talleyrand had already extorted money from most of the nations with which France had diplomatic relations.

When President Adams made public a report on the affair in which the French agents were identified as "X," "Y," and "Z," anti-French feeling swept the country. "No! No! Not a sixpence!" one of the commissioners, a South Carolina Federalist named Charles C. Pinckney, was supposed to have told the French agents. An imaginative newspaper editor transformed his retort into the wildly popular, "Millions for defense, but not one cent for tribute!"* With the Federalists leading the charge, the country prepared to fight to preserve its independence. George Washington was recalled from retirement to take command of an expanded American army, and Congress authorized the newly organized U. S. Navy to capture French vessels on the high seas.†

Once again, spy fever spread through the nation, and rumors of subversion and foreign intrigues swirled in the air like leaves in a gale. Foreshadowing the future, the Federalists created their own evidence of conspiracy. William Cobbett, the fiercely Federalist editor of *Porcupine's Gazette,* warned that on May 9, 1798, which had been ordained as a day of fasting by Adams, "desperate villains" would set fire to Philadelphia and massacre the citizenry. Nothing happened, but Cobbett continued to rage. "Take care," he thundered, "when your blood runs down the gutters, don't say you were not forewarned of the danger." Jefferson, now vice-president, was accused of being in contact with the Directory and resorted to cipher to protect the privacy of his correspondence.

It was perhaps inevitable that this frenzied atmosphere would produce the beginnings of domestic espionage in the United States. In a scene that would be replayed again and again in American history, domestic politics and constitutional issues became enmeshed with foreign affairs and threats to security both real and imagined. Federalists took to spying on their rivals and, more openly, met the alleged threat with restrictive legislation intended to put an end to their activities. In June and July of 1798, they rammed a series of laws through Congress— the Alien and Sedition Acts—that were supposedly aimed at subversives but that struck at the heart of American civil liberties. These laws placed restrictions upon aliens, particularly French and immigrant Irish, most of whom gravitated toward the anti-British Republicans, and bridled home-grown radicals, especially pro-Republican journalists.

In all, about twenty-five persons were arrested in what Jeffersonians

---

*Everyone conveniently forgot that the United States was paying millions in tribute to the Barbary pirates to protect its commerce in the Mediterranean.

†Neither France nor the United States observed the formality of a declaration of war, however, and the two-year (1798–1800) naval conflict that followed is known as the Quasi-War.

called the "Federalist Reign of Terror." Most were newspaper editors who were silenced by heavy fines or jail terms.* Matthew Lyon, a Republican congressman from Vermont, was convicted of sedition, fined one thousand dollars and sentenced to serve four months in jail. Vice-President Jefferson claimed he was being shadowed by Federalist agents. Apologizing to a hostess for being late to tea, he told her that "he was himself dogged and watched in the most extraordinary manner" and had taken a circuitous route to her home "to elude the curiosity of his spies."

When the "Tub Plot" was uncovered in Charleston, the Federalists flaunted it at as proof positive of the need for the Alien and Sedition Acts. "Americans! Unite, rally round your government," exhorted a pro-administration paper. "BEWARE OF FRENCH IMMIGRANTS!" But when the bottom fell out of the "conspiracy," the credibility of the Federalists and their persistent charges of "plots—fire plots—itinerant Jacobin plots—Talleyrand plots" were called into question. Meanwhile, President Adams became alarmed at the stormy seas into which the American ship of state was drifting. In no sense a democrat—Adams regarded Jefferson's belief in the innate virtue of the common man as sentimental nonsense—he was equally hostile to anything that smacked of dictatorship.

Peace feelers were being received from the French, and Adams seized the chance to send commissioners to Paris to negotiate an end to hostilities. The Federalists were thunderstruck. Without a war with France there would be no opportunity to discredit the Republicans and no conquest of New Orleans and the Floridas. But the president courageously put the nation's welfare above that of his party. Fully realizing that peace would probably cost him reelection, he pressed ahead with the talks. The corrupt and arrogant Directory, which had provided the excuse for war, had been ousted by Napoleon Bonaparte, and the new First Consul had no reason to continue a conflict that could only drive the United States into the arms of Britain. Seven months of negotiations ended in a settlement that, as Adams had forecast, pricked the balloon of Federalist popularity. In 1800, Republican Thomas Jefferson defeated him for the presidency, and the Federalists were swept from power—never to return.

■ ■ ■

For the next half century, the American West was the focal point of conspiracies and spy threats. The operational climate—as modern intelligence officers would put it—was highly favorable for clandestine operations. British, French, and Spanish spies vied with each other, and the area seethed with plots to detach vast tracts from the control of the

---

*In New Jersey, a tavern loiterer was jailed for expressing the hope that the wadding of the cannon fired in President Adams's honor would lodge in his backside.

United States. Perhaps the American government's only sources of reliable intelligence were the Indian agents who had the delicate task of negotiating treaties with the Indians. They also served as the government's eyes and ears in these remote areas. Wrote Captain William Henry Harrison to the War Department: "The times are such as, in my opinion, to make it the duty of every friend of the country to keep a true lookout &, if possible, discover & expose to the detestation of the world those traitors, who, acting under foreign influences are plotting schemes destructive to the interests of their country."

Within a few months after Jefferson walked through the muddy streets of Washington to his inauguration in the uncompleted Capitol on March 4, 1801, the nation was engulfed in fresh intrigues. Like most Americans, the new president wanted an end to the ever-present threat to national security posed by the presence of European colonies on its flanks. Scheming to obtain control of the territory, he planned to send a secret expedition into Louisiana to spy out the land and its inhabitants.

■ ■ ■

In requesting funds for the expedition—to be led by two regular army officers, Captain Meriwether Lewis and Lieutenant William Clark—Jefferson told Congress that it was "for the purpose of extending the external commerce of the United States." This cryptic language masked a covert military intelligence foray into lands belonging to a nation with whom the United States was at peace. Lewis and Clark were instructed to discover who lived in the vast area beteen the Mississippi and the Pacific, to make surveys, and to pick sites for fortifications. They were to conceal their identities, and if apprehended by the Spanish authorities or the British in the Pacific Northwest, were to claim they were searching for the fabled Northwest Passage.

Before the expedition was fully organized, however, Jefferson was shocked to learn that Spain had secretly conveyed possession of Louisiana back to France. If Napoleon reestablished the French empire in the New World, a barrier would be erected to the continued expansion of the United States. The situation worsened when it was learned that, in preparation of the transfer, the Spaniards had closed the port of New Orleans, which was vital to Western trade coming down the Mississippi. Acting quickly to meet the emergency, Jefferson sent James Monroe to Paris to join the American minister, Robert R. Livingston, with orders to speed up desultory negotiations already underway to purchase New Orleans and both Floridas. Monroe was authorized to make an offer of ten million dollars. If the French refused, three-quarters of this sum was to be offered for New Orleans alone. If they still balked, the president authorized the American representatives to proceed to London and open discussions for an alliance with Britain.

Shortly before Monroe's arrival, on April 11, 1804, Talleyrand, who had adroitly survived every change in the French government, unexpectedly asked Livingston: "What will you give for the whole of Louisiana?" Unable to believe what he had heard, Livingston, who was partially deaf anyway, replied that the United States was interested only in New Orleans and the Floridas. Less than three weeks later, however, with Monroe on hand, the Americans agreed to pay fifteen million dollars in cash and claims for roughly a million square miles of land. It was the greatest real estate bargain in history. As soon as Congress ratified the Louisiana Purchase, Lewis and Clark were dispatched on their expedition—no longer a covert intelligence operation but now a legitimate mission of exploration.

■ ■ ■

Another intrigue involving Western lands starred a character few Americans have heard of, but one who deserves a place in the front rank of any rogues' gallery: General James Wilkinson. To this liar and conspirator belongs the distinction of working as a spy for a foreign power while serving as commanding general of the United States Army.

Wilkinson launched his career in duplicity during the War of Independence. Rising to the rank of colonel at the age of twenty—through his ability to ingratiate himself with superiors rather than any military capacity—he was on the fringes of a cabal to depose George Washington as commander in chief and was removed as clothier general because of "gross irregularities" in his accounts. Undoubtedly thanks to the influence of the Biddle family of Philadelphia, into which he had married, Wilkinson managed to avoid dismissal from the service.

With this preparation, Wilkinson entered into intrigue on an international scale. Overwhelmed with debt and renowned as a drunkard, he moved to Kentucky, where he became active in politics and land speculation. Soon he was deeply involved in the so-called Spanish Conspiracy. The Spaniards were fearful of the American frontiersmen who were greedily eyeing their territory, and Wilkinson sensed an opportunity to turn these fears to his own profit. Floating down the Mississippi to New Orleans in a flatboat, he suggested to Estaban Miró, the Spanish governor of Louisiana, that the area west of the Alleghenies be pried away from the control of the United States and a buffer state created under Spanish protection. Miró approved the plan, and in 1787 Wilkinson secretly took the oath of allegiance to Spain. Designated in Spanish reports from this time onward as "Agent Number 13," he was provided with "one of the most incomprehensible ciphers"—and a yearly pension of two thousand dollars plus extras, payable in silver dollars.

Despite this windfall, Wilkinson's extravagance kept him teetering on the brink of bankruptcy. Perhaps to increase his value to his Spanish paymasters, he obtained a commission in the newly organized U. S. Army. Through adroit public relations, he gained a reputation as an Indian fighter, although President Washington caustically observed that "little can be said of his abilities as an officer . . . whether he is sober or not is unknown to me." Rumors of Wilkinson's connections with the Spaniards* reached the president, who, his old spymaster's antennae twitching, wanted them checked out. But no one else took the reports seriously—except for the traitor himself. "For the love of God and friendship enjoin great secrecy and caution in all our concerns," he wrote frantically to the Spanish authorities in Natchez. "Never suffer my name to be written or spoken. The suspicion of Washington is wide awake."

Wilkinson rode out the storm and was made general in chief of the army. Having ingratiated himself with Jefferson, he was named governor of the Louisiana Territory as well. All the while he was still working for the Spaniards. They were worried about the Americans' intentions, for the purchase agreement had left the boundaries of Louisiana obscured in a mist of vague language. "You have made a noble bargain for yourselves, and I suppose you will make the most of it," Talleyrand had replied enigmatically when asked by Livingston about the precise boundaries of the purchase. Was the southern border of the Territory on the Rio Grande, as the Americans claimed, or was it along the Sabine River, as the Spaniards said? Did it include West Florida?

In return for a lump sum payment of twelve thousand dollars,† "Agent Number 13" supplied the Spanish with a memorandum outlining President Jefferson's future plans. To keep the Americans from profiting from their new possession, Wilkinson suggested that the Spaniards hold on to West Florida and arrest Lewis and Clark should the expedition venture into territory claimed by Spain. He also proposed that they fortify the borders of Texas and Florida—even though as commanding general of the U. S. Army he might be called upon to lead his men against those same fortifications.

Flush with Spanish funds, Wilkinson came east. Mounted on a blooded mare, gaudy in a major general's uniform of his own design, with spurs of gold and a leopard skin for a saddlecloth, he added a flash of color to the drabness of Washington. There he renewed his acquaintance with Vice-President Aaron Burr, with whom he had served on the staff of Benedict Arnold during the Revolution. With his term coming to an end and under indictment for murder in New York and New Jersey for having killed Alexander Hamilton in a duel, Burr was looking for new fields of

*These rumors would not be confirmed until the opening of the Spanish archives a century later.

†Wilkinson had already received about twenty-six thousand dollars from the Spaniards for his services.

conquest. Soon the pair were poring over maps of Florida, the Louisiana Territory, and Mexico.

Burr is the black sheep of the revolutionary generation. Although a man of great wit, charm, and intelligence, he casts a shadow across the pages of American history only a bit less sinister than that of Arnold. Grandson of the Puritan theologian Jonathan Edwards, son of a president of Princeton, brave soldier, able advocate, and skillful politician: Burr had all the credentials for admission to the charmed circle of the Founding Fathers. But he could never dispel the aura of brimstone that seemed to swirl about him.* Perhaps his infamy can be traced to his delight in his own notoriety. In the public mind, he stands convicted of a calculated attempt to steal the election of 1800 from Jefferson, of having killed Hamilton to avenge a political slight, and of plotting to separate the vast territory to the west of the Appalachians from the rest of the country and make himself its ruler.

Just what plans Burr developed for the West with Wilkinson and Jonathan Dayton, a former senator from New Jersey—and whether they were treasonous, as later charged—is uncertain, for his story varied according to his audience. In its most ambitious form, he envisaged an empire in the Southwest based on the splitting away of the area from the Union and the conquest of Mexico. This is the version presented to Andrew Merry, the British minister in Washington, in an attempt to obtain half a million dollars in financing and Royal Navy support for what was, in effect, a covert attempt to destabilize the United States. To others, Burr presented a less grandiose plot, a freebooting expedition aimed merely at "liberating" Mexico from Spain.

Merry was a cautious professional diplomat whose bland manner belied his name. (One American observed that if he were asked the time, Merry would probably refuse a reply until he had checked with his government.) Nevertheless, he was receptive to Burr's proposal, which reached him through Charles Williamson, a British secret agent close to the vice-president. Williamson was as outgoing as Merry was reserved. After serving in the British army in America during the Revolution, he had worked for the Secret Service in Egypt and Turkey, and in 1791, returned to the United States, where he became a naturalized citizen. But despite Merry's prodding and a visit to London by Williamson to make a personal plea for British support of Burr's plan, the Foreign Office refused to divert forces from the war against Napoleon.

■ ■ ■

Wilkinson was an active participant in the conspiracy, and when Burr toured the West, he provided the vice-president with transportation

---

*The description that accompanied the warrant for Burr's arrest on treason charges noted that his eyes "sparkled like diamonds."

and introductions to prominent residents. He also dispatched an expedition headed by Lieutenant Zebulon M. Pike into Spanish territory to reconnoiter what became the Santa Fe Trail. Pike sighted the peak named for him—which he did not climb—and was detained by Spanish troops for violating Spanish sovereignty. Noting that Burr had inquired about routes to Santa Fe, some observers believe Wilkinson had more than scientific objectives in mind in ordering out the expedition.

In the summer of 1806, Wilkinson received several cipher letters notifying him that Burr and his followers were ready to move. But the slippery general was having second thoughts; loyal Westerners had warned Jefferson of the proposed expedition. To protect himself, Wilkinson betrayed Burr just as he had betrayed everyone else with whom he had ever been associated. He dispatched a lurid letter to the president denouncing "a deep, dark wicked and widespread conspiracy," and, to prove his loyalty, conducted a wave of arbitrary arrests of suspected conspirators in New Orleans. Neglecting no opportunity for personal gain, Wilkinson had the effrontery to request a reward of two hundred thousand dollars from the Spaniards for preventing an invasion of their territory!

Jefferson considered Burr, whom he suspected of having tried to steal the presidency from him in 1800, capable of almost any treachery. "I never . . . thought him an honest, frank-dealing man," he later declared, "but considered him a crooked gun, or rather a perverted machine, whose aim or shot you could never be sure of." Pouncing upon the opportunity to even old scores, Jefferson ordered Burr arrested on charges of treason.

Burr's trial in Richmond before Chief Justice John Marshall was anticlimactic. Wilkinson, who only narrowly escaped indictment himself, was the government's star witness, and a cipher letter he claimed had been written by Burr was the most damaging piece of evidence produced by the prosecution. Jefferson bent every effort to ensure a conviction, but Marshall, an ardent Federalist, made certain that the constitutional definition of treason—"'levying war against the United States or adhering to their enemies"—was strictly observed. The jury brought in a verdict of "not proved," and Burr was a free man.*

Unwilling to face other charges that were still pending and harassed by creditors, Burr fled to Europe, where he remained until a few years before his death in 1836. Unrepentant and debonair, he sired two illegitimate children in his seventies and wins the laurel for virility, being divorced at eighty on grounds of adultery. And what of James Wilkinson? As a reward for turning on his fellow conspirators, Jefferson allowed the

*Recent research indicates that Jonathan Dayton rather than Burr wrote the cipher letter. Even if Burr had written it, the document proves only that he was guilty of organizing a filibustering expedition against Mexico rather than treason against the United States. Luckily for Burr, however, his correspondence with Andrew Merry did not become public until a half-century after his death.

old reprobate to keep his post in the army. During the War of 1812, he proved his incompetence for command and was finally relieved from duty. Soon after Mexico declared its independence from Spain, he went south to see what he could scavenge from the upheaval and died there in 1821. He had claimed to be representing the American Bible Society.

■ ■ ■

The Louisiana Purchase whetted the American appetite for the Floridas. Thrusting deep into the Gulf of Mexico, East Florida had great strategic value because it was a constant threat to the lines of commerce and communication between New Orleans and the Atlantic seaboard. West Florida attracted American attention because it controlled the area around New Orleans and the rivers that flow through what is now Mississippi and Alabama. The Floridas were also a thorn in the side of the United States because hostile Indians used the area as a base from which to launch raids across the frontier, while escaped slaves found a haven there.

President Jefferson and James Madison, his secretary of state, argued that Louisiana included West Florida, but the Spaniards rejected their claims. Undismayed, the Americans tried to bribe Napoleon into twisting Spain's arm to cede the territory to the United States. A euphemistically worded resolution was approved by a secret session of Congress appropriating two million dollars for "defraying any extraordinary expenses which may be incurred in the intercourse between the United States and foreign nations." The plot failed, but Jefferson and Madison kept their eyes steadfastly fixed on the prize. "We must have the Floridas and Cuba," Jefferson declared just before Madison followed him into the presidency.

Today, Madison is revered as the "Father of the Constitution," but he also fathered presidential deniability and active American intervention into the affairs of other nations in the hemisphere. Usually regarded as a precise, even timid man unlikely to be stirred by reckless passion, he uncharacteristically threw caution to the winds as he intrigued to add the Floridas to the United States. In 1810 he saw the opportunity for which he was waiting. Spain, which had been allied with Napoleon, switched sides, King Ferdinand VI was a French prisoner, and the Spanish peninsula was torn by a savage guerrilla war. As Spain's grip upon her colonies in the New World loosened, France, Britain, and the United States hovered over the expiring empire, snatching at bits and pieces.

Taking advantage of Spain's distress, Madison decided the moment was ripe to seize West Florida. William C. Claiborne, the expansionist-minded governor of New Orleans, was summoned to Washington, where the two men examined their options. Agreeing that an open American invasion of West Florida would create serious domestic and international complications, they worked out a more subtle scenario. "Patriotic" Americans living in West Florida would be encouraged to proclaim their independence and then to request assistance from Washington—which, of course, would be immediately forthcoming. By the time the Spaniards realized what had happened, West Florida would be part of the United States.

Even before leaving Washington, Claiborne, in modern parlance the case officer for the operation, began rounding up support. On June 14, 1810, he wrote William Wykoff, a prominent American living near Baton Rouge, in West Florida, who had expressed an eagerness to lead such a "patriot movement." In his letter Claiborne outlined the details of the plan to subvert Spanish control of the territory, noting that "it would be more pleasing that the taking possession of the country be preceded by a request from the inhabitants." To create a semblance of a popular movement, he suggested that a convention of kindred spirits be called to extend an invitation to the United States to intervene.

The "patriots" had already jumped the gun, however. A month before Claiborne's letter, they had called for just such a convention to protest against high taxes, exorbitant fees, and rampant corruption in the Spanish administration. With the hope of keeping an eye on it, the Spanish governor gave permission for the meeting, which was gaveled to order on July 25, 1810. The delegates organized themselves as a legislature, but after a few weeks of deliberation accused the governor of stalling on reforms until reinforcements could arrive from Havana to put down the rebellion. On September 23, some eighty "patriots" attacked the fort at Baton Rouge. Shouting "Hurrah! Washington!" they swarmed through the undefended gate and captured the place without losing a man. The Spanish flag was torn down and replaced by the banner of the "Republic of West Florida"—a blue field with a lone silver star.

The convention now put the next part of Madison's plan into effect by dispatching a declaration of independence to Governor Claiborne in New Orleans. The declaration was transmitted to the State Department on October 3 with a note requesting "immediate and special protection as an integral and inalienable portion of the United States." The "patriots" did not have long to wait. Little more than a month after the revolt, on October 27, 1810, the gratified Madison issued a proclamation incorporating West Florida into the United States and extending the nation's boundary to the Perdido River.

The ink of the proclamation was hardly dry before the French minister demanded a meeting with Secretary of State Robert Smith. The French were angry because the Americans had beaten them to an area upon which they had their own designs. "I swear on my honor as a gentleman . . . that we are strangers to everything that has happened," Smith blandly replied. To make the annexation seem less contrived and to cover the secretary of state's bold lie, the president falsified the date he had received the note requesting American protection, making it two weeks later than it actually was. Madison's artful sleight of hand was not discovered until fifty years later, when a historian examined the State Department records.

The Spaniards vehemently protested this naked grab but were too deeply involved in the conflict against Napoleon to consider war with the United States over West Florida. Britain was also displeased, and her minister in Washington denounced the occupation as "contrary to every principle of public justice, faith and national honor." Most nations, however, accepted it as a fact of international life. When John Quincy Adams, the embarrassed American minister to Russia, tried to explain how his country had suddenly acquired the territory of its neighbor, Tsar Alexander I shrugged and replied pleasantly: "Everybody is getting a little bigger, nowadays."

Although he is not usually remembered as a master of espionage, George Washington's skillful spying activities during the American Revolution helped us win the war against the British and helped get him elected first President of the United States. Photo courtesy of The National Portrait Gallery, Smithsonian Institution, Washington, D.C.

As founder of the Culper Ring and member of a prominent Long Island family, Colonel Benjamin Tallmadge organized one of the most successful spy rings of the War for Independence. His family connections helped him secure inside information about British maneuvers on New York City and Long Island. Photo courtesy of The Library of Congress.

An all-around renaissance man, Benjamin Franklin—diplomat, author, scientist, inventor—was also a master of intrigue. With his complex and astute mind, he was a skilled manipulator of men and ideas. Having lived in Europe for twenty years, he was sent to France during the American Revolution to set up a spy network which facilitated the funneling of arms from France to America. Photo courtesy of The National Portrait Gallery, The Smithsonian Institution, Washington, D.C.

Benedict Arnold, branded as a traitor during the American Revolution, is pictured here persuading John Andre, his wife's ex-love interest, to aid him by concealing papers in his boot. The motive for Arnold's misplaced loyalties was financial gain. Photo courtesy of the author's collection.

This bronze statue of Nathan Hale awaiting execution commemorates his futile and amateur attempt at transmitting news of British troop maneuvers in the Revolutionary War. He was executed 10 days later and has since become America's most famous patriot spy. Photo courtesy of The National Archives.

General James Wilkinson was one of the great rogues of American history. He was a Spanish spy while serving as Commander in Chief of the U.S. Army and was involved with Aaron Burr in a conspiracy to detach the Southwestern territories from the United States. Photo courtesy of The National Archives.

As a self-styled spy, shown here in the field, Allan Pinkerton was the nation's first real detective and headed an intelligence operation during the Civil War. His work for General McClellan of the Union Army helped uncover Confederate spies like Rebel Rose Greenhow. Photo courtesy of The National Portrait Gallery, The Smithsonian Institution, Washington, D.C.

Pinkerton's successor was General Lafayette Baker, self-styled head of the Secret Service with a reputation for terrorizing the nation by running a ruthless campaign against disloyalty in the government. His post-war activities included helping to impeach Andrew Johnson. Photo courtesy of The National Archives.

A former New York City policeman, Timothy Webster was Allan Pinkerton's top operative and most effective agent but following his capture by the Confederates, was the first American to be hanged as a spy since Nathan Hale. Photo from the author's collection.

The Union Army's spymaster in Europe and the American Minister to Belgium during the Civil War, Henry S. Sanford tried to discredit the reputation of the Confederacy and halt European aid and trading. Under his supervision, covert operations in England and Europe were put into effect so that pro-southern sympathies would be countered and all Europe's ties with the Confederacy completely severed. Photo courtesy of The Library of Congress.

As chief of the Bureau of Military Information, Colonel George H. Sharpe directed all intelligence operations for the Union Army. This was the most sophisticated American Intelligence Service of the Civil War. Sharpe's Agency was a completely equipped intelligence organization and by the end of the War he employed about 200 spies and scouts. Photo courtesy of The National Archives.

Elizabeth Van Lew "listened in" at the Jefferson Davis household through a Negro girl she had freed, educated in the North, and placed there as a waitress. Photo courtesy of the Elizabeth Van Lew Papers; Rare Books and Manuscript Division, The New York Public Library Astor, Lenox and Tilden Foundations.

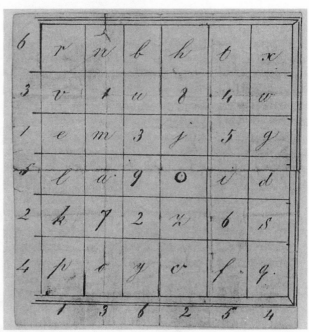

Miss Van Lew wrote dispatches in cipher to General Grant with a colorless liquid which became visible with the application of milk. She kept this key to the secret code folded in her watch case until she died. Photo courtesy of The New York Public Library, The Elizabeth Van Lew Papers, Manuscripts and Archives.

Pictured here with her daughter in the Old Capitol prison, Rose O'Neal Greenhow, alias Rebel Rose, was an ardent secessionist. She knew everyone worth knowing in Washington through her marriage to Dr. Robert Greenhow, a Virginia lawyer, and obtained information from those contacts. The information she supplied to the confederacy helped them to win the Battle of Bull Run. Photo courtesy of The Brady Collection, The Library of Congress.

Grandson and namesake of Ethan Allen, Revolutionary war hero General Ethan Allen Hitchcock carried on the tradition by masterminding and scouting Mexicans to form an entire spy ring for the U.S. Army, thus helping America to win the Mexican War. Photo courtesy of The National Archives.

5

Nobody Here But Us Patriots

Covert action—with all its ambiguities, operationally and morally—became an important instrument of United States foreign policy as the nation extended its reach across the continent in the first half of the nineteenth century. Then as now, secret maneuverings were used with varying degrees of success to further policy goals that could not be pursued openly—and sometimes ended in embarrassment as well as failure.

Elated by the success of the bloodless coup in West Florida, James Madison turned his attention to East Florida. Covert action had worked so well at Baton Rouge that he decided to use similar tactics to win control of the adjoining territory. The president laid the groundwork for the operation by sending Congress a secret message on January 3, 1811, requesting authority to incorporate East Florida into the United States should Spanish officials make such a request or a foreign power try to seize the territory. Twelve days later, Congress gave Madison a blank check for covert action by approving a secret resolution "to enable the President of the United States, under certain circumstances, to take possession of the country lying east of the river Perdido and south of the state of Georgia and the Mississippi Territory and *for other purposes* [italics added].*

Congress also authorized the president to "employ any part of the

*Similar language was used in the National Security Act of 1947 to authorize the Central Intelligence Agency to run covert operations. This act directed the agency to "perform such services of common concern as the National Security Council [NSC] determines can be more efficiently accomplished centrally, and *other such functions* and duties relating to intelligence affecting the national security as the NSC may from time to time direct" [italics supplied].

Army and Navy which he may deem necessary" should a foreign power try to occupy East Florida and provided the then substantial sum of one hundred thousand dollars to finance the operation. Immediately following approval of the resolution, Madison appointed General George Mathews, the 72-year-old former governor of Georgia, case officer for the project. The general's instructions were ambiguous, probably purposely so. Mathews was to take possession of East Florida if the Spanish governor or "the existing local authority should wish it." If the Spaniards accepted the proposal, a provisional government was to be established; if they refused Mathews' conduct was to be "regulated by the dictates of [his] own judgement." If he needed the assistance of the military, he was authorized to apply to the nearest army and navy commanders, who would be given orders from Washington to cooperate.

Like the Central Intelligence Agency's war against Nicaragua's Sandinista government in our own day, Mathews' operations in East Florida may have been covert, but they were far from secret. Assuming that it was President Madison's intention to secure control of the province by any means, he set to work with a will. Mathews told the Spanish governor that the British were greedily eyeing the colony and suggested that if he accepted the protection of the United States, the Americans would return the territory to Spain when the imprisoned King Ferdinand VII was restored to the throne. When these broad hints were rejected, he wasted no time in taking direct action to subvert the colony.

Returning to Georgia, Mathews recruited an army of some two hundred timber poachers, cattle rustlers, and slave smugglers, all of whom were promised large tracts of land in return for joining the expedition. On March 16, 1812, these self-styled "insurgents" crossed the St. Marys River, the boundary between the United States and East Florida, and united with a "patriot" army under Colonel John McIntosh for an attack on the town of Fernandina, on Amelia Island. McIntosh, a wealthy plantation owner, had been handpicked by Mathews to head the "local authority" that was to request the United States to take the territory under its protective custody.

Under the watchful eye of a flotilla of American gunboats, the "insurgents" demanded the surrender of Fernandina. The Spanish commandant dispatched a message to the commander of the vessels asking if he intended to assist the attackers. Receiving an affirmative answer, the commandant capitulated to the "patriots" without a shot. The newly invented Republic of East Florida thereupon declared its independence from Spain and raised its flag, a white field emblazoned with a soldier in blue charging with fixed bayonet and the legend *Voce Populi, Lex Suprema*—"The Voice of the People Is the Supreme Law."

Following the previously arranged script, McIntosh, as the head of the "consititued authorities of East Florida," swiftly delivered the town and the surrounding territory to Mathews, who had followed on the heels of the invaders with two companies of U. S. Army troops. The ebullient old war horse accepted the new territory in the name of the president of the United States and notified Madison of his success. While awaiting rewards and accolades from Washington, Mathews issued orders for an advance on St. Augustine, the stronghold of Spanish power in East Florida.

■ ■ ■

Unknown to Mathews, however, the Madison administration was embroiled in controversy, and there had been a sea change in its attitude toward the East Florida operation. Far from being a cause for rejoicing, the unexpected news of his success created consternation in Washington. On April 4, 1812, as the "patriot army," supported by U. S. gunboats and troops, took up positions before the walls of St. Augustine, James Monroe, now secretary of state, disavowed the seizure of Fernandina and Amelia Island. Writing to Mathews, he coldly told him that he had exceeded his orders.

"The measures which you appear to have adopted for obtaining possession of Amelia Island and other parts of East Florida are not authorized by the law of the United States under which you have acted," Monroe declared. It was not "the purpose of the Executive to wrest the province forcibly from Spain, but only to occupy it, with a view to prevent its falling into the hands of a foreign power." With expressions of appreciation for his zeal and integrity, and a vague promise of future rewards, Mathews was summarily dismissed as a presidential agent.

When he received Monroe's letter a month later, Mathews was outraged. Regarding the disavowal as nothing short of betrayal, he threatened to go to Washington and expose the perfidy of the president and the secretary of state by providing the newspapers with a full account of the background of the operation, including his private conversations with Madison. He ranted that he would shoot Monroe on sight or at least horsewhip him through the capital's streets. Governor David Mitchell of Georgia, who had been chosen to take the reins of the operation, finally managed to calm Mathews down with assurances that once the dust had settled, he would be named governor of East Florida.*

Mitchell was instructed to restore Amelia Island to Spanish control, but these orders were for public consumption only. They were carefully hedged by a requirement that U. S. troops were not to be withdrawn until the safety of the "patriot army"—now stalled in the pine barrens and salt marshes near St. Augustine—was guaranteed by the Spaniards. Inter-

---

*Fortunately for the peace of mind of both Madison and Monroe, Mathews died before he could come to Washington to tell his side of the tale.

preting this instruction as a pretext to hold on to the conquered territory as long as possible, Mitchell used it as an excuse to keep control of Fernandina. In June, a declaration of war against Britain rendered these instructions moot. Spain was Britain's ally, and East Florida was now fair game for open military conquest.

But the insurgents had made the mistake of antagonizing the Seminole Indians and runaway blacks, who feared enslavement under the American flag. Taking up arms to defend their land and liberty, in mid-1813 they drove the "patriots" and the supporting Federal troops from East Florida. Fourteen months after Mathews' ragtag force had crossed the St. Marys River, the curtain was rung down upon the American government's disastrous first adventure in covert action.

In the end, however, diplomacy succeeded where both covert and overt action had failed. In 1819 the United States surrendered its shadowy claim to Texas (based on the Louisiana Purchase) and assumed five million dollars in claims held by Americans against Spain, receiving in exchange a clear title to both East and West Florida.

■ ■ ■

What lay behind Monroe's repudiation of George Mathews' operations in East Florida? Word of American connivance in the "revolution" had leaked. The Spanish and British ministers were asking embarrassing questions, and the plot was being denounced in Congress. "I say this is not only war, it is an offensive war, not only an offensive war but an unjust war," declared Senator William Hunter, a Rhode Island Federalist. "I am for the honor of my country forced to say . . . it is a wicked war, it is robbery." More importantly, a tangled intrigue hatched by Madison and Monroe to pin the label of traitor on the Federalists had also boomeranged. It was hardly the moment to risk exposure of their own plot to steal East Florida from Spain.

On March 9, 1812, just as Mathews was getting ready to begin the invasion of East Florida, the president sent a dramatic message to Congress. He charged that three years before, the British had employed John Henry, a former U. S. Army officer, to conspire with prominent Federalists with the aim of destroying the Union and eventuallly bringing New England back into the British Empire. The message was accompanied by copies of Henry's instructions from Sir John Craig, the governor-general of Canada—marked "most secret and confidential"—as well as a number of his reports to Craig. To heighten the dramatic effect, some passages had been removed and replaced by asterisks, giving the impression that the papers had been "sanitized."

Madison's message created a sensation. The Senate demanded an investigation. Republican legislators called for the release of the names of

Henry's co-conspirators, confident that they would include those of lead-ing Federalists. Pro-administration newspapers beat the drums for a spy scare that rivaled the Tub Plot of a decade before. Caught badly off balance, the Federalists could only claim that the papers were forgeries.

As for the British, Edward Coles, a presidential secretary, reported that he had run into A. St. John Baker, the secretary of the British legation, on the steps of the Capitol just after he had delivered the message. The secretary asked Coles what the message was about.

"Nothing," Coles replied. "Just the communication of the correspon-dence of a man named Henry."

"With Sir James Craig?" gasped the horrified diplomat.

Coles merely smiled icily.

Madison and Monroe had obtained the documents from Henry by way of a bald, bearded Frenchman who styled himself the Comte Edouard de Crillon and claimed to be a Knight of Malta as well a former member of Napoleon's staff. In reality, he was a Gascon adventurer and swindler named Soubiran who had been cashiered from the army for misappropriating funds and was wanted by the police of a half-dozen countries. Arriving in Boston on Christmas Eve, 1811, along with Henry whom he had met in Europe, the amiable "Crillon" ingratiated himself with local officialdom, including Governor Elbridge Gerry, a personal friend of the president. Having obtained a letter of introduction to Madison from Gerry, the Frenchman left Henry behind—he was making the rounds of the Boston taverns—and went to Washington, where he was cordially received by Madison.

■ ■ ■

Not long afterward, the bogus nobleman confided to the president that he had a friend who had possession of documents proving the existence of a Federalist-British plot to dissolve the Union. Eagerly rising to the bait, Madison referred him to Monroe to work out the details for obtaining the papers. Both Madison and Monroe were easy marks for the smooth-talking confidence man. Like most victims of such schemes, they did not have to be sold a bill of goods because they sold themselves. They were convinced the documents would not only destroy the Federalists once and for all but also ensure Madison's reelection.

Once he had whetted the appetite of the American officials, Crillon craftily set a ridiculously high price for the papers—twenty-five thousand pounds, or about $125,000, sight unseen. Monroe was downcast, for the Secret Service Fund contained only $50,000. But instead of using some of this money to investigate the Frenchman, Monroe offered him the entire fund. Playing his catch like an expert angler, Crillon reported that Henry, who had come to Washington, had flown into a rage when offered such a paltry sum and threatened to burn the papers rather than accept it. But, he added, after a night of pleading on his part—and the offer of his own estate at St. Martial in Gascony to sweeten the deal—his companion had agreed to accept the proposal. As a French patriot, Crillon confided to Monroe, he did not wish to see "perfidious Albion" escape punishment merely for lack of a few dollars. In addition to the money, Monroe agreed to provide Henry with free transportation to France in a U. S. Navy warship and not to publish the papers until he was safely out of the country.

John Henry sailed for France on March 7, 1812, with fifty thousand dollars in gold—less six thousand he had lent the "count." Two days later Madison transmitted the sheaf of documents to Congress, accompanied by a covering letter from Henry stating that he had given the papers to the government without payment out of pure, disinterested patriotism. Monroe had insisted upon the note to cover the more sordid aspects of the affair. For the money—almost equal to the cost of a fully armed sloop of war—Madison and Monroe bought papers that contained no military or naval secrets, no evidence of a plot, no names, and nothing to incriminate anyone. The suppressed passages did not contain the names of Henry's co-conspirators; probably Crillon had deleted them to give the papers a more sinister cast. Under the circumstances, Madison and Monroe, rather than submitting the entire batch to Congress, would have been cleverer to leak only a few and keep the Federalists guessing what else they had.

The Federalists squirmed in agony over the disclosures but quickly regained their balance. Careful analysis made it clear that the documents failed to prove that the men with whom Henry had talked had known he was a British secret agent or had had culpable relations with him. A vigorous probe of the affair, directed by Josiah Quincy, a Federalist member of Congress from Boston, soon produced evidence that held the administration up to ridicule. By tracing the Treasury warrants, Quincy discovered that the president had lied in saying that no payment had been made for the documents and was even able to reveal the actual price. Moreover, he forced Monroe to admit that he had no list of persons guilty of conspiring with Henry.

Worse was yet to come. Monroe wrote to Joel Barlow, the American minister in Paris, begging him to obtain from Henry the names of the Federalists who had conspired with him. The letter crossed one from Barlow informing the secretary of state that Henry, upon his arrival at the legation, had denounced Crillon as an impostor and angrily complained that the St. Martial estate was nonexistent. Monroe must have blanched at the news, for he had given the Frenchman, who had since left the country, a draft upon Barlow for five thousand dollars that was obviously intended as compensation for the noble sacrifice of his ancestral home.* Madison and Monroe were now faced with the awful realization that the public would soon know that they had not only used public funds for partisan ends but been fleeced in the bargain. Little wonder that the mortified officials tried to cover up George Mathews' covert operations in East Florida. How could they charge the British with intriguing to divide the United States when they were engaged in similar operation in Spanish territory?

■ ■ ■

Even though the exposure of the "Henry Plot" had misfired, the episode aggravated American bitterness against Britain and added to the clamor for war, which was declared officially on June 18, 1812. Impressment of American citizens into the Royal Navy, interference with neutral trade, and British intrigues with the Indians were cited by Madison as the causes of hostilities. The real cause was the pressure brought to bear by the Western "war hawks," who saw war as an opportunity to wrest Canada from Britain. "Agrarian cupidity, not maritime rights, urges the war," declared John Randolph of Roanoke. "We have heard but one word—like the whip-poor-will, one eternal monotonous tone—Canada! Canada! Canada!"

Although the U. S. Navy's handful of frigates did surprisingly well in individual ship-to-ship duels with British naval vessels, the War of 1812 was a disaster on land and marked the nadir of the nation's intelligence efforts. Intelligence veterans who had worked for George Washington during the Revolution were still available for service, but they were not called upon to lend their talents. In fact, virtually no intelligence or espionage activities of any importance were conducted at any level during the war. The United States was so unprepared with respect to war-related intelligence that maps of the Canadian border areas were unavailable, even though the conquest of Canada was a major objective of the conflict. Further, the War Department had little information on British troop strength in Canada, only a hazy idea of the location of these forces and their Indian allies, and no information at all regarding their intentions.

The only exception to the U. S. Army's general disinterest in intel-

---

*More astute than his masters, Barlow refused to give Crillon and Henry another cent. The "Count," who apparently had hoped for a profitable place in the French government in reward for stirring up trouble between Britain and the United States, instead was clapped into jail for forgery and impersonation. He disappeared from view in 1816. Henry surfaced in 1820 as a paid informer sent to Italy to gather evidence of misconduct against Queen Caroline, whom King George IV wished to divorce. He died in Paris in 1853 after what appears to have been a long and profitable career of spying for both Britain and France.

ligence was the establishment of a topographical engineer unit of sixteen officers. In addition to their surveying and mapping duties, these officers were instructed "to accompany all reconnoitering parties sent out to obtain intelligence of the movements of the enemy or his position, etc.; to make sketches of their route, accompanied by written notes of everything worthy of observation."

The invasion of Canada was under the command of Brig. Gen. William Hull, Nathan Hale's good friend. As a young soldier during the Revolution, Hull had shown boldness and skill, but now he was rusty and lacking in energy. The British learned of the declaration of war before he did, getting the news from John Jacob Astor, the fur magnate, who was in business with Albert Gallatin, the secretary of the treasury. For its part, the War Department sent the message notifying Hull of the commencement of hostilities to the postmaster at Cleveland through the regular mail, with the request that it be forwarded to him. Ignorant of the existence of a state of war, Hull sent a schooner carrying his baggage and papers across Lake Erie to Detroit, and the British captured it, giving them access to his plans.

That was merely the beginning of Hull's misfortunes. Launching the invasion without intelligence—Napoleon had once observed that any general who neglected his intelligence service was a general "ignorant of his trade"—he blundered about the border area, unable to locate, let alone pin down, the enemy. In the meantime, General Isaac Brock, the British commander, who was fully aware of Hull's weaknesses, adroitly outmaneuvered and harassed his foe. When Hull turned back to protect his extended line of communications and sought safety at Detroit, Brock craftily played upon the old fellow's fears. Newly recruited Canadian militiamen were dressed in the red tunics of British regulars and sent to parade where they could be seen by the besieged Americans. Brock also planted letters where they could be captured by the Yankees. One purported to be a message to a British officer at Mackinac, directing him not to send any more Indians to Detroit because there were "already 5,000" on hand.

Hull swallowed the bait. With a little more than a thousand men fit for duty, he estimated that he was faced by a superior army, including a large number of British regulars and at least five thousand Indians. Actually, the two forces were about equal in strength, and the Americans had the advantage of being protected by fortifications. Thoroughly duped, Hull ordered a white flag raised over Detroit, ending the American attempt to invade Canada. The hapless general was, as much as anything else, the victim of an intelligence failure—and of British disinformation.

Before long, the country was reeling from a succession of military disasters, the ports were under an ever-tightening blockade, Washington was put to the torch by British invaders, and the government was bankrupt. In New England, where "Mr. Madison's War" was highly un-popular, there were rumblings of treason. Captain Stephen Decatur charged that warnings of his attempts to escape the blockade of New York in the frigate *President* had been flashed to waiting British ships by blue lights on the Connecticut shore, an accusation that gave rise to the highly descriptive phrase "Blue-light Federalist." A lively smuggling trade developed to supply the British army in Canada and British ships offshore. Nantucket declared its "neutrality," and once again the spectre of secession haunted the nation.

Andrew Jackson was the only successful American military com-mander of the war—and perhaps the only one with a keen understanding of the role of intelligence in military operations. The self-taught general placed considerable emphasis on the need for accurate and timely reports on enemy troop strength, supplies, and battle plans. Jackson made good use of spies and scouts; as a recent biographer notes, "his intelligence operation was quite advanced and extremely valuable." One of his most detailed military letters is a review of intelligence on British troop and naval movements received "thro a confidential channel"—possibly a spy at Pensacola, which was occupied by the British.

Foreshadowing the later ties between the Mafia and the CIA, Old Hickory also made an alliance with gangsters for intelligence purposes. In return for the promise of pardons, Jean Laffite and his pirate band served under Jackson during the New Orleans campaign. The pirates spied on the British as the invaders advanced upon the city through the bayous and played an important role in the smashing Yankee victory. Although the famous battle was fought two weeks after a peace treaty had been signed—in Ghent, Belgium, on Christmas Eve, 1814—it restored American confidence after years of bitter defeat and humiliation. Nothing was done, however, to improve the nation's intelligence ca-pability.

■ ■ ■

Unable to afford the expense of a significant diplomatic establish-ment, the United States often resorted to the use of secret agents during the three decades between the Peace of Ghent and the Mexican War. The most bizarre undoubtedly was George Bethune English, who comes about as close to the image of James Bond as any secret agent in the history of American intelligence. Decked out in turban and flowing robes, English conspired on behalf of the United States in exotic surround-ings—the palaces and teeming bazaars of far-off Constantinople.

In the 1820s trade between the Ottoman Empire and the United States amounted to more than a million dollars annually, and John Quincy Adams, secretary of state in the cabinet of President James Monroe and America's first professional diplomat, wished to protect it by establishing a diplomatic mission in Constantinople. The Turks indicated a willingness to negotiate, but Adams wanted to obtain copies of their treaties with other Western nations to make certain that the United States obtained equal privileges. English was an old family friend, and Adams turned to this flamboyant adventurer to carry out the mission.

English was a rarity among Americans, a man who not only spoke Turkish and Arabic but was thoroughly familiar with the customs of the Ottoman Empire. Born in Cambridge, Massachusetts, in 1787, he was described as "a smart, active, handsome young man" at the time of his graduation from Harvard at the age of twenty. Having switched to the Harvard Divinity School after he became bored with the study of law, he was licensed to preach, but his study of Hebrew caused him to doubt the revelations of the New Testament. He expressed his doubts in a book published in 1814 that created a furor across New England—particularly after it was determined that he had plagiarized a good part of it. So ended English's career in the pulpit.

To make a new beginning, the former preacher went West, where he edited a newspaper and showed a flair for languages, picking up several Indian dialects. (Later on, he amazed a Cherokee delegation to Washington with his fluency in their tongue.) Next, he decided to see something of the world and obtained a commission as a lieutenant in the U. S. Marine Corps. While he was serving in the Mediterranean Squadron, his ship put into Alexandria, then part of the Ottoman Empire. Immediately captivated by the East, English resigned his commission, converted to Islam, and entered the Egyptian army under the name of Mohammed Effendi.

■ ■ ■

Becoming a good friend of Ismail, the third son of Mohammed Ali, the pasha of Egypt, English accompanied him in 1820 on a campaign along the Upper Nile and into the Sudan. He was placed in charge of the expedition's artillery—ten light field guns, a pair of howitzers, and a mortar, all transported on the backs of camels. One of the first white men to venture into the Sudan, English later wrote a book about the expedition that still makes good reading. Because of the oppressive heat during the day, the army marched at night to the beat of kettledrums, the soldiers following a route laid out by an advance party that lit fires and sent up rockets to guide those who followed. The Sudanese tribesmen resisted bravely, but they were no match for English's cannon.

Through it all, English remained loyal to his native land and was receptive to being tapped for Adams' secret mission upon a visit to the United States in 1823. Returning to Constantinople, he took a small house and resumed his Turkish name and dress. Most Europeans living in Constantinople regarded him as merely another Western romantic who had donned native clothing to be better able to see the sights. But, as he told Adams, "Under favor of this garb, I penetrate almost everywhere, and have opportunities of learning the mode of transacting public business at the Ottoman Porte which European dress would infallibly exclude me from." Through means he did not disclose, English obtained a copy of the treaty between the Ottoman Empire and France "quietly and without observation." He also struck up a friendship with the Capudan Pasha, the Turkish grand admiral, and persuaded him to advance American interests.

After English had greased the way, Adams sent agents to Constantinople to conduct negotiations for the American-Turkish treaty. To prevent Britain and France from disrupting the talks—neither wished to share the lucrative trade of the Ottoman Empire with the United States— Adams insisted upon the tightest secrecy. "As the success of this measure may depend upon the secrecy with which it will be managed," he told his agents, "you will use every precaution for observing it." The courier carrying these dispatches was given a false name and smuggled on board a ship bound for the Mediterranean. English suggested that presents—a euphemism for bribes—were to be given to the Turkish officials, so Adams wrote in his own hand a "secret and confidential" memorandum transferring twenty thousand dollars from the Secret Service Fund to the Navy Department for the use of the negotiators.

■ ■ ■

While English's mission demonstrates that the young nation already had global interests, particular attention was being paid—then, as now— to developments nearer its shores. Fearing attempts by the European powers to regain their colonies in the New World, the United States kept a watchful eye on Latin America. If the despots were allowed to regain a foothold in the hemisphere, would not the United States' own security be endangered eventually? In 1823, President Monroe sent an operative named Alexander McRae to Europe to pick up intelligence regarding European intentions toward South America. Modern intelligence officers would find McRae's instructions surprisingly familiar: "You will assume no public character, but take passports as a private citizen of the United States . . . And you will take all proper precautions for avoiding any appearance or suspicion of your being employed on a public agency." Another secret agent was sent to Cuba to observe conditions on the island; he claimed to be a tourist seeking a health cure.

Secret agents were dispatched not only to Europe and Latin America but to East Asia as well. In 1832, President Andrew Jackson sent a New Hampshire sea captain named Edmund Roberts to arrange commercial treaties with Siam, Muscat, Burma, Cochin China [Indochina], and Japan. The mission was kept secret to block interference by nations "whose interest it might be to thwart the objects the President has in view." As cover, Roberts was rated as "captain's clerk" on the sloop *Peacock,* on which he sailed; only the vessel's commander knew his true status. The State Department had so little information on the countries he was to visit—in some cases it did not even know the name of the ruler—that Roberts was given a sheaf of blank passports and letters of accreditation so that he could make the appropriate entries on the spot. In view of the escapades in Florida and elsewhere, his instructions to emphasize the virtues of the United States, as compared with the other nations dealing with the East, were unintentionally ironic: "We never make conquests or ask any other nations to let us establish ourselves in their country as the English, the French and the Dutch have done."

In Indochina, Roberts learned he had to have titles to make an impressive showing. Resourcefully he began reeling off the names of the counties of his native New Hampshire and was proceeding to the towns, rivers, and lakes when a halt was called. Despite his daunting list of "titles," Roberts was rebuffed in Indochina, because he refused to kowtow—or touch his forehead to the ground in the presence of the country's ruler, a gesture Westerners regarded as degrading. Over the next four years he did succeed in negotiating treaties with Siam and the Sultan of Muscat. He died in Macao just as he was about to embark on his first visit to Japan.

While presidents dispatched agents around the globe, from time to time there were rumblings in Congress about the public's "need to know" the uses to which the unvouchered Secret Service Fund was being put. In 1831, Senator John Forsyth, later secretary of state under Presidents Jackson and Martin Van Buren, provided the first full public statement of the purpose of the fund. "It was given for all purposes to which a secret service fund should or could be applied to the public benefit," he declared. "For Spies, if the gentleman pleases . . ."

The issue erupted again in the wake of the Webster-Ashburton Treaty of 1842, which settled the long-disputed boundary between the United States and Canada. Congress charged four years later that Daniel Webster, the secretary of state, had used about seventeen thousand dollars from the Secret Service Fund for propaganda in American religious newspapers to win support for the highly unpopular treaty and demanded the records of all expenditures from the fund during Webster's tenure. Although President James K. Polk was a Democrat and Webster a Whig, Polk rebuffed the congressional investigators by echoing George Washington:

> The experience of every nation on earth has demonstrated that emergencies may arise in which it becomes absolutely necessary for the public safety or the public good to make expenditures, the very object of

which would be defeated by publicity . . . . In no nation is the application of such funds made public. In time of war or impending danger the situation of the country will make it necessary to employ individuals for the purpose of obtaining information or rendering other important services who could never be prevailed upon to act if they entertained the least apprehension that their names or their agency would in any contingency be divulged. So it may often become necessary to incur an expenditure for an object highly useful to the country . . . . But this object might altogether be defeated by the intrigues of other powers if our purposes were to be made known by the exhibition of the original papers and vouchers . . . .

■ ■ ■

President Polk had good reason to defend the integrity of the Secret Service Fund—and to include "rendering other important services" as well as "obtaining information" among the functions it supported—for he was deeply engaged in covert activities designed to ensure that Texas and California became part of the United States. Cuba and those parts of Mexico adjacent to the United States had long been regarded by many Americans as part of their domain. "We will have New Mexico and California!" trumpeted a New Orleans paper. "We will have old Mexico and Cuba! The isthmus [of Panama] cannot arrest—nor even the St. Lawrence! Time has all this in her womb."

The United States had been eyeing Texas ever since the Lone Star Republic had won its independence from Mexico in 1836, but had stopped short of annexing the territory because successive presidents feared to arouse anti-slavery zealots. In an attempt to block U. S. expansion, British agents offered the Texans support for their continued independence and were active in California as well. The annexation issue slumbered until April 1844, when an unpopular president, John Tyler, having nothing to lose, seized upon it to improve his chances in the coming presidential election. Tyler was defeated, but Congress annexed Texas anyway. Mexico, which had never recognized the independence of Texas, angrily broke relations with the United States.

In the meantime, Polk received alarming reports about stepped-up British activities in California. Political gravity had been expected to drop California into the waiting hands of the United States. The connection between the province and the far-off and chaotic Mexican government was tenuous, and hundreds of Americans had drifted into California. A successful separatist movement like the one in Texas was considered inevitable. But in late 1845, Thomas O. Larkin, the able and alert American consul in Monterey, informed Washington that the British-owned Hudson's Bay Company had offered the government in Mexico arms and money to equip an expedition to reassert its control over California.

Meanwhile, a secret agent in Mexico City reported that the Mexicans might cede California to Britain in case of war with the United States. Polk immediately deputized Larkin as a confidential agent to oppose the "transfer of California to Great Britain or any other Power."

Larkin's instructions were delicately phrased.* On the one hand, he was to inform the Californians that the United States would provide no clandestine assistance for a revolt against Mexico. On the other hand, he was to assure them that "should California assert and maintain her independence, we shall render her all the kind offices in our power, as a sister Republic." And if the question of annexation arose, he was to say that the United States had no such plans but that California would be welcomed into the Union if it were "the free and spontaneous wish of the independent people of [the] adjoining territory."

In such sensitive matters as paving the way for rebellions in other countries, orders are rarely unambiguous or explicit. To a man of Larkin's probity, however, the president's intentions were crystal-clear.

■ ■ ■

As with wars before and since, the start of the conflict with Mexico was misrepresented to the American people. Polk wanted a war to gain possession of California and the Mexican border area, but it was highly doubtful that Congress would oblige him with a declaration unless the Mexicans attacked first. To bring this about after the annexation of Texas, the president ordered a detachment of the U. S. Army under General Zachary Taylor to the Rio Grande. Ostensibly the detachment's mission was to protect the new state; in reality it was to provoke the Mexicans, who claimed that the southwestern boundary of Texas was on the Nueces River, north and east of the Rio Grande. Angrily the Mexican government charged that the occupation was a wanton violation of its country's territorial integrity. On April 25, 1846, Mexican troops crossed the Rio Grande and surprised a squadron of American cavalry, killing and wounding sixteen men. Polk now had the incident he needed.

■ ■ ■

Proclaiming that the Mexicans had "invaded our territory and shed American blood upon American soil," the president sent a war message to Congress that was approved after a long and angry debate. Supporters of Manifest Destiny were elated, but the war was not universally popular. Abolitionists condemned it as an "unholy, unrighteous and damnable"

*To keep Larkin's instructions secret, they were entrusted to Lieutenant Archibald H. Gillespie of the Marine Corps. Gillespie had a perilous trip across Mexico and had to destroy his papers. He finally reached Larkin in Monterey in April 1846, after having been forced to travel by way of Hawaii.

conspiracy to create new slave states, and an Illinois congressman named Abraham Lincoln questioned Polk's assertion that hostilities had begun on American territory.

Once again the country was ill-prepared for war from the standpoint of intelligence. Improvement in the U. S. Army's intelligence capabilities in the years since the War of 1812 had been minimal. The topographical engineers had continued their surveys of the American interior, and for the first time an effort had been made to keep abreast of foreign military developments. Although no permanent American military attachés were sent abroad until 1889, a few officers had gone to Europe as observers. Colonel Sylvanus Thayer visited several European military schools and later based the pivotal reforms he made as superintendent of the Military Academy at West Point on what he learned. Other officers picked up information that improved the army's artillery and cavalry tactics. Nevertheless, the War Department still lacked an agency to collect, analyze, and coordinate intelligence, and most American military commanders had little appreciation of the importance of intelligence operations.

The conquest of Mexico was the biggest enterprise on which the American military had ever embarked, but no preparations had been made for conducting a war. General Zachary Taylor, a rough-and-ready old soldier whose idea of war was marching, charging, and shooting rather than staff work, had made no attempt to gather intelligence while occupying the disputed territory between Mexico and the United States. When his army crossed the Rio Grande into Mexico, the terrain and local conditions were enshrouded in a dense fog of ignorance. "We are quite in the dark," observed Colonel Ethan Allen Hitchcock. "The General may have information which he keeps to himself, but I know him too well to believe he has any."

Upon being asked for a map of the Southwest, the best the War Department could provide was one of doubtful accuracy that had been torn from a commercial atlas. The topographical engineers had prepared a much superior map, but it had been filed and forgotten. The president, who had never seen northern Mexico, expected Taylor's army to live off the countryside. Quartermaster General Thomas S. Jessup bluntly summed up the situation: "There was no information at Washington, so far as I was informed, to enable me or the War Department to determine whether wagons could be used in Mexico."

Expecting no serious resistance, General Taylor advanced on Monterrey, the key to northeastern Mexico, at a deliberate pace, making no attempt to learn the enemy's strength or the nature of any defenses he would encounter. He rejected a suggestion to recruit spies and informers from the ranks of disgruntled Mexican *contrabandistas*, or smugglers and other rough border types, on the grounds that they could not be trusted. Much to the ill-informed general's surprise, Monterrey turned out to be strongly fortified. Although the assault succeeded, the price of Taylor's ineptitude was severe casualties among the attacking troops. The hard-won victory at Monterrey was followed by a strange interlude of secret diplomacy. Polk wanted a short war, and as soon as California and the Rio Grande boundary were secured, he was ready for an accommodation with Mexico. In November 1846, Moses Y. Beach, the publisher of the pro-expansionist New York *Sun*, informed the president that he was going to Mexico on private business. Pointing out that he had good contacts with the Mexican military and the Catholic Church, Beach suggested that he be named a confidential agent to negotiate a peace treaty that would ratify the American conquests. Polk decided to take the chance. Although Beach was formally instructed to merely gather information, Polk hoped that he would bring back a treaty. "Should he do so and it is a good one," the president confided to his diary, "I will . . . submit it to the Senate for ratification. It will be a good joke if he should assume the authority and take the country by surprise and make a Treaty."

Although Beach was not a British citizen, he traveled to Mexico on a British passport and with instructions "never to give the slightest intimation, directly or indirectly, that you are an agent of this Government" except under extraordinary circumstances where it might "smooth the way to peace." He was accompanied by Jane McManus Storms, a beautiful and vivacious woman who wrote editorials for his paper and spoke Spanish.* Indeed, Storms—who had a flair for the dramatic and had once tried to found a colony in Texas—may have dreamed up the mission.

Upon their arrival at Veracruz on the Gulf coast, the party was arrested by Mexican officials, who searched their baggage and questioned them for several days. At first Beach feared that his cover had been blown, but the Mexicans were merely suspicious of all foreigners. Released from custody, Beach and his companion continued on their way to Mexico City, where they promptly became involved in the capital's political and social life, and sounded out several prominent Mexicans on the subject of peace. But they made the mistake of meddling in a clerical uprising against the Mexican dictator, General Antonio López de Santa Anna,* who was in the north fighting against Taylor's army. When Santa Anna unexpectedly returned to Mexico City—falsely claiming to have

---

*Twelve years before, Mrs. Storms had been named co-respondent in the divorce case against Aaron Burr.

*Paradoxically, Santa Anna had been placed in power through another of Polk's failed intrigues. Shortly before the declaration of war, Santa Anna, then exiled in Havana, had informed the president that if he were allowed to return to Mexico, he would make peace with the United States and sell the Americans the desired territory. On Polk's orders, he was allowed to slip through the U.S. Navy's blockade of Veracruz. As soon as he reached Mexico, however, Santa Anna rallied the nation against the invader.

routed the invaders—the coup collapsed, along with any hope for a quick peace. Beach and Storms wisely fled the country. Later, Beach claimed to have made progress toward a treaty, and Polk, at least, appeared to believe him, for the president gave him $2,609.95 for expenses from the Secret Service Fund.

■ ■ ■

As the war dragged on, Polk became increasingly dissatisfied with the progress of Taylor's campaign. The old soldier had won several victories, but to Polk they amounted to lopping off branches rather than striking at the trunk of Mexican resistance. The president and his advisers also feared that Taylor might be the Whig presidential nominee in 1848. With the hope of putting a quick end to the war—and blocking Taylor's political ambitions—an army under the command of General Winfield Scott was landed at Veracruz in March 1847 with orders to strike into the enemy's heartland and capture Mexico City. Less than a month later, Scott began his march on the Mexican capital some three hundred miles away, taking the same route that Cortez had followed three centuries before.

Uncertain about the position, plans, and strength of Santa Anna's forces and traversing unfamiliar and menacing terrain with his supply lines trailing behind him through a hostile population, Scott realized he needed swift and accurate intelligence. In the absence of reliable maps, he used engineer officers for special reconnaissance missions, thus giving such future leaders as Captain Robert E. Lee and lieutenants Pierre G. T. Beauregard, George G. Meade, and George B. McClellan a taste of intelligence work. Unlike General Taylor, Scott saw the value of using Mexican irregulars as scouts and spies, and Colonel Ethan Allen Hitchcock, the army's inspector general, was detailed to organize a clandestine service. The grandson of Ethan Allen, a Revolutionary War hero, Hitchcock was a West Point graduate who had served in the war against the Seminoles in Florida as well as on Indian patrol in the Northwest, where he had learned the value of such scouts firsthand.*

When the army reached Puebla, about halfway between Veracruz and Mexico City, Hitchcock ordered the arrest of a bandit chief named Mañuel Dominguez, who was living openly in the town. In return for his freedom, Dominguez accepted an offer to spy for the Americans. To test the bandit's reliability, Hitchcock gave him a message to deliver to General Scott's headquarters. "If he performs this service faithfully, I shall further employ him," the colonel wrote in his diary. Two weeks later,

*Hitchcock was also a student of philosophy who delighted in metaphysical researches and wrote fat volumes on alchemy and other recondite subjects. Obsessed by the conviction that many writers clothed their true meanings in symbolism, he discovered in Dante, Shakespeare, and the Gospels an esoteric wisdom not discernible to the ordinary reader.

Dominguez returned with a response. Reassured, Hitchcock instructed him to recruit five of his fellow bandits to scout enemy positions and to serve as guides, couriers, and spies.

Hitchcock was fascinated by Dominguez and developed a rough affection for him. Although the Mexican appeared rather portly for a man in his profession, he was, the colonel reported "'bold as a lion' or an honest man." An American who lived in Mexico and had been hired by the army as a translator immediately recognized Dominguez as the bandit who had robbed him of five dollars and then given him a pass to protect him from other robbers who—surprisingly—had honored it. Dominguez's own account of himself was that he had been an ordinary weaver until he was robbed and beaten by a Mexican officer, at which point he had turned brigand to exact revenge from the government.

Before long, Hitchcock had a dozen of Dominguez's compatriots released from the local jails. Amid shouts and embraces, they swore eternal fidelity to each other and the United States. Dominguez was paid three dollars per day and the others, two dollars. Eventually the band— the first foreign mercenaries recruited by American intelligence—grew to about a hundred men and was officially designated as the Mexican Spy Company. To the rest of the army they were known as the Forty Thieves.

"They rode along singing ribald songs, discharging their *escopettes* [short muskets or carbines] every few minutes, and behaving in the most unsoldier-like manner," reported one American officer. "They had a few women along with them who seemed to be as thoroughly steeped in vice as the men. Each man carried a lance and wore a wide red band around his hat . . . . On first seeing them, I thought very much, as one of our Irish soldiers did, 'may the devil fly away wid 'em for a set of ragamuffins.'"

Irregular though they were, the members of the Spy Company served Scott well. They scouted enemy positions, supplied the army with information on enemy movements, and provided security for the march- ing columns and their supply lines. Dominguez himself "persuaded" guerrillas who were working for Santa Anna to switch sides by seizing their chiefs at gunpoint while turning aside the Mexican leader's at- tempts to bribe him to abandon the Americans. One band captured a Mexican general and his staff; others infiltrated Mexico City disguised as market people and mapped its defenses. To identify his spies to American officers, Hitchcock gave them bits of tissue paper carrying his signature and the words "Trust the Bearer." The bandit-spies hid the tissue in a seam of their clothes or in a lock of matted hair until it was needed.

Unhappily, and not for the last time, once the war was over the U. S. government was not as loyal to its foreign intelligence assets as they had been to it. Following the capture of Mexico City and the end of the fighting, the Mexican Spy Company was disbanded. Each man was paid twenty dollars and left to his own devices. Dominguez, who told Hitchcock he would be "killed like a dog" if he remained in Mexico, was taken to New Orleans with nine members of his family. "There," the colonel angrily reported, "he was left to support his family as he could—to live or die as he could." Hitchcock persuaded Senator Jefferson Davis of Mississippi to introduce a bill in the Senate for the relief of Dominguez, but it never got out of committee.

In establishing an espionage network in the field, Hitchcock had performed a notoriously difficult task—a rare achievement, for American intelligence operations during the war with Mexico were generally lacking in flair. Nevertheless, after a poor beginning and with limited resources, the U. S. Army made better use of intelligence than at any time since the Revolution. Intelligence did not win any battles, but the experience gained by some officers in reconnaissance and the improvements in the gathering of tactical intelligence would prove to be of value in the Civil War—to both sides.

6

Amateurs at War

With a solemn countenance, Abraham Lincoln gazed from the tall windows of the White House to the hills of Virginia on the other side of the Potomac. What was going on over there? What was the newly mustered Confederate Army up to? Three months had passed since the Southern secessionists had bombarded and captured Fort Sumter in Charleston harbor, and now, early in July 1861, a battle was looming between the raw and untrained armies. How many men did the rebels have? How much artillery? The president's questions went unanswered, for the Union had entered the war without an organized system for gathering intelligence. Anxiety and uncertainty gnawed at the president's spirit, and the bright summer sunshine seemed to mock him.

Washington, set in an area of disloyalty that reached through southern Maryland into Virginia, was threatened from within and without. Treason lurked everywhere; shadows whispered. Rebel couriers and spies circulated freely. Heavily armed bands were expected to clatter over the Potomac bridges at any moment to raid the disorganized capital. There were rumors that spies had penetrated the upper reaches of the Federal government. Civil war—with its complex interlacings of loyalties and betrayals—was giving espionage an incestuous cast. Mrs. Lincoln discovered that one of the White House guests "was in the habit of listening about the cabinet room doors." As a Kentuckian with a brother and three half-brothers serving in the Confederate Army, the First Lady was herself suspected of treason. When the president gave his sister-in-law a pass to go south, the lady carried "her weight almost" in quinine, a drug desperately needed by the Confederacy. And still the Union's commander in chief lacked the most basic information about the resources and intentions of an enemy only a few miles away.

The solution to Lincoln's need for intelligence presented itself in the unlikely person of William Alvin Lloyd, a publisher of railroad and steamboat guides to the Southern states. An acquaintance of the president, Lloyd came to the White House seeking a pass that would enable him to go through the lines and continue his work. To Lincoln he must have seemed the answer to a prayer. He was the ideal man to collect intelligence in the Confederacy: widely known in the South as a transportation expert, Lloyd could move about easily and ask questions without attracting attention as he inspected steamboat and railroad lines. His occupation was a perfect cover for espionage.

Seizing this heavensent opportunity, the president told Lloyd of his desperate need for information. As Lloyd's family would later put it, in a claim for payment, "The Government at that time was without any reliable or responsible agents in the rebellious states, and he was greatly in need of some trustworthy, competent person who had complete and thorough knowledge of the geography and topography of the States in rebellion." When Lloyd protested about the danger, Lincoln replied coolly that he would not be given a pass unless he undertook the mission. Needing to go South to stay in business, Lloyd was over a barrel. Eventually he agreed to become the president's personal secret agent. Before he left Washington, on July 13, 1861, Lincoln gave him a contract calling for a monthly salary of two hundred dollars plus expenses.

Unfamiliar with the basic principles of intelligence work, neither Lincoln nor Lloyd thought of establishing a line of secret communication. Like Nathan Hale, Lloyd had no code or cipher and was forced to carry masses of incriminating information around with him until he could find a messenger to take it to the president. Incredibly, he even took the contract bearing Lincoln's signature with him, though eventually he wisely destroyed the incriminating document. Often suspected by the Confederates of spying, Lloyd was arrested several times during the four years he spent in the South—but unlike the unfortunate Hale, he managed to evade the noose.

A reluctant and untrained amateur, Lloyd nevertheless proved a resourceful spy. On one occasion, he persuaded the general who commanded the defenses of Richmond, the Confederate capital, to take him on a personal tour of the fortifications that ringed the city. He was even permitted to talk with some of the battery commanders. Lloyd also supplied Lincoln with information regarding the strength of General Robert E. Lee's army, obtained from an indiscreet staff officer. During one of his stretches of captivity he managed to turn his imprisonment into a boon to his intelligence activities. Taken for questioning to Castle Thunder, a Confederate military prison in Richmond, he managed to open a secure channel of communication with the White House. Nobody thought of searching prisoners of war who were about to be exchanged— after all, they had been confined since capture—so, just before a group of

Yankees were about to be released, Lloyd slipped one of the men the secret dispatches he wanted delivered to the president.

For his part, Lincoln kept Lloyd's activities secret to the end. None of his reports can be found today, indicating that the president may have destroyed them after passing on the information. Indeed, so well did he conceal the fact that he had employed his own secret agent that his activities as a spymaster have escapted the attention of all his major biographers.* Inexperienced though he was in such matters, Abraham Lincoln understood the importance of a steady and reliable flow of intelligence in the conduct of war—and of the secrecy required to protect it.

■ ■ ■

Probably no subject in American history is more wrapped in romantic myth and melodrama than Civil War espionage. Intelligence gathering is at best a shadowy business, and many of the spies who provided important services to both sides are lost to history. Records were haphazardly maintained, and some spies wished to remain anonymous even after the war. In the case of the South, the bulk of the documents pertaining to intelligence operations were destroyed when the Confederacy collapsed. In the absence of documentation, tales of cloak-and-dagger adventures by both Federal and Confederate spies abound, many of them involving pretty women galloping across the lines with vital secrets concealed against their heaving bosoms. Unhappily, as Edwin C. Fishel pointed out in a trailblazing article, "The Mythology of Civil War Intelligence,"* most of these tales have less than a nodding acquaintance with the truth. More often than not, they are imaginative products of the "moonlight and magnolias" school of history.

---

*The Lloyd affair was to have long-lasting ramifications. The agent died in 1868 without having been paid $9,753.32 in salary, although the War Department did give him $2,380 in expenses. Lloyd's family filed suit in the United States Court of Claims for payment of the amount owed. In its October 1875 term, the Supreme Court heard an appeal from a Court of Claims ruling upholding the government's refusal to pay the salary promised by Lincoln. The case established the precedent that an intelligence agent cannot recover against the government for secret services rendered. "Agents . . . must look for their compensation to the contingent fund of the department employing them, and to such allowance from it as those who dispense the fund may award," the Court declared (*Totten, Administrator, v. U.S.* [92 U.S. 105]).

This decision also contains the roots of the so-called "Glomar defense," in which intelligence agencies, when asked to divulge secret information, have taken the position that whether or not such information exists—and the agency isn't saying if it exists, it's classified. The court's statement is as follows: "It may be stated, as a general principle, that public policy forbids the maintenance of any suit in a court of justice, the trial of which would inevitably lead to the disclosure of matters which the law itself regards as confidential, and respecting which it will not allow the confidence to be violated."

*See Bibliography. More than two decades later, Fishel's article is still basic to the study of Civil War intelligence.

For example, Belle Boyd is usually portrayed as the "Cleopatra of the Secession" who provided Stonewall Jackson with the information that made possible the victory over the Federals at Front Royal, Virginia, that triumphantly climaxed his Valley campaign of 1862. In point of fact, she could only have provided a few last-minute tidbits, because the general had been diligently collecting intelligence about the Yankee positions for two weeks. "Jackson was possessed of these facts before we left New Market, and based his movements upon them," observed General Richard Taylor, one of his subordinates. Further, Belle is usually depicted as a beauty who twisted Yankee officers around her fingers, but photographs show that she had a longish nose and protruding teeth. Although Belle Boyd did serve as a Confederate courier on several occasions, in truth her main value to the cause was the propaganda engendered by her supposed exploits.

The stark reality is that in four years of war, neither side created a national intelligence system capable of collecting and analyzing intelligence or conducting counterintelligence operations on a systematic basis. Intelligence staff work in both armies was rudimentary, and there was no means through which the high command and civilian leaders in Washington and Richmond could get a clear picture of what was happening on "the other side of the hill."

In the North, the War Department was hamstrung by the inept administration of Simon Cameron, the Republican boss of Pennsylvania, who had been named secretary of war in reward for his support of Lincoln at the Republican convention of 1860. To fill the gap, the Navy and State departments attempted to field their own agents, creating a hodgepodge of overlapping efforts that often operated at cross purposes. Spies were hired, projects devised, and missions assigned without any attempt to consult the "parallel" services.

Two rival intelligence organizations—each claiming to be the "Secret Service"—operated in Washington during the first eighteen months of the war. One, headed by Allan Pinkerton, the nation's first private detective, reported to General George B. McClellan, the commander of the Army of the Potomac. The other, headed by Lafayette C. Baker, reported first to General Winfield Scott, the Army's superannuated general in chief, then to William H. Seward, the secretary of state, and finally to Edwin M. Stanton, Cameron's successor as secretary of war. Upon at least two occasions, members of one organization were arrested by the other. Similar conditions prevailed in the South, where the Confederate president, Jefferson Davis, personally ran intelligence and counterespionage operations.

Various generals established localized spy networks that produced worthwhile intelligence, but their achievements pale next to George Washington's activities during the Revolution. The "Lost Order" episode, the greatest intelligence coup of the War, was not the result of spy activity but a gift of sheer luck. On September 13, 1862, two Indiana soldiers found a copy of General Lee's Special Order No. 191, which detailed forthcoming operations in western Maryland, wrapped around three cigars. The order was turned over to General McClellan, but he failed to act fast enough to exploit the opportunities offered.

On both sides, the usual hazards of espionage were multiplied by the inexperience and incompetence of staff officers assigned to intelligence duties. Codes and ciphers were usually rudimentary and so transparently contrived that they accomplished little besides certifying the guilt of those who carried them. Spies sometimes gathered important information at considerable danger to themselves, only to find their reports ignored. Security was almost nonexistent. Brig. Gen. John H. Winder, the provost marshal of Richmond, had the responsibility for counterintelligence in the rebel capital but was overburdened with the task of keeping order in the overcrowded capital. Amazingly, he kept a list of all the regiments defending Richmond and their strengths chalked on a board in his office that was open to public view.

■ ■ ■

Civil War espionage may have been badly coordinated, but there was plenty of it. The Confederates had a head start in establishing their intelligence networks. Although the most outspoken Southern zealots departed from Washington after the attack on Fort Sumter, less visible sympathizers stayed behind. One of them was Thomas Jordan, a U.S. Army captain who lingered in the Yankee capital for another month, setting up a spy ring that reached into the upper levels of the Federal government. A graduate of West Point, where he had shared a room with William Tecumseh Sherman, Jordan was on the staff of General Scott, a position that provided him with an excellent vantage point for studying the Union's war plans. By the time he left Washington, he had created a network of spies that included professional men, government clerks, shopkeepers, bankers, and politicians. Jordan, however, was partial to the use of female spies, and the binding knot in his skein of espionage was one of Washington's more prominent hostesses—a woman known to her Southern admirers as the Rebel Rose.

A Maryland aristocrat* and an ardent secessionist who was related to the Lees, Randolphs, and Calverts, Rose O'Neal Greenhow was ideally placed to gather intelligence. Through her marriage to Dr. Robert Green-

*Rose Greenhow's sister married James Madison Cutts, Dolley Madison's nephew. Her niece and namesake, Rose Cutts, was the wife of Senator Stephen A. Douglas, who had been defeated by Abraham Lincoln for the presidency in 1860.

how, a scholarly Virginia lawyer, linguist, and State Department official, she knew everyone worth knowing in Washington. Senator John C. Calhoun of South Carolina, the paladin of states' rights, was her mentor. She had nursed him during his final illness, when, black eyes burning in his wasted face, he had uttered his prophecies of the impending breakup of the Union. "I am a Southern woman, born with revolutionary blood in my veins," Rose Greenhow was to say, "and my first crude ideas on State and Federal matters received consistency and shape from the best and wisest man of this century."

Long before the war broke out, Greenhow showed a taste for politics and a talent for intrigue. Following her husband's death in 1854, she engaged in a discreet form of influence peddling. Even though her youthful beauty had faded, men found her fascinating. Her influence was at its height during the administration of President James Buchanan, the courtly bachelor who preceded Lincoln into the White House. Neighbors peering out from behind lace curtains noted that Buchanan was a frequent—and frequently late-departing—visitor to the Widow Greenhow's narrow brick house across fashionable Sixteenth Street from St. John's Church. With the coming of the war, old friends became cabinet officers, such as Senator Seward of New York, who was named secretary of state. In Greenhow's parlor ranking military officers resplendent in braid and colorful sashes mixed with statesmen in sober broadcloth. Her warm lips smiled readily at those from whom she sought to pry information, and they babbled secrets into her sympathetic ear.

The most ardent admirer of the Rebel Rose seems to have been Senator Henry Wilson of Massachusetts—a very useful friend for a Confederate spy, for he was chairman of the Senate Military Affairs Committee.* Letters preserved in the National Archives indicate their relationship was hardly platonic. "You will know that I love you—and I will sacrifice anything," states one feverish note signed "H" and written on U.S. Senate stationery. "You know that I *do love* you. I am suffering this morning, in fact I am sick physically and mentally, and you know that nothing would soothe me so much as an hour with you. And tonight, at whatever cost I will see you . . .. I will be with you tonight, and then I will tell you again and again that I love you."†

Jordan later said that it was knowledge of an "intimacy" between the senator and Greenhow that led him to recruit her for his espionage ring. According to a Union officer, Jordan also claimed that he had "estab-

---

*Later, Wilson was linked to the Credit Mobilier scandal that accompanied the building of the Union Pacific Railroad but managed to survive a congressional investigation. He served as vice-president during President Ulysses S. Grant's second term.

†The letters are preserved fragments of an envelope bearing the words, "letters from H. Not to be opened—but burnt in case of death or accident."

lished relations with the widow on the same footing" and "induced her to get from Wilson all the information she could."

By the latter part of May 1861, Jordan was confident that the spy network could operate without his presence and changed his blue coat for a gray one. He was commissioned a colonel and assigned to intelligence duties as adjutant general on the staff of General Pierre G. T. Beauregard, commander of the Confederate forces gathering across the Potomac. Before departing, he provided Greenhow with a simple cipher he had devised and instructed her to send her dispatches by courier to Thomas J. Rayford, the alias he had chosen for himself. These arrangements, Beauregard said later, enabled him "to receive regularly, from private persons at the Federal capital, most accurate information, of which politicians high in council, as well as War Department clerks, were the unconscious ducts."

Rebel couriers moved back and forth across the Potomac with ease. The war had interrupted mail service across the river, and volunteer messengers quickly filled the communications gap. Physicians were particularly useful couriers because they could go anywhere at any time without arousing suspicion. Moreover, every doctor carried his own medicines with him, and rarely would anyone be inspired to search their black bags. This was the beginning of the highly effective "Doctors' Line" that, augmented by "safe houses" and clandestine ferrymen, served the Confederacy as a communications link throughout the war.

The tavern operated by John H. Surratt at the crossroads hamlet of Surrattsville, about ten miles south of Washington, was one of these "safe houses" and became a regular stop for rebel spies, scouts, and blockade runners on the way to and from the capital. As Thomas Conrad, a leading Confederate agent, recalled, Surratt was "full of intense prejudice and hate toward the Yankees—as was almost everyone in lower Maryland— and outspoken in his Southern convictions, and proud of every Southern victory." When Surratt died in 1862, his son, John, Jr., took over the management of the way station. Eventually, he became a Confederate courier, a position that probably brought him to the attention of another Yankee-hater, John Wilkes Booth.

■ ■ ■

In Washington, Rose Greenhow operated with seeming impunity. Soldiers were encamped everywhere, marching about the dusty streets and overflowing the saloons and brothels, so their movements could hardly be kept secret. On one occasion, she toured the fortifications surrounding the city in the company of a Union officer. Before long, Jordan had detailed information on the strength and weaknesses of the redoubts and an accurate count of the number, calibre, and range of their cannon. Learning that a group of captured Confederate soldiers had been imprisoned in the Old Capitol Building—where an aunt had operated a boarding house and where she had grown up—the widow immediately appeared with baskets of food and bundles of clothing to replace their tattered uniforms.*

But the Rebel Rose's greatest contribution to the Confederate cause was in supplying information that helped make possible the victory at Bull Run, the war's first major battle. In the wake of the attack on Fort Sumter, Lincoln had called for 75,000 three-month volunteers to put down the rebellion. Ever since, president, press, and public alike had vociferously demanded an advance on Richmond. Realizing that his army was little more than an armed rabble, General Irvin McDowell had tried to forestall the assault so that his troops could receive more training. "This is not an army," he confided to a friend. "It will take a long time to make an army."

With the enlistments of the volunteers running out, McDowell succumbed to the pressure to launch an attack. The equally raw rebels were concentrated at the railroad junction at Manassas, some thirty miles southwest of Washington. McDowell would field about thirty-five thousand men against General Beauregard's twenty thousand troops at Manassas. Sixty miles away, Confederate General Joseph E. Johnston commanded twelve thousand men in the Shenandoah Valley. The success of the Yankee attack might well depend on whether the Southern forces united in time to meet it.

Beauregard received the first of Rose Greenhow's warnings of McDowell's advance on July 10, 1861. The means through which it came into his hands was right out of a romantic novel. On the preceding day, Betty Duvall, a pretty young friend of the widow's had crossed the Chain Bridge from Washington, dressed as a country girl in calico and bouncing on a produce wagon. At the home of a Virginia friend, she changed into a trim riding habit and rode off the next morning on a borrowed horse toward a Confederate advance post at Fairfax Court House. Taken before General M. L. Bonham, Betty removed a comb from her glistening black hair. As it fell about her, she drew from the back of her head a small package, about the size of a silver dollar, that had been sewn up in silk. In it was a message from Rose Greenhow, brief and very much to the point: McDowell would advance in mid-July.**

---

*The rambling building had been used by Congress as a meeting place while the Capitol, burned by the British in 1814, was undergoing reconstruction. Many of the most important lawmakers, including Senator Calhoun, lodged there while it was used as a boarding house. The site is now occupied by the Supreme Court Building.

**Senator Wilson has usually been suspected as the source of this information, but Colonel Jordan told Judah P. Benjamin, the Confederate secretary of war, that it came from John F. Callan, the clerk of the Senate Military Affairs Committee, who was apparently a member of his spy ring.

Greenhow's report confirmed information supplied by other informants, newspaper accounts, and statements made by a Federal prisoner. Thus warned, Beauregard deployed his army behind a winding, sluggish stream called Bull Run. But he wanted more information. Early on the morning of July 16, a former Land Office employee named George Donellen called at Greenhow's home. Awakened by a maid, the widow asked him for identification. Donellen replied that he came from "Mr. Rayford of Virginia" and produced a scrap of paper with a cipher message reading "Trust bearer." Satisfied, Rose passed on a message that McDowell was advancing that day upon Manassas by way of Fairfax Court House and Centerville.

Hiding this message in the heel of a boot, Donellen made his way by buggy and relays of horses through secessionist southern Maryland and back across the Potomac. By nightfall, Beauregard was in possession of the message. He sent an urgent telegram to Richmond urging that Johnston's forces in the Shenandoah Valley be ordered to join him. On the night of July 17, Greenhow sent her third vital message—a warning that the Yankees would attempt to cut the railroad from Winchester to Manassas to prevent Johnston from reinforcing Beauregard. The attack was thwarted, and the timely arrival of Johnston's troops on the battlefield of Bull Run on July 21 transformed what looked like a Union victory into a rout that did not end until the fleeing troops reached the safety of Washington.

For about a month after Bull Run, Rose Greenhow basked in the afterglow of what she regarded as a personal triumph. Although she probably exaggerated her role in the victory, it was not inconsequential. From Jordan came a note reading: "Our President and our General direct me to thank you. The Confederacy owes you a debt." Following the Battle of Bull Run, Rose continued to supply Jordan with information, including, she claimed, "verbatim reports from cabinet meetings." But suspicion soon focused on the Widow Greenhow, and her house was placed under round-the-clock surveillance.

■ ■ ■

This watch was established by order of Allan Pinkerton, who had been summoned to Washington by General McClellan to organize his secret service. There could have been no greater contrast than that between the dour, Glasgow-born detective and the arrogant society matron. Born in poverty, Pinkerton was apprenticed as a boy of eight to a cooper, or barrel maker. After coming to America as a young man, he made his home in a farming community on the Fox River near Chicago, where he worked hard, saved his money, and opened a cooperage of his own. Out one day on a river island cutting wood for his barrels, he chanced upon the hideaway of a gang of counterfeiters and led a raid upon it. Soon Pinkerton began dabbling in detective work, and news of his success in running down the counterfeiters and sundry horse thieves reached Chicago. In 1849, he was hired as the booming city's first police detective. Within a year or so, weary of political interference with his fight against crime, he resigned to open his own detective agency. After that Pinkerton's rise was meteoric. He chose as his trademark a staring eye, and businessmen and railroad managers eagerly sought the services of the "Eye."

Early in 1861, Samuel Felton, president of the Philadelphia, Wilmington & Baltimore Railroad, learned that rebel sympathizers planned to blow up the bridges and tunnels around Baltimore, which was boiling over with secessionism, and block the main line between Washington and the North. Pinkerton, a strong Union man, infiltrated the rebel "secret societies" that operated openly in Baltimore. In the process he uncovered, so he claimed, an even more sinister plot: a plan to assassinate Abraham Lincoln as he passed through the city on the way to his inauguration.

Lincoln was reluctant to credit the conspiracy but finally abandoned his schedule when he received a similar warning from General Scott. On the night before he was due to arrive in Baltimore, he boarded a special train in Philadelphia designed to speed him through danger. The telegraph line was cut, and Pinkerton operatives were stationed along the way to signal if there was trouble ahead. All went well until the train reached Baltimore, where in the early morning hours the president-elect was to transfer to the regular train to Washington, which departed from Camden Station on the other side of town. The heavily muffled party reached the station without difficulty, but the Washington train was delayed. For two hours, Lincoln entertained the nervous Pinkerton and his other companions with tall tales from his bottomless stock of anecdotes. Outside, on the platform, a drunk sang "Dixie" over and over again. Pinkerton must have been relieved in more ways than one when the train finally pulled into the station.

Opposition newspapers poked fun at Lincoln's surreptitious arrival in Washington—he was caricatured as sneaking into town disguised as an old woman or in an outsize Scotch plaid bonnet—and he was never certain whether Pinkerton had saved his life or persuaded him to make a fool of himself. Historians have likewise been unable to make up their minds about the Baltimore plot, but less than two months later, events tended to support the detective's story. A Massachusetts militia regiment was attacked by a secessionist mob as it passed through Baltimore along the same route that was to have been followed by the president-elect. Several soldiers and citizens were killed in the melee. Bridges were burned, telegraph lines were cut, and for several days the city was cut off from the outside world. Clearly, Baltimore was ripe for violence—and four years later, Lincoln was assassinated in a plot as fantastic as any reported by Pinkerton.

Pinkerton spent the opening months of the war running a spy network in the region south of the Ohio River on behalf of General McClellan, who as a railroad official had previously employed him.* Called to Washington to assume command of the Army of the Potomac after saving western Virginia for the Union, McClellan brought Pinkerton along with him. In the beginning, the detective served under Colonel Andrew Porter, the provost marshal, or chief of military police. Later he reported directly to Thomas A. Scott, another former railroad man who had been named assistant secretary of war. Using the name "Major E. J. Allen," Pinkerton immediately began operations against Confederate spies in the capital, particularly Rose Greenhow. "She knows my plans better than Lincoln and the cabinet," McClellan is supposed to have complained bitterly.

This cat-and-mouse game had its comic-opera moments. Checking on the Greenhow house one night in mid-August 1861, Pinkerton found the blinds on the front windows were drawn, although a sliver of light shone through. His curiosity aroused, he joined his men in keeping watch through a driving rain. Their soggy vigil paid off when a visitor arrived at the house. Even though he was wet to the skin, Pinkerton was determined to see what was going on. With two of his men, he sidled up to the house. Taking off his boots, he stood on the husky shoulders of his companions and peered through the blinds into a parlor. To his suprise, he saw a young officer he recognized as a captain in the provost guard huddled with the mistress of the house over a map of the defenses of Washington. Before Pinkerton could make out what they were saying, several pedestrians approached. Jumping down from the human pyramid, he hid with his men in the shadows. By the time he resumed his perch, the room was empty. An hour later, the couple reappeared at the front door, arm in arm, to exchange goodnights and "something that sounded very much like a kiss."

Without waiting to pull on his boots, Pinkerton padded down the wet street after his quarry. Obviously aware that he was being followed, the officer abruptly ducked into a building at Pennsylvania Avenue and Fifteenth Street. In a flash, four soldiers confronted Pinkerton, fixed bayonets leveled menacingly at his chest. Resistance was useless, and the shoeless detective was hustled into a provost guard house. Much to his chagrin, he found himself being questioned by the very man he had been stalking. Pinkerton refused to supply any information except for his

---

*McClellan was one of the few commanders on either side with a semblance of intelligence training. He had served as an observer during the Crimean War and had submitted an outstanding report before resigning from the army in 1857 as a captain.

name—"E. J. Allen"—and was locked up with some drunks and minor criminals. During the night, he bribed a guard to deliver a message to Assistant Secretary of War Scott, who ordered the prisoner brought to his home for questioning. Mud-stained and still in his stockinged feet, Pinkerton explained what had happened. At once Scott summoned the officer. Faced with the detective's report, the man confessed that he had given Rose Greenhow the map and was placed under arrest.

The Widow Greenhow was taken into custody about a week later. As she returned from a morning promenade along Sixteenth Street, two men accosted her at the door of her home and, with a mumbled authority, placed her under arrest. One of them, a man with a face like a clenched fist, identified himself as Major E. J. Allen.

Greenhow looked on with disdain as Pinkerton and his detectives searched beds, drawers, and wardrobes, tumbled out soiled clothes, and ransacked the papers in her desk. The men worked quietly, hoping her accomplices might call if no alarm was raised. Then efforts were foiled by the widow's eight-year-old daughter, Rose, who ran outside, climbed a tree and shouted to passers-by: "Mother has been arrested! Mother has been arrested!" The little rebel was dragged back into the house in tears.

There could be no doubt about Rose Greenhow's guilt, but chivalry still reigned. Rather than being hanged, she was held under guard in her own home, which became a detention center for women picked up in Pinkerton's dragnet. The house, dubbed "Fort Greenhow," turned into one of the sights of the capital as tourists flocked there in hopes of catching a glimpse of the famous spy. Greenhow later contended that she contrived to keep open her clandestine correspondence with the South, but Pinkerton may have allowed it to continue with the hope of entrapping her associates. Eventually, the widow and little Rose were taken to the vermin-ridden Old Capital Prison, where, in a final irony, her cell was the same room in which she had nursed the dying John Calhoun. Securely confined, throughout the dreary winter of 1862 she complained incessantly while obviously enjoying her martyrdom at the hands of the Yankees. Meanwhile, with the Widow Greenhow out of the way, Pinkerton rolled up the remainder of Jordan's spy network.*

Pinkerton and his operatives never succeeded in completely erad-

---

*Greenhow was released in June 1862 and sent through the lines to Richmond, where she was hailed as a heroine. Later she went to Europe to arouse support for the Confederate cause. In France she was received by Napoleon III, while in London she was presented to Queen Victoria. A book, *My Imprisonment and the First Year of Abolition Rule at Washington,* a highly colored account of her adventures, was favorably received. In 1864, she decided to return to her beloved Confederacy on a blockade runner. The ship ran aground off Wilmington, North Carolina. Fearing recapture, the Rebel Rose asked to be set ashore with the dispatches she was carrying. Her small boat capsized in the surf, and—weighted down by a bag of gold sovereigns fastened to her waist—she drowned. Her body washed ashore the next day and was buried in Wilmington with full military honors.

icating Confederate espionage in Washington, but the quality and timeliness of intelligence received in Richmond declined distinctly during the period he was in charge of counterintelligence operations. In mid-1862, a pair of spies managed to get into the capital, but the information they supplied on the Union army was incomplete and erroneous on every major point. The dispatches of General Lee also indicate that during this period he was in the dark about the organization of the Federal forces opposing him.

■ ■ ■

Undoubtedly the most effective of Pinkerton's agents was Timothy Webster, a former New York City policeman. "No danger was too great for him," the detective chief said, "no trust too responsible." Pinkerton first encountered Webster while visiting the Crystal Palace Exhibition in 1853 and was so impressed that he invited him to join the agency. Webster not only was a man of great physical strength but also had the gift of easily tailoring his personality to fit conditions as they arose. This talent was an asset in what proved to be his wartime role: serving the Union as a double agent. While providing the Confederacy with impressive-looking but harmless "chicken feed," he gathered valuable information for the Union.

Webster's first assignment was in Baltimore, where, according to Pinkerton, he played a prominent role in uncovering the conspiracy to assassinate Lincoln. Posing as a rabid rebel, Webster infiltrated a band of night riders and learned of their plans to burn railroad bridges and to cut telegraph lines to make certain the "tyrant" did not pass safely through the city. Later he returned to Baltimore, representing himself as "a gentleman of means and leisure" with plenty of money to spend in the local saloons. Once again he was welcomed into the Confederate fifth column. This time he was invited to join the Knights of Liberty, an organization that had been established to sabotage the Union war effort.

Webster had a narrow escape when one of the gang claimed to recognize him as a Yankee detective. Indignantly denying the charge, he called his accuser "a no-good liar." When the man sprang at him, the spy knocked him sprawling, but the rebel scrambled to his feet with a knife in his hand. Webster ended the fracas by pulling out a revolver and holding the cocked weapon to the man's head as he dared him to repeat his accusation.

That incident was enough to elevate Webster into the upper ranks of the organization. Not long afterward, while he was giving a fiery speech at a secret meeting, Federal troops battered down the doors and captured most of those present. The right of habeas corpus had been revoked by presidential order, and those arrested were unceremoniously thrown into Fort McHenry, which had been turned into a prison. Webster managed to "escape"—it was he who had alerted the troops in the first place—thereby increasing his reputation for daring among the rebels.

Early in the fall of 1861, Webster informed the Baltimore secessionists that he was going to Richmond to shake Federal detectives who were hot on his trail. They provided him with letters of introduction to Confederate officials and gave him messages for friends and relatives in the South. Before going on to Richmond, he stopped off in Washington, where this "mail" was inspected by Pinkerton. Upon arriving in the Confederate capital, Webster found that security was lax, and he strolled about the city undisturbed as he delivered the messages he had brought with him. Volunteering his services as an informant to the Richmond *Enquirer*, he was introduced to Secretary of War Benjamin and became an almost daily visitor to his office. When he passed back over the Potomac, he carried a pass from Benjamin and letters for the Baltimore Confederates. In addition to this new batch of Southern mail, Webster provided Pinkerton with a thirty-seven-page report containing the most minute military details.

Back in Baltimore, Webster was such a well-known rebel that he was arrested by other Federal agents who were unaware of his true identity. Once again, Pinkerton arranged for his escape: while the prisioner was being taken to Fort McHenry, he jumped from the wagon and disappeared. Webster's reputation was secure among Confederate partisans as well. When a young Southern sympathizer from Maryland was mistakenly arrested in Virginia on suspicion of espionage, a word from Webster to the authorities was enough to obtain his release. During one of the spy's visits to Richmond, Secretary Benjamin gave him a pass that allowed him to accompany a government contractor who was buying leather for the Confederate government through the heartland of the South, to Knoxville, Chattanooga, and Nashville.

Usually, Webster traveled to Richmond alone, but once he went in company with John Scobell, a former slave. Aware of their stake in the outcome of the war, many slaves did what they could to speed a Union victory—some by joining the Union army, others by acting as informants. "After all, they had been spies all their lives," noted one Federal officer. Born in Mississippi, Scobell had been the property of a kindly Scotsman who saw that he received an education and freed him. Among his talents was the ability to sing Highland ballads complete with a Scottish accent. Because blacks were not suspected of spying, he moved about freely, at various times adopting the role of a dull servant attending a "female" agent, a minstrel, and a steamboat roustabout.

Waiting to cross the Potomac at Leonardtown in southern Maryland, Webster and Scobell split up temporarily. Webster was introduced by the manager of his hotel to a Dr. Gurely, who confided to him that he was carrying dispatches to Richmond and needed the assistance of the well-known Confederate courier. Webster offered it with alacrity but told the physician that he must first take care of a pressing errand. Upon his return, the two men had a few drinks in the bar before Dr. Gurely left to pack. Webster was still in the bar when the doctor staggered in, his clothes muddied and disheveled. He told of being set upon in the dark by an assailant who had stolen his luggage. What about the dispatches? Ashen-faced, Gurely replied that they were gone. Webster commiserated with the unfortunate doctor awhile and then said he had to be off to Richmond. By then, of course, the dispatches were on their way to Washington with John Scobell.

In the spring of 1862, General McClellan launched his long-awaited offensive against Richmond with an attack up the peninsula between the York and James Rivers. The general was desperate for information, but there was no news from Webster. The spy had gone to the Confederate capital accompanied by Mrs. Hattie Lawton, another Pinkerton operative,* and his report was long overdue. Worried about his best agent, Pinkerton decided to send two other operatives, Pryce Lewis and John Scully, to locate him. It was a fatal blunder. Both men had been engaged in counter intelligence work and were known to rebel sympathizers who had been flushed out and deported to the Confederacy. The use of the same agents to gather intelligence and engage in counter intelligence illustrates one of the major failings of Pinkerton's wartime operations, although he contended that the practice allowed him to work with fewer operatives.

Upon their arrival in Richmond, Lewis and Scully went to the Spotswood Hotel, where Webster usually stayed. They were shocked by what they found. Webster had been stricken with inflammatory rheumatism. Unable to leave his bed, he was being nursed by Mrs. Lawton. With Webster incapacitated, she had been unable to contact Pinkerton in Washington but had loyally remained with the sick man. The newcomers were still trying to work out a plan of escape when they fell under suspicion and were taken into custody. Confederate sympathizers they had interrogated in Washington identified the pair as Federal agents. Sentenced to hang, the two men were imprisoned in separate cells. Lewis managed to escape, only to be recaptured on the outskirts of the city.

Taking a last, desperate gamble, Lewis and Scully appealed to the British consul in Richmond for assistance on grounds that they were British subjects. Hoping for recognition by Queen Victoria's government, the Confederacy was unwilling to anger the British, so the consul managed to obtain a stay of execution while an examination of the claim was

---

*Some reports say they traveled as brother and sister, others as husband and wife.

made. Scully broke under the strain, however, and implicated Webster. Taken from his bed and placed on trial as a spy, Webster steadfastly denied the charges, but Scully wound the noose around his colleague's neck as he untied it from his own.*

At Pinkerton's urging, President Lincoln and other Union officials appealed for Webster to be spared. The Confederates, however, were adamant. Barely able to stand because of his arthritic pains, Timothy Webster went bravely to his death on April 29, 1862—the first American to be hanged as a spy since Nathan Hale.

■ ■ ■

Worse was yet to come. Pinkerton spent the spring and summer of 1862 at McClellan's headquarters on the Peninsula as the "Young Napoleon" tried to push on to Richmond. Given the task of determining the strength of the Confederate forces, Pinkerton established an elaborate organization that gathered information from "prisoners of war, contrabands [escaped slaves], loyal southerners, deserters, blockade-runners and from actual observations by trustworthy scouts."

While Pinkerton's prewar activities proved to be an excellent foundation for counterintelligence operations, they were no preparation for analyzing military information. The detective's estimates of Confederate troop strength were wildly inaccurate—he sometimes had the enemy's forces more than twice as large as they actually were—and only fed McClellan's own deep-grained sense of insecurity. Although he had a good strategic sense and was a brilliant organizer and trainer of troops, McClellan was a reluctant warrior. In Lincoln's exasperated words, he "had the slows." McClellan consistently overestimated the strength of the forces opposing him, a tendency Pinkerton's grossly inflated reports did nothing to correct.

Early in the Peninsula campaign, Pinkerton informed McClellan that General Joseph Johnston had between 100,000 and 120,000 men opposing him at Yorktown. In reality, the Confederates could barely muster 50,000 men, and Johnston was imploring President Davis to strip the southern coastline bare of troops and send them to him. Six weeks later, Pinkerton insisted that the rebels had 200,000 men before Richmond; the actual number was less than half that. Taking Pinkerton's reports as gospel, McClellan convinced himself that the enemy outnumbered him, when the truth was just the reverse. Under a more aggressive commander, the Union army might have stormed into Richmond. Instead, the result was defeat and retreat—and the downfall of both McClellan and his intelligence chief. Following McClellan's dismissal,

*Scully and Lewis were released after serving twenty-three months in prison; Hattie Lawton spent a year behind bars.

Pinkerton departed from Washington and spent the remainder of the war ferreting out bounty jumpers and war-related corruption and fraud.

Pinkerton hardly deserves the sole blame for the disaster in the Peninsula, however. In fact, his overblown calculations of Confederate strength may well have been irrelevant.* Even if he had furnished Mc-Clellan with accurate information, the supercautious general probably would have conjured up other equally persuasive reasons for failing to take the offensive. Nevertheless, Pinkerton's misadventures point to an important lesson. Had Pinkerton's data been given serious review at McClellan's headquarters, questions might have been asked about the hordes of men he claimed were present in the enemy ranks. In short, intelligence *analysis* needs to be kept separate from intelligence *collection*.

It was a lesson the American intelligence community never completely absorbed. Exactly a century later, the CIA committed a similar blunder by failing to keep the planning and operational aspects of the Bay of Pigs invasion of Cuba in separate hands.

■ ■ ■

With the fading of Allan Pinkerton from the national intelligence scene, the star of Lafayette C. Baker was in the ascendancy. No man in the history of American intelligence has a more unsavory reputation. A taciturn man with a heavy reddish-brown beard and cold, searching eyes, Baker has often been charged with riding roughshod over constitutional guarantees and installing a reign of terror in the nation. A congressional report labeled him "a miserable wretch" entitled to "an unenviable immortality." These charges were grossly exaggerated and stemmed primarily from his postwar activities on behalf of the radicals trying to impeach Lincoln's successor, Andrew Johnson. Probably a majority of those caught in Baker's ample dragnet deserved to be detained.*

Baker began his career in espionage as what would now be called a "walk-in." In July 1861, he volunteered his services to General Scott, who—according to Baker—promptly accepted the offer. Scott instructed him to determine the location and strength of the enemy forces between Washington and Richmond and gave him 10 twenty-dollar gold pieces to finance the operation. Ominously, Scott told him that of five men previously assigned this task, two had been killed and the others probably taken prisoner.

*So argues Edwin C. Fishel, the authority on Civil War intelligence.

*Most of the material written about Baker is completely unreliable. His own ghostwritten *History of the United States Secret Service*, published in 1868, is often exaggerated and untruthful. The only biography, by Jacob Mogelever, is based on Baker's own work compounded by innuendo and suggestion (see Bibliography).

In order to pass through the Union lines without revealing his role as a spy, Baker claimed, he purchased a broken camera and tripod and pretended to be an itinerant photographer. He was immediately arrested as a rebel agent and sent back to headquarters. General Scott chuckled and told his neophyte spy to try again. Next, Baker tried to mingle with a large body of troops that were crossing the Long Bridge into Virginia but was immediately collared and hauled out of line by an angry officer. On his next try, he got rid of the camera and went to southern Maryland, where he gave a black farmer one of his gold pieces to row him across the Potomac.

Not long after he had landed, Baker was arrested by a Confederate patrol and taken to General Beauregard's headquarters at Manassas. He claimed to be "Sam Munson," a young Tennessean he had known in California, but Beauregard suspected that he was a spy and threw him into the guardhouse. "Sam Munson" was passed up the chain of command to Richmond, where he was interrogated by President Jefferson Davis. Davis pressed "Munson" for information on Yankee troop placements around Washington. Baker said he provided him with a few scraps of information that would not harm the Union cause. But the interrogation unexpectedly took an ominous turn. So your name is Munson and you come from Knoxville? the president asked. Who are some of the people you know there? Perspiring heavily, Baker dredged up a few names he had heard the real Munson mention. Finally, the president summoned a clerk and handed him a note.

Obviously, thought Baker, the rebels had located someone who knew Sam Munson. Fortunately, he had noticed that before a visitor was ushered into Davis's office, the president was given a card with the visitor's name written on it. When the clerk summoned by Davis returned and placed such a card on the president's desk, Baker managed to get a quick look at the name. Upon entering the room, the visitor was nearly bowled over by an effusive greeting.

"Why, how do you do, Brock?" Baker declared, jumping up and vigorously shaking the visitor's hand. When the man stared blankly at him, Baker added, "Don't you remember Judge Munson's son who went to California?"

"What, Sam Munson!" Brock cried, enthusiastically slapping Baker on the back.

Two days later, Davis released "Munson" after he gave his parole not to leave Richmond. Once more, by his own account, Baker spied on the Confederacy while in Confederate hands, moving unnoticed among the crowds wildly celebrating Bull Run and pinpointing troop dispositions and strong points. As soon as he had seen enough, he obtained a temporary pass to Fredericksburg and kept on heading north. Following several narrow escapes, he made his way back to Washington and reported to General Scott.

Pleased with Baker's performance, Scott referred him to Secretary of State Seward, who considered himself first among Lincoln's cabinet members—or "Premier"—and was fulfilling the State Department's traditional role in gathering intelligence. Seward's "Treason Bureau" sent a handful of agents to Canada, Europe, and into the Confederacy, but his major concern was stamping out disloyalty and subversion in the North. Persons suspected of rendering assistance to the Confederacy were subject to arbitrary arrest; in the opening months of the war, upward of a thousand political prisioners were taken into custody and—with the right of habeas corpus suspended by presidential order—held without trial.

Seward's campaign to stamp out subversion was supported by the rabidly anti-Southern Representative John P. Potter of Wisconsin, the chairman of the House Committee to Investigate Government Employees. Embracing methods that were to be emulated nearly a century later by another Wisconsin lawmaker, Senator Joseph R. McCarthy, Potter waged a ruthless campaign against disloyalty in government offices. Using anonymous tipsters, he claimed to have smoked out several hundred secessionists. Potter's efforts were supported by President Lincoln, who established a stiff loyalty oath for government employees. Taking the position that the Constitution was not a suicide pact, Lincoln contended that the government had the right to defend itself—even if doing so meant violating the nation's fundamental law.

Seward now assigned Baker the task of breaking up Confederate lines of communication and blockade-running operations in southern Maryland. With no formal rank and riding a borrowed horse, Baker led three hundred Indiana cavalrymen on a raid through Prince Georges, Charles, and St. Mary's counties that he claimed resulted in the arrest of several spies and couriers. In his wake he left an outraged populace.

Not long afterward, Baker's operations were formally transferred to the War Department. Officially, Baker, who established his headquarters at 217 Pennsylvania Avenue, was designated a War Department provost marshal with the honorary rank of colonel.* But in dealing with civilian police agencies, to whom his true title would mean little, he called his operation the National Detective Police. Baker's annual budget never exceeded $65,000 and his own force was limited to about thirty operatives, but he had the support of numerous informers, both volunteer and paid, who were all too eager to whisper secrets in his ear with the hope of gaining favor. Files on suspected Confederate agents were built up, and Baker instituted the practice of including photographs in them

---

*The rank was made official in June 1863, when he was allowed to organize a cavalry battalion that became known as Baker's Rangers.

for identification. Before long, his tentacles reached to New York, where he opened an office, and to other major cities as he cultivated contacts with local police departments. He also kept an eye on Confederate activities in Canada and placed men in the Post Office, where they read the mail.

For the most part, Baker operated in the realm of criminal investigation and counterintelligence and had only a negligible role in gathering "positive" intelligence. These activities are encrusted with myth, however. Baker is said to have ordered arrests to be made at night when suspects were likely to be more confused and unable to obtain help. A pounding on the door would be followed by a peremptory arrest. Interrogations in the Old Capitol Prison, it is said, smacked of brainwashing. Baker had the first shot at the prisoner. If the captive refused to crack, William P. Wood, the prison superintendent, would take over. He played the role of the "good cop", trying to cajole the suspect into confessing to avoid another session with Baker. With especially difficult prisoners, interrogation might continue around the clock for days on end. Baker was also said to be not above bringing in one of his men as an accusing witness to frighten the suspect into confessing. Prisoners were allowed only intermittent sleep, and incriminating information would be inserted in their statements, which they were ordered to sign. Sometimes, it is claimed, prisoners signed merely to escape the nightmare.

Baker had a ready answer for critics of his methods, one that would echo repeatedly in times of perceived national peril. "War," he said, "is a last and terrible resort in the defense of even a righteous cause, and sets at defiance all of the ordinary laws and customs of society." The aura of romance that had hung about Civil War espionage had been ripped away.

7

War by Other Means

Early in the morning of June 4, 1861, James D. Bulloch pushed open a heavy office door and abruptly strode into the Liverpool banking house of Fraser, Trenholm & Company. The clerks looked up from their ledgers to see a bulky man with an air of command and a luxuriant mustache that flared back into muttonchop whiskers. The visitor asked to see Charles K. Prioleau, the resident partner. Within a few minutes, he was ushered into the banker's private office. He carried no papers or letters of introduction, for the Confederacy's chief secret agent in Europe was on an undercover mission of extreme importance to the embattled South.

Bulloch's arrival in Liverpool triggered a clandestine international struggle that was almost as vital to the fate of the Confederacy as the fighting on the battlefields of Virginia. Lacking the industrial capacity to produce the arms, munitions, and ships needed to wage war, the South sought to procure them abroad, while the North fought to prevent the rebels from winning foreign support. Over the next four years, propagandists, spies, double agents, diplomats, and saboteurs engaged in a war in the shadows, a struggle in which Bulloch was a central figure. Few men would be worth more to the Southern cause.

Little more than a month before, Bulloch, a former U.S. Navy officer, had been a captain of a commercial mail steamer on the New York to New Orleans run. A native of Georgia, he had offered his services to the Confederacy immediately after the fall of Fort Sumter. In response, Secretary of the Navy Stephen R. Mallory summoned him to Montgomery, Alabama, then the Confederate capital. Their meeting was brief and direct. Expecting to be assigned to the Mississippi River defenses below New Orleans, Bulloch had barely introduced himself when Mallory declared: "I am glad to see you: I want you to go to Europe. When can you start?"

"I can start as soon as you explain what I am to do," the surprised Bulloch replied.

Mallory told him that he was to go to England and purchase or build a half-dozen commerce raiders, man and arm them, and get them to sea to harass the Union's substantial maritime trade. It was the most important and challenging secret mission of the war. Two weeks before, President Lincoln had proclaimed a blockade of the long sweep of the Southern coast, from the Potomac to the Rio Grande. If the Confederacy was prevented from exchanging its cotton for the tools of war, the rebellion would be effectively throttled. Mallory was determined to prevent such an eventuality and believed the depredations of the raiders would force the Union to divert ships from the blockade to pursue them.

Bulloch was informed that a credit of one million dollars would be deposited to his account at the Liverpool offices of Fraser, Trenholm, the financial agents for the Confederate government in Britain. Other agents were to be sent abroad with an additional two million dollars earmarked for the construction or purchase of a pair of powerful ironclad warships in England or France that would be able to break the blockade. That night, Bulloch left Montgomery by train, traveling by way of Detroit to Montreal, where he boarded a packet for Liverpool. As he crossed over into Union territory, Bulloch, who had been given no military rank, destroyed all his papers so there would be no incriminating evidence should he be arrested.

Bulloch was an excellent choice for such a sensitive operation. Possessed of sound business judgment, he was also discreet and could be relied upon to safely navigate the shoals of the British neutrality laws. A member of a prominent Georgia family that made its home at Roswell, about nineteen miles north of Atlanta,* he had entered the Navy as a midshipman at the age of sixteen. Promotion was slow, and fourteen years later he was still only a lieutenant. In 1853 he resigned his commission to join the commercial mail service. Bulloch made his home in New York City, near Martha, his younger half-sister, who was married to a businessman and philanthropist by the name of Theodore Roosevelt, Sr. The couple had a sickly three-year-old son, also named Theodore, who called Bulloch Uncle Jimmy and who was later to become the twenty-sixth president of the United States.

■ ■ ■

Bulloch found Liverpool seething with pro-Confederate sentiment. More Rebel flags were said to be flying there than in Richmond. The city

---

*The family plantation at Roswell was sacked by Sherman's army as it marched through Georgia, but Bulloch Hall survived the Civil War and is now a museum. Local legend has it that Margaret Mitchell, who knew the house, used it as the model for Tara in *Gone with the Wind*.

was the center of the cotton trade, and its financial and business interests were closely tied to the South. Before the war, the Mersey had been crowded with ships unloading cotton while others took on goods consigned to the South. Anger over the Union blockade ran high, and blockade running was already a lucrative business. "The people here undoubtedly desire to see the Southern Confederacy established," observed Thomas H. Dudley, the American consul. "Their sympathies for the South and dislike for the North are too open and apparent to be mistaken."

Wasting no time, Bulloch immediately began inspecting the ships available for purchase. As an experienced naval officer, he had a clear idea of the qualities he wanted in his commerce raiders—above all, "speed, speed, speed," because they had to be able to outrun any vessel they could not outfight. They also had to be sizable enough to carry sufficient coal and supplies for a long voyage, for they would have to be largely self-sustaining. They had to combine the best of sail and steam—canvas for cruising, steam for action—and, although built of wood to facilitate repairs in isolated ports, strong enough to sustain the weight of heavy guns.

To procure such ships Bulloch would have to overcome legal hurdles: the Foreign Enlistments Act prohibited the fitting out of armed ships in Britain. When an attorney retained by Bulloch pointed out that the law was silent on the question of vessels built in British yards and armed elsewhere, Bulloch seized upon the loophole and sailed his ships through it.

None of the available vessels met Bulloch's exacting standards, so he decided to have two raiders built from the keel up. The first, which became the *Florida,* was laid down in the Liverpool yards of William Miller & Sons. Handy and fast, she had three sharply raked masts and twin funnels that gave her the illusion of speed even when she was riding at anchor. Passersby along the Merseyside could see her hull rising on the stocks, so Bulloch gave her the faintly Italianate cover name *Oreto* and had the dockyard workers told that she was being built for a firm doing business in Palermo. The builders asked no questions, and Bulloch volunteered no information. If there was trouble later on over a violation of Britain's neutrality laws, they could honestly say they had no knowledge of the vessel's intended use as a rebel raider.

With work underway on the *Oreto,* Bulloch crossed the Mersey to Birkenhead, where he signed a contract with the highly respected Laird shipyard for the construction of a slightly larger cruiser. She was built along the lines of a yacht, and everyone thought she was among the most graceful vessels they had ever seen. In accord with shipyard practice, a sign was set up at the head of the building ways designating her as "Number 290." Although New York newspapers later claimed angrily that this indicated that a syndicate of 290 British investors had financed the vessel, it signified merely that she was the 290th ship built at the Birkenhead yard. For a brief time she was known as the *Enrica;* to history she is known as the *Alabama.*

■ ■ ■

Even before Bulloch arrived in Britain, his counterpart from the Confederate War Department, Captain Caleb Huse, was already engaged in scrambling for arms before the supply was cornered by Yankee agents. In all, it has been estimated that the Union agents had some ten million dollars at their disposal for this purpose. On his first day in Britain, Huse hurried to the London Armory Company to purchase twelve thousand rifles of the latest pattern, only to find that a man he suspected of being a Union purchasing agent had gotten there first. Waiting until the other fellow left "to flank his movement," Huse offered to buy the firm's entire production for a year with the right to renew the order. Company officials replied that they had just signed a contract with the Federal agent for their complete output. But Huse bribed a clerk, who told him the order was a comparatively small one that would be quickly filled. As soon as it was met, Huse closed a contract for *all* the guns the company could produce, effectively preventing the Union man from getting his foot in the door again.*

Next, Huse was off to Vienna, where he placed an order with the Imperial Austrian Arsenal for one hundred thousand rifles, sixty cannon, and a supply of ammunition. When the American minister protested, the Austrians blandly replied that the services of the arsenal had been offered to the United States government and they had received no reply. The minister then offered to buy the whole consignment, but the proposal was rejected. "I confess to a glow of pride when I saw those sixty pieces of rifled artillery with caissons, field forges, and battery wagons . . . all drawn up in array in the arsenal yard," Huse noted with considerable understatement. The guns were delivered to a ship in Hamburg, which carried them to Bermuda. There they were transferred to a blockade runner and slipped into the Confederacy.

Despite such early successes, the Confederate agents in Europe operated under severe handicaps. They were often short of funds, their instructions were unrealistic, and they found themselves immersed in intrigue. To his "utmost astonishment as well as chagrin," Bulloch read a complete account of his mission in the *The Times* of London even before

---

*Huse was a Northerner, born in Newburyport, Massachusetts. Following his graduation from West Point, he spent much time in the South and at the time of the outbreak of the war was commandant of cadets at the University of Alabama. Undoubtedly because of his Yankee background, Huse faced periodic charges of misappropriating government funds, but there appears to be no reason to doubt his integrity.

he had begun his operations. Everything was there—the details of his assignment, the amount of money allotted to him, the banks and commercial houses with which he was to deal—as if the information had been copied from his instructions. As a result, he wrote Secretary Mallory, everyone who had contact with him was suspected of being in the Confederate service and was under surveillance by detectives employed by Northern officials.

The timing of this dispatch is clear evidence of Bulloch's problems with security. Although he had been in England since early June, it was not until mid-August that he felt he had found a safe line of communication with Richmond. "Three gentlemen have at different times consented to take verbal messages, but no one has been willing to run the risk of attempting to carry anything in writing," he declared. Even then, fearing that his letter might fall into the wrong hands, he omitted the names of the contractors with whom he was doing business.

In truth, Northern counterintelligence had surrounded Bulloch and other Confederate agents with spies and informers. In October 1861, the Liverpool newspapers reported that a well-known businessman was being systematically watched by a detective and could not leave his office without "this odious double . . . shuffling about the doorway." Goods that he consigned to America were illegally opened and inspected; friends who traveled to New York and Boston were searched and, in some cases, imprisoned. Two months later, the London *Chronicle* revealed that "a system of espionage of the most extensive and searching character has been for some time going on in England, and that every move of a warlike character has been immediately reported to the Government of the United States." This system had been in operation for about four months, the paper added, and agents were stationed at all British seaports to learn the destination and cargo of every vessel leaving port.

These covert operations were in the hands of Henry S. Sanford, the American minister to Belgium. Sanford did not act like a spymaster, however. Elegantly dressed and sporting a heavy, gold-headed cane, he invited attention rather than displaying the passion for anonymity that is the mark of the good intelligence operative. Independently wealthy, he maintained a luxurious home, entertained lavishly, and kept a fine carriage and horses. Casual observers dismissed him as a rich dilettante, but few Americans had more diplomatic experience. Sanford held a doctorate in laws from Heidelberg, was fluent in French, German, and Spanish, and had served in several diplomatic posts abroad.

Even before the attack on Fort Sumter, Secretary of State William H. Seward had written Sanford that "the most important duty of the diplomatic representatives of the United States in Europe will be to counteract by all proper means the efforts of the agents of the projected Confederacy at their respective courts." Sanford eagerly took up the challenge. He established a wide-ranging espionage network, engaged in propaganda activities, and purchased supplies to deny them to the Confederates. Using diplomatic and consular posts as a center, Sanford's apparatus spread into textile mills, shipyards, ports, financial houses, and factories throughout Europe. Postal and telegraphic offices and other government agencies were also infiltrated by his agents.

Sanford's first covert effort was an attempt to counter pro-Confederate sympathies in the notoriously venal European press. Originally, he had expected Federal victories to speak for themselves, but the debacle at Bull Run meant stronger measures would be needed to influence public opinion. Editors and writers willing to publish pro-Northern material were given "support" from his secret service fund. For example, A. Malespine, one of the leading French journalists of the day, was guaranteed a monthly stipend to write articles for the popular press supporting the Union. Sanford also had more ambitious plans. He sought permission from Secretary Seward to secretly purchase control of one of the large-circulation newspapers or, failing that, to establish a central news bureau in Paris to funnel releases to journals throughout the Continent. When Seward refused, he launched an abortive campaign to collect the funds from Northern businessmen.

Clerks in the offices of the leading manufacturing firms in Liège, the industrial center of Belgium, were bribed by Sanford to supply tips on purchases being made by rebel agents. "I have uncovered a mine of rich Rebel Ores," he told a friend. To deny these supplies to the Confederates, he offered slightly higher bids than those made by Southern emissaries and obtained the right of first refusal on all contracts for guns and cloth. He also bought up all the saltpeter available for purchase in Europe and chartered a steamer to carry it to the United States. Once he managed to snatch a contract for sixty thousand rifles from under the noses of Confederate purchasing agents. "I hope they will be effective in destroying the Rebels for whom they were intended," he observed jubilantly.

Sanford displayed an even greater enthusiasm for the organization of his spy network. "I am determined if possible to get at the operations of these 'Commissioners' through their own papers," he told Seward on July 4, 1861. "How it will be done, whether through a pretty mistress, or an intelligent servant, or a spying landlord is nobody's business; but I lay great stress on getting you full *official* accounts of their operations here." To supplement the efforts of American diplomats and consuls, he urged Seward to increase the amount of secret service funds available and hired or authorized the employment of numerous private detectives and informers throughout Europe.

Early in July 1861, Sanford obtained the services of Ignatius Pollaky, a private detective with his own team of operatives, to monitor the activities of Confederate agents in England. Pollaky pinpointed no fewer

than seventeen active rebel conspirators and placed them under surveillance. Postmen were paid a pound a week to furnish the names of the
towns on the postmarks of letters received by the rebels. When several
letters came from a seaport, a detective was dispatched to locate a ship
that might be loading cargo for the South. Telegraph offices were
watched, and in some cases messengers were invited into pubs for free
drinks and relieved of the telegrams they were carrying. Pollaky's agents
also tracked down the warehouses where goods purchased by the Confederates were awaiting shipment and obtained the names of British
companies that were doing business with the Confederacy.

■ ■ ■

James Bulloch soon became the primary target of Sanford's apparatus. "He is the most dangerous man the South have here and fully up to
his business," he told Seward in a confidential dispatch. The watch on
him was doubled, and 150 pounds a month was spent on this activity
alone. "So dangerous do I consider this man that I feel disposed when he
comes to the continent, to have him arrested on some charge or other and
as he would have no papers, he would get no diplomatic protection &
might *be sent home for examination,*" Sanford added. In plain language,
given the opportunity he intended to have Bulloch kidnapped. "Unless
vigorous measures are taken for discovery and effective suppression of
the enterprises of the Rebels here," he noted, "we shall soon have . . .
more serious losses on the seas than any we have suffered."

Sanford's fertile imagination hatched numerous schemes for thwarting Bulloch and the other rebel agents—called "B. & Co." by his men. He
suggested bribing one of the clerks at Lloyd's insurance office to supply
information about the sailing of ships bound for Southern ports. If the
evidence secured by Pollaky's agents and the consuls proved insufficient
to justify seizure of these vessels, pettifogging lawyers should be retained
to delay them from clearing harbor with legal motions. With adequate
funds, Sanford told Seward, he could arrange to have ships sabotaged
before they got out of harbor. Referring to the British-owned blockade
runner *Thomas Watson,* which had recently sailed with a cargo of arms
for the South, he said: "5000 would have sunk her; accidents are so
numerous in the channel, you know."

At one point Sanford proposed placing Yankee agents as super-
cargoes on vessels carrying war materiel to the South. The agents would
bribe members of the crew to join them in seizing control of these ships
on the high seas. He also tried to buy a fully laden blockade runner before
she could put to sea. The plot miscarried, however, when the Federal
government failed to put up the fifty thousand pounds required to make
the purchase. Another Union agent, B. W. Saunders, who had infiltrated
the Confederate apparatus, told Secretary Seward that the Southerners

had nearly two million dollars worth of war material stockpiled in European ports awaiting shipment through the blockade. He suggested that he be supplied with funds to purchase a ship to be placed at the Confederates' disposal; the ship would then sail into the waiting arms of a Federal warship. As with Sanford's similar proposal, the plan was never put into effect.

In October 1861, Pollaky's operatives discovered that Bulloch had purchased the fast steamer *Fingal,* which was to become the first blockade runner owned by the Confederate government. Tracing shipments of firearms from London to Liverpool to Greenock, Scotland, they discovered that the *Fingal* was taking on a cargo of fourteen thousand Enfield rifles, four hundred barrels of gunpowder, a load of medical supplies, and other equipment—the largest military shipment yet destined for the South. Having pinpointed the vessel, one of Pollaky's agents secured a place at the Old Sailor's Home in the town and moved unmolested among the men doing the loading. As he reported, "After cruising amongst 'an immense assortment of multifarious goods' . . . I fortunately observed *the cases.*" He was referring to cases of rifles, marked with the name of Isaac Campbell & Company, the purchasing agents used by Caleb Huse.

Although the *Fingal* was to sail under the British flag and with a British captain and crew, Pollaky learned that Bulloch intended to command her. But the Confederate agent was nowhere in sight when the vessel left Greenock on October 9, 1861. Aware that Northern spies were watching the ship, Bulloch gave the detectives who were watching him the slip and boarded the *Fingal* at Holyhead, down the coast. The voyage almost ended before it began. Making port in a heavy gale to pick up Bulloch, the *Fingal* rammed and sank a collier, or coal-bearing ship, at the harbor's mouth. Unwilling to be delayed by a lengthy investigation, Bulloch left word for Fraser, Trenholm to make a settlement and ordered the captain to put to sea. "I thought of the rifles and sabres in the hold, and the ill-armed pickets on the Potomac, waiting and longing for them," he said.

■ ■ ■

Perhaps the most bizarre operation hatched by Union operatives in Europe was a scheme to recruit Giuseppe Garibaldi, the liberator of Italy, as a general in the U.S. Army. The idea was the brainchild of James W. Quiggle, the American consul in Antwerp, who was about to be replaced and saw an opportunity to save his job with a bit of enterprise. Learning that Garibaldi, then in semi-exile on the island of Caprera, was receptive to the idea of going to America if the United States government requested his services, Quiggle passed the idea to Washington, where it arrived just after the debacle at Bull Run. President Lincoln and Secretary Seward eagerly grasped the opportunity to recruit the renowned Italian leader in hopes that his presence would give sagging Northern morale a much-needed shot in the arm.

The proposal was not as farfetched as it seems today. Garibaldi was regarded by many Americans as the "Washington of Italy." Newly organized regiments of the Union army were proudly donning the red shirt that was the symbol of his legions and calling themselves "Garibaldi Guards." As for Garibaldi himself, he had lived in the United States for three years, during which he had become an ardent abolitionist, and he regarded himself as an adopted American citizen. With the newly installed Italian king, Victor Emanuel II, refusing to go along with his plan to free Rome from the control of the pope, Garibaldi now found himself in restless retirement at Caprera.

On July 27, 1861, Seward bypassed Quiggle and instructed Henry Sanford to enter into communication with the "distinguished Soldier of Freedom" and offer him a commission as a major general, then the highest rank in the Union army. President Lincoln's name was not mentioned, but only he could have approved such a proposal. Unfortunately, when Sanford went to Italy to open negotiations with Garibaldi, he told Quiggle of his mission. The consul hastened to inform Garibaldi that he was to be offered "the highest army commission which it is in the power of the President to confer"—leading the general to think that he was to be made supreme commander of the Union army.

Garibaldi, whose ambitions centered on Rome rather than Richmond, craftily tried to use the American offer to force King Victor Emanuel to support a march on Rome. Unless the monarch acceded to his wishes, the hero threatened, he would accept the American offer. Much to his surprise, Victor Emanuel called his bluff by giving him permission to leave Italy. Sanford, having learned of the king's rebuff, was convinced that Garibaldi would now accept the American offer as the only means of salvaging his self-respect. Deciding to continue the delicate negotiations in person, he chartered a small steamer in Genoa under an assumed name and set out for Garibaldi's rocky and windswept island.

Upon meeting the potential savior of the Union on September 8, 1861, Sanford found that he hardly looked like the part. The general was recovering from rheumatic fever and had not been out of his cottage in nearly four months. Nevertheless, having been misled by Quiggle, Garibaldi made demands that Sanford was not authorized to meet. He would go to America only if he were made commander in chief of the Union army and given blanket authority to free the slaves—conditions that only the president could grant. Sanford replied that a commission as a major general was the highest rank he was authorized to offer and expressed a willingness to underwrite a visit by Garibaldi and his entourage to the United States so he could personally survey the situation before making a final decision. The proud general took an all-or-nothing position, however, and declined the offer.

It was just as well. Had Garibaldi accepted, he would have aroused considerable jealousy among American officers, and past events made it clear that he was temperamentally incapable of being a subordinate or of cooperating with others in ways required by modern warfare. The episode did serve Garibaldi's purposes, however. When the Italian people learned that their liberator had considered abandoning the country because of the King's reluctance to support his plans, there was a tremendous groundswell of support for Garibaldi's cause. As far as he was concerned, that was the primary objective of his negotiations with the Americans.*

■ ■ ■

Several months after the abortive Garibaldi affair, the clandestine war in Europe entered a new phase. Having successfully run the Union blockade in the *Fingal,* James Bulloch returned to England in March 1862 with a commission as commander in the Confederate Navy. In his absence, work had nearly been completed on the *Oreto,* and she had attracted the attention of Northern officials—particularly Thomas Dudley, the American consul in Liverpool.

A Quaker and an abolitionist from New Jersey—he had once gone South to rescue a kidnapped black woman and her three children—Dudley had, says one writer, "the aggressiveness of a terrier and the tenacity of a bulldog." Dudley had hired a private detective named Matthew Maguire, who poked about the pubs and dockyards of the Merseyside in an effort to learn more about the mysterious vessel. Maguire discovered enough information to convince the consul that the ship was indeed intended as a rebel commerce raider. Late in February 1862, just before Bulloch's return to England, an informant claimed to have seen two gun carriages taken on board the *Oreto.* Dudley passed the report on

---

*Garibaldi had a hypnotic effect on American officials. Following a fresh series of reversals, Theodore Canisius, the American consul in Vienna, wrote Garibaldi in September 1862 on his own initiative, offering him a place in the Union army. Canisius had been the editor of a German-language newspaper in downstate Illinois that had been secretly purchased by Abraham Lincoln to support his presidential candidacy in 1860. In return for winning German votes for Lincoln, he had been given the consulship. Garibaldi, who was under arrest and recovering from a wound received in an abortive attempt to capture Rome, showed fresh interest in fighting for the Union. This time, however, he did not demand the top command. Canisius, who had expressed support for Garibaldi's march on Rome, gleefully leaked word of the general's interest to the press, whereupon the government of King Victor Emanuel protested against this intervention in Italy's domestic affairs. An embarrassed Seward immediately fired Canisius on grounds that he had exceeded his authority. But as soon as the heat was off, the president restored him to his post in Vienna—perhaps to keep him quiet about Lincoln's ties to the German newspaper.

to Charles Francis Adams, the American minister in London. Immediately Adams called upon Lord John Russell, the British foreign secretary, to demand that the ship be detained for violating the neutrality laws.

Lord Russell made an inquiry, but British officials learned nothing more than Bulloch had originally told the *Oreto*'s builders. On March 4, a customs inspector with the striking name of J. Mudie Searcher examined the ship and found no guns. The fact that her sides were pierced for cannon was of no concern to him. "She had no gunpowder or even a signal gun, and no colors save Marryatt's code of signals and a British ensign," he reported. Much to the frustration of Adams and Dudley, Russell informed them that there was no legal justification for preventing the ship from sailing. Bulloch had done his work well.

Bulloch was nevertheless worried about the *Oreto*'s safety and pushed the final preparations for getting her to sea. Dudley was still nosing about, and no one knew what he might come up with. On March 22, 1862, the *Oreto* left port under British colors and with a British captain and crew. Bulloch had spread the news that she was going out for a trial run, and several guests were on board, including a few women. But before the vessel cleared the harbor, the ladies and all but one of the visitors were sent ashore in small boats. The remaining passenger was Master John Low of the Confederate navy, who was in secret command of the ship. Low had instructions from Bulloch to take the *Oreto* to Nassau in the Bahamas and turn her over to Commander John Newland Maffitt. Only the ship's officers knew her destination; the crew thought they were going to Palermo. Several days before, the steamer *Bahama*, which had been chartered by Bulloch, had preceded the *Oreto* to sea from Hartlepool, on the other side of England, carrying the four 7-inch rifled guns, ammunition, and other supplies that would turn her into the commerce raider *Florida.**

■ ■ ■

Bulloch now turned his attention to No. 290, the vessel under construction in the Laird yards at Birkenhead. Construction had proceeded slowly because of the builders' meticulous craftsmanship and his own absence in America, and he was concerned that attempts would be made to detain her. For his part, Thomas Dudley, angry at the failure of the British to seize the *Oreto*, was determined to prevent "290" from escaping. A network of detectives, shipyard workmen, and dockside idlers was recruited to keep an eye on the vessel. Over the next several months, Bulloch and Dudley tried to outmaneuver each other as work went ahead on "290." Everyone knew she was intended as a Confederate commerce

*Under Maffitt's command, the *Florida* captured or destroyed thirty-seven Yankee vessels valued at some $3.7 million. In October 1864, she was captured off Bahia by a Union warship that violated Brazilian territorial waters.

raider, but Dudley found it difficult to obtain evidence of neutrality-law violations that would satisfy British officialdom. No matter how many sworn affidavits he presented to Samuel Price Edwards, the collector of customs at Liverpool, the answer was always the same: "Not sufficient evidence."

The ship was finally launched on May 15, 1862, and was named the *Enrica*, the Spanish equivalent of the name of the unidentified lady who christened her. She was immediately towed to a graving dock for the installation of her engines and the fitting of masts and other equipment. A month later, the *Enrica* sailed on her sea trials under the command of an English master. Dudley's spies reported that a number of "American gentlemen" were on board the vessel as she was put through her paces and that they seemed exceedingly pleased with her performance. To keep from violating British laws, Bulloch had already decided that the *Enrica* would receive her armament at Terceira in the Azores, an island he had visited during the voyage of the *Fingal* the year before. A small steamer named the *Agrippina* was purchased and loaded with guns and ammunition in London.

Expecting to take command of the *Enrica* himself as soon as she was out of British waters, Bulloch made preparations to sail. "Every aspiration in my heart is bound up in her, and I pray God to help me use her profitably in our country's cause," he declared. Coal bunkers were topped off, supplies were stowed, and a staff was appointed from among the Confederate officers in Britain, including Bulloch's 16-year-old half-brother, Irvine, who was given a midshipman's warrant.* But Bulloch then received what must have been the most disappointing news of his life. Secretary Mallory informed him that the *Enrica* was to be given to Captain Raphael Semmes, who had commanded the *Sumter,* the South's first commerce raider, on a successful cruise against Yankee shipping. Mallory told Bulloch that his "services in England are so important at this time, that I trust you will cheerfully support any disappointment you may experience in not getting to sea." As soon as the *Enrica* was turned over to Semmes, his next task would be to obtain two more cruisers and several ironclads.

Meanwhile, Federal agents were closing in on Bulloch's pride and joy. Not long before, a Southerner named Robinson, who had been paid off from a blockade runner, took up lodging in a boarding house owned by Matthew Maguire, the detective employed by Dudley. Primed, no

---

*Irvine Bulloch commanded the gun that fired the last shots in the *Alabama*'s final battle with the U.S.S. *Kearsarge*—a fact that was not lost upon his nephew, Theodore Roosevelt, when he campaigned for the presidency in the South forty years later. "One would suppose that the President, himself, fired the last two shots from the *Alabama* instead of his uncle," wrote a Washington *Star* reporter. "Mr. Roosevelt's relationship with a Confederate officer is accepted as practically equal with having fought for the cause himself."

doubt, by several drinks supplied by Maguire, Robinson let slip that he had heard the blockade runner's officers talking about a cruiser being constructed for the Confederacy at Birkenhead under the direction of someone named Bulloch. Information was also obtained from a foreman at Laird's shipyard, who said the vessel was larger than the *Oreto* and could carry eleven guns. Once again, Dudley dropped his affidavits on the desk of Price Edwards, the customs chief in Liverpool, insisting that "everything about the vessel shows her to be a war vessel—she has well constructed magazines—she had platforms already screwed to her decks for the reception of swivel guns." Once again, Edwards brushed off his complaints.

An angry Dudley took his affidavits to London, where Charles Francis Adams sent them to Lord Russell, the foreign secretary, with the urgent demand for the seizure of the *Enrica*. The Foreign Officer passed the buck to the Treasury, which had responsibility for the Customs Office, but its man in Liverpool—who happened to be Price Edwards—replied that there was no evidence the vessel had taken on arms and ammunition or enlisted men for the Confederate navy. Adams was not to be put off so easily. The similarity between the American minister and his chief adversary, Lord Russell, was striking. Both were aloof, cool, and aristocratic—Adams was the son of John Quincy Adams and the grandson of John Adams—and neither was a man to be trifled with.

To press the American claims, Adams discussed the situation with Robert R. Collier, one of Britain's leading attorneys. Following a review of the evidence, Collier told Adams that it would be difficult to make "a stronger case of infringement of the Foreign Enlistment Act." If Lord Russell allowed the *Enrica* to sail, he said, the Americans would have a valid claim for damages. On July 26, 1862, Russell, who was uneasy about the case, sent the documents to Sir John Harding, one of the Queen's Law Officers, for an immediate opinion. Inasmuch as it was a Saturday, the papers were delivered to his home. But no answer was forthcoming over the weekend. Unknown to everyone, Harding had suffered a nervous breakdown, and his terrified wife had told no one about his condition.

Somewhere along the line there was a leak. Bulloch received a telegram that Saturday from a source he never identified warning him that it would not be safe for the *Enrica* to remain at Liverpool for more than forty-eight hours.* Immediately Bulloch issued orders for the *Agrippina* to sail with her cargo of arms and the finishing touches to be put on the *Enrica*. Word was passed that she was to undergo further trials on Tuesday, July 29.

---

*The informant is now thought to have been a young Foreign Office clerk named Victor Buckley, who appears to have been a member of Bulloch's organization.

To allay suspicion, the *Enrica* carried a large party of visitors and was dressed with flags as she glided down the Mersey to the open sea, trailed by a tug boat. Following a pleasant sail and lunch, Bulloch announced that he had decided to keep the vessel out overnight. Before returning to Liverpool in the tug with his guests, he told the vessel's commander, Captain Butcher, that he would rejoin the ship the next day about fifty miles up the Welsh coast with the remainder of the crew.

Back in London, two other Law Officers, having retrieved the papers from Harding's wife, determined that there were indeed sufficient grounds to detain the *Enrica*. But the ruling bounced around the corridors of Whitehall from the Foreign Office to the Treasury to the Customs Office without any action being taken. At the same time, Dudley was frantically trying to get Price Edwards to hold the ship until her status was clarified, but the official was mysteriously absent from his post. Years later, it was learned that he had speculated heavily in cotton—and a Southern victory.

Shortly after dawn on Wednesday, July 30, Bulloch arrived at the landing stage to board the tug. He faced a raucous scene. A crew of about thirty-five or forty seamen had been collected, but they were accompanied by an almost equal number of prostitutes. When Bulloch ordered the men on board the tug, the women told him it was "a case of all or none." They would not leave unless they were given the men's first month's pay for services rendered. The harassed Bulloch was trying to sort out the problem when he was informed by telegram that the Yankee steam sloop *Tuscarora* had just stood out to sea from Southampton, apparently steering for the southern coast of Ireland, where she could head off the unarmed *Enrica*.

Wasting no time on further palaver, Bulloch ordered everyone to pile on the tug. By late afternoon, when the craft came alongside the *Enrica* as she lay in Moelfra Bay on the Welsh coast, they were all soaked by a persistent drizzle. There had been nothing to eat on the tug, so the near-frantic Bulloch had to wait until food and grog had been served on the *Enrica* before he could get down to business. The ship would not return to Liverpool, the men were told. Would they sign on for a run to Havana and intermediate ports? Most agreed and were given a month's pay in advance—which was turned over to the women. It was nearly midnight before Bulloch could breathe a sigh of relief as the last of the prostitutes went over the side and the tug was case off.

It was not a good time to leave a safe anchorage—a storm was whipping up the Irish Sea—but Bulloch dared not wait for the storm to blow itself out. To avoid a brush with the *Tuscarora,* he ordered Captain Butcher to set a course around the rugged northern coast of Ireland before heading for Terceira and a rendezvous with the *Agrippina* and Raphael Semmes. Just as evening was falling on July 31, Bulloch went ashore in a fishing boat that had been hailed off Giant's Causeway. From her pitching deck, he watched the *Enrica* disappear into the rain and mist.* Returning to Liverpool, he learned that the vessel had made it to sea only by a whisker: orders to detain her had arrived from London almost immediately after she had sailed. Confusion and conspiracy played a vital role in the vessel's escape, but in the final analysis, the margin of success was the skill and audacity of James D. Bulloch.

■ ■ ■

While Bulloch was plotting to get his ships to sea, the Confederacy was trying to widen its support among the British public. This campaign was in the hands of a twenty-eight-year-old journalist named Henry Hotze. Hotze proved to be a masterful propagandist with a finesse that would have done credit to Bismarck. A native of Switzerland, Hotze had come to America as a youth but had never lost his European manner. He served as secretary to the American minister in Brussels and at the outbreak of the war was editorial writer for the Mobile *Register,* a leading Southern newspaper. Earlier, he had written a book defending slavery on anthropological grounds.

Within a month of his arrival in Britain, Hotze had successfully planted pro-Confederate articles and commentary in several prominent newspapers and had helped prepare speeches delivered by Southern partisans in Parliament. He was so resourceful that he managed to soften the impact of the loss of Forts Henry and Donelson in February 1862, contending in *The Times* that these were merely the "outer ramparts" of the Confederacy. The inner "citadel," he argued, remained unbreached.

Since most Europeans received their news of events in America through the "mendacious" Northern press, on May 1, 1862, Hotze began publishing his own weekly newspaper, *The Index,* to provide information with a Southern viewpoint.* Hotze was keenly aware that his most potent weapon was a reputation for reliability, and *The Index* rapidly became a primary source for accurate news with a Southern slant. Several leading English journalists wrote for the paper, increasing its acceptability, and they carried over their pro-Southern views to the journals that were their regular outlets. Hotze told Judah P. Benjamin, now the Confederate secretary of state, that in addition to publishing *The Index,* he supplied news items to various London papers and had seven paid writers on their staffs. He was also a freehanded source of "boxes of cigars imported from

---

*Semmes raised the Confederate flag over the vessel and placed her in commission as the *Alabama* on August 24, 1862. Over the next twenty-two months, she captured and destroyed about sixty-five Union vessels, valued at about five million dollars. Badly in need of repairs, the raider was brought to bay by the steam sloop *Kearsarge* off Cherbourg, France, and sunk on June 19, 1864.

The Index outlasted the Confederacy; its last issue was published in August 1865.

Havana . . . American whisky and other articles." Although the circulation of the paper never climbed above 2,250, it reached the most influential segments of British society, including editors, members of Parliament, and ranking government officials.

Hotze played up the advantages to Britain of an America divided between North and South, as well as the threat posed by Northern industrialization and high tariff policies. There were frequent reports on the supposed ineffectiveness of the Union blockade, complete with statistics emphasizing the number of successful voyages by blockade runners. But English sensitivity concerning slavery was a stumbling block to Hotze's efforts that he was never able to overcome, particularly after the Emancipation Proclamation became effective on January 1, 1863. Always a realist, he informed Richmond that repugnance toward the institution was too deep-seated in Britain for the country ever to come to the aid of the South.

■ ■ ■

With the *Alabama* running westward across the Atlantic, capturing and burning Yankee merchantmen, James Bulloch plotted an even more devastating blow against the Union. Plans were worked out for the construction of a pair of ironclads in the Laird yards that could break the Union blockade. Intended to be somewhat larger, better protected, and more seaworthy than the monitors in the Union navy, each vessel was to have two turrets fitted with a pair of nine-inch guns. One was to be completed in April 1863 and the other the following month. In addition to their guns, they were to be fitted with heavy, seven-foot beaks that could be driven into the sides of wooden ships. They thus became known as the Laird rams.

Bulloch's legal adviser assured him that even though the vessels were obviously being built as warships, they would not be in violation of the neutrality laws. Nevertheless, his task was complicated by the British government's anger over the escape of the *Alabama* and the redoubled determination of Union agents to prevent these even more formidable craft from getting to sea. Some observers feared that the "sea monsters" would smash the blockade and lay the port cities of the North under bombardment. Accordingly the persistent Thomas Dudley and his agents were everywhere. Spies and informers swarmed over the shipyard where the rams were being constructed—under the cover of sheds, so that the work could continue in bad weather—asking questions and offering foremen bribes in exchange for information.

Bulloch also sensed a change in British attitudes as Charles Francis Adams continued to hammer at Downing Street with claims for damages for vessels sunk and burned by the *Alabama* and *Florida*. By the end of 1862, he was beginning to show the strain and was doubtful about ever seeing the Confederate flag flying over the rams. "I fear that the Government will interfere with any attempt to get them out," he wrote Secretary Mallory. "The United States minister is pressing hard to induce the authorities to interfere. . . . However, I will go on as if still confident of success."

To add to Bulloch's problems, there was a traitor in the Confederate circle in England. At the time the *Alabama* was being fitted out for sea, he had chosen Clarence Yonge as assistant paymaster and assigned him to recruiting British seamen for the vessel's crew. A year later, having been dismissed by Captain Semmes for drunkenness, Yonge was back in England, and he was seeking revenge. He sold the information in his possession to Adams, who laid it before Lord Russell as further evidence—if it were needed—of rebel disregard for British neutrality. As the Laird rams neared completion, a race developed between Adams and Bulloch that lasted throughout the summer of 1863. Would the Confederate agent get his ships to sea before the minister persuaded a lethargic British government to seize them?

In an effort to prevent seizure, Bulloch devised a scheme to cover his tracks. Ownership of the vessels was transferred to a shady French businessman named Bravay, who in turn claimed they were being built for His Most Serene Highness, the Pasha of Egypt. Once they were at sea, they were to be taken over by Confederate naval officers—at a significant profit for Bravay and his associates. To make Egyptian ownership more creditable, the rams were given the names *El Tousson* and *El Mounassir.* The arrangement failed to deceive Adams, however. Convinced that it was a mere subterfuge, he increased the flood of protests and affidavits pouring upon the Foreign Office. Lord Russell, who had no desire to provoke the North into a war, submitted these protests to the Law Officers. They told him that the rams could not be legally seized, for the evidence would not stand up in court.

Just when things looked darkest for Adams, the situation suddenly brightened. The Confederacy suffered decisive defeats at Gettysburg and Vicksburg, shaking the faith of the British aristocracy in an eventual Southern victory. Additional help came when the British consul at Cairo, replying to a request from London, reported that the Egyptians were not the real owners of the rams. Suspicions aroused, Russell ordered the British ambassador to France to determine whether they were intended for the French government. Informed they were not, he sought information on Bravay's operations and connections.

Late in August 1863, matters came to a head. The first of the ironclads was almost ready for her sea trials, and everyone recalled that the *Alabama* had escaped under similar circumstances. An alarmed Dudley showered protest after protest upon Price Edwards, but as usual, the collector of customs did nothing. Faced with this crisis, and emboldened by Union victories, Adams took a strong stand against Britain's failure to act. "I trust I need not express how profound is my regret at the conclusion to which her Majesty's government has arrived," he declared in a note sent to Russell on September 5. "It would be superfluous in me to point out to your Lordship that this means war . . . ."

In point of fact, Adams's note was indeed superfluous. Two days before, Russell, realizing that the situation was reaching the flash point, had grudgingly ordered the rams to be detained should they attempt to put to sea—a decision that Henry Adams, the minister's son and secretary, compared in importance to the capture of Vicksburg. Over the next several weeks, as the British debated what to do about the vessels, Bulloch attempted to sneak them out of Liverpool, to no avail. On October 9, 1863, the Laird rams were seized by the British. Eventually they were taken into the Royal Navy.*

The Confederate apparatus in Europe obtained other ships, including the commerce raider *Shenandoah,* and continued to supply the South with war material throughout the remainder of the war, but the high-water marks of its efforts had already been reached. Bulloch and his colleagues had exhibited tenacity, initiative, and courage. Hindered by haphazard organization and unrealistic orders, forced to operate on a shoestring, and harried by Federal spies, the Confederate agents abroad had, nevertheless, managed to play a key role in helping the South sustain four years of arduous warfare.**

---

*The ships, named the *Wivern* and *Scorpion,* were found to be less powerful than expected. They were so unseaworthy that they were stricken from the Navy List within a few years—a fact that raises the question of whether or not they could have crossed the Atlantic to lift the Union blockade.

**Following the war, James Bulloch did not return to the United States, settling instead in Liverpool, where his family joined him. He became a cotton factor and was active in establishing maritime and technical schools in his adopted city. He died there in 1901 at the age of 77, having lived long enough to see his nephew become president of the United States.

8

"On Special Service"

Major William Norris's office was tucked away in an obscure building on Bank Street, on the fringes of Richmond officialdom. Norris was the Confederate army's chief signal officer, but his headquarters was frequented by hard-eyed men with a decidedly unmilitary look who came and went at odd hours. In reality, the office was a cover for the Confederate Secret Service Bureau, the War Department's clandestine-operations arm. Clandestine is certainly the word: Norris kept his secret so well that his apparatus remained shrouded in mystery long after the Civil War. More than a century later, some experts claimed it had never existed at all.*

By 1862, the Union and Confederacy had settled down to a long, drawn-out struggle. The war had begun to impose its own imperatives, among them the need for professional intelligence gathering and analysis. Increasing reliance was placed on signals, ciphers, and "special service"—the Civil War equivalent of cloak-and-dagger operations. These pressures led Confederate leaders to organize the Secret Service Bureau some time late that year, while the Union's most efficient intelligence-gathering organization, the Army of the Potomac's Bureau of Military Information, was created a few months later.

The 40-year-old Norris came to his secret post by a roundabout route. A Baltimore lawyer and businessman, he abandoned his home after the city was occupied by Federal troops and joined Brig. Gen. John B. Magruder on the Peninsula as a civilian aide. A decade before, Norris had served as judge advocate to the U.S. Navy's Pacific Squadron, where he observed its signal system. Now he volunteered to establish a similar operation for Magruder. Norris's system, which included flags and col-

*The observation of David W. Gaddy, who has done the most to uncover and reconstruct the activities of Norris and the Secret Service Bureau. See his "Gray Cloaks and Daggers" and "William Norris" (Bibliography).

ored balls raised on poles, impressed the general, who recommended that Norris be commissioned in the army as a signal officer.

In the mid-nineteenth century, every army was trying to speed up the communication of information. The father of visual military signaling in both the Union and Confederate armies was Albert J. Myer, a U.S. Army surgeon and one-time civilian telegrapher. While serving in New Mexico in the late 1850s, Myer noted that the Comanche Indians sent messages by holding their spears at various angles. Curiosity aroused, he studied these signals and developed an alphabet that could be transmitted by flags during daylight and by torches at night. This system was much more flexible and mobile than the semaphore towers currently in use in European armies. In 1859, a board headed by Lt. Col. Robert E. Lee endorsed Myer's scheme. The following year, the Signal Corps was organized, with Myer, who had been promoted to major, at its head.*

One of Myer's assistants, Lieutenant Edward P. Alexander, joined the Confederate army as a captain and served with considerable success as a signal officer under General Beauregard at the First Battle of Bull Run. A flag network established by Alexander "produced results that probably had more to do with the outcome of [the battle] than any other kind of intelligence activity," notes Edwin C. Fishel, the authority on Civil War intelligence. The Confederate army's Signal Corps was organized in April 1862 to operate flag, torch, and telegraphic signals, but Alexander, given the choice between a desk job as chief of the Signal Corps and field service in the artillery, chose the artillery. William Norris was ordered to Richmond and named chief signal officer, with the rank of major.

Signaling was the handmaiden of intelligence. In both armies there were two kinds of signal stations—one with the primary mission of signal communication and the other to serve as an observation station from which enemy troop movements were observed through high-powered telescopes. With signal stations fully in view of the other side, both armies tried to intercept enemy message traffic and used ciphers and "chaff," or worthless messages, to confuse the opponent. The rather simple ciphers used in the field were easily broken, however. "We always had the Federal alphabet," said one Confederate signal officer, "and I suppose they had ours." Such intercepts usually involved flag or torch

---

*The Signal Corps had a bureaucratic rival in the United States Military Telegraph (U.S.M.T.), which was created in 1861 when President Lincoln ordered all civilian telegraph lines taken over by the War Department. Myer believed the Signal Corps should have jurisdiction over all military telegraphy, a stance that brought him into conflict with Secretary of War Stanton, who regarded the U.S.M.T. as his private fiefdom. In 1863, Myer was removed from his post and did not win reinstatement until Stanton lost his power after running afoul of Lincoln's successor, President Andrew Johnson. Most of the U.S.M.T.'s operators were civilians rather than military personnel, so army officers could not order them to divulge secret messages and codes and ciphers. Lincoln frequently visited the telegraph office in the War Department to get the latest news from the fighting fronts and expressed keen interest in the operators' efforts to break Confederate ciphers.

communication rather than wire telegraphy, according to Fishel, who points out that even though both sides often suspected their lines were tapped, documented cases of telegraph interceptions are rare. One of the more novel innovations of the war was the Federal use of captive observation balloons.

Readily grasping the intelligence implications of these activities, Norris urged the War Department to establish a clandestine organization—the Secret Service Bureau—under his command. Among the bureau's responsibilities were reconnaissance, surveillance, interceptions of enemy communications, and deception through false communications, as well the management of the cipher systems of the Confederate army. The bureau observed enemy troop movements and naval operations on the Potomac River; acted as an official courier service; and procured newspapers, books, technical publications, and other materials sought by Confederate ordnance and engineering officers. As is true today, much of the intelligence-gathering activity involved patient collection of data available to anyone rather than cloak-and-dagger espionage. Uncensored Northern newspapers, for example, were a prime source of information about Yankee troop movements. "From them," observed a Confederate intelligence officer, "we learned not only of all arrivals, but also of assignments to brigades and divisions, and, by tabulating these, we always knew quite accurately the strength of the enemy's army."

The bureau's most important function was to operate what Norris described as secret lines of communication on the Potomac. A new "Secret Line" grew out of the old "Doctors' Line" and extended from Richmond through Washington, Baltimore, and New York, and on to Canada. A chain of safe houses and way stations was established in southern Maryland, where the back roads led down to Pope's Creek, Allen's Fresh, the Port Tobacco River, and other streams that sluggishly meandered into the Potomac. Boats were kept hidden along marshy banks, and on moonless mights men slipped across the river in the darkness. The usual practice was to wait for low water when landing on the Maryland side so that the next tide would obliterate footprints. One Yankee officer ruefully reported that even the women and children of the area "vied with each other in schemes and ruses by which to discover and convey to the enemy facts which we strove to conceal."

John. H. Surratt, Jr., later involved with John Wilkes Booth in the Lincoln conspiracy, was a key operative in southern Maryland. As Norris recalled after the war, Surratt "frequently forwarded important military intelligence (in cypher) from our friends in Washington and assisted our messengers in passing to & fro between Richmond & the Northern Cities." Booth, who may also have worked for the Secret Service, may have been the last person conducted over the Secret Line, for many of the people who assisted him as he attemped to escape after fatally wounding the president had been part of this network.*

The Secret Service Bureau was never a central military intelligence agency in the modern sense, however. It had no counterintelligence functions, and there is no sign that Confederate military leaders considered its information superior to that emanating from other sources. But it kept its secrets well. Today it is impossible to obtain a detailed picture of its operations, although it is known to have had agents in the major cities of the North and Canada. Following the war, Norris returned to Baltimore, where he lived quietly until his death in 1896. He never wrote about his experiences, and most of his papers were destroyed in a fire a few years before his death.

■ ■

Thomas N. Conrad was one of the most resourceful and daring Confederate agents who traveled the Secret Line. The Virginia-born Conrad was a Methodist lay preacher and private-school principal in Georgetown at the outbreak of the war. An outspoken secessionist, he was arrested during the spy scare that swept Washington after the attack on Fort Sumter but was then released. Rather than leaving the city, Conrad remained behind for another two months, apparently plotting to assassinate General Winfield Scott, a fellow Virginian who had remained loyal to the Union. As soon as the Confederate government learned of the plan, however, it was scotched.

Returning home, Conrad was commissioned a captain and appointed chaplain of the Third Virginia Cavalry, part of the command of General J. E. B. Stuart, the dashing Confederate cavalry leader. But Conrad spent little time ministering to the spiritual needs of the troops, for he soon began reconnoitering behind the Union lines while posing as a Federal chaplain. He had a talent for disguising himself merely by changing the style of his beard and mustache. Preaching to the Yankees on such

---

*Surratt brought the actor to the boarding house run by his mother, Mary Eugenia Surratt, on H Street in downtown Washington, setting in motion a train of events that ended with her execution as one of the Lincoln conspirators. Many historians regard her as a victim of the hysteria of the times. Surratt was involved in a plot hatched by Booth—possibly with official confederate backing—to kidnap Lincoln but not in the assassination conspiracy, which Booth is believed to have cooked up on little more than the spur of the moment. Following the arrest of his mother and fearing for his life, Surratt fled the United States and joined the Papal Guard in Rome. Eventually recognized, he was extradited and tried in Washington in 1867 on charges of having participated in the murder of the president. Unlike the other alleged conspirators, who were judged by a military commission, he was tried before a civilian jury, which was unable to agree on a verdict. Surratt lived until 1916 but said little in later years about the plot against Lincoln and his role as a Confederate courier. Recently, I asked a descendant whether any family documents that added to the story had come to light in the last few years and was told nothing new had been found.

edifying themes as "The Christian Soldier" and "The Power of Prayer," he gleaned information about the state of affairs in their camps and on proposed Union movements.

Before long, Conrad later claimed, Confederate Secretary of War Judah P. Benjamin sought his services. He was instructed to go to Washington and contact two commissioners, one British and the other French, who had arrived to negotiate a loan of three million dollars to the Confederacy, and to conduct them to Richmond.* Posing as ordinary travelers, they were said to have come by way of Washington because that was considered safer than trying to run the blockade into the Confederacy. Conrad was provided with a War Department pass that he dictated himself: "The bearer, who may be known by a gash in his tongue and a scar upon the index finger of left hand, has the confidence of this department."

Making his way across the Potomac, Conrad went to the Surratt tavern, where he obtained a horse, and rode into Washington dressed as a Maryland farmer. He found the foreign agents registered at Willard's Hotel, showed them his secret pass, stuck out his tongue, and exhibited his scarred finger. Next, according to his story, he took their most important papers and their boots to a trustworthy cobbler, who hollowed out the boot heels and hid the documents in them. Before leaving the city in a hired carriage, he drove his charges past General McClellan's headquarters and the White House, smiling as he "peered into the mansion of 'Father Abraham.'"

Not long after, Conrad returned to Washington. Rebel sympathizers who held jobs as clerks in the War Department had confirmed reports that McClellan was planning his advance up the Peninsula to Richmond, and the Confederate high command wished to know the strength of the Union force. One of Conrad's spies had access to these figures but, fearing that he was under suspicion, dared not be seen consulting the secret documents. He told Conrad, however, that the War Department was preparing a summary of regimental-strength reports that he thought he could obtain. After an anxious three-day wait, Conrad received word that he would find the report on the spy's desk if he came to the War Department at a certain time the next day. Conrad, who knew exactly where to go, winked at the spy, who was on his way to lunch, as they passed in the corridor. Later, he claimed the pirated report was an important factor in turning back McClellan's attack on Richmond.

Conrad was in and out of Washington so often that he established headquarters in the old Van Ness mansion, not far from the White House

---

*No record of such a mission has been found, but John Bakeless points out in his *Spies of the Confederacy* that Conrad's narrative of his adventures can in general be regarded as reliable. The fact that the incident is not mentioned in any existing documents "proves only that sometimes secret missions really stay secret," says Bakeless.

and the War Department.* He even claimed to have an agent within Lafayette Baker's headquarters who was to alert him should Baker get wind of his presence in the city. Conrad also had a hideout in a shanty on a bluff on the Virginia side of the Potomac—called "Eagle's Nest"—where agents were stationed around the clock to receive messages from the other side of the river. Mines were planted in the adjoining creeks and coves to keep prying Yankee gunboats at a safe distance. "In less than twenty-four hours," Conrad boasted, "I could send a reliable dispatch from Washington to the Confederate capital."

For a few brief hours during the Second Battle of Bull Run, at the end of August 1862, Conrad may have held the fate of Washington in his hands. He learned that the Federals had sent almost every available man to the assistance of the hard-pressed General John Pope, leaving only a skeleton force to defend the capital. Escaping from the city, he tried to find Jeb Stuart and pass on this vital information, but he was unable to locate the cavalry leader. Not long afterward, Conrad met the general, who assured him that, had he known of the situation, "he would have dashed into Washington with his whole command and made the White House his headquarters." Less than a year later, a similar opportunity to capture the nearly defenseless capital during the Gettysburg campaign also misfired. The city's fortifications were manned by civilian clerks hastily called out to replace the troops sent to meet Lee's invading army. Once again, luck was against Conrad, who failed to make contact with Stuart by only the narrowest of margins.

In between these two lost opportunities, Conrad claimed to have scored one of his most brilliant coups. Late in November 1862, he said, he informed Confederate officials within twenty-four hours of the event that McClellan had been replaced as the head of the Army of the Potomac by General Ambrose E. Burnside. But it was not enough to know the name of the new enemy commander. What were Burnside's intentions? Would he advance upon Richmond by crossing the Rappahannock at Fredericksburg, or would he come by way of Culpeper, to the west of the Confederate capital? Conrad put his agents in the War Department to work and quickly provided the answer: Burnside would attack at Fredericksburg—a message he delivered to General Lee's headquarters in person. Burnside's army was confronted by the well-entrenched forces of Lee and Stonewall Jackson, and the hapless Yankees were slaughtered as they assaulted the heights behind Fredericksburg.

Conrad also hatched one of the numerous plots to kidnap Abraham Lincoln that flourished in Washington. To escape the pressures of the White House, the president visited a cottage on the grounds of the Soldiers' Home, just outside the city. Even though his route passed

---

*Near the present site of the Organization of American States building.

through dense woods that provided ideal cover for sharpshooters or kidnappers, he was only lightly guarded. Conrad said he planned to nab Lincoln while the president was on his way to the Soldiers' Home and smuggle him across the Potomac into Virginia. He claimed not only to have had the approval of Secretary of War James A. Seddon but to have received a letter from him on September 15, 1864, ordering John S. Mosby, the Confederate guerrilla leader, to cooperate with the plot. The plan was abandoned after word apparently leaked out about one or another of the conspiracies against Lincoln and a cavalry detachment began accompanying the president to the Soldiers' Home.

Conrad continued to pass back and forth between Richmond and Washington throughout the remainder of the war, but with diminished effectiveness after his identity became known to Lafayette Baker's men. Arrested upon one occasion and fearing that his disguise would be penetrated, he feigned the symptoms of smallpox. The ruse got the spy out of one danger but plunged him into another. Conrad's captors gingerly deposited him in a camp for smallpox victims, confronting him with the possibility of contracting the disease. The guards naturally kept their distance, however, and Conrad managed to slip away to his hiding place on the Potomac.

Conrad's flair for disguise, so useful to him during the war, nearly proved fatal just as the war was ending. Crossing over into southern Maryland, he was arrested by Union troops who were combing the area in search of John Wilkes Booth. By an odd coincidence, Conrad related afterward, he had recently chosen the same hair style and mustache worn by the presidential assassin.* Mistaken for the famous actor, he was taken to the Old Capitol Prison, where things might have gone hard for him had he not established his identity. William P. Wood, the prison superintendent, introduced him to Colonel Baker, who had been trying to catch him for more than a year. Following a cordial chat, the detective gave Conrad an official pass that allowed him to return safely to Virginia.

■ ■ ■

After Burnside's bloody fiasco at Fredericksburg, President Lincoln wearily brought another general, Joseph E. Hooker, through the revolving door that was the command of the Army of the Potomac. Hardworking if not brilliant, "Fighting Joe" set about rebuilding the dispirited army. He was an excellent organizer, and one of his most important innovations

---

*Was Conrad's choice of disguise really a simply coincidence? Inasmuch as Booth was actively assisted in his attempt to escape by some of the men who had served as Conrad's agents, might not the presence of a man in southern Maryland who resembled Booth have been intended as a decoy to confuse the assassin's pursuers and enable him to shake them off? Even though Conrad denied any knowledge of the assassination and there is no evidence linking him to the conspiracy, the question is worth considering in view of the murky circumstances surrounding Booth's flight.

was the establishment of an efficient intelligence service. General Daniel Butterfield, his chief of staff, later declared that at the time Hooker took command of the army, there was not a document or record of any kind available at headquarters from which information concerning the enemy could be learned. "We were almost as ignorant of the enemy as if they had been in China."

Early in 1863, Brig. Gen. Marsena R. Patrick, the army's provost marshal-general, was authorized to establish a "secret service" to coordinate the intelligence received from the gaggle of detectives, secret agents, amateur spies, and scouts that clustered about the army. Patrick had graduated from West Point in 1835 and served in the Seminole and Mexican wars before resigning his commission and returning home to upstate New York, where he became first president of the New York State Agricultural College, now part of Cornell University. Following the outbreak of the Civil War and service in the Peninsula, he was appointed the army's chief policeman. A gruff old fellow with flowing white hair and whiskers, he piously held prayer meetings in his tent every morning and then went forth—so his men said—to bite the heads off ten-penny nails.

Much to his consternation, Patrick found security almost nonexistent. Billy Yank and Johnny Reb were well-meaning, garrulous fellows, as Patrick discovered when he found one Pennsylvania regiment in flagrant communication with the enemy. "Any signs of a move?" a rebel picket had called across a stream. A Pennsylvanian replied: "Yes, we've got eight days' rations and we expect to move in a few days." When the rebel asked what direction the move would take, he was obligingly told it would be upstream and to the right. As a bonus, the Yankee gratuitously added that the regiment was going to use pack mules, which meant it would not be following the line of the railroad. Such breaches of security were not confined to the ranks. A naive army surgeon supplied the newspapers with detailed statistics on the number of sick and disabled among the army's personnel from which Lee computed the size of the Union army. What chance, thundered General Patrick, did the army have to deceive the enemy when such vital information was being bandied about so freely?

Tightening security, Patrick ordered a daily roundup of deserters and stragglers within the Union lines. Large numbers of rebels were bagged as well, and the general took over the questioning of these prisoners himself. Civil War armies imposed no code of silence on prisoners, and Patrick learned a great deal about Confederate activities from these interrogations. Soon he was trading information with other commands and providing intelligence to headquarters. For once in an army, organizational logic prevailed, and "secret service" matters were added to Patrick's responsibilities.

Patrick selected a handsome former lawyer, Colonel George H.

Sharpe of the 120th New York Volunteers, as chief of the new Bureau of Military Information. Sharpe, who was given the title of deputy provost marshal-general, was a fortunate choice. He exhibited unusual skill in directing a wide-ranging intelligence operation while avoiding many of the pitfalls that had engulfed Allen Pinkerton.* Although the Bureau of Military Information is largely unknown today, it became the most sophisticated and highly developed American intelligence service of the war—and the best since George Washington's day. "For the first time," stated Douglas S. Freeman, General Lee's biographer, "the Federals knew more about what was happening on the south side of the Rappahannock than Lee knew of what was taking place north of the river."

Sharpe's bureau was a complete tactical intelligence organization. By the end of the war, he employed some two hundred spies and scouts—listed as "guides" for payroll purposes—and had both transient and resident agents in Confederate territory. His soldier-agents sometimes pretended to be deserters or smugglers and remained in the enemy camp for days on end, picking up estimates of Lee's numbers and dispositions. The work was extremely dangerous. Capture meant almost certain death, for spies could expect to be hanged from the nearest tree. And if they evaded capture, they had a fair chance of being shot by Yankee pickets as they tried to make their way home.

Sharpe placed particular emphasis upon the speedy transmission of intelligence. Long and unnecessary delays in forwarding information to headquarters had often destroyed its value, and a general order was issued specifically instructing the officers and men of the army to communicate intelligence promptly to the provost marshal-general. Adopting the cover name "Colonel Streight" to confuse the Confederates in case some of his communications fell into their hands, Sharpe obtained information from spies, scouts, cavalry, balloonists, Signal Corps observation posts, signal intercepts, and newspapers, as well as from interrogations of prisoners, refugees, and deserters. From this mountain of raw data, Sharpe and his aides distilled accurate intelligence estimates, making Hooker the best-informed of any Union general who had taken the field. Meanwhile, the irascible Patrick jealously guarded the independence of the bureau from interference, particularly from Lafayette Baker. He engaged in a running feud with Baker throughout the war, at one point

*Sharpe was born in Ulster County, New York, in 1828 and graduated from Rutgers University and Yale Law School. For several years he lived in Europe and served in the American legations in Vienna and Rome. Returning home, he was admitted to the New York bar in 1854. Following the war he was sent by the State Department to London in an attempt to bring about the extradition of former Confederate Secretary of State Judah P. Benjamin, who had taken refuge in England. The government believed Banjamin had a hand in Lincoln's assassination but could not make the charges stick. Sharpe later became active in New York politics and was awarded the plum of Surveyor of the Port of New York. He died in 1900.

issuing orders that persons visiting the army with passes from Bakers' headquarters were to be immediately sent back to Washington.

While the Bureau of Military Information concentrated on gathering combat intelligence, it had counterintelligence functions as well. In the spring of 1863, as Hooker began the elaborate series of maneuvers that marked the start of the Chancellorsville campaign, Lee found it so difficult to penetrate the Union screen that he told President Davis, "I have no means of ascertaining the truth." Patrick himself noted that "the rebels have not the slightest idea what we are about." Even their pickets "know nothing about it," he crowed. The collection of intelligence by the Confederates was also hampered by a ludicrous mishap. A courier arrived in Richmond bearing a cipher message but could not remember the key to it. In contrast, one of Sharpe's agents returned from Richmond with remarkably accurate information on the size and disposition of Lee's forces.

Lee recovered from these intelligence failures, however, and soon had accumulated information on the strength of the Army of the Potomac thanks to the untiring efforts of his cavalry, scouts, messages intercepted by his signal corps, and the always accommodating Washington newspapers. Hooker also failed to put his intelligence to proper use. Prior to the devastating Confederate attack on his exposed right flank at Chancellorsville, the uneasy German troops in the area sent headquarters repeated warnings of rebel movements, but their reports were ignored by staff officers who spoke in a superior manner of "a rolling reconnaissance." This failure to take prompt action on important intelligence resulted in another resounding Union defeat.

Buoyed by his victory, Lee launched an invasion of the North that was first detected by the Bureau of Military Information. Although Union cavalry is usually credited with providing the earliest word of the Confederate offensive, Edwin Fishel states that it actually resulted from routine interrogation of a refugee by one of Sharpe's agents. "The Confederate army is under marching orders," Sharpe told Hooker. "An order from General Lee was very lately read to the troops, announcing a campaign of long marches and hard fighting. . . . All the deserters say the idea is very prevalent in the ranks that they are about to move forward."[*] The rebel host was under continual observation as it approached the Potomac, forded the river, and advanced into Maryland and Pennsylvania.

Later, information gleaned from the interrogation of rebel prisoners captured at Gettysburg provided General George G. Meade, Hooker's

*This report, dated May 27, 1863, is an excellent example of the detailed information on the composition and disposition of the Confederate forces supplied by Sharpe. Lee's biographer, Douglas S. Freeman, states that the report was correct in almost every detail (Freeman, *R. E. Lee*, vol. 3, p. 24, note 30).

successor, with decisive intelligence when he faced the choice of retreating or holding his ground as the fighting wound down. Meade feared that Lee would renew the attack on his battered forces, but, according to Fishel, Sharpe correctly informed him that the rebel army was too worn out to mount such an offensive. Meade maintained his positions on the corpse-strewn battlefield as the exhausted Confederates began the long retreat into Virginia.

Meade had turned back the gray tide, but he lacked aggressive spirit. Unwilling to take chances, he sparred cautiously with the rebels. For some reason, he lost faith in the Bureau of Military Information that had served him so well at Gettysburg, and it was relegated to the trivia of military police work. Before long, Meade, whose own fuse was as short as Patrick's, clashed head-on with the provost marshal. When Patrick raged at his impotence and threatened to resign his post and seek a combat command, Meade claimed Sharpe's bureau was "good for nothing," and "furnished no information not already furnished thro' the Cavalry."

The appointment of Ulysses S. Grant as general in chief of the Union forces in March 1864 breathed new life into both the Army of the Potomac and its combat intelligence arm. Grant had learned the value of systematic intelligence in his victorious campaigns in the West, and Sharpe and his apparatus were transferred to his headquarters.* Revitalized, the bureau sent scouts in every direction and reestablished contacts with spies in Richmond and elsewhere. Patrick proudly demonstrated the depth of his information in the wake of the fighting at Spotsylvania Court House. More than three thousand Confederates were taken prisoner, most of them from Virginia and North Carolina units. Their officers "were very much disgusted," the general wrote, "when they found that I knew their organization & called out their Regts. as readily as I would our own & formed them, to march off by Brigade, under their own officers."

■ ■ ■

In the West, General Grant's chief intelligence officer had been Grenville M. Dodge, who was later to achieve fame as the builder of the continent-spanning Union Pacific Railroad. A New Englander by birth, Dodge became a railroad surveyor and engineer before settling down in Iowa as a railroad promoter. When the war broke out, he secured a colonelcy in the state militia, distinguished himself in combat, and was promoted to general. General John C. Frémont, the Union commander in

*For an example of the thorough reports received by Grant, see the extensive account provided by a young immigrant named Louis Trager on his travels through the Confederacy in 1863 in *Official Records of the Union and Confederate Armies in the War of the Rebellion,* Series 1, vol. 30, part 4, pp. 4–8.

Missouri, gave Dodge his first intelligence assignment late in 1861, assigning him to run down rumors of rebel activity in the district.

As a result of his railroad work, Dodge was familiar with the techniques of frontier scouts and detectives. He dispatched cavalry into all parts of Missouri and Arkansas and established a network of spies in the area. He also hit upon a novel method for estimating the size of an enemy force by noting the amount of space it occupied upon a road. Before long, he was receiving information on rebel troop movements throughout the Southwest. The effectiveness of his network was proven in March 1862, when Dodge's scouts warned of the advance of a strong Confederate force and saved the Union army from defeat at Pea Ridge in Arkansas.

When Grant assumed command of Federal troops in the West, he inherited a loose and disorganized intelligence system. Uncertainty was rife about the size and disposition of Confederate forces, and Union commanders were leery of the intelligence reports furnished them. Having learned of Dodge's work, Grant gave him responsibility for reorganizing the army's intelligence system. Dodge organized the First Tennessee Cavalry, a regiment of Southern Unionists, and pressed its members and their relatives into his clandestine spy network. Indistinguishable in manner and appearance from the locals, they could live and travel in the region without arousing suspicion. He also employed escaped slaves as messengers, because enemy pickets rarely questioned them. Later, he reported that these blacks had been proven completely trustworthy; not one had betrayed a spy or a secret.

Dodge placed considerable emphasis on topographic information. He kept huge maps of the area of operations, adding data as he received it. If someone casually mentioned the location of a stream or a hill, Dodge noted it in its proper place. Although primarily designed as a positive intelligence service that collected information on the Confederate armed forces, Dodge's organization could—and did—detect rebel spies. At its peak, his apparatus fielded about a hundred agents, whose identities were kept secret. Even trusted staff members knew them only by code number, and all dispatches were destroyed after being read.*

In case of capture, Dodge told his agents to tell the rebels enough to save themselves but not enough to endanger the Northern cause. Before the war ended, about half of his spies were captured or killed. Some were court-martialed and executed, but none betrayed the Union—although a few pretended to do so to save their lives. One agent who was forced to

*Three years after the war, a War Department bureaucrat peremptorily ordered Dodge to make an itemized accounting of his expenditures for spies. Dodge referred him to a report filed by Grant's provost marshal. Nineteen years later, Dodge received the following reply: "Your secret service accounts for the years 1863 to 1865, amounting to $17,099.95, have been examined and adjusted, and are now closed on the books of this office."

join the Confederate army proved to be such a good soldier that within a short time he was made first sergeant of his company. Dodge believed the man was dead, but at the first opportunity, the spy slipped through the lines and reported for duty still dressed in his rebel uniform. "The secret service men were braver than the average soldier," noted the general.

Philip Henson, a thirty-five-year-old Mississippian, was one of Dodge's most talented operatives. Unlike the other members of his family, he was an ardent Unionist. He kept his own counsel until Federal troops pushed into the northern part of the state and then secretly went to work for the Union. Tall, shambling, and deceptively slow of speech and manner, Henson did not arouse rebel suspicions. Assigned to find out what General Sterling Price was up to, he rode into the Southern lines, chatted with the sentries and hung about Price's headquarters. When he learned all he wanted to know, he waved goodbye to the sentries and was soon telling his story to a Union officer. No one recognized Henson's talents more than General Nathan Bedford Forrest, the great Confederate cavalry leader, who called him "the most dangerous Federal spy operating in the Confederacy"— and always regretted a missed opportunity to hang him.

Early in 1863, General Dodge sent Henson into Vicksburg as Union forces were closing in on the strategic Mississippi River town. The spy solved the problem of passing through the closely guarded Confederate defenses by asking a neighbor with several sons in the rebel army whether he wanted to visit them. The man gladly accepted Henson's invitation, along with the offer of a horse. Halted by Confederate patrols, the two men explained they were "Goin' to see our boys in Vicksburg" and were waved on. Upon his arrival in the town, Henson sought out General John C. Pemberton and passed on information regarding the harsh treatment meted out to Southerners in Yankee-occupied territory. Impressed, Pemberton suggested that he tell his story to the troops in order to stiffen their will to fight. Eager to oblige, Henson circulated unhindered through the fortified perimeter of Vicksburg, talking to the soldiers—and taking mental notes on everything he saw. General Dodge was so pleased with Henson's report that he gave him a fine horse.

■ ■ ■

From all points of the compass, delegates to the Democratic convention poured into Chicago in the last days of August 1864, confident that they were about to nominate the next president of the United States. Republican Abraham Lincoln had grown increasingly unpopular as the war dragged on. General Grant's offensive against Richmond had bogged down in bloodletting at Cold Harbor, while General William Tecumseh Sherman's thrust into the heartland of the Confederacy was stalemated outside Atlanta. The North, the excited delegates believed, was ready for a change in leadership.

A group of well-dressed young men coolly observed the bustling crowds of delegates from the sidelines. Their leader was a black-haired, almost effeminate-looking Kentuckian named Thomas H. Hines. Hines and some of his companions made their headquarters at the Richmond House, where they hung a sign reading "Missouri Delegation" on the door of their suite. But they were not mere convention delegates. Hines was a hard-bitten Confederate cavalry captain and the leader of a covert operation intended to touch off an uprising in Chicago that would create havoc throughout the North.

For some time, the Confederacy had been planning to exploit unrest in the North. Lee's repulse at Gettysburg and the fall of Vicksburg had spurred the leaders in Richmond to turn to clandestine operations in hopes of reversing the slide toward defeat. They saw fertile ground for action in the Old Northwest, the states lying above the Ohio River, where Copperheads, or antiwar Democrats, were stirring up opposition to the war. Many Northerners were dissatisfied with the arbitrary measures adopted by the Lincoln administration; others feared that the freed slaves would provide competition for jobs. The Northwest was said to be ripe for revolution, and well-armed secret societies, such as the Sons of Liberty, were rumored to be preparing to create a "Northwestern Confederacy" of disaffected states eager for a speedy termination of the war.

By the middle of 1864, the Confederates had assembled a band of daredevils across the border in Canada—most of them escapees from Northern prisoner-of-war camps—under the leadership of a veteran political intriguer named Jacob Thompson, one-time secretary of the interior under President Buchanan. Thompson and Clement C. Clay, Jr., a former senator from Alabama, had the vague title of "special commissioners of the Confederate States Government in Canada" and a blank check for action from Jefferson Davis.* "I hereby direct you to proceed at once to Canada," the president guardedly wrote Thompson, "there to carry out such instructions as you have received from me verbally in such manner as shall seem most likely to conduce to the furtherance of the interests of the Confederate States of America."

Escaping through the blockade, Thompson established his headquarters in Toronto, where Captain Hines became his chief of operations, while Clay remained in Montreal. Lurid plans were hatched to transform the Copperheads into a "fifth column" and an effective spearhead for revolt against the Federal government. These plans included staging

*Shortly before Thompson's appointment, the Confederate Congress had appropriated five million dollars for secret service operations. Of this, one million was earmarked for operations in Canada.

raids across the border, seizing shipping on the Great Lakes, burning Northern cities, and liberating thousands of Confederate prisoners being held in camps throughout the Middle West. Plainly, these were the tactics of terror, but the rebels justified their actions by the atrocities alleged to have been planned or committed by the Yankees.*

Early in June, Thompson and Hines met with Clement L. Vallandingham, leader of the Sons of Liberty, at Windsor, Ontario, to plot strategy for the so-called Northwest Conspiracy. Vallandingham, a former Democratic congressman from Ohio, had been banished to the Confederacy for opposing the war and the draft. He agreed to muster his followers for an uprising timed to coincide with the start of the Democratic convention on August 29. The Sons of Liberty claimed a membership of more than two hundred thousand—eighty-five thousand in Illinois alone. With the aid of Confederate agents led by Hines, the Copperheads were to put the city to the torch. While police and firemen were fighting the flames, the rebel prisoners held at nearby Camp Douglas and Rock Island would be freed. Banks would be looted, City Hall occupied, and police headquarters captured. Once the Union's second largest city was under rebel control, the rebellion was to spread all over the Northwest.

Wearing a false beard, Vallandingham slipped across the border to his old district in Ohio. Breathing fire, he warned of "a vast multitude" of men determined to defend their constitutional rights against a dictatorial administration. Federal agents kept an eye on Vallandingham's movements, but the government refused to fulfill his wish for martyrdom and did not arrest him. Buoyed by an enthusiastic reception, Vallandingham went to Chicago, where large numbers of Sons of Liberty mixed with the crowds thronging the city. Hines and his men were there, too, armed and ready for action. The prisoners at Camp Douglas had been alerted to expect an attempt to free them, while an arsenal of arms—some in cases marked "Sunday School Books"—and an incendiary concoction known as "Greek Fire" had been stockpiled.*

The plot collapsed as Hines was making the final arrangements. Federal agents had penetrated Hines's team, and Felix Stridger, the grand secretary of the Sons of Liberty in Kentucky, turned out to be a Union spy. Forewarned, the authorities sent additional troops to Chicago, and the

---

*Especially an abortive raid upon Richmond in March 1864, led by Colonel Ulric Dahlgren. Dahlgren was killed, and the Confederates claimed to have found papers on his body indicating that the raiders intended to kill President Davis and sack and burn the city. Modern researchers are now convinced that the documents are authentic. See Jones, *Eight Hours before Richmond* (Bibliography).

*"Greek Fire" was an ancestor of the Molotov cocktail. It was described by a Confederate agent as "a clear liquid resembling water, put up in four-ounce bottles and smelt like rotten eggs." When a bottle was thrown against the wall of a building, there would be a dull explosion followed by a great sheet of flame—but not until the thrower had time to escape.

guard at Camp Douglas was reinforced. "He ruined us all," was Hines's bitter comment on Stidger. But the conspiracy had little prospect of success from the very beginning. The Confederates had erred in accepting the militancy of the Copperheads at face value. Bold talk of striking a blow for freedom was loudly cheered as long as it remained talk, but the Copperheads' eagerness for action oozed away when they were faced with the prospect of being shot or jailed. With the plot collapsing about him, Hines made a desperate effort to rally support. If only five hundred men would join him, he offered to lead an attack upon the prison camp at Rock Island. The proposal was met with silence. Finally realizing that the Sons of Liberty would rather talk than fight, he contemptuously dismissed them "as harmless as an association of children."

■ ■ ■

Undaunted by the fiasco in Chicago, Thompson and Hines pressed on with a series of cloak-and-dagger operations. Northern newspapers were subverted, with the editor of the New York *Daily News* accepting twenty-five thousand dollars to preach the cause of peace with the Confederacy. Perhaps double that amount was earmarked for an unsuccessful effort to elect James C. Robinson, the candidate of the "peace" Democrats, to the governorship of Illinois. Meanwhile, an attempt was made to touch off a financial panic by upsetting the gold market through speculative attacks on the value of the dollar and by flooding the country with counterfeit greenbacks.

In the hope of filling the depleted ranks of Lee's army,[*] an ambitious scheme was concocted to free the thousands of Confederate prisoners languishing in Northern prison camps. The focal point was the camp at Johnson's Island, near Sandusky, Ohio. Once liberated, the prisoners were to arm themselves with captured weapons and march upon Cleveland, which was to be burned. The rebels would then cut their way through to the Confederate lines in Virginia. Before the plan could be put into effect, however, the armed steamer *Michigan,* the only warship on Lake Erie, would have to be taken. Thompson selected a man named Charles H. Cole, who claimed to be a lieutenant in the Confederate Navy, to command the expedition.

Lavishly supplied with funds, Cole spent some time traveling about the area in the company of a woman he had met in Buffalo. Eventually he

[*]To prevent the Confederacy from obtaining sorely needed reinforcements, the Federal government had reversed a previous policy and now refused to exchange prisoners. The mass of Yankee captives in Confederate hands was also believed to be a drain on the South's resources. Contrary to popular myth, Union prison camps were deadlier than those in the South. Hudson Strode points out in *Jefferson Davis* (p. 113) that despite the atrocity stories about Andersonville, only 8 percent of Union POWs died in Southern camps, while 12 percent of Confederate prisoners died in Northern camps. These figures are telling, because the North had no shortage of provisions and other supplies.

informed Thompson that he had ingratiated himself with the officers of the *Michigan* and planned to sponsor a "wine-drinking party" on the vessel on the evening of September 19, 1864. Cole suggested that a raiding party should come alongside in another craft when the revelry was at its height and capture the warship. The plan was approved, and a heavily armed band led by John Yates Beall, an acting master in the Confederate Navy,* seized control of a lake steamer and approached the *Michigan* as she lay off Johnson's Island. Instead of a party in full swing, Beall found the *Michigan* with her steam up and guns run out ready for action. Obviously, something had gone wrong. Beall's men refused to carry out the attack, and he was forced to abandon the project. Later it was learned that Cole had been betrayed by an informer while on a drunken spree and was himself imprisoned on Johnson's Island.

The Confederates in Canada also launched a series of attempts to burn Northern cities, beginning with a fire in Louisville that destroyed several warehouses full of supplies for the Union army. This was followed up by a similar blaze in Mattoon, Illinois, and a fire that destroyed or damaged several transports on the St. Louis waterfront. Raids on towns close to the border were planned with the hope of causing panic. A bank robbed here, a town burned there—such incidents might relieve pressure on the South by forcing the Yankees to withdraw troops from the fighting fronts to defend the northern frontier.

On October 19, 1864, about twenty men led by Lieutenant Bennett H. Young, a twenty-one-year-old cavalryman, robbed a trio of banks in St. Albans, just over the border in Vermont. Having swept up some $220,000 in loot, they galloped up and down the main street, shooting at anyone who showed himself. Bottles of Greek Fire were hurled at the principal buildings, and the dull thud of explosions was followed by spurts of flame. Pursued by a hastily organized posse, the raiders escaped into Canada. The fires were quickly extinguished, but one citizen had been killed and another wounded. In the wake of this spectacular raid, panic raced along the border from Maine to Michigan. There were rumors that the marauders were the advance party of a Confederate army ready to launch an attack from Canada. To mollify the frightened citizenry, a few companies

---

*Beall was later hanged after being captured while trying to wreck a train in upstate New York so that some captured Confederate officers could be freed.

*The St. Albans raid had serious international complications. Young and thirteen of his men were arrested by the Canadian authorities and jailed to await extradition to the United States. The others got away with the bulk of the loot, which was never traced. Northern newspapers demanded the return of the raiders so they could be hanged. American officials charged they were guilty of carrying on "unlawful war," while the prisoners argued that they were Confederate soldiers acting under orders. Thus, even in that day, one man's freedom fighter was another man's terrorist. Following two trials, the Canadian courts ruled on April 5, 1865, that Young and his men were soldiers of a nation recognized by Britain as a belligerent, and they were freed. Four days later, Lee surrendered at Appomattox.

of troops were dispatched to reinforce the home guards, and there were no more raids.*

The Confederates next turned their attention to a plot to create havoc in the North on November 8, 1864—Election Day. Uncertainty about the reelection of President Lincoln had vanished following a series of Union victories that autumn, including the capture of Atlanta and Mobile. Thompson and Hines hoped to revitalize the Confederate cause by sparking an uprising in the Union rear. This time, however, they operated independently of the timorous Copperheads. Massive riots were set for Chicago and New York, while fires and other disturbances were to be started in Cincinnati and Boston to divert the attention of the authorities from the main centers of action. Hines was to be in command of operations in Chicago, with Colonel George St. Leger Grenfel, a British soldier of fortune who was serving the Confederacy, as his second in command.*

Once again, fate was against the Confederates. Late in October, word of the proposed assault on Camp Douglas reached Colonel Benjamin Sweet, the camp commander. He had only about eight hundred men, most of them disabled veterans like himself, to guard more than eight thousand prisoners. Sweet appealed for reinforcements; when they had not had arrived by November 6, he altered his tactics. He sent for Lieutenant John J. Shanks, the prisoner in charge of the camp's medical dispensary, who was said to have fallen in love with a widow who brought fruit and other delicacies to imprisoned rebels. Sweet promised that in return for discovering the headquarters of the conspirators, Shanks would be paroled in her custody.

Shanks was permitted to "escape" by hiding in a garbage wagon. Two of Sweet's men shadowed him as he made the rounds of Chicago's hotels in search of the plotters. Grenfel was found registered under his own name at the Richmond House. The unsuspecting Englishman recruited Shanks into the conspiracy. Shanks immediately passed the details to Colonel Sweet, and early the next morning, all the ringleaders were rounded up—all, that is, except for Hines. He escaped the detectives who ransacked the boarding house where he staying by slitting the large box mattress of his bed and hiding in it.

Upon reading the alarming news of the Chicago arrests in the newspapers, the New York conspirators decided to postpone the attempt to burn the city. Election Day passed peacefully, and Lincoln won another term in the White House, along with a greatly enlarged Unionist majority

---

*Even before his service in the Confederate army, Grenfel had had an adventurous career. He had run away from his aristocratic family to join the French army in North Africa, where he served against the Moors, then had joined the Moors and fought against the French. Next, he was employed by the governor of Gibraltar to wipe out a band of pirates who infested the coast of Morocco. He then served with Garibaldi in South America. Returning home, he settled down, but country life soon lost its appeal. Accepting a commission in the British army, he served in the Crimea and helped put down the Sepoy rebellion in India.

in Congress. Foiled in their plan for an uprising, Colonel Robert M. Martin and his men decided to set New York ablaze on the evening of November 25, 1864, to "give the people a scare, if nothing else, and let the government at Washington understand that burning houses in the South might find a counterpart in the North."

On the day before the fires were to be set, Lieutenant John W. Headley, Martin's second in command, picked up a valise full of bottles of Greek Fire from a mysterious old man in the basement of a house on the west side of Washington Square. Boarding a streetcar for the trip uptown to the conspirator's headquarters, Headley placed the heavy valise on the floor. The vehicle hit a bump, and the valise began to exude the odor of rotten eggs. Headley did his best to look unconcerned as his fellow passengers held their noses. "There must be something dead in that valise," commented one man. Fortunately for Headley, the odorous valise made it safely to its destination.

Each of the plotters was given ten bottles of Greek Fire and assigned to set fire to the three or four hotels where they were registered under false names. Headley touched off the first fire at the Astor House shortly after seven o'clock in the evening. "I hung the bedclothes loosely on the headboard and piled the chairs, drawers of the bureau, and washstand on the bed," he related, "then stuffed some newspapers about among the mass and poured a bottle of turpentine over it all. . . . I opened a bottle [of Greek Fire] carefully and quickly, and spilled it on a pile of rubbish. It blazed up instantly and the whole bed seemed to be in flames before I could get out. I locked the door and . . . left the key at the office as usual."

Headley set similar blazes at three other hotels. In all, the Confederates started fires in nineteen hotels, at Niblo's Gardens, and in Barnum's Museum, where several people were trampled in the scramble to escape. Alarm bells rang all over the city as fire companies dashed through the streets from one blaze to another. Rumors spread of an imminent rebel attack, and mobs threatened to hang the arsonists to the nearest lamp post. Panic almost broke out in the crowded Wintergarden Theatre, adjacent to one of the hotels that had been set afire, where the three Booth brothers—Edwin, Junius, Jr., and John Wilkes—were appearing together in a benefit performance of *Julius Caesar.* Edwin Booth brought this dangerous situation under control by stepping out of character to assure the audience that there was no danger, and the play continued.*

By midnight, it was clear that the conspiracy had failed. Most of the blazes were readily extinguished, and there was little damage. Some people theorized that the incendiaries had blundered by setting the fires

---

*The performance, staged to raise funds to erect a statue of Shakespeare in Central Park, was the only time the three Booth brothers appeared together on the same stage.

in hotel rooms; with the windows closed, the flames were smothered once the oxygen supply had been consumed. For their part, Headley and his disappointed colleagues, who remained in the city for several days to check on the effects of their handiwork before leaving for Canada, were convinced that the supply of Greek Fire had been tampered with.

The attempt to burn New York City was among the last efforts mounted by the Confederacy's clandestine-operations directorate. Despite the bravery, ingenuity, and large sums invested in these projects, they created little more than a series of petty annoyances for the Union. The agents were courageous, but they were also boyish and somewhat absurd. They regarded covert operations as a lark and a break with ordinary routine. Federal counterintelligence agents had no difficulty in penetrating their operations. Jacob Thompson claimed that about sixty thousand Federal troops were diverted from the fighting fronts to guard the northern frontier in the wake of these operations, but even if this figure is accurate, the number of troops was far too small to have had an important bearing on the conduct of the war.

■ ■ ■

While the Confederates in Canada plotted to turn the tide with some grand gesture, General Grant's forces were inexorably closing in upon Richmond. Grant, himself, General Meade, and many members of the staff were almost removed by the Confederate Secret Service. An agent planted a time-bomb at the massive Union supply base at City Point, Virginia, that destroyed the facility on August 9, 1864, and killed 58 men.

Throughout the final year of the war, Grant was kept informed of events within the rebel capital by a formidable collection of fifth columnists, spies, black-market operators, and secret agents who infiltrated the most important government agencies and even the Confederate White House itself. Like the Culper Ring of the War of Independence, these underground networks cut across class lines and racial barriers. Undoubtedly, the most successful ring was the one headed by the improbable figure of Miss Elizabeth Van Lew. A tiny, birdlike spinster thought by many of her fellow townspeople to be mad, "Miss Lizzie" was the Union counterpart of Rose Greenhow. But she was a far more successful secret agent than the Rebel Rose. Despite several narrow escapes, she evaded arrest throughout the war.

"By almost every standard her operations must be rated a resounding success," says Edwin Fishel. And Colonel George H. Sharpe, the head of the Bureau of Military Information, noted: "For a long, long time she represented all that was left of the power of the United States government in Richmond. . . . The greater portion [of our intelligence in 1864–1865] in its collection and in good measure in its transmission, we owed to the intelligence and devotion of Miss Van Lew."

By every rule of birth and background, Elizabeth Van Lew should have been an ardent secessionist. A member of a prominent Richmond family, she lived in a splendid mansion across the street from the church where Patrick Henry had called for liberty or death, and she always spoke of Virginians as "our people." Yet, defying convention, she was an uncompromising abolitionist and an open supporter of the Union. Perhaps the explanation for her conduct lay in the fact that the Van Lews were originally Northerners. John Van Lew, her father, had come to Richmond from Long Island as a young man and had prospered in the hardware business, while her mother was from Philadelphia. Elizabeth, who was born in Richmond in 1818, was educated in her mother's home town and her neighbors later insisted that she must have acquired her abolitionist sympathies there.

As a girl, Elizabeth was said to have been pretty, "a pleasing pale blond" with ringlets about her face and lively blue eyes. Even then, she was a lady with a cause. Following her father's death, she liberated the nine family slaves. Whenever she learned that children or relatives of former Van Lew slaves were being sold by other owners, she purchased and freed them, too. "Slave power degrades labor," she wrote in her journal. "Slave power is arrogant, is jealous and intrusive, is cruel, is despotic, not only over the slave, but over the community, the state." Friends knew her views, but thought they would pass. They were wrong. By the time the war came, she was an old maid living with her widowed mother in the house on Church Hill, isolated from the world about her—but no less a dedicated abolitionist.

The Van Lew ladies shocked the city by regularly visiting the Yankee prisoners crammed into the old warehouse—now known officially as Libby Prison—that was located below the bluff upon which their home stood. They supplied the captives with food, clothing, bedding, and medicines, and persuaded Confederate doctors to transfer sick men to the hospital. Some prisoners later credited the Van Lews with saving their lives.

Before long, the women's activities attracted unfavorable attention from the newspapers. One paper reported: "Whilst every true woman in this community was busy making articles for our troops, or administering to our sick, these two women have been spending their oppulent means in aiding and giving comfort to the miscreants who have invaded our sacred soil, bent on rapine and murder."

Rebel patriots would have been even angrier had they known that Elizabeth Van Lew was receiving military information from the prisoners. In the beginning, she had difficulty in sifting or even comprehending the intelligence passed on to her, but she made contact with Union agents who slipped in and out of Richmond, and they understood the meaning of the information. Questions and answers were hidden in baskets of food or wrapped up with bottles of medicine passed back and forth. Sometimes, while other prisoners watched the sentries, she interviewed men who had just been captured and who provided firsthand accounts of battles as well as estimates of rebel strength. Ordered not to converse with the captives, Van Lew took to supplying them with books. When the books were returned to her, they contained tiny pin pricks that spelled out messages. She also passed notes in a double-bottom dish designed to hold hot water. When a suspicious guard wanted to inspect the dish, she readily handed it out from under her shawl. He howled in pain and let it go, for she had filled the bottom with boiling water.

To turn aside suspicion, Miss Lizzie began to trade on her reputation as an eccentric. She stopped tending her hair, wore shabby and unkempt clothing, and was often seen talking to herself. People looked at her and shook their heads. They called her "Crazy Bet," but her feigned madness probably saved her from arrest. The worst official rebuke she received was the revocation of her permit to visit the military prisons. Like Rose Greenhow, however, she had friends in high places. She appealed the order to an old family friend, General John H. Winder, the provost marshal of Richmond, who wagged a fatherly finger in reproof of her activities—and signed a new permit. When the War Department began confiscating horses from civilian owners, she hid the family's last horse in the smokehouse. Fearing the animal would be found, she led him into the house and into her study, where straw had been spread on the floor. He was "a good, loyal horse," she said, and there was no pawing or loud neighing.

As the war continued, Elizabeth Van Lew's intelligence activities increased in scope and sophistication. She was given a cipher and kept the key to it in her watch case. Papers were hidden in the hollow tops of the andirons in her bedroom. Union couriers used her home for a safe house, and some townspeople were certain she also hid escaped Yankee prisoners in a secret room. Rebel agents kept the house under surveillance. "I have turned to speak to a friend and found a detective at my elbow," she later related. "Strange faces could be seen peeping around the columns and pillars of the back portico." Learning that Libby Prison was to get a new commander, Van Lew hit upon an ingenious plan to forestall surprise searches. Housing was in short supply in wartime Richmond, so she hospitably offered the newly arrived officer and his wife quarters in her home. The officer, a Captain Gibbs, gratefully accepted the offer—and was oblivious to everything going on about him.

Van Lew's most strategically placed agent was Mary Elizabeth Bowser, a young black woman who worked as a servant in the Confederate White House. Formerly a slave, she had been freed by Van Lew, who was impressed with the girl's intelligence and sent her North to be educated. Following the outbreak of the war, she asked Mary Elizabeth to return to Richmond, inducted her into her spy ring, and obtained a job for the girl in Jefferson Davis's home, where she could eavesdrop on the president's table talk and rifle his papers. Van Lew was discreet about the activities of her agents, and no record has survived of the intelligence supplied by Mary Elizabeth Bowser, but she was never suspected of being a spy.

Other members of the Van Lew ring included Walter S. Rowley, a Virginia farmer whose place was used as a safe house; Frederick W. E. Lohmann, the owner of a German restaurant and a black-market operator; Charles Palmer, a well-to-do merchant; and Martin M. Lipscomb, a purveyor of supplies to the Confederate army who ran unsuccessfully for mayor of Richmond in 1864, while spying for the Union. The enterprising Miss Van Lew claimed to have informants in the Confederate War and Navy departments as well.

Five way stations were established between the Van Lew house in Richmond and Union headquarters. In the first leg, Van Lew or one of her black servants would carry messages to a small farm south of Richmond owned by the family. From there, another courier carried it on to the next station. Sometimes a message was hidden in a hollow egg or stitched into the pattern of a dress. Other couriers carried letters that seemed innocent enough: an exchange of family news and other matters between Miss Eliza Jones and her "Dear Uncle," James ap Jones, who lived behind the enemy lines in Norfolk. In reality Miss Jones's letters were intended for the eyes of General Benjamin F. Butler at Fortress Monroe. Written between the lines in invisible ink was information about the numbers, positions, and movements of Confederate troops in the Richmond area, transfers of Federal prisoners, and the activities of rebel secret agents. And as the Union army closed in on Richmond, General Grant received fresh flowers every morning for his breakfast table from the Van Lew gardens—along with the latest intelligence from within the rebel capital.

Overlapping the Van Lew apparatus—and including some of the same members, was another espionage ring, operated by Samuel Ruth, superintendent of the Richmond, Fredericksburg and Potomac Railroad. The line was a vital link in supplying Lee's army, but the general was increasingly dissatisfied with its operation. The flow of reinforcements and supplies was inadequate, and there were always shortages of locomotives and boxcars and seemingly endless delays in repairing bridges. Early in 1863, Lee asked President Davis to remove Ruth, but the president refused with a defense of the railroad man's loyalty. Lee, however, was right: Ruth was doing his best to sabotage the Confederate war effort and was one of the Bureau of Military Information's most highly prized informants.

Two years later, Ruth was jailed in Castle Thunder on suspicion of treason. No evidence could be found against him, however, and he was released almost immediately. At war's end, he was still transmitting vital intelligence to Colonel Sharpe. In March 1865 alone, Ruth and his collaborators alerted the Union army to Lee's last-ditch attempt to break Grant's grip on Richmond, which was thrown back with heavy losses; to a rebel plan to exchange tobacco for black-market bacon; and to the location of considerable R. F. & P. rolling stock, which was captured or destroyed by Yankee raiders.

Lee's thin line around Richmond finally cracked under Grant's hammering, and the Confederate government abandoned the city on April 2, 1865. Warehouses full of munitions and supplies were set afire by the retreating rebels. Richmond was rocked by explosions, and flames leaped from building to building. Yet Elizabeth Van Lew was unafraid; the day she had prayed for had come at last. She broke out a large American flag that had been hidden in her home and unfurled its thirty-four stars from the roof—the first Union flag to fly in Richmond in four years. Pent-up hostility overflowed and a mob gathered, threatening to rip down the banner and set fire to the house. But Miss Lizzie stood her ground. Defiantly she pointed out the faces of those in the crowd that she knew and warned that if anything happened to her, Federal troops would take their revenge. Thwarted, the mob melted away in the darkness.

General Grant had not forgotten his spy in Richmond. Even before the city was occupied by his troops, he ordered an advance guard into the town to protect Van Lew. She was found performing a final task for the Union—poking through the ruins of the Confederate capitol in search of secret documents that had escaped the flames. Soon after his own arrival in the city, Grant paid a formal call upon her. They sat quietly on the colonnaded portico of the Van Lew home, talking politely and having tea. The war seemed very far away.*

---

*Grant, who admired Van Lew, appointed her postmistress of Richmond when he became president. He also endorsed an award of fifteen thousand dollars to compensate her for sums she had spent for the Union during the war, but Congress failed to approve it. In later years, Van Lew was dependent upon funds collected by friends of the prisoners she had assisted. She remained in Richmond until her death in 1900.

II

THE SPY AS PROFESSIONAL

9

The Beginnings of Professionalism

Everything seemed tranquil as Lieutenant Albert Gleaves, skipper of the torpedo boat *Cushing,* prepared to turn in for the night. It was the evening of February 15, 1898, and the *Cushing* was docked at the Navy Yard in Key West, Florida. In the forward compartments, the crew were slinging their hammocks while the slim, cigar-shaped vessel rocked gently, the black water lapping against her steel hull. Shortly after ten o'clock, the tropic calm was broken by raised voices on the dockside, followed by the tap of a watch officer on the door of Gleaves's cabin. He was told there was a civilian who insisted upon seeing him.

"I went on deck immediately," Gleaves later reported, "and found our secret agent." The visitor was Martin L. Hellings, manager of the International Ocean Telegraph Office in Key West. "I have a most important message from our agent in Havana!" he declared.

Gleaves hastily scanned the few lines by the flickering light of an oil lamp. The message was brief and ominous: the battleship *Maine* had just blown up in Havana harbor, only ninety miles away. But Gleaves was skeptical. There had been numerous false alarms since the *Maine* had been dispatched to Cuban waters the month before to protect American lives and property during another of the periodic rebellions against Spanish rule that flared on the island. Only a few days earlier, rumors had circulated that Fitzhugh Lee, the American consul, had been murdered and the consulate sacked.

But Hellings was insistent. The report had come from a source "who has never failed us." Even though he was a civilian, Hellings could not be brushed off. Not only was he well-connected and a longtime friend of Captain Charles D. Sigsbee, the *Maine's* commanding officer, but he had been providing the Navy with secret information from Havana for

155

months. His key agent was Domingo Villaverde, a Cuban telegrapher, who had apparently evaded the Spanish censor long enough to get off the brief message before the line was closed down.

Gleaves sought the advice of Lt. Cmdr. William S. Cowles, the senior naval officer at Key West.* The three men went to the cable office on Greene Street, where the night operator told them nothing had come from Havana since the original message. They stared at the silent telegraph, barely resisting the temptation to ask Villaverde to confirm his report and to furnish details. Realizing that such an inquiry might alert the Spaniards to the telegrapher's work as an American spy, they could only wait. Finally, at about eleven o'clock the telegraph receiver began to clatter. It was Captain Sigsbee's first report to the secretary of the navy in Washington: "*Maine* blown up in Havana harbor at nine-forty tonight and destroyed. Many wounded and doubtless more killed or drowned. . . ."

In all, 266 of the *Maine's* 354 officers and men lost their lives in the explosion, and many of the survivors were seriously injured. Although Sigsbee praised the rescue efforts of the Spaniards and cautioned that "public opinion should be suspended until further report," the jingoistic "yellow" press, spoiling for a war with Spain, immediately charged the Spaniards with having blown up the ship. "This means war!" declared William Randolph Hearst, publisher of the New York *Journal*. Others pinned responsibility on the Cuban rebels who doubtless hoped to provoke a war between Spain and the United States that would lead to the island's independence.*

Over the years, the United States had expressed keen interest in Cuba, and several attempts had been made to purchase or annex the island. The latest Cuban revolt against Spain had flared in 1895, and Americans overwhelmingly sympathized with the Cubans. Even though Yankee investments on the island were significant, the major reason for intervention was not imperialistic greed, but a human, if misguided, desire to alleviate the sufferings of the Cuban people and to help them win their independence. Although President William McKinley tried to avoid a conflict, the American people were whipped up to a frenzy. On April 19, 1898, with the clarion call "Remember the *Maine!* To Hell with Spain!" ringing in its ears, Congress was stampeded into a joint resolution that was tantamount to a declaration of war.

In contrast to previous conflicts, both the U.S. Army and Navy entered the Spanish-American War with the rudiments of professional

---

*Cowles was the brother-in-law of Theodore Roosevelt, the assistant secretary of the navy.

*The cause of the blast has never been conclusively determined. In 1976, Admiral Hyman G. Rickover theorized, on the basis of modern technical studies, that a fire resulting from spontaneous combustion in a forward coal bunker—a common enough occurrence in that period—set off ammunition in an adjoining magazine.

intelligence services in place. The organization of these agencies—the first designed for the systematic collection of information about the military affairs of foreign governments—had been part of a technological and intellectual revolution that produced profound changes in both the Army and Navy in the latter years of the nineteenth century. In the world of American espionage, the era of the flamboyant amateur performing duties ad hoc in wartime was beginning to give way to the era of the intelligence professional.

■ ■ ■

Following a familiar pattern, the Army and Navy that had saved the Union were rapidly demobilized at the end of the Civil War, along with the intelligence organizations that had been so painfully developed. Weary of war and burdened with debt, the American people eagerly turned to filling out the nation's frontiers and exploiting its rich resources. Reduced to little more than a constabulary of twenty-five thousand men, the Army was assigned the task of enforcing the government's Reconstruction policy in the defeated South and then of pacifying the western Indians. The Navy was slashed from nearly seven hundred ships to forty-eight outmoded wooden vessels that Admiral David D. Porter likened to "ancient Chinese forts on which dragons have been painted to frighten away the enemy."

The Army's task during Reconstruction was thankless and difficult. General Lee's surrender proved to be only a truce as Southerners renewed the conflict against federal authority in an attempt to preserve white supremacy and political power. Although the Army was assigned, along with the Freedmen's Bureau, to protect the rights of the newly liberated blacks, it lacked the force to control the violence that spread across the South less that two years after Appomattox. As lawless bands such as the Ku Klux Klan terrorized blacks and their white allies, the Army was unable to put a halt to their activities. There were not even the rudiments of an organization to gather information on the terrorists and their plans for action. The only governmental agency familiar with undercover operations was the Secret Service, which had been established by the Treasury Department following the Civil War,* but it was assigned to track down forgers and counterfeiters and was not called in to assist the Army in the South.

Similar problems faced the Indian-fighting army. Irregular warfare demands effective intelligence, but small units often found themselves fighting for their lives at unexpected times and places. To compensate for the lack of intelligence, the Army recruited friendly Indians to serve as scouts and to collect information. One general estimated that an Indian

---

*William P. Wood, the former superintendent of the Old Capitol Prison, was named the first chief of the Secret Service.

scout unit was more valuable than six cavalry troops, but many officers hesitated to rely upon Indians. Even when good intelligence was available, communications were often too unreliable to ensure offensive success or to prevent surprise. Would an intelligence service have made a difference? Later experience against guerrillas in the Philippines, Central America, and Vietnam suggests that adequate intelligence would have been of considerable value in identifying and locating hostiles and taking action against them.

Although the U.S. Army was in limbo, it was fortunate to be commanded from 1869 to 1883 by William T. Sherman, one of the most cerebral of American soldiers. Whereas most Army officers of the period knew how to command a troop of cavalrymen and little more, Sherman was a keen observer of the military innovations that accompanied Prussia's spectacular victory over France in 1870. Breechloading rifles and artillery had received their first large-scale test in combat, and the Prussians had introduced such concepts as a general staff to plan for war, a highly trained professional army that could be quickly expanded by the mobilization of reservists, and a prearranged system for using the nation's rail network to deploy this massive army.

The United States was on the far periphery of these developments, but Sherman laid the groundwork for a military renaissance. West Point began to shake its strictly engineering orientation, the works of the German military theoretician Carl von Clausewitz were translated into English, and postgraduate schools were opened to teach the science of war. Sherman's reforms were personally exemplified by Emory Upton, one of the Civil War era's prodigies. Graduating from West Point in 1861, Upton was at war's end a thrice-wounded major general of 26. He returned to the Military Academy as an instructor, developed a more fluid system of infantry tactics to deal with the problem of the massive firepower of breechloading arms, and established a reputation as an innovative and thoughtful officer.

In 1876, Sherman sent Upton on a world tour to study international military developments. Told to pay particular attention to British operations in India, with the hope that something could be learned that could be of use in campaigns on the western frontier, Upton was fascinated instead by what he saw in Germany. Upon his return home, he produced an influential report and began work on a book, *The Military Policy of the United States*. Facing enforced retirement because of poor health, Upton committed suicide in 1881 before the book was completed. It nevertheless became one of the most important works in American military history.*

---

*The manuscript was preserved and edited by one of Upton's fellow officers, and its recommendations were well-known throughout the Army before it was published under War Department sponsorship in 1904.

Upton argued that the United States had blundered through most of its wars at an enormous and unnecessary cost in blood and treasure due to civilian interference, a lack of preparation, and dependence upon untrained militia. In stark contrast, the German general staff operated largely free of civilian restraints and made preparations in peacetime for war, including the gathering of intelligence about potential enemies. To prevent a repetition of past folly, Upton called for the creation of a general staff in the German mold and an enlarged regular army that would be the cadre, or skeleton, for an expandable force to be filled out by reservists in time of war.

These proposals ran up against the American prejudice against a large standing army, but Upton's ideas had a profound influence on the nation's military. Senior officers, who were turning their attention to foreign developments and America's future role in international affairs, agreed upon the need for a general staff to remedy traditional weaknesses in planning and policy. In every country, a cardinal feature of such staffs was an intelligence bureau to collect, store, and retrieve information, and American military leaders began to discuss the organization of a similar agency as a foundation for rational planning. However, it was not the Army, but the Navy, that took the lead and established the first permanent American intelligence office.

■ ■ ■

While the U.S. Navy was weighed down with obsolete ships and outmoded equipment in the years following the Civil War, navies in other advanced countries were undergoing radical change. Improved armor plate, self-propelled torpedoes, and large-calibre rifled guns were adopted by all the maritime powers. Even the navies of Denmark and Chile were more modern than that of the United States. Frustrated American naval officers were chagrined to find that their vessels were a source of amusement to foreigners. In one of Oscar Wilde's satirical stories, an American girl who told the Canterville Ghost there were no ruins or curiosities in her country was admonished: "No ruins! No curiosities! You have your navy and your manners!"

About 1880, the tide began to turn. The spirit of Manifest Destiny, dormant since the Civil War, was again abroad in the land. Latin America and the Far East were being eyed as areas where the great surpluses pouring from America's farms and factories could be disposed of at a profit. Unlike their predecessors, the new imperialists did not envision colonizing these lands but merely wished to exploit them commercially and bring the benefits of American civilization to the benighted natives. A modern navy was a corollary to an expansionist policy, and in 1881, Congress authorized the construction of the U.S. Navy's first steel warships. The following year, on March 23, 1882, Secretary of the Navy

William H. Hunt issued General Order No. 292, which established an Office of Naval Intelligence (ONI) in the Bureau of Navigation "to collect and record such naval information as may be useful to the Department in wartime as well as peace."

The Navy had a significant intelligence heritage. Naval officers had always collected routine information during peacetime cruises in foreign waters, including data on the state of port facilities and the condition of channels and anchorages. Throughout the nineteenth century, the Navy had also mounted scientific expeditions that charted foreign coastlines and sounded the seas. Strictly speaking, these were not intelligence missions, but the information obtained had military value. Periodically, missions were sent abroad to observe the progress being made by other navies and to collect information on naval modernization and reform. Unfortunately, much of the data collected was wasted. The Navy Department had no office to collate the information or central planning authority to organize the scattered reports and apply the findings to larger policies. Key reports often disappeared into the files of one or another of the eight bureaus that operated like independent satrapies, never to be seen again.

Thirty-four-year-old Lieutenant Theodorus B. M. Mason, who had shown a flair for intelligence work, was detailed as the Navy's first chief intelligence officer. Previous to his appointment, Mason had traveled in Europe collecting ideas about naval intelligence. He had been particularly impressed by the French system. "Officers showing great proficiency are detailed as a sort of intelligence bureau, furnishing material for general improvement," he observed. Mason hoped to attract men of similar quality to his fledgling command, but for the most part, the officers assigned to assist him were an undistinguished crew.

With the establishment of the intelligence office, every ship's commanding officer was ordered by the Bureau of Navigation to appoint an intelligence officer who was directed to make reports to ONI on harbors, fortifications, and foreign vessels. These officers were inexperienced, and some complained that the additional paperwork interfered with watch-keeping and other duties. One officer who objected that he knew nothing of intelligence work was told by his skipper: "Neither do any of us." Nevertheless, reports filtered back to Washington from wherever the U.S. Navy's scattered ships were assigned. Most were routine, but there were reports on the French attempts to build a canal across the isthmus of Panama, the purchase of a new torpedo boat by Argentina, and the military and economic importance of Capetown on the southern tip of Africa.

In the tiny office allocated to him in the State, War and Navy Building,* Mason and his staff laboriously transferred data to file cards,

*Now the Executive Office Building.

along with material in the Navy Department Library that had been turned over to ONI, articles from newspapers and journals, and any reports that could be pried loose from the jealous bureaus. A year later, the first naval attaché was assigned to the American legation in London. Reflecting European power alignments, others were posted within a few years to Paris, Berlin, Rome, Vienna, and St. Petersburg.

Soon the heavy wooden file cabinets and bookshelves were crammed with data on the speed and armament of the world's warships, proposed new ship construction, and foreign naval budgets. Political conditions, national resources, iron and steel manufacturing capacity—anything relating to naval affairs was likely to appear in these burgeoning files. ONI also contributed to the modernization of the Navy by providing data on contemporary techniques to hull design and construction, ordnance, and engines. "Direct help from the intelligence office figured in every one of the [the U.S. Navy's] first steel warships," concludes one authority.*

■ ■ ■

Not to be outflanked by the Navy, the U.S. Army created its own intelligence bureau in October 1885. The beginnings of this agency are rooted in legend. Secretary of War William C. Endicott is said to have requested information on a European nation, possibly Germany or Russia, from the adjutant general, R. C. Drum, who was expected to have it. To Endicott's surprise, not only did Drum lack the data, he lacked the means of acquiring it. This story may be apocryphal, but the incident is said to have provided the stimulus for Drum to create an intelligence bureau in the Office of the Adjutant General, which constituted the nearest eqivalent to a general staff in the U.S. Army. The new Military Information Division (MID) was to collect "military data on our own and foreign services which would be available for the use of the War Department and the Army at large."

In the beginning, military intelligence was assigned to the Miscellaneous Branch of the Military Reservation Division, headed by Major William J. Volkmar. Apparently, the logic behind this move was that the new agency would be concerned with the topography of foreign countries and therefore belonged under the jurisdiction of the office responsible for all Army-held land. By every account Volkmar was a conscientious officer, but with only a single clerk and limited authority, there was little that he could accomplish. Some field commanders completely ignored his requests for reports.

In less than a year, Volkmar was replaced by Captain Daniel M. Taylor, who was in reality the Army's first intelligence chief. Taylor had the complete backing of General Drum, but with limited funds and personnel available, the two men realized that only centralization and

*See Dorwart, *The Office of Naval Intelligence,* p. 20.

efficiency would meet the War Department's need for information. Reluctant commanders were directed by the adjutant general to cooperate with the Military Information Division, and a data bank similar to that of the Office of Naval Intelligence was established. In 1887, the Army posted its first attachés, to Berlin, Paris, London, Vienna, and St. Petersburg. They were instructed to "examine and report upon all matters of a military or technical character that may be of interest and value to any branch of the Department and the service in general."

While the overt branch of military intelligence was becoming established, a curious type of covert intelligence gathering was already in use—the "Hunting and Fishing Leave." The War Department used this ruse to send officers to sensitive areas to conduct terrain reconnaissance; if they were caught, it provided a degree of official deniability.* The Canadian border territory was a magnet for such operations, General Drum sent a secret letter to selected post commanders directing reconnaissance of areas adjacent to the United States by "officers carefully selected for their tact and ability" to assist in the preparation of a military map for use in case of hostilities. Captain Taylor, the new head of MID, had conducted such a survey along the St. Lawrence River in 1881. Nine years later, in 1890, Lieutenant Andrew S. Rowan made a secret inspection of the entire line of the Canadian Pacific Railway.

This interest in Canada grew out of the strong animosity between the United States and Britain that was a legacy of the Civil War. Americans blamed the British for the depredations of the *Alabama* and other Confederate commerce raiders and for allowing Canada to be used as a springboard for clandestine activities. Flushed with victory, they talked confidently of pouring across the frontier and taking over Canada in partial redress of the wrong suffered at the hands of John Bull. Anglo-American relations were further embittered by the activities of the Fenians, an Irish secret society whose goal was the independence of Ireland. Using the United States as a base, the Fenians planned to conquer Canada, perhaps involving America and Britain in a war that would result in Irish freedom. Irish veterans of the Union army were recruited for several forays into Canada that ended ignominiously but alarmed Canadian authorities.*

---

*"Hunting and Fishing Leave" remained part of Army regulations in one form or another until 1928.

*The Fenians were spied upon by Thomas Beach, an Englishman who had served in the Union army under the pseudonym of "Henri Le Caron" and then had been recruited into the movement. Beach was both an agent of the British Secret Service and a ranking officer in the Fenians for more than a decade. On one occasion, he visited President Andrew Johnson in the White House in his role as a loyal Fenian to make a plea for support of Irish freedom. Beach told his own story in *Twenty-five Years in the Secret Service;* for a modern account, see Cole, *Prince of Spies* (Bibliography).

For a while it looked as if Canada might fall into the hands of the United States without effort. The spirit of disunion was widespread throughout the country, particularly in British Columbia, where more than a hundred residents petitioned the United States for annexation. In 1867, a bill was actually introduced in Congress making provision for the admission of Canada into the United States. Two years later, President Grant dispatched a secret agent, James W. Taylor, to investigate conditions in the Red River Valley in what is now Manitoba, where the French-Canadian residents had risen in rebellion. "All your proceedings under this commission are to be strictly confidential, and under no circumstance will you allow them to be made public," Taylor was told by Secretary of State Hamilton Fish. "This injunction includes the fact of your appointment." American hopes of acquiring additional territory were soon punctured, however. Rather than leaving Canada, the Manitoba rebels merely wished to establish a western Quebec.

■ ■ ■

Gradually, the need for increased intelligence was recognized at the highest levels of government. In 1885, President Grover Cleveland endorsed the sending of military and naval attachés abroad in a message to Congress. "We must have a [Navy] Department . . . supplied with all the talent and ingenuity our country affords, prepared to take advantage of the experience of other nations," he proclaimed. Within their respective services, both the Army and Navy intelligence agencies gained at least grudging acceptance, even though they were kept on a short rein when it came to funding and personnel.* Intelligence was not regarded as a specialty, however, and officers in both services were only temporarily detailed to it. The best that can be said about these fledgling efforts is that they represented an attempt to meet the need for systematic intelligence gathering.

For the most part, ONI and MID collected and disseminated technical information and prepared maps, although political information was also transmitted by military and naval attachés. Some was "obtained in such a way that not a little trouble would be caused should the fact be known abroad," the adjutant general acknowledged. For example, Captain Henry D. Borup, the military attaché in Paris, purchased the plans for the fortifications of Toulon from an official of the French Ministry of Marine. Incredibly, when the traitor was caught, Borup openly boasted of his complicity in the plot and had to be recalled by the War Department. In 1891, MID was able to summarize the numbers and types of arms in

---

*There was still reluctance on the part of some officers to cooperate. One naval officer reported that he could not comply with ONI's requests for information because his Chinese servant had thrown all his intelligence forms overboard with the garbage.

the arsenals of eleven European countries and was at work on maps of Canada, Mexico, and Cuba, as well as the first military maps of the United States (a project finally completed in 1915). Both agencies also made use of photography for intelligence purposes; one officer sent ONI twenty-nine pictures of the coastal defenses of Valparaiso, Chile.

From the outset there was considerable rivalry between the nation's intelligence services. Commander Charles H. Davis, Jr., chief of ONI in 1890, lashed out at Army intelligence as "a good deal of a nuisance to us as it is continually pestering us for assistance and information." When an Army officer was discovered borrowing a report from his files without permission, the irascible Davis declared: "Such an incident as this served to make me doubly cautious, especially in dealings with these people, who in matters of tact or discretion seem to me to be a lower order of intellect than the mule."

Worried that confidential material sent by commercial telegraph to the Navy Department was subject to leaks, ONI began developing a Navy secret code. The project proceeded slowly because of the inexperience of the officers working on the code, and an expert—known only as "Mr. Hawke"—was imported from Europe to assist them. Even at this early date the press and the intelligence community were wary of each other; the naval attaché in London was warned to remain silent about Mr. Hawke "because if it gets out it will at once be published in the newspapers and used as a means of attack upon the Navy Department which would ruin the whole business." Nearly two years passed before the codemakers completed their task, the results of which were embodied in a cumbersome three-volume work. Cryptographic responsibility was thereafter entrusted to the Bureau of Navigation, where it remained until 1917.

This formative period also saw the beginnings of the symbiotic relationship between American business and the intelligence community. Having learned that several European nations were manufacturing smokeless gunpowder—said to be far superior to the black powder still being used in the United States—the War Department asked the du Pont family, America's leading powder makers, to obtain information about the process. Early in 1889, Alfred du Pont, one of the family's younger and more unorthodox members, arrived in Paris with a letter to French officials from Secretary of State James G. Blaine and a disarming smile. The French refused to make the process available to du Pont, but the young man picked up useful information. To protect the secret, he discovered, smokeless powder was manufactured in four separate areas of France. And he learned that 2½ grams of the stuff would propel a bullet through a target that would only be dented by a bullet propelled by five grams of the Du Pont company's powder.

Having heard that a Belgian firm, Coopal & Co., was also producing smokeless powder, young du Pont slipped over the frontier into Belgium. Handing out bribes with abandon, he was smuggled into Coopal's powder works as a laborer. Keeping his mouth shut and his eyes open, du Pont stole the secret for which he had come. Just as he was about to leave for home, he confronted the startled Belgians. Either sign contracts permitting the Du Pont company to manufacture smokeless powder in America, they were told, or Du Pont would manufacture the explosive without paying royalties—and drive them out of business. Unable to prove that the young man had engaged in espionage, the Coopal firm reluctantly accepted his buccaneering proposition, and he returned home to the Brandywine in triumph—to be rewarded with a ranking position in the family business.

The final proof of the growing importance of intelligence to the American military was that fact that MID had become a prize worthy of bureaucratic struggle over its control. Brig. Gen. A. W. Greely, the chief signal officer, launched this power play with the doubtful argument that MID should be under his control rather than the adjutant general's because the Signal Corps had been given the responsibility for "collecting and transmitting information for the Army." In beating back this attempt at empire building, the War Department strengthened MID by broadening its mission and increasing its staff. Besides collecting information, it was given authority over the military attaché program, directed to organize the mobilization of volunteers and militia in the event of war, and told to develop contingency plans for operations against "our neighbors"—presumably, Mexico and Canada.

For its part, Naval intelligence conducted its most comprehensive intelligence-gathering operation during the Sino-Japanese War of 1895. In this conflict fleets of modern warships were engaged in battle for the first time, and naval officials wanted to evaluate the effects of new guns and shells on improved armor plate. Extensive reports were filed by American naval officers on the scene, including Lieutenant William S. Sims, who compiled a report containing over four hundred pages of notes, sketches, and maps, in the process developing a case of writer's cramps that bothered him for the rest of his life.

■ ■ ■

War with Spain did not burst unexpectedly upon America's intelligence agencies. Both the Office of Naval Intelligence and the Military Information Division had been keeping an eye on developments on the war-torn island for some time. MID was headed by Major Arthur L. Wagner, and no officer was better fitted for the assignment. A West Pointer and veteran of the Indian wars, Wagner was known throughout the Army for his innovative instruction at the Infantry and Cavalry School at Fort Leavenworth. He was also the author of the first American book on tactical intelligence, *The Service of Security and Information*, published in 1893, which served as an Army training manual for many years.* On the naval side, Theodore Roosevelt, the pugnacious assistant secretary of the navy, took a personal interest in ONI's operations, saying its chief "has got to be the man upon whom we can rely for initiating strategic work" in the war with Spain that he considered inevitable.

In mid-1897, Captain Tasker H. Bliss, the military attaché in Madrid, provided detailed information on Spanish war plans and the strength of Spanish forces in Cuba, while Cuban insurgents supplied data concerning conditions on the island itself through their organization in New York. Maps were also being prepared on an urgent basis. Before the *Maine* was sent to Havana in January 1898, Captain Sigsbee, who had been one of the original supporters of ONI, made confidential arrangements for transmitting intelligence with Martin L. Hellings in Key West.

Hellings was remarkably well placed for such operations. A native of Pennsylvania, he was a wounded veteran of the Union army who had married the daughter of a prominent island businessman and was now manager of the local office of International Ocean Telegraph Company. This firm, a subsidiary of Western Union, operated both ends of the Havana-Key West cable. Hellings also arranged for the purser of the steamer *Olivette,* which made three round trips a week between Havana and Tampa, with a stop in Key West, to serve as a secret courier for messages between these points. But Hellings' most important service was to recruit Domingo Villaverde, one of the Cuban telegraph operators in Havana, into the ring. Not only did official cables to and from Madrid pass through Villaverde's hands, but he was in a position to eavesdrop on ranking government officials: the Havana cable office happened to be located in the governor-general's palace.

In the period between the sinking of the *Maine* and the formal declaration of war, Assistant Secretary Roosevelt, often bypassing John D. Long, the secretary of the navy, instructed naval attachés to arrange for purchases of warships, equipment, and coal if required, and to keep an eye on Spanish war preparations. To avoid British neutrality laws, one shipment of rapid-fire guns was labeled machinery, while torpedo compressors purchased in Germany were disguised as agricultural pumps. Roosevelt also required naval intelligence to provide papers on the capabilities of American and Spanish warships. For the first time, such intelligence was integrated into strategic planning.

Although most strategists envisioned the war as being limited to the

---

*Wagner regarded intelligence as an arm of military operations, and—reflecting the general attitude toward espionage within the Army at the time—had a low opinion of civilian spies. They "often deserve all the obloquy cast upon spies in general," he wrote, while cautioning that they were indispensable. Wagner also took a jaundiced view of war correspondents, calling them an "unavoidable evil." On the other hand, foreign journalists were viewed as excellent channels for spreading false information.

Caribbean, Roosevelt laid plans not only to intervene in Cuba but to seize the Philippines from the Spaniards as well. On February 25, 1898, Secretary Long, worn out by a series of emergency meetings, took the day off, leaving Roosevelt in charge of the Navy Department. Roosevelt wasted no time in sending a cable to Commodore George Dewey, commander of the Asiatic Squadron, who was in Hong Kong, ordering him to to attack the Spanish fleet in the Philippines in case of war. When war did come two months later, Dewey was ready. The squadron stood out into the South China Sea bound for Manila as the band of the flagship, the *Olympia,* played the rousing Sousa march "El Capitan."

A makeshift espionage system helped Dewey construct an estimate of the reception he was likely to receive. His primary source of information was O. F. Williams, the American consul in Manila, whose activities were protected by diplomatic immunity. To supplement Williams's reports, the commodore assigned an officer to interview the crews of vessels arriving at Hong Kong from Manila. Additionally, an American businessman living in Hong Kong—his identity has been lost—frequently visited the Philippine capital and reported his observations. From these reports, Dewey learned that the Spanish vessels were old or in poor condition and barely able to deal with a flotilla of Chinese junks.

For more than a week, the nation waited for news from Dewey, but there was only silence. It was as if the squadron had sailed over the rim of the world. As rumors of a great victory over the Spaniards filtered back to the United States, Americans were left in a fever of anxiety. Early on the morning of May 7, the silence was broken when a dispatch vessel reached Hong Kong with the commodore's official report. The encoded message was delivered to Secretary Long, who stared at it as if by sheer will power he could extract some meaning from the jumble of words that began: "CRAQUIEREZ REFRANAMS VUFVOETIG. . . ." Finally, he handed it over to a cryptographic officer, who disappeared into the cipher room.

About a half-hour later, Assistant Secretary Roosevelt emerged to confront a crowd of frantic newsmen who had gathered at the Navy Department. Six days before, Roosevelt informed them, on May 1, 1898, Dewey had crushed the Spanish fleet in Manila Bay. Every one of the enemy ships had been sunk or captured. Cheers resounded throughout the room—and, shortly, across the nation—even though many of the celebrants could have joined President McKinley in confessing that "he could not have told where those darned islands were within two thousand miles."

■ ■ ■

The primary theater of operations, however, was Cuba. As early as December 28, 1897, Colonel Wagner sent a memorandum to the secretary of war, Russell A. Alger, proposing that an observer be dispatched to the island to examine the relative fighting qualities of the Spaniards and Cubans. Although a dozen officers were ready to volunteer for the mission, he added, "I should prefer to have the detail given to an officer now on duty in MID." The suggestion was pigeonholed until ten days after the sinking of the *Maine,* when First Lieutenant Andrew S. Rowan was sent to Cuba to make contact with the leader of the insurgents, General Calixto Garcia, and to assess his value as a potential ally.

Rowan was eminently qualified for this assignment. The head of MID's Frontier Section, he was one of the division's most experienced officers and had been conducting covert reconnaissance on the Canadian border since 1890. Rowan was also the author of a book, *The Island of Cuba,* that had drawn so skillfully on his reading and interviews that no one seemed to realize he had never been there. Rowan carried no "Message to Garcia"—the popular phrase later attached to his mission.* Instead, he was to track down the Cuban leader in the jungle, determine the strength of his army and what supplies were needed, and learn whether the rebel chieftain would cooperate with an American expeditionary force.

As he took off his uniform and put on civilian clothes, Rowan might well have pondered the fate of Nathan Hale or John André, for part of his mission was to determine the state of the Spanish army. Making contact with the Cuban rebels in Kingston, Jamaica, he was put on a small fishing boat that took thirty-six hours to make the crossing to Cuba. Just off the coast, the craft was sighted by a Spanish gunboat but was allowed to pass without inspection. On the same day war was declared, Rowan landed on a beach in Oriente province, where he was met by Cuban irregulars. For the next six days, he hacked his way through the jungle while battling heat, insects, and the effects of bad water. Rowan finally reached Garcia on May 1, at Bayamo, a town on the eastern end of the island that the Cubans had under siege.

The guerrilla leader was an imposing figure. Tall and determined-looking, he had a white goatee and a deep cleft in his forehead. As a young man, he had been taken prisoner by the Spaniards and had tried to commit suicide by shooting himself between the eyes. Now this formidable warrior turned a baleful eye on the newcomer. Where were his credentials? Was this a Spanish trick? For safety's sake, Rowan was carrying no documents, but he managed to convince the Cuban of his identity by mentioning the names of his contacts in Jamaica.

Satisfied that Rowan's mission was genuine, Garcia said he needed

---

*Rowan's exploit was seized upon by a businessman named Elbert Hubbard, who made it the subject of an inspirational pamphlet, *A Message to Garcia,* which sold millions of copies. Hubbard used it as an example of pluck overcoming every obstacle, but completely distorted the nature of the mission.

artillery, munitions, and modern rifles. The American officer was so impressed by the old man that six hours later he was on the trail again, this time in the company of three of Garcia's officers. The journey out to the northern coast was even worse than the one in. Spanish patrols had been alerted, and the party dared move through the jungle only at night. After five days, they reached the coast. Discovering that the boat that had been left hidden for them was too small, they left one of the Cubans behind and set out to sea. The boat had only gunny sacks for sails, and a storm threatened to capsize the little craft, but Rowan managed to arrive safely at Nassau with his information and Garcia's promises of cooperation with an American invasion force.*

An equally daring mission was carried out by Lieutenant Henry H. Whitney, another MID officer, who made a covert survey of Puerto Rico under the very eyes of the Spaniards. Somehow, word of Whitney's mission had leaked to the press, and the enemy read about it in the newspapers. They were waiting to seize him when the British steamer on which the press accounts said he was traveling touched at Ponce. Officials conducted a thorough search of the vessel—but found no trace of an American officer. Whitney had signed on as a stoker and was working in the fire room, his identity concealed by sweat and coal dust. Later, he adopted a new disguise and went ashore as H. W. Elias, a British merchant marine officer. "The information thus obtained was of great value to our army," noted Secretary of War Alger.

The major significance of both the Rowan and Whitney missions was that they were undertaken by MID on Colonel Wagner's own authority. Neither Secretary Alger nor General Nelson A. Miles, the Army's commanding general, saw the need to direct MID to collect information on Cuba or Puerto Rico. Rather than being rewarded for such enterprise, however, Wagner lost his post and saw his career blighted. When plans for an invasion of Cuba were under discussion at a White House meeting, Wagner, better informed than his supervisors, objected. The troops would be landed during the height of the yellow fever season, he pointed out, and suggested that the invasion be delayed until it had passed. He was backed up by Surgeon General George M. Sternberg, a leading epidemiologist, but Secretary Alger had the final word. He was eager for a share of the glory harvested by the Navy in the wake of Dewey's victory at Manila Bay, and Wagner's objections were brushed aside.

Wagner then proposed the creation of a Bureau of Military Information in the Field to accompany the expeditionary force to Cuba, but General William R. Shafter, the 300-pound Civil War veteran appointed its commander, declared that he didn't need any intelligence about the

---

*Rowan was promoted to captain, but it was another twenty-four years before he was awarded the Distinguished Service Cross.

enemy. The U.S. Army's most accomplished intelligence officer was thus relegated to going to war as a volunteer aide to a division commander in Cuba, where he undertook frontline reconnaissance and caught a disabling fever. As long as Alger remained secretary of war, he blocked Wagner's promotion to brigadier general. It reached him on his deathbed in 1906.

■ ■ ■

Of immediate concern to naval intelligence was the Spanish West Indies Fleet, which was refitting at Cadiz under the command of Admiral Pascual Cervera y Topete. How strong was it? What were Cervera's intentions? Also of concern were rumors that a Spanish cruiser squadron had sailed to intercept the battleship *Oregon* off Brazil as it raced around South America to join the American fleet in the Caribbean. And there were unconfirmed reports that another Spanish squadron under Admiral Mañuel de la Camara was on its way to Manila to surprise Dewey. "What we appear to suffer from most," observed one ranking officer, "seems to be an absence of correct information from abroad."

To remedy this failure, both the War and Navy departments, in a sharp break with past procedures, sent secret agents to Europe to spy on the Spaniards. One spy, known by the name "Fernandez del Campo," checked into the best hotel in Madrid and pretended to be a wealthy Mexican with strong anti-Yankee feelings. He was taken up by Spanish officers, who invited him to their clubs, where he lost money at cards with the insouciance of inherited manners and income. Before long, he was invited to Cadiz and not only shown the arsenals and dockyards but invited to dinner by Admiral Camara himself. The spy expressed the profound hope that the "Armada" would soon sail to deliver the chastisement the Yankees deserved. In response the admiral disclosed that his ships—alas—were in such poor condition that it would take another six weeks to fit out. Having gained this vital intelligence, "Fernandez del Campo" quietly disappeared.*

Another operative, Ensign William H. Buck, posed as a rich tourist and cruised the coast of Europe on a chartered yacht in search of Spanish warships. He located Camara's ships after they had sailed and tailed them through the Mediterranean to the Suez Canal. Meanwhile, in a brilliant ruse, Lieutenant William S. Sims, the naval attaché in Paris, was instructed to spread rumors among Spanish informants that an American cruiser squadron was on its way to bombard the Spanish coast. Panicked

---

*One source states that "Fernandez del Campo" may have been Lt. Col. Aristides Moreno, a West Pointer of Spanish ancestry. During World War I, he was chief of counterintelligence on General John J. Pershing's staff in France. (See Rowan, p. 705, note 9).

officials in Madrid hurriedly recalled Camara, effectively immobilizing him. Ensign Henry H. Webb, a survivor of the *Maine,* made Cervera's squadron his target. When the Spaniards sailed, he shadowed them across the Atlantic from Spain to Madeira to St. Thomas.

While spies were dispatched on secret missions, frantic requests for information poured in upon the naval attachés in Europe. Captain John R. Bartlett, chief of ONI, told them that money was no object. "There is a considerable sum to the credit of the information department," he declared, "which can be drawn upon judiciously, say fifty thousand dollars." With unlimited funds available, the attachés hired spies with abandon and let it be known in the proper circles that they were prepared to pay for information.

The most extensive network was established by Lieutenant John C. Colwell, the naval attaché in London, who planted a spy in Madrid, and paid him $2,500 per month. Agents "E" and "F" soon followed at monthly stipends of $1,500. Agent "G" reported on the shipment of cargoes from London to Spain at the bargain rate of £10 per month. Agent "K" spied for the U.S. Navy within the Spanish embassy, and agent "L" watched the Suez Canal. In Antwerp, another operative intercepted cables and reported on shipments to Spain. In all, Colwell spent $27,000 on his spy ring. Edward Breck, a former student at Heidelberg and a champion swordsman, penetrated Spain disguised as a vacationing German physician. Taking the cloak-and-dagger aspects of his assignment seriously, Breck sported a false mustache and carried hidden pistols. Yet, like many amateur spies, he had failed to provide himself with a means of safely transmitting what little useful information he did learn out of the country.

Such less-than-professional essays into espionage were paralleled by the Spaniards. Immediately after the outbreak of the war, reports reached Washington that the former Spanish ambassador to the United States and some of his staff had gone to Montreal with the intention of organizing a spy ring to operate over the border. The Spaniards, it was said, planned to raise the holy banner among the Catholics of the United States and persuade them to sabotage the American war effort. Both ONI and MID lacked counterintelligence capability and experience, so the task of penetrating the Spanish network was entrusted to the Secret Service. John E. Wilkie, the former Chicago police reporter who headed the agency, immediately placed the Spaniards under surveillance—an easy task, because they had all been identified by the Canadian press. To throw the Americans off the scent, the Spaniards booked passage for home. At the various ports along the St. Lawrence, some of the travelers quietly left the ship and returned to Montreal, where a new spy ring was masterminded by Lieutenant Ramon de Carranza, who had been naval attaché in Washington. Unknown to the Spaniards, however, a Secret

Service man—appropriately named Tracer—had watched the entire procedure.

Carranza'a first objective was to obtain information on American coastal defenses and naval strategy. His earliest recruit was George Downing, a naturalized American of English descent who had served in the U.S. Navy as a petty officer. The inexperienced spymaster made the mistake of briefing his new agent in a Toronto hotel room without making certain that the adjoining rooms were unoccupied. One of Wilkie's operatives eavesdropped on the conversation, and Downing was shadowed as he traveled to Washington. He was arrested in the act of mailing a letter containing information about naval ship movements to a "drop" in Montreal. Two days later, Downing hanged himself in his jail cell. Disbelieving the report of suicide, Carranza bitterly raised the possibility that "they did it for him."

Unfazed by this misadventure, Carranza next tried to induce Canadians and Englishmen with military experience to join the American army and, in return for cash payments, provide reports on its equipment, training, and morale. Two jobless young Englishmen accepted the offer, but one had immediate second thoughts and confided the details of the conspiracy to the American consul in Kingston, Ontario. The Secret Service was warned to be on the lookout out for Englishmen and Canadians who tried to enlist. As a result, a man later identified as Frank A. Mellors was picked up by Wilkie's agents in Tampa after he had sent a coded telegram to one of Carranza's drops in Montreal.

Not long after, Carranza moved into a house in Montreal. Having taken only a two-month lease, he was not surprised when the rental agent sent three prospective tenants to look at the place. While Carranza was having breakfast, a maid showed the visitors through the house. One of them was a Secret Service man. He spotted a letter addressed to Carranza's cousin, an admiral in the Spanish navy, and slipped it into his pocket. The Americans claimed the document made it abundantly clear that Carranza was engaged in espionage and turned it over to the Canadian government with the demand that he be ordered to leave the country. Carranza indignantly maintained that the Americans had covertly doctored the letter in order to make it appear incriminating. Despite his protests, the Canadians sent him packing for violating their neutrality.

The breakup of the Montreal spy ring was the most effective piece of American counterintelligence of the war. In accomplishing it, the Secret Service established guideposts for the future by showing what one writer has called "a calculated willingness" to ignore legalities and constitutional guarantees.* American officials violated Canadian neutrality, committed burglary, stole a private communication, and jailed a suspect for

*See Jeffreys-Jones, *American Espionage*, p. 34.

the duration of the war without charge. Obviously, in the burgeoning world of intelligence professionalism, legal niceties were not to be allowed to get in the way of a job well done.

■ ■ ■

But where was the Spanish West Indies Fleet?

Hysteria raced up and down the Atlantic coast like fire in a ship's rigging after Admiral Cervera's ships left Cape Verde on April 29. Rumors flooded into the war room in the White House, where President McKinley, surrounded by large-scale maps studded with red pins, directed the war.* Newspapers proclaimed that the "galleons of Spain" were imminently expected to shell Boston or New York, and demands for protection inundated the Navy Department. To appease public opinion, the department divided its ships into three squadrons: the most powerful, commanded by Rear Admiral William T. Sampson, was sent to Key West; a "Flying Squadron" of fast ships under Commodore Winfield S. Schley was based at Hampton Roads, where theoretically it could deal with a Spanish fleet in either the Atlantic or Caribbean; and a third squadron consisting of armed merchant ships patrolled north of the Delaware Capes.

Calculating that Cervera would head for San Juan, Puerto Rico, to refuel, Sampson steamed there to intercept him. But the Spanish ships were nowhere to be found. While Sampson was on his way back to Key West, word was received that the Spanish fleet had arrived at Martinique. Once they had refueled, Sampson thought, the Spaniards would head for Cienfuegos, on the southern coast of Cuba, to unload arms for the Havana garrison. He ordered Schley and his Flying Squadron to join him there. But Cervera outsmarted the American naval commanders. Having been denied coal by the French, he sailed to Curaçao, where the Dutch allowed him to partially replenish his bunkers. Then he disappeared into the vastness of the Caribbean.

The first solid report of Cervera's whereabouts came from the Key West-Havana spy ring headed by Martin L. Hellings. With the outbreak of the war, Helling's operation had been turned over to the Signal Corps, and he had been commissioned a captain and detached to work at his regular post in Key West. The existence of the network was kept a secret; even Secretary of War Alger was not let in on it, for he repeatedly tried to have the Havana cable closed, saying Spanish agents in the United States might be using it to send messages. As it was, there was little that transpired in Havana that was not known in President McKinley's war room within an hour.

On May 19, Domingo Villaverde, the telegrapher in the Havana cable

---

*The map had originally been set up by Colonel Wagner while he was still chief of MID.

office, was taking down routine transmissions when a message came over the wire from Santiago, near the southeastern tip of the island:

> To the Captain-General of Cuba:
> Have cast anchor today in the harbor, whence whole squadron sends you greeting, desirous of cooperating defense of country.
>
> Cervera

Villaverde tossed the telegram to a messenger and waited until he was alone before rapidly tapping out a message to Key West.

The message created a stir in Washington. It just couldn't be true. If Cervera had taken shelter behind the batteries and mine fields guarding the narrow passage into the harbor of Santiago, his fleet was out of the war—for he would be unable to get out again once an American blockade was established. Besides, an American cruiser had arrived off Santiago at about the same time Cervera was said to have anchored, and it had reported no trace of the Spanish ships. All in all, the message was so improbable that the most important intelligence coup of the war was disregarded as the U.S. Navy continued to play blind man's bluff off Cienfuegos. It was not until the evening of May 28—nine days after Villaverde had first notified Key West of Cervera's arrival—that Sampson's squadron arrived off Santiago to put a cork in the bottle.

Admiral Sampson placed his squadron in a semicircle about six miles from the entrance to Santiago. Each night, one of his battleships edged in closer and played her searchlights on the harbor mouth. Inasmuch as the Spaniards had only ancient guns and no searchlights, the forts were unable to effectively reply to the frequent bombardments ordered by Sampson, but the Americans could not run into the harbor and destroy Cervera's ships. Sampson called upon the Army to take the forts from the rear so the passage could be swept clear of mines so he could get at the Spanish vessels.

But Sampson lacked intelligence on the exact makeup of the Spanish squadron, and there were reports that several enemy cruisers were still at large. If they got among the transports carrying General Shafter's troops to Cuba, it would be a disaster. Although the troops were already on the ships rocking on the greasy swells off Tampa, the Navy Department held up the order to sail in order to make absolutely certain that all of Cervera's vessels were actually in Santiago harbor. Lieutenant (jg) Victor Blue, executive officer of the gunboat *Suwanee*, accepted the challenge.

Met on a beach about fifteen miles from Santiago by a Cuban officer and a band of irregulars, Blue began the trek through the Spanish lines. The guides, who were said to know the positions of the enemy outposts, were dubious about the mission. "They said there was no chance of getting through—that the whole party would be captured and hacked to death with machetes," Blue later recalled. The Cuban officer drew his own machete and made it abundantly clear that if the guides did not proceed, they would not be permitted to return to camp. Shortly after sunset, the party plunged into a swamp to avoid Spanish patrols. At times they waded through waist-deep mud. Reaching dry ground, they spent the night with loyal peasants who reported that some sort of Spanish troop movement was underway in the area.

Well before daybreak, Blue and the Cubans were on their way again, sometimes following the road, sometimes off it. Enemy troops seemed to be everywhere, and the pace was kept agonizingly slow to avoid discovery. Finally, the Cuban officer crept to the top of a hill, turned and beckoned silently to Blue. Working his way up the jungle path, Blue peered over the Cuban's shoulder and adjusted his binoculars. Below him, Cervera's squadron drowsed in the tropical sun. All the vessels were present and accounted for. Packing away his glasses, Blue started back to the coast. In a matter of hours the transports carrying Shafter's Third Corps began wallowing out of Tampa Bay.

Bloody fighting was still to come on both land and sea, but for American intelligence, the remainder of the war with Spain was anticlimactic. MID and ONI had already scored their most significant coups; for them, the conflict had indeed been "a splendid little war." While many aspects of the national war effort were sharply criticized when the fighting was over, the intelligence agencies emerged from the struggle with greatly enhanced reputations. One of the most important results of this successful wartime performance was not immediately visible, however. It was the impression made on a junior officer named Ralph H. Van Deman, a man who was to become the key figure in American intelligence operations over the next two decades.

10

Prophet Without Honor

Tall and spare and with a deeply seamed face, Ralph H. Van Deman reminded some acquaintances of Abraham Lincoln. He looked worn and older than his years, but his eyes burned with the piercing intensity of a zealot. For the better part of a quarter-century, he preached the gospel of intelligence and battled official indifference, prejudice, and bureaucratic bungling to provide the nation with an efficient system of information gathering and analysis. Van Deman is regarded as the founding father of modern American military intelligence—and also of domestic snooping that has sometimes infringed upon civil liberties and threatened Constitutional safeguards.

"The most necessary and essential kind of information, without which no war plan can be made that is worth the paper it is written on, does not come of its own accord or a matter of routine," Van Deman once stated. "It must be actively sought, traced out and proved out."

Van Deman arrived at this credo by way of considerable experience and a background far different from that of most soldiers. Born in Ohio in 1865, he was a Harvard graduate and studied law for a year before switching to medical school. He served briefly as an army surgeon and then sought field service. More experienced and mature than others of his rank, he opted for intelligence on the eve of the war with Spain and was assigned to the Map Section of the Military Information Division. While other MID officers were posted to combat units after the outbreak of the conflict, Van Deman, much to his chagrin, remained in Washington, where he was in charge of the White House war map. Following the war, he was sent to the Philippines, where the United States had inherited a savage little guerrilla war along with its foothold in the Far East. Convinced that his failure to see action against the Spaniards had blighted his career, in moments of despair Van Deman considered returning to civilian life.

Then Van Deman's luck turned. Promoted to captain in 1901, he came under the eye of General Arthur MacArthur, the commanding general in the Philippines.* Unlike many senior Army officers, Mac-Arthur was "intelligence conscious" and took advantage of Van Deman's experience. Ordering Van Deman to Manila from one of the outlying islands, the general instructed him to organize the Military Information Division of the Philippines, a unit similar to the one in which he had served in Washington, although there was no link between them.

The U.S. Army had been completely unprepared for the occupation of the Philippines. In reply to a request from one military commander for information on the archipelago, MID forwarded an article copied from the *Encyclopedia Britannica*. As in Vietnam a half-century later, the good intentions of the United States led it into a conflict that became a counterinsurgency. Led by a deceptively mild young man named Emilio Aguinaldo,* Filipino guerrillas who had been fighting the Spaniards for their homeland's independence resisted a takeover by the Americans. The three-year struggle that followed was fought with a brutality that verged on savagery, while at home there was an outcry against the immorality of the conflict. Aguinaldo was finally captured in March 1901, but sporadic fighting continued.

Van Deman's intelligence bureau was active in dealing with sundry plots and counterplots hatched by the Filipinos. The Philippine MID was surprisingly modern in its scope and covered the entire spectrum of intelligence operations, from data gathering to counterintelligence. Unlike its counterpart in Washington, it enlisted undercover agents who, with the exception of one American, were all Filipinos. Among other efforts, they thwarted a plot by the insurgents to stage a raid on Manila and assassinate General MacArthur and his staff. These were heady days for Van Deman; not only could he show what could be accomplished with a coordinated intelligence effort, he was actually directing it.

The Americans' greatest fear was that the Filipinos might obtain foreign support—particularly from Japan, which was already flexing its muscles in the Far East. Signs of Japanese interest in the Philippines were abundant. At one point, the Japanese politely informed the United States that if the Americans were unwilling to administer the islands alone, they would be pleased to lend a hand. Van Deman noted that in 1895, when the Spaniards had expelled Aguinaldo and the revolutionary junta, all its members had fled to Hong Kong with the exception of one man, known as "Robinson," who had opted for Tokyo. Robinson was

---

*And father of Douglas MacArthur.

*Like Vietnam's Ho Chi Minh, who had hoped the Americans would assist the Vietnamese in winning their independence from France, Aguinaldo had originally been an admirer of the United States.

known to have had contacts with Japanese military intelligence, and there were unconfirmed reports of Japanese assistance to the insurgents.

Relations between Japan and the United States, friends since the visit of Commodore Matthew C. Perry a half-century before, rapidly soured following the Russo-Japanese War in 1905. Most Americans had cheered the victories of their Japanese protégés, and when they were near exhaustion despite their victories over the hapless Russians, President Theodore Roosevelt had stepped in to arrange a settlement. But the Japanese failed to win all their objectives at the peace table and accused the United States of thwarting their ambitions. The tension between the two countries was fanned by a wave of anti-Japanese feeling that swept California, among other incidents.

One day, Van Deman found a Japanese officer in full regalia—sword, white gloves, and all—sitting stiffly in the anteroom of General MacArthur's office. An officer from one of the visiting Japanese warships in the harbor, perhaps? Making inquiries, Van Deman was surprised to learn that the visitor was the Japanese military attaché, a Captain Tanaka. This was odd, because military attachés were accredited to embassies or legations, and Manila was only a consular post. Tanaka asked for a permit to travel about the islands. Upon examining the request, Van Deman noted that the only areas he wished to visit were those where fighting was still going on. Three days later, Tanaka was told the request was denied because the commanding general wished to place no impediments to his immediate departure from the Philippines. Later, it was learned that he was attached to the Japanese general staff and was on an intelligence-gathering mission.

Not long afterward, one of Van Deman's undercover agents discovered that another Japanese officer had arrived in Manila and was posing as an agent for a boat-building firm. An examination of his wares proved that the type of craft he was peddling in outlying areas of the archipelago was eminently unsuitable for the requirements of the Filipinos. Broad hints were dropped that his presence was no longer desired, and he quickly disappeared.

Several years later, Japanese counterintelligence turned the tables on Van Deman. Following the Boxer Rebellion in China, the United States and several other nations established garrisons in Peking and Tientsin to protect their nationals. Van Deman was assigned the task of surveying and mapping rail and road routes to the seaports in case foreigners had to be evacuated. While working out of Tientsin, Van Deman used his own name (minus any title that would indicate he was a military officer), wore civilian clothes, and lived in a boarding house. One day, just after he had returned from a lengthy field trip, he was surprised to receive a visit from the Japanese postmaster, who gave him a letter addressed to him at the American consulate. Why was he honored by this special service?

"Well, I knew the Captain had been on a trip for three weeks and I thought he would like to have his mail as soon as he return," the official said blandly. "So I bring it over."

And how had he known that the "Captain" was staying at this particular place?

"You have Japanese cook," replied the postmaster with a knowing smile.

■ ■ ■

While Van Deman was engaged in these adventures, the U.S. Army was undergoing one of the greatest organizational shake-ups in its history. The confusion that had accompanied the mobilization for the war with Spain had given fresh impetus to the demand for the reforms espoused by Emory Upton two decades before. In 1903, spearheaded by President Theodore Roosevelt and his secretary of war, Elihu Root, the reformers outflanked the old guard and persuaded Congress to authorize the establishment of a limited form of general staff. To be headed by a chief of staff, the new organization was given responsibility for planning the national defense and mobilization in case of war. Realizing that intelligence must be centrally directed to be effective, Root made MID the second division of the new general staff, familiarly known as G-2. In an effort to end the rivalry between military intelligence and the Office of Naval Intelligence, arrangements were also made to share information and resources. The Philippine MID was merged into the Washington office, and Van Deman was ordered home to head the Map Section.

This reorganization coincided with President Roosevelt's determination that the United States should exercise a role in the world commensurate with its wealth and power. The first chief executive eager to play an active role in international affairs, Roosevelt paid particular attention to events in the Pacific and Caribbean. Given this presidential blessing, MID initiated a clandestine collection of intelligence in Latin America similar to the covert reconnaissance missions to Canada and Cuba of the previous decade.

As part of this effort, several army officers were dispatched to Central America and the Caribbean. The assignment of Lieutenant Joseph W. Stilwell to a mission to Guatemala followed the typical practice. A language instructor at West Point, Stilwell was ostensibly sent to the area to improve his Spanish, but his instructions from MID indicate the true nature of his duties: "You are not expected to take anything with you in the field that would reveal your identity or in any way show that you are an agent of the government." Using an assumed name, Stilwell was to send all reports to an innocent-appearing mail drop. The lieutenant was warned that in the event he was caught, the War Department would disclaim any knowledge of his mission. The parting admonition he received was chilling in its understatement: "Discovery would be greatly to the prejudice of your military reputation," he was told.*

Worried about what he perceived as the growing Japanese threat to the Philippines, Roosevelt directed MID to provide him with a weekly summary of Japanese activities in all parts of the world. Van Deman was put in charge of preparing it. Naval intelligence also bombarded Washington with rumors of Japanese war preparations, including the purchase of a 21,000-ton battleship in Britain.* Late in the spring of 1907, Van Deman was present at a White House meeting attended by the president's military and naval advisers. Roosevelt confided that he was convinced Japan was preparing a hostile move against the United States, probably before the completion of the Panama Canal. The entire American battle fleet, he said, should be transferred immediately from the Atlantic to the Pacific.

"Mr. President, do you believe that the Japanese would dare attack the West Coast of the United States?" asked one official, rising excitedly to his feet. "Why, Mr. President, the women of the Pacific Coast would drive the Japanese into the sea with their broomsticks."

"Oh, sit down, sit down," the exasperated Roosevelt replied.

Turning to the ranking admiral present, Van Deman reports, the president asked how soon the fleet could be started around Cape Horn to the Pacific. The ships could sail in three weeks, he was told. In actuality, the movement did not begin until nearly six months later, by which time the redeployment had been transformed into the around-the-world voyage of the Great White Fleet. Roosevelt regarded this epic voyage as the crowning achievement of his administration, but to Ralph Van Deman, it represented a triumph of another kind—the acceptance of intelligence in strategic planning. MID's reports, he knew, had been instrumental in the decision to dispatch the ships.

Paradoxically, at the very moment that MID was exercising influence at the upper levels of government, it was losing a bureaucratic struggle to retain its independence. Over the years, it had developed strong ties to the Army War College, the third division of the general staff, or G-3, which was located nearby in downtown Washington. In the summer of 1907, the War College was moved to a new building at the Washington

---

*In 1911, Stilwell performed a similar task in China, a country where he was to serve several tours of duty, and became one of the few American officers who spoke Chinese. He commanded the China-Burma-India theater of operations during World War II.

*It should be pointed out that, contrary to most of the alarmist reports reaching ONI, the naval attaché in Tokyo reported that Japan had not yet recovered from the effects of the war with Russia and was not rushing work on naval construction or other preparations for war.

Barracks in a remote section of the city.* The president of the school soon complained to the chief of staff, General Franklin Bell, of being deprived of ready access to MID's files and suggested that it, too, be transferred to the War College building. MID barely had time to unpack before General Bell was told that the attempt to house two completely separate organizations under one roof was not working out. MID should be abolished and its personnel and functions merged into the War College.

Unluckily for MID, General Bell harbored a strong prejudice not only against military intelligence in principle, but against Van Deman personally. Several years before, while provost marshal in the Philippines, Bell had clashed with the intelligence chief over some papers belonging to "Robinson," the suspected Japanese agent in the Filipino revolutionary junta—a clash won by Van Deman. Angry at the rebuff, Bell never forgave Van Deman, and his reaction to the request of the president of the War College was prompt and decisive. On June 24, 1908, MID was abolished by order of the chief of staff and the War College was redesignated G-2.* As a result, the U.S. Army was left for all practical purposes without the means to gather and analyze intelligence just as mounting international tensions—from the Mexican border to Europe—made the need for sound intelligence imperative.

■ ■ ■

Sometime in 1915, the Japanese cruiser *Asama* ran aground in Turtle Bay in the Gulf of California. Japanese warships had been appearing in these waters with increasing frequency, a reflection of mounting Japanese interest in Mexico. Not long before, the grand admiral of Japan had visited Mexico City and talked of strengthening the ties between the two nations. It seemed incredible that such seasoned mariners as the Japanese could be so inept as to run a warship aground and so clumsy in refloating her. Indeed, there was some question as to whether the incident was an accident. Later on, intelligence officer Sydney Mashbir claimed that several companies of Japanese troops put ashore by the *Asama* had conducted secret exercises in northern Mexico and southern Arizona.

Mashbir, then a captain in the Arizona National Guard, said that in 1916 he had been assigned by General Frederick Funston, commander of American troops on the Mexican border, to check out persistent rumors

*Now Fort McNair, the Barracks occupied the site of the old penitentiary, where the Lincoln conspirators had been tried and hanged.

*The reorganized G-2 was divided into the Military Intelligence and War College sections. The name "Military Intelligence" was preserved merely because appropriations were made for that item, but the officers of the old MID were assigned to "current General Staff work." There were suggestions that all military attachés be recalled, and reports from those abroad were filed away unread.

of the presence of Japanese troops in the area. Two officers had already tried and failed to verify the information received from local Indians. Perhaps Mashbir, who had considerable experience in the desert, would fare better. He set out on the assignment with Funston's parting words ringing in his ears: "Remember, if they get you, we never heard of you."

Indian scouts told Mashbir that every month or so parties of about fifty "Chinos" had regularly passed through the area. Mashbir realized that not even the Japanese, incredible marchers though they were reputed to be, could make the killing trek across the Mexican desert without an assured supply of water. He surmised that they had swung north into Arizona, where a sufficient supply would be available. Following the route he thought they had taken, he found Japanese ideographs written in charcoal on the rock walls of several passes. These, he thought, obviously had been left as messages for compatriots that were to follow.

Mashbir sent laboriously drawn copies of the ideographs, along with scraps of paper and printed matter bearing similar characters, to Washington, only to be told "these papers and writings have no military significance." Someone had completely missed the point. Imagine how the Japanese would have responded to evidence indicating that American troops were probing the outer fringes of their home islands! The failure to understand the importance of *any* Japanese writing in the area was typical of the ineptitude of American intelligence in Mexico in the years preceding World War I.

Mexico had exploded into a revolution in 1910 that had driven the aged dictator, Porfirio Díaz, from the presidential palace. In the kaleidoscopic violence that followed, a strongman named Victoriano Huerta shot his way into power. Taking a moral stand, President Woodrow Wilson expressed the determination to establish "an orderly and righteous government in Mexico" and refused to recognize the "unspeakable" Huerta. A U.S. Navy squadron was dispatched to the Caribbean coast of Mexico to protect American lives and investments, valued at about a billion dollars. On April 9, 1914, several unarmed sailors were arrested by the Mexicans at Tampico. Although they were quickly freed, Rear Admiral Harry T. Mayo demanded an apology and a twenty-one-gun salute to the U.S. flag. Profuse apologies were forthcoming, but Huerta balked at the salute unless assured that the Americans would render similar honors to the Mexican colors—assurances Mayo refused to supply.

The situation deteriorated rapidly. Word was received that Germany had sent Huerta a shipload of munitions, including two hundred machine guns, which were to be landed at Veracruz. Alarm bells rang in Washington. The United States had become increasingly worried about German interference in the hemisphere, including an attempt to establish a German naval base in Lower California and machinations in Venezuela that had extended over several years. On Wilson's orders, a brigade of marines and sailors was landed near Veracruz on April 21 to capture the customs house and seize the munitions ship. The landing met determined resistance; in the ensuing battle, 126 Mexicans and 19 Americans were killed.

Veracruz and the surrounding area were occupied by American troops under General Funston, but no one had a clear idea of what they were to do there. With MID out of business, most of the information available about Mexico dated back to the Mexican War of sixty-seven years before. Funston possessed hardly any information on Mexican strength or the availability of transport should he be ordered to move inland. To obtain this information, the Americans resorted to the haphazard approach used in the old days—sending out daring officers with no intelligence background to look over the land.

Captain Douglas MacArthur, a personal favorite of General Leonard Wood, the chief of staff, was sent to Mexico as "a special intelligence agent" with instructions that allowed him to operate independently. Looking about for a mission, the ambitious young officer noted that the railroad leading out of Veracruz had plenty of cars but no locomotives. Deciding to look for engines inland, he took along a Mexican engineer and penetrated deep into the countryside on a handcar. Besides locating a number of engines, he claimed to have killed several Mexicans in returning to the American lines. The mission accomplished little except to enhance MacArthur's public reputation.*

In the end, the entire Veracruz episode was a study in futility. Wilson eagerly accepted an offer by Argentina, Brazil, and Chile to mediate the dispute, and the troops were withdrawn. The U.S. Navy had no right to hold the German munitions ship, and she was released to unload her cargo at another port. Huerta, who was overthrown a few months later, never did order the salute demanded by Admiral Mayo. Soon the landing at Veracruz faded into insignificance as Europe was engulfed by the bloodiest war in history.

■ ■ ■

As the Allied and Central Powers* squared off that summer of 1914, President Wilson called upon the American people to be "impartial in thought as well as action." It was a vain appeal: most hyphenated Americans supported their country of origin, and few maintained any pretense of neutrality. In a global conflict, neutrality was a chimera in any case. With each side attempting to starve the other into submission through

*Wood tried to obtain the Medal of Honor for his protégé, but an awards board rejected the recommendation.

*On one side, the Allied Powers of Britain, France, Russia, Serbia, and later, Italy, Romania, Greece, and Japan; on the other, the Central Powers of Germany and Austria-Hungary, joined later by Turkey and Bulgaria.

naval blockade, there was little chance that the United States could avoid becoming embroiled in the war especially after the nation became the major source of supplies for the allies. British and French purchases of war materiel in the United States lifted the nation out of an economic depression, and American financial houses invested heavily in an Allied victory. Past suspicions of German intentions in the hemisphere, continuing reports of German machinations in volatile Mexico, and a flood tide of Allied propaganda all helped turn public opinion against Germany.

Nothing did more to crystallize anti-German sentiment than the torpedoing on May 7, 1915, of the Cunard liner *Lusitania*, with the loss of 1,198 men, women, and children, 128 of them American citizens. German attempts to justify the sinking on the grounds that the *Lusitania* was in the war zone, and carrying munitions besides, were unavailing. The German government agreed to pay an indemnity and, realizing the danger of provoking the United States further, ordered U-boat captains to spare large ocean liners. Nevertheless, the sinking of the *Lusitania* convinced many Americans, including President Wilson, of the need to build up the nation's defenses. Officially the United States continued to be neutral, but it was neutral in favor of the Allies. When William Jennings Bryan, the pacifist secretary of state, resigned, he was replaced by Robert M. Lansing, who was so pro-British that he attempted to cultivate an English accent.*

Fortuitously, just as the nation was beginning to look to its defenses, Ralph Van Deman, now a major, was detailed to the general staff after several years of troop duty. Van Deman was appalled by what he found at the War College. Intelligence work had been brushed aside, and reports from military attachés and observers with the European armies were stacked, unread for the most part, on a table in an obscure corner. A similar fate befell the reports received from the intelligence officer assigned to General John J. Pershing's punitive force, which was scouring northern Mexico in search of Francisco (Pancho) Villa, a guerrilla leader

---

*Lansing's nephews were John Foster and Allen W. Dulles. Allen Dulles was an intelligence officer in the American legation in Bern, Switzerland. On April 11, 1917, he was duty officer, most of the staff having left for the day, when he received a telephone call from a man who spoke heavily accented German. The caller told Dulles that he was arriving in Bern late that afternoon and that it was vital that he speak to someone at the legation.
Regarding the caller as one of the troublesome emigrés who populated Switzerland, Dulles, who had a tennis date with a girlfriend, told him the legation would be closed at that hour and to come the next day.
"Tomorrow," said the man, his voice rising in excitement, "will be too late."
Dulles insisted that the meeting could not take place until ten o'clock the next morning, when the legation reopened, and kept his date.
The caller, Vladimir Ilyich Lenin, couldn't wait for Dulles. By ten o'clock the next morning he had already left Swizerland for Russia on a train provided by the Germans, who hoped Lenin and his Bolsheviks would take Russia out of the war.
In later years, after he became director of the CIA, Dulles often cited the incident to new recruits as an example of the folly of failing to follow up on a lead.

who had attacked the town of Columbus, New Mexico. In effect, the U.S. Army's entire intelligence operation consisted of a dead-letter office. As the only officer at the War College with training and experience in intelligence, Van Deman made it his first priority to sift through the available material to find the nuggets embedded in it while developing a system for reading and disseminating new reports as they came in. This wasn't much, he later acknowledged, but at least it was a start.*

Van Deman was convinced that America's entrance into the war was inevitable and thought it more imperative than ever to revitalize the Army's intelligence service. Random observers reporting back to Washington were no substitute for a continuous and active intelligence system. In March 1916, he put his career on the line by submitting a bluntly worded report to General Hugh L. Scott, the chief of staff, on the status of military intelligence in the U.S. Army. The report branded the existing arrangements as "useless" and provided a blueprint for reforms. Probably the most significant single document in the history of American military intelligence, the Van Deman report, has been compared to Martin Luther's indictment of the Catholic Church.

> To sum up the whole matter in a single sentence [Van Deman declared], we are no better prepared, insofar as organization for intelligence duties in the field are concerned, than we were the day the General Staff was created, and as far as military information is concerned, we are not so well prepared since much of the information on hand at that time has not since been corrected or added to and is now so old as to be practically worthless.

The official response to Van Deman's report was silence. But he had an ally in Brig. Gen. Joseph E. Kuhn, the president of the War College. With Kuhn's tacit if unofficial support and the cooperation of friends inside and outside the government, Van Deman secretly established an informal intelligence network to make certain that, when war came, the basic structure would be in place. Had President Wilson learned of his activities, Van Deman probably would have been court-martialed.

■ ■ ■

Shortly after midnight on Sunday, July 30, 1916, New York City and the surrounding area were rocked by a series of tremendous explosions. As windows shattered, people ran from their homes, fearing an earth-

---

*Not long afterward, the plan to disseminate intelligence outside Washington backfired. Van Deman claimed that someone—not himself—sent a super-secret report from the military attaché in London on British army engineering operations to the Command and General Staff School at Fort Leavenworth for publication. The British, who had made the report available only with the stipulation that it be kept under tight security, angrily clamped a lid on similar reports.

quake. Towering flames and a huge column of smoke rose from Black Tom, an island linked to the Jersey shore near Bayonne by a narrow landfill. Black Tom Island was the most important loading terminal for munitions being shipped to the Allies, and the blast set off freight cars and barges crammed with shells and high explosives. Luckily, only four people were killed, although the entire facility was leveled and claims totaling about $150 million were later submitted.

Unwilling to create an atmosphere of public alarm, the terminal's owners blamed the explosion on spontaneous combustion, but experts ruled out the possibility of accident. Rumors quickly spread that the facility had been destroyed by German agents who had rowed over from the New York side of the harbor and planted a bomb in one of the barges. No one was ever caught, however. Following the war, the German government denied any complicity, and the evidence of sabotage remains circumstantial. Nevertheless, Black Tom focused the spotlight on the "secret war" being fought on this side of the Atlantic just as Van Deman was trying to alert Washington to the storm he saw gathering on the horizon. Waged on several levels by propagandists, diplomats, secret agents, and saboteurs, this clandestine struggle was marked by intrigue and violence.

German clandestine operations in the United States were under the nominal control of the ambassador, Count Johann von Bernstorff. The ambassador deplored tactics that angered the Americans, realizing better than anyone in Berlin that despite German victories, the entry of the United States into the war would tip the balance against the Central Powers. Elegant, aristocratic, and shrewd, von Bernstorff used charm and a seeming candor to influence people and events. Women admired his suavity; men envied his skill on the golf links and at the poker table. Over the years, he had cultivated an ability to appear to listen to others sympathetically while saying little, inspiring one observer to note that the secret of his diplomatic success was a willingness to be bored.

In actuality, however, German undercover operations were directed by Captain Franz von Papen, the military attaché, Captain Karl Boy-Ed, the naval attaché, and Dr. Heinrich F. Albert, the commercial attaché. These men reported directly to Berlin, leaving to von Bernstorff the unhappy task of making explanations when their plots misfired. The dapper von Papen recruited agents from among patriotic German-Americans, disgruntled Irishmen, and East Indian nationalists for less-than-successful attempts to blow up piers, canals, railroad bridges, and other targets. Boy-Ed supplied German reservists trying to return to the fatherland with forged papers and ran guns to troubled areas of the British Empire. Albert served as paymaster for the German propaganda and intelligence network in America.

This cozy division of responsibility was upset in April 1915 by the unexpected appearance in New York of a German naval officer known as Franz von Rintelen,* who brought with him orders from Berlin to prevent American arms from reaching Europe. Von Rintelen had lived in the United States as a young man, spoke excellent English and was well connected. Both von Papen and Boy-Ed resented his "I'll take over" manner. Professing to be appalled by his grandiose schemes to sabotage ships and blow up warehouses and factories, they cooperated with him only reluctantly.

Using the name "E. V. Gibbons," von Rintelen opened an export-import company and poured a half-million dollars into a front organization called Labor's National Peace Council that was designed to instigate strikes and slowdowns among longshoremen and munitions workers. In reality, most of the money was siphoned off by a Wall Street sharper, who fed "Mr. Gibbons" rosy reports of the group's progress. Von Rintelen also established a bomb factory in the engine room of an interned German liner. One type of bomb was triggered by the revolutions of a ship's propeller; another was disguised as a lump of coal. These devices were to be slipped in among cargoes bound for Allied ports by anti-British Irish longshoremen. The effectiveness of von Rintelen's campaign of sabotage is debatable, however. Although he claimed to have sunk or damaged several ships, independent observers have questioned the overall value of his activities.

Von Rintelen's operations also reached into Mexico. If the United States was involved in difficulties on its southern border, he reasoned, American attention would be distracted away from Europe. Accordingly, he plotted the return of power of Victoriano Huerta, the strongman who had seized the government in the wake of the 1910 revolution and subsequently been exiled. One day not long after his arrival in New York, he met with the Mexican general at a Madison Avenue hotel. As they conspired together, neither was aware that the rooms flanking their suite had been engaged by a pair of men who had been awaiting their arrival. They were Czech-Americans working for the British Secret Service, and they had bugged the conference room.*

■ ■ ■

*His full name was Franz Rintelen von Kliest.

*Eventually the Germans earmarked eight hundred thousand dollars to finance Huerta's return and promised the assistance of U-boats and cruisers should Mexico become involved in a war with the United States. Late in June 1915, Huerta took the train to El Paso. The Wilson administration, fearing that another Veracruz would be inevitable if he crossed the border, had him arrested.

The head of this team was Emanuel Voska—code name "Victor"—a Bohemian nationalist who had been expelled from his homeland by the Austro-Hungarian authorities for socialist activities. Emigrating to the United States, he had prospered and used his wealth to further the cause of an independent Czechoslovakia. When war broke out, Voska offered the services of his organization, the Bohemian Alliance, to the British in hopes of helping to bring about the dissolution of the Austro-Hungarian Empire. This group, composed of about eighty handpicked members, became the nucleus of Allied counterespionage in the United States.

British intelligence—then called the Secret Intelligence Section (SIS)† had established an office in New York not long after the beginning of the war. Operating under the cover of the Purchasing Committee of the Ministry of Munitions, it was headed in 1915 by Captain Sir William Wiseman. The 32-year-old Wiseman had worked for the Kuhn-Loeb banking house in New York and joined the Secret Service after being gassed in Flanders. He was assisted by Captain Norman Thwaites, a one-time staffer on the New York *World,* and Captain Guy Gaunt, the British naval attaché. Their duties included preventing sabotage and keeping an eye on Irish and Indian troublemakers working for the Germans.

Voska and his team of Czechs and Slovaks worked their way into the missions and offices of the Central Powers. Countess von Bernstorff's personal maid was one of Voska's agents; so was the chief clerk of the Austrian embassy. Two of his men penetrated the offices of the Hamburg-America shipping company, one was chauffeur at the German Embassy, and another was an operator at the Sayville wireless station on Long Island, which handled German cable traffic. Every day, a postman brought letters addressed to German offices and businesses to Voska's headquarters on East 86th Street, where they were photostated before being delivered. Voska's agents were everywhere: in the factories, in railway and shipping offices, and on the docks, where they counter-balanced Irish influence. He was, says historian Barbara Tuchman, "the most valuable secret agent of the Allies in the United States."

Voska passed on the material gathered by his operatives to Wiseman and his associates, who in turn alerted Colonel Edward M. House, President Wilson's confidential adviser. The Americans were shocked by the information—the first authentic evidence of German intrigues and violations of the nation's neutrality. The British also made certain that it became public knowledge through leaks to the Providence *Journal,* a paper edited by the Australian-born John R. Rathom. Alarmed, the president instructed Secretary of the Treasury William G. McAdoo, whose department controlled the Secret Service, to put a watch on German and

†In 1916, it became MI6.

Austrian diplomatic personnel. Taps were placed on their telephones, and they were placed under surveillance.* In the course of this stakeout, Secret Service agents unearthed von Rintelen's sabotage operation.

On July 6, 1915, four months after his arrival in New York, von Rintelen received a telegram in the German naval code recalling him on grounds that his cover was blown. In reality, this abrupt summons may have been engineered by Room 40, the Royal Navy's super-secret decrypting operation, which was reading German naval communications and could easily have forged von Rintelen's orders with the intention of taking him out of play. (Room 40 was also reading the rather simple codes and ciphers used by the U.S. State Department.) Be that as it may, the German secured a forged Swiss passport in the name "Emil Gasche" and took passage for home on a Dutch liner. When the ship called at Southampton, his disguise was easily penetrated, and he was arrested. Extradited to the United States after America's entry into the war, von Rintelen was convicted of sabotage and spent the rest of the war in the federal penitentiary at Atlanta. He always blamed von Papen for his difficulties, describing him as "a foolish and stupid intriguer"; von Papen countered by calling von Rintelen "a man of limited intelligence." Both men may have had some claim to the truth.

Von Papen's own days in America were numbered. Not long after von Rintelen's departure, Frank Burke, a U.S. Secret Service agent, was watching the office of the Hamburg-America Line on lower Broadway when he spotted Dr. Heinrich Albert, the German paymaster, leaving the office with a bulging briefcase jouncing at his side. Albert took the Sixth Avenue Elevated uptown, and Burke followed. The German dozed off in the oppressive summer heat but suddenly awoke just as the train doors were opening at Fiftieth Street. Hurrying out, he forgot his briefcase. Burke snatched it from the seat and slipped out of the car with the frantic Albert in hot pursuit. Outracing the wild-eyed German to a trolley, he made his getaway.

The contents of Albert's briefcase, which the government leaked to the New York *World,* revealed the full range of German propaganda activity in the United States. There was nothing legally incriminating, but the papers of the "Minister without Portfolio," as Albert was mockingly called, prepared Americans for further revelations. These were not long in coming. Voska's agents tipped off the British that a courier named James F. Archibald had sailed for Europe on the *Rotter-*

---

*Some lively conversations between Count von Bernstorff and various Washington society ladies were recorded. When one caller compared him to the title character in a current play, *The Great Lover,* the ambassador protested, saying he had "stopped" his activities in that field. "Perhaps you have taken a rest, but not stopped," the caller replied, adding in a biting tone, "You *needed* a rest."

dam in the last week of August. Like von Rintelen, he was taken into custody, and the rich haul found among his luggage was turned over to the Americans.

The Archibald papers included a report from the Austrian ambassador describing strikes that had been fomented among Hungarian munitions workers in America; cancelled checks showing payments to propagandists and saboteurs; reports from von Papen and Boy-Ed on the effectiveness of their campaign of sabotage; and a letter from von Papen to his wife expressing his contempt for "these idiotic Yankees." Outraged, President Wilson demanded the recall of the Austrian envoy, and the ouster of von Papen* and Boy-Ed followed soon after.

A major effect of the affair was less public. Coming on top of the Albert case, the sinking of the *Lusitania*, and the spreading fear of spies and sabotage, it awoke the adminisration to the need to keep tabs on German activities within the nation's borders.

■ ■ ■

To prevent a repetition of the diplomatic tangle that had followed the Secret Service's crushing of the Montreal spy ring in 1898, the president assigned the task of keeping an eye on potential German espionage to the Department of State. Secretary Lansing delegated supervision of domestic intelligence to the departmental counselor, Frank L. Polk. Polk's job was not to run agents but rather to keep the various branches of the burgeoning espionage bureaucracy—the Secret Service, military intelligence, ONI, and the Justice Department's fledgling Bureau of Investigation†—from tripping over each other. Nevertheless, his responsibility represented a major shift, for it marked the beginning of the ascendancy of civilian rather than military control of intelligence.

A product of Groton and Yale and a confirmed Anglophile, Polk was the prototype of the tweedy, pipe-smoking Ivy Leaguers who were to dominate the American intelligence establishment. As with most people newly introduced to the arcane world of intelligence, at first he was like a small boy with a new toy. But he knew enough to realize that a career in New York reform politics was not sufficient background for supervising such operations and accordingly sought assistance. One day, Polk startled Sir Cecil Spring Rice, the British ambassador, with a request to be put in touch with the head of the American branch of the British Secret Service.

---

*A born conspirator, von Papen became Germany's chancellor in 1932 and helped pave the way for Adolf Hitler's rise to power the following year. During World War II, he was ambassador to Turkey, a post in which he directed Operation Cicero. Von Papen escaped punishment by the Nuremberg War Crimes Tribunal, but a German denazification court sentenced him to a term in jail. He died in 1969.

†Organized in 1908, the Bureau of Investigation was designated the Federal Bureau of Investigation twenty-seven years later.

Quickly recovering his diplomatic aplomb, the envoy assured him that no such person existed.

Not long afterward, Polk received a visit from Sir William Wiseman. They had met casually a few weeks before during a pleasant weekend at a country house on Long Island, so Polk regarded the call as a social occasion.

"The ambassador tells me you want to see the head of the British Secret Service," the urbane Englishman said after settling into a comfortable chair. "Well, so far as he exists, here he is."

"Good God!" replied the astonished Polk.

Thus began an informal alliance between the British Secret Service and the American intelligence coordinator that preceded by more than a year America's formal entrance into the war. Through Polk, the British received American assistance in dealing with suspected subsersives. For example, Voska's ring tracked down a group of Hindu nationalists who were receiving funds from the Germans to buy arms, but the British could do nothing about it. Wiseman turned the information over to Arthur Woods, the New York City police commissioner and Frank Polk's ally in reformist politics. Taken into custody, at first the Indians protested their innocence. Confronted during the interrogation with knowledge they thought no New York policeman could have of their intrigues, however, they finally confessed. In actuality, the questions were written on slips of paper by a member of the Indian Civil Service who was working with Wiseman in New York and who was hidden behind a screen during the interrogation.

The British were able to use their cooperation arrangement with the Americans to good effect in the most famous espionage incident of the war. Early in 1917, Room 40 intercepted a lengthy coded telegram from Arthur Zimmermann, the German foreign secretary, to the German ambassador in Mexico. The codebreakers could scarcely believe their eyes as they transformed blocks of numbers into words:

> We intend to begin unrestricted submarine warfare on the first of February. We shall endeavor in spite of this to keep the United States neutral. In the event of this not succeeding, we will make Mexico a proposal of alliance on the following basis: Make war together, make peace together, generous financial support, and an understanding on our part that Mexico is to reconquer the lost territory in Texas, New Mexico and Arizona. . . .

Hoping that this bombshell would finally force the Americans from the sidelines into the war, the British passed the note through channels to Frank Polk. President Wilson, furious at this example of German duplicity, directed that it be leaked to the press. The country exploded in anger, and the notorious Zimmermann Telegram helped pave the way for the declaration of war against Germany on April 6, 1917.

To protect the clandestine line of communication between British intelligence and Washington, the source of the document was kept secret. Secretary Lansing, establishing a pattern to be followed in the future, invoked the doctrine of national security to keep the press at bay. Broadly hinting that a daring American spy had obtained the note in either Germany or Mexico, he told the press that continued inquiries into its origins might endanger the life of the agent. It was a dodge that would be used repeatedly in years to come.

■ ■ ■

Ralph Van Deman seized the opportunity presented by Congress's declaration of war to persuade General Scott to reestablish a military intelligence agency. The chief of staff replied that if the U.S. Army needed intelligence, it could apply to the British and French for it. "There was no reason why we should not say to them: 'Here, we are now ready for service—we should be pleased if you hand over to us all the necessary information concerning the enemy which your intelligence services have obtained.'" Van Deman made another pitch a few weeks later and again was rebuffed. On his third try, the exasperated general curtly told Van Deman he was becoming a nuisance and forbade him from directly appealing to Secretary of War Newton D. Baker. And that, he added, was an order.

Part of the folklore of American intelligence is that not long afterward, Van Deman was assigned to escort Gertrude Atherton, a leading novelist of the day, on a tour of military training camps. Atherton was preparing a series of articles on life in the camps at the request of Secretary Baker. As they toured the facilities near Washington, the novelist mentioned having a friend in British military intelligence. Van Deman is supposed to have replied bitterly that the U.S. Army had not had a military intelligence service since 1908 and that the chief of staff had blocked him from taking the matter up with the secretary of war. Shocked, Atherton told him that she would speak to Baker herself that very day. She was as good as her word. On May 3, 1917, the secretary of war issued an order creating a new Military Intelligence Division within the War College. Van Deman, who was promoted to lieutenant colonel, was named to head it.

The Atherton connection makes a good story, but the tale may have been devised by Van Deman to cover the dependence of American military intelligence upon the British. Like Frank Polk, Van Deman turned to SIS for assistance. Lt. Col. Claude M. Dansey, an intelligence officer attached to a British mission sent to Washington immediately after the United States entered the war, was assigned to help him. Although Van

Deman does not mention Dansey by name in his memoirs, he may have revealed what actually happened in a citation prepared in 1920, when he proposed that Dansey be awarded the Distinguished Service Medal.

> Not only did he give us invaluable assistance and advice in connection with the organization plans but, what was more important and valuable at that time, exerted himself to excite and interest the Secretary of War and the Chief of Staff in the subject of Military Intelligence and probably did more than any other one man to get a hearing for those officers of the General Staff who were struggling for an opportunity to bring this most important matter to the attention of the War Department.

In the hectic weeks that followed, Dansey supplied Van Deman with a detailed outline of the organization and operations of British intelligence, both in London and in the field. Before long, the links between the two men was so close that Dansey had a desk in Van Deman's office.* He lectured and advised on all aspects of the craft of intelligence, placing special emphasis on the need for a centralized intelligence effort.

The organization established by Van Deman was pervaded with Dansey's influence. It was divided into three branches: Administration, which absorbed most of the traditional functions of intelligence collection; Information, which was responsible for what Van Deman called "secret service" (espionage, or "positive intelligence," and counterespionage, or "negative intelligence"); and Censorship, which was to cooperate with other government agencies in censoring the cable and telegraph traffic as well as the mails.

Under Van Deman's determined direction, MID mushroomed. Begun with a skeletal staff of two officers and three civilian clerks, by war's end it had become a robust organization employing 282 officers, 29 noncommissioned officers, and about a thousand civilian workers, most of them working in a converted apartment building at 15th and M streets in downtown Washington. Only six of the officers on duty at any one time were regular army officers. The rest were men whose talents had been recommended to Van Deman and who were commissioned directly from civilian life. MID had no voice in establishing the intelligence system used by the American Expeditionary Force in Europe, which was under Colonel Dennis E. Nolan, who served as G-2 on the staff of General John Pershing, but it was responsible for training intelligence officers.*

---

*Dansey, a controversial figure whose career in intelligence spanned the first half of the twentieth century, rose to be vice-chief of MI6 during World War II.

*Following the British system, every combat unit from battalion upward had an intelligence section. These sections were to provide a steady flow of information from the front back to the next higher headquarters until it reached General Headquarters, where a picture was

Before long, Nolan sent Van Deman an urgent request for fifty trustworthy men to handle counterintelligence work. The men, he said, must have investigational experience and be able to speak French. Van Deman queried the leading private detective agencies, but the results were not promising. The head of the Pinkerton agency flatly declared, "There ain't no such animal." Van Deman thereupon delegated the task of recruiting the men to one of his assistants, who in desperation resorted to a method that must have caused his chief to raise an eyebrow: he advertised in the newspapers. A remarkable range of men responded— Cajuns from Louisiana, French-Canadians, several Harvard men, a French army deserter, and even an active communist, who was later jettisoned. Following brief training in Washington, the recruits were sent to France, where they formed the nucleus of the Corps of Intelligence Police. Later, this unit became the Counterintelligence Corps and eventually the Intelligence and Security Corps.

■ ■ ■

Unlike many veterans of the old Army, Van Deman was open to new ideas. When a young State Department code clerk named Herbert O. Yardley suggested that the U.S. Army ought to have a codebreaking operation similar to those in the European armies, Van Deman immediately grasped at the idea. Yardley was commissioned a first lieutenant and assigned to organize MI-8, the military intelligence cryptographic section. The need for such a unit quickly became apparent. Dansey reported that the Germans had secured a copy of the War Department code book in Mexico the previous year and that every message sent to General Pershing in France was being read in Berlin. Immediately assigned to devise a secure code, Yardley created one that later defied every enemy attempt to break it. These efforts marked the beginning of a "Black Chamber" that was to long outlast the war.

Yardley had been born in a small town in Indiana in 1889 to a family of moderate means. Following his graduation from high school, he studied law, played poker, and solved puzzles. Aspiring to be a criminal lawyer, in 1912 he found himself instead a $900-a-year code clerk in the State Department. Yardley discovered he had a flair for cryptology and amused himself during dull stretches in the code room by deciphering the department's top secret codes. He found the task astonishingly easy,

---

formed of the enemy's dispositions, intentions, and weaknesses. Combat intelligence was gathered at the battalion and regimental level by scouts who accompanied all patrols and trench raids and by observation posts that kept track of enemy movements. Listening posts, captured documents, and prisoner interrogation provided further information at the divisional level. Information obtained from balloon and aircraft reconnaissance and aerial photography were added to the mix. All these bits and pieces were assembled, evaluated, and transferred to maps at General Headquarters.

he informed his superiors: he was able to read the private traffic between President Wilson and Colonel E. M. House the President's closest adviser, after only a few hours' work.*

Yardley was soon surrounded at MI-8 by a team of men who looked strangely out of place in army uniform. Most were mathematicians and language specialists with little knowledge of cryptography but with the ability to absorb and apply its principles. Captain John M. Manley, an authority on Chaucer at the University of Chicago, was among the most gifted. Under Yardley's leadership, MI-8 quickly expanded its field of operations. An intercepted letter in German shorthand precipitated the organization of a shorthand section that could read more than thirty systems. The discovery of a blank sheet of paper in the heel of a shoe worn by a suspected spy sparked the establishment of the Secret Ink Section. Mobile radio interception stations were placed on the Mexican border to keep track of German efforts to establish a clandestine radio station in the country, while an agent in the Mexico City telegraph office stole copies of German diplomatic messages.

MI-8 also provided the evidence that convicted the only German spy sentenced to death in the United States during World War I. The operative, Lothar Witzke, was a young naval cadet who had made his way to the United States in 1916 after his ship had been scuttled to prevent its capture by the British. Becoming involved in German sabotage operations, he was suspected of having set the Black Tom explosion but escaped to Mexico. Although he later denied under oath having taken part in the plot, elsewhere Witzke boasted of his role in it.

Following the American declaration of war, Witzke obtained a passport from the Russian consul in Veracruz in the name of "Pablo Waberski" and returned to the United States to wage a campaign of sabotage. He claimed to have set a bomb that damaged the Mare Island Navy Yard and killed five people. More ambitious plans called for sabotaging the oil fields at Tampico, fomenting a revolt among blacks in the South, and inciting members of the radical Industrial Workers of the World (IWW) to strike the Arizona copper mines.

Witzke recruited several foreign residents of Mexico into his conspiracy, including William Gleaves, an American black, and Paul B. Altendorf, an Austrian surgeon. On February 1, 1918, he entered the United States at Nogales, Arizona. As soon as he had crossed the border, waiting MID agents stuck a pistol in his side and placed him under arrest. Both Gleaves and Altendorf were double agents, and they had tipped off the Americans. Under questioning, Witzke claimed to be a Russian-born

---

*President Wilson and his wife sometimes stayed up late at night enciphering private messages for House. They used two main systems. One was a variation on the State Department code so handily broken by Yardley, the other a private cipher with such obvious designations as "Mars" for the secretary of war and "Neptune" for the secretary of the navy.

journalist and steadfastly said he knew nothing about a piece of paper with a series of ten-letter groups found in a jacket pocket.

The cipher was turned over to Yardley and Manley. The entire case against Witzke hinged on their success in deciphering the message; otherwise, the prosecutors doubted they had enough evidence for conviction on a capital charge. Yardley and Manley finally cracked the cipher after a marathon session that lasted three days and nights. Headed "Strictly Secret!" it was from the German minister to Mexico to his consuls: "The bearer is a subject of the Empire who travels as a Russian under the name of Pablo Waberski. He is a German secret agent. Please furnish him on request protection and assistance, also advance him on demand up to one thousand pesos of Mexican gold and send his code telegrams to this embassy as official consular dispatches." A court-martial quickly convicted Witzke of espionage and sentenced him to be hanged. The war ended before the sentence could be carried out, however, and President Wilson commuted it to life imprisonment in Leavenworth.*

■ ■ ■

MID became involved in an even more exciting case in November 1917, when British intelligence informed Washington that a German agent had left Madrid for New York carrying ten thousand dollars to be delivered to someone living in the city. By the time federal agents checked out the two names they had been given, both persons had disappeared. Both addresses were staked out and a cover placed on mail to be delivered to them. Before long, a letter was snared and immediately turned over to MI-8's Secret Inks Section. The chemists worked over it but discovered nothing. Soon, however, the postman rang again. Oddly, the new letter bore a man's name on the envelope even though the contents revealed that it was intended for a woman. A new reagent for the most super-secret German invisible ink was applied, and the elated chemists reported that a faint trace of German script was detected between the lines. Further work revealed that the intended recipient was deeply involved in a plot to sabotage ships and munitions works.

Meantime, investigators had gone to the return address on the envelope and found it to be a West Side boarding house. The residents were interrogated and one, a badly frightened steward from a Norwegian ship, freely admitted having mailed the letter. What did it say? He didn't know. An acquaintance had given him two letters in Oslo before his ship sailed and asked him to mail them when he reached the United States. One was

---

*In 1923, Witzke was freed, partially as a reward for his bravery in saving the lives of his fellow prisoners in a boiler explosion. Upon his return to Germany, he was decorated with the Iron Cross, First and Second Class, for his activities in the United States. He became a member of the Nazi party in 1932 but dropped out of sight sometime after 1936.

addressed to a woman, the other to a man. Why had he switched them? Bewildered, the steward replied that the switch must have occurred when he addressed new envelopes for the letters. He had carried the originals in a shoe, and they had become soiled. Who was the woman and where did she live? The steward gave his interrogators an address in the heavily German Yorkville section of the city.

Racing uptown, the agents found their target—an elderly widow. Oh, yes, she had received some mysterious letters. No, she couldn't recall what they said, for she had destroyed them.* The frustrated investigators patiently tried to prod her memory, but all the old lady could remember was a name: Victorica. Seizing upon this crumb, MID asked London and Paris whether the name meant anything to them. The British immediately cabled back that since 1914 they had been trying to arrest a female German agent named Victorica who had been engaged in political espionage. Perhaps she had now broadened her field of activity. Not long afterward, Washington was notified that a woman matching the description of their quarry had passed through passport control early in 1917, bound for New York.

The German agent, Maria de Victorica, is one of the few spies who measures up to Hollywood's standards: the daughter of a German general, she was a glamorous and beautiful blonde, well educated and fluent in several languages. Before coming to the United States, she had worked for German naval intelligence in Russia and then in South America, where she married a Chilean named Victorica who also engaged in espionage.

With the word that Victorica might be in New York City, teams of agents were assigned to check every fashionable hotel and apartment house for a stunning blonde of about thirty-five. The first trace of her was found at the Knickerbocker Hotel, but she had already checked out. The next trace turned up at the Waldorf Astoria. Once more, Victorica had left the hotel, despite having paid several months' rent in advance. This baffling performance was repeated at some other locations, and then the trail was lost.

Fresh leads from London kept the case open, however. A break came when a check of intercepted cable traffic revealed a link between Victorica and a New York banking house. Officials at the bank confirmed that they had transferred thirty-five thousand dollars to her. When the temporary address she had given the bank was checked out, she was no longer there. A number of uncollected letters were found, however, and were rushed to the laboratory for analysis.

The letters revealed that Vitorica was involved in a wide-ranging

*To evade mail censorship, the German secret service often sent letters to innocent people and then relied upon relatives and friends who were within the organization to retrieve them.

conspiracy that included not only sabotage but the landing of arms by U-boats in Mexico as well. She was also in contact with some of the most dangerous saboteurs operating in America, including one known to the police as "Dynamite Charlie" Wunnenberg. Further, she had inveigled some unsuspecting Catholic priests into helping her. Telling the good fathers that she wished to import some religious statues from Zurich, Victorica had asked for help in filling out the necessary documents. The priests were so taken in that they offered to send the order in their own name. They did not know that the holy images were crammed with "Tetra"—a powerful new explosive sought by the saboteurs.

But where was Victorica? Hoping to turn up a clue, the investigators placed everyone mentioned in the correspondence under close surveillance. Weeks went by before the next break in the case. Possibly out of sheer boredom, one of the agents noted that a schoolgirl cousin of one of the people being watched went to St. Patrick's Cathedral on Fifth Avenue at the same time on the same day of each week. Of course, there was nothing strange about the girl going to the cathedral each week to pray, but why go at exactly the same time? Did she have some kind of assignment?

In the fading twilight of April 16, 1918, the agent watched as the girl entered the church just as the clock was striking the quarter-hour, clutching a folded newspaper. Following her usual pattern, she went to the same pew as always, knelt briefly in prayer, and then rose to go. The agent was about to leave, too—until he noted that she had left the newspaper behind. Suspicion aroused, he moved toward the pew, but a prosperous-looking elderly man, also carrying a newspaper, had already taken the girl's place. He, too, prayed briefly before getting up to go with the girl's newspaper in hand. When he departed from the cathedral, the agent followed at a discreet distance. The man took a taxi to Pennsylvania Station and boarded a Long Island train. He got off at Long Beach, hailed another cab, and was driven to the fashionable Hotel Nassau on the beachfront with the agent still in pursuit.

For nearly an hour, the old gentleman sat in the lounge, contentedly smoking a cigar and idly watching the guests circulating about him. Suddenly he rose and headed for the door. The agent started to follow his quarry, but as he did so, he noticed that the man had left the newspaper on a table. Before he could decide what to do next, a well-dressed blonde, obviously a guest at the hotel, took the just-vacated seat. She brought several newspapers with her and placed them on top of the one left behind. Picking up a magazine, the woman turned the pages for about a quarter-hour or so. Then she gathered up all the papers, slowly crossed the lobby, and disappeared into an elevator.

It was the end of the trail for Maria de Victorica. Federal agents quickly placed her under arrest. Although she fenced cleverly with her inquisitors, secret writing equipment and other spy paraphernalia found in her room confirmed her profession. And the newspaper? It contained $20,000 in thousand-dollar bills from the German minister to Mexico to assist her in running her network. Victorica was indicted by a federal grand jury on charges of conspiracy to commit espionage in time of war, but was never brought to trial. Years of constant tension had taken their toll, and she suffered a nervous collapse. Moreover, like many spies, Maria de Victorica was a drug addict. Her beauty gone, she died in the prison ward at Bellevue Hospital in 1920, a victim of an agent's alert curiosity and MI-8's Secret Inks Section.

■ ■ ■

Such cloak-and-dagger exploits were only part of the story on the domestic front. Reports of German spies, sabotage, and subversion—both real and imagined—created a spy hysteria in the United States that was compounded by the government and a sensationalist press. The public began to see spies on every corner as rumors of a vast conspiracy swept the country. Any "enemy" alien was likely to be suspected of being a spy. For example, Franklin D. Roosevelt, the assistant secretary of the navy, suggested that ONI spy on the large German-American community living near the Portsmouth Navy Yard in New Hampshire because they might purchase an airplane and bomb the facility.

Vigilante groups sprang up with the intention of rooting out spies. The most active was the superpatriotic American Protective League (APL), organized by a Chicago businessman, Albert Briggs, with the encouragement of the Justice Department. Within a few weeks after the declaration of war, the APL had more than one hundred branches throughout the country and eventually was said to have 350,000 operatives. Its members were sworn to report any disloyalty, industrial disturbance, or other matter that might interfere with the war effort. Mere criticism of American policy soon became suspect; with APL agents everywhere, people had to be careful in expressing unpopular opinions.* Linked to conservative business interests, the APL regarded unions—particularly the IWW—as dangerous sources of radical propaganda. Pacifist, socialist, and labor groups, along with the IWW, were infiltrated and wiretapped. Peaceful meetings were broken up, and the right to organize and strike was curtailed.

Colonel Van Deman was also worried about internal security and told

---

*The Espionage Act of 1917 made it a crime, punishable by a fine of ten thousand dollars and twenty years in jail, to "convey false reports or false statements with intent to interfere with the operation or success of the military or naval forces of the United States." The Sedition Act of 1918, a throwback to the Alien and Sedition Acts of 1798, made it a crime to "utter, print, write or publish any disloyal, profane, scurrilous or abusive language about the form of government of the United States."

Felix Frankfurter, then a special assistant to the secretary of war, that "most of us are convinced that [German] agents and propaganda have been and are responsible for many of the conditions now obtaining here which are so seriously interfering with our preparations for war." To combat subversion within the army, MID developed a system of "silent watchers" to report any suspicious activities by soldiers or civilians. Van Deman also organized a security system for sensitive government offices, ports, and industrial plants and opened a central file of suspected subversives.*

Theoretically, these activities complemented MID's fundamental mission of identifying and locating potential enemies of the United States. But Van Deman's operations rapidly brought him face to face with the American intelligence professional's continuing dilemma: In defending a free and open society, intelligence officials must often pursue methods inimical to these very freedoms. Moreover, once the line between protection of the national security and domestic snooping is crossed, it becomes difficult to stop short of outright lawbreaking. Van Deman was not alone. The Secret Service, the Department of Justice, and naval intelligence all committed excesses in the name of national security. Vague wartime laws aimed at crushing internal opposition were stretched to the limit.

Overlapping missions and rivalries compounded the confusion. In an effort to centralize intelligence under his control, Van Deman outflanked the Justice Department and Secret Service by entering into an alliance with the APL and its enthusiastic army of amateur spy catchers. A further reason for resorting to the use of APL operatives was that MID investigators were empowered to conduct inquiries only in uniform, which put suspects on guard. To further cooperation, MID opened offices in New York, Chicago, and Philadelphia, as well as in the South and Far West.

Military intelligence used APL operatives to make loyalty checks, investigate the background of passport applicants, probe the qualifications of prospective citizens, and enforce liquor and vice control around military bases. For the most part, however, the volunteer patriots spied on their neighbors, looking for any sign of disloyalty. Although some of the information they gathered may have had minor value, most of it was little more than gossip. Emboldened by the support of military intelligence,

---

*Alice Roosevelt Longworth, Theodore Roosevelt's daughter, was among those asked to take part in these surveillance operations. MID was suspicious of a woman close to Bernard Baruch, the head of the War Mobilization Board, and asked Mrs. Longworth to ascertain the best location in the woman's home for a hidden microphone. Working with her distant cousin, Franklin hurried to call on the lady, cased the place, and suggested that a bug be placed in a hammock used by the lovers. "In between the sounds of kissing so to speak" the agents heard her "ask Bernie how many locomotives were being sent to Rumania, or something like that," Longworth related many years later. See Teague, *Mrs. L*, pp. 162–163.

APL expanded its operations and waged a reign of terror against aliens and pacifists as well as suspected radicals and subversives.

Some APL operatives went so far as to carry firearms, flaunt badges reading "Secret Service," conducted mass raids, and made arrests on dubious authority. In one case, an estimated fifty thousand people were rounded up in an effort to discover "slackers" and draft evaders. For the first time in the nation's history, ordinary Americans with no probable cause for arrest found themselves subject to repressive tactics.

Public protests over these goings-on soon poured into Washington. In the end Van Deman's venture into domestic snooping cost him his job. Seizing the opportunity to strike at him, bureaucratic rivals in the Treasury and Justice departments joined in the hue and cry against the excesses of his auxiliaries in the APL. Alarmed at the widespread campaign of repression, Secretary of War Baker ordered an end to the activities of MID's amateur sleuths. In June 1918, Van Deman was relieved as chief of military intelligence and transferred overseas. Ironically, not long after his ouster, MID was reestablished as an integral element of general staff. His successor was named a brigadier general.

11

Twilight of Intelligence

Early in the evening of June 2, 1919, Assistant Secretary of the Navy Franklin D. Roosevelt, and his wife, Eleanor, were parking their car about a block from their home on R Street, just off Washington's Embassy Row. Suddenly, a tremendous explosion shattered the facade of the house of Attorney General A. Mitchell Palmer, directly across the street from their own. Rushing home to check on the safety of his children, Roosevelt discovered the bloody pieces of a corpse on his own front steps. A terrorist intent on killing Palmer, leader of a postwar crusade against alleged radicals and agitators, had apparently stumbled and blown himself up with his own bomb.

Fear and violence stalked America that summer of 1919. The end of World War I had brought inflation, unemployment, labor unrest, race riots, a bitter fight over American participation in the League of Nations, and a hysterical fear of Bolshevism that became known as the Red Scare. Radicalism was equated with terrorism, foreigners were blamed for the nation's ills, and tempers were inflamed by the press and by government agents eager to prove their worth by ferreting out suspected subversives. Only a few weeks before, bombs had been put in the mail to thirty-six prominent Americans, including Palmer, J. P. Morgan, John D. Rockefeller, and Supreme Court Justice Oliver Wendell Holmes. Only one had been delivered; it had severely injured the wife of a former senator and her maid.

Palmer, a Pennsylvania Quaker who had entered politics as a progressive, was using the Red Scare to further his ambition to succeed Woodrow Wilson in the White House. Building on the wartime spy mania, he trumpeted the danger from radicals and aliens, seeing "a Bolshevist plot in every item of the day's news." Following the bombing of his home, the attorney general obtained a $500,000 appropriation from Congress and established an anti-radical General Intelligence Division

(GID) within the Department of Justice's Bureau of Investigation. An ambitious young bureaucrat named J. Edgar Hoover was placed at the head of the new agency, which was given primary responsibility for stamping out un-Americanism.

The war against the Red menace quickly became the Justice Department's primary occupation, absorbing an ever-increasing share of its budget and manpower. The super-patriotic American Protective League was resurrected, and GID agents infiltrated the Socialist and Communist parties, the IWW, and the American Jewish Congress.* Hoover, who had once been an indexer at the Library of Congress, established an elaborate 200,000-card file containing detailed information on every known radical organization and publication. By late 1919, this index contained the names and case histories of some sixty thousand people alleged to be dangerous subversives.

Had the existing intelligence agencies done their jobs properly, the Red Scare probably would never have occurred, but Palmer had willing allies in the military and naval intelligence agencies. If MID and ONI were to retain the expanded staffs and budgets they had won during the war, they had to remain action agencies rather than musty libraries for outdated reports, maps, and photographs. They were also concerned about competition from the State Department's newly organized Bureau of Secret Intelligence. Apart from such bureaucratic agendas, there was genuine fear of the spread of Bolshevism as reports were received from Europe that American troops were being bombarded with revolutionary propaganda.

Not to be outdone by Palmer and Hoover, General Marlborough Churchill,* Ralph H. Van Deman's successor as chief of MID, sought a half-million dollars for his own investigation of radicals and urged the War Department to train officers to deal with "radical rebel groups." Fearing that the Red menace would be "a permanent feature to be reckoned with," Churchill also developed "War Plans White" to meet the expected revolutionary challenge. Admiral Albert P. Niblack, the director of naval intelligence, warned of an alleged terrorist plot led by Emma Goldman, Alexander Berkman, and "several other Anarchists." Dredging up every bugaboo likely to arouse alarm, he claimed this campaign of terror was to be carried out by a sinister combination of German and

---

*The operations of some intelligence agencies during this period had a strong anti-Semitic cast, particularly those of the Office of Naval Intelligence. For examples, see Dorwart, *The Office of Naval Intelligence,* pp. 119–120 (Bibliography).

*Marlborough Churchill was a distant relation of the Churchill family of Britain. A one-time English instructor at Harvard, he had been commissioned in the artillery in 1901 and had no experience in intelligence at the time of his appointment as MID chief. He served through four difficult years, building upon the foundation laid down by Van Deman, and firmly establishing the agency as a functioning part of the general staff.

Russian Jews, Mexican bandits, IWW subversives, and a Japanese master spy named Kato Kamoto. "The Terror will surpass anything that ever happened in this country, and the brains of the plot are already on the Pacific Coast," Niblack declared.

Hoover and Churchill cooperated in stifling dissent. MID combed its records for evidence that critics of Palmer's activities had ties to radical groups or had assisted the IWW in any way during the war. Card indexes were compared, new files opened, and critics badgered. Undercover agents infiltrated the ranks of striking workers in the steel mills of Gary in October 1919 and in the Butte copper mines the following year. In some cases, they provoked violence that resulted in the imposition of martial law on grounds that the strikers were dangerous revolutionaries. Suspected radicals were hauled before MID officers for questioning. Some were jailed; others were threatened with deportation unless they returned to work.

In a moment of candor, Churchill acknowledged that confusion among the various intelligence agencies had led to federal troops being called out as strike breakers. "Theoretically, the civilian investigational agencies, the Department of Justice and the Secret Service of the Treasury should find out everything there is to know and tell us," he declared. "Practically, they are presently working under almost insuperable difficulties which tend to complicate the situation and make almost impossible the normal relation between civil and military authority."

The Red Scare reached it culmination with the so-called Palmer raids. Hoover instructed his undercover agents to call meetings of suspected organizations in thirty-three cities across the nation on the night of January 2, 1920, and then swooped down upon them. Mass arrests were made without warrants as federal agents broke up meetings and took everyone present into custody. Families were separated and prisoners held without charge or access to lawyers. In Detroit, about eight hundred people were imprisoned for up to six days in a dark, windowless corridor of the antiquated Federal Building, where there was but a single toilet. In Newark, a man was arrested because "he looked like a radical," while another was seized when he stopped to inquire what was going on. Nationwide, the night's haul included more than four thousand suspected radicals and aliens, including the entire leadership of the communist movement.

The public was dazzled by the raids, and for a time Palmer was hailed as the savior of the republic. The Washington *Post* declared, "There is no time to waste on hairsplitting over infringement of liberty." But the fever abated almost as quickly as it had developed. Most of those arrested were released for lack of evidence, and only a handful of wretched aliens were deported. Before long the excesses of the vigilantes soured public opinion as the realization dawned that, despite some fire behind all the smoke, no real cause for alarm had ever existed. Both military and civilian intelligence agencies were discredited, and Palmer left office in 1921 a figure of derision. H. L. Mencken jeered that he was "one of the most obnoxious mountebanks ever in public life."*

■ ■ ■

Ralph Van Deman was an interested observer of these events. Following his ouster as MID chief, he had finished out the war on General Pershing's staff and was now chief of counterintelligence for the American delegation to the Paris peace conference. The city was in a carnival mood. Every great hotel flaunted the flag of some foreign delegation—the Americans took over the Crillon—and the boulevards teemed with suitors and supplicants from all over the world. Adventurers peddled oil concessions and diamond mines, while pretenders to nonexistent thrones proliferated, along with Russian grand dukes driving taxis, secret agents, pimps, prostitutes, and cranks with shortcuts to Utopia in their briefcases. Amid this colorful confusion, a dramatic reminder of the importance of security came when an anarchist tried to assassinate the French premier, Georges Clemenceau.

With the negotiating began the spying. Every country wanted to know the fallback position of every other country. The conference was like a giant poker game, with the intelligence services as the unofficial kibitzers. For Van Deman, one of the most pleasant aspects of this interlude was the opportunity to renew his acquaintanceship with Claude Dansey, the British intelligence officer who had helped him reorganize MID in 1917 and who was now Van Deman's opposite number in Paris. They must have enjoyed the irony that as they lunched together, MID's Herbert Yardley was reading the British delegation's cable traffic, while the British were intercepting American messages.

Van Deman also continued his efforts to perpetuate MID, holding discussions with British intelligence regarding continued cooperation between the two services in the postwar era. Among other suggestions, he proposed that the United States adopt the British practice of having Passport Control Officers stationed in consulates in sensitive areas as a cover for intelligence agents. Looking to the future, Van Deman also suggested that the newly organized League of Nations should create an international intelligence agency, but no one in authority seemed im-

---

*Unlike Palmer, J. Edgar Hoover managed to survive his role in pumping up the Red Scare. Although he maintained a low-keyed effort to keep watch on radicals for several years afterward, he managed to convince even the American Civil Liberties Union that he had been an unwilling participant in the Palmer raids. In 1924, he was named to head the Bureau of Investigation.

pressed with the idea. "How under the sun they expect to function without it, I can't imagine and am sure they will have to come to it in the end," he wrote General Churchill.*

Van Deman's attention was now turning to a new target—Bolshevism—and it was to be an obsession for the rest of his life. Like most military officers, he had a strong aversion to radicalism, an attitude that was reinforced by reports of revolutionary activity throughout Europe. "Italy, particularly northern Italy, is ready to blow up; Austria-Hungary has practically gone to pieces now; Belgium appears to have been taken over; the conditions in both France and Poland are most dangerous; Holland is honeycombed as is also Sweden; the condition of Russia you know," he told Churchill. "So take it all in all, it looks as though we might be entering on a period of even greater danger to the civilization of the world than the one through which we [have] just passed."

To keep an eye on these alarming developments, Van Deman requested authority to detail intelligence officers to the American Relief Administration, which was working in Eastern Europe under the direction of Herbert C. Hoover. Official permission was denied, but his men infiltrated the missions anyway. When William C. Bullitt, a young diplomat who had been sent to Russia by President Wilson to examine conditions there, returned with the recommendation that the Allied intervention aimed at toppling the Bolsheviks be ended, Van Deman was critical of his conclusions. "Wouldn't such a peace as you recommend merely give immense prestige and moral support to the existing Soviet Government without corresponding benefit to the rest of the world?" he asked. Following an exchange of letters, Bullitt, whom Van Deman regarded as "a dangerous man," was secretly placed under surveillance.

Van Deman was particularly disturbed about the appearance of leaflets appealing to American occupation troops on the Rhine to mutiny against their officers. The leaflets were traced to Robert Minor, a leading American radical. Minor was arrested in the occupied sector of Germany, but there was insufficient evidence for a conviction. Van Deman sought assistance from Marguerite Harrison, a correspondent for the Baltimore *Sun* who doubled as an undercover MID operative. Although the use of journalists as intelligence agents is now controversial, it did not strike anyone as unusual at the time. The British had long made a practice of enrolling newspaper correspondents as secret agents, and relations between the press and government were less antagonistic than they were to become.

---

*Not all of Van Deman's concerns were so weighty, however. While searching the building at 4 Place de la Concorde, where the American delegation had its offices, he discovered a trap door that led into a sinister-looking tunnel. Tracing the passageway to its terminus, he found that it led to Maxim's restaurant. Repeated efforts to keep the tunnel sealed were unsuccessful. See Van Deman, *Memoirs*, part 3, p. 5.

Harrison was a young Baltimore society matron whose husband had died, leaving her penniless. Through friends, she obtained a job as assistant society editor on the *Sun*, moved up to music and drama critic, and finally became a general assignment reporter. Fluent in French, Italian, and German, she was sent overseas by the paper just after the armistice. With the knowledge of Frank R. Kent, the managing editor, she also agreed to be an MID agent. In Paris, she helped Van Deman keep an eye on the press corps covering the peace conference. Undoubtedly due to her intelligence contacts, she was the first American journalist to reach Berlin during the revolutionary upheavals of 1919.

To obtain evidence against Minor, Harrison, posing as a writer for a socialist paper, persuaded one of Minor's associates to give her the name of the man who had printed the incendiary leaflets. The printer identified Minor as the person to whom they had been delivered. Minor was never brought to trial, however, because Colonel House, President Wilson's adviser and a family friend, quashed the charges. In the long run, the episode was to prove more costly to Marguerite Harrison than to Minor.

Not long afterward, Harrison went to Russia in her double role as MID agent and correspondent for the *Sun* and the Associated Press. She followed in well-worn footsteps. Allied intelligence had been active in Russia since the revolution of March 1917, first in an attempt to bolster the pro-Allied provisional government† and then to undermine the Bolshevik regime that had seized power in November.

Russia was on the verge of anarchy as the journalist slipped over the frontier from Poland in 1919. White counterrevolutionary bands roamed the countryside, and an Allied economic blockade contributed to the chaos. There was some question whether the communist regime would survive much longer. Although she had no visa and foreign journalists were suspect, Harrison was allowed to remain in Moscow, the new capital of the Soviet Union. She moved about freely and interviewed some of the key government figures, including Leon Trotsky, the commissar for war and founder of the Red Army. In both her newspaper articles and her secret reports to MID—which were smuggled out by diplomats leaving the country—she provided an objective account of conditions within

---

†In July 1917, W. Somerset Maugham, who had worked for British intelligence in Switzerland, headed a joint Anglo-American mission, which included Emanuel Voska, that was sent to Russia to help keep the country in the war by exposing Bolshevik intrigues with the Germans. "The work appealed both to my sense of adventure and my sense of the ridiculous," he said later. In his reports—signed "S" or "Somerville"—Maugham emphasized the growing strength of the Bolsheviks. As early as September 1917, he reported that the provisional government's days were numbered. The war-weary Russians were demanding peace, famine was beginning to appear with the approach of winter, and the army was mutinous. The whole project became moot when the Bolsheviks seized power. The mission's only result was to provide Maugham with background for his collection of espionage stories, *Ashenden, or the British Agent*.

Russia, including her opinion that the Soviets would not be overthrown. She also supplied military intelligence with the names of Russian agents dispatched to the United States.

Several months after her arrival in Russia, Harrison was arrested by the Cheka, the Soviet secret police,* and taken to the dreaded Lubianka prison for questioning. Before the revolution, the building had been an insurance company office, and she noted with grim amusement a sign over the doorway: "It is prudent to insure your life." Much to her surprise, she learned that the Cheka had known of her links to American intelligence all along. When she protested her innocence, the interrogators showed her an article from the *Army and Navy Journal* describing her work in the Minor case and a copy of one of her reports that obviously had come from MID's own files. She did not need reminding that the penalty for espionage was death.

The Cheka, however, offered her an alternative to the firing squad. If she would provide information on other members of the foreign colony, she would be allowed to continue her work as a correspondent. Feeling utterly trapped, Harrison agreed. "In that moment I renounced everything that hitherto made up my existence," she later recalled. "It was finished—and I felt as if I had already died and had been born into a new nightmare world." To herself, she resolved to provide only partial or misleading information in the hopes of staying out of prison to gather more intelligence.

Harrison was allowed to remain free for a few months, a period in which she scored her most important intelligence coup. The Russians had hired an American expert to make a detailed assessment of Soviet industry but then rejected his report as overly pessimistic. Because of the sensitivity of the information possessed by the American, he was denied permission to leave the country. Expecting to be arrested at any moment, he slipped Harrison a copy of the report. She persuaded a Latvian diplomatic courier to carry it out of the country in his pouch, and it was safely delivered to the American military attaché in Riga. "I knew this procedure could not continue indefinitely, though," she said later.

Not long afterward, there came the long-expected knock on the door in the middle of the night. Once again the Cheka bundled Harrison off to the Lubianka, this time to be imprisoned for more than a year despite efforts of the American government and her journalistic employers to obtain her freedom. All denied that she had been a spy. She was not mistreated, but conditions for all the prisoners were harsh. Eventually, she was released because the Russians hoped to receive American food supplies to alleviate the famine that was ravaging the country.

*The Cheka became the OGPU in 1923, the NKVD in 1934, the MVD in 1946, and finally the KGB in 1953.

Upon her return to Washington, Harrison was debriefed by General Churchill, who told her she had provided MID "with more information about Russia than any other agent." The intelligence chief also explained that the dispatch that had incriminated her had probably been given to the Russians by a reserve officer later discovered to be a communist sympathizer. And the *Army and Navy Journal* article? Churchill shook his head. That one he couldn't explain.

■ ■ ■

With the exception of a few outstanding personalities and operations, the period between the two world wars was a time of dissolution and decay for American intelligence. The intelligence community was largely dormant as isolationism became the keynote of American foreign policy. Post-World War I national security goals shrank to two basic elements: defending the continental United States and its overseas possessions and deterring European intervention in the affairs of the Western Hemisphere. "National policy must depend upon correct predictions concerning the international future," noted Marlborough Churchill, but the United States failed to heed his warning. The intelligence apparatus fell victim to the same indiscriminate demobilization as the rest of the armed forces.

In 1921 stringent economies forced the recall of military attachés from Belgium, Czechoslovakia, Ecuador, Holland, Hungary, Sweden, and Switzerland. Both the Bureau of Investigation and the Secret Service abandoned counterintelligence work, and the State Department abolished its intelligence operation. The number of personnel at MID headquarters shrank from a peak of 1,441 in the final year of the war to 90 in 1921, while the annual budget plummeted from $2.5 million to $225,000. Further cuts were made during the Great Depression; by 1937, the United States was spending less than 10 percent of the amount earmarked for intelligence purposes by the Soviet Union and Japan. "Prior to World War II," observed General George C. Marshall, the chief of staff during that conflict, "our foreign intelligence was little more than what a military attaché could learn at dinner, more or less over the coffee cups."

In the interwar years, noted President Dwight D. Eisenhower, a former army officer, only officers with independent means sought assignment as attachés because of the shortage of government funds. "Usually, they were estimable, socially acceptable gentlemen; few knew the essentials of intelligence," he recalled. Intelligence had so little standing that the major task assigned to intelligence officers on some U.S. Navy ships was to keep track of the laundry in port. Although the Soviets labeled the American embassy at Riga, which served as a window on Russia during the 1920s, "a sinister espionage center," George F. Kennan, one of the

State Department's leading Kremlinologists, knew better. He noted caustically that "the United States Government had not yet advanced to that level of sophistication."

Ralph Van Deman's formal ties to intelligence were also severed. Assigned to troop duty upon his return from Europe, he spent most of the remainder of his service in the Philippines, retiring in 1929 as a major general after thirty-eight years in the Army. Only one part of the wartime MID survived the cutbacks: Herbert Yardley's code- and cipher-breaking operation. Unwilling to return to the drudgery of the State Department's code room, the flamboyant Yardley told everyone who would listen that if the country was to remain on an equal footing with other important nations the work of the Cipher Bureau must be continued. "In no other manner could the United States obtain an intimate knowledge of the true sentiments and intentions of other nations," he declared.

Yardley estimated that such an operation would cost about one hundred thousand dollars per year. The State Department agreed to furnish forty thousand dollars out of its "special" funds, provided that the Navy Department was excluded (the department refused to share its secrets with the Navy). MID managed to pry the remaining sixty thousand out of Congress after congressional leaders were let in on the secret. There was a joker, however. The State Department's secret funds could not be legally expended within the District of Columbia, so Yardley moved his staff—mostly recruited from MI-8—to New York City.

This was the beginning of the American Black Chamber, which commenced operations in a townhouse at 3 East 38th Street on October 1, 1919. Little more than a year later, it moved to new quarters in a four-story brownstone at 141 East 37th Street, just off Lexington Avenue. The narrow rooms were crammed with dictionaries, language statistics, files of newspaper clippings, maps, and other paraphernalia needed for code-breaking. All open connection with the government was severed. Everyone was placed on a secret payroll with Yardley receiving $7,500 annually. Security was tight. The office locks were changed periodically, and Yardley's name did not appear in the telephone book. "We were to read the secret code and cipher diplomatic telegrams of foreign governments—by which means as we could," Yardley recalled. "If we were caught, it would be just too bad!"

Among the unit's first tasks was the deciphering of messages between a Russian agent in Berlin and his masters in Moscow. The agent was apparently running part of the Soviet Union's espionage network abroad, and one of the documents mentioned an operative named Guralski who had been dispatched to America. These messages created a sensation in Washington, Yardley reported, "for they were the first authentic documents that came into the government's possession dealing with international Soviet activities."

Soon, however, Japan became the Black Chamber's major target. Although the United States and Japan had been allies during the war, friction between them continued unabated. The Japanese felt that the Americans were blocking their legitimate aspirations in East Asia, while the United States was worried about Japan's ambitions in China and her plans for the tiny islands in the central and western Pacific that she had been awarded as League of Nations mandates. Even more ominous was the gigantic naval race in which the United States, Britain, and Japan found themselves despite the end of the war. Each was building battleships at a frantic pace and was afraid to stop as long as the others were continuing to build. Talk was rife on all sides of an "inevitable" war in the Pacific.

Yardley was given the task of breaking the Japanese diplomatic codes and in a burst of enthusiasm promised either a solution or his resignation within a year. He quickly regretted his rash promise, for his efforts almost foundered on the intricacies of the Japanese language. The State Department supplied Yardley with about a hundred intercepted Japanese code messages, which he worked over with a language expert named Frederick Livesey, who taught himself Japanese as he went along. But the work went slowly. Frustrated after several months' work, Yardley considered breaking into the Japanese consulate in New York in the desperate hope of getting a peek at the code books. Reluctantly, he gave up the idea as impractical and again took up his pad and pencil.

Night after night, Yardley climbed the stairs to his apartment on the fourth floor and fell into bed, exhausted and discouraged, only to awaken a few hours later with a brilliant idea—which always ran into another blind alley.

> By now I had worked so long with these code telegrams that every telegram, every line, even every code word was indelibly printed in my brain. I could lie awake in bed and in the darkness make my investigations—trial and error, over and over again. Finally, one night I awakened at midnight, for I had retired early, and out of the darkness came the conviction that a certain series of two-letter codewords absolutely *must* equal *Airuando* [Ireland]. Then other words danced before me in rapid succession: *dokuritsu* [independence], *Doitsu* [Germany], *owari* [stop]. At last the great discovery! My heart stood still, and I dared not move. Was I dreaming? Was I awake? Was I losing my mind? A solution? At last—and after all these months!

Yardley almost tumbled down the stairs in his eagerness to get to work. With trembling fingers, he spun the dial of the safe where he kept his files and rapidly began working over his papers. An hour's effort convinced him that he was on the right track at last. Racing back upstairs, he awakened his wife, and they dashed out to a speakeasy to celebrate. Yardley had only driven an opening wedge into the Japanese coding system, but the breakthrough eventually enabled the Black Chamber to read sixteen different variations of the Japanese diplomatic code, including the most super-secret version.

The Black Chamber scored its greatest coup at a disarmament conference that convened in Washington in November 1921 with the aim of ending the battleship race. Attended by representatives of the United States, Britain, Japan, France, and Italy, the meeting sought to limit the number of capital ships—warships of the largest class—by establishing a tonnage ratio between each nation. Each of the participants tried to obtain the most favorable level for itself, with the Japanese demanding a ratio with the United States and Britain of 10:10:7. American naval strategists worried that such a ratio would confirm Japan's dominance of the western Pacific, because the Japanese fleet would make up for its numerical inferiority by operating near its bases.

Unknownst to the Japanese negotiators, Yardley and his team were reading their instructions. ONI had already discovered hints that, despite their seeming bellicosity, the Japanese were not yet ready to offend the United States, because they still lacked the economic and industrial base of a modern naval power. A cable deciphered by the Black Chamber on November 28, 1921, confirmed these reports. The Foreign Office in Tokyo had instructed the Japanese delegation to adopt a fallback ratio of 10:10:6 if their original proposal met determined opposition. Armed with this vital information, American negotiators held out for the lesser tonnage ratio, and the Japanese capitulated. Yardley was awarded the Distinguished Service Medal for his work.

In its nearly ten years of existence, the Black Chamber solved over forty-five thousand coded messages and broke the codes of twenty nations, including Britain, France, and the Soviet Union as well as Japan. In an effort to disguise the source of the deciphered material, traffic between the Black Chamber and the State and War departments was passed in the form of "bulletins" that began with the noncommital phrase "We learn from a source believed to be reliable that . . . ," followed by a slightly paraphrased text of the intercept. Most of the intercepted cables were obtained through secret arrangements with ranking officials of the Western Union Telegraph Company and the Postal Telegraph Company.

And then it was all over. In 1929, Yardley was worried by the highly moralistic tone adopted by the newly elected president, Herbert Hoover, and was certain that Hoover would not tolerate the existence of the Black Chamber. His worst fears were confirmed when Secretary of State Henry M. Stimson was informed of Yardley's activities. Expressing total disapproval, Stimson ordered State Department financing for the Black Chamber discontinued immediately. He regarded the reading of the diplomatic messages of another country as a dirty business and a violation of the spirit of mutual trust in which he conducted his personal business and foreign policy. "Gentlemen," he is supposed to have said, "do not read each other's mail."*

On October 31, 1929, the Black Chamber was shut down. Yardley and his staff were dismissed with three months' wages as severance pay. "This fine gesture," observed the *Christian Science Monitor*, "will commend itself to all who are trying to develop the same standards of decency between Governments as exist between individuals." In practice, however, gentlemen continued to read other gentlemen's mail. MID, which had supplied 60 percent of the Black Chamber's funding, merely resorted to another cover. The work that had been performed by Yardley's operation was turned over to a newly created, super-secret Signal Corps unit, the Signal Intelligence Service, headed by William F. Friedman, a onetime plant geneticist and brilliant cryptologist who had been working for the Army since World War I.*

■ ■ ■

Throughout the years leading up to World War II, naval intelligence was haunted by the possibility that the Japanese were secretly militarizing the coral atolls of the Caroline, Marshall, and Mariana chains that stretched across the Pacific between Hawaii and the Philippines like pearls on a string. Naval bases and air strips on these islands would be of supreme strategic importance in case of war between the United States and Japan. Persistent rumors of Japanese military preparations filtered back to ONI, but there was no way of checking them out, because the Japanese had closed the islands to outsiders. Unwanted visitors were quickly hustled away by the authorities.

In 1920, ONI tried to plant intelligence officers in an expedition that supposedly was intended to find and mark the graves of American sailors lost during Commodore Perry's mission to Japan some seventy years before. The Japanese were not taken in. They politely granted permission for observances to be held at known gravesites on Okinawa but refused to

*Stimson did not actually use these words until 1947, when they appeared in his autobiography, *On Active Service in Peace and War.* They may have been supplied by McGeorge Bundy, his collaborator. See Fishel, "Mythmaking at Stimson's Expense."

*Yardley revealed the story of his codebreaking activities in a series of articles in the *Saturday Evening Post* that were published as a book, *The American Black Chamber,* in 1931. English, French, Swedish, Chinese, and Japanese editions followed. The book created a sensation, particularly in Japan, but the State and War Departments met reporters' questions with bland denials. The manuscript of a sequel was seized on grounds that it violated a law forbidding federal employees from appropriating secret documents for their own use. In 1933, Congress passed a law aimed directly at Yardley that made it a crime punishable by a $10,000 fine or imprisonment up to ten years, or both, to publish any diplomatic code. Only slightly changed, the law is still on the books (Title 18, Section 952, U.S. Code).

allow a search of the other islands. ONI now decided that it would have to send out its own agents if the secret of the mandated islands was to be uncovered. This decision led to one of the strangest episodes in American intelligence history.

Late in the summer of 1922, Lt. Cmdr. Ellis M. Zacharias, the assistant naval attaché in Tokyo, became interested in the activities of an American salesman who had recently arrived in Yokohama. A heavy drinker, the visitor seemed to have no customers and spent most of his time in the shabbier bars and geisha houses. In his wilder moments, he claimed to be an American secret agent who had been assigned "to find out what the hell was going on" in the mandated islands. Zacharias suspected that the man was under surveillance by Japanese counterintelligence.

Not long after his arrival, the "salesman"collapsed and was taken to the U.S. Naval Hospital in Yokohama, where he was admitted with a kidney ailment. He identified himself as Lt. Col. Earl H. Ellis of the Marines, and said he was touring Japan on leave. Over the next several weeks, Ellis was in and out of the hospital. In September 1922, he was brought in with an acute case of delirium tremens. While he was drying out, he was kept in a private room under the care of Chief Pharmacist Lawrence Zembsch, who functioned more as a keeper than as a nurse. Believing Ellis was too sick to remain in Japan—as well as being a security risk—Captain Lyman A. Cotton, the naval attaché, gave him the choice of returning home immediately by commercial liner or waiting for government transport. Instead, Ellis slipped out of the hospital and vanished.

Improbable as it may have seemed, Ellis actually was on an intelligence mission. One of the Marine Corps' leading strategists, he had enlisted in 1900, fresh out of a Kansas high school, and was commissioned a year later. Following the end of World War I, Ellis became a protégé of General John A. Lejeune, the Marine commandant. The Marine Corps was searching for a new mission, and in 1921 "Pete" Ellis developed operational plans for the seizure of Japanese-held island bases in case of war in the Pacific. Although the disastrous failure of the British landing at Gallipoli in 1915 had convinced strategists that any amphibious assault on a hostile shore would be doomed to defeat, Ellis's operational plans were the model for the victorious island-hopping campaign of World War II.

Developing a strategy for a future campaign was not enough for Ellis. He had to know what the Japanese were doing in the mandated islands and volunteered to make a personal reconnaissance. General Lejeune approved his request with misgivings. While Ellis was a brilliant staff officer, he also had a lengthy history of psychological problems. Periodically, he was hospitalized for "neurasthenia" or "psychasthenia"—

vague terms then used to describe depression and other nervous disorders—and he drank heavily. Alcoholism was not generally recognized as a serious problem at the time, and he was protected by his brother officers. Still, it was obvious that he would be unable to stave off forced retirement much longer, and he probably regarded his mission in the mandated islands as his last chance to prove himself.

Several months after Ellis's disappearance from the Yokohama naval hospital, Captain Cotton was called to the Naval Ministry in Tokyo and told that the missing man had been traced to Koror, an island in the mandated Carolines, and was not expected to live much longer. Cotton requested that Ellis be returned immediately to Japan and was assured that it would be done. Certain that the Japanese were hiding something, Cotton told Zacharias that he didn't expect Ellis "back here alive—ever." Not long afterward, the Americans were informed that Ellis had died and that his body had been cremated. The ashes were at the disposal of the Americans if they wished to claim them.

Hoping to solve both the riddle of Ellis's death and that of the mandated islands, Captain Cotton sent Lawrence Zembsch, who had been the dead man's nurse-keeper, to Koror to retrieve his remains and any papers that could be found. Zembsch was also instructed to keep an eye out for signs that the Japanese were fortifying the island or building naval or air bases. Seven weeks passed before the pharmacist returned, a period of agony for Cotton and Zacharias. They were at the pier when his ship docked and were surprised when there was no sign of him. Going on board, they went to Zembsch's cabin. They were shocked by what they found. Unkempt, unshaven, and obviously deranged, he was huddled in his bunk, clasping a white box of the type used by the Japanese to carry funeral urns.

Zembsch was taken to the naval hospital, where doctors suspected he had been drugged. Under treatment, he showed signs of recovery, but he was killed when an earthquake shattered the building on Sepember 1, 1923. In the years between the wars, the Ellis-Zembsch affair became legend in intelligence circles. It was an article of faith among American intelligence officers that the Japanese had somehow done away with both men to prevent them from revealing the secret of the mandated islands, though this now seems unlikely.* Ellis appears to have died of natural causes and Zembsch was probably a victim of a nervous breakdown

---

*The Japanese had suspected Ellis of being a spy from the moment of his arrival in the mandated islands. Yet they allowed him to roam about freely, making copious notes on the tides and charts of the coral reefs. As to the bases he was seeking, Ellis found only rumor and gossip. The Japanese had no reason to hinder him, for Ellis's own conduct was self-destructive. Haunted by the mythical fortifications and probably convinced that his failure to find them had doomed his career, he drank heavily, aggravating his liver condition. This condition, not the Japanese, apparently caused his death.

caused by the strain of the mission. Ironically, when the islands were captured during World War II, it was discovered that in the 1920s the Japanese had been trying to conceal their weakness, not their strength. No fortifications were erected before 1935; most were built after 1941.

■ ■ ■

Naval intelligence's undeclared war against Japan continued despite the Ellis debacle, but the scene of operations shifted from the Pacific to the United States. Burglary, deception, and wiretapping, all skirting or exceeding legal limitations, were the weapons in this struggle. The tone was set when ONI persuaded a Philadelphia bank to allow its agents to poke about in the financial records of a scrap dealer suspected of selling to the Japanese. Other agents, on the lookout for a Japanese spy supposedly dispatched to steal naval aviation secrets, surreptitiously pilfered documents from the luggage of a visiting Japanese officer. In the process, they mistakenly rifled the baggage of an American college professor as well.

ONI also began intercepting Japanese radio traffic, and listening posts were established around the world. In 1927, Ellis Zacharias secretly monitored Japanese naval radio messages during fleet exercises and opened a monitoring station at Shanghai on the Chinese coast. Eventually a network of radio intercept stations extended clear across the Pacific.

The major targets of ONI's covert activities, however, were Japanese consular and business officers in the United States. Over five successive nights in September 1929, a team headed by Lt. Cmdr. Glenn Howell, the district intelligence officer in New York City, burglarized the offices of the Japanese Inspector of Machinery. They cracked the office safe and photographed code books and secret documents containing valuable information on Japanese aircraft and weaponry. "The grand thing about the whole performance," Howell confided to his diary, "is that they haven't the slightest suspicion that we have this stuff, for they are still using the same old secret code, and of course we are getting first hand information as to what they are saying and planning." A similar raid was made against the offices of the Imperial Japanese Railway in Manhattan.

Howell did not confine his activities to the Japanese. The offices of the pacifist Federal Council of Churches were also burglarized, as were those of the Communist party. Prompted by an investigation of suspected communist subversion of Navy enlisted men, the raid turned into an orgy of vandalism. Files were rifled and strewn about, desks were ransacked, and the safe was forced open. "We even swiped the check books and bank books to create even more trouble," Howell crowed.

With the onslaught of the Great Depression, President Hoover slashed government spending, and the armed forces were forced to trim

manpower, lay up ships, and reduce activities. But ONI's activities continued—and in behalf of the embattled Hoover. As a highly moralistic
Quaker, the president was hardly the type of person to make use of
Howell's freewheeling methods, but battered by personal attacks and
political pressures, he succumbed to the temptation. In 1930, Hoover was
told that a Democratic politico named O'Brien had accumulated information believed to be so damaging that it would destroy his reputation if
released. Despite his usual moralism, Hoover resolved to obtain access to
the files.

The president turned to Louis L. Strauss,* a former private secretary,
for assistance. Strauss, now a partner of Sir William Wiseman in the Wall
Street banking firm of Kuhn, Loeb and a naval reservist with close ties to
ONI, selected Howell for the mission. "Strauss told me that the President
is anxious to know what the contents of the mysterious documents are,"
Howell wrote after a secret meeting with the banker in May 1930. For a
brief moment, however, even the exuberant Howell had second thoughts.
Until now, his clandestine operations had been directed against potential
enemies of the United States; this project involved a burglary for political
purposes. "I am going to tackle it, of course, but it's a devilish awkward
job, and I may very readily find myself in a hell's brew of trouble," Howell
noted.

Foreshadowing the Watergate break-in more than forty years later,*
Howell and a civilian assistant, Robert J. Peterkin, a former New York
City police inspector, staked out O'Brien's office and broke in late one
night. Much to their surprise, the place was empty. The chagrined secret
agents tracked down O'Brien, after shadowing him for a time, they began
to doubt that he could discredit anyone. "I came to the conclusion that no
President of the United States need be afraid of a ham-and-egger like this
O'Brien," Howell said. He informed Lewis Strauss of his findings, and on
June 30, 1930, the project was called off.

The performance of military intelligence during this period, like that
of ONI, was less than brilliant—particularly in its handling of the Bonus
March. World War veterans had been promised a bonus payable in 1945,
but as the economic crisis deepened in 1932, thousands of jobless veterans—dubbed the Bonus Army—descended upon Washington, demanding that Congress approve immediate payment of the bonus. Many
people feared that radicals were behind the movement, and military
intelligence sent corps commanders a coded message: "With reference to
any movement of veteran bonus marchers to Washington originating or

---

*Following World War II, Strauss, who had risen to the rank of admiral in the Naval Reserve,
became chairman of the Atomic Energy Commission.

*Into the offices of another O'Brien—Lawrence F. "Larry" O'Brien, chairman of the Demo-
cratic National Committee.

passing through your corps area, it is desired that a brief radio report in secret code be made to War Department indicating presence, if any, of communistic elements and names of leaders of known communistic leanings."

Most of the reports received were reasonably realistic, if none too astute. The Ninth Corps Area was unable to discover when the Oregon detachment had left Portland, although the event had been reported in the newspapers. Accurate reports were filed, however, of the political views of Royal W. Robertson, the leader of the Californians, and his men. The absence of communists was noted, and Robertson was said to be "firm in stand that [communists] will not be tolerated." But in the adjoining Eighth Corps, paranoia prevailed. Intelligence officers at Fort Sam Houston in Texas were convinced that the Californians were dangerous Reds and that Metro-Goldwyn-Mayer was financing the march on Washington. To ensure that his superiors understood the significance of this information, Colonel James Totten added: "Metro-Goldwyn-Mayer Picture Corporation is known to be 100 per cent Jewish as to controlling personnel, and . . . high officers of the company are in politics. An unconfirmed rumor circulated many months ago stated that agents of the U.S.S.R. had contacted motion picture companies in California and contributed to some of them with a view to inserting propaganda and support of U.S.S.R. policies."

Other reports mentioned machine guns in the hands of the marchers. An intelligence officer in Philadelphia claimed that a Chicago pawnbroker was selling forged discharges for fifty cents. Another reported that Walter W. Waters, the leader of the Bonus Army, had the "assistance of gunmen from New York and Washington . . . [and] that the first blood shed by the Bonus Army in Washington is to be the signal for a communist uprising in all the large cities."*

And blood *was* shed that summer on the streets of Washington. After Congress rejected a bill approving an immediate bonus, the Bonus Army began to melt away, with most of the veterans accepting the offer of free railroad tickets home. A few thousand remained behind, however, most encamped in shacks and tents on the Anacostia mud flats south of the Capitol; they had nowhere else to go. Official Washington grew uneasy. The gates of the White House were chained and the nearby streets cleared. On July 28, federal troops were ordered to disperse squatters at an encampment on lower Pennsylvania Avenue. Resplendent in full uniform and decorations, General Douglas MacArthur, the chief of staff,

*Such reports convinced some observers of the truth of the old Army adage that the brainy go to the engineers, the brave to the infantry, the deaf to the artillery, and the stupid to intelligence. In the Navy, the saying was that there were three kinds of intelligence: human, animal, and naval.

assisted by an aide, Major Dwight D. Eisenhower, took personal charge of the operation.

As a force of some eight hundred troops—cavalry under the command of Major George S. Patton, infantry with bayonets fixed, and a handful of light tanks—approached the disputed area, they were greeted by cheers from the veterans and several thousand spectators. Suddenly, there was a kaleidoscope of violence. Cavalrymen charged into the crowd with drawn sabres; infantrymen hurled tear-gas bombs. Men, women, and children were trampled and choked. Scattering veterans and spectators alike, the troops drove across the bridge to the Anacostia flats, where the camp was set afire. Throughout the night, the Capitol dome was outlined by the glow of flames and the Bonus Army was in full retreat in all directions.

■ ■ ■

Within a few months of the crushing of the Bonus Army, Adolf Hitler was catapulted into power in Germany. The rise of Hitler was accompanied by increasing aggressiveness on the part of his Italian and Japanese allies. Rejecting the Versailles treaty, the Nazis launched a massive rearmament program. Japan, planning the conquest of China, announced that it would no longer be governed by the limitations of the Washington Naval Treaty of 1921, while Italy invaded Ethiopia in defiance of the League of Nations. Once again the world was sliding down the slippery slope to war.

In the United States, espionage activity intensified. Spies infiltrated aircraft factories and naval shipyards, trying to obtain secret data on experimental airplanes and other information. In March 1936, a former U.S. Navy officer named H. T. Thompson was arrested for selling naval secrets to the Japanese. Three months later, another ex-Navy officer, John S. Farnsworth, was convicted on similar charges. There was talk of a spy alliance between Japan and Germany. The Abwehr, the German military intelligence organization, was to supply agents to be employed in areas where Japanese spies would be too conspicuous, and the countries would pool the results. Newspapers warned of sinister Japanese activities in the Panama Canal Zone and along the Mexican border with California. Following U.S. recognition of the Soviet Union in 1933, the Russians actively engaged in espionage in the United States, using Soviet trade and military missions as fronts for their operations, while Soviet naval attachés demanded free access to naval shipyards, ships, bases, and civilian factories producing equipment for the U.S. Navy.

In the White House, President Franklin D. Roosevelt, whose interest in intelligence matters reached back to his service as assistant secretary of the navy during World War I, was alarmed by these signs of widening subversions. On August 24, 1936, he summoned J. Edgar Hoover, head of the Federal Bureau of Investigation, to the Oval Office for a private meeting. Formerly called the Bureau of Investigation, the new FBI boasted a reputation refurbished by Hoover's successful pursuit of such Depression-era desperados as John Dillinger and Pretty Boy Floyd, and the "G-man" had become a popular figure in American folklore. Now Roosevelt had a different mission in mind for Hoover and his agents.

Looking up from the papers on his cluttered desk, Roosevelt waved Hoover to a chair. "I called you over," the president said, "because I want you to do a job for me and it must be confidential."

Roosevelt explained that he wanted to know what the various communist and fascist groups operating within the United States were up to. Wasn't there some way he could obtain a broad picture of these activities?

Hoover later told a friendly chronicler of the FBI's exploits that he replied that the bureau had been out of the counterintelligence business since the Red Scare, and he had no authority to make such inquiries. But he also pointed out that under existing law, the FBI could undertake an investigation if the secretary of state requested the attorney general to authorize it.

Roosevelt was unhappy with this report. He didn't want to work through the State Department, because it was prone to leaks. Finally, the president agreed to approach Secretary of State Cordell Hull informally. To make certain everything was legal, he would place a handwritten memorandum of his request in his personal safe.

The following day, Hoover returned to the Oval Office to meet with the president and the secretary of state. Roosevelt told Hull that he was concerned about the lack of information concerning subversive activities in the United States and that he wanted the FBI to make an inquiry in cooperation with military and naval intelligence and the State Department.

"Edgar says he can do this," the president added, "but the request must come from you to make it legal."

With his white hair and ascetic face, Hull projected a saintly image, but he had the temper and vocabulary of a feuding Tennessee mountaineer.

"Go ahead and investigate the bastards!" he snapped.

12

Enemies Within . . . and Without

Gulls wheeled over the German liner *Bremen* as she eased into her berth on the North River early in October 1937. Standing at the rail, Major Nikolaus Ritter watched the pewter-gray towers of Manhattan loom out of the autumnal mist with satisfaction. In a way, he was returning home. For ten years, Ritter had operated a textile plant in the United States, and he spoke "American" English and enjoyed a wide circle of American friends. Balding and wearing a conservative suit and tie, he could easily pass for an ordinary businessman, but he was now engaged in a more sinister trade. As chief of the aviation section of the Abwehr, Germany's military intelligence organization, he had returned to the United States with a single purpose in mind: to steal the Norden bombsight, the most highly valued secret in the American military arsenal.

On the crowded pier, a customs inspector showed only a perfunctory interest in Ritter's two battered suitcases but was intrigued by his umbrella. It was encased in a wooden sheath and looked like a cane. He asked Ritter to demonstrate how it worked. "A pretty slick gadget for a spy," the inspector said with a grin. Ritter joined in the laughter at this little joke.

Over the next few days, Ritter established his cover as a representative of several German textile firms. Then he began to create a new identity. He checked out of his midtown hotel, made reservations in the name of "Alfred Landing" at a small hotel on Riverside Drive, and mailed letters to "Landing" so he could have them in his pocket to verify his identity. Finally, he rented a safe deposit box and placed his German passport and papers in it. For the time being, Nikolaus Ritter had ceased to exist.

On the second Sunday after his arrival in New York, "Landing" went

221

to the Brooklyn home of Henry Sohn, one of his informants, for a previously arranged meeting with a man known only as "Paul." Four months before, Sohn had sent a routine shipment of documents to the Abwehr office in Hamburg, the branch that controlled espionage in the Western Hemisphere. A set of drawings of a series of squares and circles connected by dotted lines attracted some attention but were laid aside when no sense could be made of them. Later, Sohn advised the Abwehr that the drawings had come from a mysterious fellow who called himself "Paul" and worked in the Norden bombsight factory on Lafayette Street in Manhattan. "Paul," he said, was eager to furnish further information if a special envoy were sent from Germany to deal with him.

The Norden bombsight! The device had already taken on legendary proportions on both sides of the Atlantic. Invented by Carl. L. Norden, a civilian working for the U.S. Navy, the bombsight was said to make it possible to conduct precision bombing from high altitudes. Air power enthusiasts claimed it was so accurate that a bomb could be dropped into a pickle barrel from twenty-five thousand feet. The Luftwaffe, or German air force, had been trying to obtain one for some time. Ritter was immediately dispatched to America to deal with "Paul."

"Paul" was Hermann W. Lang, a soft-spoken 35-year-old machinist and naturalized American. The most ordinary of men, he lived with his wife and daughter in a lower-middle-class suburb on Long Island and seemed to have no interests other than his family and his job as an assembly line inspector at Norden. Yet he became the most successful German secret agent ever to operate in the United States. Why had he become a spy? Lang knew little about Adolf Hitler, did not ask Ritter for money and claimed to find no fault with his adopted country. He provided Ritter with the drawings of the fabled Norden bombsight because he considered himself a German patriot.

One of Lang's duties at Norden was to collect the secret drawings of the bombsight from the other inspectors at the end of the day and place them in a safe. Instead, he took them home. While his wife and child slept, he worked through the night, making tracings in the kitchen. Lang could not provide a complete set of plans, but he assured Ritter that German engineers should be able to work out the missing details.

There was only one problem. The drawings were too large for Ritter or a courier to carry on board the *Bremen* without attracting the attention of American customs agents. Ritter solved the problem by wrapping the drawings around his umbrella and replacing it in its wooden sheath. Following several meetings with Lang, he met with his courier, a steward on the liner, and explained that he wanted the umbrella transported back to Germany. But the courier objected. He had left the ship without an umbrella; if now he returned with one, he would have to show it to the inspectors. He proposed meeting again before the *Bremen* sailed. He would leave the ship with an umbrella that would be checked out when he left the ship. He would then exchange it for Ritter's, since his umbrella would not be inspected again upon his return.

The next day, the courier showed up at Ritter's hotel on Riverside Drive leaning heavily on an old umbrella. "I had to have a reason for carrying this damned thing on such a beautiful sunny day," he explained, "so I told them I had sprained my ankle and had only this umbrella to help me in walking." On October 31, 1937, the plans for the super-secret Norden bombsight limped out of the country.*

■ ■ ■

The theft of the Norden bombsight was the most spectacular German intelligence coup of the Hitler era. For the most part, however, German espionage in the United States was undermined by careless recruiting, inadequate planning, faulty execution, and rivalries among parallel organizations. The Abwehr—headed by Admiral Wilhelm Canaris, an enigmatic figure who had worked in intelligence during World War I—was responsible for military-intelligence gathering, counterespionage, and sabotage.† But it was challenged by the Nazi party's Security Service, generally known as the SD, which was responsible to such leaders as Reinhard Heydrich and Heinrich Himmler. The Foreign Office also had its intelligence-gathering organization, and the navy and Luftwaffe maintained still other offices. Suspicious and jealous of each other, these agencies often intruded upon competing operations and vied among themselves for assets as the Germans hastily assembled an enormous but inefficient global intelligence network.

American fears of widespread spying by German agents were confirmed in 1938 by the breaking of a Nazi spy ring that had been operating in Manhattan. The case began when a postman in Dundee, Scotland, noticed that Jessie Jordan, a middle-aged hairdresser, received a great deal of mail from the United States, France, Holland, Canada, and South America. MI5, the British counterespionage service, was alerted, and a cover was placed upon the lady's mail.

*German engineers managed to build a facsimile of the Norden bombsight but failed to exploit it because of production difficulties. American authorities did not learn about the theft until 1941. Lang received a reward of $3,500, which was credited to an account in his name in Germany.

†A product of the wealthy upper-middle class, Canaris was urbanely cosmopolitan rather than obsessively Aryan and openly contemptuous of Nazism's working-class adherents. On the other hand, he was a supporter of Hitler as a proponent of law and order and an admirer of Francisco Franco, the Spanish dictator. Ultimately Canaris became disillusioned with Hitler. Suspected of having taken part in the July 20, 1944, attempt to assassinate the German dictator, Canaris was hanged by the Nazis just before the war ended. There have been reports that he also slipped information to the British about Hitler's plans to invade England.

It turned out that Jordan was running a mail drop for the Abwehr.* Although the envelopes bore her name and address, the enclosed letters were written to an "N. Spielman," in Bremen, obviously a German spymaster. Several were postmarked in New York City and were from someone who called himself "Crown." MI5 alerted the American military attaché in London, who cabled copies of the letters to MID in Washington. Lacking the resources to launch an investigation of its own, the Army turned the matter over to the FBI, which had been given the authority for such inquiries by President Roosevelt.†

The "Crown" letters revealed that the Nazis were conspiring to steal the plans for the defense of the East Coast, secret codes and maps belonging to the Army Air Corps, and the blueprints of the U.S. Navy's newest aircraft carriers, the *Enterprise* and *Yorktown*. The only clue the FBI had was the name "Crown" typed at the bottom of the letters to "N. Spielman."

These letters were turned over to Leon G. Turrou, an agent in the FBI's New York field office. Turrou was hardly the typical FBI agent. Born in Poland in 1895, he was orphaned at three months and adopted by family friends in the importing business, who took him to Egypt and China. Later, the boy lived in Odessa, London, and Berlin before emigrating to the United States. In 1915, he returned to Europe to enlist in the Czarist army. Following the war, he worked on an anti-Bolshevik Russian-language newspaper in New York and served in the Marines. Next, he was employed as a department store detective and postal service investigator before joining the FBI in 1929. Among other cases, he had worked on the notorious Lindbergh kidnapping-murder.

From the letters Turrou proceeded to construct a profile of "Crown." The German agent lived in New York and was a man of some education, fluent in both German and English. He had served as an officer or noncom in the U.S. Army, was married with at least one child, and was chronically in need of money. With this profile in hand, the hunt was on. But no trace of "Crown" was found. "Every moment we expected the telephone to ring and bring word of a spectacular spy coup," Turrou recalled. "It was a harassing, nerve-racking period."

Turrou got the break he had been praying for when New York City detectives turned over a man who had been arrested on suspicion of

*Jordan was convicted of espionage and sentenced to four years in jail.

†In the year and a half since the chief executive and J. Edgar Hoover had met in the Oval Office, the bureau had handled nearly 650 cases of alleged espionage, in contrast to previous years, when the number of such incidents had averaged about 35. Hoover also flooded the president with daily reports, much of it little more than gossip; the FBI chief never recognized that the essence of good intelligence is the evaluation and interpretation of raw information.

trying to steal some blank passports while posing as a high-ranking official of the State Department. The man, who called himself Gunther Gustav Rumrich, protested vigorously that he had been collared by mistake. The real culprit was a man named Weston, whom he had met at a midtown bar. Weston had promised to pay him for picking up a package; that was all he knew. Through three days of questioning by police, Rumrich stuck to this story. Convinced that he was lying but uncertain what to do with him, the police finally turned the case over to the FBI.

As he sparred with Rumrich, Turrou noted that the suspect fitted the profile of the elusive "Crown." Born in Chicago in 1911, Rumrich was the son of a member of the Austrian consular service. He had been taken home by his family before World War I, but at the age of eighteen he claimed American citizenship and returned to the United States, where he knocked about for a time before joining the Army during the depths of the Depression. Despite an attempt at desertion, he was promoted to sergeant in the Medical Corps fourteen months later. In 1935, while serving in Montana, he married a pretty young farm girl. Instead of settling down, however, he became restless. After embezzling funds from the base hospital, he fled to New York, where he landed a job teaching German at a language school. Eventually he was joined in New York by his wife and a newborn child.

Turrou decided to take a gamble. Without warning, he flung several of the "Crown" letters down on the table in front of Rumrich and shouted: "Stop trying to paint a picture of yourself as a fool. I'll tell you what you are: you're a damned important spy—'Crown!'"

Eyes widening in shock at hearing himself called by his code name, Rumrich leaped from his chair. Then he seemed to collapse. The game was up, and he knew it. "All right, Mr. Turrou," he declared wearily. "Let me see my wife so I can arrange for her to go home to her folks—and I'll talk."

Gunther Rumrich's career as a Nazi spy had begun in the New York Public Library. Browsing through the books on espionage one day early in 1936, he discovered a copy of the memoirs of Colonel Walter Nicolai, the chief of Imperial Germany's military intelligence service during World War I. The book gave him an idea. Why not put his military experience to work and make his fortune by spying for Germany? Lacking Nicolai's address, Rumrich wrote him in care of the *Volkischer Beobachter,* the Nazi party newspaper in Berlin, and offered his services to the Fatherland.* Rumrich claimed to be an officer in the U.S. Army and asked Nicolai to forward his offer to the proper authorities. If they wished to take advantage of his services, a classified advertisement was to be

*In actuality, Nicholai had died in 1934.

inserted in the Public Notices column of *The New York Times*, addressed to "Theodor Koerner."

For the next several weeks, Rumrich anxiously scanned the column, but there was nothing for him. Then, on April 6, 1936, the name "Theodor Koerner" leaped out at him from among the announcements of meetings and pending divorce actions: "Letter received, please send reply and address to Sanders, Hamburg 1, Postbox 629, Germany."

Immediately Rumrich wrote to "Sanders," giving his real name and puffing up his importance. He was anxious to serve Germany, he said. Money was no object, although, of course, there would be expenses.

The ad had been placed by the Hamburg office of the Abwehr. When Rumrich's response was received, he was contacted by Karl Schluter, ostensibly a steward on the liner *Europa* but in reality an Abwehr courier and the top Nazi on the ship. The two men met in one of the German cafes in Yorkville, and Rumrich passed muster. The first tasks assigned him were modest—such as identifying the Army units stationed in the Panama Canal Zone, where he had once served—and his payment was equally modest, a mere forty dollars. Over the next twenty months, however, his assignments increased in importance. He was given the code name "Crown" and instructed to maintain communications with "N. Spielman" through the Scottish mail drop. "Spielman" was a cover for Lt. Cmdr. Erich Pheiffer, the head of the naval section of the Abwehr.

Rumrich found it astonishingly easy to spy in America. There was not even a system for classifying information. When the Germans sought data on the rate of venereal diseases in the U.S. Army, he telephoned Fort Hamilton, claiming to be "Major Milton" of the Medical Corps. He had come up from Washington to deliver a lecture on VD in the Army, he said, but unfortunately he had forgotten his notes. Would the clerk gather the data on the number of officers and men stationed at Fort Hamilton and the number of those who had contracted such diseases and deliver it to him on a street corner in Brooklyn? Quickly assembling the data, the clerk gave it to a private, who took a taxi to the location given by "Major Milton." Rumrich gave him a dollar for the thirty-cent fare and told him to keep the change.

The ease with which "Crown" provided such information whetted the appetite of the Abwehr for more complex intelligence. In November 1937, he was requested to obtain a copy of the signal code used for communication between shore batteries and the fleet offshore. Rumrich got it from Private Erich Glaser, a man he had known in the Canal Zone who was now stationed at Mitchell Field on Long Island. He gave Glaser thirty dollars for the code. Schluter told Rumrich that "Spielman" wanted blank American passports for agents being sent into Russia. A special price tag of one thousand dollars had been placed on the operation. A thousand dollars! This was the biggest prize ever dangled before Rumrich, and he determined to win it. Instead, he blew the lid off German espionage operations in America.

■ ■ ■

The next time the *Europa* docked in New York, Turrou was there to meet it. Hoping to arrest both Karl Schluter and Johanna Hofmann, a pretty young hairdresser in the beauty salon whom Rumrich had identified as Schluter's assistant, Turrou found that Schluter had not made the trip. Hofmann, however, was taken into custody. Badly frightened, she confessed to being a Nazi courier after a bundle of letters in code was found among her effects. She decoded the letters for the FBI, named other members of the spy ring, and identified a prominent Yorkville physician, Dr. Ignatz T. Griebl, as the head of German espionage operations in America.

Pudgy and bespectacled, Dr. Griebl was the picture of injured innocence. After serving as an artillery officer in the German army during World War I, he had come to the United States in 1925 and obtained his medical degree. Following the rise of Hitler, he became a leader of the Nazi movement in America and was often seen in the company of Fritz Kuhn, the fuehrer of the German-American Bund. But, Griebl pointed out to Turrou, he was also a patriotic American citizen; why, he even held a commission in the U.S. Army Reserve. Confronted by Johanna Hofmann, who accused him of spying, he unleashed a torrent of obscenities at her, but continued to maintain that the charges were ridiculous.

Griebl's composure faded when Turrou discovered a matchbook cover in his office bearing the same code used by the hairdresser. Layer by layer, his explanations were peeled away. Finally Griebl admitted his guilt. Unveiling the entire pattern of Nazi spy activities in the United States, Griebl claimed to have agents in several airplane plants and naval shipyards who supplied him with information on experimental aircraft as well as on a new class of destroyers.

In all, the cracking of the Griebl ring led to the indictment of eighteen persons on charges of spying for Germany. Most were in Germany, where they could not be prosecuted—among them, Lonkowski, Schluter, and Commander Pheiffer, or "N. Spielman." Dr. Griebl, too, was out of reach. Much to Turrou's anger, the spymaster had been released on bail following his interrogation. Evading FBI surveillance, he jumped bail and fled the country on the *Bremen*. In the end, only four persons were actually brought to trial: Rumrich and Erich Glaser, who were each sentenced to two years in federal penitentiary; Johanna

Hofmann, who received four years; and another spy, Otto H. Voss, who got six.

■ ■ ■

The Rumrich trial created a sensation. It confirmed the worst fears of many Americans that the nation was honeycombed with Nazi agents and emphasized the expanding threat of the dictators to the United States. Indirectly, the case also reveals the depth of American ignorance about Nazi intelligence operations. In a book Leon Turrou wrote after leaving the FBI,* he confused the Abwehr with the Gestapo and called it the "National Geheim Abwehr," which he said was headed by a "Colonel Busch." Moreover, the escape of so many of the defendants reopened the long-running debate over the need for improved coordination of the various intelligence services.

Indeed, the thread that runs through the history of U.S. intelligence in the years leading up to American entry into World War II is the attempt to bring order to the intelligence community. Warning that appeasement and neutrality would be no defense against aggression, President Roosevelt had ordered a buildup of the nation's armed forces, particularly the Navy. But the approach of war found American intelligence woefully unprepared for a global conflict. MID's entire staff in Washington consisted of just sixty-six people, including stenographers and clerks, and there were only a handful of attachés. ONI was in equally poor shape. "A real undercover foreign intelligence service, equipped and able to carry on espionage, counterespionage, etc. does not exist," observed Rear Admiral Walter S. Andrews, the director of naval intelligence.

One of the most significant intelligence failures of the interwar period was ONI's inability to pierce the veil of secrecy surrounding the construction of two new Japanese battleships, the *Yamato* and *Musashi*, which were laid down in the late 1930s after Japan renounced the limitations imposed by the Washington Naval Treaty. When rumors that the Japanese were building super-battleships appeared in the Italian press, ONI asked Lieutenant Edwin T. Layton, the assistant naval attaché in Tokyo, to make inquiries. The Japanese reply was a masterpiece of doubletalk: the Navy Ministry said it would not comment on "speculation in the Italian press over matters of no concern to the Italians." Layton was advised by his superiors to discontinue the inquiries, and the Navy remained in the dark about the super-ships. At 68,200 tons, they were the largest battleships ever built and were armed with 18.1-inch guns that completely outclassed the 16-inch weapon mounted on the new American capital ships, which were built within the treaty limitations. ONI also failed to produce data on the Imperial Navy's extremely effective

---

*The book, *Nazi Spies in America,* was a best-seller and was made into a popular movie as *Confessions of a Nazi Spy.*

"Long-lance" torpedoes as well as on the Zero fighter.

Apart from the sheer inadequacy of American intelligence efforts, Roosevelt was deeply troubled by the snarled lines of responsibility in the intelligence community. As if to underscore the need to rationalize intelligence operations, the president's efforts to coordinate the fight against subversion touched off a major bureaucratic row. Late in 1938, Roosevelt had approved a $50,000 appropriation for the FBI—increased by Congress to $300,000—to expand its counterintelligence operations. Since no other nonmilitary organization had received similar funds, J. Edgar Hoover regarded his agency as having primacy over the other civilian organizations. He worked out arrangements to exchange information with ONI and MID, but the State Department, the Treasury, and the Post Office refused to relinquish their intelligence roles. Hoover, one of the most accomplished bureaucratic infighters in Washington, took his case directly to the White House.

President Roosevelt needed little encouragement to intervene. Hitler had already absorbed Austria and Czechoslovakia and was now making demands on Poland. Italy had invaded Albania, while the Japanese had proclaimed a "Greater East Asia Co-Prosperity Sphere" in the Far East. With the Axis powers on the move, Roosevelt regarded the situation as too perilous to permit prolonged bickering over the control of counterintelligence. On June 26, 1939, the president issued a confidential directive intended to resolve the jurisdictional squabbling by placing "all espionage, counterespionage, and sabotage matters" in the hands of the FBI, MID, and ONI. He followed up this order with more funding for intelligence and gave the FBI authority to carry out counterintelligence and security operations against Axis agents in Latin America, generally regarded as the nation's soft underbelly.*

These moves came none too soon. War became a certainty after Hitler and Soviet premier Josef Stalin—who for years had bitterly denounced each other—stunned the world by signing their infamous nonaggression pact on August 23, 1939.† Secret clauses in the treaty divided Eastern Europe between Germany and the Soviet Union. Having isolated

---

*American military planners were haunted by the possibility of German subversion in Latin America. Upon being warned by the British in 1940 that the Nazis had sent six thousand men to Brazil to join Fascist elements in the country in overthrowing the pro-American regime of Getulio Vargas, FDR directed the chief of naval operations to devise plans for "de-establishing" any Fascist government that might be established. The resulting operational plan, Pot of Gold, called for moving ten thousand troops to Brazil by air, to be followed by one hundred thousand men to be transported by sea. In reality, however, the United States lacked the trained manpower for such an effort, and the Navy could not have moved the troops or their equipment. See Watson, *The United States Army in World War II*, pp. 94–97 (Bibliography).

†The United States was warned of the forthcoming pact by an anti-Nazi German diplomat in Moscow, but Washington did not pass these warnings on to the British and French. See Bohlen, *Witness to History*, chapter 5.

Poland, the Nazis geared up a campaign of propaganda and faked frontier incidents in preparation for an attack. The White House went on a permanent emergency routine, and Army and Navy intelligence officers began daily briefings of the president that lasted throughout the war. On September 1, 1939, German tanks knifed into Poland with Stuka dive bombers blasting the way. Two days later, Britain and France declared war.

■ ■ ■

Communications intelligence—particularly the War Department's top secret Signal Intelligence Service (SIS)—was one of the first beneficiaries of the emphasis on improved intelligence that accompanied the approach of war. The increasing reliance on radio communications by armed forces and other branches of government had provided new opportunities for gaining reliable information by listening in on this traffic. Intercept stations using sophisticated radio direction-finding and communications equipment were established, and more money and personnel were channeled to the codebreakers at SIS.

Under William F. Friedman, the Army's chief cryptanalyst, this organization had taken up where Herbert Yardley's Black Chamber had left off, but its work was infinitely more difficult. Over the years, intelligence gathering had undergone a revolution. A variety of electromechanical enciphering systems had been introduced, most of them—such as the German Enigma machine—using multiple rotors that produced ciphers and codes of far greater complexity than any dreamed of before. The new machines could generate more combinations of letters and numbers than the human mind could track. To make the cryptanalyst's task even more difficult, the machine's opposite number had to be properly set to unscramble a message. In every country, security was so tight that each government agency—diplomatic, army, and navy—had its own ciphering system, which usually could not be read by the other services.

The Japanese Foreign Office had been developing new ciphers ever since Yardley had disclosed that its codes had been broken. Early in 1939, Friedman observed that the Foreign Office had adopted a complicated new cipher for its most secret communications with embassies abroad. The Japanese called the machine that produced this cipher the Alphabetical Typewriter 97; the Americans dubbed it "Purple." Friedman immediately made breaking the Purple cipher his top priority, but the task looked hopeless.

Purple used two typewriters connected by a plugboard from which a complex system of electrical wires ran into each machine. Unlike Enigma,* which used rotors in its enciphering system, Purple worked

*Most writers have stated erroneously, that the Purple machine was a direct derivative of Enigma.

like a telephone switchboard, using switches to shuffle arrangements of letters and numbers. As a code clerk typed the plaintext on one typewriter, the second typewriter automatically transformed it into cipher. Plaintext was obtained by reversing the process. The Japanese considered the new cipher unbreakable, because anyone trying to fathom it would have to build a Purple machine to duplicate the astronomical number of electrically guided combinations.

William Friedman had been devising and unraveling codes and ciphers with dazzling success since World War I. Born in Russia in 1891, Friedman was the son of a Jewish translator employed in the Czarist postal system. The family emigrated to the United States and settled in Pittsburgh, where Friedman's father sold sewing machines while his son attended the public schools. Caught up in a "back-to-the-land" movement that excited many young Americans, Friedman enrolled at the Michigan Agricultural College, the chief attraction of which was that it was free. The young man soon discovered that farming held little interest for him. Upon learning that tuition was also free for students of genetics at Cornell, he switched schools and courses.

After his graduation in 1915, Friedman was hired by "Colonel" George Fabyan, a rich eccentric who maintained laboratories in acoustics, chemistry, and genetics on his estate, Riverbank, near Geneva, Illinois. Originally employed to improve the farm's strains of grain and livestock, Friedman soon became involved in another of Fabyan's projects: an attempt to prove through clues hidden in the texts of Shakespeare's plays that they had been written by Francis Bacon. His newfound interest in cryptology was matched only by his interest in one of the cryptologists, a young woman named Elizabeth Smith. Married in May 1917, they became the most famous husband-and-wife team in the history of cryptology.

As the only established cryptology operation in the country, Riverbank was pressed into service by various government agencies when the United States entered World War I. The most important case handled by Friedman involved a group of Hindus who were seeking German aid for a revolt against British control of India. He quickly solved the number code used by the Indians to communicate with Berlin, and his testimony led to their conviction. Both Friedmans were subsequently brought to Washington to work for the War Department, and William ended up serving overseas on General Pershing's staff.

Between the wars, Friedman was chief of the Signal Intelligence Service, where he recruited a team from scholars in such areas as mathematics and linguistics to be trained as codebreakers. At the same time, Elizabeth worked as a cryptanalyst for the Coast Goard, solving the codes of Prohibition-era rumrunners. Brilliant but insecure—jealous of his prerogatives, insistent about being addressed always as "Mister Friedman," natty in coat and tie—William Friedman became the nation's premier crytanalyst. One day, along with three subordinates, he solved between 11:12 A.M. and 2:43 P.M., with fifty minutes out for lunch, a cryptogram touted as unbreakable.

For eighteen months, Friedman and a team of assistants struggled to clone the Purple machine. Working from intercepted messages, they tried to discover some pattern in the jumble of enciphered letters that would allow them to puzzle out the laws behind these patterns. Hour after hour, day after day, they endured the mental torture of seeing solutions appear, only to fade away. Friedman could not eat and spent much of the night pacing the floor. He could not discuss his problems with his wife, for the project was veiled in secrecy. One of his associates likened this period to being "engulfed in an interminable polar night."

Finally, in August 1940, Friedman and his team produced a crude contraption consisting of a hodgepodge of multicolored wires, switches, and contacts that sometimes emitted clouds of sparks. Without ever having seen the original, they had accomplished the seemingly impossible feat of constructing a working replica of the Purple machine. Not long afterward, Friedman suffered a nervous collapse as a result of the agonizing pressure. For the rest of his life—he died in 1969—he was not allowed to work more than a few hours at a time. But in a burst of furious energy, Friedman and his colleagues had forged a mighty weapon for America's arsenal.

In a rare display of interservice cooperation, the Navy's cryptanalytic and radio traffic service—the Communications Security Unit, or OP-20-G,* headed by Commander Lawrence F. Stafford—assisted the Army in making the breakthrough. The Navy unit took over all other decoding work in order to free Friedman's team for the attack on Purple, supplied money, and helped build four additional Purple machines, receiving one for its own use. The Navy's network of radio intercept stations—spreading from the Aleutians to Hawaii, Samoa, Guam, and the Philippines—provided the raw material for the decrypters. To avoid duplication of effort, intercepts were divided by date of origin in Tokyo, with the Army doing the decrypting and translating from the Japanese into English on the even days and the Navy taking the odd days.

The decrypted intercepts were known as MAGIC and were closely held. Recognizing that the penetration of Japan's most secret diplomatic code would last only as long as the Japanese were unaware that their mail was being read, General George C. Marshall, the Army's chief of staff, drew up a "Top List" that limited distribution of MAGIC to the president, the secretaries of state, war, and navy, and a handful of top-ranking Army

---

*OP-20 stood for the 20th division of the Office of the Chief of Naval Operations; the "G" was for the Office of Naval Communications. ONI was OP-16.

and Navy officers. Despite several scares, the Japanese never did discover that Purple had been broken. In its pride of accomplishment, the Foreign Office continued to believe that the cipher produced by Alphabetical Typewriter 97 was impregnable.

■ ■ ■

Not long after the outbreak of war in Europe, a German-American aircraft mechanic named William G. Sebold opened a firm called Diesel Research Company in the Knickerbocker Building at Broadway and 42nd Street in Manhattan. Although the firm seemed to do little business and Sebold spent much of his time at a house in Centerport, near the tip of Long Island, he never appeared to have money problems. In reality, he was a German spy—codenamed "Tramp"—and the Diesel Research Company was his cover. The Centerport house was the site of a radio transmitter. Undeterred by the blowing of the Griebl apparatus, the Abwehr had established a new spy network in the United States, which was already a major source of supplies for the Allies.

Sebold, whose real name was Debowski, had jumped ship in Galveston in 1923 after serving in the German army during World War I. Drifting west, he had married, become an American citizen, and taken a job with the Consolidated Aircraft Corporation in San Diego. Early in 1939, he returned to his home in Mühlheim, an industrial city in the Ruhr, to visit his mother and to convalesce from an ulcer operation. Not long afterward, "Herr Debowski" received a letter from the Gestapo instructing him to appear at its office in nearby Düsseldorf.

Protected by his American passport, Sebold ignored the summons. But the letter that followed alarmed him. The Gestapo had discovered that he had been imprisoned in Germany on smuggling charges before leaving the country, a fact he had concealed in applying for American citizenship. If he did not cooperate, Washington would be informed, and he would be stripped of his citizenship for lying about his criminal record on his application. A Gestapo officer issued an ultimatum: Either return to America as a German spy or be sent to a concentration camp after the Americans lifted his citizenship. "I accepted his proposition one hundred percent after that," Sebold later recalled.

Sebold was turned over to a "Dr. Rankin" from Abwehr headquarters in Hamburg—actually Nikolaus Ritter—who was engaged in establishing a series of radio transmitting stations in the United States. Assured by the Gestapo that Sebold was a volunteer and had been checked out, Ritter arranged for him to attend a spy school in Hamburg.

"How long will that take?" asked Sebold.

"Well," replied Ritter, "maybe three or four months."

Sebold objected. He had been planning to return to the United States much sooner. If he was going to be away that long, he had better make arrangements to send his wife some money. Ritter assured him that the matter could be taken care of, but Sebold insisted on handling everything himself: "I think I'd better do it through the American Consul in Cologne. That way we'll avoid all suspicions."

At the spy school, Sebold proved an apt pupil. Within seven weeks, he had learned coding and decoding, the use of secret inks, how to make microfilms, and how to operate shortwave transmitters. Before leaving for the United States, he was given a thousand dollars in cash and told that another five thousand had been deposited to his credit in a Mexican bank. He left Germany supplied with the names and addresses of the "collectors" he was to contact upon reaching New York. For the most part, his job would be to radio the intelligence they gathered to Hamburg or to microfilm it for transmission through the mails.

Hermann Lang, who had supplied Ritter with the plans of the Norden bombsight, was among the agents who brought information to Sebold's office in midtown Manhattan. The others included Lilly Stein, a Viennese-born artist's model who recruited agents and served as a cutout, or go-between for couriers; Everett M. Roeder, a draftsman at the Sperry Instrument plant who had access to the firm's famed gyroscope; and Frederick Joubert Duquesne, a swashbuckling Boer who harbored an insatiable hatred of the British and who had served as a German spy in World War I.

Early in 1940, Sebold began transmitting the information supplied by these operatives to Hamburg. His code was based upon the best-selling novel *All This and Heaven, Too.* The numbers of the day and month the message was being sent were totaled, and twenty was added to the sum. The resulting figure indicated the page of the book on which the message was based; other information picked out the exact words. One of the ring's major coups was the discovery that the United States had given Britain access to the Norden bombsight. Another was the revelation that President Roosevelt had secretly inspected the British battleship *King George V* not long after it arrived off Annapolis with a new ambassador on board.

The Germans broke a fundamental rule of intelligence operations, however, by failing to keep their parallel organizations separate. "Tramp" operated so reliably that other Abwehr officers and those of the rival S.D. instructed their agents to transmit their messages through him. As a result, Sebold had contact with many of the German operatives at work in the United States. They included a mechanic employed on the New York piers, an ironworker in a ship repair yard, a clerk in a steamship office, and a chef on the liner *America,* who passed on the blueprints for converting the vessel into a troopship should the United States enter the war. Hardly a ship entered or left the Port of New York without escaping the scrutiny of German agents. The agents passed on information of great value to U-boat skippers lying offshore in wait for prey. All together, Sebold's operation transmitted more than three hundred messages to his employers.

Suddenly, the entire operation collapsed. On June 29, 1941, the FBI swept up all the major and minor members of the ring in a series of lightning raids that J. Edgar Hoover proudly called "the greatest spy roundup" in American history. To the chagrin of the Abwehr, the subsequent trials revealed that Sebold had been working with the FBI all along. He had tipped off American officials that he was being blackmailed into becoming a German spy during his visit to the U.S. consulate in Cologne. Instructing him to play along, the FBI had placed him under surveillance the moment he had arrived in New York City.

German agents who visited Sebold in his Manhattan office were secretly filmed by the FBI from behind a one-way mirror. The room was arranged so that a clock and a calendar were visible in the photographs to document the time and date of each meeting, while hidden microphones recorded every word spoken. Government agents examined each bit of data to be sent to Hamburg to make certain it was only of minor importance or to alter it if it was potentially damaging. They even built and operated the radio station at Centerport after learning to imitate "Tramp's" touch on the Morse key.

In contrast to the Griebl case, everyone arrested in the Sebold raids was convicted and given substantial jail terms. German espionage in the United States never recovered from the blow. Although Nazi spy rings continued to operate in the period before Pearl Harbor, they accomplished little. Few were unknown to the FBI. "It was like shooting fish in a barrel," said one FBI agent.

■ ■ ■

The Sebold case unfolded against a background of Nazi triumphs in Europe that stunned the American people. Without warning, Hitler occupied Denmark and Norway shortly after "Tramp" arrived in the United States. Belgium, Holland, and France were crushed by the German blitzkreig in the summer of 1940, and Britain stood alone against the Nazi fury. The nation's sense of vulnerability was heightened by wild tales of the effectiveness of German fifth columns operating behind enemy lines. In reality, subversive activities had played only a minor role in the Nazi triumph, but many people accepted these reports as gospel, and there were urgent demands for similar activities against the Germans.

Realizing the danger a Hitler victory posed to the United States, Franklin Roosevelt dropped all pretense of neutrality. In the months ahead, he expanded his executive authority—sometimes stretching legal limits—to support the beleaguered British. This decision was taken at a time when his own reelection to an unprecedented third term was far from certain and isolationists were charging him with surreptitiously leading the country into war.

Roosevelt had always sought information outside official channels. Now he spread his personal intelligence net even wider. "Roosevelt delighted in ignoring departmental procedures, preferring to work informally through men chosen by him and responsible directly to him," explained Robert Murphy, a diplomat who was often asked by the president to undertake secret missions. The presidential informants ranged from Bernard Baruch to Marine Captain Evans F. Carlson, the assistant naval attaché in China. Well-known public figures who were unlikely to be suspected of spying were also requested to secretly gather information. Novelist John Steinbeck was among them, reporting back to the president on what he saw and heard in Mexico, where he was working on a book. Through such observers, Roosevelt picked up intimate details about personalities and events that would never have reached him through official channels.

One of the major reasons the president turned to outside sources of intelligence was his distrust of the State Department. Like some future presidents, he saw the department as rigid in its thinking, prone to leaks, and instinctively opposed to his policies. For example, Joseph P. Kennedy, the American envoy to London, doubted Britain's ability to withstand Hitler. The State Department was also poorly equipped to provide intelligence. "Techniques for gathering information differed only by reason of the typewriter and the telegraph from the techniques which John Quincy Adams used in St. Petersburg and Benjamin Franklin was using in Paris," observed Dean G. Acheson, a future secretary of state. Often *The New York Times* was a better source of foreign intelligence. The president also distrusted the State Department's notoriously unreliable Gray Code, which, in fact, was being read with ease by the Germans.*

Roosevelt had good reason to be wary of regular diplomatic channels, as the case of Tyler G. Kent proved. Kent, a young cipher clerk in the American embassy in London, had strong isolationist and anti-Semitic views. A secret exchange of messages between the president and Winston S. Churchill, then the First Lord of the Admiralty, led him to fear that Roosevelt was conniving with Churchill to bring the United States into the war. Thinking it his duty to warn the U.S. Senate of the danger, Kent made copies of the correspondence between the two leaders.

In the meantime, MI5 discovered that the German ambassador to Italy was providing Hitler with copies of messages from the files of the U.S. embassy in London, including the highly sensitive Roosevelt-

---

*The Gray Code was so compromised that in the 1920s the American consul in Shanghai made his retirement speech before the entire diplomatic community in Gray.

Churchill messages. These documents were traced to the Italian naval attaché, who had received them from a White Russian woman named Anna Wolkoff. The woman was placed under surveillance, and Tyler Kent was discovered to be consorting with her. With the consent of Ambassador Kennedy, Kent's diplomatic immunity was lifted and he was arrested by the British on May 20, 1940, ten days after Churchill became prime minister. British intelligence searched Kent's flat and discovered some 1500 confidential messages, including some of the exchanges between Roosevelt and Churchill. Kent was tried under the Official Secrets Act on charges of "obtaining information for a purpose prejudicial to the safety or interests of the state" and sentenced to prison for seven years.*

Early in 1941, Roosevelt established an irregular intelligence and research operation in the White House under the direction of John Franklin Carter, who wrote a pro-administration syndicated column under the name of Jay Franklin. Carter's journalistic cover made it easy for him to come and go at the White House without arousing suspicion, and he also had connections with American corporate executives who could provide information about conditions in Axis countries where they had plants and offices. Roosevelt financed Carter's operation with secret funds, and ultimately the journalist deployed a staff of more than a hundred people working completely outside established intelligence channels.

Carter investigated everything from the loyalty of key government employees to a Nazi fifth column supposedly based on the French Caribbean island of Martinique. He roamed the West Coast in search of signs of a potential uprising among Japanese-Americans in case of war with Japan and studied population trends in the Middle East. Among his confidential sources was Ernst "Putzi" Hanfstaengel, Hitler's Harvard-educated, one-time court jester, who had fled Germany. Some of Carter's reports were unintentionally comic, such as the breathless revelation that the Nazis were behind incidents in South Africa in which "foul-breathed women" spat at British soldiers. In all, he prepared 660 reports for the president before 1945 and directed several secret studies.

Roosevelt's most intimate confidential agent, however, was Vincent Astor, a Dutchess County neighbor and distant cousin.* A commander in the naval reserve and an intelligence buff, Astor became close friends with Roosevelt in the 1920s when he invited his cousin to exercise his

---

*Isolationists later constructed a conspiracy on the Tyler Kent affair. They charged that Kent was arrested as a matter of political expediency and tried in secret and news of his case was suppressed until 1944 to hide Roosevelt's dealings with Churchill. In fact, reports of his arrest and sentence were published in the British press in 1940.

*Roosevelt's older half-brother, James Roosevelt, had married Helen Astor, daughter of *the* Mrs. Astor.

polio-damaged legs in the heated indoor pool on the Astor estate at Rhinebeck, a few miles north of the Roosevelt home at Hyde Park. Later, he became an important contributor to Roosevelt's political campaign chest and placed his luxurious motor yacht, the *Nourmahal,* at the president's disposal for deep-sea fishing expeditions. Often, they were accompanied by Kermit Roosevelt,[†] second son of Theodore Roosevelt, and others of the same social set, who were bound together by ties to a curious organization called the "ROOM."

Formed in 1927 by Astor, Kermit Roosevelt, and Kermit's older brother, Theodore, Jr., this group was composed of about twenty wealthy and well-connected men, including banker Winthrop Aldrich, Marshall Field III, David Bruce (a future ambassador to London and Peking), and C. Suydam Cutting, a well-known explorer. Some were intelligence veterans and had current contacts. The president was not a member of ROOM, but he knew most of the members from their cruises together on the *Nourmahal.* Undoubtedly Astor and Kermit Roosevelt offered ROOM's services to the president as a private intelligence network.

Astor, who maintained close ties with ONI, was a valued presidential informant. Under the guise of a Pacific cruise, he sailed his yacht among the Japanese-mandated Marshall Islands in 1938 to gather information on docks, fuel stocks, and air strips on Eniwetok and Wotje. Following the outbreak of war in Europe, he provided the president with inside information on the intelligence activities of belligerents and neutrals in the United States. Using his position as a director of Western Union, he ordered intercepts of cable traffic sent by Axis agents to Latin America. Winthrop Aldrich, a fellow ROOM member and a director of the Chase National Bank, supplied him with data on the account of Amtorg, the Soviet trading company and espionage front. Other members—all equally pro-British through family, social, and business ties—sat on the boards of important banks and companies and provided similar information, which Astor then funneled to the president. "Espionage and sabotage need money," he observed, "and that has to pass through the banks at one stage or another."

Backed by the White House—the president informed ONI that he wanted Astor to coordinate intelligence activities in the New York area— the amateur intelligence chief rapidly expanded his operations. Early in 1940, Astor made contact with William S. Stephenson, the shrewd and resourceful Canadian head of the British Security Coordination in New York City, the hub of British intelligence activities in the Western Hemisphere. Together, Astor and Stephenson blocked an attempt by the pro-

†Kermit Roosevelt was the only member of the Oyster Bay branch of the family close to FDR. The others regarded him as a usurper trading on Theodore Roosevelt's name and fame.

German Vichy government of France to establish a powerful radio station on the island of St. Pierre, off Newfoundland, that would have enabled Axis agents to bypass British monitors. With the permission of British officials, Astor also engaged in such clandestine activities as ransacking diplomatic pouches belonging to neutrals as they passed through Bermuda.

But Astor's star dimmed as quickly as it had flared into prominence. Rivalry, intrigue, and jealousy on the part of the established intelligence agencies clouded his efforts at coordination, and he also fell victim to Roosevelt's mercurial personality. The president bestowed his favor with notorious fickleness, and like so many others, Astor was dropped from the charmed circle without even knowing why he had fallen from favor. As his banner fell, it was replaced by that of William J. Donovan.

■ ■ ■

Bold, adventurous, and unpredictable are words commonly used to describe "Wild Bill" Donovan. Throwing off ideas like a human pinwheel—some good, others wildly impractical—he became the most significant figure in the history of American intelligence since Ralph Van Deman and cast the intelligence establishment in his own image. Fittingly enough, his portrait hangs in the entrance hall of Central Intelligence Agency headquarters. William Casey, a Donovan protégé and later CIA director, wanted to replace the statue of Nathan Hale outside the building with one of Donovan.

Donovan seemed an unlikely choice as President Roosevelt's confidential agent. As an unreconstructed Republican from upstate New York, he had fought the New Deal; as an Irish-Catholic, he should have been suspect to the British, who were still smarting from the defeatism of Ambassador Kennedy. But Donovan was a special man for a special job. Fifty-seven years old, with silvery hair and a silky charm, he was a much-decorated war hero and a millionaire Wall Street lawyer with global connections. He and Roosevelt had been classmates at Columbia Law School, though the ties between them were hardly as close as the president would pretend when he spoke of "my old friend and classmate, Bill Donovan." They were brothers under the skin, however. Both were activists who were convinced that America could accomplish anything—a legacy of growing up in the ebullient shadow of Theodore Roosevelt.

Donovan picked up the name "Wild Bill" while serving with General Pershing's punitive expedition to Mexico in 1916. Reportedly, when some of his men complained about a long march, their captain replied: "Look at me. I'm not even panting. If I can take it, you can." From the rear rank came a plaintive cry. "We ain't as wild as you, Bill." Donovan liked the name, and it stuck. Later he served in France as a lieutenant colonel in the Sixty-ninth Regiment—the "Fighting Irish." Thrice wounded, he was the only World War I soldier to be awarded the Medal of Honor, the Distinguished Service Cross, and the Distinguished Service Medal.

Although Donovan harbored political ambitions—perhaps to become the nation's first Catholic president—the interwar years brought disappointment. In 1922 he was defeated in his political debut, as the Republican candidate for lieutenant governor of New York; ten years later he would lose again when he ran for governor. Nevertheless, public service beckoned, and in 1924 Donovan went to Washington to become assistant attorney general in charge of the Criminal Division of the Department of Justice. One of his subordinates was J. Edgar Hoover, newly promoted to head the FBI—in later years, a bitter bureaucratic rival.

In the summer of 1928, Donovan served as acting attorney general. Everyone expected him to be named to the post permanently by his good friend, Herbert Hoover, who was elected to the presidency later that year. But Hoover never made the appointment. (Some observers attribute his reluctance to the distaste of the Republican hierarchy for the idea of a Catholic in the cabinet.) The failure to be named attorney general, Donovan's wife, Rose, acknowledged many years later, was "the greatest disappointment in his life."

Picking up the pieces of his shattered ambition, Donovan established a prosperous Wall Street law firm. Yet so adventurous a spirit could scarcely rest content with a stuffy corporate practice. Periodically, he left the office in the hands of his partners and toured the battlefronts of the Italian-Ethiopian conflict and the Spanish Civil War. He attended German army maneuvers, inspected the defenses of France and Britain, and kept a watchful eye on the advance of totalitarianism. Many of his clients were opposed to the New Deal, but when war broke out, Donovan's views on foreign policy coincided with those of the President. He urged American preparedness and argued against giving foreign nations "the impression that under no circumstances will we fight. . . . In an age of bullies, we cannot afford to be a sissy."

Donovan was drawn into the presidential orbit by Roosevelt's need for bipartisan support. In June 1940, the president moved to outflank the isolationists by naming Henry L. Stimson secretary of war and Frank Knox secretary of the navy. Both men were Republican elders, who supported all-out aid to the British. Stimson had been secretary of state under Hoover, and Knox was the GOP's vice-presidential nominee in 1936. Immediately upon assuming office, Knox suggested to the president that Donovan be sent to examine how the British dealt with the fifth-column menace and to make a general appraisal of their ability to withstand the Nazis. Undoubtedly, Donovan's high spirits and fertile imagination appealed to Roosevelt, and Wild Bill's career as a confidential presidential agent was launched.

The British rolled out the red carpet for Donovan. He was introduced to King George VI, had several conversations with Churchill, and asked "a million questions." Wherever he went, he saw well-equipped and well-trained troops ready to repel an invasion—all an elaborate deception carefully arranged to persuade him that the British possessed not only the will but the means to fight on. The British warily did not make Donovan privy to ULTRA, the super-secret deciphering operation at Bletchley Park that was just beginning to unravel the mysteries of the German Enigma machine.* Donovan returned home optimistic about Britain's chances of beating off the German attack if given logistical support by the United States. The colonel's report helped convince the hesitant Roosevelt to go along with Churchill's request for the loan of fifty World War I vintage destroyers to combat the increased threat of the U-boats now that the Germans controlled the coasts of Norway and France.

In December 1940, Donovan was on another confidential mission for the president, this one to the Mediterranean and the Balkans. On the first leg of the trip, he was accompanied by William Stephenson. "There is no doubt we can achieve infinitely more through Donovan than through any other individual," Stephenson told his superiors. "He is very receptive . . . and can be trusted to represent our needs in the right quarters."

Both Donovan and Stephenson were men of action, and they became good friends. As a World War I fighter pilot, the Canadian had destroyed several enemy planes, won the amateur lightweight world championship in boxing, and escaped from a German prison camp after being shot down, swiping the camp commander's favorite photograph of himself as a souvenir. After the war, Stephenson invented an improved technique for transmitting pictures by radio and was a millionaire before he was thirty. Upon this base he built an industrial empire—and, through his interest in German steel production, had an insider's look at Hitler's preparations for war. In the late 1930s, he supplied Churchill, who was then engaged in the Cassandra-like task of warning the world of the dangers of Nazism, with detailed information on German rearmament.

Shortly before the fall of France, Churchill sent Stephenson to New York—first under the cover of British Passport Control Officer and then as head of British Security Coordination—to carry out what were euphemistically called "special operations."* Using the code name "Intrepid," Stephenson directed a wide-ranging intelligence apparatus from Room

*The Americans were not let in on the secret of ULTRA until February 1941.

*The word "special" continues to be a giveaway from clandestine operations when used by a government agency.

3603 of the RCA Building in Rockefeller Center. Like Sir William Wiseman in World War I, he presided over anti-sabotage and counterintelligence operations as well as propaganda activities designed to influence American public opinion. Stephenson's business contacts, easy personality, and remarkable capacity for dry martinis won him a broad range of contacts, and he maintained a friendly working relationship with American officials. Fear of the ubiquitous Nazi fifth column made U.S. officials eager to cooperate with the British. The FBI had enjoyed a close peacetime liaison with MI5, and J. Edgar Hoover was perfectly aware of the true function of the Passport Control Office in New York and its successor.*

In intelligence circles, the quiet, slightly built Stephenson became known as "Little Bill," while Donovan was called "Big Bill." Eventually, the Canadian was to play a role in relation to the American that corresponded to the one Claude Dansey had performed for Ralph Van Deman in the previous war. In fact, he later claimed credit for suggesting to Donovan that the United States should establish an agency to conduct worldwide clandestine operations. Donovan, however, needed no prodding. He was already thinking about an American secret service to counter the Nazi challenge. In London, he had held lengthy conversations with Colonel Stewart Menzies, the head of the Secret Intelligence Service, or MI6, and Rear Admiral John Godfrey, director of naval intelligence. When he returned from Europe in March 1941, he was ready to lay a forthright case before the president.

"Although we are facing imminent peril," Donovan warned Roosevelt, "we are lacking an effective service for analyzing, comprehending, and appraising such information as we might obtain . . . relative to the intention of potential enemies." Radical changes had occurred in the nature of war, and the current mechanism for collecting intelligence was clearly inadequate. "It is essential that we set up a central enemy intelligence organization which would itself collect . . . pertinent information concerning potential enemies," he continued. This new agency should have sole charge of intelligence work abroad, be empowered to coordinate the activities of military and naval attachés and other collectors, and have the responsibility for evaluating information and preparing analyses for the president's use.

Fearing that Donovan's proposed "super" agency would submerge or even obliterate their organizations, ONI, MID, and the FBI tried to block the proposal. Donovan was too freewheeling to be a team player, they complained. "If there's a loose football on the field," observed General George V. Strong, head of MID, "he'll pick it up and run with it." But a counteroffensive was mounted by "Little Bill" Stephenson, who had

*Stephenson was rewarded with a knighthood in 1944.

direct access to the White House, and Admiral Godfrey, who journeyed to Washington to lend his support.* With other problems to worry about—Hitler widened the war on June 22, 1941, by attacking his erstwhile Russian allies—Roosevelt tacked back and forth on the issue. Finally, on July 11, he appointed Donovan as Coordinator of Information "with authority to collect and analyze all information and data, which may bear upon national security . . . and to make such information and data available to the President." The United States had taken the first step toward the establishment of a central intelligence agency.

■ ■ ■

Someone once observed that Bill Donovan had the "power to visualize an oak where he saw an acorn." Even though he held no military rank and received no salary as intelligence coordinator, Wild Bill swept through the Washington bureaucracy like a whirlwind. The Bureau of the Budget, believing that the Coordinator of Information (COI) would require only a small staff and limited financial resources, had earmarked about $450,000 in unvouchered funds for the agency and assigned it three obscure rooms in the old State, War and Navy Building next to the White House.* One of the rooms had a plaque commemorating the "services and sufferings" of the 243,135 horses and mules used by the Army during World War I. Visitors were even more startled by the receptionist who greeted them. Heavily made up and with brightly dyed red hair, she "sat in the gloom like Frankenstein's daughter, directing spies, safecrackers, wiretappers, and important men to their various destinations."

Since the United States was starting from scratch in strategic intelligence, Donovan recruited his own version of the best and brightest. This elite included James P. Baxter, the president of Williams College, who was made director of Research and Analysis (R & A); William L. Langer, a Harvard diplomatic historian, who headed R & A's blue-ribbon Board of Analysts, which Donovan dubbed "the College of Cardinals"; the Librarian of Congress, poet Archibald MacLeish; Robert E. Sherwood, Pulitzer Prize-winning playwright and presidential speechwriter; Edward Buxton, a one-time textile manufacturer who served in the thankless post of assistant director; James Warburg, a New York investment banker; Atherton C. Richardson, the "pineapple king" of Hawaii; James Roosevelt, the president's eldest son; David Bruce; Estelle Frankfurter, daughter of Supreme Court Justice Felix Frankfurter; and John Ford, the movie director.

---

*Godfrey was accompanied by one of his aides, Lt. Cmdr. Ian Fleming, later the creator of James Bond.

*Now the Executive Office Building.

Within a few months, the Budget Bureau was rubbing its eyes in astonishment at Donovan's feats of empire building. The COI staff had mushroomed to more than six hundred people and occupied space all over town and in New York as well. If an employee missed a day at work, according to the joke, he might need two to find where his office had been moved. And that was merely the beginning. Donovan was aiming at a staff of 1,300 and a $14 million budget. Brushing aside civil-service regulations, he recruited a team of scholars, lawyers, journalists, and businessmen with dizzying speed. Most of them knew nothing about intelligence work—or even such basics of bureaucratic life as how to obtain typewriters, ribbons, and paper clips.

Ultimately, Donovan's influence over the intelligence community extended well beyond the war years and indeed into our own time. Four future heads of the postwar Central Intelligence Agency began their careers in the COI or its successor, the Office of Strategic Services (OSS). Allen Dulles, who worked in Switzerland in World War I, returned to Bern late in 1942 to run a spy ring that reached into the upper echelon of the German government. Richard Helms, a former wire service reporter who once interviewed Hitler, helped organize clandestine operations against Germany. William E. Colby parachuted into both Norway and occupied France on guerrilla and sabotage missions. William Casey organized and directed the team that penetrated Germany.*

Throughout the existence of his agency, Donovan engaged in bureaucratic tugs of war with ONI, MID, the State Department, and the FBI as they vigorously resisted his efforts to move in on their turfs. A shrewd Washington infighter, he won some of these battles and lost others. Sherwood's radio propaganda unit, the Foreign Information Service, became embroiled in a jurisdictional dispute with Nelson A. Rockefeller, the coordinator of inter-American affairs. And J. Edgar Hoover, who called COI "Roosevelt's folly," blocked it from operating in Latin America. The brashness of some of Donovan's staffers ruffled the feathers of the military, who claimed this "bunch of faggots" had no sense of security and held back secret data.

COI had two separate wings, one overt and the other covert. Scholars were enlisted for the agency's research and analysis branch and for the first time scholarly research techniques were applied to intelligence. The academicians of R & A, who worked in a cluster of decrepit buildings in Washington's Foggy Bottom area that had once housed the laboratories of the National Institute of Health, were lampooned by German propaganda as "fifty professors, twenty monkeys, ten goats, twelve guinea pigs

*Among other top-level CIA officials who got their start in the OSS were James Jesus Angleton, the agency's longtime counterintelligence chief; Ray Cline, who rose to be deputy director for intelligence; Lyman E. Kirkpatrick, Jr., the agency's first inspector general; and Frank C. Wisner, the impresario of Cold War clandestine operations.

and a staff of Jewish scribblers." They monitored Axis radio broadcasts and pored over agricultural reports, obscure technical journals, and local newspapers, seeking to establish an accurate picture of what was happening in German-occupied Europe.

The agency's covert wing, or "secret division," was patterned on the British Special Operations Executive, which engaged in such irregular activities as sabotage and guerrilla warfare behind German lines. ONI's shadowy "K" organizations, which had been running secret agents under the direction of a hunchbacked businessman named William B. Phillips, was taken over from the Navy and became the core of this effort. Eventually, the COI and OSS had five special branches: Secret Intelligence (SI), to conduct espionage; Special Operations (SO), to conduct sabotage and subversion; Counterintelligence (X-2); Morale Operations (MO), to create and disseminate "black," or covert, propaganda; and Operational Groups (OG), to train, supply, and land guerrilla forces in enemy territory.

These units were backed up by divisions that handled finance, developed a communications system, and operated recruiting and training divisions. There was, of course, a research and development (R & D) division, composed of inventors and scientists who were assigned to develop the tools of intelligence, sabotage, and subversion. They turned out counterfeit currency and identification documents for penetration agents and produced a number of special weapons, including a noiseless, flashless .22-calibre pistol for silent killing and a wide variety of explosive devices. One ingenious gadget, called the "Casey Jones," was intended for railroad sabotage. It was fitted with a magnet to hold it to the underside of a locomotive and an electric eye so the bomb would explode only in a tunnel, where it would do the most damage.

Stanley P. Lovell, the chief of R & D, was a dour New Englander whose solemn features masked a sardonic sense of humor and a mastery of dirty tricks. Upon learning that Hitler was a vegetarian, Lovell, whom Donovan nicknamed "Professor Moriarty" after the evil genius of the Sherlock Holmes stories, produced a bizarre scheme to inject the Fuehrer's vegetables with female sex hormones so his moustache would fall out and his voice become soprano. The Japanese were said to be fanatics on personal cleanliness, so Lovell invented "Who, Me?"—a compound that simulated the effects of a loose bowel movement. Small tubes of the stuff were to be slipped into Japanese-occupied cities in China, where children were to sidle up behind Japanese officers on the crowded streets and spray a shot of "Who, Me?" on their trouser seats. This would cause the Japanese to lose face, according to Lovell.

In establishing the special operations division of COI, Donovan drew heavily upon the British for advice and support. William Stephenson made experts available, including his deputy, Colonel Charles H. Ellis, an Australian-born SIS man who was called "Disk" by his friends. "Without

[his] assistance, American intelligence could not have gotten off the ground in World War II," said David Bruce, Donovan's secret intelligence chief. Ellis was awarded the U.S. Legion of Merit for his work. Recently, however, charges have surfaced—though they have been disputed—that Ellis was a German *and* Soviet spy at the time he was helping to organize America's wartime intelligence agency—and in a position to compromise every agent and operation.*

Away from the prying eyes of other intelligence agencies, British experts tutored the Americans at "Camp X," a training school on the Canadian side of Lake Ontario. There the Americans received instruction in the tradecraft of the covert operator: mapping, weapons, demolition, communications, and the art of killing enemies silently. "How well I remember them arriving like *jeune filles en fleur* straight from finishing school, all fresh and innocent, to start work in our frowsy old intelligence brothel," recalled Malcolm Muggeridge, a one-time intelligence agent. "All too soon they were ravished and corrupted. . . ."

■ ■ ■

As Donovan was slashing his way through the bureaucratic thickets, an undeclared shooting war was being fought in the Atlantic. Late in the summer of 1941, the U.S. Navy was ordered to escort convoys bound for Britain and began attacking prowling U-boats. The Germans struck back, torpedoing the destroyer *Kearney* and killing several of her crew. In an emotional Navy Day speech on October 27, the president bitterly denounced this attack as "piracy."* Reviving memories of the Zimmermann Telegram of 1917, he referred to a secret map in his possession that provided irrefutable proof that the Nazis had designs on the Panama Canal and planned to take over Latin America and amalgamate the fourteen existing republics into "five vassal states."

The map had been funneled by Stephenson to Donovan, who had passed it on to the White House. Newsmen clamored to inspect the evidence, while Berlin denounced the map as a crude forgery. But Roose-

---

*These charges were first publicized by Chapman Pincher, a British journalist and specialist in intelligence affairs, who claimed that Ellis had been furnishing information to the Germans since well before the outbreak of the war—including the "order of battle" of MI6. According to Pincher, the Soviets blackmailed him into serving them, as well. He states that Ellis fell under suspicion after the flight of Soviet "mole" Harold A. R. "Kim" Philby and that he was interrogated by MI5 in 1966 and acknowledged his guilt. Ellis was not charged, Pincher states, because coming on top of the Philby case, the scandal would have further discredited SIS. "Informants have told me there is a strong belief in the CIA that Ellis functioned as a Soviet agent during his wartime sojourn in the U.S.," Pincher adds Ellis died in 1975, before Pincher's charges were made public. His friends, including Sir William Stephenson, flatly deny the allegations.

*The attack on the *Kearney* was followed up by the sinking of another destroyer, the *Reuben James*, with heavy loss of life.

velt sidestepped all inquiries, stating that to make the map public would "dry up the source of future information." Obviously, he suspected this was one gift horse that would not bear close public inspection.[†]

Peace or war hung in the balance during the final months of 1941. Isolationism was still strong, and any effort to secure a declaration of war would certainly divide the nation. To unite the country behind his leadership, Roosevelt, like Abraham Lincoln in 1861, had to maneuver his opponent into firing the first shot. Relatively powerless to shape events, he could do little but wait for Hitler to provide some dramatic provocation. Intelligence estimates downgraded the possibility of war with Germany, however. In October, the Army's War Plans Division declared that Germany "will not be in a position to attempt major offensive operations in the Western Hemisphere for at least a year, and then only if she acquires large numbers of British ships."

Donovan was a frequent visitor to the Oval Office during this twilight period. The president appeared satisfied with his efforts. "Bill [is] doing a pretty good job on propaganda and something of a job in terms of intelligence," he told Assistant Secretary of State Adolf Berle. Donovan kept Roosevelt supplied with a steady stream of reports, including talk of a "peace overture" from the German General Staff, an estimate of losses in Soviet industrial production, and a daily summary and analysis of Nazi shortwave broadcasts to America. Curiously enough, at no time does either man appear to have discussed the possibility of a conflict with Japan. But as the United States girded for war across the Atlantic, the blow fell in the Pacific with the swift finality of an executioner's sword.

†The latest evidence indicates that the "secret map" was indeed faked by British Security Coordination. One set of researchers contend that it was a British reworking of a map exhibited in the German embassy in Buenos Aires that was intended to show the new territory to be allotted to Argentina, Brazil, and Mexico if they joined the Axis. (See Bratzel and Rout, "FDR and the 'Secret Map.'") In another version, an ex-BSC agent named Ivar Bryce says he created the map himself. (See Bryce, *You Only Live Twice*.)

13

The Road from Pearl Harbor

Lt. Cmdr. Edwin T. Layton was a worrier. And as 1941 drew to a close, the U.S. Pacific Fleet's intelligence officer had much to be worried about. War in the Pacific appeared imminent, and on December 1 the Japanese navy had suddenly changed the radio call signs of all its ships. This shift, the second in two months, was ominous because the Communications Intelligence Unit at Pearl Harbor plotted the position of the Japanese fleet by intercepting these signals. Traffic analysts quickly identified the most commonly used new calls but were unable to locate a single Japanese aircraft carrier. Worse, none had been picked up since November 25. It was as if the flattops had vanished into thin air.

The Navy's network of radio intercept stations was still vainly searching for the carriers when Layton conducted an intelligence briefing for Admiral Husband E. Kimmel, the commander of the Pacific Fleet, on the morning of December 2. Layton presented the admiral with a summary showing the approximate position of Japanese fleet units based on radio traffic. Kimmel noted that a large naval force accompanied by troopships was reported to be moving along the coast of Thailand but that there was no trace of either of the Imperial Navy's two carrier divisions.

"What!" he declared. "You don't know where the carriers are?"

"No, sir," Layton replied. "That's why I have 'Homeland waters' with a question mark. I don't know."

"You mean they could be coming around Diamond Head, and you wouldn't know it?"

"I hope they would be sighted before now," the unhappy intelligence officer replied.

A "war warning" had been sent by Washington on November 27 to American commanders in the Pacific, including Kimmel and Lt. Gen. Walter C. Short, the Army commander in Hawaii. Negotiations with

Japan had broken down, and an attack was expected on the Philippines, Malaya, Thailand, or Borneo within the next few days. Although both commanders were ordered to execute "appropriate defensive deployment," there was nothing to indicate that Pearl Harbor was a target. Short took no action except to mass his aircraft to prevent sabotage. Kimmel ordered a partial alert but failed to order sustained around-the-compass aerial patrols. He considered sending the battle fleet to sea but decided against the idea because the only two American carriers in the Pacific had been detached to deliver planes to Midway and Wake Island. Torpedo nets were unavailable because the Navy Department thought torpedoes would be ineffective in the shallow waters of Pearl Harbor.

The day before the "war warning" was issued, six carriers flying the sunburst flag of Japan had slipped into the dense fog of the North Pacific. Their air crews were specially trained, and the planes were fitted with torpedoes modified to run true in shoal water. Maintaining strict radio silence and avoiding contact with other ships, the carriers steamed undetected toward Hawaii. Layton repeatedly warned of trouble in the offing—in the Far East, not Pearl Harbor—but the operational officers tended to regard him as an alarmist. "Here comes Layton with his usual Saturday crisis!" cried one man as Layton joined the staff for lunch on December 6.

Early the next morning, wave after wave of Japanese planes struck the unwary American base. Surprise was complete. Nineteen ships, including almost the entire battle line of the Pacific Fleet, were sunk. Neatly lined up as if for inspection, an estimated 256 aircraft were destroyed. More than 2,400 sailors, soldiers, and Marines were killed. It was the worst disaster in American military history.* A spent bullet struck Admiral Kimmel in the chest, and he murmured: "Too bad it didn't kill me."

The surprise at Pearl Harbor was echoed by shock and disbelief at home. What had happened? Why had there been no warning? Who was responsible for failing to anticipate the attack?

Pearl Harbor was more than a failure of intelligence; it was a failure of command and leadership at almost every level of government. Short and Kimmel were relieved of their commands, yet in vivid contrast, General Douglas MacArthur escaped censure even though his forces in the Philippines were caught by surprise nine hours *after* the attack on Pearl Harbor. Obviously, Kimmel and Short, whatever their failures, were

---

*The Japanese made a serious mistake in not destroying the oil tanks and repair shops at Pearl Harbor, which were vital to continued American naval operations in the Pacific. All but two of the sunken battleships were raised and returned to the fleet. Even more important, the U.S. Navy's two carriers survived to become the spearhead of the American offensive against Japan.

singled out as convenient scapegoats to cover errors of commission and omission in Washington.

■ ■ ■

Over the years, mythologists have built an industry on attempts to prove that President Roosevelt had foreknowledge of the Japanese attack and deliberately sacrificed the Pacific Fleet to bring the United States into war against Nazi Germany through the back door. Conspiracy theorists charge that the master plotter in the White House deliberately ignored clear signals of an impending attack on Hawaii to unite the American people behind him. Most researchers reject the conspiracy theory, but it is a myth that will not die. For example, in 1982 John Toland charged in *Infamy* that FDR knew about the impending attack because, along with other information, he had received "a detailed plan" of the raid from a British double agent known as "Tricycle." Unable to discover this "smoking gun" in the files, Toland surmised that the key documents had been purged as part of a cover-up designed to deflect the blame for the Pearl Harbor debacle from the White House to the naval and military commanders.

"Tricycle" was a Yugoslav playboy-adventurer named Dusko Popov, who had been recruited by the Abwehr to spy on England. Popov immediately defected to the British and became a double agent. In the summer of 1941, the Abwehr sent him to the United States to establish a spy ring. He was given a list of questions to guide him that were hidden in a microdot glued to a telegraph form. Much of the questionnaire dealt with general matters such as shipping, aircraft production, and troop movements, but fully a third of it revealed a strong interest in Pearl Harbor and the surrounding airfields and defenses. Obviously, this information was being sought by the Germans for their Japanese allies.

Upon his arrival in the United States, Popov was interviewed by J. Edgar Hoover, and Toland suggests that the FBI passed the text of the questionnaire, with all its references to Pearl Harbor, to FDR. Besides calling the questionnaire "a detailed plan," Toland left readers with the impression that it was almost wholly concerned with Pearl Harbor by editing the version published in his book to omit a good portion of the other data.

In reality, however, Hoover largely ignored the microdot because he disliked Popov on moral grounds and did not trust him. Toland could not find his "smoking gun" because the FBI director sent the White House only about a quarter of the questionnaire and did not even include the part that mentioned Pearl Harbor. Apparently he merely regarded it as a curiosity that might interest the president. Nor did Hoover provide the full text to ONI or MID.

Although Pearl Harbor certainly rescued Roosevelt from an impossible dilemma, it is hardly likely that he would have offered up the entire Pacific Fleet as a sacrifice, when he would need those same ships to win the war. Roosevelt, the cabinet, and the Army and Navy chiefs did have a great deal of intelligence regarding Japanese movements in the months leading up to Pearl Harbor, but most of it was conflicting. The conventional wisdom held that the Japanese, bogged down by the long-running war in China and cut off from vital petroleum imports by an American embargo, were likely to try to grab the oil and mineral resources of Southeast Asia and the Dutch East Indies. Perhaps they would seize the Philippines to protect their flank on the drive southward. Other analysts predicted a Japanese strike against the Soviet Union, which was reeling under the German onslaught. Although Pearl Harbor had been successfully surprised during U.S. Navy fleet maneuvers, the possibility of a real raid was ruled out because it was believed the Japanese lacked the capacity to mount the operation.

Racism had much to do with this lack of foresight. Americans regarded the Japanese as bucktoothed, bespectacled little yellow men, always photographing things with their ever-present cameras so they could copy them. "Japan has been energetic in her efforts to create naval aviation, but she is usually a phase behind," wrote Captain William B. Puleston, a former ONI director, in 1941. "She cannot match in numbers the planes carried on American carriers, and what is equally important, her personnel cannot send planes aloft or take them aboard as rapidly as American personnel."

Information poured in upon Washington from a variety of sources: the MAGIC decrypting operation, which was reading the supposedly impregnable Purple traffic between Tokyo and Japanese emissaries in Washington; messages in the lower-priority J-19 code; the tracking of Japanese naval vessels by their call signs; reports from American diplomats in Tokyo; and the observed movements of Japanese troops and vessels. Random clues to the Pearl Harbor raid were embedded in this mass of information, but the volume was so overwhelming that cryptanalysts were unable to immediately determine what was significant and what was irrelevant.

Only later, in the brilliant light of hindsight, were the relevant hints seen as heralds of a forthcoming Japanese attack. For example, not long after Admiral Isoroku Yamamoto, commander in chief of the Japanese Combined Fleet, first began the secret planning for the Pearl Harbor raid in January 1941, the project was nearly blown. Joseph C. Grew, the American envoy to Japan, notified Washington that the Peruvian minister had learned "from many sources, including a Japanese source, that in the event of war breaking out between the United States and Japan, the

Japanese intended to make a surprise attack against Pearl Harbor." The information was relayed to Kimmel—but with an assessment that read: "Naval Intelligence places no credence in these rumors."

"After the event a signal is always crystal clear," observes Roberta Wohlstetter in her account of the intelligence background of Pearl Harbor. "We can see what disaster it was signalling, since the disaster had occurred. But before the event it is obscure and pregnant with conflicting meanings. . . . In short, we failed to anticipate Pearl Harbor not for want of the relevant materials, but because of a plethora of irrelevant ones."

One of the primary hazards of intelligence work is the tendency to rely too heavily on a single source. Like Sir Henry Clinton, who convinced himself in 1781 that he possessed a copy of George Washington's plans, the president and his advisers believed MAGIC provided them with an infallible key to the maze of Japanese intentions. Other sources were downgraded or ignored. But Purple revealed only the information being passed on by the Foreign Office to its key representatives abroad. The most secret naval codes had not been broken, and Purple provided little information on the activities of the Imperial Navy. Indeed, MAGIC gave no hint of an impending Japanese attack on Pearl Harbor. Thus, MAGIC was a double-edged sword. While it gave American policymakers inside knowledge of Japanese intentions, it also created overconfidence. The fetish for security surrounding MAGIC and the limited circulation of these decrypts were also self-defeating. Neither Kimmel nor Short was privy to MAGIC, which would have allowed them to monitor the progress of the Japanese-American negotiations underway in Washington. In effect, Washington took the position that diplomatic intelligence was none of their business.*

The misuse of MAGIC lay at the heart of the Pearl Harbor disaster. There was no clearinghouse where all the raw information on Japanese intentions could be assembled, analyzed, and assessed in totality. All the individuals cleared for MAGIC had to be their own intelligence officers and make their own analyses and interpretations of the raw intelligence—a process in which they had little or no experience. Moreover, each message represented only a single frame in a lengthy motion picture, and they never saw the entire film. The intelligence process was tightly compartmentalized, and each agency and department processed the information it collected. Only rarely was information from one source weighed against material from another.

While MAGIC was silent on the subject of Pearl Harbor, messages in J-19 betrayed an abnormal interest on the part of the Japanese consulate in Honolulu in both Pearl Harbor and the movements of the Pacific Fleet.

---

*A Purple machine was to have been sent to Pearl Harbor in the summer of 1941, but it went to Britain instead.

But MAGIC had a higher priority than the J-19 traffic. American decrypters devoted most of their efforts to MAGIC, and it often took up to two weeks for a J-19 dispatch to be read, translated, and distributed. On September 24, 1941, the consulate was instructed to divide Pearl Harbor into five alphabetically coded zones and to report the exact positions of the ships of the Pacific Fleet as they lay at anchor. Incredibly, no special importance was attached to this message in Washington, and it was not passed on to Hawaii.

"I'm sure that had we seen messages that had to do with Pearl Harbor, then there would have been a different evaluation of those items of intelligence," Layton later declared. "There's an old Indian saying that the snake in your corner is the largest. This is true in intelligence. If you receive intelligence that has to do with where you are, you give it greater significance. In the late autumn of 1941, Washington was too involved with the shipping war in the Atlantic to take proper notice of intelligence related to the Pacific. Had MAGIC decrypts been available to us, they would have at least alerted us to the possibility of an attack on Pearl Harbor."

Having failed to provide Kimmel and Short with access to MAGIC, Washington was at fault for not keeping them informed of changing conditions. High-level officers in the Army and Navy also blundered by not making certain that the military commanders in Hawaii were on the alert. Sound military doctrine holds that a field commander should be given all pertinent information upon which to base his decisions. Failing that, he should be given explicit orders. Kimmel and Short received neither.

Internecine struggles within the Navy Department over the ultimate control of the intelligence aggravated the problem. There was a long-running feud between the Office of Communications and naval intelligence for control of the evaluation and dissemination of radio intelligence. In the months running down toward Pearl Harbor, this bitter rivalry was augmented by the attempts of Admiral Richmond Kelly Turner, the abrasive and aggressive director of the War Plans Division, to usurp control of the Office of Naval Intelligence. Although Turner had little knowledge of the intelligence process, he felt his judgment was superior to that of ONI when it came to analyzing and interpreting strategic intelligence. In May 1941, Captain Alan C. Kirk, the director of naval intelligence, wrote Turner a warning that "the Japs will jump pretty soon." In the margin, the admiral scrawled: "I don't think the Japs are going to jump now or ever!"

Had there been a sophisticated centralized system for evaluating all the intelligence pouring in upon Roosevelt and his inner circle, the danger signals might have been separated from the surrounding noise. William Friedman later declared that the Pearl Harbor disaster occurred because "there was *nobody* in either the Army or the Navy intelligence staffs in Washington whose most important, if not sole duty, was to study the whole story which the MAGIC messages were unfolding . . . nobody whose responsibility it was to try and put the pieces of the jigsaw puzzle together." This was a task that the Coordinator of Information's Board of Analysts—the "College of Cardinals"—might well have performed, but William Donovan was not on the Top List of persons receiving MAGIC intercepts. The military were too suspicious of the civilian intelligence service to trust it with MAGIC.

■ ■ ■

While the Japanese were bombing Pearl Harbor, Bill Donovan was watching a football game between the New York Giants and Brooklyn Dodgers at the Polo Grounds. The Dodgers had just made a first down on the Giants' four-yard line when an announcement was made over the loudspeaker: "Attention please! Here is an urgent message. Will Colonel William J. Donovan call Operator 19 in Washington, D.C." The call was from Jimmy Roosevelt, who told Donovan of the emergency and asked him to return to Washington immediately to meet with the president.

Upon his arrival in the capital, Donovan convened a meeting of the "College of Cardinals" to prepare an estimate of the situation for the president and the cabinet. But they were unable to present an opinion on future Japanese intentions, because ONI and MID, hopelessly bewildered and groping for facts themselves, ignored all of Donovan's pleas for information. Shortly before midnight, Donovan and Edward R. Murrow, the radio news correspondent, were ushered into the Oval Office. Roosevelt had still not recovered from the shock of the raid. "They caught our ships like lame ducks! Lame ducks, Bill!" he declared. "It's a good thing you got me started on this [intelligence operations]," the president added during the half-hour meeting. The main topic of discussion was the mood of the American people and whether Pearl Harbor would unify them against the Axis. Donovan thought it would.*

Over the next several months, Japanese forces fanned out over the Pacific like the rays of the rising sun. Guam and Wake Island were seized; the Philippines, Singapore, and the Dutch East Indies fell. Meanwhile, U-boats torpedoed tankers within sight of the American coast. In North Africa and Russia, the Germans drove relentlessly ahead. Wild reports circulated that German and Japanese saboteurs were descending upon American shores. Security became everybody's business. Roosevelt's own

*The United States declared war on Japan on December 8, 1941. Roosevelt still faced the problem of Germany, but Hitler solved it by declaring war on the United States on December 11. The Japanese attack on Pearl Harbor was as much a surprise to him as it had been to the Americans, however, and the German high command had no contingency plans for a war with the United States.

intelligence man, John Franklin Carter, asked for more operatives and more money to check "on certain groups in this country." The FBI expanded its counterespionage activities and placed alleged subversives under surveillance.

Panic and prejudice against Japanese-American residents of the West Coast reached hysterical levels. Rumors of an imminent Japanese invasion of Hawaii and of hordes of disguised Japanese soldiers lurking on the Mexican border with California swirled about. Although there was no evidence of serious disloyalty or cases of espionage—ONI concluded that Japanese-Americans were not a security threat—local leaders such as Earl Warren, the attorney general of California and later Chief Justice of the United States, pressured the Army to forcibly relocate them. "A Jap's a Jap, and I don't want any of them around here," declared General John L. De Witt of the West Coast Defense Command.*

Donovan tried to temper the anti-Japanese hysteria by providing the president with statements from leading West Coast citizens attesting to the loyalty of Japanese-Americans. Ralph Van Deman, who lived in San Diego, termed the plan to relocate the Japanese unnecessary, impractical and "about the craziest proposition that I have heard of yet."† These voices of reason went unheeded, however, and in April 1942 Roosevelt signed the order authorizing the internment of some 120,000 Japanese—two-thirds of them American citizens. COI and the Navy prudently moved their Japanese-American translators out of the restricted area.

Both ONI and MID were on the defensive as the post-Pearl Harbor search for scapegoats widened. General Dwight D. Eisenhower, the chief of the Army's planning staff, stated that due to "accumulated and glaring deficiencies" MID was unable to provide information essential for deter-

---

*The only spies arrested in Hawaii after Pearl Harbor were a German father-and-daughter team, Bernhard and Ruth Kuehn. They were assigned by the Abwehr to spy for the Japanese in Hawaii in 1935. Pretending to be an anthropologist and linguist, Kuehn moved freely about the islands, often accompanied by his adopted daughter, who assisted him in his espionage activities. In 1939, Ruth opened a beauty shop that catered to the wives of naval officers and listened in on their conversations. Both father and daughter reported to the Japanese consulate in Honolulu, which passed their information on to Tokyo. The Kuehns were arrested when they were caught signaling to Japanese submarines during the attack. Kuehn was sentenced to death by a military commission, but the sentence was commuted to fifty years in prison after he cooperated with American authorities. Ruth received a lighter sentence. Both were deported after the war.

†Following his retirement from the U.S. Army in 1929, Van Deman had operated a private intelligence agency aimed at combatting communist subversion. He had the apparent support of MID, ONI, and the FBI, as well as contacts with several local police forces, especially the Los Angeles Police Department's Red-baiting Intelligence Bureau. He ran a nationwide network of agents, and infiltrated the Communist party, labor unions, and church groups. Van Deman's card files contained more than one hundred thousand entries relating to persons he believed to be communists, communist sympathizers, or Nazis. In December 1941, Van Deman became an intelligence adviser to the War Department. He was awarded the Legion of Merit in 1946 at the age of 81. He died in 1952.

mining the intentions and capabilities of the Axis nations. "The chief of the Division could do little more than come to the planning and operating sections of the staff and in a rather pitiful way ask if there was anything he could do for us." Admiral Turner, head of the Navy's War Plans Division, seized upon the fumbling by ONI to further his campaign to take it over. And Admiral Ernest J. King, who had been named chief of naval operations and commander in chief of the U.S. Fleet in the wake of Pearl Harbor, brushed ONI aside and ran his own intelligence service. ONI was relegated to the status of little more than an archive and a lending library.

No scheme seemed too wild for consideration during this period of confused activity. Donovan urged the president to send half the remaining Pacific Fleet and ten to fifteen thousand commandos—which the United States did not have—to raid the Japanese home island of Hokkaido. John Carter suggested that the U.S. might be able to bury Japan in lava and ash by bombing her volcanoes and causing them to erupt. When an informant told Roosevelt the Japanese were in deadly fear of bats, the president gave serious consideration to a scheme to drop bats on Japan and demoralize the population. "This man is *not* a nut," the president told Donovan. Without checking to see whether the Japanese were really terrorized by bats—they were not—plans were laid to parachute bats into Japan. Most froze to death at high altitudes before they were released.

Some of the material based on travelers' reports that Donovan sent to the Oval Office was worthwhile. An American businessman who had left Germany in November 1941 supplied an early account of the first stage of the Final Solution—the deportation of Jews to Eastern Europe. But much of the material was erroneous. The Japanese did not run convoys to Chile to obtain copper; the Germans did not invade Morocco by way of Spain in the spring of 1942. And feuding broke out between Donovan and Robert Sherwood, chief of COI's Foreign Intelligence Service, underscoring the difficulty of combining intelligence and propaganda functions in the same agency. Even Roosevelt's zest for intrigue cooled and in April 1942 he suggested that Donovan might be assigned to "some nice quiet, isolated island where he could have a scrap with the Japs every morning before breakfast."

COI was also engaged in a war within the war with its bureaucratic rivals. J. Edgar Hoover had become resentful of William Stephenson's freewheeling activities in America, and in March 1942 Senator Kenneth McKellar of Tennessee introduced a bill that would have forced Stephenson to divulge the identity of his agents and other data to the FBI. The bill would have put the British Security Coordinator out of business and damaged COI's operations as well, and it was vetoed by the president. Even so, the canny Stephenson decided the time had come to pay more respect to American law, so he turned some of his agents and tasks over to

Donovan. One of the projects involved the periodic burglarizing of the Spanish embassy in Washington, in which code books and other documents belonging to the pro-Axis Franco government were secretly photographed. This material was sought by the codebreakers at Bletchley Park, who were reading the German Enigma cipher.

Getting wind of these "black bag" jobs, Hoover was angered because they infringed upon his territory. But the FBI director did not file a formal complaint with the White House. Instead, one night after Donovan's COI agents had made a foray into the darkened Spanish embassy, two FBI cars pulled up, turned on their emergency lights, and sounded their sirens full blast. Lights snapped on all over the neighborhood, and the startled COI men fled the building—only to be arrested by the police and turned over to the FBI. Donovan angrily protested to the president, but instead of reprimanding Hoover, Roosevelt ordered the project transferred to the FBI.

Throughout the spring of 1942, COI battled for its life. When Roosevelt was dissatisfied with an agency, his usual practice was to create a new one. "Roosevelt's normal way of reorganizing a Department was to split it down the middle," observed one authority. In an effort to end snarls and foul-ups, the president now considered abolishing COI and distributing its functions among other agencies. Research and Analysis was to go to the State Department, Secret Intelligence to MID. A commando unit then in the process of being organized was tentatively earmarked for the Marine Corps.

But Donovan had a surprising ally in the fight to save his organization from cannibalization. He convinced the Joint Chiefs of Staff (JCS), the nation's top military commanders, of the need for an organization to wage secret war against the enemy. Traditional American military doctrine relied upon a crushing application of force to defeat an enemy, but Donovan argued that the American public would not tolerate a repetition of the heavy casualties of World War I. Instead of a strategy of annihilation, he urged a strategy of indirection to keep the enemy off balance. Hitler and the Japanese would be forced to disperse their strength so that in trying to be strong everywhere, they would be weak everywhere.

Finally, after considerable infighting, the president issued executive orders on June 13, 1942, scuttling the COI, spinning off its propaganda service to the newly created Office of War Information and establishing the Office of Strategic Services. The vaguely worded directive creating the OSS gave it only two functions: the collection and analysis of strategic intelligence for the Joint Chiefs and the planning and direction of such special operations as the JCS might require. The OSS had only half the manpower of its predecessor and reported to the Joint Chiefs rather than having a direct line to the Oval Office. Nevertheless, Donovan had outflanked the enemies who had been trying to get rid of him. The new

Director of Strategic Services was none other than Colonel William J. Donovan.

■ ■ ■

While the gears of the American war machine ground with confusion and friction, the triumphant Japanese solidified their conquests. But Admiral Yamamoto was under no illusions about a final Japanese victory. Having seen America's industrial might at first hand while a naval attaché in Washington, he argued that Japan had to win a decisive victory before this power could be mobilized. "If I am told to fight regardless of the consequences, I shall run wild for the first six months or a year," he declared, "but I have utterly no confidence for the second and third years of the fighting." Obsessed with the need to complete the work of Pearl Harbor by smashing the remnants of the U.S. Pacific Fleet, Yamamoto chose Midway Island, about 1,100 miles to the west of Hawaii, as the site of this climactic battle.

Like most Japanese naval planning, the Midway operation was a complex blend of stealth, ruse, and division of forces intended to keep an enemy off balance. Yamamoto divided his fleet into three major divisions: a striking force of four carriers; a dozen transports carrying five thousand troops to occupy Midway, escorted by two battleships and a light carrier; and the main body, consisting of seven battleships, including his flagship, the giant *Yamato*. This armada was preceded to sea by a diversionary force of two carriers assigned to raid Dutch Harbor in the Aleutians and to seize Adak, Attu, and Kiska. The Aleutian raid was intended to lure the U.S. Pacific Fleet to the north while Midway was being occupied. When the Americans learned of the ruse and hastened south, they would be destroyed by Yamamoto's carriers and battleships.

The Japanese had an overwhelming preponderance of force, but Admiral Chester W. Nimitz, successor to the hapless Husband Kimmel as commander of the Pacific Fleet, was aware of much of their operational plan. The Combat Intelligence Unit at Pearl Harbor, commonly called Station Hypo, had broken the Japanese naval code used for communicating between ship and shore, designated JN25 by the Americans. Hypo was one of three cryptanalytic stations operated by the Navy that were trying to read a new edition of the code, JN25b.* The others were Station Negat in Washington and Station Cash which had been at Cavite, in the Philippines, and was evacuated to Australia.

Hidden away behind locked steel doors in the windowless basement of the Administration Building of the Fourteenth Naval District at Pearl

---

*"JN" stood for Japanese navy, "25" for the twenty-fifth code Hypo worked on, and "b" for its second edition.

Harbor, Hypo was under the command of Lt. Cmdr. Joseph J. Rochefort. Tall, lean, and caustic, Rochefort had enlisted in the Navy during World War I and had stayed on after being commissioned. In 1925 he joined OP-20-G, the Navy's first cryptographic unit, and became one of the Navy's pioneer cryptanalysts. Rochefort and Edwin Layton, who had been kept on as the fleet's intelligence officer by Admiral Nimitz, were old friends, having served together as language students in Japan. Unlike many cryptanalysts, Rochefort also had considerable service at sea, an experience that gave him an understanding of fleet operations.

Rochefort had personally assumed a large measure of the blame for Pearl Harbor. Believing that it was the duty of an intelligence officer to keep his chief informed of enemy intentions, he felt he had failed Admiral Kimmel. To make up for it, he drove himself and his staff of cryptanalysts, translators, and clerks unmercifully. For the better part of three months, they worked around the clock amid an ever-rising tide of paper and the deafening clatter of IBM tabulators and sorters. Lt. Cmdr. Thomas H. Dyer, Rochefort's deputy, had pioneered the use of this equipment to take over some of the mind-numbing drudgery of cryptanalysis. When more manpower was needed, the bandsmen of the crippled battleship *California* were among those pressed into service. The musicians proved to be particularly adept at cryptanalysis.

Rarely leaving his underground domain, Joe Rochefort stood sixteen- and twenty-hour watches and had a cot installed so he could be on call around the clock. The air conditioning was erratic, and he sometimes wore an old smoking jacket belted over his uniform to ward off the chill while he padded about in felt slippers. Everyone worked closely together, sharing their findings and their hunches. Dyer was as dedicated as his chief, alternating twelve hours on duty and twelve hours off for days at a time. Physically drained, he periodically scooped up Benzedrine pills from a basket on his desk like jelly beans. It was "not necessary to be crazy to be a cryptanalyst," Rochefort later declared, "but it always helps."

Unlike the Purple diplomatic cipher or the German Enigma, JN25 did not involve the use of a machine to encipher messages. To save money, the Imperial Navy relied instead upon printed code books and cipher tables that were distributed throughout the fleet. The code consisted of some 45,000 five-digit numbers that represented words and phrases. Before sending a message, a communications officer would encipher it by randomly choosing a five-digit number from the cipher table and subtracting it from the code number for the first word of the message. The next cipher number would then be subtracted from the next code number, and so on until the message was completed. To enable the recipient to decipher the message, the page, column, and line at which the sender had begun picking the cipher numbers from the table was included in the message.

The flaw in the Japanese system was that the code books and cipher tables were changed only after they had been in use for several months. This practice enabled the cryptanalysts at Pearl Harbor to observe that the same numbers were frequently used in the same sequence. They were also assisted by radio direction finders that helped locate ships transmitting messages and the ability of some of Rochefort's staff to recognize individual Japanese radio operators by the manner in which they transmitted signals. An operator on the carrier *Akagi*, for example, had a touch so heavy that it was said he kicked the key with his foot.

Little by little, Hypo broke into JN25. By the spring of 1942, the unit was reading about 30 percent of this traffic. As the isolated fragments of information grew denser, enlarged, and touched each other, the cryptanalysts began to make educated guesses about Japanese fleet operations from them. If a small ship usually operated with carriers, there was the strong possibility that it was a tanker. Each time the carriers summoned the tanker, code groupings appeared that could be "refuel" and "rendezvous," along with the names of favored locations for refueling. Not every message could be read—as in baseball, it was the batting average that counted—but the codebreakers made giant strides in creating their own versions of the Japanese code books. Following British practice, the information obtained from these decrypts was classified as "ultrasecret" and codenamed ULTRA.

Toward the middle of April, Admiral King requested Station Hypo to provide a long-range estimate of Japanese intentions. Rochefort predicted that the Japanese would launch a campaign aimed at capturing Port Moresby, in the eastern New Guinea area, to isolate Australia. Later that summer, a larger operation would be conducted in the Central Pacific. Admiral Nimitz countered the New Guinea expedition, and the resulting Battle of the Coral Sea, the first fought solely by carrier planes, was also the first in which a Japanese offensive was blunted. Although the U.S. Navy suffered heavy losses, a Japanese carrier was sunk, and two others were so badly mauled they were unable to participate in the upcoming Central Pacific operation.

In the meantime, Rochefort had pinpointed Midway as the target of the coming operation and presented his findings to Nimitz. Few naval commanders have been confronted by a deeper strategic dilemma. The Japanese movements could be a ruse to cover another attack on Pearl Harbor or even upon the West Coast. In fact, Admiral King's staff in Washington was convinced that these were Yamamoto's objectives. But Layton and Rochefort argued forcefully that there was a mountain of evidence pointing to Midway. The admiral staked all his chips on Rochefort's analysis and committed his outnumbered forces to the defense of Midway. On May 25, Hypo provided him with the most important intelligence yet.* Rochefort personally delivered a long intercept to headquarters that contained much of the battle order and the date and position from which the Japanese would launch their attacks.

Nevertheless, there were skeptics in Washington, and Rochefort and his staff searched for a way to convince the doubters. They noted that enemy radio traffic made numerous references to "AF," which was believed to be Midway. To nail down the identity of "AF," Lt. Cmdr. W. J. Holmes suggested that Midway be instructed to send a message in plain language that its fresh-water distilling plant was out of order. The Japanese swallowed the bait like a hungry shark. Two days later, Hypo intercepted a Japanese message reporting that "AF" was short of fresh water.

As a showdown neared, Nimitz ordered his three carriers up from the Southwest Pacific and stationed them to the northeast of Midway, on the flank of the Japanese fleet, where he hoped they would not be observed. And then the screen went blank. The May 25 intercept was the last JN25b message that Hypo managed to unravel before the battle, because the Japanese made the long-delayed switch to an updated code, JN25c. Months elapsed before Rochefort's team was again able to read the radio traffic in any detail. The next contact with the Japanese occurred in the fog-shrouded Aleutians, where on June 3 enemy bombers attacked Dutch Harbor. Totally disregarding the intelligence provided him, the commander of a cruiser force that had been dispatched by Nimitz was outmaneuvered by the Japanese, who landed troops on bleak Attu and Kiska.

While the attack on Dutch Harbor was underway, a patrol plane was droning over the sea about seven hundred miles west of Midway in search of the advancing enemy. Suddenly, the heavy cloud cover parted momentarily, and the pilot sighted the Japanese transports and their escort spread out below him. "Do you see what I see?" he asked his copilot. The report was flashed to Pearl Harbor, where Admiral Nimitz greeted the sighting with "a bright, white smile," according to Edwin Layton. The curtain had gone up on the Battle of Midway.

Outnumbered, outgunned, but not outfought, the U.S. Navy won an incredible victory. Within a few hours, American dive bombers sank four of the Japanese carriers as well as several other vessels in exchange for one flattop and some smaller ships. The battle marked the high tide of Japanese conquest, and Japan now faced the prolonged war that

---

*Many writers have erred, however, in stating that this intercept revealed the entire makeup of the Japanese fleet. Layton has emphasized that it did not include the battleships commanded by Admiral Yamamoto himself. Had the Battle of Midway gone the other way, Layton observed, the omission of these ships would have caused it to have been branded another intelligence failure. See Layton, *Reminisences*, pp. 125–127.

Yamamoto had warned against. Midway, observed Nimitz, "was essentially a victory of intelligence. In attempting surprise, the Japanese were themselves surprised."*

Midway had a bizarre aftermath. To protect the security of its codebreaking operation, the Navy assigned the credit for its successes to information supplied by patrol planes and submarines. But a few days after the battle, Washington was stunned by a front-page story in the Chicago *Tribune* disclosing that the U.S. Navy had known in advance of the strength and dispositions of the Japanese fleet. Stanley Johnston, a *Tribune* war correspondent, had been shown a copy of Yamamoto's deciphered operational plan by a friendly naval officer, and he included much of it in his story. Fearing that its codebreaking operation had been compromised, the Navy insisted that a reluctant Justice Department prosecute Johnston and the *Tribune* for espionage. One admiral was said to be so irate that he threatened to send Marines to occupy the Tribune Tower.

The case raised a thorny issue that has surfaced repeatedly in recent years—the media's degree of responsibility in reporting on sensitive intelligence matters. As a federal grand jury was empaneled, Colonel Robert R. McCormick, the *Tribune's* owner-publisher, charged that the inquiry was intended to punish the paper for its isolationist stand before Pearl Harbor and denounced it as an encroachment on the First Amendment and a free press. The case collapsed, however, when for security reasons the Navy decided against divulging the work of its cryptanalysts to the grand jury. In the glare of publicity, the Navy also had much to fear from its friends in Congress. Taking to the House floor to denounce the *Tribune,* Representative Elmer J. Holland declared: "Somehow our Navy had secured and broken the secret code of the Japanese Navy. . . ." Navy codebreakers were frantic, but luckily, the Japanese did not read the *Congressional Record.*

■ ■ ■

*The Navy's treatment of Rochefort and his staff was shabby in the extreme, however. Nimitz recommended that the codebreakers be decorated for their work, with Rochefort to be awarded the Distinguished Service Medal. But the recommendations were turned down by Admiral King as a result of internal Navy politics. Following the battle, Rochefort vigorously protested the efforts of the Office of Naval Communications to take over control of Hypo and angrily talked of "seceding" from it. Rochefort's rising prominence—and fierce independence—had aroused jealousy at Station Negat in Washington even before Midway. Now his enemies portrayed his conduct as verging on insubordinate. Resenting the awards to the Hawaiian codebreakers, they convinced Admiral King that Station Negat, which had incorrectly predicted an attack on Hawaii or the West Coast, had played the key role in breaking JN25 and deserved the bulk of the credit for Midway. Rochefort requested sea duty—and spent most of the rest of the war in command of a floating drydock in San Francisco Bay. He received the Legion of Merit, which was finally upgraded to the Distinguished Service Medal in October 1985, nine years after his death. But an effort to have a destroyer named for him was turned down.

In mid-June 1942, as Americans were still hailing the victory at Midway, Nazi Germany—on Adolf Hitler's direct orders—launched a campaign of sabotage against the United States. Two teams of four saboteurs each were landed by submarines on the American coast, one at Amagansett, toward the eastern tip of Long Island, and the other near Jacksonville, on the Florida coast. Sent by the Abwehr to mount an attack on American industry, each team carried a large amount of cash and a supply of explosives and sophisticated timing devices sufficient to last for two years.

The new teams were sent in because every active German agent in the United States had been swept up by the FBI in the wake of the Sebold affair. The man in charge of the project was Walther Kappe, a one-time leader of the German-American Bund who had returned to Germany in 1937 to become a lieutenant in the Abwehr. Kappe picked his prospective saboteurs from among men who had lived for some time in the United States and who were fluent in English and familiar with American customs. Ranging in age from twenty-two to thirty-nine, each man had a trade that would enable him to attain a job in American war industries, and each had been examined for his loyalty to nazism. With a touch of irony, Kappe called the project Operation Pastorius, after Franz Daniel Pastorius, the leader of a community of German Mennonites who had emigrated to Pennsylvania in 1683.

The eight men were given two months' training at a sabotage school near Berlin, where they were instructed in the properties and use of explosives, fuses, and timing devices. They learned how to immobilize machinery with abrasive materials and memorized the locations of industrial plants vital to the American war effort. Aircraft and aluminium plants were given the highest priority, although railroad lines and bridges were also targeted. They were warned against renewing associations with old friends and rehearsed the life stories they had been provided like actors learning a role. To document these "legends," as such cover histories are known, they carried forged birth certificates, draft deferment, and Social Security cards, and automobile drivers' licenses. The team leaders were given a $50,000 general fund and another $20,000 to be divided among their men if needed. Each man also carried a money belt containing $4,000 and a wallet with $400 in small bills. In all, the saboteurs were allotted the then considerable sum of $175,000, most of it in $50 bills. Once they reached the United States, they were to split up into pairs and make their way to their assigned targets.

Immediately after a team headed by George Dasch landed on a fog-shrouded beach near Amagansett near midnight on June 12, 1942, they began changing into civilian clothes from the German navy fatigues they had worn on the submarine. Suddenly, Dasch saw a hazy cone of light approaching from across the dunes. He froze in fright. As the light came closer, he gradually made out the shadowy figure of man in a Coast Guard uniform with a flashlight. Seaman 2c. John Cullen of the Amagansett Coast Guard Station was making the midnight beach patrol.

"What's going on here?" he demanded. "Who are you?"

"There's nothing wrong," said Dasch casually. "We're fishermen [from East Hampton]. Our boat ran aground and we're going to wait here until daylight."

Daylight was still four hours away, Cullen pointed out, and he told Dasch to come with him to the station to identify himself. Dasch left his companions and walked up the beach with the sailor for a short distance. Realizing that the young man was unarmed, Dasch refused to go farther. When Cullen insisted that he come to the station, the German growled, "How old are you?"

"Twenty-one," the Coast Guardsman replied.

"Do you have a father? Do you have a mother?"

Cullen nodded yes to both questions.

"Well, I wouldn't want to have to kill you," said Dasch. "You don't know what this is all about. . . . Forget about this and I'll give you some money and you can have a good time."

Now thoroughly frightened, Cullen declined the money and looked about nervously with the hope of breaking away. But Dasch stuffed a wad of bills into his hand and held him tightly by the arm.

"Look into my eyes!" he commanded. "Look into my eyes! You'll be meeting me in East Hampton sometime. Do you know me?"

"No, sir," replied Cullen, "I never saw you in my life." He backed away slowly and then ran into the fog.

Dasch returned to his companions, and the team hastily buried their uniforms and boxes of equipment in the dunes and began walking toward the village of Amagansett. Back at the Coast Guard station, Cullen roused his mates and told them what had happened. He showed them the money—$260—as proof. At daybreak, they returned to the beach and found footprints that led them to the cache of explosives and German uniforms. The FBI was notified, and a search was launched for the infiltrators.

In the meantime, the saboteurs had made their way to Manhattan. Dasch and Ernest Burger shared a room at the Governor Clinton Hotel, while the other two men checked into another hotel. Dasch and Burger began to consider their position. For reasons that have never become entirely clear, they decided to betray the operation to the FBI. Dasch later claimed to have been anti-Nazi all along, while Burger, a one-time storm trooper, had gotten into trouble with the Gestapo. Perhaps they realized that the encounter with the Coast Guardsman made them hunted men and that they faced the death penalty if they were caught. Or perhaps they hoped to get away with the money they carried. Whatever the reason, Dasch went to Washington on June 19 and turned himself in to the FBI.

Without coaxing, Dasch eagerly poured out his story, including the intended arrival of another sabotage team on the Florida coast. The four men had, in fact, landed two days before. He identified the members of both teams now on the loose and provided the FBI with the names of his contacts in the United States. Using the records of investigations of persons who had returned to Germany before the outbreak of war, FBI counterintelligence agents located friends and relatives of Dasch's companions and placed them under surveillance. Disobeying their instructions, several of the saboteurs renewed their contacts and were arrested before they had a chance to put their plans for sabotage into effect.

Every one of the eight saboteurs was in FBI custody within fourteen days after the first team landed on Long Island. They were tried before a secret military commission on sabotage charges, and all were convicted and sentenced to death. Six died in the electric chair at the District of Columbia Jail on August 8, 1942; Dasch's and Burger's sentences were commuted to long prison terms. Following the war, both were deported to Germany. Upon being informed of the dismal failure of Operation Pastorius, Adolf Hitler angrily denounced the Abwehr for its bungling incompetence. Admiral Canaris's days as Germany's spymaster were clearly numbered.

Two years later, the Germans tried again. On November 29, 1944, a pair of agents—William G. Colepaugh, a native-born American of German ancestry, and a German national named Erich Gimpel—were put ashore in Frenchman Bay, Maine, from a submarine. This operation was run by RSHA, or Reich Security Administration, which had absorbed the Abwehr. Colepaugh and Gimpel were instructed to transmit technical data on shipbuilding, aircraft production, rockets, and similar information that could be picked up from such open sources as newspapers and magazines. They carried sixty thousand dollars in cash and ninety-nine small diamonds that they were to sell in order to support themselves during what was supposed to be a two-year mission in enemy territory.

Once ashore, Colepaugh and Gimpel, who lacked hats and warm clothes, walked heads down through a snowstorm to the main highway, where they flagged down an automobile. The car turned out to be a taxi, and the driver took them into Bangor. After traveling to New York by train, the two men took an apartment on Beekman Place on the East Side.

The spies may have felt invisible in the huge metropolis, but the FBI was already on their trail. On December 3 a British freighter had been torpedoed near Mount Desert Island—the first ship lost off American shores in some time—and the FBI surmised that the attacking U-boat might have used the opportunity to deposit spies on the lonely Maine coast. A team of counterintelligence agents fanned out over the area. Several residents, including an 18-year-old Boy Scout, reported having spotted two men trudging along the road and thinking it odd that they should be out in such weather without hats and heavy coats.

Meantime, the FBI's quarry began halfhearted preparations for their intelligence mission. They purchased a radio, which Colepaugh intended to convert into a transmitter, but spent most of their time shopping, dining in expensive restaurants, and going to movies. Then Colepaugh, like George Dasch before him, got cold feet. Giving Gimpel the slip, he went to the home of a friend in Queens and told him that he was a Nazi spy. Following several days of indecision, the friend called the FBI. Colepaugh was taken into custody the day after Christmas.

Colepaugh readily confessed and furnished the FBI with Gimpel's description and the address of the apartment they had shared. But Gimpel had fled. FBI agents checked hotels and rooming houses all over the city and kept an eye on a Times Square newsstand where Colepaugh told them his companion often bought newspapers. He also told them Gimpel had the habit of keeping spending money in the breast pocket of his jacket. On December 30, 1944, two agents who were keeping the newsstand under surveillance spotted a man who matched Gimpel's description. Having selected a paperback, he reached into the breast pocket of his jacket for a bill to pay for it. The agents nodded to each other and moved in. Both Colepaugh and Gimpel were convicted of espionage by a military court and sentenced to death, but the sentences were commuted to life imprisonment. They, too, were deported after the war.

The abortive Colepaugh-Gimpel mission was the swan song of German efforts to spy on the United States. Like most of the previous attempts, it failed because of poor selection of personnel and carelessness in details, such as the failure to provide Colepaugh and Gimpel with clothing that would not attract attention during the Maine winter. Unlike World War I, the Axis was never able to establish a viable espionage-sabotage apparatus in America. In all, the FBI investigated 19,649 cases of suspected sabotage during the war, but every one was determined to have been an ordinary industrial accident caused by fatigue, carelessness, or spite against employers.

■ ■ ■

Throughout the first two years of the war, the question of opening a second front in Europe dominated relations between the Allies. Stalin, desperately in need of relief from the German onslaught, pressed for an immediate invasion of Western Europe that would force Hitler to divert troops from the eastern front. Haunted by the bloodletting of World War I, Churchill resisted a direct assault because he feared a major landing in

France was risky at best and might result in tremendous casualties. Instead, he urged a peripheral strategy designed to wear down the Germans by attacks in Norway and the Mediterranean while massive bombing raids destroyed German industry. Roosevelt was more in tune with Stalin, but was unable to make good on the promise of a second front until 1944 because of shortages of shipping and equipment. For the time being, he opted for the Churchillian strategy. Stalin contemptuously dismissed these arguments, and his conspiratorial mind seethed with suspicion that the Soviet Union and Germany were being allowed to destroy each other so that the capitalists could dominate postwar Europe.

Two weeks after Pearl Harbor, Churchill flew to Washington to confer with the president at what became known as the Arcadia Conference. He pressed for an immediate invasion of French North Africa to trap the German Afrika Korps between two Allied forces and to reopen the Mediterranean to Allied shipping. Besides taking pressure off the Russians, the invasion might knock Italy out of the war and give the Allies an enormous boost in morale. American military leaders regarded the Mediterranean as a "sideshow," but Roosevelt eventually was won over. Eager to have American troops in action before the end of 1942, he gave his approval to the plan, and Operation Torch was launched with a late October or early November deadline.

The projected invasion was to be the testing ground of America's new intelligence organization. "Our whole future may depend on the outcome of Torch and the accuracy of our estimates," Donovan told his staff. Washington's knowledge of conditions in North Africa was almost nil, however. "My opposite numbers [in military intelligence] in the fall of 1941 didn't know the difference between Algeria and French Equatorial Africa," observed Sherman Kent, a senior OSS analyst. Asked for information about the water supply of Libya, they pulled out a folder containing "one cable, dated about 1927, one page out of the smut section of a Hearst Sunday supplement which was entitled 'Thirst in the Desert,' a travel folder with a picture of an oasis and two date palms. . . . This was the information in the file on the water supply of Libya."

Worried by German activity in French North Africa, the United States had kept an eye on conditions in the area since well before Pearl Harbor. Since the defeat of France, the country and its colonies had been governed by the pro-Nazi Vichy regime of Marshal Henri Pétain. In February 1941, the Americans had allowed the Vichy regime to import limited quantities of American cotton and petroleum products in exchange for an observation post. Twelve vice-consuls were stationed in key North African cities to make certain that none of the supplies fell into Axis hands. These "food control officers" assumed positions at Algiers and Oran in Algeria, Tunis in Tunisia, and Casablanca in Morocco. In reality, their primary task was to gather intelligence as they moved about the ports or mingled in the gambling casinos with German and Italian officers, spies, informers, double agents, and high-priced prostitutes.

The Twelve Disciples, as they became known, were an oddly assorted lot. Picked by ONI and MID with the cooperation of the State Department, they had only one thing in common: they spoke French fluently. Consular officials who were not privy to their real duties complained that they did no work. The Germans guessed immediately that they were secret agents, but contemptuously dismissed them. "All their thoughts were centered on their social, sexual, or culinary interests; petty quarrels and jealousies are daily incidents with them," the Gestapo reported. "We can only congratulate ourselves on the selection of this group of enemy agents who will give us no trouble."

The Nazis erred, however. Within a few weeks of arriving in the summer of 1941, the amateur spies began transmitting vital information to Washington through Robert Murphy, the consul general at Algiers and chief American political agent in the region. They gathered data on the battle-readiness of the French colonial army and the French navy, which included the battleship *Jean Bart,* mapped harbor defenses and port facilities, and assessed local sentiment toward the Vichy regime. They also organized a network of informers and secret radio transmitters. Following the Anglo-American decision to invade North Africa, this underground operation was turned over to the COI and its successor, the OSS.

Donovan posted Colonel William A. Eddy, a highly decorated World War I Marine, to supervise the North African intelligence apparatus. Eddy, whose cover was naval attaché in the consulate-general at Tangier, was ideally suited for the job. Born in Syria of American missionary parents, he spoke fluent Arabic and French and had headed the English Department at the American University in Cairo, where he introduced basketball to the Egyptians.

In the beginning, Eddy had more trouble with the British, who resented American poaching on their territory, than with the Germans.* The chief of MI6 in Tangier was a man "who would sell his country, his soul, or his mother for a peseta," wrote Eddy, and was so jealous of the Americans that he supposedly plotted to poison his own assistant for being "too straightforward" with the "cousins."

Would the French military in North Africa welcome or resist an Allied invasion? The senior officers had sworn an oath of personal allegiance to the aged Marshal Pétain, the head of the Vichy regime; to

---

*The British secret agents included a beautiful young blonde secretary who kept an "open bed" for amorous Spanish generals, according to Eddy.

renounce it would be, in their eyes, an act of treason.* Other Frenchmen, who considered France to be still at war with Germany, supported General Charles de Gaulle, the leader of the Free French. Although de Gaulle was backed by the British, he was disliked by the Americans. Robert Murphy, who had been placed in charge of the operation, sought a leader elsewhere and selected General Henri Giraud, a courageous but unimaginative soldier who had escaped German captivity, as the man who could best appeal to all sectors of French society.

While Murphy was juggling the various French factions, Eddy, armed with a $2 million fund provided by Donovan, created a clandestine network that vastly expanded the existing French underground. Two OSS agents—Carleton Coon, a Harvard anthropologist, and Gordon Browne, who had once worked in the wool and leather business in Casablanca—enlisted the support of several local leaders. Among them were an adventurer codenamed Tassels, whose Rif tribesmen roamed the mountainous coastal region of Morocco, and a Moorish religious leader called Strings, who mobilized his thousands of followers to gather information for the Americans. Arms and ammunition were shipped in diplomatic pouches from the British arsenal at Gibraltar to Tangier, and smugglers delivered them to Casablanca. A supply of hand grenades left over from the Spanish Civil War was brought in from Spanish Morocco by mule pack, disguised as contraband tea and sugar.

Although there were a few foul-ups, Eddy's agents provided a large volume of detailed information on beach conditions, fortifications, and the strength of French forces. Supplemented by ULTRA decrypts and other reports, they gave General Eisenhower, who had been named to head the expedition, an unusually detailed picture of operational conditions. In August 1942, Eddy was called to London to brief Allied leaders. Limping from an old wound and wearing his Marine uniform with five rows of ribbons, he was a striking figure. "The son of a bitch's been shot at enough," declared an admiring General George S. Patton. Even General Strong, the head of MID and a bitter critic of Donovan's secret warriors, was impressed by his depth of information.

Eisenhower's staff was unenthusiastic about some of Eddy's more unorthodox operations, however. Once the landings had begun, he urged that the senior members of the German administration in North Africa, many of them Gestapo agents, be assassinated. The proposal was "squashed at a higher level," and the OSS fell back upon a contingency plan: a British-educated black African who quoted Shakespeare in clipped Oxbridge English agreed to lace the drinks of the Nazi officials with

*Naval officers, in particular, were loyal to Vichy. They could not forgive the British for having bombarded the French fleet in Oran in 1940 to prevent it from falling into German hands.

knockout drops. In another operation, Eddy smuggled out the chief harbor pilot of Port Lyautey, an expert on the North African coast and its winds and tides. Hidden in the trunk of an OSS agent's car, the man nearly asphyxiated as he was driven over the frontier to Tangier.*

No expedition that included an army of one hundred thousand men, their supplies and equipment, and an armada of ships could be kept secret, so an elaborate campaign of deception was organized to confuse the Germans about the Allied target. False reports were spread by OSS agents that the expedition was headed for Dakar, on the coast of French West Africa, about 1,500 miles to the south of Casablanca. To account for the large number of ships in Gibraltar harbor, word was spread that the vessels were destined for the relief of beleaguered Malta. These reports merely confirmed the Germans' own analysis. Like the Americans who had dismissed the possibility of an attack on Pearl Harbor in the belief that the Japanese lacked the capability to strike such a blow, the Germans were certain that the Allies did not have the strength to carry out a North African invasion.

■ ■ ■

On November 8, 1942, President Roosevelt was at Shangri-La, his retreat in the Catoctin Mountains of Western Maryland. Visitors noted that he seemed on edge, as if awaiting important news. Eventually, a telephone call came through from the War Department in Washington. Roosevelt's hand shook as he took the receiver from a secretary. He listened intently until he had heard the message through and then burst out: "Thank God! Thank God! That sounds grand. Congratulations."

The president dropped the phone and turned to his guests with a broad smile.

"We have landed in North Africa," he declared. "Casualties are below expectations. We are fighting back."

The Germans and Vichy French were stunned by the invasion. They realized the landings were underway only when they heard the engines of the landing craft, throbbing like thunder, bringing the assault teams to the beaches. Initial resistance was light, but soon stiffened. Fighting was particularly heavy in the port areas, where the navy remained loyal to the Pétain government. The landings were to coincide with an uprising by the OSS-directed French underground, but in many places the operation misfired. Promised arms and explosives failed to arrive, some resistance groups were not warned of the invasion in time to mobilize, and there were last-minute defections at the top. Troops were landed on the wrong

*The OSS was criticized for bringing the Port Lyautey pilot out, on the grounds that his disappearance might tip off the Germans to one of the points where the Allies intended to land, but the project had been approved by General Patton. The pilot proved to be so valuable that he was awarded the Navy Cross and the Silver Star for his services during the landing.

beaches, and control of Algiers, the capital of French North Africa, see-sawed back and forth between the resistance and Vichy forces before the Americans could fight their way into the city.

Still, some of the special operations succeeded. The invaders were met by friendly guides as they splashed ashore and were provided with maps and information on roads, the number of planes at the airfields, and the strength of fortifications. OSS agents accompanied the troops, advising on terrain and the location of French and German headquarters. An OSS agent prevented the Vichy forces from blowing up the vital tunnel connecting Oran with the port of Mers el Kebir by removing the caps from the demolition charges the night before. And while the invasion was taking place, seven squadrons of German aircraft fruitlessly circled over Cap Bon, some three hundred miles to the east, having been decoyed out of position in pursuit of a Malta-bound convoy that never existed.

Widespread street fighting continued into the next day. Efforts by General Giraud, who had been brought out of France to persuade the Vichy forces to cease fire, were unavailing. Murphy now turned to Admiral Jean Darlan, Pétain's second in command, who by chance was in Algiers. Although Darlan was a notorious collaborator, Murphy and Eisenhower regarded him as the only man who could win over the pro-Vichy elements and end the bloodshed. The admiral allowed himself to be persuaded. Informed that the Germans had occupied those areas of France under Vichy rule, Darlan announced that Hitler had violated the 1940 armistice and declared his readiness to work with the Americans. Eisenhower recognized Darlan as French high commissioner in North Africa, and in exchange Darlan ordered the Vichy forces to lay down their arms on November 10.*

The "Darlan deal" tarnished the military success of Operation Torch. Under the Darlan regime, French officers who had actively assisted the Allies were punished, anti-Semitic Vichy decrees remained in force, and supporters of General de Gaulle were rounded up and thrown into con-centration camps. While President Roosevelt justified the arrangement as "only a temporary expedient," liberals denounced it as a squalid sellout of the democratic ideals for which the war was being fought. Anger ran especially high among OSS officers who had worked with the anti-Vichy forces in North Africa before the landings. Many had come from academia, where hatred for fascism was strong, and they skirted the edges of insubordination in protesting the betrayal. In Washington, Donovan was equally disturbed by Darlan's appointment, for it undermined the Allied appeal to resistance forces in occupied Europe. "We have before us the very practical problem of eliminating the political leadership of Darlan," he wrote. "We cannot wait too long to find a solution."

---

*American casualties totaled 1,469 killed, wounded, and missing, while those of the French were estimated at 4,500.

Whether Donovan was contemplating "executive action" against Darlan—to have him assassinated—or merely a political change is unclear. The problem was resolved for him not long afterward: on December 24, 1942, Admiral Darlan was shot to death by a fanatical young Frenchman. The assassin, executed with uncommon haste less than two days later, was variously described as a Gaullist and a monarchist supporter of the Comte de Paris, the pretender to the French throne. To the intense relief of the Americans, General Giraud was named to replace Darlan as high commissioner.

A wave of suspicion swept North Africa following the assassination. Fingers were pointed at various secret services, including pro-Gaullist elements in the OSS. When the assassin was revealed to have been a member of the Corps Franc d'Afrique, a commando unit being trained under the direction of Carleton Coon of the OSS, Coon's activities attracted the attention of the police. He had been in the vicinity of the scene of the assassination, owned a pistol of the type used to kill Darlan—a Colt Woodsman—and shared the hostility toward him. Moreover, he was an advocate of assassination as an instrument of policy.* Coon denied having had anything to do with the murder, but Colonel Eddy hastily dispatched him to the Tunisian front. "For the sake of others as well as himself, it seemed a good idea for Coon to drop out of sight," he said.

By and large, however, the Office of Strategic Services emerged from the North African campaign with increased prestige. Not all its special operations had been successful, but it had provided vital intelligence during both the period of preparation and the actual invasion. Partially as a result of its work, the vaunted Afrika Korps was ground between the British pursuing the Germans from Egypt and the Americans advancing from Algeria. The Allies had also won bases from which an invasion of southern Europe could be mounted. These accomplishments helped the new organization to win wider acceptance and support not only in Washington but among suspicious military commanders as well. The military discovered that the OSS could be a useful partner in conducting operations and that they could work with it. This new climate strengthened the agency for the serious challenges that lay ahead.

---

*Upon his return to Washington, Coon gave Donovan a report on his mission to North Africa that included an appendix advocating the formation of an elite corps of assassins. "If such a body had existed in 1933 its members could have recognized the potential danger of Hitler and his immediate disciples and killed this group," the anthropologist wrote. The only organizations with the ability to organize such a unit were the OSS and the Special Operations Executive (SOE), the British unit responsible for sabotage and subversion. "It seems therefore to me not too wild, too visionary, or too improbable a thought to suppose that from these two groups a smaller can be selected; a group of men, sober-minded and without personal ambition, men competent to judge the needs of our world society and to take whatever steps are necessary to prevent this society from permanent collapse." There is no record of Donovan's response. See Brown, *The Last Hero*, pp. 269–270.

Following the sinking of the Maine, Lieutenant Andrew Rowan was sent to Cuba to ascertain the ability of the Cuban guerrillas to assist the U.S. Army in defeating the Spaniards. Photo courtesy of The National Archives.

General Ralph H. Van Deman was the father of modern American military intelligence and is accused of originating the type of snooping policies now considered to be infringements upon our civil liberties. After being eyed by Gen. Arthur MacArthur, he was appointed head of the Military Information Division in the Philippines during our occupation of the islands. Photo courtesy of The National Archives.

Lt. Colonel Earl H. Ellis was one of the Marine Corps' leading strategists and masterminded plans to seize a Japanese-held island in the Pacific in case of war. These plans eventually became models for campaigns during World War II. His career, however, was marred by alcohol dependency and related psychological problems. Photo courtesy of The National Archives.

After World War I, Herbert O. Yardley and his team, the American Black Chamber, were responsible for breaking Japanese diplomatic codes. Yardley once even considered breaking into the Japanese Consulate in New York City to get a close look at their code books. That attempt never materialized. Photo courtesy of The National Archives.

George Dasch (right) shown here awaiting the verdict on sabotage charges was one of the eight German saboteurs landed in the United States during World War II. Six were executed and Dasch and another man were given long prison terms. Photo courtesy of The National Archives.

William F. Friedman, head of the U.S. Army's Signal Intelligence Service, broke the Japanese Purple Code after a superhuman effort. Photo courtesy of the Library of Congress.

DOING *HIS* BIT

This cartoon, which appeared in the Brooklyn *Daily Telegraph* on May 25, 1917, shortly after the Declaration of War against Germany on April 6th, depicts America being set ablaze by German followers of the Kaiser. Photo courtesy of The Library of Congress.

Major General William J. Donovan was America's Chief of Intelligence during World War II and as the head of the OSS started a trend of covert operations that continued through William Casey's reign as head of the CIA. He was watching a football game at the Polo Grounds in New York City when Pearl Harbor was bombed and President Roosevelt summoned him to Washington. Photo courtesy of The National Portrait Gallery, The Smithsonian Institution, Washington, D.C.

William Colby parachuted in France and Norway during World War II. Director of Central Intelligence during one of the CIA's most difficult periods, he prevented the agency from being dismantled but was fired by President Ford in 1976. Photo courtesy of the Central Intelligence Agency.

Richard Helms began his career as a member of the OSS. During the turbulent Vietnam years he tried to keep the CIA's intelligence independent despite President Johnson's insistence on having every branch of government support his policies. Photo courtesy of the Central Intelligence Agency.

George Bush, Colby's replacement as head of the CIA, was hand-picked by President Ford because of his steadfastness and reliability in pulling no surprises. Generally amiable and well-liked by his colleagues, Bush later said "it's the best job in Washington." In 1976, after only 10 months, he was dismissed by Jimmy Carter who distrusted Washington insiders and the CIA in particular. Photo courtesy of the Central Intelligence Agency.

William J. Casey, not your typical CIA head, was an Irish street pug who made his first million before the age of 40. Under the Reagan administration, the CIA, headed by Casey, underwent a renaissance with new employees and an expanded federal budget. But his mastery of questionable covert activities in foreign policy eventually led to Casey's downfall and damaged the reputation of the CIA and the Reagan presidency. Photo courtesy of the Central Intelligence Agency.

On the heels of the Iran-Contra affair, William H. Webster, present head of the CIA, has the job of steering the agency into a new era of cooperation with Congress and reversing the 'wildcat' policies begun by Donovan and continued through Casey. His job is to restore faith in the CIA and to bridge the gap between the CIA and its rival agency, the FBI. Photo courtesy of the Central Intelligence Agency.

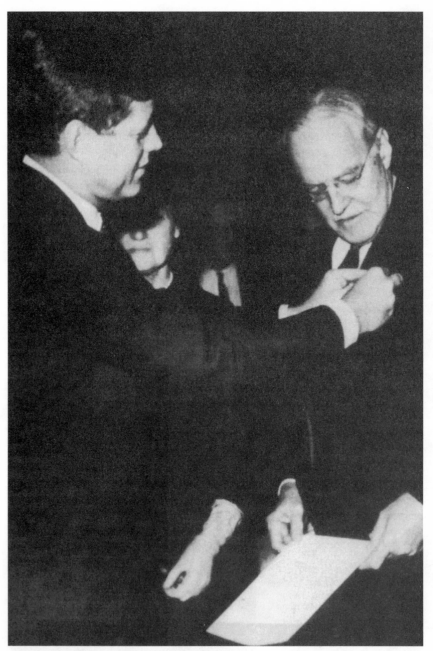

Allen W. Dulles, here being awarded the Distinguished Service Medal of the CIA by then-President Kennedy, was perhaps the most senior veteran of America's 20th century spies. Having served as the Director of the CIA under Kennedy, his spy roots go back through Donovan's OSS to Switzerland in World War I, where he had been a consular agent and spy. Photo courtesy of the Central Intelligence Agency.

14

The Unsecret Service

The parachutes snapped open with a reassuring jolt. Billowing like giant white blossoms, they silently guided a dozen men down toward a small clearing in the jungles of Japanese-occupied Burma. If a man missed the drop zone, he might dangle helplessly in the high branches of a tree until he starved to death or was eaten alive by jungle ants. Landing safely, the combat team hid their chutes in the bush and scrambled to retrieve the canisters of weapons, supplies, and explosives that had also been dropped. It was January 27, 1943, and Detachment 101, a fledgling guerrilla force fielded by the Office of Strategic Services, was launching its first mission against the Japanese.

Four months before, General "Vinegar Joe" Stilwell, commander of the China-Burma-India Theater, had only grudgingly agreed to give Detachment 101 a chance to prove itself. "All I want to hear from you are booms from the Burma jungle," he snapped to Major Carl Eifler, the unit's chief. Stilwell had been driven out of Burma by the Japanese—"We got a hell of a beating," he acknowledged—but was determined to return. The retreating Allied force had been harried by night attacks and ambushes that had sapped their strength, and Detachment 101 was dispatched to give the enemy a dose of its own medicine.

Eifler faced a formidable task. Detachment 101 contained exactly twenty-five officers and men originally intended for duty in China. No one had any experience in jungle warfare, and northern Burma was described by Winston Churchill as "the most formidable fighting country imaginable." Range after range of jungle-covered hills reached to the horizon. Giant leeches and malarial mosquitoes made an intruder's life miserable and the monsoon-sodden jungles abounded in man-eating tigers and venomous kraits, snakes whose bite meant almost instantaneous death. Uniforms and boots rotted quickly; weapons fouled if not constantly attended to. And the Japanese were skilled jungle fighters.

273

A bear of a man who weighed 250 pounds and stood well over six feet tall, Eifler was cast in the adventurous mold of Wild Bill Donovan. Stilwell once described him as the U.S. Army's "Number One thug." He was skilled in judo and boxing, flew his own plane, was a crack shot, and during service as a border patrolman had picked up the tricks of the smuggler and covert operator. One of his favorite methods of impressing new recruits was to order them to punch him in the stomach as hard as they could while he took the blows without flinching. As soon as OSS headquarters in Washington decided to create a unit to conduct guerrilla operations in Asia, Eifler was summoned from Hawaii and given a free hand in selecting his own team. "Men were expected to volunteer blindly," he later recalled. "They were advised they likely would be signing their own death warrants. . . .

Eifler established a training camp at a tea plantation at Nazira, on the Indian frontier, and recruited hundreds of Kachin tribesmen—small, wiry men with teeth blackened from chewing betel nut and with few equals as jungle fighters—who became the backbone of Detachment 101. For generations they had inhabited the Golden Triangle where Burma, Thailand, and Laos meet, sustaining themselves on opium smuggling and mercenary service to local war lords. From them, the Americans learned to survive in the jungle: to eat termites and wild bees and to kill wild pigs with a hidden crossbow and trip line, a technique that worked equally well against the Japanese. The Kachins' favorite weapon, however, was the *panji*, bamboo stakes that had been sharpened to a needle point and planted along both sides of a trail ahead of an approaching enemy patrol. Ambushed, the Japanese would dive into the jungle for cover and impale themselves on the fire-hardened stakes.

Faced with the complexity of the machine gun, the Kachins balked: they preferred shotguns. Eifler accordingly sent a request to Washington for five hundred of the weapons. The requisition seemed odd to the bureaucrats, who demanded an explanation. "I prefer muzzleloaders," Eifler cabled back, with scarcely veiled sarcasm. "The natives can make their own black powder and use nuts and bolts from wrecked vehicles for ammunition." Taking these sardonic comments at face value, the literal-minded War Department shipped five hundred Springfield muskets that had been stored in an Army warehouse since the Civil War. The Kachins carried them proudly throughout the campaign.

Four months after receiving his orders from General Stilwell, Eifler decided Detachment 101 was ready to provide the commander with his booms in the jungle. Able Group was to be parachuted into northern Burma to sabotage the rail line between Mandalay and the main Japanese base at Myitkyina. This team consisted of eight Westerners and four Kachins who had never even seen an airplane until a few weeks before. Parachute training was rudimentary and the equipment makeshift. The back- and chest-pack parachutes used by airborne infantry were unavailable, so the men had to use the seat-cushion type worn by air crews. The drop zone was a tiny clearing that had been hacked out of the jungle by teak cutters.

Once safely on the ground, Able Group established a base camp where half the team remained while the other six men, loaded with food, arms, and a supply of Composition C, an explosive impervious to rough handling, began their trek to the railroad. Their target was about fifty miles away on the map but double that over winding hill trails that disappeared in the jungle. At one point the trail divided. The Kachin headman plucked a hair from his head, tossed it into the air and watched as it slowly drifted down onto the left fork. "The Japanese are down there," he said.

The men reached their objective two days after leaving the base camp and succeeded in laying explosive charges at several points along the tracks. Just as they were completing their work, they were discovered by a Japanese patrol. One man was killed in covering the escape; the others took cover in the jungle, the heartening sound of explosions ringing in their ears as they fled. Five months later, long after hope for them had been abandoned, the eleven survivors made their way back to the Nazira camp, having narrowly escaped capture by the pursuing Japanese. They had destroyed several miles of track and a couple of bridges, temporarily knocking out the railroad.

This episode, which marked the beginning of one of the longest and most arduous guerrilla campaigns of the war, illustrated how clandestine activities could substitute, to some degree, for larger forces when they were unavailable. By late 1944, Detachment 101 was operating all over Burma, sabotaging Japanese communications, harassing enemy patrols, and rescuing downed Allied airmen from the jungle. At top strength the unit mustered 566 Americans and some 10,000 Kachins. They inflicted an estimated 5,500 casualties on the enemy and rescued over 200 airmen. Only 15 Americans and fewer than 200 Kachins were lost in action.

General Stilwell was skeptical of the Kachins' body count, however. One day, he asked a Kachin how his people could keep such accurate records. The tribesman opened a tube tied about his waist and emptied a collection of what seemed to be dried fruit before the general.

"What's that?" Stilwell asked.

"Japanese ears," replied the Kachin.

■ ■ ■

Beginning as little more than a figment of Bill Donovan's fervid imagination, the OSS spread around the globe. By the end of the war it employed nearly sixteen thousand men and women, the equivalent of a small army division. Its budget soared to about fifty-seven million dollars, much of it from unvouchered secret funds, and Donovan himself sported the two stars of a major general. For many of those who served in the OSS, the experience was the high point of their lives. "We were gentlemen volunteers on our honor," recalled Carleton Coon. "We were never under orders. We were always asked, 'Would you like to . . . [e.g., get yourself killed]?' To which we always said 'yes.' "

OSS agents came from all walks of life. They were Ivy League academics, Wall Street bankers, bartenders, lawyers, professional athletes, polo players, White Russian princes, missionaries, movie stars, emigré intellectuals, more or less reformed second-story men, and some of the most attractive women turned out by the Seven Sisters colleges. Prospective recruits were also found among those from less exalted backgrounds who had knowledge of a foreign language or of an area of the world, or who had a skill Donovan deemed important. "There were men who did careful, scholarly work; men who did sensationally dangerous work; and men who did absolutely nothing except travel around the world on a high priority at government expense," noted Stewart Alsop, a one-time OSS man.

Among the better-known recruits were Stirling Hayden, the movie actor, who ran guns to Yugoslav partisans; Kermit Roosevelt, a grandson of Teddy Roosevelt; Jumping Joe Savoldi, a Notre Dame fullback and professional wrestler; Arthur J. Goldberg, a Chicago attorney, who ran the OSS Labor Desk and was to become a Supreme Court justice; Moe Berg, a catcher for the Boston Red Sox, who parachuted into Yugoslavia and Norway; Ilya Tolstoy, grandson of the Russian novelist; John W. Gardner, later a cabinet secretary; John K. Fairbank, founder of the Center for East Asian Studies at Harvard; Henry Ringling North, of the circus family; Ralph Bunche, later a deputy secretary-general of the United Nations; and Rene Dussaq, a Hollywood stunt man who won the Distinguished Service Cross for his work with the French underground.

There were so many Social Register names on the rolls—Mellon, Bruce, Guest, Ryan, du Pont, Vanderbilt, Morgan, and Rutherfurd, among others—that critics jibed OSS really stood for "Oh, So Social." Others might have countered that it stood for "Oh, So Socialist," for at the other end of the political spectrum it veered far leftward. Marxist philosopher Herbert Marcuse and Paul Sweezy, an equally radical economist, were on the payroll, along with several avowed Communists.* When the chief of the Latin American section of Research and Analysis closed the doors to outsiders, Arthur Schlesinger, Jr., then a young Harvard historian, joked to a colleague that a "cell meeting" was probably underway. Veterans of the Communist-sponsored Abraham Lincoln Batallion,

---

*Elizabeth T. Bentley, a one-time courier for a Soviet spy ring, later told the FBI that at least five members of the OSS had been members of her ring.

who had served on the Loyalist side during the Spanish Civil War, were enlisted as guerrillas and fought behind enemy lines. When an aide objected to the recruitment of these leftists, Donovan shrugged off the criticism. "I'd put Stalin on the OSS payroll if I thought it would help defeat Hitler," he replied.

The OSS was also known for its freewheeling atmosphere. In Yugoslavia, a colonel asked a lieutenant in the American mission to Tito to immediately encode a special message and was told that it would go out the next day during the regular radio contact.

"I'll admit it's not much fun coding but that's true of a lot of things in the Army," the colonel said.

"Army?" replied the lieutenant. "Did you say Army? Hell, man, were not in the Army. We're in the OSS."

One of Donovan's most important accomplishments was the marrying of scholars and scholarly research techniques to intelligence. "We did not rely on the 'seductive blonde' or the phoney moustache,'" he said. "The major part of our intelligence was the result of good, old-fashioned sweat." The OSS established the practice of enlisting academic talent for intelligence work—an alliance that was later soured by the war in Vietnam—and its area studies were the forerunner of similar programs that became firmly established in American universities. "But above all, in the study of the capabilities and intentions of foreign powers, I think we went far beyond anything previously known or previously attempted anywhere else," recalled William L. Langer, chief of Research and Analysis.

As the OSS expanded, R & A expanded with it. Teams were sent to the various theaters of war, where they pinpointed likely targets for bombing, provided combat briefings, and interrogated prisoners. Reconnaissance parties combed the African and European battlefields for wrecked German tanks and copied down their serial numbers, which in the hands of experts became a dependable gauge of German tank production. OSS economists applied the techniques of their discipline to strategic bombing and carried out cost-benefit analysis on the relative merits of bombing factories that made aircraft engines versus those that assembled planes or produced ball bearings. At one point they argued that planes should be shifted from bombing railroad marshaling yards, which, they said, could be swiftly repaired, to attacking synthetic oil plants in order to disable German planes and trucks. The Supreme Command, however, refused to listen.

■ ■ ■

Just as the Vichy French were closing the border with Switzerland in the wake of the American landing in North Africa in November 1942, Allen Dulles slipped over the frontier and made his way to Bern, the Swiss capital. Tweedy, urbane, and puffing on his ever-present briar pipe, he looked more like an Ivy League professor than a spymaster. Traveling under the title of Special Representative of the President of the United States, he carried a battered suitcase containing a pair of suits—and a $1 million letter of credit. Although Dulles later said a good spy should have a passion for anonymity, he took a fine apartment in a picturesque building overlooking the Aare River, hired a housekeeper-cook—who turned out to be a German spy—and, having leaked word of his presence to the local press, waited for informants to contact him.

Dulles was no stranger to the shadowy world of cloak-and-dagger operations. He had been an American consular agent and spy in neutral Switzerland during World War I and a member of President Wilson's staff at the Paris peace conference, and he had held several diplomatic posts abroad. In the 1930s, along with his brother, John Foster Dulles, he became a senior partner in the Wall Street law firm of Sullivan & Cromwell. Always a romantic about the espionage business, Dulles accepted eagerly when Bill Donovan asked him to head COI's New York City office in 1941. His relations with Donovan and David Bruce were uneasy, however. As the nearest thing to an American intelligence professional, Dulles saw himself as the future chief of a centralized intelligence agency—and the other two men as possible rivals.

Following the formation of the OSS, Dulles agreed to go to Switzerland to open a listening post. With direct civilian air service to both Berlin and London, the neutral capitals—Bern, Lisbon, Madrid, Stockholm, and Istanbul—were major sources of intelligence. In Bern, Dulles made contact with the large colony of expatriate anti-Nazi politicians, businessmen, and intellectuals living there. But the intelligence product initially forwarded by OSS/Bern to Washington was found to be flawed when checked against the ULTRA decrypts of German cipher traffic. "All news from Bern these days is being discounted one hundred percent by the War Department," Donovan told Dulles on one occasion. Not long afterward, he emphasized the need for Dulles to use "greater care in checking all your sources." Normally, the proud and ambitious Dulles would have bridled, but he was already developing an intelligence source he later described as "one of the best secret agents any intelligence service ever had."

The source was Fritz Kolbe, an obscure bureaucrat who served as assistant to Karl Ritter, the German Foreign Ministry's liaison to the supreme command of the Germany army, the Wehrmacht. Each day, he sifted though the cables that poured into Ritter's office from German embassies and intelligence posts around the globe and prepared a digest. This highly sensitive post provided Kolbe, a devout Roman Catholic and dedicated anti-Nazi, the opportunity to help destroy the Third Reich. Originally he had hoped that the "Black Orchestra"—an anti-Hitler conspiracy of German generals and members of the Abwehr—would result in the Nazis' downfall. Recognizing in the summer of 1943 that only Germany's defeat would bring this about, he decided to act on his own. "It is not enough to clench one's fist and hide it in one's pocket," he later declared. "The fist must be used to strike."

Bulging briefcase clutched tightly to his chest, Kolbe slipped into the British legation in Bern on August 23, 1943, and asked to see the military attaché. By pulling strings, he had got himself appointed a Foreign Office courier, a position that allowed him to make frequent trips to Switzerland. Eventually shown in to see a bored junior aide, Kolbe told him that he had just arrived from Germany with important information. Eyeing the balding, unimpressive fellow shifting nervously in a chair, the young man decided his visitor was either a crook or a crank and unceremoniously showed him the door. Kolbe then decided to go to the Americans. Unwilling to chance another rebuff, this time he made his approach through a friend, an anti-Nazi emigré living in Bern.

Undoubtedly recalling his failure to meet with Lenin in 1917, Dulles agreed to a rendezvous with Kolbe. "I want to see Germany defeated in this war," were Kolbe's first words. "It is the only way to save my country. I think I can help in securing that defeat." Dulles was impressed both by the man and by the 186 pages of top-secret documents that Kolbe produced from the briefcase resting on his knees. Picking up a typed sheet at random, Dulles found it to be a general-staff report on the effectiveness of super-secret V-weapons, or flying bombs and rockets, against Britain. Another was a military attaché's report from Tokyo on a planned Japanese offensive in Burma. None of the papers was more than two weeks old; most were dated only a few days before. And that was merely the beginning, because Kolbe promised many more.

The Americans were elated by this treasure trove. But were the documents authentic? Was Kolbe a legitimate defector or a German plant? Even if the documents were authentic, they might be chicken feed—genuine information handed over by the Germans to lull the Allies into a false sense of security so that they would accept deliberately misleading information later on. All of these possibilities crossed Dulles's mind, for he was too experienced a secret agent to accept Kolbe's largesse at face value. The documents were divided up between the Americans and British for examination. Comparison with decrypts of the ULTRA traffic determined that they were not only authentic but too important to have been used for bait in a deception plot, though some officials continued to suspect Kolbe was a plant.*

Kolbe was given the code name "George Wood," and the material he supplied was known at OSS headquarters in Washington as the "Boston

---

*Following the war, captured German intelligence archives and debriefings established Kolbe's bona fides. He lived on a CIA pension until his death in Switzerland a few years ago.

Series." Over a period of fourteen months, he provided OSS/Bern with about 1,600 top secret documents from the Foreign Ministry files. To Dulles, unaware of the existence of ULTRA, Kolbe's information was extraordinarily revealing. A cable from the German embassy in Buenos Aires supplied the departure date and projected course of a large American convoy about to depart the Atlantic coast of the United States. The sailing date was changed, and the convoy avoided the wolf pack of U-boats lying in wait for it. Another cable confirmed reports that the Franco regime in Spain was shipping tungsten, used to temper steel, to Germany disguised as oranges. The documents also revealed that there was a German spy, codenamed "Cicero," working in the British embassy in Turkey.*

For the first few months, Kolbe delivered documents during his visits to Bern. When the Germans tightened their security, Kolbe was issued a miniature camera and instructed to photograph any new material and send the microfilm to a "girlfriend" in Switzerland—in reality, an OSS agent. With the help of a physician friend, Kolbe did his photography in the basement of a Berlin hospital, frequently working by the light of a flashlight during Allied air raids. On one occasion, Heinrich Himmler, the Gestapo chief, arrived unexpectedly at the Foreign Ministry and requested to see a document that at that very moment was being photographed by Kolbe. Notified at the hospital, he dashed back to the office and slipped the paper into the files as he pretended to be searching for it.

As Allied interest shifted to the Far East, Washington was increasingly eager to see reports from the German military attaché in Tokyo for their insight into Japanese intentions. But Dulles had no way of communicating these demands directly to Kolbe. Eventually, he hit on the idea of sending him a postcard signed by his Swiss "mistress." The card said she wished to give her son "some of those clever Japanese toys which the shops here used to be full [of]. . . . I wonder if there might be some in Berlin?" Kolbe read between the lines, and his next batch of documents included reports direct from the German embassy in Tokyo. Although Kolbe's reports ceased after the failure of the plot against

---

*"Cicero's" presence is thought to have been first established through ULTRA decrypts of the cable traffic between Berlin and the German embassy in Ankara. The spy was later identified as Elyesa Banza, an Albanian who served as valet to the British ambassador. Upon learning of the security breach, the Secret Intelligence Service dispatched several agents to Ankara to track down the spy. They concentrated on the embassy rather than the residence, where Banza was employed, and failed to discover the identity of "Cicero" before Banza left the envoy's service. Recent claims that SIS uncovered "Cicero" and used him to transmit false information to the Germans appear to be untrue. Banza provided the Germans with information regarding Allied attempts to pressure neutral Turkey into the war and on the plans for the coming invasion of Europe, including the code name for the operation (Overlord). Ironically, senior German officials were convinced that "Cicero" was a pawn in a British deception plot and were disinclined to credit the authenticity of his information. Banza received three hundred thousand pounds from the Germans for his efforts, but the bills were counterfeit.

Hitler's life on July 20, 1944, he managed to dodge arrest and escaped to Switzerland early in 1945.

Dulles established direct contact with the anti-Hitler conspirators through Hans Bernd Gisevius, an Abwehr agent with the cover of German vice-consul in Zurich. Six feet, six inches tall, myopic, and with manners as stiff as his starched white collar, Gisevius was a member of a conservative Prussian family and despised the Nazis. "I will not demean myself by being a common thief, stealing trivia from office filing cabinets," he told Dulles, "but I will give you a list of every general in Germany who wishes to see Hitler dead, and I will help you communicate with them."* As a demonstration of his trustworthiness, Gisevius warned Dulles that the codes used by both the American and British ministers in Bern had been compromised, and read from a notebook the texts of several of Dulles's most recent dispatches to Washington.

So began an association that over the next eighteen months provided OSS/Bern with a ringside seat on the plotting against Hitler.* Gisevius usually came to Dulles's apartment whenever he returned from visits to Berlin. The American gave his housekeeper the night off on these occasions, but one evening she returned for a mislaid scarf and spotted Gisevius as he was arriving. Taking his hat, she saw the initials "H. B. G." in the inside band. The next day, she reported to officials at the German legation that Dulles had met for some time the previous evening with a tall German and gave them his initials. The identity of the man was obvious, and two senior members of the legation staff attempted to question Gisevius. Feigning anger at their interference, he told them he had dined with Dulles because the notorious American spymaster was one of his best sources of information. If they told anyone of the contact, he threatened, he would have them summarily dismissed from the diplomatic service. They humbly apologized to Gisevius for bothering him.

■ ■ ■

*Throughout the remainder of the war Dulles was a keen observer—if not an active participant in—the many plots against Hitler. Dulles's maneuverings ranged beyond Gisevius and the generals, however, to include the liberals of the Kreisau Circle, German communists, religious groups, and even representatives of Gestapo chief Himmler.

*Dulles gained his greatest renown as a spymaster as a result of Operation Sunrise, his effort to bring about the surrender of German forces in northern Italy. But a close look at the incident raises serious questions about Dulles's judgment. Late in 1944 Karl Wolf, the SS chief in Italy, put out a surrender proposal, and Dulles eagerly grasped it—at least partially to prevent Communist partisans from seizing power. Dulles seemed oblivious to the facts that Wolf was deeply involved in war crimes and really had nothing to surrender. The ultimate decision was in the hands of Field Marshal Albert Kesselring, who detested Wolf. In the final analysis, the negotiations were useless, for the German surrender in Italy came only a few days before VE-Day. The affair accomplished nothing except to arouse the anger and suspicion of Stalin, inspiring sharp exchanges between the Russian leader and Roosevelt and Churchill. Dulles also swallowed the tales of an "Alpine Redoubt" where the most fanatical Nazis would fight on to the end.

Reflecting Bill Donovan's own passion for irregular warfare, the OSS was more widely renowned for its cloak-and-dagger operations than for its contributions to strategic intelligence. Special Operations (SO) teams operated in all parts of the world except the Pacific, where the Navy and General Douglas MacArthur refused to allow them to gain a foothold. Teams of OSS men operated behind enemy lines with the French *maquis*, and Italian anti-Fascists as well as with the Kachins in Burma and the Mafia in Sicily. Extensive operations were carried out in China, sometimes with the Nationalists and sometimes with the Communists. In Indochina, OSS personnel worked with a small faction of Communists led by a wispy fellow named Ho Chi Minh and an OSS medic was credited with saving Ho's life.

The SO teams were small—three to five men—and usually parachuted in at night or landed from fishing boats. They joined the local underground, maintained clandestine radio contact with OSS headquarters, and arranged for air drops of supplies and munitions. Downed Allied fliers were assisted in escaping. Bridges, roads, and power lines were blown up to keep the Germans on edge and to hinder their movements. In Greece, the OSS supplied the partisans with a mobile field hospital that was hauled from village to village by a pack train of mules. Yugoslav partisans assisted the OSS in constructing a 600-yard-long airstrip that was used to evacuate more than four hundred downed airmen. Later, these SO teams were supplemented by larger and more heavily armed Operational Groups of thirty to forty men trained as rangers, who fought alongside local guerrilla forces against German units that had been cut off by the rapid advance that followed the Allied breakout from Normandy.

To get his agents into the field, Donovan had to overcome the opposition of Britain's Secret Intelligence Service, which blocked the OSS from using Britain or its colonies as a base for conducting independent clandestine operations. Both President Roosevelt and General Donovan were outspoken anti-imperialists, and SIS—including Sir Claude Dansey, Ralph Van Deman's old mentor, who was now its deputy chief—suspected that OSS activities would hasten the spread of anticolonialism. While the Anglophiles in the top echelon of OSS/London enjoyed their clubs, relations between the SIS and the OSS in the field grew icy, even hostile, particularly in such outposts of the Empire as Delhi, Cairo, and Ceylon. Fear was also expressed that the supposedly unsophisticated American "cousins" might "blow" ongoing operations, while the affluent Americans' ready access to unlimited resources aroused British envy and resentment of their former pupils.

In an attempt to keep tabs on the Americans, Dansey suggested that SIS and OSS share the same communications system. Donovan was not taken in by the proposal. The British would know everything the OSS was up to, while SIS kept its own activities under wraps. For his part, Donovan was determined to run his own intelligence and sabotage operations in Western Europe. Eventually, an informal arrangement was worked out with kindred spirits in the Baker Street headquarters of the Special Operations Executive (SOE), the British unconventional-warfare unit, which had also tangled with SIS. By the end of 1943, Donovan had independent agents in place in France.

The Jedburghs were the cream of Donovan's paramilitary force. A joint enterprise of OSS and SOE, these three-man teams consisted of an American, a Briton, and a native of the country in which the team was to operate. Beginning in May 1944, Jedburgh units parachuted into France to organize underground resistance in support of the forthcoming Normandy invasion. Timing was vital. If the uprising occurred too soon, the Germans might put it down; if it flared too late, it would be of no help to the Allies. Once the landings had been made, the resistance forces created chaos behind the German lines, disrupting communications, ambushing troops and convoys, and trying to prevent the retreating enemy from destroying key installations. Their basic strategy was straightforward: "Surprise, kill, and vanish."

Danger was the fourth member of every "Jed" team. A few weeks before Normandy, the Germans broadcast a warning: anyone of any nationality or uniform who was caught participating in sabotage or terrorism, or inciting revolt, would be summarily shot. The leader of one of the first Jed teams dropped into France, Major Jack Bonsal, was stopped at a German checkpoint, identified, and executed on the spot. Failures in planning were often as great a hazard as the enemy, however. Briefing data were sometimes incomplete and drop zones incorrect. One unit that was to be parachuted into Brittany was assured the area would be free of German troops, but the men were dropped right into the middle of the German Second Parachute Division. Poorly trained air crews sometimes dropped the teams far from their intended targets or alerted the enemy to their presence. Apart from the possibility of capture, traitors had infiltrated the underground, and betrayal was an ever-present danger.

In all, eighty-two Americans participated in Jedburgh operations, and fifty-three were awarded the Distinguished Service Cross, Navy Cross, Croix de Guerre, Legion of Merit, Silver or Bronze Star, or the Purple Heart—said to be the highest percentage of citations awarded to any unit during World War II. Indeed, resourcefulness and courage were the hallmarks of the Jeds. After Captain Paul Cyr and his band of *maquis* had guided several American and British airmen to safety in Allied territory, Cyr returned to the German side of the lines when he learned that important intelligence could be picked up: a member of the resistance who was employed as a cleaning woman at German headquarters had obtained a copy of the enemy's plans for the defense of the Loire, including the fortifications of the port of St. Nazaire. The Gestapo had a detailed description of Cyr, and he was risking recognition and immediate execution. Nevertheless, he passed through the German lines twice to obtain the information and deliver it to the U.S. Army.

Some of the OSS agents operated with a swashbuckling insouciance. Jack Hemingway, the son of Ernest Hemingway, jumped into France with a trout rod strapped to his leg. Captain Douglas Bazata, a dashing soldier of fortune who addressed colonels as "Sugar," eluded a German search party by disguising himself as a French peasant and creeping across a field on his hands and knees as if he were searching for mushrooms. Finding a stolid German soldier blocking his path with legs spread wide, Bazata yielded to an irresistible urge and crawled through the German's legs before vanishing into the woods.

During the Normandy invasion, the OSS participated in a massive deception operation that convinced the Germans that the landing was a diversion, and the real Allied Thrust was to be made in the Pas de Calais to the north of the Seine. Wireless messages were beamed to the resistance in the area. Minesweepers and torpedo boats operated off the coast. There was intensive activity in the English harbors and rivers opposite the Pas de Calais. The ruse was so successful that the Germans kept the entire 15th Army—22 divisions— from the Normandy front. In the week after D-Day resistance teams cut the rail lines behind the Germans in a thousand places. Road movement became virtually impossible because of fallen trees and blown bridges. The elite *Das Reich* panzer division, ordered to Normandy from Toulouse, normally a three-day trip, arrived at the front 15 days late.

In addition to working in tandem with the Normandy invasion, the OSS played a key role in the Allied landings in the south of France two months later. OSS agents run from Algiers provided accurate intelligence on the location of German coastal gun emplacements and mine fields, and pinpointed fuel and ammunition dumps. (Two days before the landing, an agent cycled from Cannes to Hyères for a last-minute inspection of the invasion area.) Operating well in advance of American forces, one OSS team fell in with some 700 former Russian soldiers who had been released by the Germans to fight the French resistance. One night they shot their German officers and went over to the other side. Still wearing the German army uniforms, they fought several pitched battles with other German units. When the rest of the American troops caught up with them, the OSS men were angered to learn that the U.S. had agreed to turn all former Red Army units back to the Russian authorities. Col. William Quinn, the Seventh Army's G-2, quickly resolved the problem. He enrolled the Russians in the French Foreign Legion and they continued to fight the Germans. Overall, OSS operations in Southern France were so successful that they earned a rare testimonial from the British, as well as accolades from General Alexander M. Patch, commanding general of the Seventh Army, who congratulated Donovan on the "extraordinary accuracy" of the intelligence provided by OSS.

■ ■ ■

Behind the scenes, however, an espionage revolution was reducing the value of cloak-and-dagger operations. MAGIC and its British counterpart, ULTRA, raised the curtain on a new era in which signals intelligence—the interception, decryption, and interpretation of enemy radio communications—eclipsed spies as the primary means of collecting intelligence. The greatest intelligence successes of World War II resulted from the solution of German and Japanese ciphers rather than from the work of clandestine operators. Reports supplied by signals intelligence (SIGINT) were fresher and more voluminous than spy reports, and they were regarded as more trustworthy by policymakers and strategists. For the most part, the spy became of no more importance to the intelligence-gathering process than the individual foot soldier was in a war of rival technologies. General George C. Marshall, the Army's chief of staff, declared that "the conduct of General Eisenhower's campaign [in Europe] and all of our operations in the Pacific are closely related in conception and timing to the information we secretly obtain through these intercepted codes."*

ULTRA enabled the British to control every Nazi agent in Britain, thereby helping fool the Germans about the location of the expected Allied invasion of Europe. Once the Allies were ashore, ULTRA warned them of German counterattacks. Its most spectacular success was achieved early in August 1944, when the Americans broke out of the Normandy hedgerows and began pouring through a narrow gap in the German defenses at Avranches. The bottleneck created a target that tempted Hitler, who ordered the German commander to pull four armored divisions out of the front line and hurl them against it. The Fuehrer's orders were intercepted and read by the codebreakers in the quonset huts at Bletchley Park in time for the Allies to prepare to check the German attack. "We've got them," one of General Omar N. Bradley's commanders declared. And they had. The failure of the German attack marked the end of Hitler's hopes of halting the invaders near their beachheads and staving off the downfall of Nazi Germany. No spy could

*For example, Baron Oshima, the Japanese ambassador to Berlin, had frequent meetings with Hitler and other ranking German officials, and his reports, sent in the broken Purple code, were read by the Americans for information regarding German intentions. Oshima reported in October 1943 that Hitler had told him he believed the Allies would land in the Balkans. The discussion also included German fallback positions in Russia. On another occasion, Oshima and the Japanese military attaché inspected the Atlantic Wall and reported in depth on German defenses against an Allied invasion.

have furnished such top-grade information with such speed and accuracy—or had it accepted with equal trust.

Signals intelligence played a vital role on every front, but codebreaking and intelligence alone could not vanquish the enemy: the war still had to be won on the field of battle. A question often asked about World War II is why the Allies didn't win more quickly if they were able to read German and Japanese codes. One answer is that they did. Another is that no matter how much information Allied generals possessed about Axis intentions and strength, they had to gather men, ships, and aircraft, supply them with weapons, ammunition, and food—and inspire them with a will to win.

■ ■ ■

Nowhere were these factors more evident than in the Battle of the Atlantic. At first the entry of the United States into the war provided a rich harvest of American shipping for the German U-boats, for the U.S. Navy was ill-prepared to meet the challenge of the Nazi submarine offensive. Escort vessels were in short supply, and there were delays in establishing inshore convoys. Thick oil from blasted tankers soon covered the Atlantic beaches, and in little more than two weeks a significant portion of the nation's coastal tanker fleet was sent to the bottom. Supported by "milch cow" submarines that supplied fuel oil and torpedoes, the predators remained on station for weeks. When inshore convoys were finally organized, Admiral Karl Dönitz, the mastermind of German submarine operations, moved his boats back to the North Atlantic sea lanes.

Codebreaking was the key to victory in the Atlantic war. At first, the Germans held the edge. B-Dienst, the German navy's radio interception and codebreaking service, had broken the British naval codes at the start of the war. As a result Dönitz had at his fingertips a remarkable array of information about the Royal Navy's operations, including the daily convoy report that gave not only the position, course, and speed of every convoy but the admiralty's estimated position of all U-boats. B-Dienst eavesdropped on this traffic until July 1943, when the British realized what was happening and changed the code. On the other hand, the cryptanalysts at Bletchley had difficulty breaking into the German naval ciphers. The navy version of the Enigma enciphering machine was more complex than the versions used by the army and Abwehr; settings were changed every twenty-four hours, a practice that virtually required the enemy to break a new cipher every day.

Fortunately, Bletchley received a gift from the sea in mid-1941. The submarine U-110, which had attacked a convoy off Greenland, was badly damaged and blown to the surface by depth charges. She was abandoned by her panicked crew but remained afloat, and a British boarding party made for the wallowing craft in a small boat. Suddenly realizing that the scuttling charges had not exploded, the U-boat's captain desperately tried to swim back to complete the job before the British got on board. Before he could pull himself up the submarine's slippery sides, he was shot dead by the boarding party. The British sailors cautiously descended into the conning tower in the eerie blue light of the emergency lamps, expecting the sub to blow up or sink under them at any moment. They were amazed to discover an Enigma machine in place, along with documents giving the daily rotor settings for three months. To protect this coup—one of the most significant intelligence breakthroughs of the war—the admiralty reported that the U-110 had been sunk.

For all its effectiveness, the German system had an Achilles heel. Admiral Dönitz insisted on directing the movements of all submarines from his headquarters at Kiel, and such tight control required a considerable volume of radio traffic. Positions and weather reports, convoy movements and sightings, and reports on the consumption of fuel and torpedoes flowed back and forth. Now that the British had an Enigma machine and its rotor settings, they were able to plot the positions of individual U-boats and wolf packs and take steps to avoid them. As the effectiveness of the U-boat campaign suddenly dropped, Dönitz, never suspecting the truth, launched an intensive but fruitless search for spies in the U-boat command.

The Enigma decrypts that clattered into the admiralty's Submarine Tracking Room over a secure line from Bletchley—called Special Intelligence rather than ULTRA—enabled the British to read all the cards in Dönitz's hand. These intercepts were not continuous or complete, however, and sometimes there were gaps of days or weeks. Beginning in February 1942, a ten-month blackout occurred when the traffic could not be read because the Atlantic U-boats were using a complex new cipher known as Triton. This blackout coincided with the entry of the United States into the war. Exacerbated by American unreadiness to deal with the submarine menace, the blackout period was the most costly and savage phase of the Battle of the Atlantic.

The struggle against the U-boats reached its zenith at the end of 1942. Even though Bletchley was beginning to read Triton, the toll in sunken ships mounted to over half a million tons per month, a much faster rate than could be offset by new construction. Bad weather in January and February 1943 reduced Allied losses, but in March the toll shot up again to 567,000 tons, against the destruction of only six enemy submarines. Convoys escaped from one wolf pack only to fall into the clutches of another. "The Germans never came so near disrupting communications between the Old World and the New as in the first twenty days of March 1943," the admiralty reported.

The crisis was deepened by the discovery that the Germans had adopted a new version of Enigma, this one with four rotors rather than three. In mid-March, the Tracking Room gloomily acknowledged that it had no clear idea where German submarines were positioned. The Battle of the Atlantic hung in the balance as the decrypters worked to solve the latest version of Enigma. Somehow, Bletchley managed to break into the new cipher, and the tide began to turn. The Secret Intelligence decrypts supplied advance warnings of impending submarine operations, allowing some convoys to be diverted away from lurking wolf packs while escort vessels were concentrated about threatened convoys. The number of ships lost began to drop, and there was a corresponding increase in U-boat kills. Convoy ON-5, a slow procession of forty-two westbound ships, is generally accepted as the turning point of the Battle of the Atlantic. In early May four wolf packs totaling fifty-six U-boats attacked the convoy despite bad weather. Twelve merchantmen were lost, but ten submarines were sunk. This dramatic triumph was merely the beginning. Forty-one U-boats—a third of all those at sea—failed to return from combat patrols in May 1943.

Defeated in the North Atlantic, Dönitz shifted his boats southward, where the seas were teeming with transports and cargo ships crammed with men and equipment for the invasions of Sicily and Italy. This time, the U.S. Navy, which had the major responsibility for protecting these convoys, was ready. Antisubmarine warfare had been centralized under the Tenth Fleet. This "fleet" had no ships and only limited personnel, but it provided coordinated direction of the campaign against the U-boats, including a steady flow of intelligence from Enigma decrypts.* The information from these intercepts was augmented by the timely arrival of sophisticated radar and direction-finding equipment and the increased availability of long-range aircraft that could keep a convoy under surveillance during an entire voyage. In time, "hunter-killer" groups built around small escort carriers searched out and sank the "milch cows" and then turned upon the attack boats. They were directed to enemy submarines by decrypts of the considerable traffic passing from the U-boats to base and back again. These groups built up a remarkable record of kills, accounting for thirteen U-boats in a two-month period.

Although the antisubmarine war continued for nearly another two years, it had been reduced to the level of a running skirmish. Ultimately the victory should be credited to the phlegmatic courage of Allied merchant seamen and the skill and gallantry of the escorts, but these might

---

*U.S. Army and Navy officers were also being filtered into the codebreaking staff at Bletchley for training. Some remained to be absorbed into the existing teams; others were detailed as intelligence officers to American military commanders. Among those who remained were Alfred W. Friendly, a future managing editor of the Washington *Post,* and William Bundy, who became an assistant secretary of state and editor of *Foreign Affairs.* "There was an amazing spirit at the place," Friendly later recalled. "Morale was high because everyone knew the fantastically successful results of our daily-and-nightly endeavor. It was one place in the military where there was no sense of futility, of useless work or of nonsense."

not have been enough without the assistance of the codebreakers at Bletchley.

■ ■ ■

SIGINT also played a vital role in the American offensive in the Pacific. The offensive began on August 7, 1942, when some sixteen thousand men of the First Marine Division splashed ashore at Guadalcanal and Tulagi in the southern Solomons. Resistance from the surprised Japanese was light, and the invaders quickly secured the un-completed airfield on Guadalcanal, the key to the control of the Solomons. But the swampy, fever-ridden island and the surrounding seas soon became the scene of a fierce struggle.

The campaign for Guadalcanal was bedeviled by the difficulties of Station Hypo (now known as the Fleet Radio Unit, Pacific, or FRUPAC) in breaking into a new version of the JN25, the Japanese naval code, that had been placed in service that summer. With decrypts running about a week behind current intercepts, the solutions were often useless, and American commanders had to rely mainly on aerial reconnaissance and Australian coast watchers for operational intelligence. Sometimes the available intelligence was disastrously inadequate, and the surrounding waters soon became known as Ironbottom Sound because of the number of ships sunk there. The worst case occurred on August 9, 1942, when a Japanese task force that had maintained radio silence surprised the American and Australian squadron covering the Guadalcanal landing. Four cruisers were sunk and another severely damaged in a daring night attack. It was the worst combat defeat ever suffered by the U.S. Navy. By early in 1943, however, FRUPAC had broken into JN25c, and throughout the remainder of the Pacific war there were only sporadic periods when Japanese radio traffic could not be read.

Early in April, these intercepts revealed that Admiral Yamamoto had established his headquarters at Rabaul, the main Japanese base in the Southwest Pacific, so that he could personally direct an all-out naval air offensive against American bases in New Guinea and the lower Sol-omons. On April 7, he was on hand to wave good luck as nearly two hundred bombers and fighters took off to raid Guadalcanal. Four days later, the Admiral decided to inspect Japanese bases in the area. FRUPAC had been keeping a special watch on the Rabaul radio circuits since Yamamoto had moved his headquarters ashore, and this vigilance paid off when a signal giving his itinerary was intercepted and decrypted. It was to be his death warrant.

The times of Yamamoto's arrivals and departures were given to the minute for each location the admiral was to visit. A glance at the map showed that the initial leg of the tour would bring him just within range of American fighters on Guadalcanal. Should an attempt be made to intercept him? Intense discussion took place at Pacific Fleet headquarters. Paradoxically, in a war in which millions died, initially there was a reluctance to consider the assassination of an opposing military leader, but it soon gave way to Admiral Nimitz's more pragmatic question: could the Japanese replace Yamamoto with a more effective fleet leader?

Edwin Layton spoke up. As a language student in Japan, he had known Yamamoto, and he now assured Nimitz that there was no one of equal skill or daring to replace him. His loss would also be a blow to Japanese morale, because in the eyes of the public he was the reincarnation of Admiral Hideki Tojo, who had destroyed the enemy fleet in the Russo-Japanese war of 1905. In short order, the admiral's fate was sealed. The ambush was assigned to a squadron of U.S. Army Air Force P-38 fighters, which had the range to reach the target area. To protect the security of the codebreaking operation, intelligence about Yamamoto's movements was credited to coast watchers in the Rabaul area. There was a succinct one-line addition to the cable: "Tally Ho. Let's get the bastard."

The interception was flawless. Two type-Betty Japanese bombers were droning over the sea toward Bougainville on April 18 when sixteen P-38s suddenly dropped out of the sun with guns blazing. Most of the twin-tailed Lightnings kept an escort of a half-dozen Zeroes occupied while a pair of American fighters concentrated on the bombers. One came up behind a Betty and riddled it with a long burst. Flames erupted from an engine, a wing broke off, and the plane smashed into the jungle at the tip of the island. The other bomber quickly followed, crashing into the sea.

Yamamoto's death was a symbolic event for both sides, for it marked the beginning of the end of the struggle in the Pacific.* Although the Japanese continued to resist every step of the way, the Americans moved with growing assurance from defense to counterattack. The march across the Pacific was supported by a vast armada of new ships and aircraft pouring from America's yards and factories, an output the Japanese could not hope to equal. Signals intelligence, which had become increasingly sophisticated and fruitful, continued to play a vital role as the island-hopping campaign advanced toward the Japanese homeland.

*Recently released records in the National Archives reveal that the chattering of the pilots assigned to the mission caused the Japanese to suspect their naval code had been broken. After the attack they changed the code, and it took the Americans four months to break it again. This information is in a top secret Air Force message of March 15, 1945, containing the itinerary of an unnamed Japanese admiral. The message suggests that no attack be made because the officer was "not worth the loss of the code."
"Past experience when message intercepted of scheduled flight Japanese Admiral Yamamoto proved disastrous," the message continues. "Allied pilots in radio breach while waiting for Admiral's plane gave Japanese tipoff on compromise of their codes. Japanese code changed immediately resulting in four-months silence Japanese naval messages. Suggest no attack unless all security precautions to insure no tipoff to Japanese regarding the source of this information."

Signals intelligence also guided submarine operations that devastated Japanese commerce. As an island nation, Japan was dependent on merchant shipping for the oil and raw materials that fueled her war machine and for the commerce between the home islands. It was thus particularly vulnerable to the lethal effects of prolonged submarine warfare. In World War I, the United States had denounced unrestricted submarine warfare, but immediately after Pearl Harbor the U.S. Navy launched a similar campaign to cut Japan's strategic jugular. In the early stages of the war, radio intelligence was used to try to plot the movements of Japanese warships so they could be attacked, but the effort met with only indifferent success. It was difficult to direct submarines from a long distance to an attack on fast-moving, well protected naval units.

Early in 1943, however, FRUPAC broke the so-called *maru* code used by Japanese merchant ships to relay their positions each day at noon. The codebreakers were now able to plot Japanese convoy routes and to flash up-to-the-minute data to American submarines on war patrol. The efficiency of the subs was thereby vastly increased, because they no longer had to make long and often fruitless searches for targets of opportunity. The number of Japanese ships sent to the bottom shot upward, reaching some 300,000 tons per month early in 1944. Japanese shipyards found it impossible to replace these losses, and the nation was all but strangled before the war was ended by the blinding flash of the atomic bomb. In all, American submarines accounted for 4,861,000 tons of Japanese merchant shipping. The severance of Japan's seaborne communications was one of the most important causes of the Japanese defeat.

■ ■ ■

Even before the war in Europe and the Pacific ground to an end, rumbles of another conflict began to be felt—the Cold War. In France, Italy, Greece, and Yugoslavia, where they worked with Communist partisans, OSS agents were unwilling witnesses to the advent of the postwar struggle. The resistance in these countries was bitterly divided between pro- and anticommunist forces, and the struggle between them was often fiercer than that with the Germans.* As the struggle for control of the postwar world took shape; the OSS was caught in the crossfire between

*In Indochina, OSS operatives urged support for Ho Chi Minh and his movement against France's attempts to reimpose its colonial rule as the Japanese withdrew. President Roosevelt had always taken a dim view of French policy in the area, saying: "France has had the country—thirty million inhabitants—for nearly a hundred years, and the people are worse off than they were in the beginning." He envisioned a trusteeship leading to independence, but died before it could be implemented. Harry S. Truman, his successor, was preoccupied by European problems, where a reborn France and the alliance with Britain were important factors, so the United States supported the revival of British and French colonialism. See Patti, *Why Viet Nam?*.

left and right at home as well. Conservatives charged that leftists in the OSS were strengthening the Communists for the coming East-West confrontation by diverting arms and other assistance to them. With equal vehemence, liberals claimed that the leadership of the OSS was tipped sharply to the right and that the organization was in the forefront of the postwar anticommunist crusade.

In point of fact, the OSS's views were colored more by the pragmatic desire to win the war than by any ideology. Rather than laying the groundwork for the Cold War, Donovan tried to maintain a working relationship with the Russians until the end of the war. Indeed, cooperation with Soviet intelligence was pioneered by the British, who went so far as to parachute a few agents of the NKVD, the Soviet secret police, into Germany and the Balkans. Some officials, however, had serious misgivings about these arrangements. "Oh dear, I am not at all pleased about this," the officer in charge confided to his diary.

Initially, Donovan, an Irish-Catholic with links to the American hierarchy, was cautious in his dealings with the Soviets. While he accepted tips on enemy subversives from the American Communist Party without telling the FBI, he did not broach the subject of cooperation between the OSS and NKVD until he visited Moscow at the end of 1943 with the hope of obtaining intelligence on Japan and the Balkans. The usually secretive Russians surprised him by agreeing readily to an exchange of missions and "gadgets," or spy equipment.

But Donovan had not reckoned with J. Edgar Hoover. Upon learning of the proposal, the longtime Red-hunter denounced it as "highly dangerous" because it would "establish in the United States a unit of the Russian Secret Service which has admittedly for its purpose the penetration into the official secrets of various government agencies." Hoover also told Attorney General Francis Biddle that NKVD agents were "attempting to obtain highly confidential information concerning War Department secrets." This was an oblique reference to the atom bomb, which was then under development by the Army's Manhattan Project.

Undoubtedly afraid that Hoover would leak the news to the rightwing press, President Roosevelt countermanded the agreement. In lieu of it, Donovan and the Russians agreed to swap intelligence. A number of reports were supplied to the NKVD, most of them from R & A, though they included one from Allen Dulles that underestimated German strength on the eve of the Ardennes offensive.* The Russians furnished a

*A tight radio blackout kept ULTRA from providing advance warning of the massive German breakthrough in the Ardennes Forest on December 16, 1944. Conventional intelligence failed as well because as the Germans fell back on their own borders, there were no resistance groups to provide information about a secret military buildup. Troop movements were made at night, and bad weather prevented Allied photoreconnaissance planes from flying. Before the ensuing Battle of the Bulge was over at the end of January 1945, 76,800 American troops were reported killed, wounded, or missing. German losses totaled 120,000 men.

smaller number of reports, some of which were said to be of high quality. Toward the latter part of 1944, however, friction developed in the Balkans, where the OSS brushed up against the conquering Red Army. An anti-Nazi coup in Rumania in August had provided the agency with a window of opportunity to rescue Allied prisoners of war—and to gather intelligence on the Balkans and Germany. With the cooperation of the Russians, a hastily thrown together airlift evacuated some 1,300 prisoners. When the air rescue teams left, the secret agents remained behind.

OSS/Bucharest was headed by Lt. Cmdr. Frank Wisner, a thirtyish former Wall Street lawyer with a Mississippi drawl and the code name "Typhoid."* Using the cover of the Allied Control Commission, a quasi-diplomatic unit, he had a front-row seat for the ruthless Sovietization of Rumania and the rest of the Balkans. The Russians looted factories and hospitals, seized American- and British-owned oil equipment, and contemptuously brushed aside democratic elements as they set about establishing a Communist dictatorship.

Wisner discovered that in their haste to escape the advancing Russians, the Germans and their Rumanian allies had left behind most of their intelligence files. Expecting to be expelled by the Russians at any minute, Wisner and his team collected the names of German agents and Rumanian collaborators who had worked for the Nazis against the Russians—and who might be willing to collaborate again, this time for another paymaster. The following year, in 1945, the Russians ordered the OSS detachment to leave Bucharest.

The Soviets' cynical betrayal of the uprising by the Polish underground in Warsaw in August 1944 also alarmed Donovan about the future of relations between East and West. While the Poles fought and died in the blazing ruins of their capital, the Russian armies deliberately stalled outside the city, allowing the Germans to suppress the rebellion—and to spare the Soviets the problem of dealing with Polish nationalism. Agonized over the fate of the Poles, Donovan prepared a massive airlift of arms and supplies in Britain and pressed Moscow for permission for the planes to use Russian airfields to refuel. The Soviets ignored every request, and the loaded B-17s sat silently on their runways. Then, on September 12, just as Polish resistance was collapsing, Stalin suddenly gave approval for the planes to land in the Ukraine after completing their mission. More than a hundred aircraft participated in the airlift, but when they arrived over Warsaw, only a few succeeded in making drops, because the city below them was engulfed in flames and smoke. Not long afterward, the Poles surrendered.

The OSS continued to cooperate with the NKVD, but these episodes

---

*Wisner had been a partner in Carter, Ledyard & Milburn, the firm in which Franklin Roosevelt had begun his career as an attorney in 1907.

and others like them convinced Donovan that a confrontation with the Soviets was inevitable. So, when the Finns, who had been allied with Germany against the Soviet Union, offered to sell the OSS four Russian military and diplomatic codes as well as some 1,500 secret documents, Donovan jumped at the offer. Much to his surprise, both President Roosevelt and Edward R. Stettinius, who had recently replaced Cordell Hull as secretary of state, were less than pleased about this coup. Donovan was ordered to immediately return the codes and other material to the Russians without telling them how they had been obtained. Before doing so, Donovan made copies of the badly damaged code books and turned them over to the FBI. Years later, they were instrumental in the cracking of the Rosenberg spy ring and the detecting of the British traitor Donald Maclean.

On its face, Roosevelt's order to return the code books to the Russians appears to be another example of his alleged naiveté in dealing with the Soviets. To return the codes to the Soviets at the very time the United States needed to be fully aware of Moscow's intentions appears to be the height of irresponsibility. But the president faced a larger problem. He was preparing to attend a Big Three meeting with Stalin and Churchill at Yalta; if the Finns or their former German ally chose to leak word that the United States had secretly obtained the Russian codes, Stalin, who was already suspicious of the Western powers, could use these reports to disrupt the conference.*

Nevertheless, the need to plan for the coming struggle remained. Not long after the failure of the Warsaw uprising, Donovan warned the president that recent developments in the Balkans "show that the Russians intend to dominate this area." And Major General Edwin L. Sibert, General Omar Bradley's chief of intelligence, felt the increasing presence of another intelligence service that was more proficient than that of the Germans. "That was the apparat of the old Communist International, which Lenin formed back in 1919 to spread the world revolution of the proletariat. Those apparats were everywhere, even in our own ranks and those of the Allied Armies."

Early in November 1944, Roosevelt asked Donovan to prepare a plan for a permanent postwar intelligence agency. It was an opportunity the OSS chief had been eagerly awaiting. Undoubtedly, the president was influenced by reports from congressional investigating committees that partially blamed the Pearl Harbor disaster upon the failure to coordinate prewar strategic intelligence, but uneasiness over Soviet policy also played a role. The request was a clear indication that Roosevelt intended to use more than personal charm in future dealings with the Russians.

*This is exactly what happened in 1960 when Soviet Premier Nikita Khrushchev stormed out of a summit meeting with President Eisenhower in Paris after a CIA-operated U-2 spy plane was shot down over Russia and Eisenhower admitted knowledge of the mission.

Two weeks later, on November 18, Donovan sent the president a top secret memorandum calling for the establishment of a permanent intelligence agency that was very much like the OSS, to be headed by a man very much like himself. "Though in the midst of war, we are also in a period of transition which, before we are aware, will take us into the tumult of rehabilitation," Donovan wrote Roosevelt in a covering letter. "An adequate and orderly intelligence system" would contribute to "informed decisions" and eliminate the confusion, waste, and unnecessary duplication pervasive in wartime intelligence operations.

The draft directive proposed the creation of an "organization which will procure intelligence both by overt and covert methods and will at the same time provide intelligence guidance, determine national intelligence objectives, and correlate the intelligence material collected by all government agencies." Like the OSS in its earlier days, the new agency was to be under the direct control of the president rather than the Joint Chiefs of Staff. Its functions would include espionage, research and analysis, counterespionage, political subversion abroad, and "such other functions and duties relating to intelligence" as the president might direct. The administrative framework would include an advisory board consisting of the secretaries of state, war and navy and "such other members" as the president might appoint to advise and assist—but not control—the director. The agency itself would coordinate the activities of other intelligence services. In an effort to head off objections from the FBI, Donovan emphasized that the proposed agency would have "no police or law enforcement functions, either at home or abroad."

Realizing the delay would permit opponents to marshal their forces against the plan, Donovan tried to kindle a sense of urgency in the White House. "We have now in the Government the trained and specialized personnel needed for the task. This talent should not be dispersed. . . . You may desire to lay the keel of the ship at once." The president, however, chose to test the atmosphere before making a final decision, and the proposal was shunted aside in the confusion of the Ardennes setback, Roosevelt's fourth inauguration, and preparations for the Yalta conference. Word of it leaked out, and, as Donovan had feared, resistance stiffened all along the line, not only to the idea of a centralized intelligence agency but to his participation in it. The opposition of J. Edgar Hoover, who had been drafting a plan for the FBI to control all overseas intelligence and was already filtering agents into Paris and other liberated European capitals, was particularly strong. John Franklin Carter had also hatched a plan that he was urging upon the president.

The storm finally broke on the morning of February 9, 1945, when the anti-Roosevelt Chicago *Tribune* and Washington *Times-Herald* spread the details of Donovan's plan all over their front pages. "Donovan Proposes Super Spy System for Postwar New Deal; Would Take Over FBI,

Secret Service, ONI and G-2," proclaimed the banner headlines. The accompanying article, written by Walter Trohan, a reporter close to Hoover,* told of the "creation of an all-powerful intelligence service to spy on the postwar world and to pry into the lives of citizens at home." The resulting furor pushed all discussion of the creation of a postwar central intelligence agency onto the back burner. As General Marshall warned, it would be "inexpedient and undesirable to take action now," because to do so would result in congressional hearings that could "endanger our best sources of intelligence"—ULTRA and MAGIC.

Franklin Roosevelt's death two months later, was also the death knell of Donovan's plan for a centralized, independent intelligence agency with himself as its director. Harry S. Truman, who followed Roosevelt into the White House, was not privy to any of the private arrangements between the late president and the OSS chief, and he had more pressing matters to attend to as the war with Germany and Japan drew to a victorious end and the explosion of the atomic bomb over Hiroshima and Nagasaki heralded a new and terrifying age. In addition, repeated warnings about an "American Gestapo" had transformed the OSS into a political liability. Despite the threatening clouds already gathering over relations with the Russians, few Americans saw any need for an all-powerful intelligence agency in the postwar world.

Donovan tried to make a personal sales pitch to the president but was rebuffed by the Missouri palace guard surrounding Truman. Influenced by the generals and admirals and Harold D. Smith, of the Bureau of the Budget, who had long resented Donovan's freewheeling ways, the president issued an executive order on September 20, 1945, abolishing the OSS as of October 1. To soften the blow, he expressed his appreciation to Donovan for "the capable leadership you have brought to a wartime activity . . . which will not be needed in time of peace" and assured him that "the postwar intelligence services of the government are being erected on the foundation" created by Donovan's organization.* With a stroke of Truman's pen, the Office of Strategic Services, America's first centralized intelligence agency, passed into legend.

■ ■ ■

Red-eyed and worn out—he had not slept much since Truman's order—Wild Bill Donovan rose to address a farewell gathering of OSS

---

*Trohan later claimed that the source of the leak was Steve Early, FDR's press secretary, rather than Hoover, but this may have been an attempt to deflect suspicion from the FBI chief.

*Research and Analysis was transferred to the State Department, while the Secret Intelligence and Counterintelligence branches were turned over to the War Department. Members of these two units threatened to resign en masse upon hearing a rumor that they were to be placed under FBI control.

veterans at a roller-skating rink near the agency's Foggy Bottom headquarters on September 28, 1945. The service, he told them, had been "an unusual experiment," one that had clearly demonstrated that "a group of Americans constituting a cross-section of racial origins, of abilities, temperaments and talents, could risk an encounter with long-established and well-trained enemy organizations. . . . You can go with the assurance that you have made a beginning in showing the people of America that only by decisions of national policy based upon accurate information can we have the chance that peace will endure."

In fact, Donovan's agency had revolutionized American intelligence. Until the coming of the OSS, intelligence was a military backwater with little prestige and even less dynamism. More often than not, it was a refuge of the inept and the second-rate. Hospitable to civilian talent, Donovan almost singlehandedly transformed intelligence into a professional career for adventurous and clever civilians. And during his tenure intelligence became a basic ingredient in the making of American strategic policy.

But the agency created in Donovan's image and likeness left other bequests as well—foremost among them, the glamorous aura surrounding its more publicized exploits, an aura only imperfectly related to their true value. The bravery of individual OSS agents and the dedication of its spymasters are unquestioned. Nor does anyone deny that OSS harmed America's enemies and buoyed the morale of people in Axis-occupied territories. Some OSS missions did contribute significantly to positive military results, such as those that preceded the North African and Normandy landings, while others led to the rescue of downed airmen and forced the Germans to spread themselves thin. Overall, however, OSS's impact on the outcome of World War II was minimal. Most of its operations were mere pinpricks. Was the destruction of a bridge or a small section of railroad track that were quickly repaired worth the lives of the brave men who carried out these missions? Or the lives of the local civilians executed by the Germans or Japanese in reprisal or as a deterrent?

Take the highly publicized OSS penetration of Germany in the closing months of the conflict, an operation run by William J. Casey, a future head of the Central Intelligence Agency. Only a handful of agents were parachuted into the already crumbling Third Reich. For the most part, they reported on such minutiae as troop movements and the location of military installations. Obtained at extreme personal risk, their reports led to the bombing of a power station here or the destruction of a troop convoy there, but none contributed intelligence that was vital to Allied strategy. Casey himself best summed up these operations. "All we could do was pop a guy into Germany with a radio and hope to hear from him," he later acknowledged.

The fact is that cloak-and-dagger derring-do has only a modest role to play in modern, total warfare—or peacetime geopolitics. Yet the tidal wave of "now it can be told" books and articles about the OSS that followed the war concentrated almost exclusively on dramatic tales of hair-raising adventures behind enemy lines. The glamorous aspects of OSS resistance and guerrilla operations were emphasized, while the day-to-day slogging of clandestine collection and analysis was all but ignored.

The long-term effects of these tales upon the popular view of the OSS—and intelligence operations in general—was devastating. Within the intelligence profession, a tension developed between those engaged in determining an enemy's intentions and ability to carry them out and the swaggering paramilitary and covert operators, a tension that was to become a consistent theme in American postwar intelligence. More broadly, the way was prepared for serious strain between those who saw the issues dividing the world's people in political terms and those who were quick to pull the trigger on clever and daring covert operations.

Raw activism has always appealed more to the American temperament than the patient assembly of small pieces of evidence into a complex mosaic. When a central intelligence agency was finally created, it paralleled the OSS experience, and the "cowboys" held the dominant role. Often they would resort to paramilitary action to resolve what were essentially political problems. The fact that OSS operations had been conducted in a unique wartime climate would be brushed aside. The Jedburghs and other Allied agents who parachuted into Western Europe had the support and cooperation of indigenous resistance groups; there was even a modicum of such support in China and Southeast Asia. The same objective conditions were lacking in the postwar world, and the domestic and international climate were often inhospitable to large-scale covert operations. Too often—as in the case of the Bay of Pigs and the Nicaraguan contra operation—the failure to make such distinctions resulted in badly conceived operations, if not outright disaster.

In short, the legacy of Donovan's OSS was powerful, rich—and mixed.

THE SPY AS BUREAUCRAT

15

Onward Cold War Soldiers

Klaus Fuchs walked into history carrying a white tennis ball in his hand. Thin and sallow and with watery eyes that peered out from behind thick lenses, he looked faintly ridiculous as he searched the sidewalks of New York's Low East Side on a winter day early in 1944. He was looking for a man who carried a pair of gloves and a book with a green cover. Then Fuchs spotted his quarry—a nondescript, middle-aged fellow with a round face. Following an exchange of a few words, they hailed a cab. The stranger gave the driver the address of a restaurant on Third Avenue.

"I am 'Raymond,'" Fuchs's companion said when they had been seated at a table far enough away from the other patrons to avoid being overheard.

Fuchs, a German-born Communist who had become a British citizen, had recently arrived in America to work as a physicist at Columbia University on the super-secret Manhattan Project that was developing an atom bomb. As "Raymond" listened intently, Fuchs provided him with information on the efforts of a joint Anglo-American team to produce a large quantity of fissionable uranium, the key to the success of the project. Fuchs promised to furnish specific details later on. After arranging a recognition signal for their next meeting, the two men parted, one leaving after the other.

In those few fleeting minutes Klaus Fuchs had unlocked the door for the Soviet Union to the most closely guarded secret in the Western arsenal. Subsequently he met at least four more times with "Raymond" in New York. After Fuchs was transferred to the laboratory in Los Alamos, New Mexico, where the bomb was being built, the courier traveled twice to New Mexico to pick up vital information. The information was then passed on to "Raymond's" NKVD control, Anatoli Yakovlev, codenamed "John," whose cover was Soviet vice-consul in New York.

Uncertain of Stalin's intentions, President Roosevelt and Prime Minister Churchill had been wary of sharing atomic secrets with their Russian allies. Through a variety of sources, however, the Russians were aware of the British and American efforts to perfect an atom bomb, and Stalin had directed the "Organs"—Soviet intelligence—to launch a major effort to rob the West of its lead in atomic research. There was no "secret" to the bomb itself; the theory of atomic weapons was widely known among scientists. The engineering and production problems, however, were overwhelming for any nation except an economic and technological superpower such as the United States.

Fuchs was a cog in a larger machine. Some of its members rationalized their cooperation with the Soviet Union with the notion that "ideas know no boundaries." Others were ideological spies, either dedicated communists or disillusioned men and women who despaired of the ability of Western democracy to combat the ravages of the Great Depression and fascism and who looked toward an idealized Soviet Union for salvation. This last group included Donald Maclean, first secretary of the British embassy and a member of the Combined Policy Committee that coordinated American, British, and Canadian efforts to build the bomb.*

To exploit the data stolen by Maclean and Fuchs, the Russians had the services of Bruno Pontecorvo, a brilliant Italian nuclear physicist who had worked on the Manhattan Project, and Allan Nunn May, a member of the National Research Council of Canada. Thus, when President Truman casually informed Stalin at the Potsdam conference that the United States had a new weapon of unusual destructive force that was to be used against Japan, the Soviet dictator expressed only a flicker of interest. In reality, he was almost as well informed about the progress of the atomic bomb as the American president himself.

Independently of Fuchs, "Raymond" also served as a conduit for David Greenglass, an Army technician at Los Alamos, to whom he was directed by Anatoli Yakovlev. The courier was instructed to use the password "I come from Julius." Greenglass supplied "Raymond" with basic data on the triggering mechanism of the bomb. Later he provided several crude drawings of the weapon to Julius Rosenberg, his brother-in-law. Julius, along with his wife, Ethel, had adopted communism with a chilling fanaticism and masterminded a network that specialized in industrial espionage.

*Walter Krivitsky, a Soviet defector who claimed to have been a high official in the GRU (Soviet military intelligence) in charge of Western Europe, is said to have told the British in 1941 that there was a young Scotsman in the Foreign Office who had become involved with communism while a student at Cambridge in the early 1930s. In equally vague terms, he added that a British journalist had been sent by the Russians to spy in Spain during the Civil War. Not until a decade later did anyone note that these shadowy clues pointed to Maclean and Harold A. R. "Kim" Philby. Krivitsky was found shot to death not long afterward in a Washington hotel. The Metropolitan Police ruled his death a suicide, but he had previously declared that the NKVD might murder him and make it look like suicide.

The atom spy ring operated undetected until 1946, when Fuchs returned to Britain to take an important position in the British nuclear establishment at Harwell and Greenglass refused to cooperate any further. By then the network had supplied the Russians with the data that enabled them to build their own bomb far more quickly than American experts had thought possible. Undoubtedly the ring's most valuable contribution was precise information on American failures. Because of its financial, technical, and scientific wealth, the United States could afford to try many alternative solutions to developmental problems concurrently, thus saving considerable time. The information supplied by the spies permitted the Russians to avoid the costly dead ends and trial-and-error mistakes of the Americans.

■ ■ ■

Fear and suspicion divided the United States from its Soviet ally even before the guns of World War II had cooled. The Russians, paranoid after three nearly fatal invasions from the West and ideologically committed to world revolution, rapidly moved to fill the strategic vacuum left by the collapse of Europe and the old colonial order in Asia. Alarmed, the United States committed itself to the defense of the West from Soviet ambitions. Each of the superpowers saw the other, in mirror image, as a predator. Repeated alarms, inflamed rhetoric, and confrontational attitudes on both sides set the stage for the Cold War—and for the apparent need to maintain a permanent intelligence and espionage capability. In this changed atmosphere, many Americans were convinced that the nation was riddled with Soviet spies—a conviction seemingly borne out by events.

Early in 1945, an OSS official discovered that *Amerasia,* a left-wing magazine devoted to Asian affairs, contained an article on American-British rivalries in Thailand that quoted verbatim from a classified OSS report. Suspecting a leak, OSS security men broke into *Amerasia's* offices and "found them literally strewn with confidential government documents."* The FBI secured a warrant and followed up with a raid in June, in which some seventeen hundred classified documents were seized. Six persons were arrested on charges of conspiring to pass secrets to a foreign power, including Philip Jaffe, the magazine's editor, a naval intelligence officer, and John Stewart Service, a State Department expert on China who was critical of the Nationalist Chinese regime. Jaffe and an assistant pleaded guilty to possessing classified documents and were fined, but a grand jury refused to return an indictment against the

---

*Willis George, the head of the OSS team that carried out the burglary, later revealed that he had taken part in some two hundred "black bag" jobs while working for OSS and the Office of Naval Intelligence.

others.† The *Amerasia* case fanned public hysteria about spies and the "climate of treason" alleged to prevail in Washington.

The revelations of Elizabeth T. Bentley, a self-confessed courier for a Soviet spy ring, fanned the fires of suspicion. In 1945, she supplied the FBI with the names of more than a hundred people allegedly linked to the Soviet underground. Twenty-seven were employed by the U.S. government—among them, Harry Dexter White, assistant secretary of the treasury, and Alger Hiss, a rising young State Department official.

Hiss had been fingered as a possible Communist at least three times before. In 1939, Whittaker Chambers, a one-time Soviet courier, had warned Assistant Secretary of State Adolf Berle that Hiss, then Berle's assistant, was a Communist, but the charges were dismissed as those of a crank. At about the same time, William C. Bullitt, the U.S. envoy to Paris, told Stanley Hornbeck, Hiss's superior at the State Department, that French intelligence had information naming Hiss and his brother Donald as Soviet agents. Hornbeck asked Hiss if he was a Communist; upon receiving a denial, he promptly forgot the matter. In 1945, Igor Gouzenko, a GRU code clerk in the Russian embassy in Ottawa who had defected to the West, reported that an assistant to Secretary of State Edward R. Stettinius was a Soviet agent. By process of elimination, the trail seemed to lead to Hiss, but once again the charges were ignored. No one in authority seriously doubted the loyalty of a man with Hiss's impeccable credentials. Along with the others named by Bentley, he was placed under surveillance, but the FBI was unable to establish evidence of ongoing espionage activity. In 1946 Hiss left the State Department for the prestigious job of president of the Carnegie Foundation for International Peace.*

Persistent rumors circulated that the Manhattan Project had been infiltrated by Soviet spies, rumors that were given substance in 1946 by the arrest of Allan Nunn May. Unmasked by Igor Gouzenko, May acknowledged that he had spied for the Soviets. Unrepentant to the last, he accepted a ten-year sentence rather than reveal his associates. The FBI, which had launched an investigation on its own, was stymied. But in the

†Service returned to duty at the State Department, but in 1950 Senator Joseph R. McCarthy revived the *Amerasia* case as part of his compaign against "Communists in government." McCarthy questioned Service's loyalty because of his criticism of the Nationalists, who were driven from the Chinese mainland by the Communists in 1949. Following prolonged loyalty and security hearings, Service was dismissed from the State Department. He filed suit and won reinstatement in 1957. The *Amerasia* case was also investigated by two congressional committees, but the source of the documents found in the periodical's files was never disclosed. Jaffe was in contact with a Soviet agent and was amenable to passing secret information to him, although there was no evidence he ever did so.

*After two trials, Hiss was convicted of perjury in 1950 for denying under oath before a congressional committee that he had ever known Whittaker Chambers or given him secret documents from State Department files. Harry Dexter White died in 1948 shortly after Bentley went public with her charges against him.

summer of 1949, a combination of hard work, good luck, and Russian carelessness assisted American codebreakers in cracking the Soviet cipher that Wild Bill Donovan had secretly purchased from the Finns. It revealed that the laboratories at Los Alamos had indeed been penetrated by foreign agents.

The Russian cipher was relatively simple compared to the machine-enciphered Enigma and Purple codes. It was based on 999 five-digit numbers, each of which corresponded to a single letter, word, or key phrase. Unfortunately, the code book recovered by the Finns had been badly burned, and many of the five-digit numbers were unintelligible. To make the cryptanalysts' task even more difficult, the code was to be used with special note pads, each page of which contained a different series of additives that were added to the original numbers to produce an endless series of variations on the basic system. Known as "one-time pads," they were issued to Soviet operatives throughout the world with the instruction that each page was to be used only once and then destroyed.

The FBI got an unexpected break when it burglarized the New York offices of the Soviet Purchasing Commission, a well-known front for espionage activities, and made off with a number of documents. When this lode was examined, FBI counterintelligence specialists were delighted to find that it included a set of the "one-time pads." The used pages had been disposed of in accordance with orders, but copies of some messages—in both cipher and plaintext—were found in the files. Working with these shards of information, the Armed Forces Security Agency,* America's newly created communications intelligence and security organization, reconstructed all 999 entries of the code book. Soon the cryptanalysts were reading the mounds of messages that had been monitored over the years but had gathered dust in the files because they could not be read.

Included among them was a copy of a cable from Churchill to Truman that had obviously come from the files of the British embassy in Washington. Further investigation provided even more shocking disclosures. Not only had a Soviet spy been able to obtain access to a private communication between two heads of state but there had been a massive hemorrhaging of secrets from both the embassy and Los Alamos. All together, there were about two dozen references to the embassy source—codenamed "Homer"—in the decrypts, but the FBI was unable to make much progress in identifying him.

In the meantime, Robert Lamphere, an FBI counterintelligence agent, poked into the mountain of decrypts and discovered a report from Klaus Fuchs on the progress of the Manhattan Project. Lamphere did not regard this as positive proof that the physicist was a spy, however. Per-

*The Armed Forces Security Agency was the predecessor of the National Security Agency.

haps the report had merely fallen into the hands of a Soviet agent. But another decrypt mentioned a British atomic spy whose sister was attending an American university. "Walking back the cat"—reconstructing Fuchs's background—revealed that his sister Kristel had been a student at Swarthmore College and that Fuchs himself had been a member of the German Communist Party before fleeing Hitler.*

Later Lamphere ruefully recalled that he passed these discoveries on to "Kim" Philby, the MI6 liaison to Washington and one-time head of British counterintelligence operations against the Soviet Union. Philby must have approached his meetings with Lamphere with a mixture of euphoria and dread, for he was a long-time Soviet mole. On the one hand, he had a ringside seat for the FBI's inquiry; on the other, the decrypts might at any moment supply clues to the identity of "Homer"—Donald Maclean—or to his own treason. Masking whatever concern he felt, Philby blandly made suggestions for dealing with Fuchs while informing the Russians that the FBI was on his trail. Regarding the physicist as expendable, Moscow decided to sacrifice him, probably to keep from blowing Philby's cover.

Under questioning by British intelligence, Fuchs appeared almost eager to admit his guilt. Since his return from America, he had become disillusioned by the Soviet Union's postwar policies in Eastern Europe and had been fitfully trying to break off his relations with the Russians. He did not seem to understand the magnitude of the charges against him, apparently hoping that if he owned up, all would be forgiven and he would be allowed to remain at Harwell. Luckily for Fuchs, British law, unlike that in the United States, made·a clear distinction between spying for a wartime ally and an enemy, and he escaped with a fourteen-year jail sentence.

The single clue the FBI had in its search for Fuchs's Soviet contact was his vague description of "Raymond." Middle-aged . . . pudgy . . . not a physicist or employed in the atomic establishment . . . knew something about chemistry . . . perhaps a chemist? Combing its lists of possible suspects, the FBI found that the description of "Raymond" matched that of Harry Gold, a Philadelphia chemist previously identified by Elizabeth Bentley as a Soviet courier. Gold readily acknowledged having been Fuchs's contact and implicated David Greenglass in the conspiracy. Badly frightened, Greenglass accused Ethel and Julius Rosenberg of persuading him to steal atomic secrets for the Russians. In short order the Rosenbergs were arrested, along with Morton Sobell, a friend and former college classmate of Julius Rosenberg.

Unlike the other suspects, the Rosenbergs and Sobell vigorously

---

*MI5, British counterintelligence, had known of Fuchs's Communist background at the time he was sent to the United States, but had ignored it. Some authorities contend this was no mere oversight but a deliberate action by Soviet agents who had infiltrated MI5.

denied having engaged in espionage, and the case became one of the most disputed in American history. To protect its most secret source, the government withheld the most damaging evidence against the couple: the Russian cipher traffic. The Rosenbergs were identified in it only by a codename, but the picture of a husband-wife team that emerged from the decrypts matched them precisely, including the fact that the woman had a brother involved in the conspiracy. Even without this evidence, a jury chose to believe Gold and Greenglass. The Rosenbergs were sentenced to death in the electric chair and executed in 1953. Gold and Sobell were each sentenced to thirty-year jail terms; Greenglass got ten years.

The Rosenbergs went to their deaths supported by the knowledge that their case had provoked a worldwide outcry of protest. The verdict was attacked not only by those who regarded the Rosenbergs as blameless victims of Cold War hysteria and an ugly undercurrent of anti-Semitism, but by those who thought them guilty but deserving of nothing worse than the jail sentence given the other conspirators.

Judge Irving Kaufman justified the death penalty on grounds that the Rosenbergs' crime was uniquely repugnant. They not only were responsible for giving the Russians the atomic bomb, he declared, but had "caused . . . the Communist aggression in Korea with the resultant casualties exceeding fifty thousand . . . and who knows but that millions more of innocent people may pay the price of your treason?" Many observers regard Kaufman's remarks as exaggerated, but in its entirety the atomic spy ring was undoubtedly the most effective ever to operate in the United States.* As a direct result of the information supplied by this network, the Russians were able to shorten the time required to develop and produce their own bomb by at least three to four years—and to reshape world history.

■ ■ ■

The United States launched its own postwar intelligence effort in an atmosphere of farce. On January 24, 1946, Fleet Admiral William D. Leahy and Rear Admiral Sydney W. Souers were ushered into the Oval Office to find themselves the centerpieces in a bizarre ceremony. Two

---

*Ronald Radosh and Joyce Milton conclude in *The Rosenberg File* that Julius Rosenberg ran a spy ring whose members were in a position to steal top secret data in the areas of radar and aeronautics even before he began trading in atomic secrets. Ethel Rosenberg probably knew of and supported these activities. None of this, however, validates Judge Kaufman's statements in sentencing the couple to death. They did not steal the "secret" of the atom bomb and certainly did not cause the Korean War. The only use the Russians could have made of the crude sketches supplied by the Rosenbergs was to confirm the sophisticated data supplied by Klaus Fuchs. According to Radosh and Milton, the real reason the federal government pushed the case against the Rosenbergs to the limit had nothing to do with the crime for which they were tried. Rather, the FBI and the prosecutors hoped to pressure Julius Rosenberg into producing the names of other active spies. In fact, they claim, Ethel Rosenberg was prosecuted on the flimsiest of evidence so she could be used as a hostage to pressure her husband into confessing.

days before, Leahy had been named the president's personal representative on the newly organized National Intelligence Authority, while Souers had been chosen director of the Central Intelligence Group, the predecessor of the CIA. Now each man received a black hat, a black cloak, and a wooden dagger as President Truman read a mock proclamation: "By virtue of the authority vested in me as Top Dog, I require and charge Front Admiral William D. Leahy and Rear Admiral Sidney W. Souers to receive and accept the vestments and appurtenances of their respective positions, namely as personal snooper and as director of centralized snooping. . . ."

Within a few months after the end of World War II, Truman realized he had made a serious mistake in dismantling the OSS. Lacking experience in foreign affairs, he was confused by the conflicting "intelligence" pouring in upon him from the State Department, the military services, and the FBI. For example, J. Edgar Hoover is supposed to have reported the death of Stalin not long after the end of the war. As Truman himself might have said, the rumor was greatly exaggerated. The president wanted "somebody, some outfit, that can make sense out of all this stuff," but there was no one to sort out the "signals" from the "noise."

With tension between the superpowers rising and the lesson of Pearl Harbor fresh in mind, everyone agreed that the nation needed a better way to handle intelligence. There agreement ended, for a bitter fight ensued over the question of who should be in control. This clash was linked to a larger battle over the reorganization of the postwar military establishment. Should the services be subordinated to a single chief of staff or, as the Navy insisted, should there be a composite Joint Chiefs of Staff whose members were equals? As numerous options were explored, the State Department and the military continued their squabbling over control of the intelligence function. The situation was so confused that Harold D. Smith, the budget director, tartly observed: "I'm not so sure that we are not approaching the subject of intelligence in a most unintelligent fashion."

Finally, on January 22, 1946, the president issued an executive order establishing a National Intelligence Authority (NIA), which was to make policy, and under it, a Central Intelligence Group (CIG), which was to carry it out. The members of the NIA were Secretary of State James F. Byrnes, Secretary of War Robert W. Patterson, Navy Secretary James V. Forrestal, and Admiral Leahy. Admiral Souers, one-time owner of the Piggly-Wiggly stores and a reservist who had become deputy chief of naval intelligence, was named head of the CIG and the nation's first Director of Central Intelligence (DCI).

The Central Intelligence Group was to coordinate and reconcile information being produced by the twenty-five American agencies involved in intelligence gathering and was responsible for providing the president and his national security advisers with a unified intelligence "product." But there was little of a centralized intelligence agency about CIG. It did not fit rationally into the structure of government and had no mandate. It was completely dependent upon the military and State Department for its budget and had a staff pegged at about one hundred professional and clerical workers. Souers's own reluctance to assume his post—he wanted to return to civilian life as soon as possible—further limited the agency's clout in the bureaucratic wars. CIG devoted much of its effort to the preparation of a daily intelligence summary for the president. Even so, its access to the Oval Office was challenged by the State Department, which insisted on supplying the president with its own digest of foreign policy issues.

In March 1946, the Army, Navy, and Air Force intelligence services were directed to join with CIG in producing the first major postwar evaluation of Soviet military capabilities. The project quickly revealed the depth of the chasm dividing the intelligence community. The military flatly refused to provide data to CIG on the grounds that it was a breach of security to supply such information to a civilian agency. Moreover, the military was interested only in those aspects of the project that served its own purposes. The Air Force, for example, trumpeted the need for a "catch up" campaign of aerial expansion, despite the fact that there was no one to catch up with. The Air Force's own secret intelligence estimates showed that the Russians were years behind American air power.

Under Lt. Gen. Hoyt S. Vandenberg, who succeeded Souers in June 1946, CIG increased in size, if not effectiveness.* The nephew of Senator Arthur H. Vandenberg, the influential Republican chairman of the Senate Foreign Relations Committee, the general was aggressive and ambitious and regarded CIG as a stepping-stone to a fourth star and the soon-to-be-created post of chief of staff of the Air Force. Awaiting these developments, he passed the time in empire building. Vandenberg persuaded the National Intelligence Authority to permit CIG to generate its own intelligence rather than depend upon the limited generosity of the other agencies and to carry out research and analysis that were "not being presently performed" by them. When aides supplied him with a proposal for an Office of Research and Evaluation to perform this function with a staff of eighty, the general promptly bucked it back with an order to come up with an operational plan for eight hundred employees.

Vandenberg also won the right to collect intelligence in Latin America, formerly the exclusive bailiwick of the FBI. His most important acquisition, however, was the remains of the old OSS secret intelligence and counterespionage units that had been transferred to the War Depart-

---

*Souers later returned to Washington as a civilian assistant to President Truman specializing in intelligence and national security affairs.

ment. Renamed the Office of Special Operations, these units gave the CIG clandestine intelligence capabilities and brought with them about one thousand employees, most of them in seven field stations. Among the inherited personnel were such old OSS hands as Richard Helms, who was in Germany, and James Jesus Angleton, in Rome. But despite the presence of individual professionals, the overall quality of the CIG and its "product" was mediocre. "It was a disorganized assembly of parts, not a working machine," noted one observer. Many of the personnel were military officers of questionable merit who had been foisted off on CIG.

For advocates of a centralized intelligence agency, the CIG was merely a way station toward that goal. Wild Bill Donovan, Allen Dulles, and other influential former OSS officers lobbied extensively for the creation of such an organization. Donovan called the existing operation the "Orphan Annie of the services" and warned that "intelligence must be our first line of defense." But it was mounting fear of the Soviet Union that clinched the agreement. Late in February 1947, President Truman sent Congress the draft of a proposed National Security Act calling for reorganization of the armed services. Included in its provisions was the establishment of the Central Intelligence Agency.

The congressional hearings focused largely on the changes in the defense structure, but there was also concern about the dangers of a large peacetime intelligence establishment. Witnesses warned against importing the evils of the European police state. There was talk of "an American Gestapo." To allay these fears, supporters emphasized that the agency's purpose was to collect, evaluate, and disseminate intelligence from overseas, not to engage in clandestine political operations at home. "The purposes of the Central Intelligence [Agency] are limited definitely to purposes outside of this country, except the collation of information gathered by other government agencies," Navy Secretary Forrestal assured the doubters.

The National Security Act, eventually passed on July 26, 1947, was one of the most far-reaching pieces of legislation in American history. In addition to creating the Central Intelligence Agency, it established the office of Secretary of Defense, mandated an independent Air Force,* and organized the National Security Council (NSC) under the chairmanship of the president, with the secretaries of state and defense as key members. Both the Joint Chiefs of Staff and the Director of Central Intelligence were to report to the NSC. For the first time, the United States had formally recognized the importance of intelligence to national security in both peace and war and centralized the intelligence process in an independent department.

To a remarkable extent, the new structure resembled the plan

---

*As he had hoped, General Vandenberg was named the first chief of staff of the U.S. Air Force. The Department of Defense was not created as a department until 1949.

William Donovan had given President Roosevelt back in 1944. Although Donovan expressed the faint hope that he would be appointed to head the CIA, he had too many enemies. The post went instead to Rear Admiral Roscoe H. Hillenkoetter, who had a background in naval intelligence and had replaced Vandenberg at CIG a few months before.

The CIA's mandate was to collect and analyze intelligence and to prepare finished estimates for the nation's top policymakers. To avoid the "Gestapo" pitfall, it had "no police, subpoena, law-enforcement powers, or internal security functions," and was not to supersede other departments and agencies in the gathering, production, and dissemination of intelligence. But the new agency was vested with extraordinary powers nonetheless. It was authorized to protect its sources and methods and to perform "such other functions and duties" relating to the national security as the NSC might direct. Like the "commerce clause" of the Constitution, this "other functions" proviso came to encompass activities only tacitly hinted at in the law. Inasmuch as the agency's charter clearly entailed a large measure of secrecy, a subsequent law, the Central Intelligence Act of 1949, exempted the CIA from all federal laws that required the disclosure of the "functions, names, official titles, salaries or number of personnel employed by the Agency." It also gave the authority to spend money by voucher—carrying on a secret procedure that began in the administration of George Washington.

Somewhat disingenuously, President Truman later complained that he had no idea that the CIA would engage in covert activities on a massive scale. "I have been disturbed by the way the CIA has been diverted from its original assignment," he wrote in 1963. "It has become an operational and at times a policy-making arm of the government. . . . I never had any thought when I set up the CIA that it would be injected into peacetime cloak-and-dagger operations. . . . This quiet intelligence arm of the President has been so removed from its intended role that it is being interpreted as a symbol of sinister and mysterious intrigue." Perhaps so. But it was under Harry Truman that the CIA first engaged in such operations.*

■ ■ ■

*Independent of the CIA, Truman also appears to have backed a plan for government inspection of private cable communications on grounds of national security. During World War II, RCA Global, ITT World Communications, and Western Union International had made some of the traffic involving foreign targets available for scrutiny by military intelligence. Over the years, however, the government began to look at telegrams sent by American citizens about whom it had suspicions. James Forrestal, who had been appointed secretary of defense, renewed the arrangement in 1947 under the code name Shamrock. The three companies were assured that the procedure had the approval of the president and Attorney General Tom C. Clark. Hundreds of thousands of communications were scanned before Shamrock was terminated by Defense Secretary James R. Schlesinger in May 1975. Truman may have been the only president to have known of its existence. See U.S. Congress, Senate, *The National Security Agency and Fourth Amendment Rights,* pp. 57ff.

Today it is impossible to recreate the surrealistic atmosphere in which American policymakers operated during the Cold War years. A mood of foreboding and despair hung over Europe, and the Western allies were convinced that a Soviet attack was imminent. Russian troops occupied the Iranian frontier province of Azerbaijan, a civil war erupted in Greece, Communists seized power in Poland, Hungary, and Romania. In the Philippines, the government was under assault by the Huks, a Communist-led guerrilla group. In France, Communists were said to be plotting a rebellion that was to spill over into Spain. The United States responded with a multipronged counterattack. Among its elements were the Marshall Plan, designed to provide massive aid to America's allies as they rebuilt their war-shattered economies, and covert action designed to frustrate Soviet ambitions without provoking open warfare.

A murky war of spies was already underway in Berlin and Vienna, and covert actions had been under consideration in Washington since late 1946, when a cabinet-level committee discussed them with the OSS experience as background. But there was bickering over who was to have responsibility for these operations. A proposal to put them under the State Department was rejected by Secretary of State George C. Marshall on the grounds that discovery of the department's links with such activities would discredit American foreign policy. For his part, Admiral Hillenkoetter believed covert operations were not worth the risk; if direct action was required, it should be a function of the military. These arguments were soon made moot by the flow of events. In February 1948, Communists seized control of Czechoslovakia, Communist-led strikes rocked Italy and France, and it was feared that the Communists would win the Italian parliamentary elections scheduled for April.

Alarmed by these developments, Forrestal and other hard-liners pressed President Truman to use the CIA as an active Cold War weapon. If Italy went the way of Czechoslovakia, warned George F. Kennan, the head of the State Department's Policy Planning Staff, "our whole position in the Mediterranean, and possibly in Europe as well, would probably be undermined." The National Security Council ordered Hillenkoetter to ensure that the pro-Western Christian Democrats remained in power. Reluctant to become involved in covert operations, the admiral requested a legal opinion from Lawrence R. Houston, the CIA's general counsel. Did the agency have statutory authority for such operations? Houston thought that it did not. Pressed further, he amended his view, telling the admiral that the CIA could indeed become involved in these activities if directly ordered to do so by the president or the NSC. And the NSC had already spoken.

Backed by ten million dollars in secret funds, the CIA's Office of Special Operations (OSO) launched a well-coordinated propaganda campaign intended to raise fear among Italians of a Communist takeover.

James J. Angleton, drawing on his previous experience in Italy, played a leading role in the operation. Politicians were bought and sold with impunity. Tens of thousands of Americans of Italian ancestry were persuaded to appeal directly to relatives and friends at home to cast their ballots for centrist parties that would cooperate with the United States. President Truman threatened to withhold economic assistance from any Italian government that included Communists. Hints were also dropped that should the Communists win the election, the United States would extend clandestine backing to a pro-Western military coup. In the end, the Christian Democrats managed to win a large enough majority to keep the Communists out of the government—and the CIA received much of the credit for the victory.

The success of the Italian operation brought demands for similar actions elsewhere. Washington was swept by a wave of near-hysteria as a result of a cable from General Lucius D. Clay, commander of U.S. forces in Europe, warning of the imminent danger of war with the Russians. "I have felt a subtle change in Soviet attitude which I cannot define but which now gives me a feeling that it [war] may come with dramatic suddenness," Clay told the head of G-2. No hard evidence existed to indicate the Russians were actually planning to attack, but the war scare intensified Cold War attitudes.

Operating against this turbulent background, George Kennan produced a plan in May 1948 for a permanent agency to do worldwide what OSO had done in Italy. The CIA would continue the routine collection and interpretation of intelligence, while this new "directorate," euphemistically called the Office of Policy Coordination (OPC), was to engage in back-alley struggle against the Soviet Union. OPC's charter, National Security Council directive 10/2—issued six days before the Russians imposed a blockade on Berlin—was sweeping. The agency was authorized to counter the Soviet threat with propaganda, economic warfare, sabotage, and paramilitary action, including assistance to underground resistance groups in Eastern Europe. The only limitation was deniability—the proviso that, if any OPC operations were blown, the president should be able to deny any knowledge of them.

OPC was a bureaucratic anomaly. Its personnel were on the CIA payroll, and the CIA furnished logistical support and cover for its operations, while policy guidance was supposedly provided by the secretaries of state and defense. In practice, however, OPC "political action" programs emanated almost entirely from Kennan's own Policy and Planning Staff, which functioned as the operational arm of the NSC. This relationship was not surprising, for Kennan was the author of the policy of "containment" of Russian expansion, and Robert Joyce, the State Department liaison officer with OPC, was a former OSS agent who had served with the Yugoslav partisans. The director of central intelligence was completely bypassed, even though, in theory, he was to coordinate all intelligence operations. The net result was that *nobody* had ultimate authority for riding herd on OPC, and an activist director could do almost anything he wanted.

And that is exactly what Frank Wisner did.

■ ■ ■

Balding and fleshy though not yet forty, Frank Wisner looked like the prosperous Wall Street lawyer he was, but few Americans had more experience in the black art of covert operations. After being expelled from Rumania by the Soviets, he had served briefly with the OSS in Germany and then returned to his legal practice after the war. Finding the world of estates and trusts too tame, in 1947 he readily accepted the post of deputy assistant secretary of state for occupied countries, an intelligence rather than a diplomatic assignment.

Wisner was appointed director of OPC—his title was actually assistant director for policy coordination—at the suggestion of Dean G. Acheson, the under secretary of state, who recommended him to Secretary of State Marshall. By background, training, and temperament, he was ideally suited to run a secret war against the Soviet Union, but the appointment stirred opposition—particularly from military intelligence, which regarded Wisner as "another Donovan who'll run away with the ball." But Wisner had strong backing from Forrestal, General Clay, and Allen Dulles, all of whom espoused a "liberationist" doctrine aimed at rolling back the Soviet presence in Eastern Europe.

Wisner bears roughly the same relation to Cold War covert operations that Edward Teller does to the hydrogen bomb. Experiences in the Soviet-occupied Balkans and postwar Germany had left him with an obsessive hatred of communism and the conviction that a conflict with the Soviet Union was inevitable. Energetic, adventurous, and something of a romantic, he bristled with ideas to wage unconventional warfare against Moscow and its satellites and created OPC in the activist image of the OSS. To him, the CIA under Admiral Hillenkoetter was "a bunch of old washerwomen exchanging gossip while they rinse through the dirty linen."

As a bulwark against Communist encroachment upon Western Europe, OPC subsidized anticommunist politicians, such as West Germany's Willy Brandt and Alcide de Gaspari of Italy, as well as journalists and student and labor leaders. Discontent among the oppressed peoples of Eastern Europe was to be fanned to the point where they would rise up against their Communist masters. Guerrilla bands, backed up by secret arms caches, were to be organized and held in readiness to sabotage and slow up any Russian offensive against the West. Unaware that OSS operations had been marred by a high degree of failure, American policymakers confidently expected Wisner to repeat the fabled successes of World War II.

Soon the dilapidated "tempos" near the Reflecting Pool where OPC had its headquarters were crowded with bright young men and women from Ivy League campuses with socially impeccable backgrounds. Joining the CIA was considered a glamorous and even fashionable thing to do. Stewart Alsop called Wisner's recruits "Bold Easterners"; less admiring observers dubbed them Ivy League dilettantes. They included old OSS hands like Kermit Roosevelt, Tom Braden, Tracy Barnes, and William Colby, as well as recruits such as Desmond FitzGerald, Cord Meyer, William F. Buckley, Jr., and E. Howard Hunt. OPC, Colby observed, operated "in the atmosphere of an order of Knights Templars, to save Western freedom from Communist darkness—and from war."

With World War III apparently imminent, the need for intelligence on Russian capabilities and intentions was urgent. Harry Rositzke, a longtime CIA officer, recalls a 1948 meeting at the Pentagon that began with an Army colonel banging his fist on the table and shouting: "I want an agent with a radio on every goddamn airfield between Berlin and the Urals!" An Air Force officer demanded that the agency immediately supply him with a Soviet TU-4 strategic bomber for examination, preferably complete with pilot. But the Soviet Union was a "denied area," closed to the West, and the United States lacked intelligence resources behind the Iron Curtain. No current information was available on Soviet scientific and technological progress or on the huge armies that Stalin was said to be preparing for the assault he intended to launch as soon as he checkmated the American atomic bomb by developing one of his own. Even the most elementary facts on roads, bridges, and the location and productive capacity of factories were unavailable. Lacking the time for the patient building of networks and support organizations, Wisner tried to fill the gap with the assets at hand.

Reinhard Gehlen, Germany's wartime Soviet expert, was a key figure in his plans. As chief of the eastern military intelligence section of the German armed forces' high command, Gehlen had earned a reputation for accurate estimates of the Russian situation, even risking the anger of Hitler with truthful reports when the tide turned against the German invaders.* Gehlen had also worked closely with the puppet governments in Nazi-occupied areas and the "stay behind" networks the Germans had established in the Soviet rear as they were driven back by the Russians.

---

*Early in 1945, General Heinz Guderian, the chief of staff on the eastern front, presented Hitler with an estimate of the deteriorating military situation prepared by Gehlen. "Completely idiotic!" Hitler shouted, and he demanded that Gehlen be committed to an insane asylum. Guderian angrily defended his intelligence chief and the report. "If you want General Gehlen sent to a lunatic asylum, then you had better have me certified as well," Guderian retorted. Hitler relented, but both Guderian and Gehlen were placed on his black list.

Realizing at war's end that he would be sought by the Soviets for punishment even though he claimed never to have been a Nazi, he made plans to ensure his survival.

Like many Germans, Gehlen was convinced that it was only a matter of time before the alliance between the Russians and the West unraveled. In anticipation of that day, he microfilmed his files, stored them in steel boxes—some fifty in all—and buried the boxes in the Bavarian Alps, directly in the path of the advancing Americans, to whom he and his staff surrendered in May 1945. Gehlen offered his interrogators—among them, Frank Wisner and Allen Dulles, then OSS station chief in Germany—not only his files but access to his networks in Soviet territory. The Americans, already worried about a confrontation with the Soviets, accepted with alacrity. Gehlen was brought to America for further interrogation and then sent back to Germany in July 1946. As head of the American-subsidized ORG (Organisation Gehlen), he directed espionage activities against the Soviet Union and its satellites. Gehlen thus became the only Wehrmacht general to function in the postwar era with his wartime staff almost intact.*

From his archives, Gehlen provided Wisner with the dossiers of Eastern Europeans who had served the Nazi puppet governments in the Baltic states, Byelorussia, Georgia, the Ukraine, and other German-occupied territories in Eastern Europe. Most were hiding out in displaced-persons camps in Germany; some were accused of having massacred thousands of Jews as well as their own countrymen. Wisner also combed old OSS political intelligence files, including those he had compiled in Bucharest, for Nazi collaborators. Soon, anticommunist zealots from all over Eastern Europe were enrolled in his spy networks and guerrilla armies. They were the nucleus of the underground liberation army that was to roll back the Iron Curtain.

■ ■ ■

In the dark of the moon of September 5, 1949—a few days after the Russians had exploded their own atomic bomb—an unmarked C-47 took off from an airfield in West Germany and headed across Eastern Europe.

---

*Gehlen warned the Americans of Stalin's plans to drive the Western allies out of Berlin, but his reports were not believed until the Russians blockaded the city. Long before anyone else, he reported that the Russians were planning to transform their zone of occupation into the German Democratic Republic, which would have its own army, complete with tank divisions, and its own air force. By piecing together bits of information obtained from interrogations of returning German prisoners who had worked in Soviet factories and mines, or rebuilding dams and highways, Gehlen was able to deduce significant information about the state of Soviet reconstruction. One POW brought back with him an ordinary-looking piece of ore that turned out to be a fragment of radioactive uranium pitchblende, which was thought to be unknown in the Soviet Union. Another provided a soup bowl made out of a piece of special aircraft metal; the bowl enabled Gehlen to make a precise estimate of the level of development of Soviet metallurgical processes.

Over a drop zone in the Carpathian Mountains, two men bailed out to join a Ukrainian partisan army, once encouraged by the Nazis, that was still fighting to prevent Soviet reoccupation of their territory. The mission was the first deep penetration of the Soviet Union launched by OPC.

Over the next five years, until well after Stalin's death in 1953, OPC made repeated efforts to infiltrate agents behind the Iron Curtain. Wisner also created a gaggle of "National Committees of Liberation" and "research institutes" that served as fronts for former officials of Nazi puppet governments.* Some were admitted to the United States even though they were wanted by war crimes tribunals. The emigrés claimed to have operatives behind the Iron Curtain, but in reality the Soviets had long since rolled up whatever networks they had. Most were mere paper mills churning out "intelligence" fabricated from newspapers, old books, radio broadcasts, and gossip. They had little popular support in their homelands because they had been responsible for savage atrocities while working for the Nazis. Nevertheless, Wisner was pleased by the flood of supposedly inside information. One of the biggest coups scored by Kim Philby was the unloading of several emigré groups infiltrated by Soviet agents upon the all-too-eager Americans. Pleading a lack of funding from Britain's impecunious postwar government, Philby agreed to turn them over to Wisner in exchange for OPC's financial support. The sardonic Philby must have smiled to himself as Wisner eagerly took control of these hollow shells.*

The displaced-persons camps were fertile ground for recruits for Wisner's guerrilla army. Hundreds of thousands of young refugees—Byelorussians, Poles, Balts, Ukrainians, and anti-Stalinist Russians—lacked both work and the prospect of emigration. The "special forces" provided good pay and living conditions, and there was the chance of later being allowed to go to the United States. Schools were established where American and former Wehrmacht and Waffen-SS instructors provided training in the use of small arms, wireless operation, and demolition. Secret agents to be dropped behind the Iron Curtain were provided with legends, forged documents, and miniature radio transmitters, as well as a few thousand rubles and small bags of gold coins for use in case of emergency. Some were assigned to contact guerrilla groups that were still supposedly active, while others were to take jobs in Soviet industry and report on what they found.

---

*Funding came from the American Committee for Liberation from Bolshevism, originally a subsidiary of the National Committee for a Free Europe, which was financed through the "private" fund-raising efforts of the Crusade for Freedom. In actuality, over 90 percent of its income came from the unvouchered accounts of the CIA. The money had been laundered through such groups as the Rockefeller and Carnegie Funds and the Ford Foundation's Russian Research Committee.

*In his memoirs, published after his flight to the Soviet Union, Philby dismissed Wisner as "a young man for so responsible a job, balding and running self-importantly to fat."

Wisner saw nothing vicious in using Nazi collaborators in what were perceived to be the legitimate needs of national security. Imbued with the anticommunist spirit of the Cold War, American intelligence officers believed moral ends justified possibly immoral means. They were not alone, for the British and the French—and the Russians as well—perverted the hunt for war criminals into a pretext for recruiting Nazi scientists and intelligence operatives, almost racing to see who could hunt down the most valuable assets. In fact, Klaus Barbie, the so-called Butcher of Lyons, was employed by the British before he was picked up by American military intelligence for use as an informant on secret Communist cells in Western Europe. Asked why he made use of someone like Gehlen, Allen Dulles tartly expressed the prevailing point of view: "There are few archbishops in espionage. He's on our side and that's all that matters. Besides, one needn't ask him to one's club."

Wisner's aggressive tactics brought him into conflict with the rest of the intelligence community. In 1949, OPC fielded a staff of 302 officers in five stations and commanded a budget of $4.7 million. By 1952, it had mushroomed to about 4,000 employees in forty-seven stations, and the budget had climbed to $82 million.* Most of its personnel were tucked away in embassies, consulates, and military and trade missions, where to the casual observer they seemed indentical to their bona fide diplomatic colleagues. They had diplomatic titles, appeared to have legitimate duties, and enjoyed all diplomatic privileges, including immunity from arrest. Wisner's ability to stuff embassies with intelligence agents togged out as diplomats was a measure of OPC's clout.

To a considerable extent, Wisner's empire building came at the expense of OSO, the clandestine arm of the CIA. OSO personnel regarded themselves as intelligence professionals and looked down upon OPC operatives as "cowboys" whose noisy, high-risk operations endangered their efforts to collect information. OPC and OSO squabbled over jurisdiction, stole each other's agents, and trod upon each other's operations. Interagency raiding was also not uncommon. One military intelligence officer recalls being offered a high-paying job by OPC with the stipulation that he bring the Army's list of assets with him. He refused, but others did not. OPC was envied, feared, and resented by other intelligence agencies because of its power, influence, and apparently limitless financial resources.

OPC operations often had an Alice in Wonderland quality about them. A team of Ukrainians who were parachuted behind the Iron Curtain were supplied with folding bicycles—and were arrested by the

---

*This figure is cited by the Church Committee (U.S. Congress, Senate, *Final Report*, Book 4, pp. 31–32), but it may be an understatement. Other sources say OPC accounted for perhaps as much as half of CIA's budget and in the early 1950s was spending more than $100 million annually in Eastern Europe alone.

first policeman they came across, because folding bicycles were unavailable in the Soviet Union. One day, John Bross, a member of OPC's Eastern European Division, was asked by a colleague: "How many guerrillas do we deploy in Poland by D plus thirty?" (that is, thirty days after war began). Pulling a figure out of the air, Bross answered, "Thirty-seven thousand." Much to his surprise, this offhanded estimate became the accepted goal.

Even more surprising, it unexpectedly seemed attainable. An organization called Freedom and Independence (known as WIN, from its Polish initials), which claimed to be the remnants of the old Polish underground that had fought the Germans, made contact with OPC and sought assistance in fighting the Russians. CIA counterintelligence advised caution, but OPC, in its eagerness to gain guerrilla capability in Eastern Europe, pressed ahead. Substantial amounts of money, arms, and equipment were airdropped to WIN over the next two years. Then, in December 1952, Warsaw announced with much fanfare that UB, the Polish security agency, had rolled up a plot to overthrow the government. Further investigation revealed that WIN was controlled by UB from the beginning.

A few of OPC's early attempts to infiltrate Eastern Europe were successful and provided information for a brief time, but for the most part, the record was bleak. Agents were quickly captured and executed. Some were "turned" by the Soviets and transmitted false information; others proclaimed themselves as having been Soviet agents at staged press conferences. The Gehlen organization and the "special forces" school were later discovered to have been riddled with Soviet agents. Philby tipped off the Soviets to planned infiltrations. A force of five hundred Albanians recruited by Wisner slipped over the frontier from Greece to depose the Communist dictatorship of Enver Hoxa, only to be ambushed. And a failed attempt to parachute reinforcements for the Ukrainian partisans prompted a macabre epitaph from Philby: "I do not know what happened to the parties concerned. But I can make an informed guess."

■ ■ ■

The performance of CIA analysts also drew mixed reviews. Intelligence analysis is more of an art than a science, for the analyst must often move out of the realm of the factual into the arena of speculation to determine the intentions of a foreign leader. Nevertheless, expectations remain high. "America's people expect you to be on a communing level with God and Joe Stalin," observed General Walter Bedell ("Beetle") Smith, who became director of central intelligence during the war in Korea. "They expect you to be able to say that a war will start next Tuesday at 5:32 P.M."

The reality fell considerably short of such expectations. For the most part, the CIA's summaries in its early years offered little that could not be found in the dispatches of seasoned newspaper correspondents, because the agency lacked inside information from behind the Iron Curtain. And its extrapolation from the hard data was not always the height of accuracy. In 1948, the quarrel between Tito and Stalin that resulted in the expulsion of Yugoslavia from the Communist International seems to have taken the CIA unawares even though Moscow and Belgrade had been openly feuding for some time. Once the split had occurred, CIA analysts correctly predicted that it would probably result in a disruptive purge of Communist ranks, but added a trifle optimistically that it would "complete the elimination of communism as a formidable political movement in Western Europe." The agency was also severely criticized for its failure to provide warning of the *Bogotazo*, a savage antigovernment, anti-Yankee riot that swept Bogotá, Colombia, during a meeting of hemispheric foreign ministers in April. Admiral Hillenkoetter contended that the CIA had indeed warned the State Department of unrest in the Colombian capital but that the warning had been ignored.

Estimates of the situation in East Asia were also spotty. The Communist victory in China in 1949 created an urgent need for intelligence in the region, but the task was made difficult by the fact that the CIA, like the OSS, had been barred from the Far East command by General Douglas MacArthur. In fact, the agency had only three men in all of Japan, and they worked out of a Tokyo hotel room because MacArthur would not allow them to open an office. The outbreak of war in Korea on June 25, 1950, surprised both the CIA and General Charles Willoughby, MacArthur's G-2, who controlled Far Eastern intelligence and tailored his estimates to fit the known desires of his superior.

The North Korean invasion across the 38th parallel, the line dividing the two Koreas that had been created in the aftermath of World War II, soon had the outclassed South Koreans fleeing from their capital at Seoul. Despite assistance from the United Nations, most of it American, it appeared that the entire country would soon be overrun. Truman and his aides saw the North Korean attack as a test of America's will to resist communist expansion everywhere. Failure to respond would influence Chinese and Soviet policy throughout East Asia.

The intelligence background of the attack resembled the preliminaries to Pearl Harbor. Throughout the spring of 1950, the CIA reported that the North Koreans were building up their forces and were sending guerrillas into the South but discounted the possibility of an invasion. Willoughby also scoffed at field reports of large North Korean tank and troop movements and the clearing of farmers from the border zone—both clear invasion signals. In Washington, a similar lack of concern about an invasion prevailed. On June 20, Dean Rusk, assistant secretary of state for Far Eastern affairs, told a congressional committee: "We see no present intention that the people across the border have any intention of fighting a major war for that purpose." As in 1941, American officials realized the enemy had the capacity to attack but paid too much attention to what they hoped it would do and not enough to what it was capable of doing.

Dissatisfied with the CIA's performance, President Truman dismissed Admiral Hillenkoetter and appointed "Beetle" Smith in his place. Brilliant and acerbic, Smith had been General Eisenhower's chief of staff during World War II and was regarded as the driving force behind the Allied victory in Europe. A postwar tour as envoy to Moscow had left him with a hatred of communism and the Soviet Union. He was, it was said, the most even-tempered man in the world—always angry—and stomach ulcers had done nothing to soothe his temper.

Before Smith could settle into his new post, there was fresh controversy over the adequacy of intelligence estimates in Korea. Regaining the initiative, UN forces under General MacArthur had driven the North Koreans back over the 38th parallel, and the question was whether Communist China would intervene if MacArthur's army pushed on to the Yalu River border with China. Regarding China as little more than a Soviet satellite, CIA analysts took the position that the Chinese would intervene only if it suited the Russians. "While full-scale Chinese Communist intervention must be regarded as a continuing possibility, consideration of all known factors leads to the conclusion that barring a Soviet decision for global war, such action is not probable in 1950," the agency reported.*

But as MacArthur's forces approached the Yalu, reports intensified of a Chinese buildup and the presence of Chinese "volunteers" in the war zone, and the CIA's reporting took on a note of urgency. The most accurate intelligence was provided by a former Chinese Nationalist officer who slipped into Manchuria, where he had served before the Communist takeover. From close observation, augmented by information supplied by former colleagues now serving in the People's Liberation Army, he was able to establish the number and order of battle of Chinese Communist troops along the Manchurian-North Korean border. Coupled

---

*Beginning in the autumn of 1950, MacArthur began complaining to Washington that his "strategic movements" were being relayed to the Communists. At this time Philby was active in Washington, Guy Burgess was a second secretary in the British embassy, and Donald Maclean was head of the American Department of the Foreign Office in London. Commonwealth troops were fighting in Korea, so considerable traffic concerning the war passed through the embassy to London, and the trio of traitors would have had access to it. Before his death in 1983, Maclean indicated that he had provided Moscow with a copy of an order from Truman to MacArthur forbidding the general to cross the Yalu into China or to use atomic weapons against a Chinese attack, thus relieving the Chinese from the fear of such retribution.

with other sources of information, these reports provided the UN high command with a warning of an imminent Chinese crossing of the Yalu. The reports were made available to MacArthur, but it was already too late. On November 24, he launched a general offensive with the typically grandiloquent statement that the war would be over by Christmas. Wave after wave of Chinese troops surprised the outnumbered UN forces two days later and sent them reeling in a retreat that did not end until all of North Korea had been abandoned.

When the battle line was ultimately stabilized near the 38th parallel and truce talks began in July 1951, OPC replaced the UN "police action" with "boom and bang" operations against North Korea and the Chinese mainland designed to keep the Communists off balance. Directed by Hans Tofte, an old East Asia hand who had served in the OSS, these operations ranged from creating an evasion and escape network for downed fliers to sending a force of about 1,200 guerrillas into North Korea. At least a half-dozen agents infiltrated the Soviet naval base at Vladivostok, where they kept an eye out for any sign of possible Russian intervention into the war. Tofte also cut the telephone cable under the Yellow Sea used by Chinese troop commanders in Manchuria to communicate with their headquarters in Peking. With this link severed, the Chinese were forced to use radio communications—which were monitored by the Armed Forces Security Agency.

Tofte's boldest operation was an unabashed act of piracy—the seizure on the high seas of a shipload of medical supplies and equipment desperately needed by the Chinese Communists to deal with an epidemic that was felling thousands of their troops. The supplies, including three field hospitals, were furnished by the neutralist government of Indian prime minister Jawaharlal Nehru and were being carried on a Norwegian freighter. OPC/Washington's orders were blunt: Although the ship flew the flag of a friendly nation, the cargo must be prevented from reaching China. Tofte planned to sabotage the vessel when it put into Hong Kong for supplies, but the port was bypassed. After hurried arrangements were made with the Nationalist Chinese, armed but unmarked vessels intercepted the freighter off Formosa. While a team of OPC officers masterminded the operation from below deck, the Chinese transferred the cargo to their own vessels. The crew of the freighter were allowed to proceed on their way, believing they had been the victims of China Sea pirates.*

In the years following the Korean War, more than a hundred Chinese agents were recruited and trained for guerrilla operations on the mainland, and several teams were parachuted in or landed on the coast. They found no sign of the "extensive resistance elements" that the Chinese

---

*Tofte was a controversial figure and was fired by the CIA in 1966 following a flap in which it was charged that he kept a stock of classified documents in his home.

Nationalists claimed were fighting the Communists. Similar pinpricks continued to be made until about 1960, resulting in little but the capture of the CIA officers running them and the death of their operatives. The agency also supported a 10,000-man Chinese Nationalist army in Burma that invaded China in 1952 and was routed. Retreating into Burma, the army's remnants settled down to the more profitable business of producing opium. In Asia as in Eastern Europe, the CIA's efforts to topple Communist regimes left them unshaken and intact.

■ ■ ■

Under the vigorous leadership of General Smith and the pressures of the Korean War, the CIA expanded rapidly from about five thousand employees in 1950 to fifteen thousand in 1955, as well as thousands of contract employees and foreign agents. The war had globalized the Cold War, and the United States now had bases in thirty-six countries. Impatient with jurisdictional arguments within the agency and the intelligence community as a whole, Smith brought his prestige to bear to increase its effectiveness. Various study commissions had repeatedly criticized the agency's failure to produce authoritative estimates and to coordinate the intelligence activities of the rest of the community. Too often, it was charged, it acted as just another intelligence agency in competition with the others.

To improve the quality of CIA intelligence estimates, the general persuaded William Langer, who had headed the Research and Analysis section of OSS, to take a leave of absence from Harvard to establish the Office of National Estimates (ONE). Under Langer's guidance, the office prepared papers that were vastly improved in quality. They provided assessments of enemy intentions and a full range of options for the president's consideration. To prevent end runs by those peddling their own line, Smith insisted that these estimates be presented to Truman without contrary briefings from other agencies; objections to the agreed text were to be stated in footnotes. ONE also showed initiative by producing reports on subjects for which no specific request had been made. In a similar vein, Smith acted to regularize the intelligence analysis section of the agency by creating a deputy directorate for intelligence (DDI), headed by Robert Amory, a Harvard Law School professor. For the first time, the CIA began to fulfill the task for which it was originally created: to coordinate the intelligence-gathering programs of the various government agencies and to inform and advise the nation's policymakers.

Less than a week after assuming office, the general took decisive steps to bring OPC under his control. Before they had time to object, Smith told the secretaries of state and defense that he was assuming full control of the organization. From now on, they were to channel policy guidance through him rather than Frank Wisner. In January 1951, he brought Allen Dulles in from the wings, where he had served as an unofficial adviser to successive DCIs, and made him deputy director for plans, with instructions to arrange a shotgun marriage of OPC and OSO. Not long afterward, Dulles was named deputy director of central intelligence.

The proposed merger proceeded slowly, and late in the summer of 1952 Smith called a meeting of all the officers involved. Lyman B. Kirkpatrick relates that the usual objections were voiced, whereupon the general's legendary temper flared. Abruptly, he cut off discussion, announced that the merger would take place whether everyone liked it or not, and stalked out. Smith had recently lost fifty pounds following an ulcer operation, and one of the officials now leaned over and whispered to Kirkpatrick: "My God, if he is that terrifying now, imagine what he must have been at full weight!" The merger did take place, with OPC and OSO combined into the Deputy Directorate for Plans (DDP), to be headed by OPC's Frank Wisner. Richard Helms, drawn from OSO to strike a balance, was named his second in command, or chief of operations. In addition to DDI and DDP, Smith created a third unit, the Deputy Directorate for Administration (DDA), to consolidate such functions as budget, personnel, security, and logistics.

But "Beetle" Smith's stay at CIA was brief. Immediately after his inauguration in 1953, President Eisenhower appointed his old comrade under secretary of state, and Allen Dulles moved up to DCI. Nevertheless, in his three years in office, Smith had left an enduring mark on the agency, establishing the basic structure and scale that were to prevail for the next two decades. The centralized intelligence agency envisioned by Wild Bill Donovan nearly a decade before was now a functioning reality.

16

The Struggle for the World

Everyone was surprised by the telephone calls. Late in the afternoon of April 25, 1956, the entire West Berlin press corps was summoned to a briefing in the Soviet sector of the divided city. Such an invitation was unprecedented, and the hall buzzed with rumors as Colonel Ivan A. Kotsyuba, acting commandant of the Soviet military garrison, took the rostrum. Kotsyuba announced that the Russians had just discovered a secret tunnel leading from West to East Berlin. The Central Intelligence Agency, he charged, had been using the tunnel to tap Soviet military communications—an act of "criminal espionage." Brushing off questions from the excited reporters, he announced that they would all be taken to the site for a personal inspection.

Flanked by motorcycle outriders with sirens screaming, a convoy of fully loaded buses sped off through the falling darkness to the suburb of Alt-Gliencke, where, close to the Western quarter of Rudow, they halted at a large hole surrounded by searchlights. The head of a Soviet officer poked out, and he genially called to the journalists to join him. "Come along, gentlemen, come closer. Climb down to me." The reporters clambered down a ladder leading into a subterranean chamber, and the Russian showed them around.

The curved walls of the underground room were lined with banks of amplifiers that were hooked up to three large telephone cables. The officer explained that a tunnel, some five hundred yards long and fifteen feet deep, had been dug from West Berlin to this interception room, where taps had been placed on the trunk lines that carried the three hundred telephone circuits linking Red Army headquarters in East Berlin to Moscow. Boosted by the amplifiers, the captured messages were sent back through the tunnel to West Berlin, where they were recorded on tape. Through slits in a steel door at the other end of the tunnel, the journalists could see flickers of light and clearly hear snatches of conversation in American-accented English.

The Russians claimed the tunnel had been discovered four days earlier by signal troops assigned to make routine repairs to the cables. After digging down six feet, they discoverd a steel door bearing an inscription in German and Russian: "No Admittance by Order of the Commanding Officer." The puzzled soldiers called their headquarters and, after some delay, received orders to break in the door. The startled Americans on the other side of the door fled so suddenly that they left a pot of coffee percolating on a burner.

The Berlin tunnel—Operation Gold—was a combined project of the American, British, and West German intelligence services and was intended to close a dangerous gap in their coverage of Soviet communications. To prevent the West from listening in on their radio messages, the Russians had switched to ultrahigh frequencies that could not be monitored. Western intelligence tried to overcome this setback by tapping Russian telephone lines, but the Soviets began using scrambler phones that defied eavesdropping. Fortunately, a scientific wizard working for the CIA, Carl Nelson, had recently discovered that a trace of the actual voice transmission remained on a telephone line for a split second after being scrambled and that this "shadow" could be picked up.

Not long afterward, one of Reinhard Gehlen's agents came up with drawings showing that the East German telephone cables ran tantalizingly close to the American-occupied sector of Berlin. But they were six feet underground. How could a tap be installed without alerting the Russians and East Germans? William K. Harvey, head of the CIA's Operations Base in Berlin, suggested digging a tunnel to the cables. As a precedent, he cited a tunnel the British Secret Intelligence Service had used in 1951 to tap the circuits leading from Soviet headquarters in Vienna to Moscow.* The Berlin project would be an infinitely more complex undertaking, however. The tunnelers would have to dig under a heavily patrolled border through hundreds of feet of soft soil that was prone to cave-ins.

Through the force of his personality, Harvey, a tough-talking ex-FBI agent, badgered Washington into reluctantly approving the project. Harvey was something of a legendary figure within the CIA. During the war, he had been an FBI counterintelligence agent working against the Soviet spy apparatus operating in the United States. Frustrated by his inability to prove the truth of Elizabeth Bentley's charges against Alger

*As a cover, MI6 established a shop selling imported Harris tweed, certain that it would not attract enough customers to interfere with the operation of the tap. But Harris tweed proved to be surprisingly popular with the Viennese, and the secret agents found themselves spending an ever-increasing amount of time tending the shop. Overwhelmed with orders, they finally closed the business.

Hiss and others, Harvey ran afoul of J. Edgar Hoover. In 1947, he resigned to join the newly organized CIA. With his fund of knowledge about Soviet espionage, he was placed in charge of Staff C, a small counterintelligence unit, and was credited with being the first to point an accusing finger at British mole Kim Philby.*

To add to his mystique, Harvey had an appetite for drink and women. His liquor capacity was prodigious, and he once told an acquaintance that he had been to bed with a woman every day of his life since he was twelve. He was the only CIA officer who always carried a pistol, which he sometimes left in open view on his desk. "If you ever know as many secrets as I do," he declared, "then you'll know why I carry a gun."

Indirectly, Operation Gold was also an attempt by the CIA to maintain its position as a sophisticated collector of intelligence by technological means in the face of the encroachments of the National Security Agency (NSA). The CIA had been offered the opportunity to become the nation's principal communications interception center, but "Beetle" Smith had rejected the proposal on the grounds that the agency's role in this field should consist primarily of analysis. As a result, the NSA had been established by executive order in 1952 on the structure of the old Armed Forces Security Agency. Within a few years, NSA, which was later installed in a sprawling glass and concrete complex at Fort Meade, Maryland, had grown into the largest single intelligence factory in the free world.

The tunnel was dug by U. S. Army engineers, who burrowed into East Berlin only a few feet at a time so the noise would not be heard on the surface. The British, who had developed the art of tunneling upward, drove a vertical shaft up to the telephone cables from the control chamber. As cover for the project, the Army leaked word that it was building a radar station to observe traffic at the nearby East Berlin airfield at Schönefeld. The work proceeded with difficulty. At one point, the tunnelers struck water; at another, they ran into a foul-smelling drainage field for septic tanks. The tunnel was finally completed on February 22, 1955, and the 150 sound-activated tape recorders began siphoning off their stolen secrets.

Processing the take was a monumental task. Except for the circuits

---

*Early in 1951, Philby had learned that the Americans were on the verge of identifying Donald Maclean as the Russian source "Homer" and warned him to flee through Guy Burgess, whom the Foreign Office had recently ordered to return to London from Washington because of his outrageously homosexual conduct. Assisted by Anthony Blunt, another member of the ring, Maclean made plans to slip behind the Iron Curtain. In a moment of panic, Burgess fled with him. Blunt, who had given up spying, was ordered by the Russians to defect as well, but he refused. Philby, recalled to London under suspicion of being the "third man" in the Burgess-Maclean affair, bluffed his way through an investigation and remained on the MI6 payroll until 1963, when he, too, fearing he was about to be unmasked, turned up in Moscow.

of the East German police, which were monitored on the scene for clues that the taps had been discovered, everything was shipped to Washington. Teams of translators worked round the clock in T-2, one of the World War I temporary buildings on the Mall, trying to keep up with the bales of incoming messages. Considerable information on the Soviet order of battle—the precise locations of Russian military units and their movements—mingled with such tidbits as the fact that the Soviet commander's wife was dealing in oriental rugs on the black market. The backlog was so great that the processing of information was not completed until September 1958, more than two years after the tunnel was sealed.

Several times the tappers thought they had been discovered. At one point, heat radiating from the interception chamber caused the ice directly above to melt, but it began to snow again before the Soviets noticed anything suspicious. And early one morning, the tappers were alarmed by the sound of heavy thuds overhead. Just as they were ready to abandon their posts, someone checked outside and saw that the East German police had established a temporary checkpoint directly over the chamber. Some of the guards were stamping their feet to keep warm.

"Harvey's Hole" kept a finger on the Soviet pulse for eleven months and eleven days. When at last it was exposed, the ingenuity of the Americans in putting one over on the Russians was widely admired. Indeed, the CIA ranked the Berlin tunnel high among its Cold War triumphs. Allen W. Dulles, then director of central intelligence, described it as "one of the most valuable and daring projects ever undertaken" by the agency, and Harvey received its highest award, the Distinguished Intelligence Medal.

To a remarkable degree, Operation Gold neatly sums up some of the most significant aspects of the American intelligence experience. Courage, imaginative planning, and technical brilliance were found in abundance, but the operation's contribution to the national security was problemical. As it turned out, the Russians had known all about the Berlin tunnel from the moment of its inception. George Blake, one of the British intelligence officers who participated in the planning of the operation, was a Soviet mole.

Originally named Georg Behar, Blake had served in the Dutch resistance and the British cloak-and-dagger Special Operations Executive during World War II. Afterward he became a British citizen and joined the diplomatic service. He was serving in Seoul, South Korea, when the North Koreans overran the country in 1950, and was held prisoner for three years. While in captivity, he either was brainwashed or shifted allegiance of his own free will. Returning to Britain a dedicated Communist agent, he was assigned to MI6 in West Germany, where in addition to alerting the Russians to the Berlin tunnel, he betrayed several West German agents operating behind the Iron Curtain.*

Although Blake was unaware of Carl Nelson's technique for picking up the shadows of scrambled telephone calls, he alerted the Russians to the threat to the security of their communications. Faced with the alternative of scotching the project and blowing the cover of an important source, the Russians chose instead to allow the operation to continue. It seemed a fair trade-off. The KGB maintained its penetration of Allied intelligence, while the CIA sank money and labor into processing the reams of trivia it sucked off the tapped lines.

■ ■ ■

Allen Dulles presided over what was later viewed as the golden age of the CIA. In his eight years as DCI, the agency not only expanded its operations but assumed an influential role in the conduct of American policy. Power flowed toward Dulles because of his reputation as a World War II master spy and his close working relationship with his older brother, Secretary of State John Foster Dulles. Together, the Dulles brothers had a firm grip on the making of American foreign policy. Problems could be sorted out with a single telephone call or a chat over drinks or dinner.

President Eisenhower had been elected on a stridently anticommunist platform that called for "rolling back" communism in place of the "passive" containment policies of the Truman years. But policymakers believed the nature of the Soviet threat had changed in the wake of the Korean war and the death of Stalin. Instead of outright military interventions, penetration and subversion of governments were considered the weapons likely to be used by the Russians to achieve their global ambitions. Accordingly, the CIA became the clenched fist of the Eisenhower crusade against communism. Increasing reliance was placed upon covert operations and paramilitary action, activities that gave the agency an institutional identity it has never been able to shake.

This role coincided with Dulles's own personal inclinations. If communists threatened to take over a country, he told associates, he wouldn't "wait for an engraved invitation to come in and give aid." Reflecting his service in both world wars, Dulles was fascinated by the operational side of intelligence and showed scant interest in the unglamorous business of preparing analyses and situation estimates. Ray Cline, who served in the Directorate for Intelligence during those years, declared that Dulles probably spent about three-quarters of his time and energy on the "dirty

---

*In 1961, Blake was caught as a result of a tip from a Polish defector and sentenced to forty-two years in prison. He served only six years before escaping to the Soviet Union, where he was awarded the Order of Lenin and the Order of the Red Banner.

tricks" side of the CIA. The clandestine branch of the agency absorbed about 54 percent of the billion-dollar annual budget between 1953 and 1961, and it gained nearly two thousand new employees. Up to his neck in the intricacies of specific operations, Dulles—who was known as the Great White Case Officer—was happiest when plotting with Frank Wisner, a friend from OSS days, or discussing the latest wrinkle in tradecraft. The bureaucratic details of day-to-day administration of the agency were left to Air Force General Charles P. Cabell, the deputy director.

Dulles was a sharp contrast to the glowering, monosyllabic "Beetle" Smith. Jovial and bluff and with an explosive "ho-ho" Santa Claus laugh, he reminded many people of a prep school headmaster. Tousled white hair, an ample mustache, and his ever-present briar pipe completed the portrait. He exuded charm and—much to the despair of his long-suffering wife, Clover—had an eye for attractive women. Sometimes he disposed of business while playing a sharp game of tennis with his aides; at other times recurrent gout forced him to pad about his office in carpet slippers. Although his doctor urged him to diet, he loved good food, fine wines, and the Georgetown party circuit too much to comply.*

Unlike previous directors, Dulles delighted in his reputation as a master spy and issued a steady stream of speeches, articles, and books. He liked to personally welcome new recruits to the CIA with a colorful recounting of the embarrassing tale of his missed rendezvous with Lenin in Switzerland during World War I. He insisted that proposals submitted to him be confined to a single sheet of paper; those that met his approval were authorized with an off-handed "Let's give it a try."*

■ ■ ■

The mood of the Eisenhower White House in those tense Cold War years is best reflected in a top secret report submitted by General James H. Doolittle that recommended an expansion of covert operations:

*Someone is supposed to have polled a group of ex-CIA officers as to which former DCI would they like to have at their side if they were stranded on an island. If there was an ample supply of good food and drink available, Allen Dulles was the overwhelming choice; if conditions smacked of danger, Richard Helms or William Colby won the nod.

*Dulles also earned the respect of his staff because of his stand against the Red-baiting tactics of Senator Joseph R. McCarthy. Unlike his brother, who allowed McCarthy to cut a wide swath through the State Department, Allen Dulles was uncowed when McCarthy went after William P. Bundy, an assistant to the deputy director for intelligence and son-in-law of Dean Acheson. Learning that Bundy had contributed to Alger Hiss's defense fund and implying that Bundy might be another Hiss, McCarthy demanded that Bundy appear before his Permanent Subcommittee on Investigations. Dulles firmly replied that the CIA had its secrets to protect and would investigate its own personnel. McCarthy was told by fellow Republicans on his subcommittee that he would not have their support if he pursued Bundy and the CIA. Cord Meyer was another officer shielded by Dulles from the McCarthy inquisition.

It is now clear that we are facing an implacable enemy whose avowed objective is world domination by whatever means and at whatever cost. There are no rules in such a game. Hitherto acceptable norms of human conduct do not apply. If the United States is to survive, long-standing American concepts of "fair play" must be reconsidered. We must develop effective espionage and counterespionage services and must learn to subvert, sabotage and destroy our enemies by more clever, more sophisticated and more effective methods than those used against us.

This "Anti-Communist Manifesto" was followed by National Security Council directives† giving the Directorate for Plans the green light for a no-holds-barred covert war against communism. With unlimited funds at his disposal, Wisner constructed what he called his "mighty Wurlitzer," a propaganda machine that vastly expanded the initiatives of the Truman years. He could produce any theme he wished from his network of journalists, subsidized publications,* and "agents of influence" in political parties, labor unions, and world student associations. Radio Free Europe and Radio Liberation augmented these efforts by beaming propaganda at Eastern bloc nations believed ripe for revolt.

The rumble of the mighty Wurlitzer was intended to be the accompaniment to nothing less than a mass uprising against Soviet domination. Millions of dollars were poured into training dissident East Europeans to be the spearhead of the great revolt, which was codenamed Operation Red Sox/Red Cap. Sometime late in the 1950s, the plan decreed, simultaneous revolts were to be incited by dissidents in each of the major cities of Eastern Europe, to be followed by civil war among the various ethnic and religious minorities within the Soviet Union itself. Within hours, Wisner's "liberation armies" would attack Soviet garrisons. Once the Soviets had been sufficiently weakened, North Atlantic Treaty Organization (NATO) troops would be dispatched as a peacekeeping force, with the declaration that they would remain only long enough to restore order and conduct the democratic elections that Stalin had pledged at Yalta in 1945.†

Wisner's plans were wildly romantic and absurdly impractical, and some of his colleagues were skeptical. Lyman Kirkpatrick and Richard

---

†NSC 5412/1 and 5412/2.

*Including the respected intellectual magazine *Encounter.* The CIA claims that it cut its ties to American journalists following the post-Watergate disclosures.

†In June 1953, anti-Soviet rioting unexpectedly broke out in East Berlin and spread throughout East Germany. The CIA station in Berlin requested permission to distribute arms to the demonstrators, but Washington turned thumbs down on the request because it would be futile without open American support of the rioters. There was considerable criticism of the CIA's failure to create more trouble for the Russians, and Wisner resolved to be ready the next time an opportunity presented itself.

Helms, among others, viewed large-scale covert operations as a threat to the security of local agent networks. Besides, the chances of success were uncertain at best. Kirkpatrick described covert operations as being as volatile as nuclear weapons and thought they should never be attempted unless complete secrecy could be guaranteed "from inception to eternity." And Operation Red Sox/Red Cap was compromised from the start, for the Gehlen organization that was to supply the core of the recruits had been penetrated by Communist agents.

For one thing, Heinz Felfe, Gehlen's liaison to NATO headquarters and an ex-Nazi, was a Soviet mole. There was no secret in NATO's files to which he did not have access, including the plans for Red Sox/Red Cap. Wisner even brought Felfe to America for consultation. Because of his Nazi background the German was not eligible for a visa, but that was no problem; Wisner merely created a legend for him. Felfe's KGB controllers must have smiled at Wisner's convoluted efforts to smuggle a Soviet mole into the United States.

■ ■ ■

With the lines of the Cold War firmly drawn in Europe, the Soviet-American confrontation shifted to the developing nations of the Third World. The stakes in this worldwide struggle were high. These countries were rich in raw materials and for decades had served the needs of the industrial nations. But the volatile conditions in the emerging countries did not permit easy management by either Moscow or Washington. Many of their leaders were anticolonial revolutionaries. Nationalism was intense, poverty endemic, and politics chaotic. Despite the United States's own revolutionary tradition, the Eisenhower administration stubbornly equated nationalism and "neutralism" with communism and assumed that much of the trouble in the Third World was inspired by the Russians.

The first American-sponsored subversion of a government outside the Soviet orbit occurred in Iran, where Premier Mohammed Mossadegh had nationalized the British-owned Anglo-Iranian Oil Corporation in 1952. Unable to get their own agents into the country, the British turned to the United States for help in getting rid of Mossadegh. A crafty old fellow given to alternate bursts of weeping and demagoguery, Mossadegh was no communist, and nationalization was popular. The influence of the Moscow-dominated Iranian Communist Party, the Tudeh, was mounting, however, and the Eisenhower administration feared that the Russians would gain a stranglehold on Iran's huge oil reserves. More positively, the administration saw an opportunity to extend American commercial interests into what had been a British sphere. President Eisenhower and his advisers accordingly decided that the time had come for Mossadegh to go. Kermit Roosevelt, the head of the CIA's Middle East division, was named field commander of the operation, which was codenamed Ajax.

Kim Roosevelt, then thirty-seven, was the grandson of Theodore Roosevelt and had served with the OSS in the Middle East and Italy. Fascinated by the Arab world, Roosevelt had traveled and written extensively about the area before returning to intelligence work in 1950. As one observer has said, "For the next eight years he helped mold, and largely dominate, the CIA's Mideastern policies."*

Mild-mannered and looking more like the history professor he had once been than James Bond, Roosevelt slipped across the frontier into Iran in July 1953 to orchestrate the coup against Mossadegh. A semiliterate border guard mistook the description on his passport for his name and transcribed it as "Mr. Sear on Right Forehead." Keeping out of sight because he was known in Teheran, Roosevelt worked from the basement of a safe house in the suburbs with a skeleton staff of CIA operatives. He met several times in secret with the young shah, Mohammed Reza Pahlavi, and stiffened his will to resist by assuring him of American and British support. Simultaneously, anti-Mossadegh Iranians were at work within the army, spreading cash, directing a stream of propaganda tying the premier to the Communists, and stirring up street mobs to counter those of the Tudeh party.

The climactic chain of events began with a decree signed by the shah on August 13, dismissing Mossadegh and naming General Fazlollah Zahedi, the handpicked candidate of the CIA, as prime minister.* The officer carrying the decree was arrested, and Tudeh mobs poured into the streets to support Mossadegh. At Roosevelt's suggestion, the shah left the country in order to dramatize the situation. For two anxious days, Roosevelt lost contact with his Iranian agents, and the situation was chaotic. Communist mobs controlled the streets, portraits of the shah were torn from government buildings, and the mention of his name in the morning and evening prayers of military units was forbidden. Tudeh party stal-

*Among his assignments was to try to persuade King Farouk of Egypt to get rid of corrupt advisers and to make reforms aimed at bringing the country into the twentieth century. When the weak-willed monarch failed to take these steps, Roosevelt, realizing Farouk's days on the throne were numbered, sought out among the young officers plotting to overthrow the monarchy the man most likely to succeed. The chosen one proved to be Gamal Abdel Nasser. The two men were soon on a "Gamal" and "Kim" basis. Nasser is said to have once suggested jokingly that Roosevelt become Egypt's ambassador to the United States, while his own man, who constantly made excuses for the Eisenhower administration's erratic Middle Eastern policies, should represent the United States in Cairo. Later on, when the Eisenhower administration soured on Nasser and asked Roosevelt to take charge of a coup against the Egyptian leader, he resigned from the CIA.

*During World War II, Zahedi had been arrested by the British, who occupied Iran along with the Russians, because he was suspected of being pro-German. The arresting officer reported finding the following items in Zahedi's bedroom: German automatic weapons, silk underwear, messages from German parachutists operating in the hills, and an illustrated register of Teheran's more attractive prostitutes. The general's son, Ardeshir, who also took part in the coup, later became the shah's son-in-law and free-spending ambassador to Washington.

warts began destroying statues of the shah and his father, the founder of the Pahlavi dynasty.

Early on August 16, Roosevelt ordered his Iranian agents to get their own "cast of thousands" into action. Led by giant weightlifters recruited from the bazaars, crowds swarmed into the streets chanting "Zindabad Shah! Zindabad Shah!" ("Long live the shah!) Swelled by peasants who were trucked in from the countryside armed with daggers, picks, and bicycle chains, the mob surged toward the center of Teheran, sweeping all before it. Troops ordered out to disperse the rioters joined them instead. General Zahedi emerged from hiding and, riding on the top of a tank, led the march on Parliament Square. By noon, it was all over. Mossadegh had fled, his ministers were under arrest and Tudeh had been crushed.

The shah returned in triumph to Teheran. "I owe my throne to God, my people, my army—and to you," he told Kim Roosevelt.

The grateful ruler ended Anglo-Iranian's monopoly and granted a consortium of American oil companies a 40 percent share of the nation's petroleum output. The coup had been achieved at a remarkably low price, about one million dollars in CIA funds.* In the final analysis, however, the agency had little to do with the success of Operation Ajax. Mossadegh was weak, and little effort was needed to topple him once the shah and his military supporters regained their nerve. But the Iranian operation, to all appearances a spectacular success, created a legend of CIA invincibility in the minds of American policymakers.†

Upon his return to Washington, Roosevelt sensed that the Eisenhower administration had failed to grasp the underlying reasons for the success of the Iranian coup. While presenting a briefing on Ajax at the White House, he noted with dismay that John Foster Dulles's "eyes were gleaming; he seemed to be purring like a giant cat. Clearly he was enjoying what he was hearing, but my instinct told me he was planning [another operation] as well." As the acknowledged expert on covert operations, Roosevelt felt it his duty to warn his audience—which included President Eisenhower—that similar coups would not be succesful unless the "people and the army want what we want. If not, you had better give the job to the Marines."

*Bribery was part of the CIA's stock-in-trade in the Middle East. General Mohammed Naguib, the front man for the coup that ousted Egypt's King Farouk, reputedly received $12 million; the mother of King Hussein of Jordan is supposed to have gotten an equal amount; Hussein himself was given $750,000 a year; an estimated $40 million is said to have gone to King Saud of Saudi Arabia; and a smaller amount to his brother, Prince Faisal. When Naguib and Nasser fell out, Nasser confiscated Naguib's funds. A portion of them was used to build the Cairo Tower, a structure familiarly known as Roosevelt's Erection.

†The CIA, with the assistance of Israeli intelligence, later known as Mossad, was also invited by the shah to organize and guide SAVAK, the Iranian security and intelligence service, which became notorious for its brutality.

But the secretary of state did not wish to hear what Roosevelt was saying. "He was still leaning back in his chair with a catlike grin on his face." Roosevelt's concern was well founded. Within a few weeks, he was offered field command of an operation designed to overthrow the leftist government of Guatemala. A quick check of the planned operation disclosed that it did not meet his requirements, and he declined the offer.

■ ■ ■

Three years before, Jacobo Arbenz Guzmán, a one-time army colonel who espoused a fuzzy socialism, had become Guatemala's first democratically elected president. Building upon the economic and social reforms of his predecessor, Juan José Arevalo, Arbenz was determined to do something about the lopsided ownership of land. Only 2 percent of the landowners owned 72 percent of the arable acreage, while most of the people barely survived at subsistence levels. The illiteracy rate was 75 percent, and the life expectancy of the Indians forty years. But Arbenz's agrarian reform program alienated conservative landholders as well as the U. S.-owned United Fruit Company, a huge banana exporter with powerful friends in Washington. Arbenz expropriated 234,000 acres of the company's uncultivated land and offered it $600,000 in compensation, based upon the value of the land as stated by the company itself for tax purposes. Flatly rejecting the offer as unrealistic, the company demanded $15 million.

Not surprisingly, the company received strong backing from the State Department for its claim. For its friends in Washington were powerful indeed: John Foster Dulles had been United Fruit's legal counsel; Allen Dulles was a stockholder; General Robert Cutler, the president's representative on the NSC, was a director; "Beetle" Smith later became a director; and the brother of John Moors Cabot, assistant secretary of state for inter-American affairs, had been its president. The company also had the backing of Thomas G. Corcoran, an aide to Franklin Roosevelt, who had become Washington's most influential lobbyist. "Tommy the Cork" had strong ties to the CIA as counsel to the Civil Air Transport Company (later Air America), an agency front.

United Fruit gathered public support by launching a high-pressure propaganda campaign designed to create an atmosphere of fear and suspicion in the United States about a Communist takeover in Guatemala. The Monroe Doctrine was trotted out, and the Soviet threat to the Panama Canal was emphasized. Arbenz was accused of being controlled by Communists, even though there were none in his cabinet or in the army—and Guatemala did not have diplomatic relations with the Soviet Union or any of its satellites. (The small but militant Communist party did control the labor movement and hold lesser government offices, however.) Rumors were also spread that Arbenz was a dope addict as well as a dupe of the Russians. John E. Peurifoy, the tough-talking U. S. ambassador who had been handpicked by Frank Wisner, reported that Arbenz "thought like a Communist and talked like a Communist, and if not actually one, would do until one came along." Late in 1953 President Eisenhower decided that Arbenz must be deposed. The president was influenced less by United Fruit than by the perceived drift of Guatemala toward Communist control.

Like most Cold War operations, the decision to oust Arbenz was the product of a bipartisan consensus and was supported by key Democrats. Wisner and Allen Dulles assumed strategic control of the project—dubbed Operation Success—and chose Colonel Albert Haney as field commander after Kim Roosevelt rejected the post. Haney, a one-time military intelligence officer, was then CIA station chief in South Korea, but he had considerable experience in Latin America. Tracy Barnes, Wisner's own assistant, served as liaison to CIA headquarters. For the role of "Liberator," the CIA chose Colonel Carlos Castillo Armas, an ascetic-looking career officer who had tunneled his way out of prison after leading an unsuccessful coup against Arbenz. Castillo Armas, who was almost unknown in Guatemala, had no ideology beyond simple anticommunism, but he could be relied upon to do as he was told—and to look after the interests of United Fruit.

Haney realized that it would be impossible for the CIA to engineer a "spontaneous" uprising in the Iranian mold; Arbenz had too much popular support. His survival, however, depended upon the loyalty of the army. Haney decided to undermine Arbenz by subverting this loyalty through a campaign of propaganda, sabotage, and commando raids that was to culminate in an "invasion" led by Castillo Armas. A budget of $4.5 million was earmarked for Operation Success, although others claimed it eventually cost about $20 million.

With the cooperation of General Anastasio Somoza Garcia, the dictator of neighboring Nicaragua,* training camps were opened for an "army of liberation" consisting of several hundred Guatemalan exiles and American soldiers of fortune recruited by the CIA. A former CIA employee named Samuel Cummings established a dummy company to supply them with arms. Soviet-made weapons were planted inside Guatemala to reinforce American allegations that the Russians were trying to establish a foothold in Central America. Secret radio stations, including one within the U. S. embassy in Guatemala City, broadcast alarming reports on the same frequencies as Guatemalan stations. E. Howard Hunt, later of Watergate fame, was in charge of this propaganda effort. Along with David Atlee Phillips, a former actor and journalist newly recruited to the CIA, Hunt prepared a steadily escalating

---

*The father of Anastasio Somoza Debayle, who was overthrown by the Sandinistas in 1979.

campaign of psychological pressure aimed at destabilizing the country. A key element in the planned coup was the CIA's air force, a motley collection of World War II surplus transports and P-47 fighters flown by American pilots under contract to the agency.

By mid-1954, the net had been drawn tight about Arbenz. The usually somnolent U. S. embassy in Guatemala City took on the aspect of a frontline headquarters as the CIA staff on the heavily guarded fourth-floor command post increased in size. Ambassador Peurifoy met openly with opposition leaders and army officers, officials were bribed to supply information from within the government, and influence was brought to bear to get suspicious American newspaper correspondents out of the area.* Labor leaders such as George Meany of the American Federation of Labor denounced Communist control of the Guatemalan unions. The Organization of American States declared by a vote of 17 to 1 that the domination of any American nation by the "international communist movement" would constitute a threat to the hemisphere. President Eisenhower warned congressional leaders that Guatemala was spreading its "Marxist tentacles" into El Salvador.*

Expecting an invasion at any moment and aware that the poorly armed Guatemalan army would be no match for a full-scale, U. S. sponsored coup, Arbenz tried to buy weapons in the United States and Western Europe, but every attempt was blocked. Turning as a last resort to the Soviet bloc, he purchased a million dollars' worth of rifles, machine guns, and ammunition from Czechoslovakia. The arrival of the *Alfhem,* the Swedish freighter carrying this cargo, at Puerto Barrios on May 15, 1954, sent a shock wave through Washington. The CIA had been searching for a pretext for "unleashing" Castillo Armas for some time. Not long before, it had planted a few boxes of Soviet arms on the Nicaraguan coast, where Somoza's police could find them and claim they had been put ashore by a previously sighted "non-American" submarine.

The day after the arrival of the *Alfhem,* Dulles convened a meeting of the Intelligence Advisory Committee, which included top intelligence officers from the military services, the State Department, and the Joint

---

*Sydney Gruson, a New York *Times* foreign correspondent whose beat included Central America, depicted Arbenz as captive of the Communists in his government, but aroused Wisner's ire by reporting that the American attacks on him were creating support among nationalists in Guatemala and other Latin countries. Dulles told a *Times* executive that the CIA had confidential information raising questions about the political reliability of Gruson and his wife, Flora Lewis. Gruson was taken off the story. He later became a vice-chairman of The New York Times Corporation; his ex-wife is a foreign affairs columnist.

*Hunt also convened a meeting of the CIA-financed "Congress against Soviet Intervention in Latin America" in Mexico City, but it turned into a public relations fiasco. With an ineptness that became a trademark, Hunt stacked it with extreme reactionaries, who spent as much time attacking the handful of liberals that had been invited for window dressing as they did Arbenz.

Chiefs of Staff. Without any evidence, they concluded that the vessel was carrying sufficient arms to enable Arbenz to sweep eight hundred miles through the neighboring countries to threaten the Panama Canal Zone. Dulles took these findings to the National Security Council and received approval for an invasion of Guatemala the following month. Meanwhile, the CIA attempted to sabotage the train carrying the arms from Puerto Barrios to Guatemala City. A team of commandos laid explosives along the tracks, but a torrential downpour soaked the detonators and only one went off, slightly damaging the track. The raiders opened fire on the train, killing a guard, and losing one of their own men in the getaway. The train rattled on to the capital undamaged.

The CIA's psychological campaign was more successful. A plot against the government was discovered, and the police rounded up a dozen suspects. Ranking army officers went to Arbenz at Peurifoy's urging to demand that the president dismiss all Communists who held posts in the government. Arbenz told them it was better to have the Communists working in the open than underground, and the officers left dissatisfied. They were further alarmed by CIA-planted rumors that Arbenz planned to disband the army and replace it with a Commnist-dominated peasant militia. The retired Air Force chief fled the country in a small plane, causing Arbenz to permanently ground his handful of aircraft.

The invasion began on June 18, with Castillo Armas leading his Army of Liberation over the border from Honduras in a battered station wagon. But there was no spontaneous uprising to greet them, and the CIA ordered the invaders to halt six miles within the country and await developments. David Phillips's Radio Liberation created the illusion of a massive invasion and beamed fake messages to a fifth column supposedly operating in the hills. When Arbenz went on the air to calm the country, the broadcast of his speech was jammed. CIA planes dropped leaflets over Guatemala City and bombed and strafed outlying towns as part of the softening-up process.

But events quickly went awry. Two CIA planes were shot up so badly they had to be written off. Another ran out of gas and crashed. Instead of knocking out the government radio station, an ex-Marine pilot destroyed a nearby station operated by American evangelists. A British freighter was mistaken for a Soviet ship and bombed. Fearing the imminent collapse of the operation, Haney pleaded with Washington to replace the lost aircraft. Two more P-47s were dredged up, but Henry Holland, the assistant secretary of state for inter-American affairs, argued that turning them over to the rebels while world attention was focused on Guatemala would have serious international repercussions.

President Eisenhower was called upon to make the final decision. On June 22, he heard Allen Dulles's appeal to send the planes and Holland's objections. What chance would the revolt have without the planes? the president wanted to know.

"About zero," Dulles replied.

"Suppose we supply the aircraft? What would the chances be then?"

"About twenty percent," the CIA chief said.

Eisenhower approved the transfer. Dulles's frankness had paid off: as he was leaving, the president told him, "If you'd said ninety percent, I'd have said no."

To provide cover for the transaction, the P-47s were "sold" to the Nicaraguan Air Force and paid for with $150,000 supplied by the CIA. Haney immediately sent the fighters on a seventy-two-hour rampage that turned the tide in the rebels' favor. Barracks were bombed and machine-gunned, ammunition and oil dumps were hit, and the population was panicked. Radio Liberation announced major rebel victories in nonexistent clashes. The Guatemalan army was demoralized by radio reports claiming the rebel force had grown to five thousand men and that its ranks were swelling by the hour. In actuality, the Army of Liberation never totaled more than four hundred men and remained close to its Honduran sanctuary so it could flee at the first sign of an attack. Kept from the "front" by a suspicious Arbenz, foreign correspondents relied completely on reports of rebel advances fed them by Peurifoy, who swaggered about the capital wearing a pistol.*

Unable to trust his officers and rattled by the fake radio reports and stories in the international press that several rebel columns were advancing upon Guatemala City, Arbenz resigned on June 2 and took sanctuary in the Mexican embassy.† The victorious Castillo Armas entered the capital to the cheers of 150,000 people and the crackle of firecrackers distributed beforehand by the CIA. United Fruit quickly regained control of the land that had been expropriated by Arbenz, some four thousand people were arrested on suspicion of Communist activity, and laws guaranteeing rights to workers and labor unions were repealed. For the four decades since then, a succession of colonels and generals have ruled

---

*One journalist, Evelyn Irons of the London *Evening Standard,* rented a mule and slipped into Castillo Armas's camp from Honduras, where the correspondent obtained a brief interview with the rebel chief. After this exclusive was published, the New York *Times* sent a "rocket" to its stringer in Guatemala City: "Get off ass—get on burro."

†Arbenz's downfall was witnessed by a twenty-five-year-old Argentine physician named Ernesto Guevara de la Serna, who had been attracted to Guatemala by the promise of social reform. Rather than surrendering, he thought Arbenz should have retreated to the mountains with a band of armed followers and fought on indefinitely. "Che" Guevara took sanctuary in the Argentine embassy after Arbenz fell and was granted safe passage to Mexico City, where he met Fidel Castro, who was planning a guerrilla war against the Cuban dictatorship of Fulgencio Batista. The treacherous conduct of the Guatemalan army officers taught Guevara an important lesson. "We cannot guarantee the Revolution before cleansing the armed forces," he told Castro after Batista's fall. "It is necessary to remove everyone who might be a danger. But it is necessary to do it rapidly, right now."

Guatemala as conditions for the majority of the people have stagnated or worsened. Not long after Arbenz's flight, Eisenhower called the CIA team that had run the operation to the White House to express his personal thanks. "You've averted a Soviet beachhead in our hemisphere," the president told them.

■ ■ ■

Inspired by the success of the Iranian and Guatemalan adventures, Eisenhower turned with increasing frequency to the CIA to prevent the spread of communism abroad. This tactic not only avoided formal avowal of an American presence in trouble spots around the world but also permitted the president to bypass the State Department and the Pentagon, which were often reluctant to become involved in Third World struggles. The Iranian and Guatemalan operations consolidated the ascendency of covert operations over espionage. By the mid-1950s, the agency was running as many as fifty covert operations at a time, and such operations accounted for 80 percent of its budget. Some were carried off as smoothly as the Iranian and Guatemalan operations; others were bungled.

The CIA's looming presence gave it a sinister reputation. A growing number of Americans insisted that it constituted an "invisible government" that operated without restraints or accountability. In much of the Third World, even the most reasonable leaders were convinced that the CIA used infiltration, subversion, and even war to accomplish its ends. This notoriety has enabled some adversaries to recover from their own mistakes. On one occasion, pro-Chinese elements in East Africa circulated a document that urged revolt against several governments. When this inflammatory message backfired, its authors promptly denounced it as a CIA forgery intended to discredit them, and their claim was widely accepted.

Air Force Colonel Edward G. Lansdale, a deceptively mild-mannered one-time OSS operative and advertising executive, was the archetypical covert operator of the period, so well known that he served as the model for characters in two best-selling novels.* In the Philippines, Lansdale, working as adviser to Ramon Magsaysay, the minister of defense, used a two-tracked system to defeat an insurgency by the Communist Hukbalahap guerrillas. Backed by a sizable infusion of American economic assistance, he promoted land reform and social development programs designed to win the peasants away from the Communists and promoted Magsaysay as a democratic alternative.

He also launched a campaign of dirty tricks to keep the Huks off

---

*The Ugly American of William J. Lederer and William Burdick and The Quiet American, by Graham Greene. Lansdale was portrayed as a hero in the former book and a bumbler in the latter.

balance. One ingenious operation played on the Filipinos' superstitious dread of vampires. Lansdale arranged for the body of a Huk killed in an ambush to be punctured on the neck in two places, drained of blood and left at a crossroads. The Huks, as frightened of vampires as anyone else, fled the area. Lansdale also pumped more than one million dollars into Magsaysay's presidential campaign. A CIA agent, masquerading as a *Christian Science Monitor* correspondent, wrote his speeches, and the agency drugged the drinks of some of his opponents so they would make fools of themselves while campaigning.

Following his success in the Philippines, Lansdale was sent to Vietnam just as the Geneva accords of 1954 marked the victorious end of Ho Chi Minh's long war against the French. The strife-torn country was to be temporarily divided along the 17th parallel until elections were held in 1956. The United States, fearing that the Communist Ho would win, disregarded the election plan and attempted to build an anticommunist Vietnamese state in the truncated southern portion of the country. American advisers and aid—about three hundred million dollars a year— poured into the country. Looking about for a Vietnamese Magsaysay, the Americans settled upon Ngo Dinh Diem, a member of a Catholic family who had lived in the United States. The French had discovered him in a monastery in Belgium and brought him to Saigon as premier.

Lansdale helped Diem eliminate political rivals and ran pacification and military training programs in the South as well as "boom and bang" operations in the North in violation of the Geneva agreement. Sabotage teams were trained in the Philippines and infiltrated into North Vietnam on U. S. Navy vessels. Most were eventually rounded up, giving the regime in Hanoi the opportunity to denounce the United States and its clients in the South for subversion.* Lansdale also helped encourage a massive flight of Catholic refugees from the north to the south. Fearful of the Communists, whole communities fled south under the leadership of their priests. Even though Catholics were a minority in the predominantly Buddhist South, they became the backbone of the Diem regime. When Diem won election to the presidency—with an embarrassingly high 98.2 percent of the vote—Lansdale was credited with another successful operation.

CIA-backed attempts to overthrow President Sukarno of Indonesia in the late 1950s were less successful. Sukarno, a shrewd and mercurial revolutionary socialist who had led his country to independence after 350 years of Dutch rule, was distrusted by the Eisenhower administration. In

---

*In 1960, CIA officers in Laos directed the stuffing of ballot boxes and engineered local uprisings to help General Phoumi Nosavan establish a pro-American government. The operation was so successful that it inspired the Russians to intervene on the side of forces opposed to him. The pro-leftists controlled the border zone near North Vietnam, and the North Vietnamese used it to resupply the Viet Cong in South Vietnam.

1956 he abandoned the semblance of representative government for a
"guided democracy" in which Communists had increasing power. Worried about the potential loss of Indonesia's rich reserves of oil, rubber, and
tin, Washington agreed to support a rebellion by a band of dissident
colonels on the island of Sumatra. "I think it's time we held Sukarno's feet
to the fire," Frank Wisner declared.

Preliminary to the revolt, the CIA tried to discredit Sukarno by
exploiting his well-known reputation as a womanizer, according to
Joseph B. Smith, deputy chief of the FE/5 Branch of DDP, which handled
Indonesian affairs. Being known for womanizing was no handicap in
macho Indonesia, but the agency spread the rumor that Sukarno had
fallen under the spell of a blonde Russian agent. The rumor achieved
some currency, and the CIA made plans to produce and clandestinely
distribute a pornographic movie showing the president engaged in his
favorite activity with a beautiful blonde. Some difficulty was encountered
in finding a Sukarno look-alike, and the film was eventually made with an
actor wearing a Sukarno mask.*

The CIA-supported colonels raised the banner of revolt on Sumatra
in February 1958, while Sukarno was out of the country. Following the
pattern established in Guatemala, pilots employed by Civil Air Transport,
CIA proprietary, carried out airdrops of arms and bombing missions in
support of the insurgents. Sukarno turned out to be more competent than
expected, however, and crushed the revolt. Before the fighting ended, the
Indonesians shot down one of the rebel planes after it had mistakenly
bombed a temple and killed most of the worshipers. The pilot, an American named Allen Pope, was captured. Both President Eisenhower and
Secretary of State Dulles claimed Pope was a soldier of fortune and
denied any American involvement. Not long afterward, Allen Dulles
ordered the CIA to disengage from the Indonesian adventure. The curtain was finally rung down on the fiasco four years later, when Sukarno
freed Pope in response to a personal plea from Robert F. Kennedy. Within
a few months of his release, he was flying again with another CIA
proprietary—Southern Air Transport, which was based in Miami.

■ ■ ■

If the degree of access that an intelligence chief has to the president
he serves is one of the key measures of his influence, then Allen Dulles
was one of the most powerful directors of central intelligence. Some

*Upon learning that Sukarno had chartered a Pan American jet for a tour of world capitals
and surmising that he was likely to proposition the stewardesses, the CIA considered
recruiting one of them, but dismissed the idea. "We already knew enough about his sex
life," reports Joe Smith, "and unless we had been able to give the girl a lot of training we
figured we wouldn't find out much of intelligence value."

DCIs, like medieval courtiers, were forced to resort to guile to get their ideas across. They dropped in when the president was about to take a nap, studied his schedule so they could run into him on his way back to the Oval Office after a public function, or suddenly appeared on a Saturday morning when the defenses erected by the White House staff might be slightly lowered.

Dulles had unparalleled access to Eisenhower, but he did not stroll into the Oval Office every morning for a chat, as is sometimes portrayed. The two men dealt with each other at arm's length rather than as intimates. Eisenhower met with Dulles twice a week and was briefed daily by lower-ranked CIA officials. By and large, he was satisfied with the intelligence product furnished him. When his advisers criticized Dulles's administrative shortcomings Eisenhower responded: "I'm not going to be able to change Allen. . . . I'd rather have Allen as my chief intelligence officer with his limitations than anyone I know."

Until 1955, the Eisenhower administration's only method of approval and control of covert operations took the form of informal understanding among the agencies involved. Nevertheless, the president, who often gave the public impression of bumbling when asked about these operations, kept an old soldier's eye upon them. "The White House," one former high-ranking CIA official has said, "made the decisions on [all] covert actions to be taken." These loose policy guidelines for controlling covert actions were deemed sufficient as long as such actions were infrequent. But this rather off-handed arrangement was plainly inadequate after the number of covert actions multiplied. To deal with the vast increase, NSC directives 5412/1 and 5412/2 established control procedures that, with a few changes, lasted for the better part of two decades.

They created a body of designated representatives of the president, the secretaries of state and defense, and the chairman of the Joint Chiefs of Staff to review and approve projects. The president was usually represented by his national security adviser; the others either attended in person or delegated someone to stand in for them. Projects were referred by the committee to the NSC for final approval. Under presidents Eisenhower and Kennedy this group was called the "5412 Committee" or the "Special Group"; during the Johnson years it was called the "303 Committee," from the number of the room in the Executive Office Building in which it met; under Nixon it was referred to as the "40 Committee," from a directive governing its activities. No matter what the name, however, the same core of people was represented.

Eisenhower also established the President's Board of Consultants on Foreign Intelligence Activities to serve as a presidential watchdog—and, partially, to head off closer congressional scrutiny of intelligence activities. The board was composed of retired senior officials and former members of the intelligence profession, such as General Omar Bradley and David Bruce. Bruce, for one, was disturbed by the ubiquitousness of CIA operations. In 1956, he headed a subcommittee that condemned "the increased mingling in the internal affairs of other nations of bright . . . young men who must be doing something all the time to justify their reason for being."* The watchdog was mostly bark with little bite, however. The board was merely an advisory group without substantive authority, and its recommendations often were ignored.

Given these fuzzy arrangements, the DCI usually could secure approval of covert-action projects without the knowledge of anyone except the president or his designated representative. The system reflected the unspoken agreement—particularly in Congress—not to delve too deeply into intelligence matters. For the first twenty years of the CIA's existence, the agency enjoyed a comfortable relationship with the senior members of the military affairs and appropriations committees charged with overseeing intelligence activities. Dulles's reputation as an intelligence professional and his amiable, outwardly friendly approach to Congress had much to do with encouraging this atmosphere of trust. Usually, he would meet informally with a congressional group and present a generalized picture of world conditions and CIA activities. Questioning was perfunctory. The most sensitive discussions were reserved for private one-on-one sessions between Dulles and individual committee chairmen.

Over the years, several attempts were made to strengthen congressional oversight of the CIA and to broaden participation in these activities. But these efforts foundered on the reluctance of many lawmakers to know too much about secret operations and the strength of the existing committee system, which forbade interference from juniors. Senator Leverett Saltonstall of Massachusetts put it best: "It is not a reluctance on the part of CIA officials to speak to us. Instead it is a question of our reluctance, if you will, to seek information and knowledge of subjects which I personally, as a member of Congress and as a citizen, would rather not have, unless I believed it to be my responsibility to have it because it might involve the lives of American citizens."

■ ■ ■

While covert paramilitary action consumed much of the CIA's efforts during the early 1950s, the one-on-one of the classic spy game operated in tandem with it. Top priority was given to recruiting penetration agents, or moles, inside Soviet intelligence. Numerous defectors had sought

---

*In one case, a CIA officer met with a source at a hotel in Singapore, plugged a lie detector into an overloaded electric circuit, and blew out all the lights in the building. The men were jailed as American spies.

asylum in the West,* but Western intelligence had been unsuccessful in recruiting moles. Allen Dulles was especially keen on such operations because he had firsthand experience of their value in Switzerland during World War II, when Fritz Kolbe had supplied him with reams of documents from the files of the German Foreign Office. Running a mole is the most dramatic and dangerous kind of espionage. Exposure is a constant threat, the psychological stresses are almost unbearable, and there is always the possibility that the spy is a double agent.

The operating advantage has always lain with the Russians. Western intelligence has found it difficult to recruit assets in the closed societies of the Eastern bloc, while the Soviets meet almost no roadblocks in making contact with Europeans or Americans willing to betray their countries. The KGB and GRU operate with impunity in the open societies of the West, and communication with Moscow Center is relatively secure and uncomplex. If the Russians wish to send a courier to Moscow from the West, or in the opposite direction, they have only to pay the air fare. Planting an "illegal" in America—a spy operating on his or her own, without diplomatic cover—is child's play compared to trying to gather intelligence in the Soviet Union or its satellites.

Under these circumstances, the most productive sources for Western intelligence have been "walk-ins" who volunteered their services. "It's the walk-in trade that keeps the shop open," observed the CIA's William Hood. As deputy chief of the CIA station in Vienna, Hood was case officer for one of the most successful of these operations. This episode began in November 1952, when an American intelligence officer returned to his parked car and found a sealed envelope that had been slipped in through a partially opened window. "I am a Russian officer attached to the Soviet Group of Forces Headquarters in Baden bei Wien," the letter inside read. "If you are interested in buying a copy of the new table of organization for a Soviet armored division, meet me on the corner of Dortheerstrasse and Stalburgstrasse at 8:30 P.M., November 12. If you are not there I will return at the same time on November 13. The price is 3,000 Austrian schillings."*

The CIA was even more eager to make contact with a Soviet officer than to obtain a divisional order of battle. Accordingly, the agency sent a Russian-speaking officer to keep the rendezvous. The informant refused

---

*In 1945, Konstantin Volkov, the NKVD representative in the Soviet consulate in Istanbul, informed the British that he wished to defect. Volkov urged that extreme caution be exercised in discussion of his case with London, because the Russians had two agents in the Foreign Office and another in British counterintelligence—obviously, Maclean, Burgess, and Philby, although he could not identify them by name. Unfortunately for Volkov, his case was turned over to Philby, who tipped off the Soviets that he was planning to defect. The hapless Russian was spirited off to Moscow and summarily liquidated.

*About $120.

to give his name but was eventually identified as Pytor Semyonovich Popov, a major in the GRU. At first suspected of being a double agent, Popov proved to be the first Soviet officer successfully recruited by the CIA. Although he received a small amount of cash, money had nothing to do with his decision. Popov apparently initiated his contact with American intelligence because of a festering anger at Soviet exploitation of the Russian peasantry from which he came.

Popov met secretly with the CIA officer in a safe house once or twice a month. Fueled by large quantities of vodka and smoked sturgeon, the major provided a wealth of information about Russian military capabilities and worldwide espionage operations. No Western intelligence service had penetrated so deeply into the nerve center of Soviet secret operations. From 1952 to 1958, Popov "trundled bales of top-secret information out of the secret centers of Soviet power," according to William Hood. "In the process, he shattered the Soviet military intelligence service, caused the transfer of the KGB chief [a four-star general and one of the most powerful men in the USSR], and saved the United States half a billion dollars in military research."

Popov also supplied the names of Russian spies in Europe and gave the CIA a priceless inside look into Soviet methods of running "illegals." In the end, however, just such a spy led to his undoing. While working in East Berlin, Popov served as case officer for a woman undergoing final training before infiltrating the United States. He fingered her for the CIA, and as soon as the woman joined her husband in New York, the couple were placed under close surveillance by the FBI. Somehow, they discovered they were being watched—or perhaps they were merely nervous—and they slipped out of the country before engaging in any illegal activity. Their report sparked an intensive inquiry by the KGB, which was only too delighted to investigate its rivals in the GRU. The probe pointed to Popov. The Soviets may have also received an assist from George Blake, their own mole within British intelligence, who discovered that the CIA had penetrated the GRU. Recalled to Moscow, supposedly to discuss an ongoing operation, Popov felt uneasy but refused an offer from his CIA case officer to assist him to defect. Not long afterward, he was arrested and executed.

■ ■ ■

To Allen Dulles, "one of the major coups" of his tenure as DCI was the CIA's successful effort to secure a copy of a secret speech delivered by Nikita S. Khrushchev, Stalin's successor, before the Twentieth Congress of the Communist Party of the Soviet Union in February 1956. For six hours Khrushchev had astounded the delegates with a blow-by-blow account of the crimes committed by Stalin during his long and bloody reign. Warnings were issued against washing the party's dirty linen in public, but rumors of Khrushchev's sensational revelations spread around the globe. References to the speech in the press made it clear that a text must be available, Dulles observed. The speech was too long and too detailed to have been extemporaneous—even for Khrushchev, who was noted for lengthy off-the-cuff remarks.

Dulles called in the chiefs of the CIA's Clandestine Services—Wisner, Helms, and Angleton—and told them that both the president and Dulles's brother, the secretary of state, were anxious to have a copy of the speech. Money was no object. A "book" message—an all-points bulletin—was to be sent to every CIA station, ordering a maximum effort to obtain the text.

Six weeks later, Angleton came up with the document. Most observers believe it was supplied by the Mossad, the Israeli intelligence agency; Angleton had handled the "Israeli account" since the establishment of the CIA.* In exchange, the Mossad is believed to have received a massive dose of financial and technical help from the CIA. The Israelis may also have wanted to burnish Angleton's reputation within the agency because of his "special relationship" with them.

Unwilling to accept this gift horse without a careful examination, Dulles insisted that an expert from outside Clandestine Services be brought in to determine its authenticity. Helms suggested Ray Cline of DDI for the job. Internal evidence indicated that the document was genuine, and Cline suggested that it be made public immediately. All the charges that the United States had made over the years about the ferocity of the Stalinist dictatorship had been confirmed by no less than the leader of the Soviet Union himself. To Cline's surprise, Wisner and Angleton resisted. They wanted to leak the speech piecemeal to encourage discontent in the Soviet satellites as part of Operation Red Sox/Red Cap. "They wanted to 'exploit' the speech rather than simply let everyone read it," Cline later recalled. He put this response down as an example of the "excessively narrow and Byzantine" covert mind in action.

There the matter lay until June 2, when Cline was working with Dulles on a speech that contained references to the Soviet Union. "Suddenly," Cline later reported, "in a way he often moved from one topic to quite an unrelated one, Dulles swung his chair around to look intently at me and said, 'Wisner says you think we ought to release the secret Khrushchev speech.' I related my reasons for thinking so, and the old man, with a twinkle in his eye, said, 'By golly, I'm going to make a policy decision!' He buzzed Wisner on the intercom box, told him he had given

*Some observers state that the CIA also obtained an abridged version of the speech in Poland.

a lot of thought to the matter, and wanted to get the speech printed." The text was sent over to the State Department, which leaked it to the New York *Times*.

Publication of the speech created a sensation throughout the Communist bloc. In the Far East, where ideological divergencies had already begun to appear, the de-Stalinization campaign widened the schism between China and the Soviet Union.* In Eastern Europe, the effects were even more immediate. On June 28, a strike flared in Poznan, Poland; forty-four workers were killed as the Russians brutally suppressed the action. The publication of the secret speech was not the sole cause of the unrest, but it contributed to an atmosphere of crisis that swept through the satellite nations. A clear sign of impending trouble was the steady stream of refugees from the East. Nevertheless, the Russians completely underestimated the strength of the demands for reform that were brought to a head by Khrushchev's speech.

Revolt swept Hungary in late October 1956. Equipped with only small arms and homemade bombs, youthful rebels overthrew the Communist regime imposed by the Soviet Union and proclaimed Hungary a free nation, neutral between East and West. There is no evidence that the CIA provoked the uprising—in fact, Washington appeared as surprised by the revolt as the Russians—although broadcasts by Radio Free Europe and Radio Liberty created the hope of American support. The situation was complicated by a nearly simultaneous Anglo-French-Israeli invasion of Egypt aimed at seizing control of the Suez Canal, which had been expropriated by the Egyptians. The Eisenhower administration opposed the Suez adventure, and on November 4 Khrushchev took advantage of the disarray among the Western allies to pour two hundred thousand troops into Hungary to put down the rebellion.*

Fighting for control of Budapest block by block, the Hungarian "freedom fighters" frantically called out to the West for help against Soviet tanks. "We appeal to the conscience of the world," Radio Rakoczi

---

*The CIA had erroneously ruled out a serious conflict between the Soviet Union and China. While its intelligence estimates conceded that the two countries had separate and potentially conflicting national objectives, the agency stated that they would nevertheless maintain a close working relationship because of common ideology and China's need for Soviet military and economic assistance. The precedent of Yugoslavia should have been given more weight. As in that country, communism had not been imposed upon China from the outside, and the Russian hold was correspondingly weak.

*President Eisenhower expressed surprise at the Anglo-French-Israeli operation, saying that he got his information about it from the press. Allen Dulles was furious. In a deliberate leak, he declared that the president would have known what was going to happen if he had read the CIA briefing papers. Washington had received information from numerous quarters that the use of force against Egypt was a likely option, and the military buildup was not a secret. But the agency's estimates seem to have been less categorical in discussing the possibility of an intervention. Thus, both Eisenhower and Dulles may have had a point in their favor.

broadcast on November 6. "Why cannot you hear the call for help of our murdered women and children? Peoples of the world! Hear the call for help of a small nation! . . . This is Radio Rakoczi, Hungary! Radio Free Europe, Munich! Radio Free Europe, Munich! Answer! . . . We urgently need medicine, bandages, arms, food, and ammunition! Drop them to us by parachute! Attention, attention, Munich!"

Frank Wisner, who had been on a tour of CIA stations in Europe, was in Vienna as these appeals for help poured in. At the first reports of the uprising he was euphoric, expecting the revolt to spread to Poland, Czechoslovakia, and East Germany. He pleaded with Washington to put Operation Red Sox/Red Cap into effect, to airlift arms and reinforcements for the Hungarians—only to be ignored. Boiling over with rage, he cursed the British, French, and Israelis, claiming the attack on Egypt provided the Russians with cover for the intervention in Hungary.

There was to be no help for the Hungarians. The shock of the Soviet counterattack jolted the Eisenhower administration. The Joint Chiefs pointed out that an airlift of weapons would require the use of military aircraft and open American intervention. Such an action might well lead to war with the Soviet Union, a war for which the United States was unprepared. Before the fighting ended, upward of thirty thousand Hungarians may have been killed; two hundred thousand fled the country. "Poor fellows, poor fellows," lamented President Eisenhower. "I think about them all the time. I wish there was some way of helping them."

The crushing of the Hungarian uprising exposed "liberation" and talk of rolling back the Iron Curtain as hollow generalities. Short of an all-out war, the United States simply lacked the means to direct or influence events in the Soviet sphere. General Lucien K. Truscott, assigned by the president to investigate Wisner's operations, found that the Hungarians had been encouraged by Wisner's operatives to believe that the American military would intervene once the revolt had started. Truscott also discovered that despite the disaster in Budapest, Wisner was pressing ahead with plans for inciting or assisting an uprising in Czechoslovakia. He persuaded Eisenhower that the outcome would be equally disastrous. The operation was closed down, and the personnel involved were dispersed.

Soon after his return to Washington from Europe, Wisner began to act erratically. He told long and pointless stories at conferences and drank more heavily than usual. Not long afterward, he was hospitalized with nervous exhaustion and a bad case of hepatitis, apparently picked up in Athens from a plate of tainted clams. Over the next few years, he suffered several nervous breakdowns. Once he had to be subdued by hospital attendants and carried from CIA headquarters as his embarrassed colleagues looked on. He was finally eased out as DDP in 1959, first to become station chief in London and then into retirement. Six years later, he killed himself at his Maryland farm with a blast from a 20-gauge shotgun.

Friends regarded Wisner as a casualty of the Cold War and blamed his death on disappointments stemming from the failed Hungarian revolt. "For about a decade," they said in a statement issued at the time of his death, "he devoted himself totally to one of the most onerous and difficult tasks any American public servant has ever had to undertake. . . ." What never can be broken is the image of Frank Wisner left with those who worked with him. He was brave yet wise, prudent yet strongly determined, and deeply American above all.

■ ■ ■

Insiders expected Richard Helms to be named the new director of plans to replace Wisner, but Dulles chose Richard M. Bissell for the post. This choice was as unexpected as it was unorthodox, for the new chief of the CIA's clandestine service was completely unlike the typical agency executive. In contrast to the coolly competent Helms, who had been involved in intelligence work since World War II, Bissell was a comparative newcomer. He had joined the agency less than five years before, when Dulles brought him in as his personal assistant. He had never run an agent and had no military or investigative background. Nevertheless, Bissell led the CIA into a sophisticated new age in which technology, electronics, and computer science dominated intelligence gathering.

"Brilliant" was the word most often used to describe Bissell, whom many of his colleagues regarded with something approaching awe. Long-legged, stoop-shouldered, and with a loping gait, he reminded observers of a giant stork. He was independently wealthy, a patrician product of Groton and Yale. After study at the London School of Economics, he had returned to Yale to pioneer the teaching of Keynesian economics in America. In World War II, he had been one of the principal organizers of the massive Allied shipping effort and later was an architect of the Marshall Plan. In fact, some observers credited the selling of the plan to Congress to Bissell's lucidity as a witness.

At the CIA, Bissell immediately exhibited impatience with the limitations of old-style intelligence. "Espionage has been disappointing," he later declared. "The general conclusion is that against the Soviet bloc or other sophisticated societies, espionage is not a primary source of intelligence, although it has had occasional brilliant successes." For Bissell, sophisticated technological snooping, not old-fashioned back-alley melodramas, was the key to discovering an adversary's intentions and capabilities.

Bissell's reputation as one of the CIA's rising stars was confirmed by his role in the development of the high-flying U-2 photoreconnaissance plane and the satellite reconnaissance systems that followed it. The secrecy in which the Soviet Union cloaked its atomic experiments, missile development programs, and military maneuvers had long been a problem for the American intelligence community. Since the onset of the Cold War, the United States had tried to penetrate the darkness by sending military aircraft over Soviet territory to collect photographic and signals intelligence. "One day, I had forty-seven airplanes flying all over Russia," boasted one Air Force general. But early in the 1950s, the Soviets developed surface-to-air missiles that made such missions a risky business, and new methods were sought to provide advance warning of a possible Russian surprise attack.

To meet the challenge, late in 1954 a presidential committee headed by James R. Killian, president of the Massachusetts Institute of Technology, recommended the development of new planes that could operate at altitudes well out of reach of existing Soviet missiles. President Eisenhower approved the proposal, and Dulles ordered Bissell to work with the Air Force, which had been studying a similar project. Instead, Bissell brought the program completely under CIA control by volunteering to pay the entire cost—an estimated twenty-two million dollars—out of the DCI's unvouchered funds. This maneuver bypassed Congress and walled off the super-secret project even from the rest of the agency.

Bissell assigned the task of building the new plane to Clarence L. "Kelly" Johnson of Lockheed Aircraft, who had already suggested a similar airborne spy system. The high-definition camera was the work of Edwin H. Land, inventor of the Polaroid camera. Experts said the project would take six years to complete—if it was possible at all—and would run well over budget. But under the driving lash of Bissell's enthusiasm, the first U-2 was rolled out of the "skunk works" at Lockheed in less than two years and at three million dollars under the estimated cost. Bissell ran the project as a private duchy independent even of Allen Dulles. Secrecy meant more than security to him; it meant absolute control—and control was power.

Over the next four years, the United States virtually owned the sky over the Soviet Union. Between mid-1956 and mid-1960, U-2s made fifty espionage flights. Piloted by former Air Force personnel under contract to the CIA, the U-2s cruised at about seventy thousand feet, giving them a safety buffer of ten thousand feet over the range of Soviet SA-1 missiles. Photographs taken by Land's camera were so extraordinarily detailed that it was said the makes of the autos on the Kremlin parking lot could be identified from them. Missile silos, launching pads, atomic plants, and airfields were kept under continuing surveillance. At the peak of the operations, Bissell had U-2s based in Turkey, Japan, Pakistan, West Germany, and Norway. With twenty-four hours notice, he boasted, "I could have a reccee plane over any part of the earth's surface." The Russians were aware of what was happening from the first overflight, but to protest would reveal the inadequacy of their defenses, and they remained silent.

It would be difficult to exaggerate the importance of Bissell's achievement. The U-2 provided invaluable data on the status of Soviet air defenses and assured American policymakers that the Russians had scarcely any operational intercontinental ballistic missiles, despite the extravagant claims of Nikita Khrushchev. Ironically, this reassuring but highly secret intelligence could not be shared with the public to deflate overestimates of Soviet capabilities. Eisenhower could only listen helplessly as Democrats charged during the 1960 presidential campaign that his administration had allowed a "missile gap" to develop in Moscow's favor.

Despite the successes of the U-2 program, the president always harbored reservations about it. "Well, boys, I believe this country needs this information and I am going to approve it," Eisenhower declared. "But I'll tell you one thing. Someday one of these machines is going to get caught and we're going to have a storm." To reduce the possibility that such an event would destroy his efforts to improve relations with the Russians, Eisenhower insisted on personally approving each series of overflights. Much to the chagrin of the CIA and the Air Force, he canceled or delayed several missions. With the possibility of a thaw in Cold War tensions following a meeting with Khrushchev at Camp David, Maryland, in the fall of 1959, the president ordered the temporary suspension of all overflights of the Soviet Union.

Pressed by the CIA to resume the flights in April 1960, Eisenhower authorized a mission for May 1—May Day, one of the most festive dates on the Soviet calendar—just ten days before the opening of a four-power summit conference in Paris. Perhaps the president mistook Soviet silence about the flights for acquiesence. In reality, Khrushchev was furious. White House fears that an overflight so close in time to the summit would be risky were met by assurances that even if a U-2 were brought down, neither the pilot nor the plane would fall into Soviet hands. All U-2 pilots had instructions to activate a delayed-action bomb that would destroy the craft immediately after they had ejected; they also carried poisoned needles for prompt suicide if faced with captivity and torture.

On the appointed day, the U-2 took off from Peshawar, Pakistan, with a CIA contract employee named Francis Gary Powers at the controls. Powers was to follow a 3,800-mile course that would carry him over the Soviet missile testing site at Tyuratam and the atomic research center at Sverdlovsk, in the Urals, before landing at Bodø, Norway. The mission was proceeding routinely and the plane had passed over the designated targets without incident when suddenly, over Sverdlovsk, Powers heard a dull thump and an orange flash lit up the sky, temporarily blinding him.

One of the Soviets' new SA-2 missiles had apparently exploded nearby, ripping the wings off the plane. Spinning crazily, the plane plunged toward the earth.

Several days later, Khrushchev announced cryptically that an American spy plane had been shot down over Soviet territory. Assuming that neither Powers nor his plane had survived, the State Department responded with a hastily contrived story that the lost plane was a weather research aircraft that had strayed into Russian territory after its civilian pilot reported difficulty with his oxygen supply. Triumphantly, Khrushchev sprang his trap. The U-2's pilot had been captured alive, he announced, and incriminating film and equipment had been found in the wreckage of his plane.*

Despite this provocation, Khrushchev implied he might be willing to proceed with the summit if Eisenhower provided assurances that he was not involved in the overflights and repudiated them. Perhaps Khrushchev reasoned that the Americans might be so embarrassed at getting caught while spying that they would make concessions at the conference, allowing him to emerge with laurels as an adroit diplomatic negotiator. In Washington, Allen Dulles privately offered his resignation so that Eisenhower could issue a plausible denial of involvement; he could tell the world he had fired the CIA director for exceeding his authority. The president rejected the proposal. Although he was angry that the U-2 incident had botched his efforts to reduce tensions, he not only accepted direct responsibility for the ill-timed flight but defended America's right to spy on the Soviet Union. To do otherwise, he reasoned, would create the impression that underlings were making the key decisions in Washington. Under attack by rivals in the Kremlin and the Chinese Commu-

*Powers later claimed he had been unable to set off the detonator and had never been told to commit suicide if captured. Following the destruction of his plane, he parachuted into the May Day celebration in Sverdlovsk. Taken to Moscow, he confessed to espionage charges and was sentenced to three years in prison and seven years in a labor camp. In 1962, he was exchanged for Colonel Rudolf Abel, a Soviet "illegal" who had been captured in New York. Abel had been sent by the NKVD to Canada and had slipped into the United States in 1948 to run a network of spies already in place and to recruit new agents for future operations. Under the cover name "Emil R. Golfus," he established himself in Brooklyn Heights as a retired photofinisher with an interest in painting and photography. Soft-spoken and outwardly friendly, Abel made several friends in the community. But hidden among his cameras and canvases were a radio transmitter, equipment for reducing documents to microdots, and other spy paraphernalia. In 1953, he was joined by an assistant named Reino Hayhaynen, whom Abel disliked because he drank and chased women. Four years later Hayhaynen was recalled to Moscow but turned up instead at the American embassy in Paris, where he fingered Abel.
The Abel affair has an elusive aspect, however. Abel denied being a Russian agent, and even though prosecutors described him as a master spy, no evidence was ever produced concerning his espionage activity. There are also indications that Hayhaynen was under FBI surveillance well before his defection. Following his release from prison, Abel returned to Moscow, where he died in 1972.

nists for softness toward the imperialists, Khrushchev seized upon Eisenhower's refusal to apologize to bolster his position, and the hostility between the two superpowers remained intense.

The irony was that the plane whose flights created all the fuss was very nearly an outmoded weapon. A few months later, the United States and then the Soviet Union shifted to photographing their adversary's territory and military deployments from orbit reconnaissance satellites in space. Well before Powers was shot down, Bissell had foreseen the possibility that Russian technology would catch up with the U-2 and had started work on satellites capable of outranging any Soviet missile and producing pictures equal in fineness of resolution to those taken by the U-2. Paradoxically, these "spies in space" have not triggered the same anxiety about foreign intrusion while providing the superpowers with the means to verify that the other side is not planning a surprise attack.

But the U-2 affair had a larger meaning. Many ordinary Americans were shocked that their own government would lie to them. The bumbling that preceded Eisenhower's acceptance of responsibility for the overflights created unease in the public mind about the secret expedients of power. For the first time, Americans realized that the United States might indeed be guilty of the same Cold War machinations they attributed to its enemies. Outside Washington, the word "intelligence" began to take on a new and sinister meaning.

17

To Bear Any Burden

Three weeks after the inauguration of John F. Kennedy, Allen Dulles was the host at a very private dinner in Washington. Exuding affability, he led a delegation of the CIA's top people to the party, to which he had also invited a dozen of the new president's ranking aides. Several rounds of cocktails lubricated relations between the two groups, and the president's men listened in fascination as the "spooks" recounted tales of some of the agency's most secret exploits. Over brandy and cigars, the old spymaster had each of his staff directors describe their work. Richard Bissell stopped the show. "I'm your man-eating shark," he declared.

Dulles gloried in being among Kennedy's first appointments—along with J. Edgar Hoover—but as a holdover from President Eisenhower's administration, he saw the need to quickly establish links with the new men in the White House. These friendships provided the CIA with a head start on its bureaucratic rivals in the State and Defense departments. Presidential aides, now on a first-name basis with the CIA hierarchy, dispensed with the usual chain of command to telephone directly when they needed information. Indeed, the CIA was made to order for the new president's vigorous, action-oriented style. "By gosh, I don't care what it is, but if I need some material fast or an idea fast, CIA is the place I have to go," Kennedy told an aide. "The State Department takes four or five days to answer a simple yes or no."

As the youngest president since Theodore Roosevelt, Kennedy believed his election not only marked the replacement of a Republican administration by the Democrats but also represented the passing of the torch from one generation to another. Projecting an image of toughness and impatience, he welcomed confrontation and personalized diplomacy into a struggle of wills. A confirmed cold warrior, Kennedy was impatient with Eisenhower's leadership and eager to test his own manhood on the world scene. To him, the old soldier had not been aggressive enough and had accepted too many limitations on America's power. Where Eisenhower had been passive, he would be active. Where Eisenhower had been cautious, he would be bold. Kennedy threw down the gauntlet in his inaugural address: "We shall pay any price, bear any burden, meet any hardship, support any friend, oppose any foes, in order to assure the survival and success of liberty."

One of the Kennedy administration's top priorities was military expansion. The American people had been startled and alarmed by the success of the Russians in sending *Sputnik*, the first artificial satellite, into space and by Nikita Khrushchev's warning that the Soviet Union could destroy the United States with intercontinental ballistic missiles (ICBMs). Kennedy had been elected with the promise to close what he had called the "missile gap."* Once in office, however, he saw intelligence reports showing that Khrushchev had been bluffing. Nevertheless, fearing to be seen as soft on communism, the new president created a missile gap of his own—about two hundred to one in favor of the United States.

Kennedy understood that the realities of the nuclear age precluded a victory over communism in the traditional sense. But rather than accept a policy of containment, he talked of spreading the "disease of liberty" into areas of the Third World held by Communists, even as Khrushchev pledged "wars of national liberation" to break the grip of imperialism. Like the Communists, Kennedy was convinced of the inevitable success of his system. And like them, he was not adverse to speeding up the process of change—both through "nation-building" schemes such as the Alliance for Progress in Latin America and through CIA covert actions.

Kennedy's first test came in Cuba. In January 1959, after three years of guerrilla warfare, Fidel Castro, a young Cuban nationalist, had succeeded in overthrowing the brutal, American-supported regime of Fulgencio Batista.* Initial enthusiasm in the United States for the revolution soon soured as Castro ordered the ruthless execution of opponents and followed up by confiscating the American-owned mining, sugar, and

---

*The intelligence community was convinced that the massive rocket used to orbit *Sputnik* and later, an astronaut, gave the Soviet Union an enormous advantage over the United States in the deployment of an ICBM. Unless the United States greatly increased its missile deployment, it was argued, a gap would develop beginning in 1963. Unable to convince the Eisenhower administration of the alleged threat, CIA sources leaked the information to the Kennedy campaign. Surveillance of Soviet territory by spy satellites beginning in 1961 revealed that the United States was, in fact, far ahead of the Russians in missile development. The huge missile that had given the Soviets their advantage in space turned out to be too big and cumbersome to serve as a practical ICBM. (Letter to the Editor from Roger Hilsman, former director of the State Department Bureau of Intelligence and Research, New York *Times*, September 26, 1987.)

*Hedging its bets, the CIA secretly channeled fifty thousand dollars to leaders of Castro's 26th of July Movement while still supporting Batista. Whether Castro knew of the CIA support has not been resolved.

utility companies that had dominated Cuba since 1898. Having alienated the United States, he turned to the Soviet Union for help, signing a trade agreement with Russia in the spring of 1960. Some authorities claim that Castro intended to establish a Communist regime in Cuba from the beginning; in any case, he began larding his speeches with Marxist rhetoric and proclaimed himself on the side of the Soviet Union in the struggle against imperialism. "This revolution is like a watermelon," remarked a disgruntled American businessman. "The more they slice it, the redder it gets."

Washington was outraged by the presence of a Soviet satellite only ninety miles from the United States. As early as December 1959, the CIA had advocated Castro's "elimination," and plans were discussed in meetings of a subcommittee of the 5412 Committee, or "Special Group," to overthrow him. In March 1960, President Eisenhower, looking back to the success of the Iranian and Guatemalan operations, approved a CIA plan to train and infiltrate company-sized bands of guerrillas into Cuba. Once on the island, they were to link up with resistance groups and destabilize the Castro regime. Allen Dulles underscored the importance of the project by placing Bissell, the CIA's resident "Wonder Boy" and his own logical successor, in charge. But Cuba was not Iran, and Fidel Castro was not Jacobo Arbenz.

■ ■ ■

Plots to assassinate Castro unfolded in tandem with the conspiracy to overthrow him. No one in authority ever actually talked openly about assassination—top-level officials are hardly likely to be so indiscreet—but the evidence indicates that President Eisenhower knew about these intrigues even if he did not actually authorize them. Such discussions took place, at least by inference, at a meeting of the National Security Council on March 10, 1960, at which Eisenhower presided. Plans were discussed to "bring another government to power in Cuba," and the official minutes state that "Admiral [Arleigh] Burke [the chief of naval operations] suggested that any plan for the removal of Cuban leaders should be a package deal since many of the leaders around Castro were even worse than Castro." Four days later, the Special Group discussed "the effect on the Cuban scene if Fidel and Raul Castro [his brother] and Che Guevara [his top aide] should disappear simultaneously."

Was this a wink-and-a-nod hint to the CIA to murder Castro? Surviving participants later told a Senate Select Committee headed by Senator Frank Church that assassination was neither considered nor discussed at these meetings. But Ray Cline, who was familiar with the terminology employed in such discussions, stated that the language used suggests that the assassination of the Castro brothers and Guevara "was at least theoretically considered." While the Church Committee concluded that

"there was insufficient evidence from which the Committee could conclude that Presidents Eisenhower, Kennedy, or Johnson, their close advisers, or the Special Group authorized the assassination of Castro," none
of them would have shed tears at his passing. Bissell, for one, never
doubted that he had been subtly directed through Dulles to arrange a
capability for assassination, or "executive action," as it became euphemistically known.

The involvement of the CIA in planning assassinations was not a
momentary aberration of a handful of rogue agents who had jumped the
reservation. The goals pursued by the agency—no matter how questionable—were those of the United States government. For at least a brief
period, political assassination was regarded as a tool of American foreign
policy.* Increasingly, the United States, as self-anointed defender of the
free world, found itself facing the question of whether or not the elimination of particular individuals would be in its own best interests and those
of its allies. In the case of Fidel Castro, Patrice Lumumba, the Congolese
leader, Colonel Abdul Kassem of Iraq, and Rafael Trujillo, the dictator of
the Dominican Republic, the answer was overwhelmingly in the affirmative.

"Killing people is wrong," Bissell later said in an attempt at ra-
tionalization of these plots, "but it happens, and if someone had polished
off Idi Amin it would have saved a lot of people a lot of grief." The task of
getting rid of inconvenient leaders fell to the CIA because its participation in paramilitary operations, coups, and rebellions had made the
agency no stranger to violence and death. In the prevailing Cold War
atmosphere, the assassination of foreign leaders was regarded as a logical
extension of these operations. Although the Church Committee found
that no foreign leader was directly killed by the CIA, it was not for lack of
trying.

Lumumba, premier of the Congo in the tumultuous period that
followed independence from Belgian rule, was marked for executive
action in the later part of 1960 because American policymakers believed
he was paving the way for chaos and a Soviet takeover. "The chain of
events revealed by the documents and testimony is strong enough to
permit a reasonable inference that the plot to assassinate Lumumba was
authorized by President Eisenhower," the Church Committee declared.*

---

*The Church Committee discovered in the early 1950s that OPC had a "special operations"
unit headed by Colonel Boris T. Pash that was to arrange for the assassination and
kidnapping of double agents if necessary. Pash denied that the unit was ever asked to
perform such services, and the committee found no evidence that it had.

*Later on, the committee hedged by stating: "Nevertheless, there is enough countervailing
testimony by Eisenhower Administration officials and enough ambiguity and lack of clarity
in the records of high level policy meetings to preclude the Committee from making a
finding that the President intended an assassination effort against Lumumba."

The official minutes of both the Special Group and the NSC contain such phrases as "getting rid of" and "disposed of" in discussions of Lumumba's fate. Dr. Stanley Gottlieb, the CIA's expert on toxins and head of the Technical Services Staff, produced vials of poison that were sent to the CIA station in the Congo for use on Lumumba. Local events forestalled the plot, however. Before the toxins could be administered to Lumumba, he was ousted by CIA-supported rivals and executed.

Colonel Kassem was also marked for a fatal dose of one of Dr. Gottlieb's poisons. In seizing power in Iraq early in 1960, he not only had murdered his predecessor and a number of foreigners, but had further antagonized the Eisenhower administration by reopening relations with the Soviet Union and legalizing the local Communist party. Richard Helms, as Bissell's deputy, endorsed Kassem's removal as "highly desirable," and a handkerchief impregnated with a toxic substance was sent to him through the mail. Before it arrived, the intended victim had already been overthrown and shot.

Trujillo, a brutal dictator originally put in power three decades before by the United States, had outstayed his welcome, and both the Eisenhower and Kennedy administrations encouraged Dominican dissidents to oust him. Although the Church Committee found no evidence of CIA participation in Trujillo's assassination in May 1961, the agency had supplied the dissidents with weapons that were probably used in the killing.

The major target of the CIA's attempts to make policy by assassination, however, was Fidel Castro. The sundry plots against his life and those of other top Cuban leaders ranged from the vague to the grotesque. The first overt attempt occurred in July 1960, when the CIA station chief in Havana was ordered by Washington to arrange an "accident" that would eliminate Raul Castro. A Cuban dissident accepted an offer of ten thousand dollars to carry out the scheme, but it was called off before an attempt could be made.

In its eagerness to eliminate Castro, the CIA entered into an alliance with the Mafia, which harbored a grudge against the Cuban leader because he had closed down the syndicate's lucrative gambling, prostitution, and narcotics operations in Cuba. Bissell reasoned that the Mafia had considerable experience in such matters and that there was little chance for the "hit" to be traced back to the U. S. government. Robert A. Maheu, a one-time FBI agent who had proved useful to the CIA—among other favors, he had produced the pornographic film intended to discredit Indonesia's Sukarno—arranged the contacts with the Mafia. Two ranking underworld figures were recruited, John Rosselli and Sam Giancana, who were only too delighted to have the government in their debt. A gangland-style killing was rejected as too dangerous; instead, the CIA's hired mobsters agreed to furnish a "contractor" who would drop some of Dr.

Gottlieb's ubiquitous potions into Castro's dinner or drinks.* Two attempts were said to have been made early in 1961. The first batch of capsules failed to dissolve in water; there is no report on the second. In the meantime, the guerrilla campaign against Castro initially approved by President Eisenhower had mushroomed into something else entirely: a full-scale invasion of Cuba.

■ ■ ■

Barely making bow waves, five rusty merchant vessels steamed single file into the ominously dark waters of the Bay of Pigs, on Cuba's southern coast, shortly after midnight on April 17, 1961. In the dawn's early light, some 1,200 men of a Cuban exile brigade recruited and trained by the CIA splashed ashore to establish a beachhead in their homeland. Operaton Zapata—the long-awaited invasion of Cuba—had begun.

But Castro was ready for the assault. With the coming of daylight, the invaders were bombed and strafed by the Cuban air force. President Kennedy had made a last-minute decision to cancel a promised D-Day air strike against the handful of Cuban planes that had survived an earlier surprise attack by the emigré air force, and Castro controlled the air over the beachhead.

Two of the brigade's ships were sunk almost immediately, one carrying the bulk of its ammunition and the other loaded with communications equipment. The invaders were pinned down between the sea and the mangrove swamps behind the beaches, and any hope of escape soon drained away. With his men dying under the fire of Castro's planes and artillery and nearly out of ammunition, Pepe San Roman, the brigade's commander, pleaded over the radio for help that never came. In Washington, the men who had organized the invasion listened numbly, openly cursing Kennedy for canceling the air strike. Seventy-two hours after the landing, San Roman radioed: "I have nothing left to fight with. Am headed for the swamp." And then the radio went dead.*

---

*Giancana was also sharing the bed of a Las Vegas "party girl" named Judith Campbell with President Kennedy. Kennedy was introduced to Campbell, an attractive brunette and Giancana's mistress, by Frank Sinatra in February 1960 while he was running for the Democratic presidential nomination. The relationship continued until J. Edgar Hoover warned the president that the liaison was widely known and could expose him to blackmail. Records were later found of seventy phone calls between Campbell and the White House. The last was on March 22, 1962, the date of Hoover's warning.
Giancana and Rosselli were both murdered in 1975 at about the time the Church Committee was taking testimony regarding their attempts to murder Castro. Rosselli was killed after he had testified; Giancana, before he could be heard. Both killings are thought to have been in revenge for having dragged the Mafia into the public spotlight.

*U.S. Navy fliers who observed the unequal battle from a distance were kept from intervening only with difficulty. About 1,500 U.S. Marines waited on a ship off the coast but were never deployed. (*Time,* June 1, 1987.)

The Bay of Pigs was a tragedy of epic proportions. Lives were lost needlessly, America's reputation was damaged, and the new administration was humiliated. To Kennedy's credit, he assumed responsibility for the disaster. "Victory has a thousand fathers," he declared, "but defeat is an orphan." Nevertheless, Bissell and Dulles were saddled with the blame for the biggest fiasco in the CIA's history. The disaster was even more damaging to the agency's reputation than the Hungarian failure, because the United States had suffered a severe defeat in the full glare of public knowledge that it had been behind the operation. "In a parliamentary government I would resign," the president told Bissell. "In this government the President can't and doesn't and so you and Allen must go."

What went wrong?

Numerous postmortems produced a flock of reasons for the dismal failure of Operaton Zapata: Kennedy's refusal to authorize the second air strike; the lack of security; the folly of trying to invade Cuba with 1,200 men when Castro had an army and militia of 200,000, rapidly increasing in quality and strength; flawed intelligence and assumptions about conditions in Cuba; CIA arrogance after its successes in Iran, Guatemala, and elsewhere. Some critics question whether the agency should have been involved in the operation in the first place. If Kennedy considered Castro a serious threat to the security of the United States, they argue, he should have sent in the Marines instead of mounting a risky paramilitary operation held together with hope and baling wire.

The plan originated in the fertile imagination of Richard Bissell. Throughout the autumn of 1960, he had watched with mounting impatience as the handful of guerrillas infiltrated into Cuba were tracked down by Castro forces. Influenced by the reports of emigrés that a major show of force would inspire the Cuban people to rise up in revolt against Castro, Bissell began preparing a full-scale invasion. Under the cover of planes supplied by the CIA, the exiles would be landed near the town of Trinidad, on the southern coast of Cuba. When the beachhead had been secured, a government-in-exile hammered together by the CIA from among the feuding exile groups in Florida would be transported to the island.* If the situation went awry, the invaders could fade into the nearby Escambray Mountains and launch a guerrilla war against Castro. Either way, uprisings against Castro were expected to follow, and the United States would recognize the new government.

*As in the Guatemalan operation, the swashbuckling Howard Hunt was brought in to create some sort of order among the various exile factions that made up the Cuban Revolutionary Council. Time had done nothing to sharpen his skills, however. On one occasion, he reportedly drank too much while on a visit to Washington and displayed all his fake CIA papers in the name of "Eduardo" to his companions. During this period and its aftermath, he became acquainted with many of the Cubans he later employed in the Watergate burglary.

Violating every precept of sound intelligence practice, Bissell ran the Cuban enterprise out of his vest pocket. The aging Dulles exercised only peripheral control and spent much of his time overseeing a project dearer to his heart: the building of a $46 million CIA complex at Langley, in the Virginia countryside outside Washington. The operation was sealed off from the rest of the agency, and assessments of the risks involved were made by the men planning it. Robert Amory, the deputy director for intelligence, and Sherman Kent, of the Board of National Estimates, found themselves cut out of the loop after they questioned the reports supplied by the exiles that the Cuban people were ripe for revolt. Their own information indicated that Castro was popular and that with most dissidents either in jail or in exile there was little possibility of spontaneous uprising. British intelligence estimates made available to the CIA also made it clear that the vast majority of Cubans were still behind Castro.

Richard Helms, sensing a disaster in the making, carefully distanced himself from the project. In fact, David Atlee Phillips, who ran the propaganda side of the operation, as he had in Guatemala, noted that Helms remained silent at the early planning sessions. Phillips thought it "incredible" that he was not asking his usual penetrating questions. Soon Helms stayed away from the meetings altogether. Tacitly, Bissell and his deputy divided up the work of the DDP among themselves; Bissell devoted full attention to the Cuban project, while Helms took charge of all other clandestine activities. On the surface, relations between them were correct, if cool; privately, Bissell urged Dulles to transfer Helms to London, while Helms referred to Bissell as "the bastard."

President Kennedy, who had assailed the Eisenhower administration for weakness on Cuba and Castro while campaigning against Richard Nixon, approved the plan to invade the island immediately after he entered office. Influenced by the CIA's previous successes in overthrowing governments—and unaware of the dissension surrounding the project within the upper levels of the agency—the Joint Chiefs of Staff and the White House accepted Bissell's assurances and failed to raise necessary questions about the deficiencies of the project.* But as the invasion neared and various newspapers and magazines published stories about American-backed Cubans training in Guatemala, Kennedy had second

*One of the most controversial aspects of the Cuban operation was whether or not the planners told the president the invasion would trigger a spontaneous revolt that would bring down Castro. Bissell and Dulles claimed that they had never contended the landing would inspire an immediate uprising. Instead, they said, they told the White House that a week or more *after* the anti-Castro government had been established, they anticipated that it would incite resistance to Castro, primarily in the form of guerrilla action. On the other hand, Arthur Schlesinger, Jr., has written, "We all in the White House considered uprisings behind the lines essential to the success of the operation; so too did the Joint Chiefs of Staff; and so, we thought, did the CIA."

thoughts about the "noise level" of the operation. Worried about the all-but-open American involvement, he made vital changes in the plan designed to give the exiles enough support to allow the invasion to succeed but not enough to make American participation obvious. On both counts he failed.

The landing site was moved eastward to the isolated Bay of Pigs, but Kennedy did not realize—nor was he told—that the site was some seventy miles from the Escambray, so that the move effectively closed out the guerrilla option. Then, on the eve of the invasion, the president scaled back the number of missions to be flown by the exile air force and canceled the vital D-Day air strike that was to knock out Castro's air power. Somewhere along the line Bissell and Dulles should have protested as Kennedy whittled away at the margin for error and perhaps threatened to resign or close down the project. But they were advocates as well as planners and pressed ahead, convinced that in the event of serious trouble events would compel the president to order open American intervention.

Could the the Bay of Pigs invasion have succeeded if Kennedy had followed through with the planned air strikes? Castro thought so. He credited his victory to the invaders' lack of air support. In his own analysis of the debacle, however, Kennedy pointed the finger elsewhere. "All my life I've known better than to depend on the experts," the angry president declared in the wake of the disaster. "How could I have been so stupid to let them go ahead?" The conventional wisdom is that CIA and the Joint Chiefs led a new and inexperienced president astray, that he depended upon their expert judgment, and they had let him down. This is nonsense. Certainly, Bissell and Dulles were guilty of sloppy planning, but they were merely telling Kennedy what he wanted to hear. The fundamental cause of the disaster was the failure of the president and other decision makers to take heed of Kermit Roosevelt's admonition that such operations could not succeed unless the "people and the army want what we want."

■ ■ ■

Undoubtedly the most important effect of the Cuban disaster was its influence on Soviet views of Kennedy. Two months later, the president met face to face with Khrushchev in Vienna. Afterward a dazed Kennedy declared: "He just beat the hell out of me. I think he did it because of the Bay of Pigs. I think he saw anyone who was so young and inexperienced as to get into that mess could be taken. . . . Until we remove those ideas, we won't get anywhere with him. So we have to act."

In his immediate rage over the mismanagement of the Bay of Pigs invasion, Kennedy reportedly vowed to "splinter the CIA in a thousand pieces and scatter it to the winds." One proposal called for reducing the

CIA's size and power by splitting the intelligence and analysis functions from the agency's "black" operations. Eventually, the president's anger subsided, but he ordered a full-scale shake-up of the agency, including an internal investigation by Lyman Kirkpatrick, then the CIA's inspector general. Kirkpatrick's report—which is still locked up in the agency's secret files—was a ruthless attack on Dulles and Bissell. Some agency officials who have read it are convinced that Kirkpatrick, who had been crippled by polio a decade before and was confined to a wheelchair, believed that his advancement had been hindered by Dulles and that the report was designed not only to gain revenge but to curry favor with the Kennedys by blaming the disaster on the CIA leadership rather than on the White House. Dulles was understood to have been especially upset by its devastating tone, because he had regarded Kirkpatrick as a protégé.*

To replace Dulles and bring the CIA under tighter Oval Office control, the president wanted to appoint his brother, Bobby, the attorney general, as director of central inteligence. The younger Kennedy protested that such a move would be poor politics; instead, he became the president's personal watchdog over the CIA—though, like many outsiders, he was soon captivated by cloak-and-dagger operations. The agency itself was humbled by investigations, its budget was cut, station chiefs were brought under the control of ambassadors, paramilitary operations were transferred to the Pentagon, and restrictions were placed on what covert operations remained.† As a counterbalance to the agency, the Defense Intelligence Agency was established to take over many of the responsibilities of the intelligence arms of the three armed services.

The appointment of John A. McCone as Dulles's successor marked the beginning of a new era for the CIA. McCone was a conservative Republican businessman who had served Truman as under secretary of the air force and Eisenhower as chairman of the Atomic Energy Commission. He found the agency in a shambles. Both internal morale and White House confidence in the CIA had been shattered. Accordingly, the new director's mission was to rebuild the agency's prestige and return it to active participation in the policy process. But his role as DCI was sharply different from that of his predecessor. Unlike Eisenhower, who had used Dulles to interpret intelligence for him, Kennedy preferred to be his own intelligence officer, so McCone would serve more as a manager than as an oracle.

---

*The gist of Kirkpatrick's report is contained in an article he published a decade afterward, "Paramilitary Case Study—The Bay of Pigs" (*Naval War College Review,* November/December 1972).

†Among the operations closed down was a secret base in the Colorado Rockies for training Tibetan guerrillas to be infiltrated into Tibet to harass the Chinese who had taken over the country in the 1950s and expelled the Dalai Lama. Like similar groups infiltrated into Cuba, the guerrillas were not a success.

Kennedy's approach suited McCone's own view of his job. Businesslike and dour—he was soon known throughout the CIA as "Jolly John"—he believed the agency should maintain a low profile and disliked being referred to as a "spymaster" by the press. Whereas Dulles had delighted in gossiping with his aides, McCone was a no-nonsense manager. Upon taking over the luxurious suite of offices his predecessor had designed for himself on the seventh floor of the new headquarters at Langley, his first step was to rip out an intercom system that allowed top assistants to reach him directly. On one occasion, he called in an aide and gave him a memo asking for a large amount of information.

"I suppose you want it all tomorrow," said the dismayed staff man as he looked over the list.

"Not tomorrow—today," replied McCone. "If I wanted it tomorrow, I would ask for it tomorrow."

Immediately upon taking office, McCone restructured the CIA's high command to remove the taint of defeat. Richard Helms took over as DDP in place of Bissell, Ray Cline became DDI, and Lyman Kirkpatrick filled the newly created post of Executive Director-Comptroller. Unlike previous DCI's, McCone was more concerned with the technical side of intelligence gathering, especially the fast-expanding satellite photo systems, than with clandestine operations. During his tenure greater emphasis was placed upon analysis and intelligence estimates than ever before in the agency's history.

But Cuba was an issue that would not go away. If anything, the Bay of Pigs debacle had intensified the Kennedy brothers' conviction that the island was a dagger pointed at the heart of the United States. Unused to the bitter taste of defeat, they harbored an irrational hatred of the bearded Cuban who had bested them. "We were hysterical about Castro," recalled Secretary of Defense Robert S. McNamara, "and there was pressure from JFK and RFK to do something about Castro." On November 30, 1961, the president authorized a wide-ranging covert program, dubbed "Operation Mongoose," that would make use of every option—including assassination—to get rid of Castro.

General Edward Lansdale, the counterinsurgency expert from the Phillippines and Vietnam, was placed in charge of Mongoose. Bobby Kennedy personally rode herd on the operation, declaring that Castro's removal was the "top priority of the U. S. government—all else is secondary. . . . No time, money, effort, or manpower is to be spared." But Mongoose was doomed to failure, because it suffered from the same faulty assumption that bedeviled Operation Zapata: that the Cuban people were opposed to Fidel Castro and would revolt if given the opportunity. Although the CIA's Board of National Estimates concluded that "it is highly improbable that an extensive popular revolt could be fomented" against Castro, the Kennedys had learned nothing from the earlier failure. In their eagerness for revenge they continued to regard Castro as an anomaly imposed upon the Cuban people, a view that betrayed both a lack of understanding of the roots of the Cuban revolution and a lack of adequate intelligence from the island.

With his usual exuberance, Lansdale spawned no fewer than thirty-three separate schemes to oust the Cuban leader. Ranging from anti-Castro propaganda to paramilitary raids and sabotage of the sugar crop, these actions were to be capped by what he called "the touchdown play"—open revolt and the overthrow of the regime in October 1962. Some of Lansdale's brainstorms had overtones of the Keystone Cops. Undoubtedly the most imaginative was aimed at convincing Cuba's Catholic population that the Second Coming was near but that Christ would bypass Cuba as long as the anti-Christ—in the person of Fidel Castro—remained in power. Once the rumors had taken root, an American submarine would lie off the Cuban coast and fill the night sky with star shells to make it appear that Christ's return was imminent, thus pushing the Cubans into deposing their cigar-smoking anti-Christ. The Special Group thought "elimination by illumination" a bit fanciful, however, and the scheme was never implemented.

William Harvey, whose credits included the Berlin Tunnel—no one pointed out that the operation had been blown from the start—was given the job of actually getting rid of Castro. Lansdale told President Kennedy that Harvey was "America's James Bond." Kennedy, an admirer of Ian Fleming's novels, raised a quizzical eyebrow when Harvey turned out to be fat, pop-eyed, and raspy-voiced. As head of a super-secret unit known as Task Force W, which operated out of the basement of CIA headquarters, "America's James Bond" ran a no-holds barred guerrilla war budgeted at fifty million dollars annually. The CIA station in Miami, run by a Harvey protégé from Berlin named Theodore Shackley, became the largest in the world. "Boom and bang" raids were made by Cuban exiles, and infiltrators tried to make up for the CIA's lack of intelligence assets on the island by establishing a network of informants. Most of these operations were pinpricks that strengthened the regime by giving it the excuse to impose tighter controls; a sizable number were penetrated by the DGI, Castro's Soviet-trained intelligence service.

Bobby Kennedy quickly grew impatient with Harvey's insistence on building up assets, and there were angry exchanges between the two men. Under Kennedy's urgent prodding, Harvey plotted Castro's murder. Bizarre schemes flourished in the crisis atmosphere. Dr. Gottlieb produced various lethal gifts for Castro, including poisoned cigars and pens and a diving suit impregnated with a toxic skin contaminant. Then there was an exotic seashell that was to be placed in Castro's favorite skin-diving area—rigged with an explosive device. As if all that were not enough, Harvey also sought technical assistance from the British. "We're developing a new capability in the 'Company' to handle these kinds of problems, and we're looking for the requisite expertise," Peter Wright, an M15 official, quoted him as saying. The Mafia connection with Johnny Rosselli was renewed as well. Harvey provided him with a $5,000 arsenal of weapons and explosives, along with the usual array of poison pills. But if an actual attempt on Castro's life ever resulted, it was unsuccessful.

In 1975 Castro estimated that the CIA had made two dozen attempts to kill either himself or other Cuban leaders. The Church Committee found concrete evidence for at least eight such plots. Some never proceeded beyond the planning stage, and those that did had the consistency of failure. Apart from assassination schemes, the agency also considered such nonlethal methods of undermining Castro's charismatic appeal as spraying the television studio where he was to give a speech with a chemical that would cause him to act erratically on the air and dusting his shoes with another chemical that would cause his beard to fall out. Needless to say, Castro outlived all these schemes with beards and charisma intact.

Although there is no direct evidence linking the president to the anti-Castro conspiracy, the closeness of the Kennedy brothers makes it likely that the attorney general kept him fully informed of developments. But as these plots were being concocted, Cuba suddenly became the center-piece of a frightening crisis that dwarfed the futile attempts to overthrow Castro—and nearly plunged the world into nuclear war.

■ ■ ■

Throughout the summer of 1962, American intelligence picked up numerous clues pointing to a Soviet arms buildup in Cuba. MIG jet fighters appeared on the air fields, the number of Russian troops increased to five thousand, and aerial reconnaissance showed that large quantities of electronic equipment were being unloaded at Mariel, a small port on the north shore of the island. Thinking that these shipments were preparatory to the arrival of IL-28 medium bombers capable of reaching targets in the United States, CIA analysts were mystified when there were no signs of the construction of landing strips capable of handling the planes. If the Cubans weren't receiving bombers, what were they getting?

The CIA was paying the price for its lack of reliable intelligence assets in Cuba. Aerial reconnaissance could keep track of Soviet arms shipments, but it could not tell what was inside the crates. The only direct information from the island came from Cuban refugees arriving in Miami. The analysts distrusted their reports, especially after some refugees told of seeing large Russian rockets being transported about the island on flatbed trucks. Such tales were regarded as preposterous. To tamp down these rumors, the CIA's Board of National Estimates issued a secret report on September 12 concluding that the Russians would not deploy offensive missiles in Cuba. They had never installed such weapons outside their own territory, the agency said, and would hardly risk a confrontation with the United States by doing so in Cuba.

This estimate was eagerly accepted by the White House. With the approach of the midterm congressional elections, Kennedy was under fire from the Republicans, who charged that the Russians were installing long-range missiles in Cuba and that the administration was doing nothing about it. But there were dissenters—among them, John McCone. Ever since he had seen aerial photographs showing surface-to-air (SAM) missile sites under construction in western Cuba, he had been convinced that they were intended to protect Soviet nuclear missiles. Common sense told him that the Russians were hardly likely to use SAMs to defend ordinary construction sites. From the south of France, where he was honeymooning with his second wife, he bombarded Langley with messages—known as the "honeymoon cables"—urging greater attention to the possibility of missiles in Cuba.

On September 20, a Cuban refugee not only told interrogators in Miami that had he seen a missile being trucked through his town but provided an estimate of its size that matched those of a Soviet medium-range missile. This report was followed by one from an agent in Cuba stating that all civilians had been evacuated from the area of San Cristobal, fifty miles southwest of Havana. The angry cables from McCone and mounting evidence from other sources spurred the CIA into a maximum effort to discover whether the Soviets were indeed deploying missiles in the island. U-2s flashed through the high, thin air over western Cuba, photographing every possible site again and again.

Photoanalysts at the CIA's National Photographic Interpretation Center discovered what they were looking for in a series of pictures taken on October 14. Huddling over the pictures of a clearing in a wooded area near San Cristobal, they traced out the sites for batteries of medium-range missiles.

"Are you sure of this?" President Kennedy asked Arthur C. Lundahl, the center's director, when the pictures were brought to the Oval Office.

"Mr. President," replied Lundahl, "I am as sure of this as a photo interpreter can be sure of anything."

Kennedy was angered and alarmed. With ranges up to 2,200 miles, the missiles could reach targets in a large area of the United States. To this day, there is no firm consensus about why Khrushchev decided to introduce strategic missiles into Cuba. Soviet officials later said he may have been trying to defend the Castro regime against the threat of invasion, to one-up critics in the Kremlin by securing a Cold War triumph, and to gain a nuclear "quick fix" that would give the Soviets the appearance of parity with America's arsenal of missiles capable of reaching his own country. But if he expected Kennedy to negotiate the withdrawal of the missiles, he badly miscalculated. After the Bay of the Pigs, the president was in no mood to back down.

Over the next thirteen days, Kennedy's top aides met as the Excom, or Executive Committee of the National Security Council, to monitor the situation and to advise the president. McCone sat in on the meetings—a clear sign that the CIA had redeemed itself by its success in detecting the missiles and the steady flow of accurate intelligence during the crisis. As U-2 photos showed that work on the missile sites was being speeded up, Excom examined its options: an immediate air strike against the missile bases before they were operational, a full-scale invasion of Cuba, or a naval blockade. Most of those present, McCone included, urged that the sites be bombed without warning, but Bobby Kennedy resisted. "I now know how Tojo felt when he was planning Pearl Harbor," he wrote in a note passed to an aide. And he did not want his brother to be remembered as a Tojo.

On October 22, President Kennedy went on television to inform the nation and the world that the Soviets had emplaced rockets in Cuba that endangered the national security of the United States. He announced a naval blockade, or "quarantine," of arms shipments to Cuba that was backed up by an ultimatum demanding that Khrushchev withdraw the missiles. To give the Russians time to weigh the consequences, the actual blockade was not to begin until the morning of October 24. Khrushchev branded the American charges as lies and warned that if the Americans carried out any act of "piracy" the Soviet Union would react accordingly.

Tension mounted as nearly a dozen Soviet freighters steamed toward the quarantine line. A U-2 was shot down over Cuba; B-52 bombers loaded with nuclear bombs were placed on aerial alert. FBI agents reported that Soviet diplomats at the United Nations were burning documents, usually a sign of an imminent rupture of relations. "There wasn't one of us who wasn't pretty sure that in a few hours we'd have to sink one of those Russian ships," a presidential aide later recalled. Suddenly, word was received that perhaps half the Russian vessels had either stopped or put about. "We're eyeball to eyeball and I think the other fellow just blinked," commented Secretary of State Dean Rusk.

Unable to sustain his bold attempt to alter the balance of power on the sly, Khrushchev backed down. In exchange for an American pledge to respect Cuba's territorial integrity, the Russians dismantled the missiles and removed them from the island. The humiliating failure was one of the major reasons for Khrushchev's ouster from power two years later.

■ ■ ■

The missile crisis restored the CIA to the foreign policy first team. Even though Operation Mongoose was a disaster and was closed down following the October settlement,* and even though the agency had fumbled the initial attempts to confirm the presence of Soviet missiles in Cuba, the White House was impressed with the blend of human and technical intelligence it had received during the crisis. Moreover, even doubters were now convinced that the nation needed a strong intelligence agency. Bobby Kennedy and McGeorge Bundy, the president's national security adviser, told Ray Cline, who had spearheaded the CIA's analytical operations, that the first U-2 pictures of the missile sites fully justified all that the CIA had cost over its entire history.

One of the CIA's most valuable assets during the crisis was intelligence received from Colonel Oleg Penkovsky, a GRU officer and mole within the Soviet high command. "Things that were photographed or overheard were explained in Penkovsky's stolen documents, as well as many things that would have been unknown altogether," Cline noted. Largely as a result of Penkovsky's information, President Kennedy was aware that Soviet missile capabilities were inferior to those of the United States and that Khrushchev was bluffing when he threatened nuclear war. Working from Penkovsky's data, CIA analysts created a precise estimate of the time it would take for the missiles placed in Cuba to become operational, a crucial factor in the timing of the American response. Penkovsky also reported that Khrushchev did not plan to apply pressure on Berlin during the crisis. Without the intelligence supplied by Penkovsky, the American position during the missile crisis would have been even more precarious than it was.

Unlike the earlier Soviet mole, Major Vladimir Popov, who came from a peasant background, Penkovsky was the son of a Czarist army officer and was a well educated man with a taste for the good life. Wounded and decorated several times during World War II, he had been promoted to colonel at the age of thirty. But Penkovsky had become disillusioned with the Soviet system, particularly with Khrushchev's leadership, and feared that the Soviet premier might trigger a nuclear war. Beginning in 1960, he desperately tried to arouse the interest of Western intelligence services. He even went so far as to approach tourists on the streets of Moscow and ask them to relay messages to the Western embassies, but these approaches only aroused suspicion that he was a Soviet plant.

*Bill Harvey was made the goat for the failure of Mongoose. At the height of the missile crisis he had ordered ten commando teams dispatched to Cuba, not to conduct sabotage but to be ready with beacons and flares should the president order an invasion of the island. Upon learning of the mission, Bobby Kennedy ordered it scrubbed, fearing that the slightest provocation might trigger a nuclear holocaust. Kennedy was furious when he was told that three of the teams were beyond recall and stormed out of the meeting while Harvey was still trying to explain. Not long after, McCone told the hapless Harvey he was through as chief of Task Force W. He was replaced by Desmond FitzGerald, the head of DDP's Far East Division, and sidetracked to Rome as station chief. William Colby, then station chief in Saigon, took over FitzGerald's previous position.

Penkovsky finally made contact through Greville Wynne, a businessman linked to British intelligence, who was in Moscow to arrange for a Soviet trade delegation to visit London. The Russian, who was to head the mission, convinced Wynne of his sincerity. Early in 1961, British and American intelligence officers began "running" him as a joint operation, even though there were those—James Angleton was one—who remained convinced that Penkovsky was spreading disinformation. Over the next eighteen months, while ostensibly a faithful officer of the GRU, Penkovsky supplied the West with thousands of copies of top secret documents, including personal data on Soviet generals as well as information on military plans, espionage activities, armaments, rockets, and space satellites.

Penkovsky had a fatal flaw for a spy—a craving for recognition. At one point he insisted upon a personal meeting with Queen Elizabeth II. He was informed that the queen did not become involved in intelligence operations and had to be content with a close-up view of her at Windsor Castle and a day with Earl Mountbatten, a royal cousin. The CIA made up for it by arranging a secret meeting with President Kennedy in the Oval Office, according to Wynn. Taking the Russian by the arm and walking with him over to a window, the president said, "Oleg Penkovsky, I want to assure you, from what I know about the situation with the Soviet Union, that I am very aware of all that you've done to help the cause of peace in the world, not only for the West, but for the sake of your own people as well."

But the KGB was on Penkovsky's trail, and he and Wynne were arrested at the moment of their greatest triumph. Taken into custody just as the missile crisis was unfolding, they were tried in May 1963 and found guilty of espionage. Penkovsky is said by the Russians to have been immediately shot. Wynne was imprisoned and eventually exchanged for Gordon Lonsdale, a Soviet sypmaster who had been caught by the British.*

■ ■ ■

Emboldened by his success in the missile crisis, President Kennedy embarked on a vigorous campaign to blunt probes by the Soviet Union and China wherever they might be met, particularly in Indochina. The two Vietnams had coexisted uneasily since 1955, when the United

---

*Lonsdale, whose real name was Konon Molody, was born in Russia but as a youth lived for nine years with relatives in California before returning to the Soviet Union. In 1954, Soviet intelligence sent him to Canada with a forged passport in the name of Lonsdale. Pretending to be a Canadian businessman, he moved to Britain and established contact with employees of the Admiralty Underwater Weapons Establishment at Portland, who provided him with information on underwater detection devices in exchange for substantial sums of money. A defecting Polish intelligence officer provided the tip that led to the roundup of the Portland spy ring in 1961. Among those arrested were Peter and Helen Kroger, later identified as Morris and Leona Cohen of New York City, suspected accomplices of the Rosenbergs.

States, in contravention of the Geneva accords, supported the establishment of the Ngo Dinh Diem regime in the South. This stand-off had continued until Diem, with American backing, tried to suppress the remnants of the Vietminh. The Vietminh, now calling itself the National Liberation Front but known as the Vietcong, struck back with a reign of terror that became a full-scale revolt in March 1960.

Unplanned, unwanted, and undeclared, the war in Southeast Asia was the logical culmination of the policy of containment. President Kennedy and his team of "can do" liberal technocrats viewed this new conflict through the Cold War prism of the great-power confrontation between the United States and Russia and China rather than as an indigenous Vietnamese struggle. South Vietnam was transformed into the "cornerstone of the Free World in Southeast Asia, the keystone to the arch, the finger in the dike," in Kennedy's mixed metaphor. Vice-president Lyndon B. Johnson anointed Diem the "Winston Churchill of Asia" adding, less elegantly, "shit, man, he's the only boy we got out there."

Although intelligence reports indicated that 80 to 90 percent of the Vietcong were recruited in South Vietnam and that most of their supplies were also obtained there rather than from the North, hawks such as Defense Secretary Robert McNamara and presidential advisers McGeorge Bundy and Walt W. Rostow insisted that the crisis was the result of Hanoi's aggression. The Americans saw themselves as defending the noncommunist half of a divided country from an attack by the other, as in Korea. By defending the Saigon regime, they would prove to the Communists that wars of national liberation did not work. In actuality, they were protecting a discredited elite composed almost entirely of the heirs of colonial rule who had squandered what little legitimacy they had possessed through corruption and incompetence. In stark contrast to the Vietcong, the Saigon regime had no background of common effort, sacrifice, or doctrine to lend cohesion to its rule and no political leaders that could capture the public imagination.

American policy in Vietnam was a fatal blend of ignorance and arrogance. Oblivious to alien patterns of thought as well as Vietnam's political and cultural complexities, the Kennedy, Johnson, and Nixon administrations successively tried to apply the traditional maxims of American military strategy and academic precepts of policy analysis to a situation where they were completely irrelevant. Although Vietnam began as the testing ground for widely heralded counterinsurgency-warfare theories, the United States injected ever larger amounts of men, money, and weaponry into the struggle, certain that superior firepower and technology would prevail. When Kennedy was inaugurated in 1961, there were about eight hundred Americans in South Vietnam. Following a mission by General Maxwell D. Taylor and Walt Rostow to Saigon late that year, the Military Assistance Command, Vietnam [MACV] was established, and the United States began stepping up its commitment. By the time of Kennedy's death, the American presence had grown to twenty-three thousand men, but the Vietcong's guerrilla campaign was unchecked and its clandestine apparatus still firmly in place.

For the American intelligence community, Vietnam was a frustrating experience. The efficiency of Vietcong counterintelligence made it impossible to penetrate the enemy's operations, leaving the Americans dependent upon South Vietnamese intelligence and police sources for information—a significant handicap. These units had been infiltrated by the Vietcong and were an unreliable—sometimes, positively dangerous—source. Only a handful of CIA case officers had more than a smattering of Vietnamese, and the one-year tour of duty they usually served there was too brief to gain knowledge of the Vietnamese mentality or an intuitive grasp of the situation.

Since 1953 Vietnam had been one of the countries included in the CIA's National Intelligence Estimates, but the policymakers reached their most important decisions without adequate study of the information available or full consultation with intelligence officials. Unlike World War II, in which strategic intelligence was a decisive factor in the making of military and political strategy, it had little impact on Vietnam policy unless it supported the version of reality preferred by the civilian and military decision makers. The skeptical assessments of the CIA's Office of Current Intelligence and Board of National Estimates about the long-range prospects for the survival of a noncommunist South Vietnam were disregarded in favor of the optimistic forecasts of the Defense Intelligence Agency, which was enthusiastically serving its constituency in the Pentagon. Moreover, the CIA doubted the validity of the "domino theory" on the grounds that national antagonisms in Southeast Asia would be a stumbling block to the expansion of communism even if South Vietnam fell.

Questioning the wisdom of escalating the American intervention, CIA analysts maintained that the North Vietnamese would increase their own infiltration of men and supplies to the South, because these troop movements could not be blocked by U. S. air power. Both the war in Korea and Ho's revolutionary struggle against the French had shown that aerial interdiction was of only limited use in underdeveloped areas. This prophetic estimate was brushed aside, however, and the buildup went ahead at a rapid pace. Increasingly regarded as the bearer of bad tidings, the CIA found itself frozen out of the decision-making process.

As the United States took over control of the war, the Americans were exposed to the hazards of "nation building." South Vietnam was a Buddhist country governed by Catholics, and Buddhist dissatisfaction exploded in mid-1963 with demonstrations against the Diem regime. Although the protests were a vehicle for nationalist sentiments, Diem ordered South Vietnamese troops to attack unarmed Buddhists and equated them with communists. In reality, the Vietcong were as surprised as Diem by the Buddhist uprising. Already having second thoughts about Diem, Washington had been trying to pressure him into broadening the base of his government, but he resisted change. The bloody attack on the Buddhists was the last straw. Several ranking South Vietnamese generals, aware that Diem was no longer in favor with Washington, asked American officials how they would respond to a coup. The new ambassador, Henry Cabot Lodge, the unsuccessful Republican vice-presidential candidate in 1960, concluded that Diem and his family were obstacles to winning the war and flashed what was, in effect, a green light for his ouster.

The CIA had a ringside seat for the plotting through Lucien Conein, who was the liaison with the Vietnamese generals.* Opinion in Washington about the advisability of a coup was divided, however, especially after the generals indicated an intention to assassinate Diem and several of his relatives. Johnson, McNamara, and McCone, among others, were opposed to overthrowing Diem. "We cannot be in a position of stimulating, approving, or supporting assassination," the CIA chief declared with unconscious irony. Echoing the basic thrust of the agency's analysis that there was no qualified replacement for Diem in sight, he told Kennedy: "Mr. President, if I was manager of a baseball team [and] I had one pitcher, I'd keep him in the box whether he was a good pitcher or not." McCone's objections went unheeded. On November 1, 1963, troops surrounded Diem's palace and, after issuing a promise of safe conduct, murdered him.

President Kennedy was conferring with aides when the report of Diem's death reached Washington. Kennedy leaped to his feet and, as General Taylor later recalled, "rushed from the room with a look of shock and dismay on his face." In Saigon, an elated Lodge invited the rebel generals to his office to congratulate them on their victory. "The prospects now are for a shorter war," he declared.

But murder was in the air. Three weeks later, on November 22, 1963, John Fitzgerald Kennedy was gunned down in Dallas.

---

*Conein, a native of France, had been an OSS Jedburgh. At the time of the French withdrawal from Indochina in 1954, he was in charge of CIA sabotage and paramilitary operations in North Vietnam.

18

All Honorable Men

Unlike John Kennedy, Lyndon Johnson was uninterested in the details of intelligence. Kennedy would often pick up the telephone and chat with CIA officials about some item on the President's Intelligence Checklist that had caught his eye, but John McCone was not certain his successor even read it. William Colby recalls that the CIA chief once pushed him forward at a White House meeting to show Johnson a photograph of a newly discovered Vietnamese installation. "But it was clear that he did not want to examine it the way Kennedy would have done, and his only reaction was to caution me sharply to be careful not to spill his coffee in his lap."

In the tumultuous period immediately following Kennedy's murder, McCone was an almost daily visitor to the Oval Office. The new president was convinced that Fidel Castro, angered by the various plots against his own life, had retaliated in kind and was behind the Kennedy assassination.* McCone assured Johnson that despite the suspicious links of the assassin, Lee Harvey Oswald, to Cuba—and to the Soviet Union, where he had lived for two and a half years—there was no sign of a conspiracy. The honeymoon between Johnson and his CIA chief was brief, however, for the president and McCone were on different wavelengths. Rather than patiently absorb briefings and staff recommendations, recalls Ray Cline, Johnson preferred to talk over issues with a few close advisers as

*Even though anti-Castro efforts were reduced in the wake of the missile crisis, the CIA had continued to plot the assassination of the Cuban leader. Desmond FitzGerald discussed the possibility of eliminating Castro with Major Rolando Cubela, a Castro confidant who was known to the agency by the code name Amlash, as late as October 29, 1963. At almost the very moment Kennedy was shot, a CIA case officer was meeting with Cubela to give him a ballpoint pen fitted with a hypodermic needle. The CIA man suggested that it be used in conjunction with Blackleaf 40, a deadly poison that was commercially available. Cubela was also promised a rifle with a telescopic sight. (Allen Dulles was a member of the Warren Commission that investigated the president's murder, but the inquiry was never informed of the CIA plots to kill Castro.)

he sought "consensus." And while Kennedy would accept unwelcome information, Johnson did not like to hear bad news.

A political wheeler-dealer from the hardscrabble Texas hill country, Johnson was uneasy with the subtleties of foreign affairs and retained Kennedy appointees Dean Rusk, Robert McNamara, and McGeorge Bundy to maintain continuity in international policy. The president shared the Cold War assumptions of most Americans, repeatedly citing the "lessons" of Munich, Greece, China, and Korea as he vowed that Communist aggression would not be permitted to win in Southeast Asia. Johnson was haunted by the fear that if South Vietnam fell to the Communists, the right wing would saddle him with the blame, just as they had done to President Truman after the Communist victory in China.

But the Johnson presidency coincided with a slippage of America's international authority. The Western allies were demanding greater independence from the United States, and the Third World was seeking increasing autonomy. Uncertain of how to respond to this era of limits, Johnson clung to the past, still believing Uncle Sam could direct events through the use of arms and aid. Urged on by the Kennedy holdovers, who had little sense of the complexities of Vietnamese politics or the limits of American power, he gradually deepened the commitment to Saigon. Despite his genuine commitment to building a prosperous and just Great Society, Vietnam came to consume his energies, his ambitions and, eventually, his reputation.

Once in, Johnson repeatedly raised the stakes in Southeast Asia with the hope of scoring a victory. The Tonkin Gulf incident in August 1964, in which a U.S. Navy destroyer reported that it was attacked by North Vietnamese torpedo boats under questionable circumstances, was followed by intensive bombing of the North, a widening American combat role, and the spread of the war to Laos and Cambodia. American forces in Vietnam rose from eighty thousand in 1965 to well over a half-million in 1968. As the CIA had forecast, the North Vietnamese matched the American escalation. Responding with a "people's war," the Communists linked their cause to deep-seated, village-based patriotism, the fruit of two thousand years of resistance to foreign domination.

Twenty years before, Ho Chi Minh had told the French: "You can kill ten of my men for every one I kill of yours, but even at those odds, you will lose and I will win." The deeper truth of Ho's calculation never changed, only his enemy. Worried that the United States was becoming mired in a ground war in Asia, McCone warned the president that in the Vietcong and North Vietnamese the United States faced implacable enemies "in a military effort that we cannot win." McCone's forecast of even greater political instability in the South following Diem's ouster also proved correct, as a succession of generals tried and failed to take control of the volatile country.

From its inception, the CIA had been intended as a central clearinghouse for intelligence and as a resource for the president to use in making policy. As the Bay of Pigs made clear, however, presidents and their intelligence agency—which had, like all governmental bodies, a life of its own—would sometimes part ways. The bureaucratization of intelligence meant that this function, however dependent it might be on elected officials for its influence, was itself a player in the game of policy and power. And at times—especially under presidents Johnson and Nixon—it would be treated as an unruly servant, if not an outright adversary.

Thus, in the case of Vietnam, the policymakers who supposedly relied on the CIA chose to ignore its views on the outlook for the war. The agency faced a formidable array of challengers, ranging from the Joint Chiefs of Staff to the State Department, each touting its own view. In the end, the president opted for those that supported his own position. Faced with another pessimistic CIA review, Johnson wearily told an aide, "Same old shit." McCone's invitations to the "Tuesday lunches" at which Vietnam policy was hammered out grew fewer and soon ceased altogether. Isolated from the center of power, McCone resigned early in 1965 and urged the appointment of Richard Helms, Ray Cline, or Lyman Kirkpatrick—all old intelligence hands—in his place. But the president, who delighted in pulling rabbits out of hats, chose a fellow Texan, Vice-admiral William Raborn, as his intelligence chief.

"Red" Raborn was a bluff old salt who had gained renown as manager of the Polaris missile program—which he brought in on time and under budget—but he had no experience in intelligence or international policy. The appointment was a sign of both the president's wish to put his own brand on the agency and his lack of interest in the analytic side of intelligence. "Johnson's only interested in dossiers on who's doing what to whom," observed an embittered CIA man. In keeping with the unwritten rule that the CIA's two top jobs were be divided between the military and civilian side of government, Helms was named Raborn's deputy, with the expectation of succeeding him.*

The admiral's tenure at Langley began on an unhappy note from which it never recovered. The same afternoon that Raborn was sworn in at a White House ceremony, the president ordered American troops into

---

*FitzGerald was appointed DDP and Cline remained on as DDI, but Kirkpatrick quickly resigned. Soon dissatisfied with Raborn's management of the agency, Cline asked Helms for a transfer and was named station chief in Frankfurt, West Germany. FitzGerald suffered a heart attack and died two years later and was replaced as DDP by Thomas Karamessines, who had once been a racket-buster on New York District Attorney Thomas E. Dewey's staff.

the Dominican Republic. Johnson first justified the intervention by the need to protect the lives of Americans trapped in a revolt against a Dominican government that had Washington's backing; later he claimed the uprising was Communist-inspired. CIA documentation was contradictory, and the new DCI was saddled with the blame for the confusion.

The professionals were unhappy with Raborn as well, because his loyalty was to the president who had appointed him rather than to the agency. The new DCI saw his task as transforming the CIA into a smooth-working instrument of the president's will. Manpower and resources were concentrated on Vietnam, and operations were increasingly militarized. The so-called secret army in Laos was a case in point. Early on, the CIA recruited small teams of Meo tribesmen to harass Vietnamese infiltrators and gather intelligence. But the military took over this hand-tooled force, expanded it to upward of forty thousand men, and used it to carry out combat operations. "This was the operational story of the mid-60s," observed Ray Cline. "Much useful work was done, but the covert action pressures upon the CIA distorted its overall effort, even as Vietnam was distorting the political life of the nation."

Insiders also protested against Raborn's brusque manner and his ignorance of world affairs. "How would the navy like it if one of us was designated Chief of Naval Operations?" CIA officials asked. Vicious little jokes about the admiral's blunders surfaced on the Georgetown party circuit and made their way into print. "Which tribe in Liberia are the oligarchs?" Raborn was said to have inquired plaintively at one staff meeting. Pointedly, he was told to bring his deputy to White House briefings and let him do the talking. Even President Johnson finally recognized that Raborn was an embarrassment. In June 1966 the admiral was replaced by Richard Helms, the first DCI to have risen through the ranks of the CIA.

■ ■ ■

Not long before his appointment, Helms was invited by the president for an overnight stay at the LBJ Ranch in Texas. At dinner, Senator Eugene McCarthy, a Minnesota Democrat with a mordant sense of humor, asked Helms if he could identify some yellow flowers on the table. Helms was unable to do so. The Senator then asked Helms if he knew the vintages of the various wines being served. Once again, Helms flunked the test.

"James Bond would have known the answers," McCarthy commented dryly.

Helms was not amused. Like most intelligence professionals, he was contemptuous of the swashbuckling spies of popular fiction. Tall, ruggedly handsome, and with the cool, appraising eye of a riverboat gambler,

Helms commanded the personal respect of the CIA establishment and was the model of the prudent professional manager of agent networks and case officers. "There will be no Bay of Pigs under Dick Helms," observed a colleague, "but there'll be no U-2 either."

As Johnson's intelligence chief, Helms faced a formidable task. On one hand, frustration was boiling over within the CIA because its advice and warnings about Vietnam were consistently ignored. On the other, the president was uninterested in dispassionate analysis, believing that the agency's function should be to help him win the war. Inasmuch as the war was unwinnable, Helms could not provide Johnson with a magic key to victory, but he managed to maintain his access to the president while keeping the agency's analysis straight and well focused.

To show that it was on the team, the CIA established or participated in numerous counterinsurgency efforts. The Phoenix program was the most notorious. Originated by a hard-driving ex-CIA analyst named Robert W. Komer, who now headed the Civilian Operations Revolutionary Development Staff (CORDS), Phoenix was designed to root out the secret Vietcong infrastructure in South Vietnam. The rationale was to beat the Vietcong guerrillas at their own game, and some impressive statistics were piled up. In 1969 alone, Phoenix claimed to have "neutralized" 19,534 suspected Vietcong, of whom 6,187 were killed. But the operation quickly soured as indiscriminate raids were launched on hamlets suspected of being sympathetic to the Vietcong. Villagers were rounded up and tortured at random to gain information, and those thought to be Communist cadres were swiftly executed. "They assassinated a lot of the wrong damn people," observed one CIA man. Phoenix gained a sinister reputation, and antiwar zealots contended that its operations confirmed their creeping paranoia about a pervasive "invisible government."*

William Colby, who had technically left the CIA to become Komer's deputy and director of Phoenix, later tried to distance the agency from these charges. Vietnamese actually carried out the operations, he explained, and the relative handful of Americans involved were primarily concerned with training and advisory missions. Nevertheless, the CIA bore the ultimate responsibility for the program. The agency, which had a lengthy history of involvement in antiterrorist activities in Vietnam, provided weapons and served as paymaster for Phoenix. Colby must have realized something was amiss, for he issued a directive that recognized

---

*The CIA's image problems were heightened by disclosures in *Ramparts* magazine and other publications early in 1967 that revealed the agency's use of foundations and corporations as conduits for subsidies to labor and student groups. Portraying these activities, which dated back to the days of Frank Wisner and his "mighty Wurlitzer," as vaguely sinister, the agency's critics charged the CIA with violating its charter, which forbade it from engaging in domestic operations.

the possibility of excesses. "If U.S. personnel come in contact with activities conducted by Vietnamese which do not meet the standards of land warfare, they are certainly not to participate futher in the activity," he declared. "If an individual finds the police-type activities of the Phoenix program repugnant . . . he can be reassigned from the program without prejudice." When Colby returned home from Vietnam, he was greeted with posters displaying his picture and the caption: "Colby— Wanted for Murder."

The agency fared better in its intelligence gathering and analysis. According to General Bruce Palmer, Jr., the deputy U.S. commander in Vietnam, the CIA's overall intelligence judgments "were generally sound and its estimates were mostly on the mark." In evaluating the effectiveness of U.S. air attacks, the agency concluded correctly that they would not shake Hanoi's will or reduce its ability to sustain the war. And it consistently reported that North Vietnam would continue the war indefinitely in the belief that it possessed greater staying power than the Americans and their South Vietnamese allies.

But accurate intelligence was not always popular intelligence, and the CIA found itself embroiled in a paper war with the military concerning the real size of the Communist forces in South Vietnam. There is no more difficult military intelligence judgment than determining enemy troop strength and the composition of the major units, or the order of battle. The task is even more difficult in a guerrilla war in which regular troops are assisted by irregulars who fade in and out of the fighting.

A bitter controversy over the order of battle erupted when a rumpled young CIA analyst named Samuel Adams examined the Army's statistics and "began to have this feeling that something funny was going on. . . . The statistics didn't make any sense." Adams was convinced that the Communist forces totaled 600,000 men, double the 300,000 claimed by the Military Assistance Command, Vietnam (MACV). The Army arrived at its estimate by refusing to categorize guerrilla and auxiliary units active in South Vietnam as part of the enemy's available fighting force. Adams charged, in effect, that General William C. Westmoreland, the American commander in Vietnam, had imposed the 300,000-man ceiling in order to convince President Johnson that the war of attrition against the enemy was being won.

Adams's analysis had a dramatic impact. If he was correct, the rosy reports of progress fed to the president by Westmoreland's command were patently false. By 1967, public support for the war was sagging. If there was no breakthrough before the presidential election the following year, Johnson's chances for reelection would be endangered. When this hot potato was dropped in Helms's lap, he ordered Adams's findings subjected to rigorous in-house scrutiny. If the CIA was going to tell the president that victory did not lie just around the corner, he wanted the agency to be able to rely on more than the report of an obscure junior analyst.

The resulting examination was inconclusive, for the Communists were not about to come through turnstiles to be counted. But the experts agreed that Adams had produced an authoritative study of the strength of the guerrillas and their auxiliaries. MACV resisted the CIA projection, and a meeting was held in Saigon in September 1967 to weigh the evidence. For three days, the participants hurled numbers and insults at each other. "Adams, you're full of shit!" shouted one Army officer. Finally, a compromise estimate lower than that of the CIA but higher than MACV's was hammered out—a compromise Helms accepted, much to the chagrin of Adams.*

When the Tet offensive exploded across South Vietnam at the end of January 1968, it essentially confirmed the validity of the CIA's estimate of Communist strength. The Americans and their South Vietnamese allies found themselves up against an enemy that was far stronger and better organized than had been officially conceded. General Palmer has observed that the compromise estimate "probably helped reinforce the feeling . . . that the enemy was not capable of conducting major, near-simultaneous, country-wide attacks." Apart from this miscalculation, Tet recalled the intelligence failure at Pearl Harbor. Like the Japanese surprise attack, the offensive was heralded by captured documents, communications intercepts, and photographic analysis that indicated an attack was being prepared. As early as December 20, 1967, Westmoreland warned Washington to expect a "maximum effort" by the enemy. But, as in 1941, no one knew precisely where or when the enemy would strike.

Most observers expected the offensive to begin before Tet, the sacred lunar new year celebrations, for it was thought the Communists would be unlikely to attack during the holiday and alienate public support by violating a truce they had proclaimed. So, when Tet approached without an enemy offensive, security was relaxed. Unfamiliar with Vietnam's

*The order of battle controversy had a curious resonance fifteen years later, when General Westmoreland sued CBS for $120 million in libel damages in the wake of a television documentary in which the network, using Sam Adams as its basic source, linked Westmoreland to a "conspiracy at the highest levels" to understate enemy troop strength prior to the Tet offensive. This deception was supposed to have not only deceived President Johnson but led to a defeat at Tet.
Like the Vietnam war itself, the trial ended inconclusively after eighteen weeks when a settlement was reached just as the case was to go to the jury. CBS issued a statement recognizing Westmoreland's "patriotism and loyalty"—which had never been at issue—and he withdrew his suit. Independent observers believe it was hardly likely that Lyndon Johnson would have been fooled for long by any subterfuge on Westmoreland's part, for the president had alternative sources of information. If he chose to share the general's optimism, it was not because he was being duped but because he needed every shred of evidence to convince critics that the war was being won.

history, most Americans did not know that the Vietnamese had launched a surprise attack during Tet in 1789 that had routed an occupying Chinese army.

Although the Communists scored some spectacular temporary successes against the totally surprised Americans—fighting their way into the U.S. embassy compound in Saigon and capturing the old imperial capital of Hue—the offensive was a costly military failure. Some forty thousand Vietcong were killed, and the guerrillas' tactical leadership was nearly wiped out. The Vietcong were never again able to launch a large operation against the Americans. Almost before the echo of the guns had died, President Johnson and General Westmoreland launched a public relations campaign that portrayed Tet as a last-gasp effort by the enemy and a smashing victory for the American forces.

But the battle appeared different on the color television screens in American living rooms. The chaotic images—Vietcong swarming into the embassy grounds, wounded and dead strewn about the streets, buildings shelled, huts in flames, refugees fleeing, women wailing in anguish—did not convey a sense of triumph. The brief penetration of the embassy compound had no military significance, but it was a dramatic event with damaging psychological fallout in the United States. Having been repeatedly assured by the president that "there was light at the end of the tunnel" in Vietnam, most Americans were shocked by the bloody spectacle. The major casualty of Tet proved to be public faith in Johnson's credibility. Antiwar fervor grew as mass demonstrations demanding a bombing halt, negotiations, and even withdrawal increased in intensity. Ironically, the North Vietnamese were taken aback by the American reaction to Tet. "In all honesty, we didn't achieve our main objective, which was to spur uprisings throughout the south," General Tran Do later conceded. "As for making an impact in the United States, it had not been our intention—but it turned out to be a fortunate result."

With Westmoreland relentlessly pressing for an additional two hundred thousand troops—which would mean calling up the reserves and extending the draft—and with the pacification program in South Vietnam in shambles, Johnson wearily asked Clark Clifford, the new secretary of defense, to convene a special study group to examine the situation in Vietnam. This was the opportunity Helms had been waiting for. Over the next three days, he supplied the group with CIA studies concluding that, even if the additional troops were dispatched to Vietnam, "our best estimate is that . . . the overall situation ten months hence will be no better than a standoff." Clifford and his study group reached similar conclusions. And the president's Senior Informal Advisory Group on Vietnam, the so-called Wise Men, recommended disengagement and withdrawal.

A key factor in the formerly hawkish Wise Men's decision was a Joint

Chiefs of Staff assessment of enemy strength that, when analyzed, showed that the number of Communists killed and wounded was larger than the total number of men the Pentagon claimed were in the enemy's order of battle. "If you have 240,000 seriously wounded plus 80,000 killed, for a total of 320,000 out of an order of battle of 230,000, General, who in the hell are we fighting out there?" asked Arthur Goldberg, the UN ambassador and one-time OSS officer. Meanwhile, Johnson also faced a political firestorm. Senator McCarthy, who had challenged the president for the Democratic presidential nomination, nearly scored a dramatic upset in the New Hampshire primary, and the polls indicated almost certain defeat for Johnson in Wisconsin.

On March 31, President Johnson went on television to announce that he was ordering an end to the bombing of North Vietnam with the hope of bringing Hanoi to the peace table. Then to the amazement of viewers and even some of his advisers, the president said he would not seek reelection. The latest casualty of the war was Johnson's own presidency.

The policy of global containment of communism, announced so forcefully twenty years before, had reached a dead end. The North Vietnamese took up Johnson's offer of negotiation, but they merely switched the zone of combat from the battlefield to the peace talks in Paris. The talking—and dying—went on long after Lyndon Johnson had been replaced in the White House by Richard M. Nixon.

■ ■ ■

Few men have come to the presidency better prepared than Richard Nixon. He had served as Eisenhower's vice-president for eight years and had a ready grasp of the complexities of world affairs. Moreover, he had demonstrated an adroitness that earned the grudging respect of even his most unrelenting enemies. Yet Nixon regarded himself as an outsider and harbored a visceral resentment toward those he felt had slighted him. He saw plots and conspiracies everywhere: in the press, in the wealthy Eastern establishment that dominated the Republican party, and in the top levels of the Washington bureaucracy, especially the CIA.

Although the new president, in a show of bipartisanship, reappointed Richard Helms as DCI—he kept J. Edgar Hoover on as well—he was suspicious of Helms as an Ivy League liberal. Indeed, Nixon distrusted not only Helms but the CIA itself, which he blamed for his defeat by John Kennedy in 1960. Many senior CIA officials were members of the Georgetown set and close to the Kennedys. In order to ensure Kennedy's victory, Nixon was convinced, they had leaked reports of a "missile gap" that had been used against him by the Democratic candidate.

Nixon arrived at the White House at a critical moment in American history. He had inherited a war not of his own making, a deteriorating international situation, a rising tide of domestic dissent, and a demoralized national security apparatus. Like Kennedy, the new president moved to concentrate power in the White House, particularly in the hands of Dr. Henry A. Kissinger, the former Harvard professor who served him first as national security adviser and later as secretary of state. In their efforts to extract the United States from the Vietnam quagmire before the 1972 elections, Nixon and Kissinger resorted to a deviousness remarkable even for Washington. They expanded the war into Laos and Cambodia and sold the escalation to the American public as a peace crusade. And they claimed that a massive bombing campaign against Hanoi was designed to force the North Vietnamese to end the fighting, when the real obstruction to peace was the Saigon regime and its insistence that the United States guarantee its survival after American withdrawal from the war.

To add to his personal antipathy toward the CIA, Nixon was dissatisfied with the quality of the intelligence supplied him. He saw the analysts as reflecting the liberal bias of the academic community and found their reports bland and overly hedged with qualifications. The agency, he charged, was incapable of providing straight answers to direct questions. "What the hell do those clowns do out there in Langley?" he complained bitterly. "They've got forty thousand people out there reading newspapers!"

Even worse, from Nixon's point of view, were repeated intelligence failures. Lacking assets in Eastern Europe, the agency had given off confusing signals prior to the Russian invasion of Czechoslovakia in the summer of 1968. The CIA also underestimated the volume of supplies being unloaded at Sihanoukville in Cambodia and transported overland to North Vietnamese forces. And, as it turned out, the military's more alarmist assessment of Soviet strength proved closer to the truth than the CIA's estimate.

The real power over the intelligence community quickly shifted to Kissinger. Ruthless, charming, cleverer than many of those he dealt with—and not averse to letting them know it—Kissinger looked like a Bronx butcher and operated with the cynicism of a Renaissance cardinal. He transformed the National Security Council from an advisory committee into a foreign operations directorate and launched a bureaucratic coup d'etat against the State Department and the intelligence community.* Asked a series of searching questions about American foreign policy, the intelligence agencies all received failing grades from Professor Kissinger. Some intelligence reports, it was claimed, were little more than rewrites of dispatches filed by newspaper correspondents. One aide re-

*As originally conceived, the National Security Council was to assist the president in determining policy and objectives. It was not intended to be another State Department or intelligence agency or to conduct operations of any kind.

members Kissinger angrily waving a National Intelligence Estimate in the air and all but screaming: "This isn't what I want!" Simultaneously, James Schlesinger, the assistant director of the Office of Management and Budget, carried out an analysis of the administrative side of the intelligence community and found duplication and disorganization.

Kissinger's power came at the expense of the formally constituted agencies and departments. To keep the CIA off balance, Helms was badgered for the files on the Bay of Pigs and the Diem slaying with the veiled threat that they would be leaked to the press to embarrass the agency if needed. Helms had difficulty in even seeing Nixon and was forced to leave notes for him at National Security Council meetings. Although Helms tried to accommodate the agency to this increasingly difficult situation, without access to the president and his thinking, the CIA was handicapped in its search for relevant information—completing a vicious circle. "There's something I've had to learn to understand," Helms once confided to an associate. "I've had to learn to understand Presidents."*

The CIA had little impact on the policymaking process in the Nixon years, especially the president's efforts to restore relations with Communist China. Kissinger made a sweeping end run around the State Department and the intelligence community in conducting the negotiations that preceded Nixon's visit to Peking in February 1972.

Both Nixon and Kissinger viewed the CIA as being primarily an instrument for the execution of secret White House initiatives, rather than a source of intelligence analysis. Thus, when it appeared that an avowed Marxist, Dr. Salvador Allende, would be elected president of Chile in 1970, the CIA was called in. Allende had won a plurality but not a majority over two other candidates in the election that September, and under the Chilean constitution the Congress was to choose the new president from between the first and second-place winners. Tradition decreed that the candidate with the greatest number of votes in the general election—Allende—be chosen in the balloting, which was scheduled for October 24. Although Allende promised to shape Chile into a Marxist state only within the framework of the nation's constitution, American multinational corporations, especially Anaconda Copper and International Telephone and Telegraph, feared nationalization. "I don't see why we need to stand by and watch a country go Communist due to the irresponsibility of its own people," rumbled Kissinger.

On September 15 Nixon summoned Helms to the White House and ordered the CIA to prevent another Fidel Castro from taking power at the

---

*In 1972, the CIA alerted Washington to the fact that President Ferdinand E. Marcos would soon declare martial law in the Philippines, but Nixon and Kissinger ignored the warning. Marcos and his wife, Imelda, contributed $250,000 to Nixon's campaign for reelection that year.

tip of South America. "One in 10 chance perhaps, but save Chile!" Helms recorded the president as saying in the notes he made of the conversation. The agency could have ten million dollars for the Chilean operation—more if needed—and the best men were to be assigned to it. The U.S. embassy in Santiago was to be bypassed. "Make the economy scream," Nixon ordered.

"The President came down very hard," Helms later told the Church Committee. "If I ever carried a marshal's baton in my knapsack out of the Oval Office, it was that day."

U.S. intervention in Chilean elections was nothing new. Back in 1964, the CIA had persuaded the opposition to Allende to unite behind the Christian Democratic candidate, Eduardo Frei, and pumped some three million dollars into the country to elect him. More money was expended the following year to elect Christian Democratic candidates to Congress. And in June 1970, John McCone, now an ITT director, had approached Helms with a proposal for a joint ITT-CIA effort in which the company would provide at least a million dollars to prevent an Allende victory. ITT had already spent substantial sums in opposing Allende, but this time the opposition refused to unite behind a single candidate. Helms, doubting the agency's ability to influence the election at this late date, refused the offer but assisted ITT in channeling funds to the opposition.

The White House authorized a dual-tracked effort to thwart Allende's election. Track I, which was approved by the 40 Committee, as Kennedy's old Special Group was now called, included bribing Chilean congressmen to vote against Allende. The super-secret Track II, which was approved by the White House without the knowledge of the 40 Committee, authorized the CIA to foment a military coup, if necessary, to block Allende from taking office. Ironically, under Helms's direction, the agency had been shedding the emphasis on covert action and paramilitary operations that had dominated its first quarter-century of existence, and there were widespread misgivings at Langley about the plot against Chilean democracy. Indeed, two years before, a National Intelligence Estimate had concluded that the forces of social change in Latin America were so powerful that they were beyond outside manipulation.*

David Atlee Phillips, a veteran of the Guatemalan and Bay of Pigs operations, was among the reluctant warriors. Placed in charge of the Chile Task Force, which ran Track II, Phillips asked, "Should the CIA, even responding to a President's ukase, encourage a military coup in one of the few contries in Latin America with a solid, functioning democratic tradition?" But Thomas Karamessines, the DDP and the agency's liaison with the White House, was adamant. "Nobody was going to go into the

*See Marchetti and Marks, *The CIA and the Cult of Intelligence*, pp. 14–15.

Oval Office, bang his fist on the table, and say we won't do it," he declared.

To no one's surprise, Track I failed, despite the distribution of at least $250,000 in bribes and warnings that military and economic aid to Chile would be cut off if Allende won. Efforts to promote a military coup through Track II were equally unproductive. Several Chilean officers plotted against Allende, but General Rene Schneider, the army commander in chief, insisted that constitutional process be followed. Unable to have Schneider retired or reassigned, the conspirators decided to get him out of the way by kidnapping him before the congressional vote on October 24.

The CIA furnished the conspirators with submachine guns and ammunition, but a pair of abduction attempts failed. Two days before the balloting, Schneider was fatally wounded as he shot it out with a band of would-be kidnappers. His killers were said to have used pistols rather than submachine guns of the type furnished by the CIA and to have been operating independently of the CIA-supplied group. Be that as it may, rather than inspiring a coup the general's death shocked Chileans into rallying around the flag of constitutionalism, and Allende was chosen president without further incident.

Nixon and Kissinger later claimed that they ordered Track II discontinued after the unsuccessful kidnapping attempts, but agency officials contended that the operation continued unabated with the full knowledge of the White House. "At least as far as I was concerned, Track II was really never ended," Karamessines told the Church Committee. The committee was unable to resolve the conflicting accounts.

After Allende's election, efforts to destabilize Chile intensified, and over the next three years the CIA provided nearly eight million dollars to the Chilean opposition. Economic pressure was also stepped up through an embargo on American aid and the denial of international credits. The Chilean economy, already tottering from governmental mismanagement, went into a tailspin. Unrest reached a fever pitch with a truckers' strike that virtually tied up the nation. There were rumors that the stoppage was financed by the CIA—rumors denied by the agency, although it is unlikely that the union's own funds could have sustained the strike for very long—and the chaotic situation was fertile ground for a coup.

The final blow fell on September 11, 1973. General Augusto Pinochet led a bloody military revolt during which Allende either was murdered or committed suicide in the smoking ruins of the presidential palace in downtown Santiago. Although the CIA denied any direct involvement in the coup, it had kept a watchful eye on the conspiracy and encouraged the plotters. The new regime was quickly recognized by the United States as a bulwark against the spread of communism and soon received the massive doses of assistance denied Allende. Once in power,

Pinochet imposed a state of siege and launched a campaign of brutal repression that was still continuing more than fifteen years later. By the time of Allende's fall, however, Richard Helms had been exiled from Washington, a casualty of the Watergate scandal.

■ ■ ■

Helms's first reaction to the Watergate scandal was to batten down the hatches against the rising storm. In the early morning hours of June 17, 1972, James McCord, a retired CIA security officer, had been arrested along with four Cuban exiles while installing wiretaps in the offices of the Democratic National Committee in the Watergate office complex. By the time Helms convened a meeting of top aides to review the situation, the number of people with CIA links who were known to be involved in the "third-rate burglary," as the White House was to characterize it, had increased to three. Besides McCord, there were E. Howard Hunt, who had retired from the agency two years before, and Eugenio R. Martinez, one of the Cubans, who was still on the payroll. "Stay cool, volunteer nothing, because it will only be used to involve us," Helms told his associates. "Just stay away from the whole damn thing."

The Watergate fiasco was rooted in the obsession of Nixon and Kissinger with the steady leakage of administration policy initiatives to the press. Already they had ordered wiretaps on the telephones of NSC staffers, White House aides, and journalists under the guise of protecting national security. In 1971, following the publication by the New York *Times* of the Pentagon Papers, a highly classified history of American involvement in Vietnam,* presidential assistant John Ehrlichman organized a Special Investigative Unit to plug the leaks. Hunt, who had been working in a routine public relations job since his retirement from the CIA, and G. Gordon Liddy, a one-time FBI agent and Justice Department official, were hired as the chief "plumbers," even though both had reputations for flamboyance—and trouble. Later they were transferred to the staff of Nixon's presidential campaign, the Committee to Re-elect the President (CREEP).

The CIA had good reason to avoid the Watergate spotlight. In the summer of 1971, it had caved in to White House pressure and supplied Hunt with spy paraphernalia, including disguises, cameras, and recording equipment used in the burglary of the offices of the psychiatrist

*The government complained that publication of the Pentagon Papers gave away secret American codes. Some officials contended that by comparing intercepted enciphered messages with the verbatim texts, an enemy could reconstruct American cryptosystems and read current secret messages. But David Kahn, a leading authority on codes and ciphers, argues that publication of the Papers "had absolutely no effect at all upon American cryptography" (*Newsday*, June 25, 1971).

treating Daniel Ellsberg, the former NSC staffer charged with leaking the Pentagon Papers to the press. The agency also prepared a psychiatric profile of Ellsberg at Hunt's request.* Helms, who knew Hunt well and was amused by his swashbuckling, personally approved these requests, probably in an effort to improve relations with the Nixon White House. But when Hunt's repeated demands caused too many questions, he had second thoughts and ordered him cut off.

President Nixon had no intention of allowing the CIA to scuttle away from the scandal. For one thing, he was convinced that the Watergate burglars' bumbling was no accident. He believed the entire escapade had been set up by old enemies within the agency—the same foes who had worked to elect Kennedy in 1960—in order to embarrass him during his reelection campaign. At the same time he saw the CIA as a way to keep FBI investigators from following the trail of secret funds that had been laundered in Mexico and funneled to the plumbers by CREEP.

On June 23, a week after the break-in, Helms was summoned to the White House along with his recently appointed deputy, General Vernon A. Walters. Walters, who built a military career on a facility for languages—he spoke eleven with some degree of fluency, and, it was said, was too loquacious in all of them—had been a Nixon favorite since 1959, when he had braved a stone-throwing anti-Yankee mob in Caracas with the then vice-president. H. R. Haldeman, the president's chief of staff, told the CIA men that the president wanted the agency to instruct the FBI to drop its Mexican inquiry because it would reveal legitimate CIA operations abroad.* Helms replied, in effect, that he knew of no such operations.

Nevertheless, Haldeman insisted that Walters discuss the matter with L. Patrick Gray III, the undistinguished New England lawyer who had unexpectedly been named acting FBI director following the death of J. Edgar Hoover the previous month. Over the next several days, Walters and Gray sparred with each other over the Mexican connection, with the FBI chief all but imploring Walters to ask him to restrict the investigation in the interests of national security. Finally, on July 6, Walters firmly told

*The OSS had begun the business of preparing psychiatric profiles by doing one on Adolf Hitler during World War II. The CIA also maintains a staff of contract psychiatrists to deal with the problems of agency personnel without the danger of confidential information reaching outsiders. Because of the tensions inherent in intelligence work, stress and alcoholism have been described as the occupational hazards of the profession.

*The ensuing conversation with Nixon, recorded by the president's voice-activated taping system, was the "smoking gun" that connected Nixon to the attempt to cover up Watergate and ultimately led to his resignation from the presidency two years later. Nixon was not the first president to record conversations in the Oval Office, however. President Hoover sometimes had a secretary surreptitiously listen in on telephone conversations and transcribe them. And both Franklin Roosevelt and John Kennedy had recording systems that could be activated by the president himself.

Gray that the investigation constituted no threat to ongoing CIA operations in Mexico. And the agency flatly rejected a White House proposal that it put up the bail and pay the salaries and family expenses of the Watergate burglars.

By taking these actions—even though they were belated—the CIA insulated itself from involvement in the cover-up and from being used by Nixon and his aides to avoid punishment for their crimes. But Helms's strategy of distancing the agency from Watergate was, as William Colby observed, a two-edged sword. By refusing to volunteer evidence and by answering questions with precision and without elaboration, the CIA generated distrust and suspicion. Each disclosure wrung or leaked from the agency fed the belief that even more sinister material was still being withheld and that somehow the CIA really was behind Watergate. On the other hand, even such severe critics as the Washington *Post* noted that the CIA "was the only agency in town that said 'No'" to the Nixon White House.

Richard Helms paid dearly for that "No." In December 1972, soon after Nixon had resoundingly won reelection, Helms was fired and packed off to Iran as an ambassador. As he left Langley for the last time, walking past the more than three dozen stars carved into the wall of the marble entrance hall that represented CIA officers who had died in the line of duty, there was a spontaneous outpouring of respect and affection from all ranks. For over six years, Helms had done his best to protect the independence and integrity of his agency.

■ ■ ■

"The nation must to a degree take it on faith that we too are honorable men devoted to her service," Helms had once declared. For a quarter-century, the American people, Congress, and the press had indeed taken it on faith that the nation's intelligence community was led by "honorable men." Senator John Stennis, the Mississippi Democrat who headed the Senate Armed Services Committee, expressed the prevailing view well: "Spying is spying," he said. "You have to make up your mind that you are going to have an intelligence agency and protect it as such, and shut your eyes and take what is coming." But Vietnam and Watergate depleted this fund of trust. Paranoia had been legitimized, and national security and secrecy were now regarded less as tools for the defense of the Republic than as convenient covers used to hide wickedness and bungling from public scrutiny.

Within the CIA itself, this hostility and suspicion were reflected in plummeting morale. It didn't help that the director's office appeared to have been fitted with a revolving door. In the four years following Helms's ouster, the CIA had five chiefs. James Schlesinger, the immediate successor to Helms, served only four months—from February to June 1973—but no one did more to shake up the CIA. Or was so heartily disliked. In fact, some observers joked that the abrasive Schlesinger was President Nixon's revenge on the CIA. Although he had no background in intelligence, Schlesinger was not a neophyte, having previously made a study of the organization and operation of the intelligence community. As DCI, he had his own agenda for reform. He was convinced that the agency had too many people, too much money, and too little real work to do* and that the cloak-and-dagger operator was an anachronism in a world of sophisticated technology.

Schlesinger saw his major task as slashing the intelligence budget, which, according to congressional sources, had increased to $6 billion by 1973, about 80 percent of it controlled by the Pentagon. The CIA received an estimated $750 million, including about $440 million for Clandestine Services, while Science and Technology and the Directorate for Intelligence received about half that amount. Other sources estimated the total budget of the intelligence community to be as much as $11 billion annually. The only certainty was that intelligence cost far more than Congress was told. Whatever the actual figure, it was entirely too much as far as Schlesinger was concerned, and, moreover, the priorities for spending it were all wrong.

Schlesinger planned to put greater reliance on the technological collection of intelligence through computers and satellite "spies in the sky" and to tie data collection more firmly to analysis. Accordingly, he lopped away at the "deadwood" in the Directorate for Plans. Too many of the "cowboys" from the OSS and the early Cold War days were still around, in his view, and he ordered William Colby, the new DDP, to carry out a major purge of the covert operators and paramilitary specialists. In little more than a few weeks, about 7 percent of the CIA's personnel, or some one thousand people, retired, were forced to resign, or simply were fired. Brutally traumatic, this pruning went far beyond the scaling-back of operations due to the winding down of the Vietnam war, but many insiders agreed that it was long overdue. In keeping with the reining-in of covert operations, the agency sold off Air America and Southern Air Transport, two of the proprietaries that had played key roles in Indochina and other areas. To further mark the decline of the clandestine mystique, Colby ordered the euphemistic name of his office changed to the more straightforward Directorate of Operations. In the same spirit, the high-

---

*He was not altogether wrong. CIA officers at the Rio de Janeiro station used safe houses for assignations with their girlfriends. Another DCI, Admiral Stansfield Turner, discovered that some DDP case officers used their expense accounts to live lavishly and maintain mistresses while doing business with arms dealers for their own profits.

way sign marking the way to the agency's headquarters was altered from "Bureau of Public Roads" to "CIA."*

The reaction against Schlesinger's purge was so intense that the DCI's personal bodyguard was augmented to protect him from his own staff. "I can't take you through there," Schlesinger told a visitor who requested a tour of the Technical Services Division, which housed the devil's workshop where hypodermic pens and nitroglycerine-primed cigars were fabricated. "I don't think either one of us would emerge alive." The joke was a pointed one.

To Colby's surprise, James Angleton, the gray eminence of counterintelligence, survived the housecleaning. Colby had strongly urged Schlesinger to fire Angleton, arguing that, despite his acknowledged brilliance, his activities were disrupting the agency and some of his advice was questionable. Angleton had insisted, for example, that the rift between Stalin and Tito was only a sham and the Sino-Soviet split a mere ruse to lull the West into reducing its defenses. The two men had long been at odds. In the late 1950s, Colby, then serving in Rome, had supported an "opening to the left" in which the ruling Christian Democrats entered a coalition with the Socialists, who had foresaken their historic ties with the Communists. Angleton, who had lived in Italy and saw Communist influence everywhere, suspected the Socialists were still secretly aligned with the Communists and derided Colby's idea as naive. Colby won that battle, but Angleton never forgot the rebuff.

A legendary figure within the CIA, Angleton cultivated his reputation as a man of mystery with the same avidity with which he pursued his hobbies of orchid growing and fly fishing. Cadaverously thin, he dressed in funeral black and had the disquieting habit of turning questions back upon an inquisitor. One officer who was summoned into his presence found him "tucked away in an inside office which was completely draped in very heavy black drapes. . . . Angleton himself was peering at some documents under a strong desk light. . . . I felt I had been admitted to an inner sanctum whose existence I must never mention to anyone. . . . It took me a day to get over the experience."

In his three decades in the looking-glass world of counterintelligence, Angleton had become obsessed with the idea that Soviet agents had penetrated the CIA. Kim Philby and Hans Felfe had risen to important posts in British and West German intelligence, and the French SEDECE leaked at every pore. Was it not likely, he reasoned, that Langley also harbored a Soviet mole? As this obsession fed upon itself, Angleton became convinced that the agency's agents and contacts behind the Iron Curtain were controlled by the KGB and that most defectors were dispatched to the West by the Russians to spread disinformation. As

---

*The agency's sometimes comic efforts at secrecy had long been publicly derided.

a result of Angleton's objections, the CIA had rejected Oleg Penkovsky's first overtures and had to be persuaded by the British to accept his information. Moreover, Angleton came to believe that some of the agency's own officers—among others—were suspect.*

Tainted with overtones of paranoia, this fixation upon KGB penetration caused Colby to observe that it "so preoccupied us that we were devoting most of our time to protecting ourselves from the KGB and not enough to developing the new sources and operations that we needed to learn secret information about the Soviets." Yet there was always the possibility that Angleton might be right. Successive CIA chiefs from Dulles to Schlesinger were fascinated by his briefings and accepted the possibility that there might be something to his darkly labyrinthine theories. And so the mole hunt went on, creating turmoil and wrecking careers. The hunt was so disruptive that some officers facetiously suggested that there was indeed a Soviet mole at Langley—and that his name was James Jesus Angleton.

Angleton's worst fears were confirmed by Anatoly Golitsyn, a KGB major who defected in Helsinki in December 1961. Claiming that the Soviets had penetrated all Western intelligence agencies, including the CIA, Golitsyn also told Angleton that the KGB and GRU would soon send false defectors to the West to spread disinformation. Not long afterward, two members of the Soviet UN delegation (codenamed Fedora and Tophat) offered their services to the FBI. Then, in 1964, a KGB officer named Yuri Nosenko defected in Geneva. Nosenko made the startling claim that he had monitored the activities of Lee Harvey Oswald, President Kennedy's assassin, while Oswald had lived in the Soviet Union, and that the KGB had not been involved with him. Part of his story was confirmed by Fedora.*

Nosenko's information pleased the FBI, which had reported that Oswald had acted alone. But three defectors in a relatively brief period of time—four, if Penkovsky is included—was too much of a coincidence for Angleton, especially in light of Golitsyn's warning and the discovery that Nosenko had fabricated his rank and status in the KGB. Other CIA officers, including Richard Helms, also found Nosenko's story that the KGB had expressed no interest in Oswald hard to swallow in view of the fact that

*Angleton once told MI5 that the CIA had evidence that Harold Wilson, the British prime minister and leader of the Labor Party, was "a Soviet agent," according to Peter Wright. But he refused to divulge details unless the British could assure him that this information would not fall into "political hands." (Washington *Post*, May 3, 1987.)

*Fedora has been identified as Aleksei Isidorovich Kulak, a KGB officer at the UN. Top Hat was Dimitri Fedorovich Polyakov, a GRU colonel. Over the years, he provided U.S. intelligence with the names of four American citizens who were spying for the Soviets and the identities of several Soviet "illegals" operating in the United States. Promoted to general in 1974, Polyakov gave the Americans the Soviet "wish list" of foreign military equipment sought by the Russians which showed the gaps in Soviet technology. Both Fedora and Top Hat also reported that the Soviet ICBM program was encountering difficulties and the United States was far ahead. See Wise, *Nightmover,* pp. 55–68.

while in the Marines Oswald had worked on the U-2. Over the next three years, Nosenko was held in solitary confinement, questioned mercilessly, and subjected to assorted physical and mental pressures. Although discrepancies were found, he stuck to the basic line of his original story.

Eventually, a small school of Nosenko believers developed among those who thought the KGB was hardly likely to give away so many secrets as he had. He fingered John Vassall, an assistant to the British naval attaché in Moscow, as a Soviet spy; divulged the bugging of the American Embassy there; and provided leads that put investigators on the trail of Sergeant Robert Lee Johnson, who supplied the Russians with valuable strategic documents while serving at NATO headquarters in Paris. All in all, the value of Nosenko's information at least matched that of Golitsyn's. In the end, he was "rehabilitated," given a new identity, and placed on the CIA payroll to train recruits specializing in Soviet affairs.

■ ■ ■

Still reeling from the Schlesinger purge, the CIA added to its troubles by failing to forecast the outbreak of war between Egypt and Israel in October 1973. The failure reduced respect for the agency's analysis at a time when it needed all the credit it could muster. Until then, it had enjoyed a record of success in the Middle East. In 1968, Helms had won President Johnson's confidence by reporting that Israel would win any war with the Arabs within seven to ten days; in fact, the Israelis surged to victory in only six. When rumblings of an Egyptian surprise attack circulated late in 1973, however, both Israeli and U.S. intelligence discounted the reports in the belief that the Egyptians lacked the capability to launch an offensive. Even if the Egyptian army managed to cross the Suez Canal, the analysts said, it would be unable to hold "even a small amount of territory . . . for as much as one week." This intelligence breakdown was compounded by a failure to foresee the oil embargo imposed by the Organization of Petroleum Exporting Countries (OPEC). And worse challenges were to come.

Upon taking over at Langley, Schlesinger had been given what he assumed was a full briefing on the CIA's involvement in Watergate. He was furious when Daniel Ellsberg's trial for leaking the Pentagon Papers disclosed that Howard Hunt had received logistical support from the agency for the burglary of the offices of Ellsberg's psychiatrist. Angrily, he told Colby that he would "tear the place apart and fire everyone if necessary" to find if there were any other skeletons hidden in the agency's closet. A directive was immediately issued ordering all past and present employees to report to the inspector general any incidents in which they suspected that the CIA had engaged in illegal or questionable activities. But it fell to Colby to deal with the problem. Soon after the directive was issued, Nixon abruptly named Schlesinger to be secretary of defense, and William Colby was chosen as his successor.

19

An Age of Uncertainty

With his bookkeeper's glasses and bland manner, William Colby looked like a colorless bureaucrat, but he was an extremely complex personality. A brave and resourceful OSS Jedburgh, he had parachuted into German-occupied France and Norway and had been decorated several times. Colby was also a devout Catholic convert with such a rigorous sense of moral integrity that some colleagues called him a "soldier-priest." The inspector general's report ordered by Schlesinger, with its 693 closely typewritten pages detailing questionable CIA activities—the report was dubbed the "Family Jewels"—gnawed at his conscience.

Operation Chaos was the most damaging. Jointly mounted by the CIA and FBI at President Johnson's orders, it had been aimed at determining whether or not the Vietnam antiwar movement was being manipulated or financially supported from abroad. Files were opened on thousands of American citizens, in clear violation of the CIA's charter, which barred it from engaging in domestic operations. No foreign links were found, but Chaos lasted well into the Nixon years. The report's other findings were scarcely less disturbing.

Journalists had been placed under surveillance in an effort to track down the sources of leaks, the White House plumbers had been provided with support, Angleton's staff had operated a long-running mail intercept program, and the agency had sanctioned a bizarre experiment called MKULTRA, in which mind-control drugs such as LSD were administered to unsuspecting victims. In the course of the experiment, one CIA officer had committed suicide. And in a separate and even more sensitive report, the inspector general summarized the assassination plots against Castro, Lumumba, and Trujillo.

The Family Jewels violated one of the cardinal rules established by Colby's predecessors: never put anything on paper that might prove embarrassing. In 1972, for example, Helms, sensing the danger inherent in Watergate of a backlash against the CIA, had ordered the original MKULTRA documents destroyed. But Colby reasoned that the best way to protect the agency and ensure its survival was to make a clean breast of past mistakes and move into a brighter future. He informed the chairmen of the Senate and House oversight committees of the details of the inspector general's report and followed up with internal directives establishing guidelines for future behavior. These ranged from flatly stating that the CIA would not engage in assassination to edicts against a repetition of Operation Chaos, mail openings, the testing of drugs on unwitting subjects, and other violations of the CIA charter.

But in the rancid atmosphere that surrounded Nixon's dying presidency—he resigned on August 9, 1974, to be replaced by Vice-president Gerald R. Ford—Colby's effort to distance the agency from its past was doomed. Late that December, Seymour M. Hersh, a Pulitzer Prize-winning reporter for the New York *Times,* informed Colby that he had information that the CIA had carried out illegal intelligence operations against antiwar activists. Rather than denying the charges, Colby tried to explain that these activities were isolated acts and that the story was being blown out of proportion. In any case, he claimed, the operations had ceased and the directives he had promulgated the previous year made it unlikely that they would be repeated.

Hersh did not agree. Three days before Christmas, the *Times* began publishing a series of articles accusing the CIA of "massive" spying and illegal activities that included domestic surveillance, break-ins, mail intercepts, and wiretapping. The obvious source of these disclosures was the Family Jewels information that Colby had furnished the congressional committees, augmented by leaks from factions within the agency eager to blow the whistle on bureaucratic rivals. The CIA was quickly enveloped in a media and political firestorm that was compounded by Colby's ill-timed but coincidental decision to finally fire James Angleton, a move that created the erroneous impression that Angleton bore the responsibility for all the alleged skullduggery.

No one was more surprised by the disclosures of CIA misconduct than President Ford. As a congressman, he had been a member of the House Appropriations Committee, which was supposed to be a CIA watchdog, but he had not known of the assassination plots until Colby gave him a briefing on the Family Jewels. In an effort to preempt demands for a wide-ranging and hostile congressional investigation, Ford appointed Vice-president Nelson A. Rockefeller to head a blue-ribbon commission composed of business and political figures—including Ronald Reagan, the former governor of California—that was to limit its inquiry to domestic abuses by the CIA such as Chaos and the mail openings. But Congress, its blood up after having deposed a president and insistent on knowing everything about the CIA, was not to be brushed aside. The Senate created a Select Committee on Intelligence Activities, headed by Senator Frank Church, an Idaho Democrat with presidential ambitions; the House, after some fumbling, established a panel headed by New York Representative Otis G. Pike. Over the next year, the nation was treated to the distinctly American spectacle of an intelligence service being scrutinized in the full glare of the public spotlight.

In reality, the assault upon the intelligence community was an attack upon the foreign policy of the United States. Because so little was known about the secret services, it was possible to make them the scapegoat for other dissatisfactions. The effort to rein in the CIA—and American foreign policy—had begun even before the inquiries were launched. Congress had reacted to reports of the agency's activities in Chile with passage of the Hughes-Ryan amendment to the Foreign Assistance Act of 1974. The first successful congressional effort to place controls on the CIA, it required the president to send written "findings" justifying the need for covert operations to congressional oversight committees in an effort to keep Congress "fully and currently informed" on all such activities.*

The most startling of the endless stream of revelations about CIA activities during what became known as the "Year of Intelligence" was leaked by President Ford himself. In an off-the-record session with the top editors of the *Times,* he let slip the fact that the investigators might discover far more sensitive matters than those revealed by Hersh.

"Like what?" one of his visitors is supposed to have asked.

"Like assassinations," the president is said to have responded.

This tidbit was far too juicy to remain secret. Soon a long file of witnesses was parading before the various investigatory panels as they attempted to untangle the story of the assassination plots. One day, Senator Church mused out loud whether the CIA had become a "rogue elephant." The catchy phrase created an image of an organization running amok, a threat to the nation's fundamental liberties. In effect, however, Church's glib phrase absolved presidents and other officials who had approved of—or ignored—CIA abuses of all responsibility for them.

Fearing that the agency was threatened with emasculation or destruction, Colby took a bold, high-stakes gamble. Rather than drawing

---

*The Hughes-Ryan requirements were a prescription for leaks, for there were eight such committees with a total of no less than 163 members. In 1980, the notification procedure was modified to require reporting to only two intelligence committees created by the Senate and House in 1976 and 1977. Nevertheless, Hughes-Ryan has proved to be of dubious value. "Findings" became mere statements by the president that he deems an operation necessary, and the definition of "fully and currently informed" has been a matter of controversy ever since.

the traditional cloak of secrecy around the agency, he was candid and cooperative with the investigators, balancing the needs of national security against Congress's right to know. The entire panoply of Mafia hoods, poisoned cigars, and exotic weapons was unveiled before a fascinated public.

The president, Henry Kissinger, Richard Helms, and many members of the intelligence community were convinced Colby went too far in lifting the veil on the agency's past. In fact, Vice-president Rockefeller pulled him aside after one hearing and said: "Bill, do you really have to present all this material to us?" Kissinger, in a joking reference to Colby's Catholicism, observed, "Bill, do you know what you do when you go up to the Hill? You go to confession." And Helms's response was heartfelt. "Who would have thought," he muttered, "that it would someday be judged a crime to carry out the orders of the President of the United States?"*

The Church and Pike committees soon found that the Family Jewels were merely the tip of the iceberg. Abuses were not confined to the CIA. From 1942 to 1968, it was revealed, the FBI had carried out 238 burglaries against "domestic surveillance targets." For twenty years, it had tried to discredit Dr. Martin Luther King, the civil rights leader, through COINTELPRO, a counterintelligence operation that included bugging and blackmail. And the national security agency disclosed the existence of Operation Shamrock, under which the international telegraph companies had for three decades supplied the government with copies of cable traffic sent and received by U.S. citizens.

As the investigations continued, occasional lip service was paid to improving performance, but that was a side issue. The investigators were really interested in exposing abuses and restricting covert operations. The CIA's covert branch "is a self-serving apparatus," Church thundered.

*Among the matters called to the inspector general's attention were discrepancies in Helms's testimony during the hearings before the Senate Foreign Relations Committee on his nomination as envoy to Iran in 1973. Questioned about rumors that the CIA had tried to overthrow the government of Chile and had bankrolled opposition candidates, he replied to both questions with an unequivocal denial. Undoubtedly, Helms reasoned that inasmuch as the CIA's activities in Chile were still classified, his confirmation hearings were not the forum to discuss them and he was justified in keeping the secret. Besides, technically speaking, the agency had not tried to overthrow the Chilean government but to block Salvador Allende from becoming president, and money had been given to political parties and organizations, not individual candidates.

Colby has stated that at first he ignored the matter but later agreed to an internal investigation. Although none of the investigators were lawyers, they concluded that Helms had committed perjury. Colby says that he sat on their report for a time but eventually sent it to the Justice Department.

In 1977, Helms was indicted for perjury. He pleaded no contest to two misdemeanors, was given a severe tonguelashing by the presiding judge, and was fined two thousand dollars, a sum raised by former colleagues in a single afternoon. In 1983, President Reagan awarded him the nation's highest intelligence decoration, the National Security Medal.

"It's a bureaucracy which feeds on itself, and those involved are constantly sitting around thinking up schemes for [foreign] intervention which will win them promotions and justify further additions to the staff. . . . It self-generates interventions that otherwise never would be thought of, let alone authorized."

The effect of these inquiries upon morale and efficiency was devastating. "With every new sensational headline, with every new damaging revelation, nerves frayed, emotions erupted," Colby later recalled. CIA officers felt inhibited in expressing candid opinions, and other intelligence agencies were uneasy about sharing secrets. Some officers, furious that men who had served the agency with loyalty and courage might now be subject to criminal prosecution, never forgave Colby for refusing to stonewall the investigations.

■ ■ ■

While congressional investigators were rummaging through its files, the CIA was engaged in one of the most active—if operationally ill-starred—periods in its history. South Vietnam finally fell to the North Vietnamese, and covert operations were launched in Iraq, which was menacing Iran, and Angola. In an effort to keep the Iraqis off balance, the U.S. and Iran jointly supported Kurdish tribesmen who were fighting to establish an independent homeland called Kurdistan. The CIA funneled about sixteen million dollars worth of captured Soviet arms to the Kurds; Iranian assistance ran much higher. Then, in 1975, the shah reached an understanding with Iraq. He not only halted aid to the Kurds but blocked free passage of CIA arms to them just as the Iraqis launched a full-scale offensive against Kurdish strong points. Anguished Kurdish pleas for American intervention were ignored. "Covert action should not be confused with missionary work," Henry Kissinger is supposed to have replied to a congressman who was critical of the abandonment of the Kurds.

Meanwhile, Nixon and Kissinger had finally extracted the last American troops from South Vietnam in 1973 while promising to ensure the survival of the Saigon regime. Promise or no, the CIA forecast that the North Vietnamese would try to take over the country in 1976. The enemy did not wait that long. Little more than eighteen months after the last American troops had left, South Vietnam quickly crumbled under a massive North Vietnamese offensive.

Panicked by the onslaught, some CIA base chiefs abandoned their Vietnamese assets and secret files. In Saigon, Graham Martin, the U.S. envoy, and Thomas Polgar, the station chief, resisted pressures to expedite an evacuation of "high risk" personnel on the grounds that to do so would touch off a stampede. Out of touch with reality, they spent their time fostering one last coup in hopes of establishing a Vichy-type regime acceptable to Hanoi. As the helicopters took off from the roof of the

American embassy during the final, frantic evacuation, many of the Vietnamese who had worked with the CIA were left behind, along with key documents that compromised them. One CIA man was captured and under interrogation provided the enemy with valuable information. Frank Snepp, a CIA analyst who served in Vietnam, resigned in anger over the debacle and went public with the charge that as many as thirty thousand people with CIA contacts were abandoned.

The Angola venture, Operation Feature, was equally disastrous. It begin late in 1975, when a civil war—based as much upon tribal and ethnic rivalries as political differences—erupted after Portugal abruptly granted independence to the African colony. Had Angola not been transformed into a Cold War battleground, it would probably have achieved independence with little notice from the outside world. But Henry Kissinger, fearing that the MPL, a faction backed by the Soviet Union and Cuba, would take over the country, ordered the CIA to launch covert operations to aid the opposing factions, FNLA and UNITA. Money and arms were channeled to the two groups, which were also supported by China and South Africa. Haunted by the spectre of another Vietnam, the 40 Committee forbade the CIA from sending American advisers into Angola, but John Stockwell, chief of the Angola Task Force, flatly stated, "We did it anyway."

Congressional critics first learned of Operation Feature through the reporting requirements of the Hughes-Ryan amendment. They were angered by the alliance of the CIA and the segregationist government of South Africa and feared that the action would discredit American policy in Africa as well as lead to a new Vietnam. When reports of CIA participation in the Angolan civil war eventually appeared in the press, Senator Dick Clark, an Iowa Democrat, introduced legislation aimed at cutting off secret aid to the American-backed Angolan factions. President Ford accused Congress of having "lost it guts," but early in 1976, it voted for the first time to close down a CIA covert operation. With the help of fifteen thousand Cuban troops, the MPL won the war.

On the other hand, Project Jenifer showed the CIA at its imaginative best. Jenifer was a salvage operation designed to recover a sunken Russian submarine from its grave sixteen thousand feet below the surface of the Pacific. At the request of the Navy, which hoped to obtain the submarine's missiles, code books, and operational equipment, the agency built a recovery ship, the *Glomar Explorer,* in conjunction with Howard Hughes, the reclusive billionaire industrialist, with whom it had previously worked.

In the summer of 1974, the *Explorer,* disguised as a deep-sea mining vessel, found the submarine and began lifting it to the surface. But the hull cracked, and half fell back to the bottom. The following year, the ship returned to the site and raised the remaining section of the submarine.

The missiles and codes were not retrieved, but a wealth of other information was recovered. With its overtones of high-tech science fiction, the operation polished the CIA's tarnished image. Whether the results justified the estimated $350 million cost was questioned by some observers, however, to whom the whole operation smacked of the Berlin Tunnel.

■ ■ ■

As the Year of Intelligence drew to an end, a backlash developed against the relentless exposure of secret operations. Senators from both parties lost their enthusiasm for curbing the CIA and fell to squabbling among themselves. The ravaging of Western nations' economies by OPEC's oil price increases and the rising threat of international terrorism raised fears that futher disclosures would damage the nation's intelligence apparatus at a time when it was sorely needed. The single most crucial event in swinging public opinion against the inquiry, however, was the assassination of Richard Welch, the CIA station chief in Athens. Welch had been identified by *Counterspy*, an underground anti-CIA journal, and the agency seized upon the opportunity provided by his murder to discredit its critics. The Church Committee was thrown into a disarray from which it never recovered by Colby's charge that the "sensational and hysterical way the CIA investigations had been handled and trumpeted around the world" had contributed to Welch's death.*

The one word that stood out in the thousands of pages of testimony, findings, and recommendations produced by the various investigations was "oversight." If there was a rogue elephant on the loose, it wasn't merely the CIA: it was the way American foreign policy was conducted. The executive branch of government had not always conducted operations within the constitutional framework provided by law; presidents had made excessive use of covert operations; insignificant attention had been paid to balancing the requirements for secrecy with the processes of democratic government and respect for constitutional guarantees. All this had occurred in part, it was felt, because Congress had failed to exercise adequate oversight of the intelligence community—and, by implication, of the president and the entire executive branch. The old unquestioning trust in honorable men would no longer suffice; oversight must be tightened and formalized.

The Church Committee went so far as to consider seeking "a total ban on all forms of covert action," but pious intentions ran up against the dangers lurking in an imperfect world. The committee concluded that

---

Counterspy claimed, however, that it had not fingered Welch. The publication pointed out that he was widely known in Athens as the CIA station chief, lived in the same home occupied by several of his predecessors, and had refused a bodyguard. In short, he owed his death, *Counterspy* claimed, to the inexcusably thin cover and lax protection provided him by the CIA.

---

the capacity to intervene secretly in the affairs of other countries should be retained, but only for use in cases in which it was "absolutely essential to the national security." To strengthen Congress's hand in dealing with the intelligence community—and to make oversight less susceptible to leaks—the investigators called for replacing the unwieldy multi-committee apparatus of the Hughes-Ryan amendment with two permanent intelligence committees, one in each house of Congress.

President Ford outpaced congressional efforts at reform. On February 18, 1976, he issued Executive Order 11905, which was basically a reworking of recommendations made by the Rockefeller Commission and the changes already ordered by William Colby. Of particular importance was the enhancement of the stature of the DCI in the intelligence community and the White House hierarchy. The director was named chairman of a three-member Committee on Foreign Intelligence that was to report directly to the National Security Committee, and hence to the president himself, as chairman of the NSC.* The old 40 Committee that had supervised covert action was replaced by a five-member Operations Advisory Group, composed of Cabinet-level officials rather than their deputies. To further strengthen outside oversight of intelligence activities, Ford also created an Intelligence Oversight Board composed of three distinguished private citizens who were members of the president's Foreign Intelligence Advisory Board, which had been advising presidents since the Cold War. Critics regarded these reforms as little more than window dressing, however, and the Pentagon retained control of at least half the intelligence budget. In the final analysis, the real power of the DCI rested upon access to the president who appointed him.

No one understood this better than William Colby. Even though he had shepherded the CIA through the most difficult period in its history, Ford dismissed him as the plethora of inquiries was finally drawing to a close. Wishing to clear the deck of politically embarrassing CIA scandals as he prepared to seek election in his own right, the president wanted his own man in the job and chose George Bush, the ambassador to China, as Colby's successor. Bush's appointment marked a turn away from the tradition that the president's top intelligence adviser should be aloof from politics. A former Texas congressman and chairman of the Republican National Committee, Bush made no secret of his presidential ambitions.

Essentially, Bush was picked because he could be trusted to provide no surprises. Amiable and well-liked by old CIA hands, he sincerely believed in the agency and its mission. Bush soothed Congress, tried to restore confidence and morale at Langley, and avoided delving too deeply

*The other two members were the president's national security adviser and a newly appointed deputy secretary of defense for intelligence affairs. The committee was given authority to control budget preparation and resource allocation, enabling the DCI to coordinate the intelligence community if he used his powers properly.

into the agency's darker recesses. "It's the best job in Washington," he later declared, with characteristic enthusiasm. He held it for only ten months, however, because Ford narrowly lost the 1976 presidential election to Jimmy Carter. While Bush expressed a willingness to stay on at Langley, the new president was deeply suspicious of Washington insiders and of the CIA in particular. For the first time, a change in administration meant a change at the top of the intelligence community.

■ ■ ■

Making a virtue of political inexperience and exuding a moral certitude that recalled Woodrow Wilson, Carter won election by running against Washington as much as against Gerald Ford. A former naval officer, successful businessman, and Georgia governor, he had less experience in foreign affairs than any previous postwar president but held strong views about international morality. In his campaign, he flailed away at what he branded as the three national disgraces—"Watergate, Vietnam, and the CIA"—and questioned the policy of secret interventions into the affairs of other nations. Carter was the embodiment of the "Come home, America" neo-isolationism that permeated the United States in the wake of the Indochina debacle. Unlike his predecessors, he was unconvinced that the ultimate intentions of the Soviet Union were hostile, even as he proclaimed that "human rights is the soul of our foreign policy."

The new president's distrust of the CIA was reinforced by his vice-president, former Senator Walter F. Mondale of Minnesota, who had been a member of the Church Committee. Carter's choice of Theodore C. Sorensen as director of central intelligence created even more unease among CIA professionals. Sorensen, John Kennedy's favorite speechwriter, was too liberal for congressional conservatives, who—undoubtedly with agency assistance—dredged up the fact that he had been a conscientious objector during World War II. Rather than face a bitter battle over his nomination, Sorensen asked that his name be withdrawn. To fend off charges of pacifism, Carter next chose Admiral Stansfield Turner, a Naval Academy classmate, as DCI. Turner accepted with considerable reluctance. A Rhodes scholar with a reputation as one of the Navy's brightest officers, he had hoped to become chief of naval operations or chairman of the Joint Chiefs of Staff and considered the CIA post a detour, if not a dead end.

Like the president, Turner had a well-honed skepticism about intelligence operations and its practitioners. "Find out what kind of mess they have out there," Carter is said to have told him, "and clean it up." Some CIA insiders charge that Turner arrived at Langley with a chip on his shoulder. Although he had little previous experience in intelligence, he regarded it as simply a problem of assessing data or, as he put it, little more than "bean counting." Having had some difficult commands in his naval career, Turner believed he could bring the agency to the same level of efficiency.

No sooner had the admiral assumed his place on the seventh floor of CIA headquarters than he ran into trouble. He claimed to have found "a disturbing lack of specificity and clarity" when he questioned senior CIA executives about their work. The written reports presented to him were "too long and detailed to be useful." Turner also professed to be frustrated by the compartmentalization of the CIA. He not only viewed this secrecy as irrational but suspected that it cloaked a wide range of unseemly activities.

Turner's suspicions were confirmed by a scandal that swirled about the unsavory figure of a one-time CIA contract officer and ONI employee named Edwin P. Wilson. Wilson was ultimately sentenced to fifty-two years in prison for supplying Libya's erratic Colonel Muammar L. Kadafi with the hardware of terrorism and for conspiring to murder two U.S. prosecutors and some of the witnesses against him. In their eagerness to make a fast buck, several ranking CIA officials had become Wilson's business associates, and the affair resulted in dismissals and forced resignations. Turner followed up by issuing a new code of conduct updating the agency's guidelines of permissible activities for retired employees, but the episode confirmed the suspicions of many Americans that intelligence was a grubby business.

Meanwhile, there had been charges that CIA estimates of Soviet strength and intentions were overly optimistic. Hardliners claimed that to conform to the Nixon-Kissinger-Ford policy of detente, agency analysts had grossly understated the possibility that the Russians were aiming for first-strike capability rather than nuclear balance with the United States. To resolve the issue, George Bush had ordered two competing teams of analysts, known as A Team and B Team, to produce independent assessments of Russian strength and intentions. A Team consisted of CIA Soviet specialists, while B Team was composed of outside defense analysts of a conservative bent. As expected, B Team concluded that the CIA had indeed underestimated Russian capabilities. Expecting its opponents to take such a position, A Team revised its original findings to produce results more "pessimistic" than its original findings, according to Richard Pipes, the Harvard history professor who headed B Team. CIA analysts disputed this claim, however, and assailed Bush for unquestioningly accepting the Team B assessment.*

*This episode had a curious aftermath involving John A. Paisley, a former deputy director of the CIA's Office of Strategic Research, who had been assigned as the agency's liaison to B Team. Richard Pipes later claimed that Paisley spied on the group on behalf of the CIA. Be that as it may, two years after the exercise, on October 1, 1978, a badly decomposed body identified as Paisley's was pulled from Chesapeake Bay a week after his unmanned sailboat was found aground on the western shore of the bay. The body was weighted with thirty-eight pounds of lead and had a 9-millimeter bullet wound behind the left ear. Both the CIA

As an outsider, Admiral Turner's basic problem was getting control of the CIA. "When the first annual budget came to me for approval, everything had been decided," he later wrote. "The three branches [clandestine operations, analysis, and support] expected me to rubber-stamp what they wanted." He claimed that the agency's branches operated as independent fiefdoms, jealously guarding their territories against poaching from outsiders. Frank Carlucci, his deputy, compared the DCI's office to the control room of a power plant—with all the switches disconnected.

On the positive side, Turner was impressed with the agency's ability to gather accurate and detailed technical intelligence through satellites and electronic sensors. With his naval background, he accepted the supposed supremacy of electronic and signals intelligence over live agents. Technology—impersonal and seemingly infallible—appeared the perfect solution to the CIA's problems of image and management. Besides, the emphasis on technology fitted in with Carter's foreign policy of disengagement, enabling the United States to take shelter behind a wall of systems and machines.

Yet, when the president asked to see "overhead" photography of a minor war in the Third World, it took a balky bureaucracy weeks to comply. Embarrassed, Turner commissioned DDO to hire a plane to fly over the battleground and take pictures. The plane crashed into a yam patch, leaving the agency with a $2 million indemnification bill. Fuming, the admiral complained that even though he was nominally chief of the best intelligence machine in the world, he could not get pictures of a "Mickey Mouse war" within a reasonable time.*

---

and Maryland State police concluded that the dead man had probably committed suicide. Questions were raised in the press after the CIA supplied wildly conflicting stories about Paisley's background. There was debate over whether the corpse was actually his and, if it was, whether he had been murdered. There were also allegations that Paisley, who had remained on the CIA payroll as a consultant following his retirement, may have been recruited by the Russians as a spy. Some journalists have claimed that at the time of his disappearance Paisley had materials on B Team on his sailboat. The CIA conducted an investigation but did not release its findings, and the circumstances surrounding the case have never been cleared up.

*Some observers say such bureaucratic problems involve more than inertia and are manifestations of a large phenomenon that could be called "deoperationalization." As a result of the thicket of safeguards imposed in the wake of Vietnam and Watergate—and perhaps the "play it safe" mentality of those attracted to government service—greater emphasis is placed upon administration than quick action. (See Edward N. Luttwak, "Ollie North Was Right," Outlook Section, Washington *Post,* March 8, 1987.)

If the CIA needed a bucket, for example, no one would simply go to the nearest hardware store and buy one because of a fear of violating one of the government's countless purchasing requirements. Instead, officials would draft memos on buckets. In due course a bucket-purchasing committee would be formed, which would eventually recommend that a contract for a bucket be given to a trading company run by a trusted ex-CIA employee who would subcontract delivery of the bucket to a hardware dealer. By then, the bucket would no longer be needed—or no one would be able to remember why it was needed in the first place.

Turner was also unhappy with the other members of the intelligence community. Although he was nominally its head, he found himself embroiled in bureaucratic infighting with the Defense Intelligence Agency and the National Security Agency. NSA withheld intelligence on the Soviet navy from the CIA on the grounds that it was "tactical" rather than "national" intelligence, and DIA officials were pressured by the Pentagon to produce reports that supported increased defense appropriations. The tug of war extended into the White House, where officials demanded that the CIA produce estimates that would help the president politically.

Critics charged that Turner used post-Vietnam manpower cutbacks to downgrade human intelligence operations in favor of technological intelligence gathering. This housecleaning, which began during the last weekend in October 1977 and fell most heavily upon the Operations directorate, became known in CIA annals as the "Halloween Massacre." Turner claimed that the actual reduction in force was minimal and that most of the 820 vacancies created were the result of early retirement and normal attrition over a two-year period. But the cutback was handled in a brutal and insensitive manner. Many of those dismissed received only a computerized note consisting of a single sentence. One longtime employee is reputed to have been given a dismissal notice while still in the hospital recuperating from a serious operation.

The simmering tension between Turner and his agency now turned into open warfare. Old intelligence hands spread the word that the admiral had fired 820 people, with some press accounts raising the toll to 2,000. The CIA's covert operations capability was said to have been "gutted" by the firing and retirement of many of the most experienced officers. For his part, Turner argued that the real reason for the outrage was his decision to challenge the traditional independence of DDO. "If I could summarily reduce the size of the espionage branch, I might next begin to supervise what it did," he declared. "The cry was over power and turf."

Turner maintained that he wanted to preserve the CIA's capability for covert action but to hold it in reserve for really significant operations. Nevertheless, intelligence priorities were radically reordered over the next three years. While major European services and Israel's Mossad earmarked about 85 percent of their budgets to the human side of collection and 15 percent to technology, the United States shifted to a reverse ratio. Critics charged that this allotment was unbalanced. While spy satellites or remote sensing devices may provide more information on Russian troop deployments than any spy network, they are unable to tell what is going on in the laboratories where a new generation of Soviet missiles is under development. "Technical intelligence often doesn't capture what you really want to know," observes George A. Carver, a former

CIA official. "Human agents can get you war plans, documents, blueprints of new weapons systems and spot political trends."

Furthermore, experts caution that technical collection provides information that adversaries have allowed to leak into the open, either because they don't know of the leak—at best, a temporary situation—or because protecting the data isn't worth the expense. It is also argued that American intelligence has become overly dependent upon a handful of vulnerable and fragile satellites that in case of war, will be the first targets for Soviet missiles.* And to an increasing extent, the rise of terrorism and international drug dealing have forced intelligence agencies to focus on problems that depend upon having a human agent in place.

Ironically, President Carter downgraded clandestine operations in the Third World precisely as the Soviets were projecting their military and political power into that area. Cuban troops were used to bolster Soviet influence in Angola, Ethiopia, and South Yemen.* Vietnam became a formal Soviet ally, providing the Russians with the unsurpassed American-built naval facilities at Camranh Bay as well as an ally against China. Soviet troops moved into Afghanistan to prop up a shaky pro-Communist regime, and Iran slid into chaos. The NSA mistakenly reported the presence of a Soviet combat brigade in Cuba, and this bit of misinformation played a direct role in preventing Senate ratification of the SALT II arms control treaty. As these troubles piled up, an obviously shaken president sent Turner a handwritten note with copies addressed to Secretary of State Cyrus R. Vance and Zbigniew Brzezinski, the national security adviser. "I am not satisfied with the quality of our political intelligence," Carter declared. It was a masterpiece of understatement.

■ ■ ■

On New Year's Eve, 1977, just as his first year in the White House was ending, Jimmy Carter was the guest of honor at a glittering dinner

*The series of disasters that struck the American space program beginning in early 1986 exposes the fallacy of relying almost entirely upon space and high technology for gathering intelligence. The loss of the Challenger space shuttle and the explosion of at least two other rockets carrying satellites into orbit were serious blows to the intelligence community. Part of the problem is the result of an earlier decision to build a few extremely sophisticated satellites rather than a fleet of less complex models. As a result, the National Reconnaissance Office, the agency responsible for spy satellites, has only been able to keep two KH-11 satellites in space at a time. One of them died of old age in August 1985; its replacement was lost in one of the explosions. The larger and even more sophisticated KH-12, which was due to be launched by shuttle, will probably be delayed for years.

*In 1979, Frank Carlucci, then deputy DCI, supervised a top secret paramilitary effort against the Marxist government of South Yemen, which was threatening to topple the ruler of the neighboring, pro-Western North Yemen. The operation ended disastrously when a CIA-trained team of about a dozen Yemenis were captured while trying to blow a bridge in South Yemen. Under torture, they betrayed their CIA sponsors.

hosted by Shah Mohammed Reza Pahlevi in Teheran. Lifting his glass in a midnight toast, the president declaimed: "Iran, because of the great leadership of the shah, is an island of stability in one of the more troubled areas of the world." No one mentioned the massive anti-shah demonstrations that had taken place in the island of stability earlier that day. The intelligence community was equally myopic. Less than a year later, while strikes and demonstrations were virtually paralyzing the country, the CIA issued a National Intelligence Estimate—a bottom-line study of conditions in Iran—stating that the country "is not in a revolutionary or even a 'prevolutionary' situation." The Defense Intelligence Agency chipped in with a prediction that the shah would remain in power for at least another ten years.

Since 1953, when the CIA had reestablished the shah on the Peacock Throne, Iran had become an American bulwark in the oil-rich Persian Gulf. Nixon and Kissinger had even expanded this role. The shah was granted unlimited access to American weaponry in exchange for his help in containing the Russians and serving as a voice of moderation in OPEC—although in reality he helped drive oil prices to astronomical levels. But anti-shah and anti-American feeling was growing in intensity. Countless Iranians objected to the shah's plans to modernize society, which in the view of the mullahs, or priests, violated fundamental Islamic law and tradition. Other were angered by widespread corruption and by the brutality of the dictatorship. The CIA failed to sense the depth of this discontent, causing one observer to remark that its information was "too much PX, too little bazaar."

Congressional investigators later concluded that the basic cause of the intelligence failure was the agency's dual role in Iran. Once again, the roles of advocacy and objective assessment intermingled, to the detriment of both. On the one hand, "the CIA has historically considered itself the shah's booster," while on the other, "it was supposed to provide sound intelligence analysis of the Iranian political situation." In 1973, the agency's chief Iran analyst wrote a report that warned that the shah's policies were "sowing the seed for popular dissidence." But this conclusion was deleted from the final version because, as a superior told him, it did not reflect American policy toward Iran. American diplomats and intelligence operatives were also handicapped by a lack of contact with the religious opposition and failed to appreciate the appeal of Islamic fundamentalism. Most of their information came from the shah, the SAVAK—his notoriously brutal secret police—and the oil companies, which ignored or dismissed the unrest. But a hallmark of good intelligence is precisely the way in which it circumvents such difficulties.

Undoubtedly the worst intelligence breakdown of the Iranian crisis was the CIA's failure to discover that the shah had incurable cancer and was being given massive doses of drugs by a team of French doctors. Weak and indecisive, he refused to order the army and SAVAK to take strong measures against the rioters, fearing that a bloodbath would make it impossible for his son to succeed to the throne after his death. Most Americans, President Carter among them, remained lulled by the shah's image as an absolute monarch. They refused to believe that he could be overthrown by street mobs pledging loyalty to an aged religious fanatic, the Ayatollah Ruhollah Khomeini, who was living in exile in Paris.

Iran boiled over at a time when the American foreign policy apparatus was already overtaxed. The last phase of the negotiations with the Russians on limiting strategic arms, the normalization of relations with China, and the need to move beyond the spectacular breakthrough in the Egyptian-Israeli conflict achieved at Camp David all had a higher priority than the plight of the shah. The full attention of Washington policymakers was not drawn forcefully to Iran until October 1978, when it was probably already too late to do anything about the deteriorating situation. "The most fundamental problem at the moment is the astonishing lack of hard information we are getting about developments in Iran," observed Gary Sick, the Iran specialist on the NSC. "This has been an intelligence disaster of the first order. Our information has been extremely meager; our resources were not positioned to report accurately."

Turner acknowledged the problem but explained that he was unable to respond to demands for information because American intelligence capabilities in Iran had atrophied. Eleven days after President Carter's note to his foreign policy advisers complaining about the quality of political intelligence, the CIA distributed a paper that attempted to explain the shah's failure to take decisive action. The paper concluded that his vacillation meant he was "continuing to cope with the problems of his regime." Sick dismissed this as "sheer gobbledygook masquerading as informed judgment." Policymakers began to seek out other sources of information—which were often inaccurate and had their own axes to grind—and were reluctant to share them, thereby adding to an atmosphere of distrust and suspicion in Washington.

The Iranian crisis reflected the conflict among Carter's foreign policy advisers. Vance followed conciliatory policies, while the Polish-born Brzezinski took a more confrontational line. Torn by a feud between those who hoped for a stable, liberal Iran without the shah and those arguing for support of a tough military government that would suppress the revolution, the administration floundered.

Unlike a quarter-century before, no Kermit Roosevelt was to be dispatched to Teheran to save the shah's throne. With his army demoralized and support crumbling, the shah fled Iran on January 16, 1979, never to return. On the way to the airport, he wistfully recalled that when he had left the country in 1953, the people had poured into the streets to demand his return. This time the crowds cheered his departure and chanted, "The Shah is gone! Now it's the Americans' turn!"

Political leaders tend to take for granted the predictability and rationality of events. In dealing with the Iranian crisis, Carter failed to take into account the irrelevance of Western models of behavior to the situation. Like his predecessors, he viewed international affairs through the prism of the Cold War and was thrown off balance by a fundamentalist religious revolution that denounced both the United States and the Soviet Union. In particular, the president failed to recognize that the glue holding together such otherwise incompatible forces as the extreme left, political moderates, and the mullahs was blended of equal parts anti-Americanism and hatred of the shah. The decision to allow the terminally ill former ruler to obtain medical treatment in the United States in October 1979—made under pressure from Kissinger and the Rockefeller interests—merged these two sentiments into one.

A one-day seizure of the American embassy in Teheran in February 1979 should have been a warning. But instead of reducing the American diplomatic presence to modest levels after this incident, Carter persuaded himself that Iran had returned to "normalcy," and the mission was enlarged. Efforts were made to portray the Ayatollah Khomeini as "some kind of saint," as UN Ambassador Andrew Young described him. This approach simply played into the hands of the Iranian fanatics. With chaos mounting and public enthusiasm running down, they were seeking a way to depose a moderate interim government and radicalize the revolution. By granting even temporary asylum to the shah—against the warnings of those on the scene—Washington provided the spark for an explosion. On November 4, 1979, militant "students" seized the embassy and took about one hundred hostages. Woman and blacks were soon released, leaving fifty-three captives, three of them CIA officers, in Iranian hands.

Throughout most of the 444 days in which the hostages were held captive, the intelligence community was without "stay-behind" assets on the ground in Teheran. Its network of agents had been in disrepair since the ouster of the shah, and the lack of resources made it difficult even to determine for certain where all the captives were being held. The militants also discovered a bonanza of secret documents in the files of what they called the "Espionage Den." Incredibly, no effort had been made to destroy or remove sensitive papers after the one-day occupation of the embassy, and millions of documents were still on hand. "One of the basic rules is to burn the damn stuff before you get into trouble," notes William Colby. Some sources say the loss of secrets was the greatest since the frantic evacuation of Saigon. Thomas Ahern, the CIA station chief, managed to destroy the bulk of his records, but most of the papers in the files of the military attaché were captured. Among them were lists of only thinly veiled DIA sources in Iran and top-priority American intelligence targets. To fan anti-American feeling, the militants published nearly sixty volumes of documents purportedly discovered in the embassy. They included photocopies of original texts as well as shredded secret documents that had been pieced together.*

The death of the shah failed to bring about the release of the hostages because his presence in the United States had been merely a pretext for holding them. The militants had more ambitious plans than they were credited with by contemptuous Americans. As long as they held the hostages, the purifying flames of the "revolution within the revolution" would continue to burn. The United States might have been wise to disengage, because it had no leverage on events. But President Carter was consumed by the Iranian crisis. He developed an intense personal commitment to the hostages, in part because he felt guilty at having left them exposed. Heightened by emotional media coverage, the hostage situation soon dominated American life.

In dealing with Iran, some critics saw the United States as Charlie Brown, a character in the comic strip *Peanuts*. Charlie repeatedly allows the mischievous Lucy to hold a football for him even though she unfailingly snatches the ball away as he tries to kick it and he takes a resounding pratfall. Tragically, the American hostages were a perfect football. Carter repeatedly tried to negotiate their release, only to have the Iranians snatch the ball away at the last minute.

By April 1980, the president had moved closer to Brzezinski's confrontational policies. The Soviet invasion of Afghanistan at the end of the previous year, aimed at propping up a Marxist regime, shocked Carter more profoundly than any other event while he was in the White House. He viewed the Soviet presence as a dagger pointed at the Persian Gulf.* Abandoning his efforts to seek a peaceful accommodation with the Soviet Union, Carter adopted a posture of enhanced military readiness and political confrontation. The downtrend in the intelligence community's budget was reversed, though not enough to make up for the 40 percent cut in funding that had occurred over the course of the decade or the 50 percent reduction in personnel. The CIA was directed to make covert assistance available to the Afghan rebels, and funds and arms—mostly obsolescent Soviet weapons purchased from the Chinese—were channeled to the insurgents through Pakistan.

Meanwhile, the Iran crisis festered as newspapers and television

*See the New York *Times*, July 10, 1986.

*The CIA provided ample warning of a Soviet military buildup, but the invasion itself was a surprise. Analysts believed direct Russian military intervention was a thing of the past; the Soviets were thought more likely to act through proxies.

counted each day of the hostages' ordeal. Worried about the effects of the hostage crisis on his chances for reelection in 1980, Carter gave the go-ahead for a military rescue mission. The CIA's role in Eagle Claw, as the operation was known, was primarily to provide support. Former Air America specialists from Laos worked on the logistical problems. An agency plane touched down briefly at the planned landing site, called Desert One, to take a soil sample. DDO's paramilitary staff furnished and installed overland navigational devices in the Marine helicopters that were to carry Delta Force, the Army Special Forces rescue team. At least seven agents were infiltrated into Iran in the months before the rescue attempt to pinpoint the location of the hostages and to gather a fleet of trucks to carry the commandos to the embassy.

But Eagle Claw turned into a nightmare. Long before any of the combat team came within striking range of Teheran, the operation had to be aborted. Three of the helicopters, always unreliable vehicles, suffered mechanical breakdowns, leaving too little lift capacity to provide a margin of error.

The scrubbed mission ended in ignominy. One of the helicopters collided with a transport plane during the hurried withdrawal, and eight crew members were killed in the fiery crash. The last shreds of Carter's credibility also perished in the flaming wreckage strewn about Desert One.

20

Once More Into the Breach

Like many Washington events, the ceremony had a subliminal message. One bright spring morning toward the end of May 1984, President Ronald Reagan crossed the Potomac to join in ground-breaking ceremonies for a massive new addition to the Central Intelligence Agency complex at Langley. Looking out over the crowd of intelligence professionals gathered before him, Reagan, with his knack for telling an audience what it wanted to hear, paid tribute to their dedication and personal sacrifice. "Without you, our nation's safety would be more vulnerable and our security fragile and endangered," he declared. "The work you do each day is essential to the survival and to the spread of human freedom."

The president's presence at CIA headquarters—as well as the $200 million new building itself—symbolized the reversal of the agency's fortunes since Reagan had replaced Jimmy Carter in the White House. Under William J. Casey, the combative one-time OSS officer and financial buccaneer chosen by Reagan as his director of central intelligence, the CIA had undergone a remarkable renaissance. The post-Vietnam orgy of investigations and restrictions had ended. With the fastest-growing share of the federal budget, large numbers of new employees, and ready access to the ear of the president, the agency had become a formidable player in the implementation of American foreign policy. "It's go, go, go," observed William Colby from the sidelines.

But these changes were made at a high price. Rather than providing the president with cool, professional evaluations of world problems, Casey, reliving the glory days of the OSS, propelled the agency into open-ended covert wars and revived fears of the CIA as a "rogue elephant." In the end, these activities were to blight the Reagan presidency.

413

Casey's record included flashes of insight, however. Several months before the death of Soviet leader Leonid I. Brezhev in November 1982, he assessed the prospects for the Soviet succession. "Chernenko peaked too soon," he told President Reagan. "Kirilenko faded in the stretch. Grishin is a dark horse, but if I had to bet money, I'd say Andropov on the nose, and Gorbachev across the board." Casey's prescient memo, with its racetrack parlance and its accurate forecast of KGB chief Yuri V. Andropov's rise to power, became CIA legend. But when Andropov died after little more than a year in power, the CIA was scooped on the news by Dusko Doder, a Washington *Post* correspondent.

It is axiomatic in the intelligence business that mishaps and mistakes are well publicized, while successes remain secret. Still, the American intelligence community suffered a number of indisputable setbacks during Casey's watch:

- American intelligence reportedly had word early in 1983 that an Iranian-connected, Syrian-protected Shiite Moslem group calling itself the Party of God planned to attack the U.S. Marines ordered to Beirut by Reagan on a peacekeeping mission, but failed to provide a precise warning of the truck-bombing that killed 241 Marines.
- The CIA has not been able to protect even its own from terrorist attack. Almost the entire Beirut station was wiped out in a bombing of the U.S. embassy early in 1983, and the agency was unable to penetrate the Islamic factions holding American hostages, including agency personnel, in the Middle East.
- CIA efforts to organize counterterrorist units for preemptive strikes against suspected terrorists backfired. One such group exploded a car bomb outside the residence of the leader of the Party of God in Beirut, killing more than eighty people and wounding another two hundred while the target was unharmed.
- The CIA botched the handling of Soviet defectors, particularly Vitaly S. Yurchenko, a top-level KGB officer who re-defected to Moscow with jibes at the unprofessional way in which he had been handled.
- CIA handprints were found all over the so-called secret war in Nicaragua.
- Despite the satellites orbiting over Russia, the CIA knew nothing of the Chernobyl nuclear disaster for three days.
- The CIA failed to detect the fact that Saudi Arabia had purchased long-range missiles capable of carrying nuclear warheads, a destabilizing factor in the Middle East.
- A flood of secrets flowed to foreign powers through greed, betrayal, and deception, in some cases from within the CIA's own ranks.

Casey survived these embarrassments because of his ties to the president. An amiable former movie actor, pitchman for right-wing causes, and California governor, Reagan arrived at the White House with only a sketchy knowledge of foreign affairs.* But he needed no coaching about the Soviet Union. As the White House's most dedicated cold warrior since John F. Kennedy, he viewed Russia as "the focus of evil in the modern world." Having defeated Carter with the promise to restore America's shattered power and prestige by "standing tall," he talked tough to the Russians, promised never to negotiate with terrorists, dramatically escalated the arms race, and took a firm anticommunist line, especially in the Third World.

Like Kennedy two decades before, the new president saw the Third World as a battleground where the tide of communism could be rolled back. Under the Reagan Doctrine, Washington provided enthusiastic support to indigenous "freedom fighters" of every stripe whose only common feature was opposition to Soviet-backed Marxist regimes. The task of translating rhetoric into reality in Nicaragua, Angola, Afghanistan, and other world trouble spots was given to Bill Casey and a reinvigorated CIA. Within a few years, at least fifty "special activities" were underway. But instead of serving as the handmaiden of foreign policy, covert action became the policy.

■ ■ ■

"You have to understand that Bill Casey is a 73-year-old man having a tremendous time," one observer noted during the height of Casey's tenure at Langley. Rumpled, stoop-shouldered, and shambling, Reagan's DCI looked more like a tired businessman on the last commuter train home than a spymaster, but he was in the direct line of succession from Wild Bill Donovan. Casey was hardly cast in the gentlemanly mold of the Ivy Leaguers who had set the tone for the OSS and CIA, however. Left fatherless at an early age, he grew up "an Irish street pug" and worked his way through Fordham and St. John's University Law School. Following Pearl Harbor, he joined the Navy and angled his way into the OSS. He attracted Donovan's attention and at war's end was running the Jedburgh teams that parachuted into Germany. One of his most cherished possessions was a letter from the general that said: "You took up one of the heaviest loads which any of us had to carry at a time when the going was roughest and you delivered brilliantly."

*During the early 1940s, Reagan played Brass Bancroft, a U.S. government secret agent, in four grade-B movies. In one, he is told: "It may become necessary for you to break the law, but you will be doing so at your own risk, with no hope of official intercession unless your life is at stake—in which case your value to the service will have ended." As a real FBI informant during the McCarthy era, he was given the code name T-10 and was assigned to inform on leftists among the board members of the Screen Actors Guild, of which he was then president.

Casey made his first million dollars before turning forty but was involved in several scrapes, raising questions about the propriety if not the legality of some of his dealings. As one friend has said, "I'm glad he's on *our* side." Over the years, he had remained an intelligence buff and had been appointed by Gerald Ford to the President's Foreign Intelligence Advisory Board. A relative latecomer to the Reagan presidential campaign, he took over just as Reagan's candidacy was on the ropes after his loss to George Bush in the Iowa caucuses. Casey devised the strategy that won the crucial New Hampshire primary, thus propelling Reagan toward the White House. Although he wanted to be secretary of state, he was rewarded instead with the top intelligence job.

Intelligence professionals were wary of Casey and thought the director's job should have gone to Admiral Bobby Ray Inman, the highly regarded head of the National Security Agency, who was named his deputy.* Critics charged that the new DCI's expertise was forty years out of date and suspected he would be a cheerleader for administration policies. Casey's choice of a Reagan campaign worker, Max Hugel, to head the sensitive Directorate of Operations also drew heavy fire. Hugel was jettisoned—and Casey nearly went along with him—when two shady operators raised questions about his business dealings and then dropped out of sight. The incident, which may have been orchestrated by CIA insiders, coincided with Casey's own involvement in a flap over the means by which the Reagan campaign obtained a copy of the briefing book used to prepare Jimmy Carter for a televised debate between the candidates. But Casey had the support of the OSS "old boy" network and President Reagan's blessing, and the Senate Intelligence Committee concluded unenthusiastically that he was "not unfit to serve."

Under Casey, the budget for the intelligence community shot up about 25 percent annually—rising at a faster rate than even that of the Pentagon—and reached an estimated twenty-four billion dollars during the 1987 fiscal year.* As much as three billion may have gone to the CIA. The seven-story addition at Langley for which Reagan broke ground doubled the size of the agency's headquarters and helped to house a

---

*Inman, unhappy with the CIA's renewed involvement in covert paramilitary operations, soon resigned. The admiral would get so nervous when Casey was lying to the Senate Intelligence Committee that he would lean over and pull up his socks—a gesture that the senators eventually realized was a solid clue to the degree of veracity in Casey's testimony.

*Most of the intelligence budget is hidden in the appropriations for defense. Half the overall $24 billion is for the National Foreign Intelligence Program (NFIP) and provides funds for the Central Intelligence Agency, the Defense Intelligence Agency, the National Security Agency, and the National Reconnaissance Office (NRO). These funds are the responsibility of the DCI. The other half, for Tactical Intelligence and Related Activities (TIRA) is under the control of the secretary of defense. About $5 billion of the NFIP budget goes to the NRO, which oversees photo reconnaissance and signals-intelligence satellites. NSA gets $4 billion, and DIA about $1 billion. The $12 billion TIRA allocation pays for the ongoing intelligence activities of the military, including Air Force reconnaissance flights, early warning satellites, and intelligence assistance to allies.

rapidly swelling payroll of some sixteen thousand employees. And if access to the president is the key measurement of an intelligence chief's effectiveness, Casey surpassed even Allen Dulles, for he was the first DCI to regularly sit in on cabinet meetings as a peer of the secretaries of state and defense. Reagan would listen for hours as Casey regaled him with tales of OSS exploits during World War II. "It can't help but boost the morale of CIA analysts to know their stuff is getting to the top," observed Ray Cline.

Even critics credited Casey with whipping the agency's estimate process into shape. Intelligence gathering was reorganized under a deputy director for intelligence and Robert M. Gates, a Soviet specialist and Casey favorite, was named to the post. Efforts were made to adjust the balance between technological espionage and human collection, and the quantity and quality of the National Intelligence Estimates and other analyses were upgraded. The number of NIE's rose to more than sixty in 1985 from only a dozen in 1980. Reflecting the A Team/B Team experience, greater emphasis was placed upon competitive analyses, and the estimates now routinely include dissenting opinions. Casey also ordered the preparation of the first-ever NIE on the future of Soviet science and extended the CIA's mandate to study such problems as terrorism and drug trafficking. Recognizing the president's limitations, he served up intelligence to Reagan in crisp mini-memo form and in ancedote-filled briefings.

Insiders complained, however, that Casey pressured analysts to tailor the intelligence product to support specific policies or political positions. "Casey comes back here from the White House looking for reports to buttress his stand," related one intelligence officer. "He does not ask us for a review of an issue or a situation. He wants material he can use to justify controversial policy or expand the agency's involvement." John Horton, the national intelligence officer for Latin America, angrily resigned in 1984 after Casey rejected his analysis of the situation in Mexico. "Casey wanted an alarmist view of Mexico's stability to rationalize U.S. goals in Central America," Horton declared. And Secretary of State George P. Shultz later said that even before the Iran-contra affair, he had "grave doubts about the objectivity and reliability of some of the intelligence I was getting" from the agency.*

---

*As usual, the CIA's record was mixed when it came to accuracy. An agency report on the Soviet oil industry issued in 1977 stated that it was in trouble and forecast that by 1985 the Soviet Union would be importing oil. Just the opposite occurred. In 1985, the Soviet Union was the world's largest producer of oil and second only to Saudi Arabia as an exporter. In 1983, the agency announced that Soviet military spending had grown by 2 percent yearly since 1977, instead of the 3 to 4 percent it had stated a year earlier. Some lawmakers were infuriated, claiming that they had been misled into supporting an increased defense budget based on a faulty estimate. On the other hand, CIA accurately clocked events in the Philippines that led to the fall of Ferdinand Marcos, whom it had originally supported, and his replacement by Corazon Aquino.

Paradoxically, Casey's greatest weakness was in the political aspects of his job. Legislative oversight had added a new dimension to the DCI's responsibilities, making him the point man for winning congressional backing for presidential policies. But the irascible Casey's aversion to legislative monitoring of his shadowy domain—even though such oversight has hardly been onerous—resulted in frequent clashes with Congress and charges that he was withholding information. "Don't brief, limit disclosure," he told associates. Under questioning, he professed ignorance of key issues or simply mumbled inaudible replies. "He wouldn't tell you your coat was on fire unless you asked him a direct question," observed Representative Norman Y. Mineta, a California Democrat.

■ ■ ■

While Casey was retooling the CIA, the Soviet Union launched a crash program to acquire the fruits of American technology. In the Cold War era, the KGB had primarily sought conventional military secrets. Now its targets were industrial, scientific, and technological processes and equipment, especially in the fields of satellites, computers, and codebreaking. The success of its operations can be measured by the fact that in 1983 investigators determined that Western technology could be found in more than 150 of the main Soviet weapons systems. Indeed, with the assistance of stolen technology, the Russians have been able to clone Western missiles and aircraft. One missile, the submarine-launched SS-N-21, so resembles the American-made Tomahawk cruise missile that the U.S. intelligence community calls the Soviet weapon the "Tomahawksi." And Western armor-piercing expertise has been used to place NATO's own tank forces in jeopardy.

Targets for Soviet industrial espionage are identified by the blandly named Military Industrial Commission, which draws up lists of desired Western technological secrets. By the mid-1980s, these lists totaled more than 3,500 items a year, and the "organs"—Soviet Intelligence—had succeeded in acquiring more than a third. According to William R. Corson and Robert T. Crowley, two former U.S. intelligence officers, Russian technical espionage operates on several levels. All pertinent scientific material published in the United States, including doctoral dissertations and postdoctoral papers, is routinely collected, and available technology is obtained through purchase and licensing. When their needs cannot be met by legal means, the Russians and their Warsaw Pact allies resort to smuggling and the use of dummy corporations to divert Western technology. They are also on the alert for possible traitors likely to trade national security secrets for cash or to succumb to the sexual wiles of attractive KGB female and male agents known as "swallows" and "ravens."

Soviet bloc countries have more than doubled the number of their spies in the West in recent years. In the United States alone, the number increased from perhaps several dozen in the 1950s to more than a thousand today. Every third or fourth person in a Soviet bloc embassy or press office in the West is probably a KGB officer or the equivalent. As many as 1,300 such agents are believed to be in the United States, placed in the Soviet and Eastern bloc embassies, in United Nations missions, and among employees of the UN itself. In addition to these "legals," an unknown number of "illegals" operate under deep cover.

The Soviet quest for new technology has turned Silicon Valley, south of San Francisco, into a spy center as notorious as Vienna. Bright young KGB agents are said to have been planted among Soviet emigrés to the United States with orders to obtain degrees from American universities and jobs with defense contractors. Soviet agents are even said to have attempted to purchase a California bank so the KGB could learn which high-tech workers were in financial difficulty and might be susceptible to its overtures. In addition to the Russians and their Eastern bloc proxies, agents from China, Japan, France, Israel, and South Korea prowl Silicon Valley and similar places in search of secrets. Their work has been made easy by a notorious lack of security among Pentagon contractors. "Our internal laxness is inexcusable," acknowledged the embarrassed chairman of Lockheed when it was learned that the company could not account for more than one thousand classified documents pertaining to the super-secret Stealth bomber.

Unlike the Cold War spies—the Rosenbergs, Klaus Fuchs, Kim Philby, and others—the traitors of the 1980s are motivated by financial gain rather than ideological solidarity with the Soviet Union. The collapse of old moral values and loyalties in the wake of Watergate and Vietnam, combined with the mushrooming of secrets and the number of people with access to them, has been a major cause of the espionage explosion. A Carter administration decision to prosecute more espionage cases rather than quietly try to use the culprits as double agents has also been a factor in publicizing the cases. The current crop of spies bears little resemblance to the intellectualized traitors of John le Carre's novels; most are low- and mid-level personnel, relatively unsupervised, discontented with their jobs, earning modest salaries, and suffering from serious financial problems. To them, espionage is merely a way to make a fast buck. Not even the CIA has escaped the recent rash of betrayals.* But the

*The most serious case involved William Kampiles, a twenty-three-year-old CIA watch officer who became bored with his job routing secret message traffic. Denied transfer to the covert branch, he angrily quit and took with him a top secret manual detailing the operation of the KH-11 photographic satellite, which he sold to the Soviets for three thousand dollars. Kampiles was arrested and sentenced to forty years after he told a former colleague he had been approached by the Russians and was considering becoming a double agent. It was later discovered that 13 other copies of the manual were also missing, reportedly, including one checked out to then CIA director George Bush.

most alarming losses of vital secrets came from a different quarter entirely.

■ ■ ■

The Year of the Spy—1985—began in May as FBI counterintelligence agents kept an eye on a van with Virginia tags that seemed to be traveling erratically over the back roads outside Washington. The vehicle pulled over to the side several times, and the driver repeatedly consulted a map as if looking for a landmark. Finally, he stopped on a deserted stretch of road, placed a paper sack topped with some empty bottles and other trash behind a telephone pole with a "No Hunting" sign, and drove off. The sack contained 129 classified U.S. Navy documents. The agents settled down to wait to see who picked it up. Aleksei G. Takchenko. a vice-consul at the Soviet embassy, was spotted driving about the area, but must have suspected something was wrong for he did not go near the "drop." Having given up on arresting the Russian, the FBI agents retrieved the bag and took the van driver into custody that night at a nearby motel.

The arrest of John A. Walker, Jr., a retired U.S. Navy chief warrant officer and communications expert, touched off the worst spy scandal in Navy history. Further investigation revealed that Walker was running a wide-ranging spy network that included his brother, Arthur J. Walker, a retired lieutenant commander and antisubmarine-warfare specialist; his son Michael, a crewman on the carrier *Nimitz;* and a friend, Jerry A. Whitworth, a retired senior chief radioman living in California. Walker had also tried to persuade his daughter, an Army communications specialist, to supply him with classified information, but she had refused. Three days after Walker's arrest, Takchenko and his family hurriedly left for Moscow.

The dimensions of the security breach caused by the "Walker Family Spy Ring" will probably never be fully determined. Over eighteen years Walker had provided Moscow with the precise details of American naval communications and other data. In exchange, he received about $750,000, which promptly sank without a trace in high living and an assortment of failing businesses. In the Navy, Walker had had a top secret "crypto" clearance and had occupied several sensitive posts. Along with Whitworth, he was in position to furnish the Russians with everything they needed to track American submarines and compromise antisubmarine operations. When asked about the extent of his activities, Walker replied, "If I had access to a secret, color it gone." His treachery was particularly unnerving because the Trident and Polaris missile submarines were regarded as the most secure of the nation's nuclear deterrents. Unlike the other two legs of the strategic triad—the aging B-52 manned bombers and land-based nuclear missiles—they were considered invulnerable to Soviet attack.

Meanwhile, Walker's brother Arthur, who worked for a defense contractor, supplied him with reports on the frequency of equipment breakdowns on U.S. ships. Much of the information provided by Michael Walker dealt with Soviet submarine movements, information that would indicate the ability of the U.S. Navy to track Soviet ships. James Bamford, a specialist in national security affairs, succinctly expressed the value of the information passed to the Russians: "For the Soviets, the Walker spy ring has meant a more transparent ocean in which to hunt U.S. undersea forces and a murkier sea to hide their own."

The most alarming aspect of the Walker case is that the spy ring might still be operating had it not fallen victim to a family squabble. Walker's divorced wife, Barbara, who had known of his espionage activities since 1968, finally tipped off the FBI late in 1984, but four months passed before the report was taken seriously and the family ring broken up.* According to Admiral James Watkins, then chief of naval operations, to offset the damage done by the ring will cost an estimated one hundred million dollars. But the most gnawing question was who else might be engaged in espionage for profit.

An answer was not long in coming. Between 1984 and 1986, twenty-seven U.S. citizens were charged with espionage. One of them was Ronald W. Pelton, a former mid-level employee of the National Security Agency, who was taken into custody on charges of selling secrets to the Soviets only a few months after Walker's arrest. For the bargain price of thirty-five thousand dollars, he had sold the Russians the key to some of the NSA's most vital communications and monitoring operations. The case was described as the most damaging to U.S. intelligence in recent memory. Pelton had resigned from his $24,500 job at NSA in 1979 after declaring bankruptcy, and his life had immediately begun to self-destruct. He left his wife, moved in with an aging ex-beauty queen, drank heavily, and ran through several jobs. Six months later, in January 1980, he approached the Soviet embassy in Washington with an offer to sell information.

From memory, Pelton provided the KGB with the details of a sixty-page report he had helped prepare that was used by several agencies to keep track of intelligence-gathering operations. Moreover, he had "a broad overview of everything going on in the intelligence community," according to testimony at Pelton's espionage trial. The government took the unprecedented step of disclosing that Pelton had betrayed a wide

*The Walker brothers received life terms. Michael Walker was sentenced to 25 years, and Whitworth got 365.

variety of sophisticated eavesdropping devices that had enabled NSA to read fifty-seven main Soviet communications systems, including Operation Ivy Bells, a super-secret submarine intelligence-collection project in the Sea of Okhotsk near the naval base of Vladivostok. An NSA official testified that the operations blown by Pelton "gave us an insight into their military forces, their relative sizes, their plans for maneuvers or training."*

Pelton had been betrayed by Vitaly S. Yurchenko, a KGB colonel who defected in Rome in August. Yurchenko told interrogators he knew of two penetrations of U.S. intelligence: Pelton, with whom he had dealt while serving in Washington and who was known to the Russians as "Mr. Long," and another man known as "Robert." Yurchenko had never met "Robert" and could not provide a physical description, but he did dredge up a clue to his identity. "Robert," he said, had met with the KGB in Austria in 1984, where he had sold CIA secrets while being trained for posting to the Moscow station.

The CIA was horrified. If Yurchenko's tale was true, it meant there was a mole in the highly sensitive Soviet/East European Division. But there had already been disquieting indications that something was wrong in Moscow. At least one major operation had been blown, and a leading expert on stealth aircraft technology, named Adolf G. Tolkachev, an important contact with almost unlimited access to Russian technology, had been arrested and shot.

Working from the information supplied by Yurchenko, the agency eventually zeroed in on a former CIA trainee named Edward L. Howard, who had been fired in 1983. Howard had joined the agency two years before, and both he and his wife, Mary, had received training preparatory to assignment to Moscow, where his mission was to handle some of the agency's prized assets. But Howard was fired after routine polygraph tests indicated that he had drinking and drug problems. He was deeply embittered against the agency even though it helped him get a job as an analyst with the state legislature in his native New Mexico and paid for his psychiatric treatment. On one occasion, as he later admitted to CIA officials, he lingered outside the Soviet embassy in Washington, trying to decide whether to go in. Incredibly, the agency failed to notify the FBI of the incident, and Howard was not ordered to turn in his diplomatic passport.

Traveling to Austria with his wife in September 1984, Howard took the spy's ultimate revenge by going over to the other side. Although only in trainee status, Howard knew enough about the Moscow station to compromise its operations. Tolkachev was shot, and several other Russian informers were reportedly arrested and executed. At least five American diplomats were expelled after being caught while allegedly engaged

*Pelton was sentenced to life imprisonment.

in espionage. "The information available to him was absolutely devastating," said one knowledgeable official. As soon as Howard was identified as a renegade, the FBI staked out his home near Santa Fe. But after agents confronted him with the charges, he put techniques he had learned in his CIA training to work and, with the assistance of his wife, gave the FBI the slip. Nearly a year later, in August 1986, Howard surfaced in the Soviet Union, where he was granted asylum.

A House Intelligence Committee report charged that the CIA had committed fundamental blunders in its handling of the Howard affair. In its haste to expand, the agency recruited a man known to be a drug user and temperamentally unsuited for a delicate clandestine assignment, gave him access to highly sensitive material early in his career, failed to keep track of his activities after he was fired, and even neglected to warn the FBI when he admitted that he had thought of selling out to the Russians. Some sources suspected, however, that Howard had not been privy to Tolkachev's activities, raising the chilling prospect that there was a mole within the American intelligence community who was still active.

The Moscow embassy itself was notoriously porous. As far back as 1940, the FBI had warned that male diplomats in Moscow were frequenting prostitutes and consorting with homosexuals linked to Soviet intelligence, while Russian nationals employed in the embassy had free run of the place. But these warnings were ignored by the State Department until a former Marine guard confessed that he had succumbed to the charms of an attractive Russian receptionist—a KGB swallow—and allegedly allowed Soviet agents free rein to prowl the embassy's most sensitive areas, read secret documents, and implant bugging devices throughout the building. Other guards were arrested as the episode escalated into the most serious sex-for-secrets scandal in American intelligence history. Navy investigators botched the inquiries, however, and all but one of the cases were dropped.

Much to the amusement of the Russians, frazzled U.S. diplomats in Moscow were reduced to writing sensitive messages in longhand because their communications facilities were thought to have been compromised, and Secretary of State George P. Shultz had to use a specially imported communications van during negotiations with Soviet officials in the Kremlin. The security breach also focused attention on the festering problem of the new $200 million U.S. embassy compound under construction in Moscow. Work had been halted in 1985 when it was discovered that prefabricated sections produced off the site, out of sight of American inspectors—with the KGB as the contractor—were riddled with sophisticated listening devices. President Reagan, among others, suggested that the building be bulldozed or abandoned and a replacement built.

Not to be outdone, the Soviets charged that a new Russian embassy compound in Washington had been bugged by American intelligence. In contrast to the site of the new American embassy in Moscow, however, which was built on low ground near the Moscow River, the Russians had been given a site on Mount Alban, one of the highest points in Washington and an ideal spot for their own eavesdropping equipment. Although the intelligence community had warned against allowing the Russians to have the site, "the State Department wouldn't listen," says Admiral Bobby Inman. The Russians were prevented from moving in until the U.S. resolved the question of what to do about their own embassy.

Beneath these spy-versus-spy maneuvers, there may have been a deeper plot at work as well. In an obvious ploy to counteract the wave of bad publicity the agency had been receiving, CIA officials leaked news of Vitaly Yurchenko's defection to the media amid much private gloating. The Russian was considered such a prime catch that he lunched with Casey in the director's private dining room at Langley where he noted that the DCI's fly was open. But after three months, he stunned the CIA by walking away from an inexperienced CIA escort while dining in a Georgetown restaurant and turning up at the Soviet embassy compound a few blocks away. Before his return to Moscow, Yurchenko told a press conference that he had been drugged by American agents in Rome and kidnapped. Rather than being meek and contrite, observers noted, he was in full charge at the conference, interrupting and overriding embassy personnel, something no ordinary defector was likely to consider doing.

Was Yurchenko a genuine defector who later soured on the prospect of life in America? Did he decide to go home as a result of poor handling by the CIA and the refusal of his girlfriend, the wife of a Soviet diplomat in Canada, to join him in exile? Or was he a plant sent by the KGB to find out as much as he could about the CIA and as a warning to prospective defectors that the Americans would be unable to provide them with a safe haven? Not long before, it is pointed out, Oleg Gordievsky, the KGB's London resident, had sought asylum in Britain. To show his bona fides, Yurchenko fingered Pelton and Howard, but by mid-1985 they were burnt assets, anyway.

While Soviet penetration of U.S. intelligence occupied center stage, another country was caught trying to steal America's secrets—Israel. In the winter of 1985, Jonathan Jay Pollard, a Navy counterterrorism analyst, and his wife, Anne, were taken into custody on charges of spying for Israel. Pollard, who had access to the computer system servicing the entire intelligence establishment, supplied the Israelis with secret information on American arms shipments to the Arabs, data on Iraqi and Syrian chemical warfare potential, and intelligence that enabled the Israelis to bomb PLO headquarters in Tunisia in October 1985. In exchange, the Pollards received fifty thousand dollars in cash from the

Israelis and the promise of three hundred thousand more over ten years. The couple lived well beyond their means, but Navy investigators didn't tumble to Pollard's activities until his repeated requests for classified documents that had nothing to do with his job attracted suspicion.

Placed under FBI surveillance, the Pollards bolted to the Israeli embassy, only to be refused admittance. They were arrested at the entrance with a suitcase full of classified documents and the family cat. Immediately afterward, three Israeli diplomats, Pollard's reputed handlers, unceremoniously fled the country to escape questioning. Israeli officials claimed that the Pollard connection was a "rogue" operation, but Pollard related to his interrogators that he had been told "the highest levels of the Israeli government" were grateful for the secrets he passed on.

The Pollard case touched off a diplomatic uproar between the United States and Israel, for it meant that U.S. counterintelligence was engaged in secret war not only with the nation's enemies but with one of its staunchest allies as well. The possibility was also raised that the Pollards had merely taken documents that had been previously described to the Israelis by a high-ranking U.S. official. If so, the Israelis had chosen to sacrifice the Pollards to protect this source.*

■ ■ ■

Years of painstaking effort and billions of dollars will be required to repair the damage caused by the epidemic of spy cases. Preliminary studies indicated that U.S. intelligence suffered serious damage to its agent networks abroad and its ability to electronically eavesdrop on key areas of the world without fear of countermeasures. Reacting to the public pressure to stem the illegal outflow of information, Congress passed a rash of legislation that ranged from reinstituting the death penalty for espionage to requiring lie detector tests for the four million government employees with access to classified material.

Counterintelligence experts pointed out, however, that the death penalty was unlikely to curb spying. Spies do not undertake clandestine missions out of confidence that they will be imprisoned rather than executed if they are caught. They do not expect to be caught at all. And the lie detector is hardly an infallible instrument for unmasking secret agents; it can be deceived by those trained to do so. It will take more than simple get-tough measures to prevent a recurrence of the Year of the Spy.

Following James Angleton's ouster, the CIA's counterintelligence staff was cut from three hundred to eighty, and the centralized files that he had created were broken up along less efficient geographic lines. Security clearances were said to be easier to obtain than an American

---

*Jonathan Pollard was sentenced to life imprisonment; Anne received five years.

Express card. In response to the rash of spy cases, experts recommended expanding the counterintelligence services of the FBI and CIA and improving coordination to make up for the cutbacks in counterintelligence budgets and personnel that had been made in reaction to congressional criticism of domestic spying. But it takes at least four years to train an effective counterespionage operative. Experts say that the best way to immediately tighten secrecy is to reduce the amount of material classified as secret and the number of people with access to it while increasing the stringency and frequency of government security checks. But late in 1988, the House Intelligence Committee reported the nation was still vulnerable to security lapses. For example, the Pentagon has a backlog of 100,000 people needing the security review required every five years. As the Senate Intelligence Committee observed, there are "too many secrets, too much access to secrets, too many spies . . . and too little effort given to combatting the very real threat that spies represent."*

■ ■ ■

The espionage cases were damaging enough, but by far the biggest controversy surrounding the Reagan/Casey CIA was its resort to covert paramilitary actions around the globe. Tales of "freedom fighters" pitted against vastly superior Soviet-backed forces—so many Rambos bucking the odds in the Afghan hills, the African bush,† and the jungles of Central America—captured the presidential imagination. "America will support . . . with moral and material assistance your right not just to fight and die for freedom but to fight and win freedom," Reagan told the "freedom fighters" in his 1986 State of the Union message.

Under Reagan, covert action became the "third option," the middle ground between ignoring communist aggression and waging all-out war. "In the late part of the twentieth century we are going to face in many countries . . . a determined effort by the Soviet Union to subvert friendly governments," explained Robert C. McFarlane, the president's national security adviser. "Now when they do that, using great violence, do the American people really want their president . . . to have no other options than to go to war or do nothing?" The administration supplied its own answer to the question, escalating the commitment to covert action and earmarking about six hundred million dollars annually for paramilitary operations in the mid-1980s.

The Afghan operation had the longest history, dating back to 1979. Unlike some of the other operations, there was a popular consensus

*The House Intelligence Committee reported in 1987 that five million Americans held security clearances—a 40 percent increase over 1980—and that there are *trillions* of classified documents.

†The Clark amendment, which had barred American intervention in Angola, was repealed by Congress in 1985.

favoring assistance to the *mujaheddin* in hopes of increasing the costs of the occupation to the Russians. Besides, the Soviet threat in Afghanistan, unlike the alleged threat in Central America, was unambiguous. More than $1 billion was earmarked for anti-Soviet activities in Afghanistan— including at least $250 million from Saudi Arabia—of which perhaps a third was reportedly skimmed off before reaching the tribesmen. The money was to be used for Soviet, Chinese, and other arms and was deposited in a CIA-run Swiss bank account, but rebel spokesmen complained that they never received half the equipment and some that did arrive was defective.*

To critics, the policy of helping anticommunist rebels wherever they might appear was too open-ended and was likely to embroil the United States in countries where there are no vital American interests. Except for Afghan rebels none of the groups receiving American support had realistic prospects of unseating pro-Soviet regimes, it was charged; furthermore, labeling them "freedom fighters" was a travesty. The former Somoza National Guardsmen leading the anti-Sandinista contras in Nicaragua, for example, were regarded as no more democratic than the Sandinistas themselves and had considerably less popular support. The Moslem insurgents in Afghanistan were defiantly anti-Soviet, but they were also religious fanatics with no love for democracy. And if the crazy-quilt situation in Angola had not been tragic, it would have been farcical. Jonas Savimbi, chief of UNITA and the recipient of the CIA's largess, could have stepped from one of Evelyn Waugh's darkly satirical African novels. Trained in guerrilla warfare in China, he was allied with the racist South African government and periodically sabotaged American-owned Chevron/Gulf Oil installations—facilities that were being protected by Cuban troops.*

Central America, however, was Reagan's main obsession. He was convinced the Sandinistas and their allies in El Salvador planned to turn the area into another Cuba that the Soviets could use both as a base in the heart of the Americas and as a platform for subversion. Moreover, he feared that chaos, or a communist victory in Central America, would

---

*In 1984, Jonathan Pollard told then New York Representative John LeBoutillier that he had evidence the CIA was diverting money intended for the Afghan rebels to the Nicaraguan contras. LeBoutillier dismissed the charge, saying such statements made him realize "I was dealing . . . with a guy who was full of hot air, full of exaggerations" (New York *Times,* November 27, 1985). This was two years before the scandal surfaced involving the diversion of profits from the sale of arms to Iran to the contras. As part of the inquiry into the Iran-contra affair, congressional investigators launched a probe of the possibility that funds intended for the Afghan rebels were diverted as well.

*Stinger and Redeye antiaircraft missiles supplied to UNITA were reported to have turned up in the black market in Zambia. Fears were expressed that they might fall into the hands of terrorists and be used to shoot down a commercial airliner. (See *Defense and Foreign Affairs Weekly,* March 2, 1987.)

inundate the United States in a tidal wave of refugees. Within a few months of taking office, Reagan signed a finding attesting to the desirability of halting the flow of arms from Cuba and Nicaragua to El Salvador, thus laying the foundation for the largest covert operation since Vietnam.

Casey eagerly took up the challenge, and the operation soon became known as "Casey's War." Initially, $19.5 million was earmarked to mobilize a force of five hundred men trained by the Argentine and Honduran military as proxies for the United States. This tactic was designed to stall off congressional opponents who were haunted by the spectre of Vietnam and warned of the danger of again being unwittingly dragged into a quagmire, this time in Central America. But the cloak of plausible deniability became increasingly threadbare, and when the Argentines angrily dropped out of the project after Washington supported Britain in the Falklands war, the CIA took over direct control of the operation.

Proprietaries that had been closed down after Vietnam were reactivated, and old-time "cowboys" with experience in similar operations in the Caribbean and Southeast Asia were recruited for the undeclared war. Several were linked to Edwin Wilson, the rogue intelligence operative. Casey handpicked retired Air Force Maj. Gen. Richard V. Secord to serve as commercial "cut-out" despite the fact that he had left the service under an ethical cloud and the CIA had qualms about him. Secord denied having worked with Wilson, but he and his business partner, an Iranian named Albert H. Hakim, had been brought together by Wilson. Thomas Clines, an ex-CIA officer and another Wilson associate, hired the pilots and air crews for the secret supply missions. There were also reports—denied by the CIA—that the agency recruited drug smugglers for use in the contra air lift.

Nurtured by Casey, the ragtag band of poorly armed ex-Somoza guardsmen was transformed into a counterrevolutionary striking force of twenty thousand men equipped with automatic rifles, mortars, heavy-calibre machine guns, and light aircraft. But as the number of contras swelled, they proved correspondingly difficult to control. Persistent reports surfaced of atrocities, internal bickering, human rights abuses, corruption, drug smuggling, and military incompetence. Even after several years of CIA support, the contras were unable to achieve any lasting signs of success.

Within the CIA itself, there were strong reservations about Casey's enthusiastic support of covert operations. John N. McMahon, the deputy DCI, resigned in February 1986 after being on the losing side of repeated battles against the expansion of such activities. He was replaced by Robert Gates, who was expected to carry out orders. McMahon objected to CIA involvement in large-scale paramilitary operations because they provoked public criticism, inspired congressional attacks, and invited media exposure. But Casey's enthusiasm for the contra cause was unabated. Impatient with the constraints imposed by Congress and the bureaucracy—including the CIA bureaucracy—he concentrated control of the operations in his own hands and those of a few carefully chosen aides, especially Duane Clarridge, chief of the Latin American desk in the Directorate of Operations.

To a remarkable extent, this freewheeling "CIA within the CIA" harkened back forty years to the glory days of the OSS. "I'm convinced that our success [during World War II] can teach us something about how we can meet our global responsibilities today," Casey told a reunion of fellow OSS veterans. "With a relatively few skilled officers and a tiny fraction of our military budget, we can introduce new elements . . . into the Third World and check Third World Marxist-Leninist regimes that are stamping out democratic liberties and human rights and posing a threat to our own national security."

U.S. ambassadors and station chiefs in Costa Rica, Honduras, and El Salvador directly assisted the supply operation by telling the crews where to make the drops and how to avoid Sandinista defenses. CIA operatives directed a raid on oil storage tanks at the Pacific coast port of Corinto and produced a primer for waging guerrilla warfare that seemingly advocated political assassination. They also carried out the mining of Nicaraguan ports, in flagrant violation of international law. Edgar Chamorro, a former contra leader, later claimed he had been awakened at 2 A.M. the following morning by a CIA official who handed him a statement in which he was to take responsibility for the mining. Allied nations, among them Saudi Arabia and Israel, were persuaded to contribute cash and arms to the contras, and the assistance of South Africa was solicited. President Reagan personally participated in the fund raising; following a meeting between King Saud and the president, the Saudis agreed to double their million-dollar-a-month contribution. The total eventually exceeded thirty million.

Increasingly uncomfortable with the not-so-secret "secret war" and with Casey's management of it, Congress was further angered by the contrast between the limited aims expressed in the presidential findings presented to it and the CIA's open-ended activities. Even Senator Barry Goldwater, who chaired the Senate Intelligence Committee and was in sympathy with President Reagan's goals, questioned Casey's candor and truthfulness. Senator Daniel P. Moynihan, the committee's vice-chairman, charged that, rather than providing prior notice of "significant anticipated activities," as required by law, Casey did not mention the mining of Nicaraguan ports until five weeks after the event.

Congress finally rebelled and in October 1984 approved the first of a series of laws, known collectively as the Boland amendment,* that specifically barred the CIA, the Defense Department, "or any agency or entity of the United States involved in intelligence activity" from using its funds to support the contras. Although funding was restored in the summer of 1986, when Congress voted one hundred million dollars in military aid for the contras, in the intervening period legal support for the contras was limited to "humanitarian assistance," which was not to be administered by either the CIA or the Pentagon.

■ ■ ■

Anyone who thought these restrictions would force President Reagan to reduce or close down the secret war in Central America obviously had not reckoned with the depth of his commitment to the Nicaraguan rebels. "The President repeatedly made it clear in public and private that he did not intend to break faith with the contras," Robert McFarlane told congressional investigators. While Reagan lobbied Congress and the American people for the restoration of military assistance—insinuating that those who opposed aid to the contras were soft on communism— Casey prepared a cover for the CIA. Whereas the agency was required by law to report its activities to Congress, the National Security Council operated out of the White House basement, without oversight from any outside authority. Accordingly, active direction of the anti-Sandinista campaign was turned over to the NSC.

Marine Lt. Col. Oliver L. North, an NSC staffer, was Casey's surrogate. Casey designed the policy; North carried it out. Boyishly handsome, intense, and patriotic, North seemed to pop up wherever there was trouble. He helped plan the invasion of Grenada, the secret mining of Nicaraguan harbors, the bombing of Libya, and the seizure of the terrorists who had hijacked the liner *Achille Lauro*. Like President Reagan, North was obsessed with the contras. Until Congress revoked the Boland amendment, he funneled assistance to them and provided military advice. Working with Casey, he presided over a network of conservative fund raisers and ex-intelligence and military operatives that reached from the jungles of Central America to the discreet world of numbered Swiss bank accounts.

Later, the Presidential Review Board headed by former Senator John Tower of Texas faulted Casey for abdicating his responsibility to advise the president of the dangers of the "privatization" of American foreign policy and said he "should have pressed for operational responsibility to be transferred to the CIA." This is exactly what Casey was trying to avoid. In fact, he needed an activist NSC to circumvent the congressional restrictions on the CIA's own operations and to keep "command control"

---

*Named for its sponsor, Representative Edward P. Boland, a Massachusetts Democrat.

of the operation tightly in his own hands. Had Oliver North not existed, Casey would have had to invent him.

The fiction of outside financing of the contras collapsed early in November 1986. The tangled story began to unravel in Lebanon, where a Beirut magazine with links to the Iranian radicals disclosed that McFarlane, who had left the NSC at the end of the previous year, had made a secret visit to Teheran in May 1986 and that the United States had supplied Iran with military hardware in an effort to obtain the release of several Americans held captive in Lebanon by Shiite terrorists. President Reagan—who had repeatedly declared that he would never negotiate with terrorists and had condemned Iran as a member of an international "Murder, Inc."—was said to have authorized the mission and other dealings with the Iranians.

Reagan flatly claimed these reports had "no foundation" and charged that by publicizing them the U.S. media had damaged efforts to free the hostages. But two days before Thanksgiving, Attorney General Edwin Meese revealed that arms had indeed been shipped to Iran in an attempt to establish links with Iranian "moderates" and obtain the release of the hostages. Further, he disclosed that upwards of thirty million dollars in profits from the sale was missing and presumably had been siphoned off to the Nicaraguan rebels. In an effort to absolve the president, Meese asserted that only Vice-Admiral John M. Poindexter, McFarlane's successor, and Colonel North had been involved in the secret plan to divert funds to the contras and that the president knew nothing about it. In the wake of these disclosures, North was fired from the NSC and Poindexter resigned.

The Iran-contra affair quickly mushroomed into the biggest Washington scandal since Watergate and undermined confidence in President Reagan. Serious questions were raised about his truthfulness and competence, especially after he claimed to be unable to remember important details and insisted, appearances notwithstanding, that he hadn't traded arms for hostages. For most Americans, the key issue was neither the shipment of arms to Iran nor the diversion of funds to the contras in violation of the Boland amendment. Rather, it was the administration's deceitfulness in lying to its own people. The secret exchange of arms for hostages made a cynical mockery of Reagan's highly publicized policy of refusing to deal with terrorists. Washington's effort to counter world terrorism was left in shreds, and the president was exposed to ridicule.

Reagan supporters contended that the scandal originated with a pair of overzealous staff members who thought they were doing what the president wanted. In effect, Reagan was a befuddled bystander—a finding accepted by the Tower Commission—and the episode was merely part of an ongoing struggle between the White House and the Congress for control of American foreign policy. But testimony before a House-Senate investigating committee later revealed that the president was deeply involved in the Iran-contra operation. Forced out of his defensive pocket of claimed ignorance and forgetfulness, Reagan now insisted that the Boland amendment did not apply to him as president or to the National Security Council. "The NSC is not an intelligence operation," he maintained. "It's simply advisory to me."

■ ■ ■

Two congressional committees and a special prosecutor began delving into the affair, and over the next eight months the nation watched breathlessly as a lurid tale of covert operations, "shredding parties," secret Swiss bank accounts, and shady international arms dealings unfolded in the newspapers and on television screens. Oliver North and William Casey were at the center of the melodrama. Three decades apart in age, they were united in their dedication to the contras and in their frustration over congressional limitations on their range of action. To North, Casey was an imposing figure—wealthy, successful, and powerful—and he later told congressional investigators that the older man had been his mentor. North had established a private network to supply the contras under Casey's guidance, and when the Iran-contra link was threatened with exposure, Casey had masterminded the attempted cover-up by instructing him to destroy all the evidence.

Casey's own version of his role and that of the CIA in the episode was murky. "The NSC was operating this thing," he declared. "We were in a support mode." Testifying before the House Foreign Affairs Committee, he replied "I don't know" to so many questions that each such answer soon drew laughter from his questioners. But a long string of circumstances contradicted his claims to know little about the operation. Soon after this appearance, Casey, who had seemed tired and befuddled, was hospitalized with a cancerous brain tumor. In February 1987, he was replaced by his deputy, Robert Gates. Three months later he died, taking to the grave the secret of his exact role in the Iran-contra affair.

Gates was the first intelligence professional to be named DCI since William Colby, and the first to come up through the analytical rather than the clandestine side of the agency. But his nomination lasted exactly twenty-nine days. When questions about Gates's own involvement in the Iran arms deal clouded his confirmation hearings before the Senate Intelligence Committee, he asked that his name be withdrawn. FBI Director William H. Webster, who had helped restore the bureau's tarnished reputation in the wake of Watergate, was named in his place, while Gates remained deputy director.

Casey's death made him a convenient scapegoat, but the entire operation was consistent with his methods. "You do not have to see each grain of sand to recognize a beach," observed Senator Daniel K. Inouye, chairman of the Senate Select Committee. But the escapade involved a much larger cast of characters than just the DCI and his sidekick.

The plight of one of the hostages in Lebanon, William Buckley, had created a special sense of urgency at Langley. Identified as a political officer in the U.S. embassy in Beirut at the time of his capture in March 1984, Buckley was actually the CIA station chief and possessed full knowledge of the agency's underground network in the Middle East. The CIA launched its own efforts to find Buckley, vainly spending at least half a million dollars on informers.

In fact, the possibility of ransoming the hostages had been first raised by others, including an old CIA hand, Theodore Shackley,* one-time deputy chief of the Directorate of Operations. In November 1984, he reported having been approached with a proposal to exchange arms for the hostages by Manucher Ghorbanifar, an Iranian wheeler-dealer who claimed to have contacts with the leaders of revolutionary Iran. U.S. officials, who regarded Ghorbanifar as a "crook," brushed off the proposal. Buckley died after a period of torture and medical neglect, and senior CIA officials are said to have wept when they learned the details of his painful and prolonged torment.

The Iranian initiative was then forgotten until the spring of 1985, when, according to congressional investigators' reconstruction of the affair, the Israelis suggested an arms-for-hostages trade. Israeli officials later acknowledged that Adnan Khashoggi, a Saudi arms dealer, had arranged a meeting between Ghorbanifar and two of Khashoggi's associates, Israeli arms dealers Adolph Schwimmer and Yaacov Nimrodi. Ghorbanifar told them that "moderate" elements in Iran wanted to buy arms and make an opening to the West.

The arrangement offered something for everyone. Iran was engaged in a bloody four-year war with Iraq and was in desperate need of arms and spare parts for the American weapons that had originally been purchased by the shah. The Israelis, who had surreptitiously supplied the Iranians with this equipment until Washington had declared an embargo, sought an advantage by helping Iran against Iraq. The United States wanted its hostages back. And the arms dealers stood to make millions by brokering the sales.

On July 3, 1985, David Kimche, the director general of the Israeli foreign ministry and former No. 2 man in the Mossad, told McFarlane that Israel had succeeded in establishing a dialogue with Iran. Iranian officials, reportedly concerned about growing pressure from the Soviet Union, were interested in opening political talks with the Americans and promised to use their influence to obtain the release of the hostages in

---

*Like General Secord, Albert Hakim, and Thomas Clines, Shackley had been linked to Ed Wilson. Some observers believe the relationship had blighted his career.

exchange for a shipment of U.S.-made TOW antitank missiles. U.S. officials, especially the president, were receptive to the Israeli sales pitch. Just the day before, Reagan had attended a wrenching ceremony at Arlington Cemetery, where he laid a wreath on the grave of an American sailor named Robert D. Strethem, who had been murdered by the hijackers of a TWA airliner.

Under Casey's guidance, CIA staffers worked up fresh analyses that held that the Khomeini regime was weakening and the Iraquis were winning the war—although other agency sources challenged this finding.* Both Secretary of State Shultz and Caspar W. Weinberger, the secretary of defense, objected to the assessment, with Weinberger penciling "This is almost too absurd to comment on" across one of the papers. Shultz warned that Israel's agenda concerning Iran "is not the same as ours" and condemned the proposal as "perverse" and "contrary to our own interests."

Lacking assets of its own in Iran, the CIA was unable to verify Ghorbanifar's claims and relied primarily on Israel. But the Israelis later acknowledged that their own intelligence was based almost entirely on information supplied by Ghorbanifar, who had earlier been judged unreliable by the CIA. Nevertheless, President Reagan, persuaded that a shipment of arms would show "good faith" and bring about the release of the hostages, gave the Israelis the green light to proceed. With Ghorbanifar and the Israelis serving as middlemen, a shipment of TOW missiles was delivered to Iran in August and September. To the disappointment of the White House, which had expected all five hostages to be released, only one was freed.

Several other shipments of missiles and spare parts were made—at least one, in November 1985, with the cooperation of the CIA. Upon learning that the shipment, carried by Southern Air Transport and described as oil drilling equipment, had contained arms, John McMahon, then Casey's deputy, told colleagues that the agency's action was illegal because there was no written authorization from the president to deliver such a cargo. To blunt these objections, Casey asked the president to issue a finding retroactively, bringing the agency's actions within the law. In the meantime, the Iranians had rejected the weapons on the grounds that they not only were obsolete but had Israeli markings. No hostages were released.

In December 1985, the disappointed president and his national

*Over the years, the CIA had conducted several covert operations designed both to curry favor with Iran and to support anti-Khomeini exiles. In 1983, it provided a list of Soviet KGB agents and collaborators to the regime, which promptly executed as many as two hundred suspects and banned the communist Tudeh party. The Ayatollah publically thanked God for the "miracle" that led to the arrests. At the same time, the agency provided six million dollars to the Iranian exile movement to finance an anti-Khomeini radio station beamed at Iran from Egypt.

security team decided to call off arms sales to Iran. Only one hostage had been released, and they distrusted Ghorbanifar, who had failed a CIA polygraph test.* Besides, both Shultz and Weinberger still opposed the operation. But on January 7, 1986, the president called his aides together for renewed discussion of the Iranian initiative, and Shultz observed that it was obvious that he was leaning toward resuming the arms shipments. "What's wrong with shipping arms?" the president asked. Casey, who brushed off Ghorbanifar's failure to pass the polygraph test administered by his own agency, enthusiastically supported the plan.

Ten days later, Reagan signed a formal finding ordering the resumption of arms sales to Iran, this time directly from U.S. arms stocks. CIA lawyers had assured him that "under an appropriate finding, you could authorize the CIA to sell arms to countries outside the provisions of the laws and reporting requirements for foreign military sales." Casey was directed to conceal this finding from the congressional oversight committees, however, because of the "extreme sensitivity" of the matter. Although Shultz and Weinberger were fully aware of what was going on, they asked no questions and were cut out of the loop.

Reagan's obsession about the hostages was the likely reason for the switch in policy. The anguish of the hostages' families weighed heavily on the president during the Christmas season, and there is evidence that he hoped to obtain the captives' release in time for his State of the Union address in 1986. According to a memorandum prepared by Admiral Poindexter, who had succeeded McFarlane as national security adviser, there was also another nudge from the Israelis, who feared Iran's position in the war with Iraq was deteriorating.

With the private arms dealers out of the picture, the CIA assumed the key role in the transaction. The agency purchased the weapons from the Pentagon for twelve million dollars, an amount considerably less than they were worth on the world market, and was responsible for flying them to Israel for transshipment to Iran. Since the CIA would have needed congressional authorization to spend funds on the deal, Casey "privatized" the operation by bringing in Secord to establish a dummy corporation to serve as a cover for the agency. Under this arrangement, Secord's "enterprise" substituted for the Israelis and made the sale to Iran. When the Iranians refused to pay in advance, Adnan Khashoggi, who had originally brought Ghorbanifar and the Israelis together, lined up several associates to put up about thirty million dollars as a bridge loan.

Once the Pentagon had received its $12 million, the remaining $18 million of the money paid by the Iranians disappeared into a Swiss bank account controlled by Secord, Albert Hakim, and Colonel North. North

*One intelligence official joked that the Iranian lied about almost everything but his name.

credited Ghorbanifar with first suggesting that these profits be diverted to the contras. North immmediately agreed that it was "a neat deal" to have the Iranians finance the Nicaraguan rebels, and, according to North, Casey gleefully accepted the suggestion. But only $3.5 million of the profits generated by the arms sales ever reached the contras, while $8 million still remained in the Swiss account at the time the operation was blown. North soon made the reason for holding the "residuals" clear. He testified that the funds gave Casey the idea for an audacious plan to establish an off-the-books entity to carry out cloak-and-dagger operations on a global basis free of congressional restrictions.

The Iranians were old hands in deviousness, however. Angry at the inflated prices they were charged for the arms—which had been marked up 400 percent—they repeatedly dangled the imminent release of the hostages before the Americans, only to withdraw the bait. With Ghorbanifar's credibility eroded by the repeated failure to arrange the release of all the hostages, North, Secord, and Albert Hakim initiated contact with another go-between, a nephew of Hashemi Rafsanjani, Iran's No. 2 man. Making foreign policy on the spot, they assured the Iranians that the United States would go to war with the Soviet Union if the Russians invaded Iran and claimed Washington would seek an end to the Iran-Iraq war on terms favorable to Iran. In exchange for five hundred TOW missiles, the Iranians promised freedom for all the hostages, but again only one captive was released.

By then, the operation was unraveling. Ghorbanifar, angry over being squeezed out of the negotiations—and the profits—was threatening to blow the whistle. Some of the wheeler-dealers who had invested with Khashoggi in the project were talking about filing suit for their money in an obvious attempt to blackmail the U.S. government. On November 2, 1986, the Beirut magazine appeared with its story of McFarlane's unsuccessful mission to Teheran, and the ill-conceived and badly botched arms-for-hostage exchange lay exposed to public scrutiny.

In all, three Americans were released, but another three were kidnapped—leaving Iran with more than two thousand missiles and other weaponry, while the extremists held the same number of captives they had had in the first place. Unprepared for the bazaar mentality of the Iranians, American officials had been utterly bamboozled. "Our guys got taken to the cleaners," observed George Shultz. Each new proof of Iranian unreliability had been met with greater gullibility and more missiles and spare parts. The picture that emerged was one of greed, duplicity, and incompetence—and of an American policy largely out of control.

■ ■ ■

"Colonel North, will you please rise? Raise your right hand," intoned Senator Inouye, as the House-Senate investigation of the Iran-contra affair finally went public on a steamy morning early in July 1987. A hush fell over the cavernous Senate Caucus Room as Oliver North, ramrod-straight in his bemedalled Marine uniform, assumed center stage in what was to become the most compelling political melodrama since Richard M. Nixon had been forced to resign the presidency thirteen years before. Although the hearing room had been the scene of some of the most memorable events in the nation's history—Teapot Dome, the Army-McCarthy hearings, Watergate—North's bravura performance rivaled all that had gone before.

"I came here to tell you the truth—the good, the bad and the ugly," North declared, and the nation was immediately transfixed by his story. Over the next six days, alternately eloquent, aggressive, and abrasive, he related a bizarre tale of secret operations, "shredding parties," Swiss bank accounts, shady arms deals, "plausible denial," and untraceable corporations.

"A covert operation, is, in its nature, a lie," North coolly declared, establishing his version of the credo of the covert operator. He raised lying to the level of policy. Lying to the Congress, lying to cabinet members, lying to the American people—all were justified by the necessity to avoid betraying operational security. If memos were sent up to the president and no answer came back, it was because plausible denial had to be maintained. In essence, North's testimony came down to the conviction that the administration had sound reasons and high motives for its actions. Faced with such sensitive circumstances, it was permissible to ignore inconvenient laws. The president was a surer, tougher, truer champion of democracy than a vacillating Congress.

One of the more startling elements of North's testimony concerned William Casey's alleged intention to establish an "off-the-shelf, self-sustaining, stand-alone entity" free of control by Congress and the intelligence bureaucracy to carry out operations that the intelligence community would not or could not undertake. The investigating committee was taken aback by this plan to establish a throwback to the OSS, but in point of fact, it already existed in the form of the "enterprise" organized by Casey to supply the contras and conduct other operations. Within two years of its founding, the "enterprise" had at its disposal a fleet of planes, air fields, ships, warehouses full of arms, secret bank accounts, and a network of businesses that extended around the globe.

In the end, the investigators found no "smoking gun" that linked President Reagan to the diversion of funds to the contras in violation of the Boland amendment. North's testimony had seemed to draw the net about him. "I have never carried out a single act, not one, in which I did not have authority from my superiors," he told the committee. But Poindexter, who exhibited a surprisingly weak memory in other matters, took the president off the hook. He authorized the diversions himself, he said, because he thought it was what Reagan wanted—but he had not told the president, so as to preserve "plausible deniability." Reagan claimed to have been vindicated, although many Americans did not believe this version of events.

Brushing up against a self-imposed deadline and wishing to avoid a constitutional confrontation with the president, the committee left the conflicting testimony and numerous unanswered questions to be resolved by the special prosecutor who was looking into the affair. On March 16, 1988, North, Poindexter, Secord, Hakim and Joseph F. Fernandez, CIA station chief in Costa Rica, were indicted on charges of lying to Congress, violation of the Boland amendment, and appropriation of government funds.

Whatever the final outcome, several points were clear. President Reagan condoned the creation of a private network outside the government to carry out a secret foreign policy. Initiatives were conducted by men of questionable background who made promises that were contrary to formal American policy. Ranking officials repeatedly lied to Congress and the American people about the extent of the administration's efforts in behalf of the contras. Deals were cut with disreputable middlemen to trade arms for hostages, and the U.S. government had been reduced to begging allies for alms and arms.

To a remarkable extent, the Iran-contra affair was the Bay of Pigs revisited. There were the same cloak-and-dagger operators, the same anticommunist crusaders, the same foolish bravado of attempting to accomplish in secret what Washington was unwilling to risk in public, the same misguided belief that the operational hand of the United States could be hidden, and the same failure to appreciate the consequences of exposure. Reagan's supporters defended the initiative with the argument that although the means may have been badly flawed, the release of the hostages and the survival of the Nicaraguan resistance justified it. The president's only fault, they maintained, was to bend an imperfectly worded law to secretly execute a policy too sophisticated to be grasped by the American people.

But that blames democracy for the shortcomings of its leaders. In the final analysis, the Iran-contra scandal was the logical result of a disdain for the sometimes cumbersome processes of democratic government—a disdain bred over decades by the easy, all-too-frequent resort to the quick fix of covert operations. The secret apparatus lay readily at hand, and the temptation to make use of it proved irresistible. Yet it is axiomatic that in a democratic society, secret policies can be successful only when they follow the same agenda as public policy. Representative Lee H. Hamilton, chairman of the House investigating committee, put it best. "Our government cannot function cloaked in secrecy," he declared." "It cannot function unless officials tell the truth. The Constitution only works when [all] branches of government trust one another and cooperate."

Epilogue

Aldrich H. Ames pulled away from his home in an upscale bedroom suburb of Alexandria, Virginia in a $50,000 wine-red Jaguar XJ6 and headed toward CIA headquarters at nearby Langley on the morning of February 21, 1994. It was President's Day—a federal holiday—so the Operations Directorate veteran had planned to remain at home to finish packing for a trip to Moscow to begin the next day. With the Cold War over, Ames was to meet with Russian intelligence to discuss joint efforts to combat narcotics trafficking in the Black Sea area. Unexpectedly, the office had telephoned asking him to come in for a discussion of some last-minute details. As he left home, he told his Colombian-born wife, Maria del Rosario Casas Ames, he would be back soon.

Ames loved the Jaguar—it was his third—and took pleasure in the car's velvety surge of power as it eased down the quiet street. Not far from home, he found the intersection blocked by a pair of vehicles, one with a right-turn signal blinking, the other apparently turning left. But neither vehicle moved. Two more cars with flashing red lights suddenly appeared in the Jaguar's, rear-view mirror, completely boxing it in. The moment Ames had been dreading for nine years, that he had feared in the small hours of the night, had finally arrived.

"You're under arrest for violating U.S. espionage statutes," an FBI agent told Ames as he was ordered out of his car. He was handcuffed and placed in the back of an FBI vehicle. The telephone call was a stratagem to get him out of the house so he could not destroy evidence. Within minutes, Rosario Ames was arrested for aiding and abetting her husband's operations.

Ames settled into the car, apparently resigned to his fate. There were no protests, no sign of fear of what may lie ahead. Instead, he hunched low in the seat, saying to himself over and over like a mantra: "Think. Think. Think."

In his nine years of spying for the Soviet KGB and its successor, the Russian SVR—part of it as head of counterintelligence in the Soviet/East

440

European [SE] Division[1]—Rick Ames had all but backed up a van to CIA headquarters and carted away its secrets. He betrayed at least eleven CIA/FBI agents in the Soviet Union, ten of whom were eventually executed. They included Dimitri Fedorovich Polyakov—codename Top Hat—the most valuable single Soviet source ever recruited by American intelligence, and Adolf G. Tolkachev, the defense researcher originally thought to have been fingered by Edward L. Howard, the rogue CIA trainee.[2] The most important asset recruited by British intelligence within the KGB only narrowly escaped capture and certain death because of Ames. Scores of agents were compromised, a hundred operations were blown and thousands of pages of top secret documents were passed to the Russians.

"Ames was without a doubt the most valuable asset the Soviets or the Russians have ever had in Western intelligence," according to one senior intelligence officer. In exchange for $2.7 million and the promise of $1.9 million more, he destroyed the CIA's entire intelligence-gathering capability in the Soviet Union, leaving it blind at a time when Communism was collapsing and democracy was struggling to find its feet. Significant CIA and NSA technical operations were also compromised, including those aimed at intercepting Soviet and Russian communications.

In the hierarchy of awful things that can happen to an intelligence agency, the discovery of a traitor in its midst is bad, the discovery that he has been operating for years is worse, and worst of all, is the discovery that the culprit was obvious all along. In retrospect, it is clear that catching Ames should have been a routine exercise once the agency's network of assets in the Soviet Union were rolled up in one fell swoop. For much of the following decade, however, the CIA refused to acknowledge that Ames was the mole, even though he matched every test for identifying a potential defector. He all but wore a T-shirt to work proclaiming "It's me! I'm the mole!"

A shy and bookish man, the son of a former CIA officer with a drinking problem, Ames was, after thirty-one years of service, far from the agency's inner circle. He held a mid-level job equivalent to a GS-14 in the Civil Service or a lieutenant colonel in the military and earned about $70,000 annually. He was "not going anywhere and no one cared," in the words of a later CIA Inspector General's report and was ranked 197th of 200 officers in his grade. Embittered by the fact that his career had stalled, and a borderline alcoholic, Ames often took six-vodka lunches and returned too drunk to work. Bumbling about like Mr. Magoo, he misplaced top-secret documents, missed appointments with contacts and was caught using a safe house for an assignation. Ames also complained to colleagues

[1]Now the Central Eurasian, or CE Division.

[2]Tolkachev was arrested on June 13, 1985, the same day Ames turned his name over to the KGB. The date is thought to be coincidental because no bureaucracy moves so quickly. It is assumed he was taken into custody on the basis of information supplied earlier by Howard. Ames confirmed his role as a CIA informant which sealed his fate. Wise, *Nightmover*, pp. 123–124.

about the financial drain of a costly divorce and was about to marry Rosario, who had expensive tastes and no more money than he.

Yet despite this uninspiring record, Ames was assigned as chief of the Soviet counterintelligence office, one of the CIA's most sensitive posts. Part of his job was to routinely meet with Soviet Embassy officials to assess them as potential assets and he used it to cover a plan to obtain money from the Russians. On April 18, 1985, following a liquid lunch, he simply walked into the Soviet Embassy and handed a duty officer a sealed envelope. In it were the names of two KGB officers who secretly worked for the CIA, a page torn from an agency directory with his own name highlighted in yellow marker and a request for $50,000.

Soon, he was raking in such huge sums from the Soviets—usually stingy with money for their informants—that he purchased a new home for $540,000 in cash, spent $100,000 on home improvements, drove a new Jaguar,[3] charged $30,000-a-month on credit cards and bought a farm and a seaside condominium in Colombia. He had his bad teeth capped and wore thousand-dollar Armani suits. Following Rosario's arrest, the FBI found 500 pairs of shoes and 165 unopened packages of panty hose in her closet. When questioned about his new-found wealth, Ames would talk vaguely about his wife's family money. A cursory check would have revealed that although they were well-connected in Colombia, they were not rich.

Yet Ames failed to attract scrutiny because of gross ineptitude and bureaucratic bumbling in the Directorate of Operations. Not only did he have unlimited access to CIA computers and everything the CIA knew about the Soviet Union, but he was placed on a promotion board where he learned the identities and duties of hundreds of other CIA officers around the world. In 1985, he was one of the debriefers assigned to Vitaly Yurchenko, and reported everything the KGB defector told the Americans to his handlers. Ames made a joke of the agency's vaunted "compartmentation" that is designed to limit the spread of information by picking up tid-bits of information while schmoozing with other officers during smoking breaks outside the building. He banked on the CIA being too stupid to catch him.

Had not Ames's activities had such tragic results, they would have had a sense of broad farce about them. To signal the Russians, he was to make a white chalk mark on a certain Washington mailbox Once, when he forgot the chalk, he ran into a nearby store, bought the nearest thing available— a white crayon—and used that instead. It took his Russian contact a half-hour to erase the signal. "Do not repeat," the Russian angrily upbraided Ames.

Curiously, the CIA did not give high priority to searching for the cause

[3]William Webster, Casey's successor as DCI, said the Jaguar was not in itself a tip-off that Ames was a potential mole because a number of people in the CIA had family money and drove expensive cars. Webster's own driver had a Corvette sports car with "double-oh-seven" license plates.

of the hemorrhaging of all its assets in the Soviet Union. Instead of turning the agency upside down to root out the traitor, the Operations Directorate waited a full year before assigning a Special Task Force to the case—and it consisted of four people, two of them retirees.[4] The DO preferred to believe the leaks resulted from a KGB penetration of CIA communications rather than a mole. Then, it tried to link the compromised cases to Ed Howard's treachery and the Marine guard scandal in Moscow. Finally, the roll-up was blamed on "poor tradecraft" by those who were caught. As this was going on, Ames was strolling out of CIA headquarters with shopping bags stuffed with secrets. No one even bothered to search him.

Several reasons have been advanced for the CIA's unwillingness to face the reality that it harbored a mole and his name was Aldrich Ames. The agency was wary of repeating the "great mole hunt" conducted by James Jesus Angleton thirty years before that had destroyed so many careers without uncovering a single spy. The "old-boy" culture prevailing in the Operations Directorate refused to accept the fact that one of its own, a member of the club, even such a lackluster one as Ames, could be a traitor.

There was also continued reluctance by the CIA to turn over its dirty laundry to its old "enemy", the FBI, despite a Memorandum of Understanding signed in 1988 by William Webster and William S. Sessions, his successor as FBI director. Designed to prevent a repetition of the Howard debacle, the agreement called for the CIA to notify the FBI if it had "reasonable belief" that a former or current employee was considering espionage or defecting to another country.

But the real reason the CIA was lax in launching a full court press in search of the mole was that *it was afraid it might actually find him*. If so, the agency would be exposed to humiliating ridicule while it was in trouble for Iran-contra and other missteps. Thus, there was a reluctance to disturb this particular sleeping dog. Over the years, even the limited effort to find the mole tapered off and the officers assigned to the Task Force were diverted to other matters. The secret was closely held by the Operations Directorate—and both Webster and Robert Gates, who succeeded him as DCI in 1991,[5] later claimed they were not told about the depth of the penetration or the magnitude of the losses. The Senate and House intelligence committees, which have the responsibility of monitoring the CIA, were also left in the dark about the rape of the agency.

In November 1989, the finger was finally pointed at Ames. Diana Worthen, who had previously worked with him, became suspicious of his

---

[4] When the Russians suggested Ames provide them with name of someone in the SE who could be fingered as the mole to draw suspicion away from himself, Ames gave them the name of Jeanne Vertefeuille, the female officer heading the Task Force.

[5] Senate Intelligence Committee hearings on Gates's nomination to be DCI were particularly stormy, with several former CIA analysts charging he had "politicized" their reports to conform with the Reagan and Bush administrations's goals. Gates vigorously denied the allegations.

free-spending habits, and having connected it to the disappearance of the CIA's spies, notified the agency's Office of Security that Ames was living far beyond his means. But the OS lived up to its reputation within the agency as a bunch of Keystone Kops and only a cursory check was made before attention was diverted elsewhere.[6] Not until the spring of 1991, more than five years after the CIA starting loosing its agents, did it tell the FBI there had been "a major penetration within the agency." Apparently, a East European source had tipped off the Americans that Ames had sold-out. In the meantime, bungling by the Office of Security allowed him to slip through a routine polygraph test even though he then was on the short list of suspected moles.

Finally, in March 1993, FBI counterintelligence launched a full-scale inquiry into Ames's activities. Dipping into its files of photographs of people going into the Soviet Embassy, it discovered several of Ames on occasions he had not reported to his superiors. Later it was determined these visits were followed by large deposits in Ames's bank account. Ames was placed under around-the-clock surveillance, his home and office were searched and bugged, papers, and typewriter and computer printer ribbons were retrieved from his trash and his personal computer was tapped. The investigators broke into his system for contacting his Russian handlers, and determined the location of the drops where messages, instructions and money were exchanged. Wiretaps of Ames's conversations with his wife also confirmed that Rosario was an eager participant in his espionage activities. Without alarming Ames, he was transferred to a less sensitive job in the CIA's new Counternarcotics Center.

With Ames scheduled to go to Moscow—and the possibility that he might choose to defect there—the FBI decided to close the case by arresting him on February 21, 1994. Ames pleaded guilty to conspiracy to commit espionage and tax fraud but showed no remorse for the men whose deaths he had caused. He was sentenced to life in prison without possibility of parole, and in exchange for his promise to cooperate, Rosario got off with five years. The red Jaguar, the house, the bank accounts for which Ames had betrayed his country, his agency, and his colleagues, were all seized by the government.

The CIA's internal assessment of the case, based on questions put to the imprisoned Ames, swiftly revealed that as suspected he had been the best source the Russians had ever had inside American intelligence. "It's like turning over rocks," said one debriefer. "Each rock has more and more crap under it."

Rick Ames had by no means ended his efforts to damage the CIA, how-

---

[6]There is a almost a pleading tone in a memo sent to the OS by the Counterintelligence Center on December 5, 1990 in which it action is sought on the reports of free spending by Ames. "Since Ames has been assigned to CIC, his access has been limited to a degree. Unfortunately, we are quickly running out of things for him to do without granting him greater access."

ever. Having already done it irreparable harm, he now heaved a custard pie in its face from behind bars. Masking his greed in a higher philosophy, he claimed in a statement to the court and in later interviews with the media, that spying was essentially an expensive game between intelligence agencies that achieved little of value and should be scrapped. "These spy wars are a sideshow, which have had no real impact on our significant security interests over the years," Ames declared.

This was a theme eagerly taken up by the CIA's critics who regarded it as a creaky and expensive relic of the Cold War. With the Soviet threat gone, it was facing a midlife crisis and desperately casting about for ways to justify its $3.1 billion budget and nearly 20,000 employees.[7] Morale was at the lowest point in the agency's history, gifted younger officers dissatisfied with the agency's loss of direction were leaving, and many of those who remained were deeply embittered. Something had to be done about the in-bred, isolated culture of the clandestine service which had permitted Ames to escape detection.

Unhappily, other traitors turned up in the wake of the Ames case. In November 1996, Harold J. Nicholson, a branch chief in the CIA's counterterrorism center, was arrested on charges of having sold out to the Russians for at least $120,000. Unlike Ames, whose career was going nowhere, Nicholson was considered an exemplary officer and his last assignment was as a training officer at CIA headquarters. The classified material that he allegedly gave the Russians included personal data on many if not all the young CIA officers he helped train for clandestine work overseas which compromised their identity.

The FBI also suffered embarrassment when it was disclosed less than a month later that Earl E. Pitts, a veteran FBI counterintelligence officer, had betrayed some of the bureau's most sensitive operations. Pitts, it was charged, had sold information on how the United States tried to protect itself from the operations of other nations for $224,000. "It's a worse-case scenario for us because he knew out operation," said a counterintelligence officer familiar with Pitt's work. "He is exactly the kind of guy that would be valuable to the Russians."

Paradoxically, the Ames case revealed that the CIA had been doing something right. Through skill or luck, the agency had successfully recruited a surprising number of ranking KGB officers and had handled these assets well—until Ames destroyed them. Had the Ames case been atypical, the agency might well have been able to ride out the storm more

---

[7]By mistake, in late 1994, a congressional budget committee published a breakdown of the estimated $28 billion allocated for the entire intelligence community which is normally hidden in the Pentagon's budget. The CIA asked for $3.1 billion; the Pentagon intelligence agencies—the National Security Agency, the National Reconnaissance Office, and the Defense Intelligence Agency—sought $13.2 billion. The Army, Navy, Air Force and Marines requested $10.4 billion for tactical intelligence. New York *Times,* November 5, 1994.

or less unscathed. But it was only the latest of a string of alleged failures that created demands from congress and the public for reform.

The CIA was under fire for being slow to anticipate the collapse of the Soviet Union,[8] and to anticipate the Iraqi invasion of Kuwait as well as the effectiveness of Iraq's secret nuclear development program. A plot to depose Saddam Hussein, the Iraqui leader, misfired at a cost of $100 million. A network of American agents was uncovered and arrested in Egypt. Efforts at economic espionage in France ended in comic opera farce.[9] Virtually all the East German and Cuban assets recruited by the agency over a decade were found to be double agents. American policy in Guatemala was subverted as the agency kept funds flowing to military officers involved in the murder of a U.S. citizen. Intelligence on armed gangs operating in Somalia at the time of the American intervention was inadequate. Networks in Iran and Ghana were rolled-up. Cover-ups, corruption and widespread sexual discrimination against female employees plagued the agency.

This litany of operational and analytical lapses was uncomfortably long, yet the list of senior officers held accountable is extremely short. R. James Woolsey, the Washington attorney and insider who had been named DCI by President Bill Clinton in 1993, merely reprimanded eleven of the twenty-three present and former senior CIA officers who were cited in a report by CIA Inspector General Frederick P. Hitz for neglect and ignoring the signs pointing to Ames as a mole. No one was demoted or dismissed. In contrast, the FBI agents blamed for allowing Ed Howard to flee the country, had been fired.

The firestorm that resulted from Woolsey's failure to discipline those responsible eventually forced his resignation and he was replaced early in 1995 by John M. Deutch, a former deputy Defense Secretary, The new DCI—third in five years—pledged to shakeup the CIA and sweep away the "old boys" who had protected Ames and cultivated a culture of unaccountability. Foremost among Deutch's promised changes was to shift intelligence priorities to gathering information for the U.S. military, and to combat international criminals, terrorists and narcotics traffickers.

[8]The CIA maintains, however, that it did not fail to forecast the Soviet collapse. See Berkowitz and Richelson, "The CIA Vindicated," *The National Interest,* Fall 1995.

[9]In 1993, the then DCI, R. James Woolsey publicly announced that gathering economic intelligence would be a major new priority for the CIA. This entailed spying on such allies as Japan, Germany and France. The French, had been particularly aggressive in spying on American executives, including bugging hotel rooms and stealing documents. The CIA's Paris station soon had five operatives at work—four officers posing as diplomats and a woman posing as the representative of an American foundation—trying to uncover French positions on world trade talks and to counter French espionage against U.S. companies. The woman began an affair with a French official and either through sloppy work or pillow talk, she revealed that she was an American spy. The operation quickly unraveled and the French gleefully expelled the accused spies, much to the embarrassment of the United States. The incident raised questions about whether spying for economic secrets is a worthy pursuit for the CIA, or should it confine its efforts to the activities of terrorists and stealing state secrets. New York *Times,* March 13, 1996.

Numerous proposals designed to increase the efficiency and accountability of the intelligence community were thrown on the table. Solutions ranged from incremental tinkering to complete abolition of the agency as advocated by Senator Daniel Patrick Moynihan, one-time vice chairman of the Senate Intelligence Committee. Steps were taken to tighten CIA security procedures—an action that had been urged for years. In an unprecedented move, Clinton, who had previously shown little interest in intelligence, ordered that the chief of the CIA's Counterintelligence Center be an FBI agent. The House and Senate intelligence committees produced their own ideas for change. Assorted think tanks peddled their versions of reform. And an Ames-shocked Congress directed the president to appoint a special commission to rethink the roles of the intelligence services, the CIA in particular.

As the United States struggles to deal with post-Cold War challenges to its security—regional, ethnic, and religious conflicts; the potential spread of nuclear, biological and chemical weapons to such rogue regimes as North Korea, Iran, Iraq and Libya; terrorism, and organized crime—most everyone agrees that the nation needs an efficient intelligence service. At the same time, it is agreed that the CIA, created primarily to monitor the Soviet Union, is too big, too bloated, and too bureaucratized to function effectively in a world in which its main target no longer exists.

The consensus proposals for fixing the CIA and making American intelligence more efficient, include "downsizing" the agency, by cutting staff by roughly 25 per cent over the next few years. Some officials believe it should be more like Britain's MI6, which is smaller and more elite. Paramilitary operations and scientific and technological research should be spun off to the Pentagon. Propaganda should be devolved to the U.S. Information Service or to private foundations similar to those used by West German political parties to aid democratic forces during the Cold War. Services and structures that are duplicated and triplicated within the thirteen U.S. intelligence agencies should be consolidated and streamlined. For example, the CIA has some 1,500 analysts and the Pentagon intelligence agencies have another 13,000 analysts.

Missions should be more focused and the agency should choose its priorities rather than tying to do everything everywhere. Inspired by the seemingly endless shopping list of intelligence data sought by policymakers, the CIA prided itself on being a global intelligence service with stations or bases in virtually every country. This is a luxury it can no longer afford. In Africa, for example, the agency is reducing its presence there from twenty-four stations to twelve. Increasingly, it is asking the basic question: What secrets do we really need to steal in Gabon, or Uruguay or Denmark?

Particular attention has been focused on the role of the Director of Intelligence who currently runs the CIA and serves as chairman of the board of all the nation's intelligence agencies. Suggestions have been made that he be placed in charge of the entire intelligence community and serve as the president's chief intelligence adviser, while the day-to-day job of running the CIA should be given to a deputy who would be on the same level as the FBI director who is to serve for a fixed six-year term to insulate the job from changes in the White House. The concentration of both positions in one person has, it is said, allowed presidents to secretly conduct foreign policy independent of the State Department and congressional consultation.

Moreover, there needs to be more stability in the DCI's office. President Clinton appointed Anthony Lake to the post at the beginning of his second term but he withdrew his name from consideration after questions were raised about his management of the National Security Council. With the appointment of George T. Tenet, who had been Deutch's deputy, five men will have held the post of DCI in six years. Because of the turnover, Senator Moynihan observed that the CIA is approaching "institutional collapse."

Past experience with the intelligence community makes it clear, however, that such attempts at bureaucratic reshuffling and organizational fine-tuning will be ineffective. No matter what flow charts are drawn or legal restrictions imposed, presidents will continue to be frustrated by the restraints upon their conduct of foreign policy and are likely to seek independent means for swift action. If the White House is determined to follow a certain course, someone with a "can-do" attitude will be found to carry it out. The counterparts of George Mathews and Oliver North are always waiting in the wings.

In these situations, good judgment and common sense rather than unquestioning obedience to orders or loyalty to the agency must be the bottom line. Policymakers—the ultimate consumers of intelligence—should ask themselves a series of basic questions whenever they contemplate such activities. Given the propensity for leaks in Washington and the aggressiveness of the media in ferreting out secrets, the obvious question is what will happen if—or, more than likely, when—the operation becomes public. Will it have the support of the American people? Does it contradict open American policy? What is the nature of those who are to receive secret American assistance? Had anyone in authority taken the time to ask these questions about the reckless decision to trade arms for American hostages in the Middle East, the Iran-contra affair could hardly have happened.

Thus, it behooves us to learn from our past. The performance of American intelligence over the course of its history has been uneven. While it pioneered in technical means of collection, it has lagged in analysis. It has been excellent at obtaining facts, but less accomplished in placing them in context, in sensing trends, assessing situations, and warning of future contingencies. Sometimes, as in the case of Vietnam, when the CIA went against the grain and argued, correctly, that the United States could not win—the policymakers did not want to hear the truth. In summary, the problem is not merely acquiring intelligence but making proper use of it.

No panaceas, no new laws, no promises of reform, no sudden breakthroughs in technology will provide better intelligence. Prosaic measures provide the best hope for genuine improvement: recruitment of promising individuals, systematic training, a constant search for improved collection and analysis, an upgrading of the quality and independence of senior staff. Moral courage is required for intelligence officials to tell presidents that their policies, which often reflect the domestic imperatives of politics, cannot be implemented because they are poorly designed or because circumstances have changed.

For their part, consumers must learn to maintain composure in the face of alarming intelligence. Too often, such findings have created panic and led to misguided action for action's sake. Policymakers can use intelligence well only if they keep an open mind about intelligence assessments, established policies, the identification of friends and foes, and definitions of national interest. They must have a realistic understanding not only of what intelligence can accomplish but also its limitations. Intelligence can only be as good as those charged with the ultimate use of it.

Furthermore, there must be accountability. The basic question is how to ensure restraint without compromising secrecy. There is a natural tension between a secret service and a democratic society. Intelligence agencies form a closed society with imperatives distinct from the purposes and standards of the rest of the nation. Working in an isolated, twilight world, intelligence operatives are notoriously subject to bouts of paranoia. They view themselves as the custodians of national security, more knowledgeable about these sensitive matters than elected officials who come and go. In this respect they are not unlike other bureaucratic professionals—and their judgments are no less in need of independent, critical scrutiny than those of others in positions of power. Ironically, the need for secrecy—which allows paranoia to mushroom and all sense of proportion to be lost—creates, if anything, a greater need for checks and balances, which in turn, imperil secrecy. There are no easy answers for this dilemma; it cannot be legislated or wished away.

In the final analysis, for a secret service to be acceptable in a democratic society, it must reflect the values of that society. But our government is not merely a government of laws but of men and women. Whatever legal and institutional safeguards we devise, there will always be an irreducible need for intelligence professionals, and for those who oversee them, to be, in that old-fashioned phrase, honorable men.

Citations

Works listed in the Bibliography are cited herein by author's last name and abbreviated title.

Chapter 1:
George Washington, Spymaster

The basic source for Honeyman's adventures is John Van Dyke's article, "An Unwritten Account of a Spy of Washington," in *Our Home* (October 1873), available on microfilm at the Library of Congress. Van Dyke states that he knew Honeyman personally and received the story from him. A modern account based on Van Dyke is Falkner's article in *American Heritage*. "I think the game": Washington, *Writings*, vol. 6, p. 398. "Expense must not be spared": ibid., p. 369.

For a full discussion of Washington as spymaster, see Sayle, "George Washington: Manager of Intelligence and Bryan, *The Spy in America*, pp. 51–53. Washington's journal entry: Washington, *Writings*, vol. 3, p. 407. "Everything, in a manner": letter to Gen. William Heath, Sept. 5, 1776, quoted in Bryan, *The Spy in America*, ibid., p. 55. "Even minutiae": *Writings*, vol. 13, p. 31. "I would not have you": ibid., vol. 9, pp. 66–67. "It is now 3 days": letter to Lord Stirling, Oct. 4, 1778, quoted in Corson, *The Armies of Ignorance*, p. 504. "If they have no": letter to Col. William Paterson, March 1, 1779, quoted in Corson, *The Armies of Ignorance*. Washington on intelligence expenditures: ibid., vol. 12, pp. 399–400; vol. 15, p. 263.

For the Revere ring, see Forbes, *Paul Revere*, pp. 224–226.

For the intelligence background of Lexington and Concord, see French, *General Gage's Informers*, pp. 9–33.

For Dr. Church and his activities, see ibid., pp. 147–201. For the Church–Wenwood affair, see also Bakeless, *Turncoats*, pp. 9–23, and Freeman, *George Washington*, vol. 3, pp. 544–552. Most accounts give the baker's name as Wainwood, but Bakeless, who says that he tracked down advertisements for his shop, states that it was Wenwood. Facsimiles of the cipher letter and the note from Church's mistress are in Freeman, *George Washington*; the originals are in the George Washington Papers in the Library of Congress. Washington's report to Hancock: Washington, *Writings*, vol. 4, pp. 10–11.

For American spies at siege of Boston, see Bakeless, *Turncoats*, pp. 87–89. For conditions in New York City, see Ford, *A Peculiar Service*, pp. 59–67. For the Hickey plot, see Van Doren, *Secret History*, pp. 13–15.

Chapter 2:
Spies Who Went Out Into the Cold

The fullest and most accurate account of Nathan Hale is in Seymour, *Documentary Life*. For New York City before the British attack, see Bliven, *Under the Guns*. "Leave no stone unturned": Washington, *Writings*, vol. 6, pp. 18–19. "I am willing to go": Seymour, *Documentary Life*, p. 318.

Hull's account: ibid., pp. 308–309. Hempstead's account: ibid., pp. 311–314. Hull's account of the meeting with Montresor: ibid., p. 310.

Lydia Darragh's mission: Bakeless, *Turncoats*, pp. 210–221.

The "merchant" affair: Boudinot, *Life of Elias Boudinot*, vol. 1, pp. 72–74. "I hope you will": Washington, *Writings*, vol. 10, p. 329. Letter to president of Congress: ibid., vol. 15, pp. 42–48.

For Tallmadge's background, see Hall, *Benjamin Tallmadge*, pp. 3–44, and Tallmadge, *Memoir*. The first complete account of the Culper Ring is in Pennypacker, *George Washington's Spies*; the most thorough is Barber, "The Tallmadge-Culper Intelligence Ring." "That year I opened": Bakeless, *Turncoats*, p. 32. "You should be perfectly": Washington to Tallmadge (August 25, 1778), in George Washington papers in the Library of Congress. "All great movements": Washington, *Writings*, vol. 14, pp. 276–278.

"I am perfectly acquainted": Pennypacker, *George Washington's Spies*, pp. 259–261. "Such excessive fright": ibid., pp. 239–241. "An intimate friend": ibid., pp. 44–45. Rivington's activities as an American secret agent were confirmed by Catherine S. Crary in her article in the *William and Mary Quarterly*.

"During this time": Pennypacker, *George Washington's Spies*, pp. 85–87. "I am engaging": ibid., p. 200. "One that hath": ibid., pp. 189–190. The link between Townsend and 355 was disclosed in Pennypacker, *Supplement*, pp. 32–42.

The most complete account of the Arnold treason plot is in Van Doren, *Secret History*, which contains the Arnold–André correspondence; also see Flexner, *The Traitor and the Spy*. A good study of Arnold's life and personality is Wallace, *Traitorous Hero*. "Surely a more active": Flexner, *The Traitor and the Spy*, p. 119. "I communicated my suspicion": Tallmadge, *Memoir*, p. 53. "Betrayed into the life": Van Doren, *Benjamin Franklin*, p. 342. "I endeavored to evade": ibid., pp. 133–134. "Hackneyed in villainy": Washington, *Writings*, vol. 20, p. 173.

Chapter 3:
"Surrounded by Spies"

For the organization of the secret committees, see Auger, *The Secret War*, chapter 4. For the Continental Congress and intelligence operations, see Sayle, "The Historical Underpinnings"; for the Bermuda operation, see Auger, *The Secret War*, chapter 3.

Bonvouloir's mission is in Bemis, *Diplomacy*, pp. 22–23, 29–34. "Europe has its reasons": Franklin, *Writings*, vol. 5, p. 231. For background on Deane, see James, *Silas Deane*. "People here": quoted in Montross, *Reluctant Rebels*, p. 117.

"He must be": Stevens, *Facsimiles*, No. 889. "Lupton's" report: ibid., No. 154. Beaumarchais' operations are discussed in detail in Auger, *The Secret War*, chapters 7 and 8.

For Franklin in Paris, see Bendiner, *The Virgin Diplomats;* New York: Knopf, 1976. For background on Eden, Wentworth, and the British Secret Service, see Auger, *The Secret War*, pp. 132–137. "I am old": Wharton, *Revolutionary Diplomatic Correspondence*, vol. 1, p. 473. "This Mr. Wentworth": Stevens, *Facsimiles*, No. 1781. Bancroft's operations are detailed in Bemis, "British Secret Service" and Boyd, "Silas Deane"; the latter includes considerable biographical data. Bancroft's own account is in the Bemis article. "A very decent house": quoted in John C. Miller, *Triumph of Freedom;* Boston: Little Brown, 1948. Franklin on security: quoted in Currey, *Code Number 72*, p. 108. For Lee's adventures in Berlin, see Stevens, *Facsimiles*, Nos. 1451–1481.

The Hynson–Nicholson affair can be followed by consulting the index (vol. 25) to Stevens, *Facsimiles*, and looking under the names of those involved. Vardill's own account of his career is in Einstein, *Divided Loyalties*, pp. 411–417. "I have ever doubted": Stevens, *Facsimiles*, No. 249. "He was an honest rascal" (note): ibid., No. 275.

The intrigues surrounding the negotiation of the French–American alliance are covered in Bemis, "British Secret Service"; Currey, *Code Number 72*, provides further detail. "*Edwards* is": quoted in Einstein, *Divided Loyalties*, p. 25. "A Gentleman who": Stevens, *Facsimiles*, No. 719. "Governors General—Privy Seals": ibid., No. 234. "Take care": ibid., No. 231. "72 received me": ibid., No. 489. "The immediate conclusion": ibid., No. 774.

That Silas Deane was poisoned by Bancroft is argued in Boyd, "Silas Deane." "Franklin used": Deacon, *History of British Secret Service*, p. 114.

Chapter 4:
A More Perfect Union

The "Tub Plot" is covered in detail in J. Miller, *Crisis in Freedom*, pp. 146–150. For Dorchester's intelligence ring, see Boyd, *Number 7*. Jay's comments are in Hamilton et al., *The Federalist Papers* (No. 64), pp. 392–393. For the contingency fund, see Wriston, *Executive Agents*, p. 695, and Sayle, "Historical Underpinnings." Washington's use of secret agents is described in Wriston, *Executive Agents*, pp. 209–212. Maclay's comments: Maclay, *Journal*, p. 396.

For the reaction of Americans to the French Revolution, see J. Miller, *The Federalist Era*, chapter 8. For Hamilton's relations with Hammond, see Boyd, *Number 7*, and Bemis, *Jay's Treaty*, pp. 142–143. For the XYZ affair, see Beveridge, *Life of John Marshall*, vol. 2. For the Alien and Sedition Acts, see J. Miller, *Crisis in Freedom*.

For the Lewis and Clark expedition as an intelligence mission, see Keats, *Eminent Domain*, pp. 11–12; the same work contains the details of the Louisiana Purchase. The best biography of Wilkinson is Jacobs, *Tarnished Warrior*. For the details of the Burr conspiracy, see Lomask, *Aaron Burr*. For the Burr trial, see Beirne, *Shout Treason*, and Levy, *Jefferson and Civil Liberties*, chapter 4.

The most complete account of the Florida affair is J. Smith, *The Plot to Steal Florida*.

Chapter 5:
Nobody Here But Us Patriots

For the Florida affair, see J. Smith, *The Plot to Steal Florida*.

Mitchell's mission is covered in detail in J. Smith, *The Plot to Steal Florida*.

The best account of the Crillon affair is in Morison, "The Henry-Crillon Affair of 1812." Coles's conversation: Brant, *The Fourth President*, p. 479.

For the causes of the War of 1812, see Horsman, *The War of 1812*. The low state of intelligence at the beginning of the war is in Powe, *The Emergence of the War Department Intelligence Agency*, pp. 4–5. Instructions to topographical engineers: Goetzmann, *Army Exploration*, p. 7. For military operations during the war, see Horsman, *The War of 1812*. "Blue-light Federalists": Bryan, *The Spy in America*, p. 116. For Andrew Jackson and intelligence, see Remini, *Andrew Jackson*, p. 236. Jackson's letter reviewing intelligence is printed in Rowan, *The Story of Secret Service*, p. 256. For Laffite and Jackson, see Remini, *Andrew Jackson*, pp. 251–254.

For George English's activities, see Wriston, *Executive Agents*, pp. 323–327; for background on English, see the *Dictionary of American Biography*.

McRae's mission: Wriston, *Executive Agents*, pp. 572–574 and 696–697. Roberts's mission: ibid., pp. 335–339. "It was given for all purposes": ibid., pp. 241–242. "The experience of every nation": Corson, *Armies of Ignorance*, p. 521.

For Larkin's instructions, see Wriston, *Executive Agents,* pp. 713–717.
For the war with Mexico, see Bauer, *The Mexican War;* for the status of intelligence in the U.S. Army at the time of the war, see Powe, *The Emergence of the War Department Intelligence Agency,* pp. 5–7. The topographical engineers map story is in Goetzmann, *Army Exploration,* pp. 109–110. "We are quite in the dark": Diary of Ethan Allen Hitchcock, William Croffut Papers, Library of Congress, Sept. 7, 1845. The most complete account of the Beach-Storms mission is in Nelson, "Mission to Mexico." For background on Jane Storms, see Wallace, *Destiny and Glory,* Chapter 12.

For the Mexican Spy Company, see Diary of Ethan Allen Hitchcock, June 5, 20, 28, and 30, 1847; June 5, 1848. The transcript of a newspaper article written by Hitchcock that contains information on Dominguez in exile in New Orleans can be found in Hitchcock, *Fifty Years,* pp. 334–345. "They rode along singing": Brackett, *General Lane's Brigade,* pp. 186–187.

Chapter 6:
Amateurs at War

Lloyd's operations are outlined in Bakeless, "Lincoln's Private Eye." Although this is the most complete account available, Bakeless fails to mention the lawsuit that followed.

For general comments on Civil War intelligence, see Fishel, "The Mythology of Civil War Intelligence"; also Powe, *The Emergence of the War Department Intelligence Agency,* pp. 8–9. For Belle Boyd, see her own account, *Belle Boyd in Camp and Prison;* the 1968 edition contains a long introduction by Curtis Carroll Davis. Also see Davis's "The Civil War's Most Over-Rated Spy."

For Washington during the Civil War, see Leech, *Reveille in Washington.* For a biography of Rose Greenhow, see Ross, *Rebel Rose.* Greenhow's own account is *My Imprisonment.* The Wilson letters are in the National Archives, RG 59. "Established relations with": Horan, *The Pinkertons,* p. 84. "To receive regularly": Ross, *Rebel Rose,* p. 116.

For a discussion of Beauregard's sources of information, see Williams, *Lincoln Finds a General,* pp. 85–86. "Our President and our General": Ross, *Rebel Rose,* p. 118.

For background on Pinkerton and his agency, see Horan, *The Pinkertons,* pp. 2–36. For the Baltimore plot, see Cuthbert, *Lincoln and the Baltimore Plot;* also Horan, *The Pinkerton's,* pp. 52–61.

For Pinkerton's watch on Rose Greenhow's house, see Pinkerton, *The Spy of the Rebellion,* pp. 156–157. The same work describes the rolling up of the Greenhow ring. For Pinkerton's effectiveness in counterintelligence, see Fishel, "The Mythology of Civil War Intelligence." For background and activities of Timothy Webster, see Kane, *Spies for the Blue and Gray,* pp. 87–108. For Lewis episode, see Horan, *The Pinkertons,* pp. 72–76, 98–114.

For Pinkerton and McClellan, see Sears, *McClellan,* chapters 7–9.

For Baker's first adventures as a spy, see his *History of the United States Secret Service,* pp. 45–72. For discussion of Seward's counterintelligence operations, see *Supplementary Reports on Intelligence Activities,* Book 6, pp. 32–34. For Potter and his committee, see Leech, *Reveille in Washington,* pp. 144–145. For Baker's operations, including purported brainwashing techniques, see Mogelever, *Death to Traitors,* pp. 109–127. Congressional criticism of Baker is in *Impeachment Investigation,* Fortieth Congress, first session, Representative Committee no. 7. U.S. Congress House Impeachment Investigation second session 39th Congress and first session 40th Congress, U.S. House Reports, Washington, 1867.

Chapter 7:
War by Other Means

The best account of Bulloch's activities is his own *The Secret Service of the Confederate States in Europe*, originally published in 1883. A 1959 reprint has an introduction by Philip Van Doren Stern that includes a biographical sketch of Bulloch. For Bulloch's meeting with Mallory and his arrival in Liverpool, see ibid., vol. 1, pp. 51–54. For the diplomatic background, see Bailey, *A Diplomatic History*, pp. 359–363. For the description of Liverpool, see Merli, *Great Britain*, pp. 61–62. For the qualities sought in a commerce raider, see *Official Records of the Union and Confederate Navies*, Series 2, vol. 2, p. 44. For contracting for the *Oreto*, see Bulloch, *Secret Service*, vol. 1, pp. 57–58; for contracting for the *Enrica*, see ibid., pp. 58–62.

Caleb Huse's account is in Stern, *Secret Missions*, pp. 75–78. Bulloch's first report: *Official Records of the Union and Confederate Navies*, Series 2, vol. 2, pp. 83–97. "A system of espionage": H. Owsley, "Henry Shelton Sanford." For background on Sanford, see Fry, *Henry S. Sanford*, chapters 1 and 2. His covert activities are covered in ibid., chapter 2, and in H. Owsley, "Henry Shelton Sanford."

For B. W. Saunders, see National Archives, RG 59, Dispatches from Special Agents, vol. 22; also Dispatches from U.S. Ministers, France, vol. 54, no. 471.

For the Garibaldi affair, see Mitgang, "Garibaldi and Lincoln." For Lincoln and Canisius (note), see Sandburg, *Abraham Lincoln*, p. 184.

For the fitting out of the *Oreto*, see Bulloch, *Secret Service*, vol. 1, pp. 57–58. "The aggressiveness of a terrier": Stern, *When the Guns Roared*, p. 102. British customs report: ibid., p. 143.

The fitting out of the *Enrica* is in Bulloch, *Secret Service*, vol. 1, pp. 230–231. For Dudley and the *Enrica*, see Stern, *When the Guns Roared*, pp. 145–146. For Adams's protests, see Merli, *Great Britain*, pp. 91–92. For the escape of the vessel, see Maynard, "Union Efforts," and "Plotting the Escape." The identity of Bulloch's informant is in Stern, *When the Guns Roared*, p. 148. Edwards's cotton speculations: ibid., p. 150. Bulloch's account of the escape: Bulloch, *Secret Service*, vol. 1, pp. 240–241.

For Hotze's activities, see Cullop, *Confederate Propaganda*. For the Laird rams, see Spencer, *The Confederate Navy*, pp. 79–86, 104–119; also Merli, *Great Britain*, pp. 178–217.

Chapter 8:
"On Special Service"

The basic sources for Norris and the Confederate Secret Service are the articles by Gaddy, "Grey Cloaks and Daggers" and "William Norris"; also see Canan, "Confederate Military Intelligence" and Taylor, *The Signal and Secret Service*. For background on Myer and his conflict with the U.S. Military Telegraph, see Scheips, "Union Signal Communications." For Lincoln's interest in the U.S.M.T. (note), see Bates, *Lincoln in the Telegraph Office*. "We always had": Bakeless, *Spies of the Confederacy*, p. 302. "From them we learned": ibid., p. 97. "Vied wth each other": Catton, *Glory Road*, p. 170.

Conrad told the story of his adventures in *A Confederate Spy.*

Butterfield's comment, ("We were almost as ignorant"): Senate, U.S. Congress, Joint Committee on the Conduct of the War, *Report I*. For the biographic sketch of Patrick, see Patrick, *Inside Lincoln's Army*. "Any signs of a move": Catton, *Glory Road*, p. 145. For biographical information on Sharpe, see Hasbrouck, "Address," pp. 25–48. "For the first time": Freeman, *R. E. Lee*, p. 24. Most writers on the Civil War have completely overlooked

Sharpe and the Bureau of Military Information, but there is a brief assessment of his work in Fishel, "The Mythology of Civil War Intelligence." The general order on the communication of intelligence is in *Official Records of the Union and Confederate Armies*, Series 1, vol. 25, part 2, pp. 197–198. "I have no means": ibid., p. 700. "The rebels have not": Patrick diary, April 28, 1863. "The Confederate Army": *Official Records of the War of the Rebellion*, Series 1, vol. 25, part 2, pg. 528. "Very much disgusted": Patrick diary, May 12, 1864.

For Dodge's intelligence activities, see Hirshson, *Grenville M. Dodge*, pp. 67–69, 80–84. For Henson, see Johns, *Philip Henson*.

Horan, Confederate Agent, is a non-too-reliable biography of Thomas Hines.

For Confederate activities on the northern frontier, see Kinchen, *Confederate Operations*. The most complete account of the St. Alban's raid is Kinchen, *Daredevils of the Confederate Army*. John W. Headley presented his account of the attempt to burn New York in *Confederate Operations*, pp. 271–280.

The basic sources for Elizabeth Van Lew's activities are her journal and other papers in the Elizabeth Van Lew Papers, New York Public Library; also see Stuart, "Colonel Ulric Dahlgren." For Samuel Ruth, see Stuart, "Samuel Ruth."

Chapter 9:
The Beginnings of Professionalism

For Gleaves and Hellings, see O'Toole, *The Spanish War*, pp. 32–34. O'Toole was the first to report the existence of the Hellings espionage ring. For background on the war, also see Trask, *The War with Spain*. For the *Maine* explosion, see Rickover, *How the Battleship "Maine" Was Destroyed*.

For the state of the American armed forces in the years following the Civil War, see Millet and Maslowski, *For the Common Defense*, chapter 8, and Millis, *Arms and Men*, pp. 131–167. For Upton, see the above and Ambrose, *Upton and the Army*.

For the organization of ONI, see Dorwart, *The Office of Naval Intelligence*, chapters 1 and 2. For the experiences of an early naval intelligence officer, see E. Morison, *Admiral Sims*, pp. 34–48.

For the early history of MID, see Powe, *The Emergence of the War Department Intelligence Agency*, pp. 11–28. For the Taylor mission to Canada, see Wriston, *Executive Agents*, pp. 738–742.

"We must have": Richardson, *A Compilation*, pp. 4923, 4936. The Borup incident is in Dorwart, *The Office of Naval Intelligence*, p. 48. For the rivalry between ONI and MID, see ibid., p. 44. For the Navy secret code and "Mr. Hawke," see ibid., pp. 26–27. For the du Pont episode, see G. Colby, *Du Pont Dynasty*, pp. 111–117. The bureaucratic struggle over MID is detailed in Powe, *The Emergence of the War Department Intelligence Agency*, pp. 20–24.

For Wagner and MID, see ibid., pp. 28–29; also Wagner's own *The Service of Security*. For background on Hellings and his ring, see O'Toole, *The Spanish War*, pp. 207–208. For Roosevelt and ONI, see Dorwart, *The Office of Naval Intelligence*, pp. 55–62. For the Navy in the war with Spain, see N. Miller, *The U.S. Navy*, pp. 203–220. For Dewey's intelligence, see O'Toole, *The Spanish War*, pp. 176–177. The atmosphere in Washington upon receipt of Dewey's message is described in Kahn, *The Codebreakers*, pp. 253–254.

For Rowan's mission, see Rowan, *The Story of Secret Service*, pp. 416–418. For Whitney's mission, see O'Toole, *The Spanish War*, pp. 353–354. Wagner's problems are discussed in Powe, *The Emergence of the War Department Intelligence Agency*, pp. 30–32, and in Van Deman, *Memoirs*, vol. 1, pp. 4–5.

The best account of the activities of "Fernandez del Campo" is in Rowan, *The Story of Secret Service*, pp. 422–423. For ONI during the war, see Dorwart, *The Office of Naval Intelligence*, pp. 63–70. The fullest account of the Montreal spy ring is in Jeffreys-Jones, *American Espionage*, pp. 29–41.

The episode of Villaverde and the Spanish fleet is in O'Toole, *The Spanish War*, pp. 212–221. Victor Blue's own account of his mission is in Bryan, *The Spy in America*, pp. 206–212.

Chapter 10:
Prophet Without Honor

For biographical data on Van Deman, see Corson, *The Armies of Ignorance*, pp. 45–47. Corson was a personal friend of Van Deman's. For background on the Filipino insurrection, see S. Miller, *Benevolent Assimilation*. For Van Deman's own account of duty in the Philippines, see Van Deman, *Memoirs*, part 1, pp. 8–13. For Van Deman in China, see ibid., pp. 16–18.

For the establishment of a general staff system, see Powe, *The Emergence of the War Department Intelligence Agency*, pp. 37–46, and Millett and Maslowski, *For the Common Defense*, pp. 309–311. For Stilwell in Central America, see Tuchman, *Stilwell*, pp. 21–22, and Powe, *The Emergence of the War Department Intelligence Agency*, pp. 48–49. The ONI and alleged Japanese war preparations are described in Dorwart, *The Office of Naval Intelligence*, pp. 83–84. Roosevelt's cabinet meeting is recorded in Van Deman, *Memoirs*, part 1, pp. 20–21. For the bureaucratic battle over MID, see ibid., pp. 13–15 and 23–26; also see Powe, *The Emergence of the War Department Intelligence Agency*, pp. 53–57.

For the *Asama* incident, see Ind, *A Short History*, p. 131. For Mashbir's account, see Mashbir, *I Was an American Spy*, pp. 5–10. For the MacArthur episode, see Manchester, *American Caesar*, pp. 73–76.

For the domestic situation in the United States during World War I, see Millis, *Road to War*, and Dos Passos, *Mr. Wilson's War*. For the Lenin incident (note), see Moseley, *Dulles*, pp. 47–48. For Van Deman's comments on the state of U.S. intelligence in 1915, see Van Deman, *Memoirs*, part 1, pp. 28–33. For Van Deman's report to Scott in 1916, see Powe, *The Emergence of the War Department Intelligence Agency*, pp. 71–75, and Corson, *The Armies of Ignorance*, pp. 47–49.

The most complete account of the Black Tom case is in Landau, *The Enemy Within*, but it should be pointed out that the author was an investigator for the American claimants. For a readable account of German relations with the United States before the American entry into the war, see Tuchman, *The Zimmerman Telegram*. Van Rintelen provided his own, less than reliable account of his adventures in *The Dark Invader*.

Voska's story is in Voska and Irwin, *Spy and Counterspy*. For British operations in America, see Willert, *The Road to Safety*, and Fowler, *British-American Relations 1917–1918*, chapter 1. For Room 40 and its work, see Tuchman, *The Zimmerman Telegram*, and Beesly, *Room 40*.

For Polk, see Jeffreys-Jones, *American Espionage*, pp. 44–47. The conversation between Polk and Wiseman is in Willert, *The Road to Safety*, p. 26. The arrest of the Indians is described in ibid., pp. 27–28. See Tuchman's *The Zimmerman Telegram* for the decoding and effect of the telegram.

For Van Deman and Scott, see Van Deman, *Memoirs*, part 1, pp. 33–35. For Van Deman and the woman writer, see ibid., pp. 35–36. For Van Deman and Dansey, see Read and Fisher, *Colonel Z*. For the organization of MID, see Van Deman, *Memoirs*, part 1, pp. 36–40. For the establishment of CIC, see ibid., pp. 63–64, and Ind, *A Short History of Espionage*, pp. 181–182.

For details on the establishment and operations of MI-8, see Yardley, *The American Black Chamber*. For background on Yardley, see David Kahn's introduction to the paperback edition of ibid. For Lothar Witzke, see Yardley, ibid., chapter 7. For Maria de Victorica, see ibid., chapter 5.

For Roosevelt and ONI, see Dorwart, *The Office of Naval Intelligence*, p. 117. For APL, see Jensen, *The Price of Vigilance*. Van Deman's words to Frankfurter are quoted in Powe,

The Emergence of the War Department Intelligence Agency, p. 94. MID and APL are in Corson, *The Armies of Ignorance*, p. 54–62. In his *Memoirs*, Van Deman makes his sacking by Baker appear like an ordinary transfer.

Chapter 11:
Twilight of Intelligence

The most complete account of the Red Scare is Murray, *Red Scare*. For the organization of the General Intelligence Division, see Lowenthal, *The Federal Bureau of Investigation*, pp. 84–92. MID's investigation of radicals is described in Jensen, *The Price of Vigilance*, pp. 274–291. Niblack's warning is in Dorwart, *Conflict of Duty*, pp. 12–13.

For Van Deman's postwar activities, see Van Deman, *Memoirs*, part 3. For Van Deman and Dansey, see Read and Fisher, *Colonel Z*, pp. 154–155, and Van Deman, *Memoirs*, p. 14 and pp. 25–26. For Van Deman and the League of Nations, see ibid., pp. 20–21. "Italy, particularly northern Italy": ibid., Appendix G. For Van Deman and Bullitt, see ibid., p. 13, pp. 20–21, and Appendix B. For Marguerite Harrison's adventures, see Harrison, *There's Always Tomorrow*; also Van Deman, *Memoirs*, part 3, p. 8.

For postwar economies, see "Materials on the History of Military Intelligence in the United States, 1885–1944." Marshall's comment is quoted in Ransom, *Central Intelligence*, p. 45. Kennan's comment is in Kennan, *Memoirs*, p. 48. Yardley told his story in Yardley, *The American Black Chamber*.

For ONI's efforts to penetrate the mandated islands, see Dorwart, *Conflict of Duty*, pp. 30–33. For Zacharias's account, see Zacharias, *Secret Missions*, chapter 5. The fullest and most reasoned account of the Ellis affair is Ballendorf, "Earl Hancock Ellis"; also see Reber, "Pete Ellis."

For ONI's efforts against the Japanese, see Dorwart, *Conflict of Duty*, pp. 38–46, and Zacharias, *Secret Missions*, pp. 102–108. President Hoover's use of ONI against political opponents was disclosed by Dorwart in *Conflict of Duty*, pp. 3–5. For MID and the Bonus Marchers, see Daniels, *The Bonus March*, pp. 159–160.

J. Edgar Hoover's version of his meetings with Roosevelt and Hull is in Whitehead, *The FBI Story*, pp. 157–158.

Chapter 12:
Enemies Within . . . And Without

For Ritter and the Norden bombsight, see Farago, *The Game of Foxes*, pp. 43–53.

For background on German espionage operations in the United States, see Trefousse, "Failure of German Intelligence in the United States." The best biography of Canaris is Hohne, *Canaris: Hitler's Master Spy*. The most complete account of the Rumrich-Griebl case is in Turrou, *The Nazi Spy Conspiracy*.

For the status of American intelligence on the eve of World War II, see Troy, *Donovan and the CIA*, pp. 3–16, and Dorwart, *Conflict of Duty*, pp. 86–124. The episode of Layton and the Japanese super-battleships is in Layton, *Reminiscences*, pp. 63–64.

For Friedman and his accomplishments, see Clark, *The Man Who Broke Purple*, and Kahn, *The Codebreakers*, pp. 18–23 and 369–393.

For the Sebold case, see Farago, *The Game of Foxes*, pp. 371–379.

For FDR's foreign policy in the prewar era, see N. Miller, *F.D.R.*, pp. 418–476. Murphy's comment is in his *Diplomat among Warriors*, p. 70. Acheson's comment is in Pettee, *The Future of American Secret Intelligence*, pp. 36–37. The Tyler Kent case is discussed in West, *A Thread of Deceit*, pp. 81–84; also see Pease, "The Putative Spy," *Foreign Intelligence Literary Scene*, March/April, 1986. Some of the John Franklin Carter Papers are in the Franklin D. Roosevelt Library, Hyde Park, N.Y. Astor's operations are discussed in Dorwart,

Conflict of Duty, pp. 163–169. There is a list of ROOM members in the Kermit Roosevelt Papers in the Library of Congress.

For Donovan's biography, see Brown, *The Last Hero.* The origin of Donovan's nickname is in Troy, *Donovan and the CIA,* p. 24; B. Smith, *The Shadow Warriors,* is less admiring of Donovan. For Stephenson and the British Security Coordination, see Hyde, *Room 3603;* this is a far more reliable account than Stevenson's *A Man Called Intrepid,* which borders on fiction. For Stephenson and Donovan, see Troy, *Donovan and the CIA,* pp. 34–36, and Brown, *The Last Hero,* pp. 147–149.

For the creation of COI, see Troy, *Donovan and the CIA,* pp. 43–70; the text of Donovan's memos are in Appendices A and B, and the text of the presidential order establishing COI is in Appendix C.

For the first six months of COI, see ibid., pp. 73–116; Brown, *The Last Hero,* pp. 168–185; and B. Smith, *The Shadow Warriors,* pp. 55–94. The description of Donovan's office is from Brown, *The Last Hero,* p. 169. For Lovell's "Special Weapons," see Lovell, *Of Spies and Strategems.* Pincher's comments on Ellis (note) are in Pincher, *Too Secret Too Long;* the charges against Ellis first appeared in Pincher, *Their Trade Is Treachery.* Also see West, *MI6,* pp. 243–245.

Chapter 13:
The Road from Pearl Harbor

Layton's activities are detailed in his *Reminiscences.* This account was expanded in his posthumously published memoirs, *"And I Was There."*

For the "Tricycle" warning, see Bratzel and Rout, "Pearl Harbor." For Roosevelt's involvement in the negotiations leading up to Pearl Harbor, see Dallek, *Franklin D. Roosevelt,* pp. 299–313, and N. Miller, *F.D.R.,* pp. 468–476. ONI's reaction to the Peruvian minister's tip is in Layton, *"And I Was There,"* pp. 73–74. Wohlstetter's comment is in her *Pearl Harbor: Warning and Decision,* p. 387. Layton's "snake in the corner" comment is in his *Reminiscences.* The struggle for control of radio intelligence is detailed in Layton, *"And I Was There."* For Turner and ONI, see Dorwart, *Conflict of Duty,* pp. 157–160, and Layton, *"And I Was There,"* pp. 96–102.

Donovan's activities at the time of Pearl Harbor are in Brown, *The Last Hero,* pp. 3–7. Further biographical details on Van Deman are in Corson, *The Armies of Ignorance,* pp. 105–106. Eisenhower's statement is in Eisenhower, *Crusade in Europe,* p. 32. ONI's difficulties are described in Dorwart, *Conflict of Duty,* pp. 187–189. The bat story is in B. Smith, *The Shadow Warriors,* p. 102. For the Spanish embassy affair, see Donald Downs, *The Scarlet Thread,* pp. 87–97. For the struggle over COI and the birth of OSS, see Troy, *Donovan and the CIA,* chapter 6, and B. Smith, *The Shadow Warriors,* pp. 117–121; the pertinent documents are in Troy, *Donovan and the CIA,* Appendices E and F.

For background on the Battle of Midway, see Lord, *Incredible Victory.* For Rochefort and Station Hypo, see Rochefort, *Reminiscences,* and Layton, *Reminiscences* and *"And I Was There."* Also see Holmes, *Double-Edged Secrets,* especially for conditions within Station Hypo and the confirmation of Midway as "AF." For the post-Midway treatment of Rochefort (note), see Layton, *"And I Was There,"* pp. 464–469. The Chicago *Tribune* case is presented in Frank, "The United States Navy v. the Chicago *Tribune."*

The most detailed account of the eight German saboteurs is in Rachlis, *They Came to Kill.* For Colepaugh and Gimpel, see Kahn, *Hitler's Spies,* pp. 3–26, and Whitehead, *The FBI Story,* New York: Random House, 1956, pp. 205–207.

For the OSS in Operation Torch, see Roosevelt, *The Secret War Report of the OSS,* pp. 134–145; Brown, *The Last Hero,* pp. 235–259; R. Smith, *OSS,* chapter 2; B. Smith, *The Shadow Warriors,* pp. 145–157; and Coon, *A North Africa Story.*

For Donovan and Darlan and the Darlan assassination, see Brown, *The Last Hero,* pp.

259–271. Coon did not include his recommendations on assassination as a government policy in his book, but discussed them later with Brown. Kermit Roosevelt ed. *The Secret War Report of the OSS*, New York: Berkley, 1976.

Chapter 14:
The Unsecret Service

For Detachment 101, see Dunlop, *Behind Japanese Lines*.

For Coon's comment, see *A North Africa Story*, p. ix. "There were men": Alsop and Braden, *Sub Rosa*, p. 26. Schlesinger's comment is in R. Smith, *OSS*, p. 14. "We did not rely": Ford, *Donovan of OSS*, p. 148.

For Dulles's operations in Switzerland, see Moseley, *Dulles*, chapter 8, and Dulles, *Germany's Underground* and *The Secret Surrender*. For "Cicero" (note), see West, *A Thread of Deceit*, pp. 99–107. For Dulles and the "Alpine Redoubt," and the German surrender in Italy (note), see B. Smith and Agarossi, *Operation Sunrise*.

For OSS exploits, see Brown, *The Last Hero*; Roosevelt, *The Secret War Report*; R. Smith, *OSS*; Ford, *Donovan of OSS*; and Alsop and Braden, *Sub Rosa*.

For the fullest account of ULTRA, see Lewin, *Ultra Goes to War*.

For signals intelligence and the Battle of the Atlantic, see Beesly, *Very Special Intelligence*.

For signals intelligence in the Pacific war, see Lewin, *Magic*, and Holmes, *Double-Edged Secrets*. For the Yamamoto ambush, see Layton, "*And I Was There*," pp. 474–476. For signals intelligence and the submarine war against Japan, see Lewin, *Magic*; Holmes, *Double-Edged Secrets*; and Blair, *Silent Victory*.

For Allied intelligence agencies and NKVD, see B. Smith, *The Shadow Warriors*, chapter 7. For OSS/Bucharest, see ibid., pp. 350–352, and Brown, *The Last Hero*, pp. 670–682. For Donovan and the Polish uprising, see ibid., pp. 621–622. The NKVD penetration of OSS is discussed in Corson and Crowley, *The New KGB*, pp. 214–222. For Donovan's report to Roosevelt, see Troy, *Donovan and the CIA*, chapter 9; the text of the letter and proposal are in Appendix M. Also see Brown, *The Last Hero*, pp. 623–633. The maneuvering surrounding the dissolution of OSS is described in Troy, *Donovan and the CIA*, chapters 10–12; Truman's order dissolving the OSS is in Appendix S.

Donovan's appearance before the meeting of the OSS is in Ford, *Donovan of OSS*, pp. 309–312. OSS operations in Germany are detailed in Persico, *Piercing the Reich*. Casey's comment is in Joseph Lelyveld, "The Director," *The New York Times Magazine*, January 20, 1985.

Chapter 15:
Onward Cold War Soldiers

The most balanced source on the atom spy ring is Radosh and Milton, *The Rosenberg File*. For the FBI version of the case, see Whitehead, *The FBI Story*, pp. 303–320. For a pro-Rosenberg version, see the Schneirs' *Invitation to an Inquest*. Stalin's reaction to Truman's announcement of the atomic bomb is in R. Donovan, *Conflict and Crisis*, p. 93.

For the *Amerasia* case, see Klehr and Radosh, "Anatomy of a Fix." Willis George's revelation (note) is in George, *Surreptitious Entry*. The best book on the Hiss case is Weinstein, *Perjury*. For codebreaking and the atomic spy case, see Martin, *Wilderness of Mirrors*, pp. 41–48, and *Newsweek*, May 19, 1980.

For the White House ceremony, see the diary of Fleet Admiral William D. Leahy, in the Library of Congress, entry for January 24, 1946. For the organization of CIG, see Troy, *Donovan and the CIA*, pp. 305–349; for the directive establishing CIG, see ibid., Appendix

U. For assessments of CIG, see ibid., pp. 351–365; Cline, *The CIA*, pp. 112–115; and Corson, *The Armies of Ignorance*, pp. 274–290. Donovan's comments are in Brown, *The Last Hero*, p. 801. For the establishment of the CIA, see Troy, *Donovan and the CIA*, pp. 377–410. For Shamrock (note), see Truman's comments in the Washington *Post*, December 22, 1963.

For events leading up to the development of OPC, see Corson, *The Armies of Ignorance*, pp. 295–302. For the founding of OPC, see U.S. Congress, Senate, *Final Report*, Book 4, pp. 25–35.

For biographical information on Frank Wisner, see T. Powers, *The Man Who Kept the Secrets*, pp. 32–33, and Wisner's obituary in the Washington *Post*, October 30, 965. For the OPC under Wisner, see Loftus, *The Belarus Secret*. Rositzke's observations are in Rositzke, *The CIA's Secret Operations*, p. 21. The best account of Gehlen's activities is in Hohne and Zolling, *The General Was a Spy*. Guderian's confrontation with Hitler (note) is in Guderian, *Panzer Leader*, p. 387.

Wisner's use of Nazi collaborators was first disclosed in Loftus, *The Belarus Secret*, which remains the fullest account. For Philby's comment on Wisner (note), see Philby, *My Secret War*, p. 193.

"There are few": Moseley, *Dulles*, p. 275. Bross's story is in T. Powers, *The Man Who Kept the Secrets*, p. 49. For the WIN affair, see ibid., pp. 49–52, and Rositzke, *The CIA's Secret Operations*, pp. 170–172.

For a discussion of CIA research and analysis before the Smith reforms, see Laqueur, *A World of Secrets*, pp. 110–117. "America's people expect you": Ransom, *Central Intelligence and National Security*, p. 41. For the intelligence background of the Korean War, see Goulden, *Korea*, pp. 37–41. For intelligence and the Chinese intervention, see Truman, *Memoirs*, vol. 2, chapter 24. The spy mission of the former Nationalist officer is discussed in Rositzke, *The CIA's Secret Operations*, p. 53. For Tofte's activities, see Goulden, *Korea*, pp. 464–475. For the Chinese army in Burma, see Corson, *The Armies of Ignorance*, pp. 321–322.

For Smith's CIA reforms, see U.S. Congress, Senate, *Final Report*, Book 6, pp. 36–38; Cline, *The CIA*, pp. 129–139; and Laqueur, *A World of Secrets*, pp. 71–75. Kirkpatrick's comment is in his *U.S. Intelligence Community*, pp. 32–33.

Chapter 16:
The Struggle for the World

For the Berlin tunnel, see Martin, *Wilderness of Mirrors*, pp. 74–92, and Hohne and Zolling, *The General Was a Spy*, Appendix B. For biographical details on Harvey, see Martin, *Wilderness of Mirrors*, and T. Powers, *The Man Who Kept the Secrets*, pp. 172–173.

For Dulles as DCI, see Cline, *The CIA*, pp. 174–178; Moseley, *Dulles*, pp. 323–325; T. Powers, *The Man Who Kept the Secrets*, pp. 103–107; and U.S. Congress, Senate, *Final Report*, Book 4, pp. 43–45.

For the Doolittle report, see ibid., pp. 52–53n. NSC 5412/1 is in U.S. Congress, Senate, *Final Report*, Book 1, p. 51. For the opposition of Helms and Kirkpatrick to covert action, see T. Powers, *The Man Who Kept the Secrets*, pp. 102–103. For the Felfe affair, see Loftus, *The Belarus Secret*, p. 132, and Hohne and Zolling, *The General Was a Spy*, pp. 280–290.

For the Iranian operation, see K. Roosevelt, *Countercoup*.

The most complete account of the Guatemalan affair is in Schlesinger and Kinzer, *Bitter Fruit*; also see Phillips, *The Night Watch*, pp. 37–68.

For Lansdale, see J. Smith, *Portrait of a Cold Warrior*, pp. 101–106, and Karnow, *Vietnam*, pp. 220–223. For the Indonesian affair, see J. Smith, *Portrait of a Cold Warrior*, pp. 205–248.

For the administration of intelligence and congressional review, see U.S. Congress, Senate, *Final Report*, Book 4, pp. 50–55. "The White House made the decisions": Rositzke, *The CIA's Secret Operations*, p. 190. The most complete account of the Popov case is in Hood, *Mole*. For Khrushchev's speech, see Cline, *The CIA*, pp. 185–187. For the Hungarian revolt and Wisner's collapse, see T. Powers, *The Man Who Kept the Secrets*, pp. 91–97, and Corson, *The Armies of Ignorance*, pp. 367–372. "Poor fellows": Alexander, *Holding the Line*, p. 180. Truscott's role in terminating Wisner's covert activities is in Corson, *The Armies of Ignorance*. The statement issued by Wisner's friends is in the Washington *Post*, October 30, 1965.

There is a good profile of Bissell in Wyden, *Bay of Pigs*, pp. 10–19. "Espionage has been": transcript of a Bissell speech included as an appendix in Marchetti and Marks, *The CIA and the Cult of Intelligence*. For the U-2 and its aftermath, see Beschloss, *Mayday*. Francis Powers told his story in *Operation Overflight*. For the Abel case (note), see Bernikow, *Abel*, and J. Donovan, *Strangers on a Bridge*.

Chapter 17:
To Bear Any Burden

Dulles's dinner party is in Wyden, *Bay of Pigs*, p. 95. For Kennedy's foreign policy, see Ambrose, *Rise to Globalism*, chapter 10. "This revolution is like": LeFeber, *America in the Cold War*, p. 139. CIA's early support for Castro (note) is in Szule, *Fidel*.

For plots to assassinate Castro and others, see U.S. Congress, Senate, *Alleged Assassination Plots*. Cline's comment is in Cline, *The CIA*, p. 209; also see U.S. Congress, Senate, *Alleged Assassination Plots*, pp. 91–93. For "executive action" capability, see ibid., pp. 181–190. "Killing people": Ranelagh, *The Agency*, p. 211.

The most complete account of the Bay of Pigs operation and its aftermath is Wyden, *Bay of Pigs;* also see Phillips, *The Night Watch*, chapter 4. Schlesinger's comment (note) is in Schlesinger, *A Thousand Days*, p. 247.

"He just beat": Halberstam, *The Best and Brightest*, pp. 96–97. "Splinter the CIA": Crile and Branch, "The Kennedy Vendetta." For post–Bay of Pigs changes in the CIA, see Schlesinger, *A Thousand Days*, pp. 428–429. For an admiring account of McCone's stewardship of the CIA, see Cline, *The CIA*, pp. 215–234. For Operation Mongoose, see U. S. Congress, Senate, *Alleged Assassination Plots*, pp. 134–169, and Martin, *Wilderness of Mirrors*, chapter 6. Castro's estimate of the number of attempts on his life is in Ranelagh, *The Agency*, pp. 336–337.

For the missile crisis, see Abel, *The Missile Crisis*, and Dinerstein, *The Making of a Missile Crisis*.

Kennedy and Bundy's comment to Cline is in Cline, *The CIA*, p. 221. For Penkovsky, see Wynne, *Contact on Gorky Street*, and Penkovsky's *The Penkovsky Papers*, a book secretly produced by CIA personnel. For an appraisal of the value of Penkovsky's work, see Cline, *The CIA*, p. 222.

For the origins of American involvement in Vietnam, see Kahin, *Intervention*, and Karnow, *Vietnam*. "Winston Churchill of Asia": Halberstam, *The Best and Brightest*, p. 167. For the intelligence community and the early stages of the Vietnam war, see T. Powers, *The Man Who Kept the Secrets*, p. 206; Cline, *The CIA*, pp. 222–223; and Laqueur, *A World of Secrets*, pp. 171–177. Kennedy's reaction to the death of Diem is in Karnow, *Vietnam*, pp. 310–311.

Chapter 18:
All Honorable Men

Colby's comment is in Colby, *Honorable Men*, p. 241. For Johnson's conviction that Kennedy's murder was a Cuban turnabout for the plots against Castro, see Janos, "The Last Days of the President." The Rockefeller Commission found no CIA complicity in the Kennedy assassination or evidence of a relationship between Oswald and the agency. See Rockefeller Commission, *Report on CIA Activities*, pp. 251–269. "You can kill": Karnow, *Vietnam*, p. 169. For McCone and Johnson, see T. Powers, *The Man Who Kept the Secrets*, pp. 210–212, and Cline, *The CIA*, pp. 223–225. For Raborn, see T. Powers, *The Man Who Kept the Secrets*, pp. 212–217, and Cline, *The CIA*, pp. 234–239.

Helms's visit to the LBJ Ranch is in Wise and Ross, *The Espionage Establishment*, p. 110. For the CIA and Vietnam under Johnson, see Cline, *The CIA*, pp. 239–240, and T. Powers, *The Man Who Kept the Secrets*, pp. 218–249. Colby's account of Phoenix is in Colby, *Honorable Men*, pp. 266–280. Palmer's comments are in Palmer, *The 25-Year War*, pp. 162–164. For the order of battle controversy, see Adams, "Vietnam Coverup"; T. Powers, *The Man Who Kept the Secrets*, pp. 236–241; and Palmer, *The 25-Year War*, pp. 78–80 and p. 164. For the Westmoreland/CBS case, see Adler, *Reckless Disregard*. For Tet, see Oberdorfer, *Tet!*; Karnow, *Vietnam*, chapter 14; and T. Powers, *The Man Who Kept the Secrets*, pp. 242–247.

For Nixon and the CIA, see Laqueur, *A World of Secrets*, pp. 82–84, and T. Powers, *The Man Who Kept the Secrets*, pp. 254–280. For the CIA and Chile, see U. S. Congress, Senate, *Covert Action in Chile* and *Alleged Assassination Plots*, both reports of the Church committee; S. Hersh, *The Price of Power*; and Phillips, *The Night Watch*, pp. 281–287.

For Watergate, see Lukas, *Nightmare*; T. Powers, *The Man Who Kept the Secrets*, pp. 320–346; and Colby, *Honorable Men*, pp. 320–338.

"The nation must": see Helms's speech of August 14, 1971, in *Vital Speeches*, May 15, 1971. Stennis's comment is in Johnson, *A Season of Inquiry*, p. 31. For Schlesinger as DCI, see Colby, *Honorable Men*, and T. Powers, *The Man Who Kept the Secrets*, pp. 356–359. For relations between Colby and Angleton, see B. Hersh, "Dragons Must Be Killed." The most complete study of the Nosenko affair is Epstein, *Legend*. For a critical view of the case, see Turner, *Secrecy and Democracy*, pp. 43–45, and Laqueur, *A World of Secrets*, pp. 134–135.

Chapter 19:
An Age of Uncertainty

Colby related his version of his tenure as DCI in *Honorable Men*, chapters 12–14. For Operation Chaos, see U.S. Congress, Senate, *Final Report*, Book 3, pp. 679–732. For the organization and operations of the Church Committee, see Johnson, *A Season of Inquiry*. Rockefeller's and Kissinger's comments are in Colby, *Honorable Men*, p. 16.

The Kurdish operation is discussed in Prados, *President's Secret Wars*, pp. 313–315. For the fall of Saigon, see Snepp, *Decent Interval*. For Operation Feature, see Stockwell, *In Search of Enemies*. Frank Snepp's charges (note) are in Snepp, *Decent Interval*. Colby discussed Project Jenifer in Colby, *Honorable Men*, pp. 413–418.

Ford's reforms are discussed in Cline, *The CIA*, pp. 260–268. For Bush's tenure as DCI, see Cline, *The CIA*, pp. 265–268, and Ranelagh, *The Agency*, pp. 631–633.

Turner's version of his tenure at Langley is in his *Secrecy and Democracy*. For a critical view, see Epstein, "Who Killed the CIA?" and Cline, *The CIA*, pp. 268–275. For Ed Wilson, see Goulden, *The Death Merchant*. For A Team and B Team, see Pipes, "Team B."

For American relations with Iran both before and after the fall of the shah, see Rubin, *Paved with Good Intentions,* and Sick, *All Fall Down.* For the critical congressional report, see *The New York Times,* January 25, 1979.

Chapter 20:
Once More Into the Breach

For an account of the CIA at the height of Casey's influence, see *U.S. News & World Report,* June 16, 1986; also see Lelyveld, "The Director," and Brock, "Spies Are Back in U.S. Arsenal." A more critical view is presented in Goodman, "Dateline Langley. For Reagan and his background, see Wills, *Reagan's America.*

Intelligence community budget figures (note) are from a confidential source. Gates's defense of CIA analyses is in the Washington *Post,* December 12, 1984. Horton made his charges in the Washington *Post,* January 2, 1985.

For Soviet technological espionage, see Corson and Crowley, *The New KGB,* pp. 366–379. For the missing Stealth bomber documents, see the New York *Times,* July 25, 1986. For the Walker case, see Bamford, "The Walker Espionage Case." The figure of twenty-seven U.S. citizens arrested is in U.S. Congress, House, *United States Counterintelligence and Security,* a House Intelligence Committee report. For the Howard case, see Wise, "The Spy Who Got Away." For secrets allegedly stolen by Pollard, see Blitzer, "Pollard."

The first detailed account of American support for the contras was in *Newsweek,* November 8, 1982. The basic sources for the Iran-contra scandal are the U.S. Congress, Senate, *Report on Preliminary Inquiry,* the Tower Commission report (John Tower chairman, *The Tower Commission Report,* New York: Bantam, 1987), and the running coverage in the New York *Times* and Washington *Post;* also see Draper, "The Reagan Junta."

Laughter greeting Casey's answers is from a confidential source. The results of Ghorbanifar's polygraph test is from a confidential source.

Epilogue:

The basic sources for the Ames case are the *Senate Intelligence Committee Report;* Abstract of the CIA Inspector General's Report; Wise, *Nightmover;* Adams *Sellout;* Weiner, et al., *Betrayal* and the running coverage in the New York *Times* and Washington *Post.*

Tip-off on Ames may have come from East European defector is from a confidential source.

Copy of letter from CIC to OS (footnote 6) was transmitted by the Senate Intelligence Committee to Woolsey on June 17, 1994.

Appendix

Directors and Deputy Directors

Directors of Central Intelligence

Rear Admiral Sidney W. Souers, USNR	23 January 1946–10 June 1946
Lieutenant General Hoyt S. Vandenberg, USA	10 June 1946–1 May 1947
Rear Admiral Roscoe H. Hillenkoetter, USN	1 May 1947–7 October 1950
General Walter Bedell Smith, USA	7 October 1950–9 February 1953
Allen W. Dulles	26 February 1953–29 November 1961
John A. McCone	29 November 1961–28 April 1965
Vice Admiral William F. Raborn, Jr., USN (Ret.)	28 April 1965–30 June 1966
Richard Helms	30 June 1966–2 February 1973
James R. Schlesinger	2 February 1973–2 July 1973
William E. Colby	4 September 1973–30 January 1976
George Bush	30 January 1976–20 January 1977
Admiral Stansfield Turner, USN (Ret.)	9 March 1977–20 January 1981
William J. Casey	28 January 1981–29 January 1987
William H. Webster	26 May 1987–31 August 1991
Robert M. Gates	6 November 1991–19 January 1993
R. James Woolsey	5 February 1993–10 January 1995
John M. Deutch	10 May 1995

Deputy Directors of Central Intelligence

Kingman Douglass	2 March 1946–11 July 1946
Brigadier General Edwin K. Wright, USA	20 January 1947–9 March 1949
William H. Jackson	7 October 1950–3 August 1951
Allen W. Dulles	August 1951–26 February 1953
General Charles P. Cabell, USAF	23 April 1953–31 January 1962
Lieutenant General Marshall S. Carter, USA	3 April 1962–28 April 1965
Richard Helms	28 April 1965–30 June 1966
Vice Admiral Rufus L. Taylor, USN	13 October 1966–31 January 1969
Lieutenant General Robert E. Cushman, Jr., USMC	7 May 1969–31 December 1971
Lieutenant General Vernon A. Walters, USA	2 May 1972–7 July 1976
E. Henry Knoche	7 July 1976–31 July 1977
John F. Blake	31 July 1977–10 February 1978
Frank C. Carlucci	10 February 1978–20 January 1981
Admiral Bobby R. Inman, USN	12 February 1981–10 June 1982
John N. McMahon	10 June 1982–28 March 1986
Robert M. Gates	18 April 1986–20 March 1989
Richard J. Kerr	20 March 1989–31 August 1991
Admiral William O. Studeman	9 April 1992–3 July 1995
George J. Tenet	3 July 1995

CIA Organization — 1997

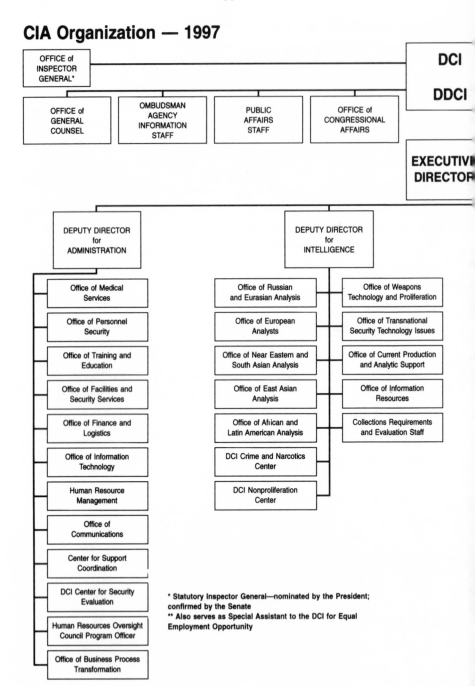

OFFICE of INSPECTOR GENERAL*

DCI

DDCI

OFFICE of GENERAL COUNSEL

OMBUDSMAN AGENCY INFORMATION STAFF

PUBLIC AFFAIRS STAFF

OFFICE of CONGRESSIONAL AFFAIRS

EXECUTIVE DIRECTOR

DEPUTY DIRECTOR for ADMINISTRATION

DEPUTY DIRECTOR for INTELLIGENCE

Office of Medical Services

Office of Personnel Security

Office of Training and Education

Office of Facilities and Security Services

Office of Finance and Logistics

Office of Information Technology

Human Resource Management

Office of Communications

Center for Support Coordination

DCI Center for Security Evaluation

Human Resources Oversight Council Program Officer

Office of Business Process Transformation

Office of Russian and Eurasian Analysis

Office of European Analysts

Office of Near Eastern and South Asian Analysis

Office of East Asian Analysis

Office of African and Latin American Analysis

DCI Crime and Narcotics Center

DCI Nonproliferation Center

Office of Weapons Technology and Proliferation

Office of Transnational Security Technology Issues

Office of Current Production and Analytic Support

Office of Information Resources

Collections Requirements and Evaluation Staff

* Statutory Inspector General—nominated by the President; confirmed by the Senate
** Also serves as Special Assistant to the DCI for Equal Employment Opportunity

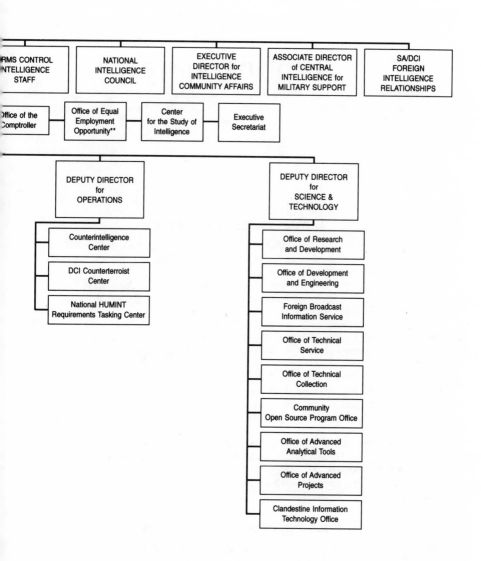

RMS CONTROL
NTELLIGENCE
STAFF

NATIONAL
INTELLIGENCE
COUNCIL

EXECUTIVE
DIRECTOR for
INTELLIGENCE
COMMUNITY AFFAIRS

ASSOCIATE DIRECTOR
of CENTRAL
INTELLIGENCE for
MILITARY SUPPORT

SA/DCI
FOREIGN
INTELLIGENCE
RELATIONSHIPS

Office of the
Comptroller

Office of Equal
Employment
Opportunity**

Center
for the Study of
Intelligence

Executive
Secretariat

DEPUTY DIRECTOR
for
OPERATIONS

DEPUTY DIRECTOR
for
SCIENCE &
TECHNOLOGY

Counterintelligence
Center

DCI Counterterroist
Center

National HUMINT
Requirements Tasking Center

Office of Research
and Development

Office of Development
and Engineering

Foreign Broadcast
Information Service

Office of Technical
Service

Office of Technical
Collection

Community
Open Source Program Office

Office of Advanced
Analytical Tools

Office of Advanced
Projects

Clandestine Information
Technology Office

Bibliography

This select bibliography lists works consulted in the preparation of this book. Sources cited by author and title in the Notes section and in textual footnotes will be found in the alphabetical listing in Part III.

I. Manuscript Collections

Carter, John Franklin. File. Franklin D. Roosevelt Library, Hyde Park, N.Y.
Donovan, William J. Collection on Intelligence History. Columbia University Library.
Harrison, Leland. Papers. Library of Congress.
Hitchcock, Ethan Allen. Diary. William Croffut Papers, Library of Congress.
Layton, Edwin T. Oral History. Nimitz Library. U.S. Naval Academy, Annapolis, Md.
Leahy, Fleet Admiral William D. Diary. Library of Congress.
Map Room Papers. Franklin D. Roosevelt Library, Hyde Park, N.Y.
"Materials on the History of Military Intelligence of the United States, 1885–1944." Unpublished document in U.S. Army Center of Military History, Forrestal Building, Washington, D.C.
National Archives RG 45, Old Army Records.
National Archives RG 59, General Records of the Department of State.
National Archives RG 226, Records of the Office of Strategic Services.
Rochefort, Joseph J. Oral History. Nimitz Library. U.S. Naval Academy Library, Anapolis, Md.
Roosevelt, Kermit. Papers. Library of Congress.
Van Demen, Ralph H. Memoirs. Russell J. Bowen Collection. Georgetown University Library, Washington, D.C.
Van Lew, Elizabeth. Papers. New York Public Library.
Washington, George. Papers. Library of Congress.

II. Encyclopedias and Bibliographies

Boatner, Mark M., 3d. *The Civil War Dictionary*. New York: McKay, 1959.
Buranelli, Vincent, and Buranelli, Nan. *Spy/Counterspy: An Encyclopedia of Espionage*. New York: McGraw-Hill, 1982.
Constantinides, George C. *Intelligence and Espionage: An Analytical Bibliography*. Boulder, Colo.: Westview Press, 1983.
Pforzheimer, Walter, ed. *Bibliography of Intelligence Literature*. 8th ed. Washington, D.C.: Defense Intelligence College, 1985.
Scholar's Guide to Intelligence Literature: Bibliography of the Russell J. Bowen Collection. Frederick, Md.: University Publications of America, 1983.

468

III. Books, Articles, and Other Sources

Abel, Elie. *The Missile Crisis.* Philadelphia: Lippincott, 1966.

Adams, Samuel. "Vietnam Coverup." *Harper's,* May 1975.

Adler, Renata. *Reckless Disregard.* New York: Knopf, 1986.

Agee, Philip. *Dirty Work: The CIA in Western Europe.* Secaucus, N.J.: Lyle Stuart, 1978.

———. *Inside the Company: CIA Diary.* New York: Stonehill, 1975.

Alexander, Charles C. *Holding the Line: The Eisenhower Era, 1952–1961.* Bloomington, Ind.: Indiana University Press, 1975.

Alsop, Stewart, and Thomas Braden. *Sub Rosa: The OSS and American Espionage.* New York: Harcourt, 1964.

Ambrose, Stephen E. *Rise to Globalism: American Foreign Policy Since 1938.* New York: Penguin, 1985.

———. *Upton and the Army.* Baton Rouge: Louisiana State University Press, 1964.

Auger, Helen. *The Secret War of Independence.* New York: Duell, Sloan and Pearce, 1955.

Bailey, Thomas A. *A Diplomatic History of the American People.* New York: Appleton-Century-Crofts, 1946.

Bakeless, John. "Lincoln's Private Eye." *Civil War Times Illustrated,* October 1975.

———. *Spies of the Confederacy.* Philadelphia: Lippincott, 1970.

———. *Turncoats, Traitors and Heroes.* Philadelphia: Lippincott, 1959.

Baker, Lafayette C. *History of the United States Secret Service.* Philadelphia: King and Baird, 1868.

Ballendorf, Dirk A. "Earl Hancock Ellis: The Man and His Mission." *U.S. Naval Institute Proceedings,* November 1983.

Bamford, James. *The Puzzle Palace.* Boston: Houghton Mifflin, 1982.

———. "The Walker Espionage Case." *U.S. Naval Institute Proceedings,* May 1986.

Barber, A. Richard. "The Tallmadge-Culper Intelligence Ring." Master's thesis, Columbia University.

Barron, John. *KGB: The Secret Work of Soviet Agents.* Pleasantville, N.Y.: Reader's Digest Press, 1974.

Bates, David Homer. *Lincoln in the Telegraph Office.* New York: Century, 1907.

Bauer, K. Jack. *The Mexican War: 1846–1848.* New York: Macmillan, 1974.

Beach, Thomas. *Twenty-five Years in the Secret Service: The Recollections of a Spy.* London: Heinemann, 1892.

Beesley, Patrick. *Room 40: British Naval Intelligence 1914–1918.* New York: Harcourt, 1982.

———. *Very Special Intelligence.* Garden City, N.Y.: Doubleday, 1978.

Beirne, Francis F. *Shout Treason: The Trial of Aaron Burr.* New York: Hastings House, 1959.

Bemis, Samuel Flagg. "British Secret Service and the French-American Alliance." *American Historical Review,* April 1924.

———. *The Diplomacy of the American Revolution.* Bloomington, Ind.: Indiana University Press, 1957.

———. *Jay's Treaty.* New Haven, Conn.: Yale University Press, 1962.

Bernikow, Louise. *Abel.* New York: Ballantine, 1982.

Beschloss, Michael R. *Mayday: Eisenhower, Khrushchev and the U-2 Affair.* New York: Harper & Row, 1986.

Beveridge, Albert J. *The Life of John Marshall.* Vol. 2. Boston: Houghton Mifflin, 1919.

Blair, Clay. *Silent Victory: The U.S. Submarine War against Japan.* Philadelphia: Lippincott, 1975.

Blitzer, Wolf. "Pollard: Not a Bumbler, but Israel's Master Spy." *Washington Post,* Outlook Section, February 15, 1987.

Bliven, Bruce. *Under the Guns: New York 1775–1776*. New York: Harper & Row, 1972.

Bohlen, Charles E. *Witness to History: 1929–1969*. New York: Norton, 1973.

Boudinot, J. J. *Life of Elias Boudinot*. 2 vols. Boston, 1896.

Boyd, Belle. *Belle Boyd in Camp and Prison*. South Brunswick, N.J.: Thomas Yoseloff, 1968.

Boyd, Julian P. *Number 7*. Princeton, N.J.: Princeton University Press, 1964.

———. "Silas Deane: Death by a Kindly Teacher of Treason?" *William and Mary Quarterly*, April, July, October 1959.

Brackett, Albert G. *General Lane's Brigade in Central Mexico*. New York: J. C. Derby, 1854.

Brant, Irving. *The Fourth President: A Life of James Madison*. Indianapolis: Bobbs-Merrill, 1970.

Bratzell, John F., and Leslie B. Rout, Jr. "FDR and the 'Secret Map.' "*The Wilson Quarterly*, New Year's 1985.

———. "Pearl Harbor, Microdots and J. Edgar Hoover." *American Historical Review*, December 1982.

———. *The Shadow War*. Frederick, Md.: University Publications of America, 1986.

Breckinridge, Scott D. *The CIA and the U.S. Intelligence System*. Boulder, Colo.: Westview Press, 1986.

Brock, David. "Spies Are Back in U.S. Arsenal." *Insight*, June 23, 1986.

Brown, Anthony Cave. *The Last Hero: Wild Bill Donovan*. New York: Times Books, 1982.

Bryan, George S. *The Spy in America*. Philadelphia: Lippincott, 1943.

Bryce, Ivar. *You Only Live Twice: Memories of Ian Fleming*. Frederick, Md.: University Publications of America, 1984.

Bulloch, James D. *The Secret Service of the Confederate States in Europe*. 2 vols. New York: Thomas Yoseloff, 1959.

Campbell, Helen Jones. *Confederate Courier*. New York: St. Martin's, 1964.

Campbell, Kenneth J. "Bedell Smith's Imprint on the CIA," *International Journal of Intelligence and Counterintelligence*, vol. 1., no. 2.

———. "Major General Ralph H. Van Deman: Father of American Military Intelligence." *American Intelligence Journal*, Summer 1987.

Canan, H. V. "Confederate Military Intelligence." *Maryland Historical Magazine*, March 1964.

Casey, William J. "Remarks before the OSS/Donovan Symposium." September 19, 1986.

———. *The Secret War against Hitler*. Washington, D.C.: Regnery Gateway, 1988.

Catton, Bruce. *Glory Road*. Garden City, N.Y.: Doubleday, 1952.

Churchill, Marlborough. "The Military Intelligence Division of the General Staff." *Journal of the United States Artillery*, April 1920.

Clark, Ronald. *The Man Who Broke Purple*. Boston: Little, Brown, 1977.

Cline, Ray S. *The CIA under Reagan, Bush and Casey*. Washington, D.C.: Acropolis, 1981.

Colby, Gerard. *Du Pont Dynasty*. Secaucus. N.J.: Lyle Stuart, 1984.

Colby, William. *Honorable Men: My Life in the CIA*. New York: Simon and Schuster, 1978.

Cole, J. A. *Prince of Spies: Henri Le Caron*. London: Faber and Faber, 1984.

Conrad, Thomas. *A Confederate Spy*. New York: J. S. Ogilvie, 1892.

———. *The Rebel Scout*. Washington, D.C.: The National Publishing Co., 1904.

Coon, Carleton S. *A North Africa Story*. Ipswich, Mass.: Gambit, 1980.

Corson, William R. *The Armies of Ignorance*. New York: Dial, 1977.

———, and Robert T. Crowly. *The New KGB: Engine of Soviet Power*. New York: Morrow, 1985.

Crary, Catherine S. "The Tory and the Spy: The Double Life of James Rivington." *The William and Mary Quarterly*, January 1958.

Crile, George, and Taylor Branch. "The Kennedy Vendetta." *Harper's*, August 1975.

Cullop, Charles P. *Confederate Propaganda in Europe*. Coral Gables, Fla.: University of Miami Press, 1969.

Currey, Cecil B. *Code Number 72/ Ben Franklin: Patriot or Spy?* Englewood Cliffs, N.J.: Prentice-Hall, 1972.

Cuthbert, Norma B., ed. *Lincoln and the Baltimore Plot.* San Marino, Calif.: Huntington Library, 1949.

Dallek, Robert. *Franklin D. Roosevelt and American Foreign Policy.* New York: Oxford University Press, 1979.

Daniels, Roger. *The Bonus March: An Episode of the Great Depression.* Westport, Conn.. Greenwood, 1971.

Davis, Curtis Carroll. "The Civil War's Most Over-Rated Spy." *West Virginia History,* October 1965.

Deacon, Richard. *A History of British Secret Service.* London: Granada, 1980.

Dinerstein, Herbert. *The Making of a Missile Crisis.* Baltimore, Md.: Johns Hopkins University Press, 1976.

Donovan, James B. *Strangers on a Bridge: The Case of Colonel Abel.* New York: Atheneum, 1964.

Donovan, Robert J. *Conflict and Crisis.* New York: Norton, 1977.

Dorwart, Jeffery. *Conflict of Duty: The U.S. Navy's Intelligence Dilemma, 1919–1945.* Annapolis, Md.: Naval Institute Press, 1983.

———. *The Office of Naval Intelligence: The Birth of America's First Intelligence Agency, 1865–1918.* Annapolis, Md.: Naval Institute Press, 1979.

Dos Passos, John. *Mr. Wilson's War.* Garden City, N.Y.: Doubleday, 1962.

Downs, Donald. *The Scarlet Thread.* London: Vershoyle, 1953.

Draper, Theodore. "The Reagan Junta." *The New York Review of Books,* January 29, 1987.

Dulles, Allen W. *The Craft of Intelligence.* New York: Signet, 1965.

———. *Germany's Underground.* New York: Macmillan, 1947.

———. *The Secret Surrender.* New York: Harper & Row, 1966.

Dunlop, Richard. *Behind Japanese Lines: With the OSS in Burma.* Chicago: Rand McNally, 1979.

Einstein, Lewis. *Divided Loyalties.* Boston: Houghton Mifflin, 1935.

Eisenhower, Dwight D. *Crusade in Europe.* Garden City, N.Y.: Doubleday, 1948.

Epstein, Edward Jay. *Legend: The Secret World of Lee Harvey Oswald.* Pleasantville, N.Y.: Reader's Digest Press, 1978.

———. "Who Killed the CIA?" *Commentary,* October 1985.

Falkner, Leonard. "A Spy for Washington." *American Heritage,* August 1957.

Farago, Ladislas. *The Game of Foxes.* New York: McKay, 1971.

Fishel, Edwin C. "Mythmaking at Stimson's Expense: What *Did* the Secretary Say (or Not Say)?" *Foreign Intelligence Literary Scene,* October 1985.

———. "The Mythology of Civil War Intelligence." *Civil War History,* December 1964.

Flexner, James Thomas. *George Washington in the American Revolution.* Boston: Little, Brown, 1967.

———. *The Traitor and the Spy.* New York: Harcourt, Brace, 1953.

Forbes, Esther. *Paul Revere and the World He Lived in.* Boston: Houghton Mifflin, 1942.

Ford, Corey. *Donovan of OSS.* Boston: Little, Brown, 1970.

———. *A Peculiar Service.* Boston: Little, Brown, 1965.

Fowler, W. B. *British-American Relations, 1917–1918.* Princeton, N.J.: Princeton University Press, 1969.

Frank, Larry J. "The United States Navy v. the Chicago *Tribune.*" *The Historian,* February 1980.

Franklin, Benjamin. *The Writings of Benjamin Franklin.* Edited by Albert H. Smith. 10 vols. New York: Macmillan, 1905–1907.

Freeman, Douglas S. *George Washington: Planter and Patriot.* New York: Scribner, 1951.

———. *R. E. Lee,* Vol. 3. New York: Scribner, 1937.

Freese, Jacob. *Secrets of the Late Rebellion.* Philadelphia: Crombarger, 1882.

French, Allen. *The First Year of the American Revolution.* Boston: Houghton Mifflin, 1934.

——. *General Gage's Informers.* Ann Arbor, Mich.: University of Michigan Press, 1932.

Fry, Joseph A. *Henry S. Sanford: Diplomacy and Business in Nineteenth-Century America.* Reno: University of Nevada Press, 1982.

Gaddis, John Lewis. *The United States and the Origins of the Cold War.* New York: Columbia University Press, 1972.

Gaddy, David W. "Gray Cloaks and Daggers." *Civil War Times,* July 1975.

——. "William Norris and the Confederate Signal and Secret Service." *Maryland Historical Magazine,* Summer 1975.

George, Willis. *Surreptitious Entry.* New York: Appleton-Century, 1946.

Godson, Ray, ed. *Intelligence Requirements for the 1980s.* 5 vols. Washington, D.C.: Consortium for the Study of Intelligence, 1979–1982.

Goetzmann, William H. *Army Exploration in the American West 1803–1863.* Lincoln: University of Nebraska Press, 1979.

Goodman, Allan E. "Dateline Langley: Fixing the Intelligence Mess." *Foreign Policy,* Winter 1984–1985.

Goulden, Joseph C. *The Death Merchant: The Rise and Fall of Edwin P. Wilson.* New York: Simon and Schuster, 1984.

——. *Korea: The Untold Story.* New York: McGraw-Hill, 1983.

Gray, Wood. *The Hidden Civil War: The Story of the Copperheads.* New York: Viking, 1942.

Greenhow, Rose O'Neale. *My Imprisonment and the First Year of Abolition Rule in Washington.* London: Robert Bentley, 1863.

Griffith, Samuel B. *In Defense of the Public Liberty.* Garden City, N.Y.: Doubleday, 1976.

Guderian, Heinz. *Panzer Leader.* New York: Dutton, 1952.

Halberstam, David. *The Best and the Brightest.* New York: Random House, 1972.

Hall, Charles S. *Benjamin Tallmadge.* New York: Columbia University Press, 1943.

Hamilton, Alexander, James Madison, and John Jay. *The Federalist Papers.* New York: New American Library, 1961.

Harrison, Marguerite. *There's Always Tomorrow.* New York: Farrar & Rinehart, 1935.

Hasbrouck, G. B. D. "Address on Major General George H. Sharpe." *Proceedings of Ulster County Historical Society, 1936–1937.*

Hatch, Robert M. *Thrust for Canada.* Boston: Houghton Mifflin, 1979.

Headley, John W. *Confederate Operations in Canada and the North.* New York: Neale, 1906.

Hersh, Burton. "Dragons Must Be Killed." *Washingtonian,* September 1985.

Hersh, Seymour M. *The Price of Power: Kissinger in the White House.* New York: Summit Books, 1983.

Higginbotham, Don. *The War of American Independence.* New York: Macmillan, 1971.

Hirshson, Stanley P. *Grenville M. Dodge: Soldier, Politician, Railroad Pioneer.* Bloomington, Ind.: University of Indiana Press, 1967.

Hitchcock, Ethan Allen. *Fifty Years of Camp and Field.* Edited by W. Croffut. New York: Putnam, 1909.

Hohne, Heinz. *Canaris: Hitler's Master Spy.* Garden City, N.Y.: Doubleday, 1979.

——, and Herman Zolling. *The General Was a Spy.* New York: Bantam, 1972.

Holmes, W. J. *Double-Edged Secrets.* Annapolis, Md.: Naval Institute Press, 1979.

Hood, William. *Mole.* New York: Ballantine, 1982.

Horan, James D. *Confederate Agent.* New York: Crown, 1954.

——. *The Pinkertons: The Detective Dynasty That Made History.* New York: Crown 1967.

Horsman, Reginald. *The War of 1812.* New York: Knopf, 1969.

Hyde, H. Montgomery. *Room 3603.* New York: Dell, 1964.

Hymoff, Edward. *The OSS in World War II*. New York: Ballantine, 1972.

Ind, Allison. *A Short History of Espionage*. New York: McKay, 1963.

Isaacson, Walter, and Evan Thomas. *The Wise Men: Six Friends and the World They Made*. New York: Simon and Schuster, 1986.

Jacobs, James Ripley. *Tarnished Warrior: Maj. Gen. James Wilkinson*. New York: Macmillan, 1938.

James, Coy H. *Silas Deane—Patriot or Traitor*. Lansing, Mich.: Michigan State University Press, 1975.

Janos, Leo. "The Last Days of the President: LBJ in Retirement." *Atlantic*, July 1973.

Jeffreys-Jones, Rhodri. *American Espionage: From Secret Service to CIA*. New York: Free Press, 1977.

Jensen, Joan M. *The Price of Vigilance*. Chicago: Rand McNally, 1968.

Johns, George S. *Philip Henson, The Southern Union Spy*. St. Louis: Nixon-Jones Printing Co., 1887.

Johnson, Loch K. *A Season of Inquiry: The Senate Intelligence Investigation*. Lexington, Ky.: University of Kentucky, 1985.

Jones, Virgil C. *Eight Hours before Richmond*. New York: Holt, 1957.

Kahin, George McT. *Intervention: How America Became Involved in Vietnam*. New York: Knopf, 1986.

Kahn, David. *The Codebreakers*. New York: Macmillan, 1967.

———. *Hitler's Spies: German Military Intelligence in World War II*. New York: Macmillan, 1978.

Kane, Harnett T. *Spies for the Blue and Gray*. Garden City, N.Y.: Hanover House, 1954.

Karnow, Stanley. *Vietnam: A History*. New York: Penguin, 1983.

Keats, John. *Eminent Domain: The Louisiana Purchase and the Making of America*. New York: Charterhouse, 1973.

Kennan, George, *Memoirs, 1925–1950*. Boston: Little, Brown, 1967.

Kent, Sherman. *Strategic Intelligence*. Princeton, N.J.: Princeton University Press, 1949.

Kinchen, Oscar A. *Confederate Operations in Canada and the North*. North Quincy, Mass.: Christopher, 1970.

———. *Daredevils of the Confederate Army*. Boston: Christopher, 1959.

Kirkpatrick, Lyman E. "Paramilitary Case Study—The Bay of Pigs." *Naval War College Review*, November–December 1972.

———. *The Real CIA*. New York: Macmillan, 1968.

———. *The U.S. Intelligence Community: Foreign Policy and Domestic Activities*. New York: Hill and Wang, 1973.

Klehr, Harvey, and Ronald Radosh. "Anatomy of a Fix." *The New Republic*, April 21, 1986.

Knightley, Philip. *The Second Oldest Profession: Spies and Spying in the Twentieth Century*. New York: Norton, 1987.

Kohn, Richard H. *Eagle and Sword: The Beginnings of the Military Establishment in America*. New York: Free Press, 1975.

Lamphere, Robert J., and Tom Shachtman. *The FBI-KGB War*. New York: Random House, 1986.

Landau, Henry. *The Enemy Within*. New York: Putnam, 1937.

Laqueur, Walter. *A World of Secrets*. New York: Basic Books, 1985.

Laqueur, Walter and Richard Breitman, *Breaking the Silence*. New York: Simon and Schuster, 1986.

Layton, Edwin T., with Roger Pineau and John Costello. *"And I Was There": Pearl Harbor and Midway—Breaking the Secrets*. New York: Morrow, 1985.

Leech, Margaret. *Reveille in Washington*. New York: Harper, 1941.

LeFeber, Walter. *America in the Cold War*. New York: Wiley, 1969.

Lelyveld, Joseph. "The Director." *The New York Times Magazine*, January 26, 1985.

Lester, Richard L. *Confederate Finance and Purchasing in Great Britain.* Charlottesville, Va.: University of Virginia Press, 1975.

Levy, Leonard W. *Jefferson and Civil Liberties.* New York: Quadrangle, 1973.

Lewin, Ronald. *The American Magic.* New York: Farrar, Straus, & Giroux, 1982.

──────. *Ultra Goes to War.* New York: McGraw-Hill, 1978.

Loftus, John. *The Belarus Secret.* Edited by Nathan Miller. New York: Knopf, 1982.

Lomask, Milton. *Aaron Burr: The Conspiracy and the Years of Exile.* New York: Farrar, Straus, & Giroux, 1982.

Lord, Walter. *Incredible Victory.* New York: Harper & Row, 1967.

Lovell, Stanley P. *Of Spies and Strategems.* New York: Prentice-Hall, 1963.

Lowenthal, Mark. *U.S. Intelligence: Evolution and Anatomy.* Washington, D.C.: Center for Strategic and International Studies, 1984.

Lowenthal, Max. *The Federal Bureau of Investigation.* New York: William Sloan, 1959.

Lukas, J. Anthony. *Nightmare: The Underside of the Nixon Years.* New York: Viking, 1976.

Maclay, William, *The Journal of William Maclay.* New York: A. & C. Boni, 1927.

Manchester, William. *American Caesar: Douglas MacArthur 1880–1964.* Boston: Little, Brown, 1978.

Marchetti, Victor, and John D. Marks. *The CIA and the Cult of Intelligence.* New York: Dell, 1980.

Martin, David C. *Wilderness of Mirrors.* New York: Ballantine, 1980.

Mashbir, Sidney F. *I Was an American Spy.* New York: Vantage, 1953.

Maynard, Douglas. "Plotting the Escape of the *Alabama.*" *Journal of Southern History,* May 1954.

──────. "Union Efforts to Prevent the Escape of the Alabama." *Mississippi Valley Historical Review,* June 1954.

McGhee, Ralph W. *Deadly Deceit: My 25 Years in the CIA.* New York: Sheridan Square, 1983.

McLachlan, Donald. *Room 39: A Study in Naval Intelligence.* New York: Atheneum, 1968.

Merli, Frank J. *Great Britain and the Confederate Navy.* Bloomington, Ind.: University of Indiana Press, 1965.

Meyer, Cord. *Facing Reality.* New York: Harper & Row, 1980.

Miller, John C. *Crisis in Freedom.* Boston: Little, Brown, 1951.

──────. *Triumph of Freedom.* Boston: Little, Brown, 1948.

──────. *The Federalist Era.* New York: Harper, 1960.

Miller, Nathan. *F.D.R.: An Intimate History.* Garden City, N.Y.: Doubleday, 1983.

──────. *Sea of Glory: The Continental Navy Fights for Independence, 1775–1783.* New York: McKay, 1974.

──────. *The U.S. Navy: An Illustrated History.* Annapolis, Md.: Naval Institute Press, 1977.

Miller, Stuart Creighton. *"Benevolent Assimilation": The American Conquest of the Philippines, 1898–1903.* New Haven, Conn.: Yale University Press, 1982.

Millet, Allan R., and Peter Maslowski. *For the Common Defense: A Military History of the United States of America.* New York: Free Press, 1984.

Millis, Walter. *Arms and Men.* New York: Putnam, 1956.

──────. *Road to War: America, 1914–1917. Boston: Houghton Mifflin, 1935.*

Mitgang, Herbert. "Garibaldi and Lincoln." *American Heritage,* October 1975.

Mogelever, Jacob. *Death to Traitors: The Story of General Lafayette C. Baker, Lincoln's Forgotten Secret Service Chief.* Garden City, N.Y.: Doubleday, 1960.

Montross, Lynn. *The Reluctant Rebels.* New York: Harper & Row, 1950.

Morison, Elting E. *Admiral Sims and the Modern American Navy.* Boston: Houghton Mifflin, 1942.

Morison, Samuel Eliot. "The Henry-Crillon Affair of 1812." In *By Land and by Sea.* New York: Knopf, 1953.

Morris, Richard R. *The Peacemakers*. New York: Harper & Row, 1965.

Moseley, Leonard. *Dulles*. New York: Dial, 1978.

Moses, Hans. *The Clandestine Service of the Central Intelligence Agency*. McLean, Va.: Association of Former Intelligence Officers, 1983.

Murphy, Robert. *Diplomat among Warriors*. Garden City, N.Y.: Doubleday, 1984.

Murray, Robert K. *Red Scare: A Study in National Hysteria*. Minneapolis: University of Minnesota, 1955.

Nelson, Anna Kasten. "Mission to Mexico: Moses Y. Beach—Secret Agent." *New York Historical Society Quarterly*, July 1975.

Neustadt, Richard E., and Ernest R. May. *Thinking in Time*. New York: Free Press, 1986.

Oberdorfer, Don. *Tet!* Garden City, N.Y.: Doubleday, 1971.

Official Records of the Union and Confederate Armies in the War of the Rebellion. Washington, D.C.: Government Printing Office.

Official Records of the Union and Confederate Navies, 31 vols. Washington, D.C.: Government Printing Office.

O'Toole, G. J. A. *The Spanish War*. New York: Norton, 1984.

Owsley, Frank L. *King Cotton Diplomacy*. Chicago: University of Chicago Press, 1959.

Owsley, Harriet C. "Henry Shelton Sanford and Federal Surveillance Abroad." *Mississippi Valley Historical Review*, September 1961.

Palmer, Bruce. *The 25-Year War: America's Military Role in Vietnam*. New York: Touchstone, 1984.

Patrick, Marsena R. *Inside Lincoln's Army: The Diary of Marsena R. Patrick*. Edited by David Sparks. New York: Thomas Yoseloff, 1964.

Patti, Archimedes. *Why Viet Nam?* Berkeley: University of California Press, 1980.

Peake, Hayden B. "The Putative Spy." *Foreign Intelligence Literary Scene*, March–April 1986.

Penkovsky, Oleg. *The Penkovsky Papers*. Garden City, N.Y.: Doubleday, 1966.

Pennypacker, Morton. *George Washington's Spies on Long Island and in New York*. Brooklyn, N.Y.: Long Island Historical Society, 1939.

———. *Supplement to George Washington's Spies*. East Hampton, N.Y.: Privately printed, 1948.

Persico, Joseph E. *Piercing the Reich*. New York: Ballantine, 1979.

Pettee, George S. *The Future of American Secret Intelligence*. Washington, D.C.: Infantry Journal Press, 1946.

Philby, Harold A. R. *My Secret War*. New York: Grove Press, 1968.

Phillips, David Atlee. *The Night Watch*. New York: Ballantine, 1977.

Pincher, Chapman. *Their Trade Is Treachery*. London: Sidgewick and Jackson, 1981.

———. *Too Secret Too Long*. New York: St. Martin's, 1984.

Pinkerton, Allan. *The Spy of the Rebellion*. New York: G. W. Dillingham, 1886.

Pipes, Richard. "Team B: The Reality behind the Myth." *Commentary*, October 1986.

Porter, Horace. *Campaigning with Grant*. Alexandria, Va.: Time-Life Books, 1981.

Powe, Marc B. *The Emergence of the War Department Intelligence Agency, 1885–1918*. Manhattan, Kans.: Military Affairs, 1975.

Powers, Francis Gary. *Operation Overflight*. New York: Holt, 1970.

Powers, Richard G. *Secrecy and Power: The Life of J. Edgar Hoover*. New York: Free Press, 1987.

Powers, Thomas. *The Man Who Kept the Secrets: Richard Helms and the CIA*. New York: Pocket Books, 1981.

Prados, John. *Presidents' Secret Wars: CIA and Pentagon Covert Operations Since World War II*. New York: Morrow, 1986.

Rachlis, Eugene. *They Came to Kill*. New York: Random House, 1961.

Radosh, Ronald, and Joyce Martin. *The Rosenberg File*. New York: Holt, Rinehart & Winston, 1983.

Ranelagh, John. *The Agency: The Rise and Decline of the CIA.* New York: Simon and Schuster, 1986.

Ransom, Harry Howe. *Central Intelligence and National Security.* Cambridge: Harvard University Press, 1958.

Read, Anthony, and David Fisher. *Colonel Z: The Secret Life of a Master of Spies.* New York: Viking, 1985.

Reber, John J. "Pete Ellis: Amphibious War Prophet." *U.S. Naval Institute Proceedings,* November 1977.

Remini, Robert V. *Andrew Jackson and the Course of American Empire, 1767–1821.* New York: Harper, 1977.

Richardson, James D., ed. *A Compilation of the Messages and Papers of the Presidents.* Vol. 10. New York: Bureau of National Literature, 1897.

Rickover, H. G. *How the Battleship Maine Was Destroyed.* Washington, D.C.: Government Printing Office, 1976.

Rintelen, Franz von Kliest. *The Dark Invader.* New York: Macmillan, 1933.

Rochefort, Joseph J. *Reminiscences of Captain Joseph J. Rochefort U.S.N. (ret.).* Transcript of Oral History, Nimitz Library, U.S. Naval Academy.

Rockefeller Commission. *Report to the President by the Commission on CIA Activities within the United States.* Washington, D.C.: Government Printing Office, 1975.

Roosevelt, Kermit. *Countercoup: The Struggle for Control of Iran.* New York: McGraw-Hill, 1979.

Rositzke, Harry. *The CIA's Secret Operations.* Pleasantville, N.Y.: Reader's Digest Press, 1977.

Ross, Ishbel. *Rebel Rose: The Life of Rose O'Neal Greenhow.* New York: Harper, 1954.

Rowan, Richard W. *The Story of Secret Service.* New York: Literary Guild, 1937.

Rubin, Barry. *Paved with Good Intentions: The American Experience and Iran.* New York: Oxford University Press, 1980.

Sandburg, Carl. *Abraham Lincoln: The Prairie Years.* Vol. 2. New York: Harcourt, 1926.

Sayle, Edward F. "George Washington: Manager of Intelligence." Paper presented at the Smithsonian Institution, November 16, 1983.

———. "The Historical Underpinnings of the U.S. Intelligence Community." *International Journal of Intelligence and Counterintelligence,* Vol. 1, No. 1.

Scheips, Philip. "Union Signal Communications: Innovation and Conflict." *Civil War History,* December 1963.

Schlesinger, Arthur. *Robert F. Kennedy and His Times.* Boston: Houghton Mifflin, 1978.

———. *A Thousand Days: John F. Kennedy in the White House.* Boston: Houghton Mifflin, 1965.

Schlesinger, Stephen, and Stephen Kinzer. *Bitter Fruit: The Untold Story of the American Coup in Guatemala.* Garden City, N.Y.: Doubleday, 1982.

Schneir, Walter, and Miriam Schneir. *Invitation to an Inquest.* New York: Penguin, 1983.

Sears, Stephen W. *George B. McClellan: The Young Napoleon.* New York: Ticknor & Fields, 1988.

"Secret Service Papers of John Howe." *The American Historical Review,* October 1911 and January 1912.

Seymour, George D. *Documentary Life of Nathan Hale.* New Haven, Conn.: Privately printed, 1941.

Shackley, Theodore. *The Third Option.* New York: McGraw-Hill, 1981.

Sick, Gary. *All Fall Down: America's Tragic Encounter with Iran.* New York: Random House, 1985.

Smith, Bradley F. *The Shadow Warriors: O.S.S. and the Origins of the C.I.A.* New York: Basic Books, 1983.

———, & Elena Agarossi, *Operation Sunrise: The Secret Surrender.* Philadelphia: Basic Books, 1979.

Smith, Joseph B. *The Plot to Steal Florida: James Madison's Phony War.* New York: Arbor House, 1983.

———. *Portrait of a Cold Warrior.* New York: Putnam, 1976.

Smith, R. Harris. *OSS: The Secret History of America's First Central Intelligence Agency.* New York: Dell, 1972.

Smolla, Rodney A. *Suing the Press.* New York: Oxford University Press, 1986.

Snepp, Frank. *Decent Interval.* New York: Random House, 1977.

Spencer, Warren F. *The Confederate Navy in Europe.* Tuscaloosa: University of Alabama Press, 1983.

Stafford, David. *Camp X.* New York: Dodd, Mead, 1987.

Sterling, Claire. *The Terror Network.* New York: Holt, Rinehart & Winston, 1981.

Stern, Philip Van Doren. *Secret Missions of the Civil War.* New York: Bonanza Books, 1959.

———. *When the Guns Roared.* Garden City, N.Y.: Doubleday, 1965.

Stevens, Benjamin F. *Facsimiles of Documents in European Archives Relating to America, 1773–1783.* 25 vols. Wilmington, Del.: Melliport Press, 1970.

Stevenson, William. *Intrepid's Last Case.* New York: Random House, 1984.

———. *A Man Called Intrepid.* New York: Harcourt, 1976.

Stimson, Henry L., and McGeorge Bundy. *On Active Service in Peace and War.* New York: Harper, 1947.

Stockwell, John. *In Search of Enemies: A CIA Story.* New York: Norton, 1978.

Strode, Hudson. *Jefferson Davis.* Volume 3. New York, 1964.

Stuart, Meriwether. "Colonel Ulric Dahlgren and Richmond's Union Underground." *Virginia Magazine of History and Biography,* April 1964.

———. "Samuel Ruth and General R. E. Lee." *Virginia Magazine of History and Biography,* January 1963.   .

Sun Tzu. *The Art of War.* Edited by James Clavell. New York: Delacorte, 1983.

Szulc, Tad. *Compulsive Spy: The Strange Career of E. Howard Hunt.* Viking: New York, 1974.

———. *Fidel: A Critical Portrait.* New York: Morrow, 1986.

Tallmadge, Benjamin. *Memoir of Colonel Tallmadge.* New York: New York Times, 1967.

Taylor, Charles E. *The Signal and Secret Service of the Confederate States.* Hamlet, N.C.: North Carolina Booklet, 1903.

Teague, Michael. *Mrs. L.: Conversations with Alice Roosevelt Longworth.* Garden City, N.Y.: Doubleday, 1981.

Thompson, James W., and Saul K. Padover. *Secret Diplomacy, Espionage and Cryptography, 1500–1815.* New York: Frederick Unger, 1963.

Toland, John. *Infamy: Pearl Harbor and Its Aftermath.* Garden City, N.Y.: Doubleday, 1982.

Trask, David F. *The War with Spain in 1898.* New York: Macmillan, 1981.

Trefousse, Hans L. "Failure of German Intelligence in the United States, 1935–1945." *Mississippi Valley Historical Review,* June 1955.

Troy, Thomas. *Donovan and the CIA: A History of the Establishment of the Central Intelligence Agency.* Frederick, Md.: University Publications of America, 1981.

Truman, Harry S. *Memoirs.* 2 vols. Garden City, N.Y.: Doubleday, 1956.

Tuchman, Barbara. *Stilwell and the American Experience in China.* New York: Macmillan, 1970.

———. *The Zimmerman Telegram.* London: Constable, 1959.

Turner, Stansfield. *Secrecy and Democracy.* Boston: Houghton Mifflin, 1985.

Turrou, Leon. *The Nazi Spy Conspiracy in America.* Freeport, N.Y.: Books for Libraries Press, 1972.

Ungar, Sanford J. *FBI.* Boston: Little, Brown, 1976.

U.S. Congress, House of Representatives. Permanent Select Committee on Intelligence. *Soviet Covert Action (The Forgery Offensive).* Washington, D.C.: Government Printing Office, 1980.

————. Permanent Select Committee on Intelligence. *United States Counterintelligence and Security, 1986*. Washington, D.C.: Government Printing Office, 1987.

————. Select Committee on Intelligence. *Recommendations of the Final Report*. Leaked to the *Village Voice* and published on February 16 and 23, 1976.

U.S. Congress, Senate. *Alleged Assassination Plots Involving Foreign Leaders*. An Interim Report of the U.S. Senate Select Committee to Study Governmental Operations with Respect to Intelligence Activities. Washington, D.C.: Government Printing Office, 1975.

————. *Covert Action in Chile, 1963–1973*. Staff Report of the Select Committee to Study Governmental Operations with Respect to Intelligence Activities. Washington, D.C.: Government Printing Office, 1975.

————. *Final Report of the U.S. Senate Select Committee to Study Governmental Operations with Respect to Intelligence Activities*. 94th Cong., 2d. sess. Six vols. Washington, D.C.: Government Printing Office, 1976 (Church Committee Report.)

U.S. Congress, Senate. *The National Security Agency and Fourth Amendment Rights*. Hearings. 94th Cong. 1st sess. Vol. 5. Washington, D.C.: Government Printing Office, 1975.

————. Joint Committee on the Conduct of the War. *Report 1*, 38th Cong., 2d sess. Washington, D.C.: Government Printing Office, 1865.

————. Senate Select Committee on Intelligence. *Report on Preliminary Inquiry*. 1987. (The Iran-contra scandal.)

U.S. Department of Defense. *The "Magic" Background of Pearl Harbor*. 8 vols. Washington, D.C.: Government Printing Office, 1976.

U.S. War Department. Strategic Services Unit. *War Report of the OSS*. New introduction by Kermit Roosevelt. 2 vols. New York: Walker, 1976.

Van Doren, Carl. *Benjamin Franklin*. New York: Viking, 1938.

————. *Secret History of the American Revolution*. Garden City, N.Y.: Garden City Publishing, 1941.

Voska, Eugene, and Will Irwin. *Spy and Counterspy*. Garden City, N.Y.: Doubleday, 1940.

Wagner, Arthur L. *The Service of Security and Information*. Kansas City: Franklin Hudson, 1894.

Wallace, Edward S. *Destiny and Glory*. New York: Coward-McCann, 1957.

Wallace, Willard M. *Traitorous Hero: The Life and Fortunes of Benedict Arnold*. New York: Harper, 1954.

Washington, George. *Writings*. Edited by J. C. Fitzpatrick. 39 vols. Washington, D.C.: Government Printing Office, 1931–1944.

Watson, Mark S. *The United States Army in World War II. The War Department. Chief of Staff: Prewar Plans and Preparations*. Washington, D.C.: Government Printing Office, 1950.

Weber, Ralph E. *United States Diplomatic Codes and Ciphers, 1775–1938*. Chicago: Precedent Publishing, 1979.

Weigley, Russell F. *The American Way of War*. New York: Macmillan, 1973.

————. *History of the United States Army*. Bloomington, Ind.: Indiana University Press, 1984.

Weinstein, Alan. *Perjury: The Hiss-Chambers Case*. New York: Knopf, 1978.

West, Nigel. *MI6: British Secret Intelligence Operations, 1909–1945*. New York: Random House, 1984.

————. *A Thread of Deceit: Espionage Myths of World War II*. New York: Random House, 1985.

Wharton, Francis, ed. *The Revolutionary Diplomatic Correspondence of the United States*. 62 vols. Washington, D.C.: Government Printing Office, 1889.

Willet, Arthur. *The Road to Safety: A Study in Anglo-American Relations*. London: Vershoyle, 1952.

Williams, Kenneth. *Lincoln Finds a General.* Vol. 1. New York: Macmillan, 1949.

Wills, Gary. *Reagan's America.* Garden City, N.Y.: Doubleday, 1987.

Winks, Robin W. *Cloak and Gown: Scholars in the Secret War, 1939–1961.* New York: Morrow, 1987.

Wise, David. "Campus Recruiting and the CIA." *The New York Times Magazine,* June 8, 1986.

————. "The Spy Who Got Away." *The New York Times Magazine,* November 2, 1986.

————, and Thomas B. Ross. *The Espionage Establishment.* New York: Bantam, 1968.

————. *The Invisible Government.* New York: Random House, 1964.

Wohlstetter, Roberta. *Pearl Harbor: Warning and Decision.* Palo Alto, Calif.: Stanford University Press, 1962.

Woodward, Bob. *Veil.* New York: Simon and Schuster, 1987.

Wriston, Henry M. *Executive Agents in American Foreign Relations.* Baltimore, Md.: Johns Hopkins University Press, 1929.

Wyden, Peter. *Bay of Pigs: The Untold Story.* New York: Simon and Schuster, 1975.

Wynne, Greville. *Contact on Gorki Street.* New York: Atheneum, 1968.

Yardley, Herbert O. *The American Black Chamber.* New York: Ballantine, 1981.

Yergin, Daniel. *Shattered Peace: The Origins of the Cold War and the National Security State.* Boston: Houghton Mifflin, 1977.

Zacharias, Ellis M. *Secret Missions: The Story of an Intelligence Officer.* New York: Putnam, 1946.

Addendum to the Bibliography

Adams, James. *Sellout: Aldrich Ames and the Corruption of the CIA.* New York: Viking, 1995.

Berkowitz, Bruce D. and Jeffrey T. Richelson. "The CIA Vindicated: The Soviet Collapse *Was* Predicted." *The National Interest* Fall 1995.

Godson, Roy. *Dirty Tricks or Trump Cards: U.S. Covert Action and Counterintelligence,* Washington: Brassey's, 1995.

———— and Ernest R. May and Gary Schmitt. *U.S. Intelligence at the Crossroads.* Washington: Brassey's, 1995.

Haass, Richard N. Project Director. *Making Intelligence Smarter: The Future of U.S. Intelligence.* New York: Council on Foreign Reltions, 1966.

Hilsman, Roger. "Downsizing the CIA." *Foreign Affairs,* September/October 1995.

Hitz, Frederick P. *Abstract of Report of Investigation: The Aldrich H. Ames Case.* Langley, Va. October 21, 1994. Unclassified version of the CIA Inspector General's Report.

Kessler, Ronald. *Inside the CIA.* Pocket Books: New York, 1994.

Shulsky, Abram N. and Gary J. Schmitt. "The Future of Intelligence." *The National Interest,* Winter 1994/1995.

U.S. Congress, Senate. Senate Committee on Intelligence. *An Assessment of the Aldrich H. Ames Espionage Case.* Washington: Government Printing Office, 1994.

Weiner, Tim, David Johnston and Neil A. Lewis. *Betrayal The Story of Aldrich Ames.* New York: Random House, 1995

Wise, David. *Nightmover: How Aldrich Ames Sold the CIA to the KGB for $4.6 Million.* New York: Random House, 1995.

Index

480